★ ★ ★

John M. Schofield
& the Politics *of* Generalship

★ ★ ★

CIVIL WAR AMERICA

Gary W. Gallagher, editor

John M. Schofield

& the Politics *of* Generalship

★ ★ ★

DONALD B. CONNELLY

THE UNIVERSITY OF NORTH CAROLINA PRESS

CHAPEL HILL

Designed by Heidi Perov

Set in Bulmer and Engraver

by Keystone Typesetting, Inc.

Frontispiece: Painting of John M. Schofield by John White
Alexander, 1914, oil on canvas. Courtesy West Point Museum Art
Collection, United States Military Academy.

The paper in this book meets the guidelines for permanence and
durability of the Committee on Production Guidelines for Book
Longevity of the Council on Library Resources.

Library of Congress Cataloging-in-Publication Data

Connelly, Donald B.

John M. Schofield and the politics of generalship /

Donald B. Connelly.

p. cm.—(Civil War America)

Includes bibliographical references and index.

ISBN-13: 978-0-8078-3007-9 (cloth : alk. paper)

ISBN-10: 0-8078-3007-0 (cloth : alk. paper)

1. Schofield, John McAllister, 1831–1906. 2. Generals—
United States—Biography. 3. United States. Army—Biography.
4. United States—History—Civil War, 1861–1865—Campaigns. 5. United
States. Army—History—19th century. 6. Civil-military relations—
United States—History—19th century. I. Title. II. Series.

E467.1.S35C66 2006

355.0092—dc22   2005031388

10 09 08 07 06   5 4 3 2 1

For my wife, Lynne

CONTENTS

MAPS & ILLUSTRATIONS

PREFACE

I have written this biography of Lieutenant General John M. Schofield with three different, but occasionally overlapping, groups of readers in mind. For the avid students of the Civil War, I hope to provide a slightly different perspective on the war than combat and battlefield command. For the scholars of civil-military relations, I hope to portray the complexity of the American experience in both war and peace. Finally, I hope current or former soldiers will appreciate the roots of their profession and recognize the dilemmas faced by an earlier generation.

In examining John Schofield's Civil War experience, I have placed special emphasis on the role of politics in the formulation and execution of military policy. I have endeavored to demonstrate that there is no easy dividing line. Political disputes about slavery or the use of African American soldiers had enormous military implications. Similarly, military efforts to suppress guerrillas, seize or destroy enemy property, and seek battle or resort to maneuver had enormous political implications. The relationship between political and military policies was even more dynamic as contending political factions attempted to promote their ideas and adherents in both the military and civil spheres.

This study also focuses on the role of military government in American history. During the Civil War and Reconstruction, military governments displaced civil authorities in numerous states. In the early days of the Civil War, Schofield helped overthrow the legal, but secessionist, governor of Missouri. As departmental commander, Schofield supervised a nearly parallel government, with its own courts and the ability to levy fines and taxes. As a military governor in Reconstruction Virginia, General Schofield replaced civilian officials, supervised elections, and drafted constitutions.

The military was also heavily involved in federal intervention in domestic disorders. In the West soldiers in the U.S. Army frequently served as law enforcement officers, while in the East they aided civil authorities in quelling labor violence. Army officers also frequently displaced civilian Indian agents in the supervision of Indian reservations. By the end of the nineteenth century, however, the army's constabulary missions had diminished as the Indian Wars subsided and the state-based National Guard took over the primary task of handling domestic disorder. The U.S. Army turned to new missions.

Throughout the nineteenth century, the U.S. Army undertook the process of professionalization. Before the Civil War, the army had developed a professional ethic of service to the nation and fidelity to the Constitution as its guiding principle. After the war, it emphasized the need for lifelong commitment to professional education and the cultivation of expertise in the art and science of war. Earlier than most of his colleagues, John Schofield recognized that soldiers could never achieve professional autonomy by separating the military from politics. Only by accommodating to politics and the nation's intentionally divided institutions could the army attain a limited professional independence.

Another major theme of this study is the changing character and demands of senior command. While Schofield was a field commander in the Atlanta, Nashville, and North Carolina campaigns, the bulk of his command experience was conducted more remotely. As commander in Missouri, he directed rather than led operations against either the Confederate army or guerrillas, much in the same way as he would later orchestrate operations during major domestic disorders, such as the Pullman Strike. Thus, his experiences in planning, directing, and administering military operations further habituated him to think in terms of a modern Chief of Staff rather than a traditional commanding general.

Yet despite these changes, this study affirms the primacy of politics, whether ideological, partisan, institutional, or personal, in the formulation of military policy. Characteristic of the checks and balances of the American political system, military authorities were divided between the states and the federal government, between the executive and legislative branches, and even among the executive departments. Traditionally, conflict over military policy among these institutions produced corresponding divisions within the officer corps. Thus, civil-military conflicts habitually consisted of groups of civil officials and military officers struggling against other civil-military factions over the control of policy.

Finally, I have characterized John Schofield as a "political soldier" both to emphasize the political environment in which military officers must operate and to differentiate him from the "political generals" of the Civil War era, such as Frank Blair, John Logan, and Samuel Curtis. Political generals, or generals appointed from civilian life, were a central feature of civil-military relations in the founding of the nation and its early wars. As the need for professional expertise became more important, the senior ranks were filled by lifelong professionals. However, professional soldiers still needed to appreciate the political implications of their actions. This study of the career of John M. Schofield, I hope, will contribute to a greater understanding of the dynamics of American civil-military relations, and especially the shift from political generals to political soldiers.

One cannot complete such a research project without incurring many debts. First, I need to thank my advisor and friend Dr. Joseph T. Glatthaar, who has patiently guided me in this endeavor from idea to dissertation to book. Next, I must thank the other members of my dissertation committee, Dr. James Kirby Martin, Dr. Frank Holt, and Dr. Richard Murray. Their examples in the classroom and in reviewing and improving my work were invaluable.

I owe a special debt of gratitude to J. Thomas Crouch, who had embarked on a dissertation of "Schofield and His Army" and produced an extensive set of notes on Schofield's years as commanding general. In addition to this gold mine, Crouch's translations of the Schofield scrawl greatly aided my own efforts. I must also thank Edward M. Coffman and Graham Cosmas for making these notes available to me. I would like to thank Schofield Gross of Riverside, Illinois, Schofield Andrews Jr. of Nova Scotia, and Stockton Andrews of Bar Harbor, Maine, for providing me information on the Schofield family.

I would like to thank the United States Army Center of Military History for a research grant and Andrew Birtle, Graham Cosmas, and Robert Wright for their research advice and assistance. I also thank the University of Houston Murray Miller Research Scholarship fund for financial support. On a more personal level, I would like to thank Dr. Cindy Gurney for letting me stay in her home during my rather lengthy research expeditions to Washington, D.C.

No researcher can succeed without the support of countless dedicated librarians and archivists. I would like to thank particularly the archivists at the United States Military Academy, Judith Sibley, Susan Lintelmann, and Deborah McKeon-Pogue; David Keough at the United States Military History Institute; and Phyllis Russell at the Proctor Free Library. The dedicated professionals at the Library of Congress and the National Archives are too numerous to name, and their expertise, whether in person or via telephone or e-mail, has been invaluable. I also owe a great debt to the librarians at the University of Houston and the San Antonio Public Library for the assistance in obtaining hard-to-find materials.

I would also like to thank my editor David Perry, Paula Wald, Bethany Johnson, and the rest of the staff of the University of North Carolina Press for guiding me through the publication process. I am especially grateful that they permitted me to retain so many of my extended endnotes, which I hope will be of interest and benefit to other researchers. I am also indebted to Dr. Gary Gallagher and Dr. Steven E. Woodworth for helping to make this a much better book.

I owe a general debt of gratitude to my friends and colleagues at the United States Army Command and General Staff College, Fort Leavenworth, Kansas. The opportunity to learn from such a talented and varied group of military historians and military professionals has been inspirational.

Finally, I want to thank my wife, Lynne, who has supported me through this long project. She has made all the difference in my life.

* * *

John M. Schofield
& the Politics *of* Generalship

* * *

Introduction

In 1888 John M. Schofield succeeded Philip H. Sheridan as commanding general of the United States Army. Schofield did not enjoy the spectacular Civil War fame of his predecessors, Ulysses S. Grant, William T. Sherman, and Sheridan, or the renown as an Indian fighter of his successor Nelson Miles. Nevertheless, Lieutenant General John McAllister Schofield (1831–1906) was an important figure in the late nineteenth-century army. In addition to serving as a departmental, corps, and army commander in the Civil War, he occupied every senior position in the postwar army, including secretary of war. From the Civil War to the "Root Reforms," General Schofield played an influential role in the formulation of American military policy and especially in shaping the American military profession.[1]

Of average height, prematurely bald, and with a tendency to plumpness, General Schofield never cut a dashing figure. Instead, he impressed people with his earnestness and intelligence, presenting a demeanor of calm courtesy and good humor. He was, by temperament, a cautious and methodical man and consciously cultivated a reputation for moderation and restraint. In his later years, some would describe Schofield as a bit of a courtier. Yet Schofield was more commonly regarded as one of the shrewdest and most politically astute officers in the army. General John Pope reportedly said that Schofield "could stand steadier on the bulge of a barrel than any man who ever wore shoulder straps."[2]

In war and peace, Schofield's experience reflected the pervasiveness of politics in military affairs. Schofield discovered the benefits and pitfalls of political affiliation and factionalism. A West Point classmate, David Stanley, described him as a good man, but who was too afraid of politicians. However, in an era when politics and personal connections suffused public life, Schofield had good reason to be attentive to politicians.[3] In learning to balance his military duties amid contending political pressures, Schofield ultimately rejected the idea that the path to military professionalism lay through a complete separation of military from political affairs. Rather than assert his independent authority and feud with the secretary of war, Schofield forthrightly subordinated himself to the secretary. Schofield's ideas and approach to command of the army laid the groundwork for the "Root Reforms," and in retirement, he energetically worked for their passage. Schofield's accommodation to the primacy of politics in military affairs was an essential element in the professionalization of the United States Army.

The professionalization of the American military had been an ongoing project for most of the nineteenth century.[4] It took place against the backdrop of major transformations in American political culture. The political spoils system retreated before increasing demands for disinterested expertise. During Schofield's lifetime, the highly localistic nature of the American polity changed dramatically. The army began the century as one of the few national institutions, yet by the end of the century there were dozens of national governmental, economic, educational, and social institutions. The heretofore personal and informal approaches to administration were transformed into highly bureaucratic structures that emphasized normative rules and procedures.

Politics and the need to conform to the American constitutional system primarily dictated the nature, speed, and direction of this movement. By the end of the century, the groundwork for a modern, professional national army had been laid, but it was by no means a finished structure. Although one may fairly claim that throughout this period there were professional soldiers, or those who took up soldiering as a lifelong occupation, that is not the same as the establishment of a military profession. There are numerous definitions of what constitutes a "profession," but historian Nathan O. Hatch has offered a useful one that is composed of three elements. First, a profession is based on "a definable body of organized knowledge that requires extensive academic preparation." Second, a profession requires "a moral commitment of service to the public that goes beyond the test of the market or desire for personal profit." Third, it enjoys a "relative independence or autonomy of professional life."[5]

In the development of American military professionalism, the criterion that was the earliest to evolve was the moral commitment to public service, or the sense of public responsibility. Historians of American professions have contrasted the class-linked rise of the professions in Britain with the seeming contradiction of professionalism's developing in an egalitarian republic, especially during the "Age of Jackson." The idea of a profession as a public service bridged this apparent gap. For the American officer corps, this meant that it had to dispense with or adapt traditions and values associated with monarchical or aristocratic views of service to republican ones. Though American military traditions were built on British foundations, the American officer corps soon developed a commitment to the nation and, more significantly, to its republican form of government. While the president as commander in chief was roughly analogous to the king, the officers of the government, military and civilian, swore an oath to the Constitution, not the president.[6]

The United States Military Academy played an essential role in developing the professional ethic of public service. The curriculum was more heavily focused on turning out military and civil engineers than on giving young men a comprehensive education in the art and science of war. The engineering orientation was itself a product of the public interest in national internal development. In addition to being highly technical, the academy was a ruthless meritocracy that stressed individual responsibility and accountability. As Schofield attested, the academy also inculcated the idea of subordination and selfless service into strong-willed young men. "Duty, Honor, Country" were not simply martial values; they were pledges to the values of the nation.[7]

Given the academy's appointment process, the officer corps tended to mirror the political and sectional divisions of the larger society. Schofield and his fellow cadets were schooled in the emerging officer ethic that celebrated the academy and the army as national institutions dedicated to a national interest. While many officers were interested in politics and most officers nurtured political connections, one historian has concluded that these alliances were personal, rather than overtly partisan. Young Schofield learned the benefits of political connections when a Democratic congressman appointed him to the academy and a Democratic senator saved him from expulsion. Throughout his life, Schofield retained his general loyalty to the Democratic Party, but that allegiance did not stop him from developing contacts with Republicans. In fact, the very volatility of American politics made it prudent for an officer to avoid identification with one political party or faction. By cultivating the attitude of seemingly disinterested national service, military officers enhanced their professional status and their ability to withstand partisan attacks. Abraham Lincoln's advice that Schofield would be doing well "if both sides . . . shall abuse you" was uncomfortable and not always successful, but it afforded a certain reassurance to political leaders who worried about the aspirations of political generals.[8]

The second characteristic of the American military professionalism to emerge was a commitment to professional education and the cultivation of expertise in the art and science of war. The establishment of the U.S. Military Academy was the beginning of this process; however, this institution did not provide a comprehensive military education. Instead, West Point socialized officers into military values and provided certain technical skills, primarily related to engineering and artillery. Schofield's education suited him for a career as a physics and engineering professor as much as a military officer. Most of an officer's military education took place in his unit or, more rarely, through private study. This approach reflected the traditional concept of the military art as one in which persons learned by experience or displayed a "natural gift."[9]

The engineering and artillery skills were part of the rapid technological and scientific advances in the nineteenth century that transformed the art and science of warfare and most professions. As technology progressed and the scope and scale of military operations expanded, the level of expertise required increased. It is unsurprising that the basic military education provided at West Point would eventually be deemed inadequate for professional officers. Sherman, Schofield, and other military professionals saw the importance of continuing military education. By the time Elihu Root created the Army War College in 1901, the army had developed a philosophy of professional education that extended from precommission education, to basic branch instruction, to staff training and culminated in the study of strategy and mobilization. It was an educational philosophy that embraced individual study and public debate.[10] General Schofield set an example in presenting papers at professional meetings. He extended the idea to "post lyceums," which became the basis of formal training programs.

In the navy, the technological developments created a division between the line officers, who emphasized the importance of sailing and tactics, and the engineers, who stressed the ability to master the modern machinery of naval warfare. The army did not experience such dramatic cleavages, but advancing technology tended to produce ever-greater complexity and specialization in military affairs. Army leaders needed to be able to integrate these units and their equipment into more complex military organizations. In turn, these ever more complex military organizations increased the need for professional education beyond one's specialty. The term "combined arms" took on greater saliency in the twentieth century. The Infantry and Cavalry School and the Cavalry and Light Artillery School began this process, and the Staff College and War College, created in 1901, raised it to new levels. As the founder and chief sponsor of the Cavalry and Light Artillery School, Schofield recognized the need for practical, as well as classroom, training and instruction.[11]

The third characteristic of a profession involves professional autonomy. In most professions, this entails a certain monopoly on the function. It also encompasses gatekeeping and the creation of internal standards of conduct and practice. Rather than autonomy, Samuel P. Huntington used the term "corporateness," or a sense that members share a common bond and constitute a group apart, one that defines and enforces its own standards. Even this formulation is extremely problematic for military professionalism, however. The idea of the military profession's having the power to regulate entry and its own internal affairs was anathema in a democratic republic, especially one in which Oliver Cromwell seemed to be part of living memory. This autonomy, or corporateness, also ran counter to the ideal of the citizen soldier as the ultimate defender of the nation's liberty. Furthermore, military renown had long been one of the important paths to high political office, and politicians were not about to let career officers be the gatekeepers to that entrée. The reconciliation of professional autonomy and political subordination was Schofield's most enduring contribution to the professionalization of the army.[12]

While the United States was not militaristic, it certainly possessed a martial spirit strongly linked to the ideal of citizenship. From the Minuteman to the Continental to the volunteer soldier, it was an article of faith that it was the citizen soldier—and not the regular—who fought and won the nation's wars. West Pointers saw the Civil War as a vindication of the academy's worth, but other Americans saw patriotism as more important than professionalism. The Civil War convinced a new generation of Americans that military leadership was not arcane, and that courage, character, and common sense remained the true requirements of command, even high command. The professional dilemma was how to maintain the popular enthusiasm and support, while gaining acceptance of professional expertise and direction.

Military reformer Colonel Emory Upton had advocated the immediate transformation of a state-based militia system into a national reserve for the regular army, but the more pragmatic Schofield paid obeisance to popular and political opinion. By maintaining a role for the National Guard, but increasingly bringing it under the tutelage and control of the regular army, Schofield and his successors, such as John McAuley Palmer, attempted to transform the old institutions. Schofield, the professional soldier, certainly valued the discipline and toughness of the regular, but he also admired the tenacity and common sense of the volunteer soldier. He sought a way to marry professional experience to volunteer numbers and spirit. The accommodations to the state-based National Guard units were not as efficient as the centralized national reserve systems of Europe, but by adapting American traditions, these units fostered a sense of public engagement and promoted local political support.[13]

In the nineteenth century the continuing republican ideology meant that politics permeated the process of commissioning officers. Initially, politicians were the gatekeepers to military careers. The selection of prominent men to lead the militia or volunteer units and the election of junior officers by the troops were ways of fostering spirit and confidence. The politically based appointment of cadets to the U.S. Military Academy reflected the commonplace practice of balancing local, sectional, and partisan interests in the allocation of national benefits. Yet, as in the case of West Point entrance exams, the military gradually instituted entry standards that constrained political choices. These professional criteria were slowly applied to direct appointments, staff appointments, and, eventually, commissioning programs in the National Guard and Army Reserve. As commanding general, Schofield was also an energetic proponent of military training at civilian universities. The military, however, did not replace politicians as gatekeepers. West Point never became the exclusive entrée to a military commission, and civilian officials continued to set the size and sources of the various commissioning programs.

Military promotion followed a similar pattern. For example, the strict promotion by date of rank was a collective response to the pervasively political environment in which the army existed through most of the nineteenth century. In the early twentieth century most army officers opposed President Theodore Roosevelt's initial efforts to permit some promotion based on merit, but soon the "corporate" answer was to adopt selection processes and criteria that tended to insulate or stigmatize overtly political choices. As for the higher ranks, there were fewer and fewer political generals, especially after the Spanish-American War. However, even the shift from political to professional standards was based on politics. The army made its case for professional expertise because it convinced the political leadership that the appointment of civilians to high military positions based on political, and not professional, considerations could be detrimental to their political health. High command became restricted to those who had made a lifelong commitment to the profession.[14]

By the beginning of the twentieth century, the ideas of professional military officers had made great strides within the constraints of the American constitutional system. The army was unable to replace the state-based National Guard with a fully nationalized army reserve, but slowly the National Guard came under the supervision of the regulars. Similarly, the army was able to set professional standards and criteria for officer appointment and promotion. If the political leaders gradually adjusted to professional military requirements, it was John M. Schofield's example of military authority—one that accommodated to political needs—that helped open the door to enhanced professional autonomy.

Schofield saw that professional development could only be achieved by subordination to, not autonomy from, politicians. The perennial conflict between the commanding general and the secretary of war often undermined the arguments of military professionals by sowing distrust, especially since the source of the conflict involved intramilitary disputes. By accepting the authority of the secretary of war, Schofield bowed to political realities that too many of his predecessors had sought to evade. Presidents, especially in peacetime, looked to their political appointees to protect their interests in the War Department. Schofield reinforced this confidence by advocating that the senior officer of the army should have a limited tenure, not unlike cabinet and other high civil officials. He further held that the commander in chief ought to have the right to select his own senior military advisor. By acknowledging that senior military officers, like civil officers, served at the discretion of the president, that their tenure should be limited, and that each president should be given the opportunity to make his own selection, Schofield strengthened the commanding general's authority. The senior military officers, through this selection process, thus shared part of the special trust and confidence that presidents placed in their cabinet secretaries.

The mutual accommodation between political leaders and military professionals at the beginning of the twentieth century was a major realignment, not a revolution, in civil-military relations. The demands of modern warfare and military professionalism required a rearrangement of the relations between civil and military authorities, but this reorganization was played out against a larger background. In an era of intense partisanship and political spoils, the concept of separating the military from politics was not simply an assertion of military power. The formation of the civil service was the civilian equivalent of military professionalization. Moreover, as the nation shifted from local to national political, economic, and social structures, it is not surprising that states would lose power over military affairs to the federal government. Congress, which had always reflected state interests, would continue to represent such interests regarding military policy. Finally, the transformation of the army was an early example of the reforming mentality that came to be known as Progressivism.

The history of American civil-military relations, even by historians, is too often infused with a high degree of "presentism" and pessimism.[15] Too many writers, unfortunately, treat both the civil and military sectors as relatively distinct and monolithic entities. They presume that the military and the political spheres can be readily delineated, and they focus primarily on the relationship between the president and the senior military chiefs. Often overlooked are the roles of the Congress, the states, and the public, as well as disparate elements and interests within the military. Most civil-military conflicts have involved struggles between one civilian and military coalition of interests versus another coalition.[16] In American history, the central question has never been whether to have civilian control over the military, but which civilians will have a say in the formulation and execution of policy.[17]

One of the reasons for this tendency among scholars and policymakers is the continuing influence of Samuel P. Huntington's concept of objective civilian control, defined as a "depoliticized professional military." Huntington contrasted this model of civilian control with what he termed "subjective control" through class, institutional, or constitutional approaches. Huntington saw subjective control as "civilianizing" the military and objective control as a way of safely "militarizing" the military. Since objective control is dependent on professionalization, Huntington argued that objective control could not and did not emerge until the late nineteenth-century professionalization of the army. In contrast, this study argues that the complete depoliticization of the military is impossible, and even dangerous. American civil-military relations depend on both objective and subjective civilian control. Objective control fosters the false belief that in matters of military policy and strategy, there are purely "political" and purely "military" decisions. It also fosters the dangerous idea that the military can be safely segregated from the constitutional ideals and social realities of the nation.[18]

The differences between military and civil officers in an era of political patronage were generally quite slender and many—like George B. McClellan, Jefferson Davis, and Ulysses S. Grant—passed back and forth between the two with remarkable facility. Though military officers saw themselves as different from many of their civilian friends and colleagues, they were not estranged. Most officers, of necessity, maintained cordial and sometimes very close relations with local elites. The supposed isolation of the army in frontier outposts was not as extreme as some commentators suggest.[19] Schofield's brother Lieutenant Colonel George W. Schofield may well have felt isolated and alone when he shot himself at Fort Apache in Arizona Territory one winter's morning. Nevertheless, over the years George had been given important and varied assignments, including duty as an aide to his brother, official travel to Europe, and collaboration with the Smith & Wesson Company. For his part, John Schofield had been at the center of most of the pivotal events of the period, and he enjoyed a diversity of friends among the political, economic, and to a lesser extent, cultural elites.

The bright line between political and military policy assumed by many commentators seldom existed in American historical experience. Politics has pervaded most military issues, and the most seemingly routine military action could have enormous political ramifications. Whether on the western frontier or in the South during Reconstruction, the army became, sometimes unwillingly, the arbiter of political disputes that had the potential to turn very violent. As "domestic diplomats," army officers frequently negotiated treaties with the Indian nations. Finally, the army's constabulary duties were inherently political. As Schofield had remarked during the Great Strike of 1877, one raw recruit could spark actions that "might do incalculable harm."[20]

In war, and especially in civil war, military policy is formulated amid the clash of political interests and perceptions. Often, especially at the early stages of the Civil War, military officers had to wrestle with issues that had profound political implications, without authoritative political guidance. While awaiting political direction, army officers had to deal with obviously disloyal persons, the advent of guerrilla warfare, and people who refused to remain enslaved. Later, the contending civil authorities provided conflicting or contradictory directions that compelled military commanders to make political choices. Schofield's participation in this facet of the war is perhaps more instructive about American civil-military relations than the more well known debates over battlefield strategies.

Civil War and Reconstruction prompted the greatest crises in American civil-military relations and reveal typically American patterns of civilian control. Schofield's service in Civil War Missouri, during Reconstruction, and as commanding general enmeshed him in struggles between the president, secretaries of war, Congress, governors, and the people. In Missouri in the spring of 1861, Lieutenant John M. Schofield, in aligning himself with Captain Nathaniel Lyon and Congressman Frank Blair Jr., became a supporting player in the extralegal mustering of federal troops, the arrest of the lawful state militia, the ouster of the military department commander, and the overthrow of the elected governor of Missouri. Promoted for his efforts, Schofield learned a few years later that simply having the support and confidence of the commander in chief was not enough. In the poisonous political environment of Civil War Missouri, Schofield could not maintain his balance between the conservative Unionists and the radical Republicans, either in Missouri or in Congress. He proved unable to follow Lincoln's admonition that "if both factions, or neither, shall abuse you, you will probably be about right."[21]

Reconstruction was the greatest crisis in civil-military relations in the nation's history.[22] First, it was a military occupation of large portions of the United States, where military rule and military law displaced the elected governments. Second, and most important, Reconstruction precipitated a fight over control of this army of occupation—a fight between the commander in chief and some like-minded generals on the one hand and the Republican majority in Congress, the secretary of war, and the commanding general on the other. Subordinate generals, like the nation, were divided; some, such as Philip Sheridan and

John Pope, supported the congressional Republicans, while others, like John Schofield and Winfield Scott Hancock, tilted toward President Andrew Johnson and the Democrats. As secretary of war, Schofield was able to maintain his political equilibrium by retaining General Grant's trust while serving in President Johnson's cabinet.

While the long struggle for army reorganization and reform was not a crisis, it further illustrates this pattern of American civil-military relations, as the contending military and civilian groups sought alliances in order to shape military policy. State and local officials sometimes opposed the efforts of army reformers, as with the National Guard; sometimes they supported the army, as in coastal defense; and sometimes both, as state and local officials splintered in their support for post realignment or the army's role in domestic disorder. Similarly, army reformers had to cope with the contending views and agendas of Congress, the administration, and those within the army itself. In the 1870s even the line officers were divided over reform; by the 1890s, Schofield was able to build a rough consensus for many important reform measures, though some ideas, such as the command of the army and the General Staff, remained controversial.

When Schofield became the commanding general in 1888, he attempted a different solution to the problem of command of the army. By subordinating himself to the secretary of war, Schofield hoped to end a futile struggle that only served the interests of the staff bureaus. In attempting to insert himself between the secretary and the staff departments, he only partially succeeded. The concept depended on good personal relationships with the secretaries. Further, many of the staff chiefs continued to go around him and often issued orders without the approval of the president, the secretary of war, or the commanding general.[23]

After his retirement, Schofield sought an institutional solution. His advice to Secretary of War Elihu Root about the General Staff Bill in 1902 demonstrates the paradox of politics and military professionalism. Schofield insisted that the Chief of Staff position be filled not simply by the senior general of the army, but by someone that the president selected. The president, Schofield contended, could only grant full authority to someone in whom he has "entire confidence." Thus, he must have the "same freedom of choice . . . as in selecting the heads of departments."[24] It is not surprising that when Root, with Schofield's help, realigned the relationship between the secretary and the Chief of Staff, their institutional adversaries—Congress and the staff departments—also adjusted their relationships. The traditional staff departments turned to Congress to protect their prerogatives and independence from a united secretary of war and Chief of Staff.

Schofield recognized that military authority and efficiency could never be achieved at the expense of the constitutional system. He understood that while the army should naturally look to the commander in chief for leadership, Congress played a vital role in laying the institutional foundations of the army, which would endure beyond the policies of any given president. As commanding general, Schofield appreciated that in the absence of crisis or consensus, only incremental reform was possible, and that the commanding general needed the active support of the secretary of war and Congress. Schofield's political education taught him to value the hidden hand of influence over the peremptory habit of command. Schofield mastered the art of bureaucratic infighting. While in many ways Schofield was a product of the "Old Army," he also foreshadowed the managerial requirements of modern military bureaucracies.

Despite the enormous passions and conflict unleashed by the Civil War and Reconstruction, the principle of civilian control was never in jeopardy. Again, the real debates were generally not civilian versus military, but shifting alliances of civilians and military men versus other combinations of civilians and military men. Schofield had learned that only a commander who possessed the trust and confidence of the political leadership, and not just the president, could survive, much less thrive. Professional competence alone was not enough for a senior general. In war or peace, civil authorities would only grant soldiers authority if they could be trusted, and they would only be trusted if they displayed some appreciation of the political implications of military policies.

Throughout most of the nineteenth century, politics shaped much of the army's institutional life, while many officers sought some way to separate the army from politics. Sherman's insistence that he was the subordinate of the president and that he, as commanding general, should control the General Staff was a misguided effort to shield the military from the "political" secretary of war. John Schofield was among the earliest professional soldiers to realize that the path to professionalization did not entail a complete separation of the military from politics. Such a separation was impossible. Instead, Schofield, the astute political soldier, saw that professional development could only be achieved by subordination to, not autonomy from, political leaders. Civilian control required accommodation to politics, not separation.[25]

ONE

Early Years

In his memoirs Lieutenant General John McAllister Schofield looked back nearly fifty years to his days at the United States Military Academy and stressed the importance of the mental discipline that West Point had provided. The academy system developed "reasoning faculties and habits of independent thought." More interestingly, he observed that "what I needed to learn was not so much how to command as how to obey." In a nation that prized equality and independence, Schofield related his painful experience of learning to "submit my opinions to those of an accidental superior in rank." In a tiny, far-flung army that demanded initiative and self-reliance from its officers, Schofield declared that "nothing is more absolutely indispensable to a good soldier than perfect subordination."[1] These views did not mean that Schofield lacked the self-confidence, ambition, or the prickly pride of most of his contemporaries; rather, these were the mature reflections of a professional soldier who had learned to value the hidden hand of influence over the peremptory habit of command.

Schofield's writings do not reveal an especially introspective man. His memoirs make occasional references to his personal life, and his voluminous papers only contain brief glimpses of his family life. Schofield was born in the town of Gerry, in Chautauqua County, New York, on September 29, 1831. His father, Reverend James Schofield, moved the family to Illinois in 1843. In 1845 Reverend Schofield established the First Baptist Church of Freeport, Illinois. In his long life, James Schofield was married three times and had sixteen children, ten of whom reached adulthood. General Schofield was the second child of the second marriage. His mother, Caroline McAllister Schofield, was the sister of James's first wife. Of his childhood, Schofield said little, but he recalled that "manly sports" and hard work on the farm left "little time or inclination for mischief." He also appreciated the "best possible opportunities for education" that he obtained in the local public schools. While his military career would take him to many faraway places, Schofield nevertheless maintained connections with New York and Illinois throughout his life.[2]

Though he was the first professional soldier in the family and by far the most distinguished, the Schofield family was well acquainted with military service. According to family tradition, the Schofields came to America well before the Revolution and settled in New England. During the Revolution, several Schofield ancestors fought against one another as patriots and loyalists. Grandfather James S. Schofield, too young to serve in the Revolution, settled in New York and served in the militia during the War of 1812. General Schofield's father, though in his sixties, served as a chaplain in the Union army from 1862 to 1865. Brother George Wheeler Schofield became the general's chief of artillery in the Civil War and died a lieutenant colonel of the 6th Cavalry in 1882. Brother Charles B. Schofield, West Point class of 1870, died of fever in Cuba in 1901. General Schofield's surviving sons, William and Richmond, both served in the army during the Spanish-American War. William died on active duty in August 1906. Richmond served in World War I and retired a colonel in 1920.[3]

John Schofield's military career came by the same combination of luck and personal affiliations that marked his entire professional life. By age seventeen, Schofield had received a solid secondary education and had decided on a law career. To earn money to pursue his legal studies, he worked as a surveyor in northern Wisconsin and as a teacher in the public school in the small town of Oneco. When the district's military academy candidate unexpectedly withdrew, the local Democratic congressman, Thomas J. Turner, needed to find a replacement quickly. Turner's brother James, who was one of the Oneco public school directors, suggested Schofield as a young man capable of meeting the stringent standards of the academy entrance exam. Years later, Schofield wryly observed that he was very fortunate that James Turner had chosen to visit his classroom on the day he was teaching mathematics rather than Latin. Had he been lecturing in Latin, the director would have had a very different opinion of his academic attainments. Nonetheless, the offer came, and Schofield believed the free education would provide a good foundation for the study of law. On June 1, 1849, he reported to West Point.[4]

Upon arrival, two fellow Illinois cadets, William P. Carlin, Second Class, and Hezekiah H. Garber, Third Class, immediately took the new Fourth Classman under their wing. Still three months short of eighteen, Schofield was already beginning to lose his hair, which gave him a more mature appearance. Schofield, therefore, experienced little hazing at the summer camp that preceded the start of classes. One night, to avoid having his clothes stolen by upperclassmen, Schofield slept outside and became quite sick. Yet, this illness proved fortunate because while in the hospital, he met Commanding General Winfield Scott, who spent his summers in West Point. Schofield sufficiently impressed "Old

Fuss and Feathers" so that some years later Scott would make an important intervention in Schofield's career.[5]

Schofield's roommates were two Virginians, Henry H. Walker and John R. Chambliss.[6] They were relieved that Schofield was not a "Yankee," but a "Western" man. The sectionalism that increasingly divided the nation was rife at West Point, creating tense moments for many cadets. Foreshadowing his future role, Schofield attempted to moderate and act as peacemaker between the sometimes hostile factions. Schofield's classmates also included the future Union commander of the Army of the Tennessee, James B. McPherson, and the Confederate commander of the Army of Tennessee, John Bell Hood. Philip H. Sheridan, who began a year earlier, would also graduate with Schofield's class.[7]

Habituation to hierarchy was not just confined to the bivouac and parade field. Most instruction was carried out in small recitation sections conducted by the assistant professors. After the instructors had demonstrated the solution to a problem, each cadet was called on to explain subsequent examples. Students usually recited daily and were graded accordingly. The sections were organized largely by order of merit, with section assignments periodically rearranged to reflect student performance. Far from what Jacksonian critics styled an aristocracy, West Point was a rather rigorous meritocracy.[8] Since mathematics was a major part of the West Point curriculum, Schofield prospered academically. In the Fourth Class year, cadets studied mathematics, French, and English. As Third Classmen, they learned mathematics, French, and drawing. Second Classmen took natural philosophy, chemistry, and drawing. The academic subjects for First Classmen were engineering, mineralogy and geology, and ethics. Although Schofield claims that he did not spend that much time with his studies, he stood eleventh in his first year, sixth in his second and third years, and seventh in his final year. While mathematics and engineering were his best subjects, his intention to study law sparked his efforts in English, philosophy, drawing, and ethics.[9]

The West Point system of daily recitation demanded that cadets keep up with their studies, yet it was not a program of rote memorization. O. O. Howard observed that those who simply committed their lessons to memory at first prospered; but over time, those who were able to systematize the principles of the subject were much better prepared for final examinations. (Howard went on to note that many officers failed with large commands because they encumbered "their minds with the detail.") Many cadets, in their letters home, complained about the abstract and theoretical content of most courses. Schofield's affinity for mathematics, law, and later physics reflected his proclivity for abstract thinking, and his military memorandums reflect this theoretical bent. Yet his intellectual interests extended beyond mathematics and science into English, history, geography, and philosophy and continued throughout his career. As superintendent and later in retirement, Schofield would champion the need for a broad liberal arts education at West Point.[10]

The formal course of instruction, while demanding, did not consume all of the energy of the young cadets. Schofield admitted to only studying an hour to an hour and a half for each lesson. His library records reveal a special interest in history and the works of Walter Scott. McPherson had similar reading habits, while young Sheridan was a voracious reader of history. From the records, John B. Hood seems to have been unacquainted with the library.[11] By Schofield's third year at the academy, however, his extracurricular reading began to wane as he became more interested in playing cards and smoking after taps. These infractions—along with visiting other cadets' rooms during study hours and cooking in the barracks rooms—were common and served as illicit pleasures for young men held under routinely strict discipline. Schofield's rebelliousness and daring even prompted him to make a bet that he could go to New York and back without getting caught. With money borrowed from Cadet Jerome N. Bonaparte and the help of famed tavern owner Benny Havens, Schofield departed during evening parade and returned before morning roll call. Characteristically, he delighted in the careful planning of the exploit, rather than the wager.[12]

Church attendance was required at the academy. While some cadets were devout and others scoffed at religion, most "totally disregarded it." As with many young students, Schofield's years at the academy altered his religious beliefs. While he still viewed the Bible as "divinely inspired," he sought more evidence. The academy chaplain's distaste for "skepticism" and his denunciation of "God-hating Geologists" prompted this son of the Baptist minister to forgo further Sunday Bible study classes. As with politics, Schofield learned to be circumspect about his religious beliefs. He remained conventionally devout, but by no means zealous in his religious convictions. No doubt influenced by his wife, he shifted from the Baptist Church of his father to the Episcopal Church. Years later as West Point superintendent, Schofield still believed that mandatory Sunday chapel services were important and should be retained. But as commanding general, he championed the right of the local garrisons to select their own chaplains based on the desires of a majority of soldiers, rather than having one appointed by the War Department.[13]

In 1878 when Sherman's son decided to become a Catholic priest, Schofield attempted to console a distraught father. "Young men of intellect and self will rarely follow their fathers," wrote the minister's son to Sherman. "May not a

Cardinal or Archbishop exert more power for good or evil than a lawyer, statesman, or general?"[14] Schofield's rather temperate view of religion, combined with having Catholic relatives himself, shaped his mild response to what Sherman clearly viewed as a calamity. Ever the moderate, Schofield's religious beliefs were carefully modulated and thoroughly conventional.[15]

By the end of his third year, in 1852, Schofield was well established at West Point. Academically he stood sixth and was appointed a cadet lieutenant.[16] In June the faculty selected him to help tutor prospective cadets in mathematics for their entrance examination. This assignment, however, nearly scuttled his West Point career. When several candidates who failed the entrance examination complained about "improper behavior" by cadet visitors to Schofield's classroom, Secretary of War Charles M. Conrad dismissed him from the academy for "breach of trust and abuse of authority whilst instructor of the candidates for admission." Faced with dismissal and disgrace, Cadet Schofield would learn the importance of having friends and political connections.[17]

Schofield, in his memoirs, declared that his conscience was clear and that he had no anxiety about the final results, but he soon discovered he was in serious trouble. An investigation by the commandant of cadets revealed that senior cadets routinely visited Schofield's section classroom. Moreover, on the Friday before the examination, several senior cadets had entered Schofield's classroom and asked some of the candidates "indecent questions," such as had they visited a bordello; the intruding cadets also ordered the candidates to draw "obscene figures" on the blackboard. Though several other sections, including O. O. Howard's English section, also had unauthorized senior cadet visitors, none had instruction disrupted in this manner. While it was unclear whether all of these episodes took place in Schofield's presence, the commandant held that Schofield had violated the superintendent's orders by permitting other cadets to "impose" on the candidates. Schofield insisted that no obscene questions had been asked in his hearing, and he argued that the candidates' statements indicated that the comments had been made "in a low tone." Schofield admitted that on the Friday in question some cadets had come in and were quizzing candidates while he was busy drilling at the blackboard his most deficient students. In defending himself, Schofield insisted that cadet visitation of the section rooms and having the candidates stand when senior cadets entered the room was the "universal custom."[18]

This "excuse" particularly infuriated Superintendent Henry Brewerton. Brewerton had worked hard to suppress the hazing of new cadets.[19] During their initial summer, new cadets were subjected to a certain amount of hazing that usually stopped once classes began in September. At summer camp, for example, senior cadets would try to steal the new cadets' clothes so that they would have to report to morning formation "out of uniform."[20] They would sneak up on new cadets during guard duty and see if they could steal their weapons. The superintendent urged plebes to use their bayonets to fend off these assaults.[21] Nearly fifty years later, Schofield admitted to a "misunderstanding" with a sentinel while acting as corporal of the guard. Upon his approach, the guard tore Schofield's coat with a bayonet, and Schofield threw him in a ditch and ruined his musket. Schofield then picked the lad up, apologized, and traded muskets with him.[22] While the scope of hazing at this time was relatively minor and would become more severe at the post–Civil War academy, it nevertheless constituted a serious public relations problem for West Point. The academy had been under continual attack from Jacksonian critics who labeled it an aristocratic institution. The entrance examination was a particular sore point for these Democratic politicians. Even Jefferson Davis, the first academy graduate to become secretary of war, rejected higher admission standards as undemocratic.[23]

Though Brewerton's report concurred with Schofield's request for a court-martial, Secretary Conrad summarily dismissed him. In the summer of 1852, Schofield traveled to Washington to plead his case. Armed with letters from his classmates, he endeavored to rally political support to overturn the decision. After several unproductive meetings with congressmen and the secretary of war, Schofield, as a "citizen of Illinois in trouble," finally gained the assistance of the "Little Giant," Senator Stephen Douglas. At first reluctant to get involved with the Whig administration, Douglas ultimately agreed that there was nothing left but to "put in the reserve." While an anxious Schofield waited outside, Douglas met with the secretary and got his promise to let Schofield return to West Point for a court-martial. Schofield recalled that this experience "taught me that innocence and justice sometimes need powerful backing. Implicit trust in Providence does not seem to justify any neglect to employ also the biggest battalions and the heaviest guns."[24]

During the fall term Schofield went about his studies with dismissal hanging over his head. His court-martial was convened on September 9, 1852, and finally published its decision on December 13, 1852. Serving on this court were such future Civil War generals and Schofield colleagues as Philip St. George Cooke, E. R. S. Canby, George H. Thomas, and Fitz John Porter. For hazing the candidates on June 18, the court found Cadets Oliver D. Green, James Wright, and David P. Hancock guilty of disorderly conduct and disobedience of orders. The court sentenced them to suspension from the academy until July 1, 1853, and then returned to the First Class. For disorderly conduct, disobedience of orders, and neglect of duty, the court sentenced Cadet John M. Schofield to be dismissed from the service. However, based on Schofield's previous good conduct and on the recommendation of a majority of the members of the court, the secretary of war agreed to remit the sentence. Sixteen years later, as secretary of war, Schofield would discover that all but two of the thirteen court members voted for remission. Significantly, the two officers who voted to dismiss Schofield from the service and end his military career were George H. Thomas and Fitz John Porter.[25]

Schofield's court-martial had little lasting impact on his career. Court-martial was a relatively common occurrence at the academy, and in the army generally. The academy inculcated an exacting standard of duty into the cadets. The leadership took neglect of duty and breaches in discipline seriously. O. O. Howard was court-martialed for fighting in the mess hall with southerner L. R. Browne.[26] Even the golden James B. McPherson did not escape the rigorous application of regulations. When he failed to prevent a group of cadets from riding on an "unauthorized" omnibus, the academy demoted him from first captain to quartermaster.[27]

Schofield's narrow escape from dismissal was not that uncommon for the academy, which combined stern standards of discipline and accountability with clemency. The same court that remitted Schofield's sentence also remitted the sentences of Cadets Stephen Weed and Ezekiel Holloway for drunkenness on duty.[28] Philip Sheridan had faced a more serious charge in September 1851. Angered at the imperious behavior of Cadet Sergeant William Terrill of Virginia, Sheridan threatened him with a bayonet. After Terrill reported the incident, an enraged Sheridan attacked him again with his fists. Instead of expulsion, Brewerton suspended Sheridan for one year, and he thus joined Schofield's class of 1853.[29]

Fighting, especially during a time of increasing sectional animosity, was a particular problem for the academy leaders. The army needed disciplined, but not docile, officers. Captain Alden, the commandant of cadets, upon noting that a hostile clique was persecuting O. O. Howard, once gave the cadet some advice. As the commandant, Alden said, he would punish Howard for any infraction of regulations. However, as a father to a son, "If I were in your place, I would knock some man down."[30]

During this fall term, Schofield roomed with the redoubtable James B. McPherson and the amiable LaRhett L. Livingston.[31] Schofield's demotion from cadet lieutenant to private, however, made it more difficult for him to avoid demerits. Smoking and lateness were his most common faults. His tactical officer, Lieutenant John M. Jones, who would die as a Confederate brigadier general leading the Stonewall Brigade at the Wilderness in May 1864, was highly respected but strict. In January Schofield applied for a transfer to Company C, where he would serve under the more lenient Lieutenant Milton Cogswell and would room with his lifelong friend, Cadet Captain Thomas Vincent. Ultimately, Schofield scraped by with 196 demerits, four short of the limit.[32]

Scholastically, Schofield continued to do well. While First Classmen studied such academic subjects as engineering, ethics, and mineralogy and geology, the final year also included military subjects. For most Civil War–era West Pointers, these classes, which were mostly low-level drills, constituted the first and last formal instruction they would receive in combat tactics. Still, Schofield was especially proud of placing first in infantry tactics, surpassing even McPherson.[33] He finished eleventh in artillery, his future combat branch, and thirty-fifth in cavalry. Hood finished number three in cavalry, his highest academic achievement at West Point. Meanwhile, Sheridan, the best battlefield commander of the class, finished twenty-fifth in cavalry, fortieth in artillery, and forty-seventh in infantry. In the final class standings, out of fifty-five cadets, McPherson finished first, Schofield seventh, Sheridan thirty-fifth, and Hood forty-fourth. McPherson, as befitted his class standing, was commissioned in the engineers, Schofield in the artillery, and Sheridan and Hood in the infantry.[34] On graduation day, the commandant of cadets twice singled out Schofield, once for graduating first in infantry tactics, and again for "not carrying musket properly in ranks."[35]

Brevet Second Lieutenant Schofield, 2nd Artillery, reported to Fort Moultrie, South Carolina, in September 1853, where he was immediately placed in charge of a battery. The guns of his battery would later fire on Fort Sumter. The young officer was fortunate to have an old sergeant to guide him in his duties; Schofield later pitied the volunteer officers who had to train raw regiments, with "not even one old sergeant to teach them anything." After a few months, the War Department reassigned him to Fort Capron, Indian River, Florida, where he was reunited with his old roommate, LaRhett Livingston. Schofield also became acquainted with Ambrose Powell Hill, U.S. Military Academy class of 1847. The winter of 1853–54 was a period of armed truce between the United States and the Seminole Nation, yet Schofield found that life there "was not by any means monotonous." In addition to hunting and fishing and courier trips back to Charleston, Schofield supervised road and construction details aimed at securely confining the Seminoles within the Everglades.[36]

Still interested in pursuing a career in the law, Schofield took Blackstone, Kent, and other law books with him. He read the entire legal code of Florida and committed much of the U.S. Constitution to memory. This intense study proved useful in his career, for military officers of his generation were frequently called upon to interpret and enforce military and civil laws. Henry Halleck, William T. Sherman, and many other senior officers were lawyers, and in the 1880s the University of Chicago would award Schofield an honorary LL.D. in law. Knowledge of the law was considered so important that in 1880, General Sherman's contribution to the new *Journal of the Military Service Institution of the United States* was a long essay on military law.[37]

By the winter of 1854–55, the War Department ordered the occupation of Fort Jupiter, the construction of several blockhouses along Lake Okeechobee, and the reopening of the old military road. Schofield was assigned to the tasks. With the advent of warm weather, fever broke out among the troops at Fort Jupiter. Schofield and nearly every man, woman, and child came down with fever, probably malaria. When he recovered, Schofield reported the situation and soon afterward the troops were evacuated back to Fort Capron. Schofield's mission ended before the Seminoles discovered the army's plans. His friend George L. Hartsuff, academy class of 1852, was not so lucky. The Seminoles attacked Hartsuff's command, killing several and severely wounding him. Hartsuff also nearly died of yellow fever. During the Civil War, Hartsuff was again severely wounded at Antietam. He, nevertheless, rose to command the XXIII Corps, Schofield's future command, before his wounds and illness forced him from active field command. He retired in 1871 and died in 1874 at age forty-four of pneumonia brought on by his wounds. "Hartsuff," Schofield wrote, "was one of the strongest, bravest, finest soldiers I ever knew . . . but, unlike myself, he was always in bad luck." While Schofield was not shy about his own achievements, in his memoirs he repeatedly acknowledged his good fortune in contrast to many of his equally accomplished contemporaries.[38]

Since there was no doctor available at Fort Capron, Schofield was placed in charge of the other twenty-five to thirty convalescing soldiers. He conducted sick call every morning by mimicking what other doctors had done to him. His patients survived. When A. P. Hill returned from Fort Jupiter on his way home for sick leave, he had a relapse and grew desperately ill. Schofield and others nursed him night and day for a long period. By the time Hill had recovered sufficiently to continue his journey home, the War Department had promoted Schofield to first lieutenant and ordered him to instructor duty at West Point. Hill and Schofield departed Florida together, but on the steamer it was Schofield's turn to have a relapse. Hill cared for him at Savannah, then Charleston, and finally at Hill's home at Culpeper, Virginia. Rest and a discreet number of brandied mint juleps prepared by Hill's father restored Schofield's health.

Nevertheless, Schofield would suffer from periodic bouts of malaria for the rest of his life. By December 1855, Schofield was recovered enough to report for duty at West Point. Hill accompanied him on the trip. It was the last time they ever met. Hill's death at Petersburg in April 1864 stung Schofield. Though now an enemy, Schofield never forgot his kind and esteemed friend.[39]

Schofield's assignment back to the academy after little more than two years pleased him greatly. As an assistant professor of natural philosophy, Schofield felt vindicated for his earlier "bad conduct." For the next four years, he served under the renowned professor W. H. C. Bartlett. Bartlett, academy class of 1826, was one of America's foremost astronomers. He had studied astronomy in Europe and continued his observations at West Point. He was the first American to employ photography when he captured a solar eclipse in 1854. Bartlett was the author of popular textbooks on acoustics, astronomy, optics, mechanics, and molecular physics. Bartlett's course was perhaps the most difficult at the academy. Unlike most permanent professors, Bartlett taught the recitation sections himself rather than let the military assistant instructors conduct them. His nervous temperament and impatience with those who lacked his passion for the subject intimidated many students.[40]

Schofield found that the "law had no longer any charms for me," and he soon learned to share his boss's passion for natural philosophy and astronomy and more. He began by mastering analytical mechanics. By 1860, he had completed a draft of a textbook on physics, which he set aside when the war began. Bartlett's second daughter, Harriet, further captivated the young assistant professor, and in June 1857 John Schofield married her. His roommate Thomas Vincent was on hand as best man.[41] John and Harriet would have five children together before she died in 1889.[42] The marriage of young officers to the daughters of their superiors was relatively common in the nineteenth-century army. (John and Harriet's daughter Mary would marry Schofield's aide-de-camp, Avery Andrews.) As a new family man, Schofield was very happy at West Point. Although he appeared a bit standoffish to new cadets, he and his wife opened their home to the friends and relatives of the cadets. Outwardly strict, Schofield was really softhearted and later admitted that he was never "compelled to report a cadet for any deficiency, nor to find one deficient in studies."[43]

By the summer of 1860, with a wife, two sons, and a budding career in science, Schofield was losing his taste for the army. After four years, he remained the nineteenth first lieutenant in his regiment. He foresaw "no captaincy in sight for me during the ordinary lifetime of man." Resolved to leave the army, Schofield accepted the position of professor of physics and civil engineering at Washington University in St. Louis, Missouri. Professor Bartlett was from St.

Louis and doubtless helped to secure the appointment. But Schofield's father-in-law was also an intimate friend of Jefferson Davis, who urged the lieutenant to retain his commission. This former secretary of war and future president of the Confederacy ironically predicted that promotion opportunities might be better in a year or two, and so Schofield applied for a military leave of absence instead. To add further irony to the situation, Commanding General Winfield Scott, a bitter enemy of Davis, gave Schofield a highly flattering endorsement of his request.[44]

As a professor at Washington University, Schofield met many of the most prominent men in St. Louis. Of special significance were Frank P. Blair, congressman and future major general, and Charles Gibson, the protégé of future attorney general Edward Bates and the nephew of the future Unionist governor of Missouri, Hamilton Gamble. While Gibson served in the Justice Department as the equivalent of solicitor general during the war, Schofield lived in his St. Louis home. In moving to St. Louis but retaining his commission, the Schofield luck persisted—in just over a year he would be promoted not just to captain but to brigadier general.[45] Indeed, Schofield's connections to Missouri political leaders would boost him to brigadier general of Volunteers by November 1861, well before his academy classmates James B. McPherson (May 1862) and Philip H. Sheridan (July 1862).[46]

Saving Missouri

The revolutionary events of 1861 proved to be the making of John M. Schofield. The crisis overturned the normal constitutional arrangements. The tiny regular army also began to splinter amid apprehension, uncertainty, and suspicion.[1] Lieutenant John M. Schofield, in aligning himself with Nathaniel Lyon and Frank Blair, became a secondary figure in the extralegal mustering of federal troops, the arrest of the lawful state militia, the overthrow of the elected governor, and ouster of the military department commander. Although Schofield was just a bit player in this initial drama, his uncharacteristic decision to join the "radicals" had a decisive influence on his career. Many senior officers who failed to respond to the crisis were pushed aside, while many junior officers advanced. After the war, most writers proclaimed General Nathaniel Lyon a hero and martyr who saved Missouri for the Union.[2] More recently, Lyon and his political ally Frank Blair have been accused of needlessly polarizing the situation and provoking the bloody civil war in Missouri. These changing interpretations cast the civil-military problems of Missouri in a new light.[3]

Missouri in 1861, like the nation, was badly divided. The state was primarily Democrat, while St. Louis, its largest city, was predominantly Republican. Although secessionists outnumbered Republicans, the vast majority of Missourians were conservative Democrats who favored the status quo. Calling themselves "Conditional Unionists," these conservatives hoped to avoid the impending conflict. They sought to stay in the Union, retain slavery, and remain neutral in "Lincoln's war" with the South. As in most revolutionary situations, the passionate men of the extremes would not accept neutrality. Missourians' desire to avoid war was understandable, if not realistic. They would be forced to choose.[4]

Foremost among the secessionist leaders were the newly elected governor of Missouri, Claiborne Jackson, and Sterling Price, major general of the Missouri State Militia. Jackson had been a stalwart of the proslavery wing of the Missouri Democratic Party, although in the 1860 election, Jackson positioned himself with a majority of Democrats and supported Stephen A. Douglas. Price, a Mexican War veteran and former Missouri governor, had initially opposed secession, but as Unionists consolidated their grip on St. Louis, he joined Jackson and was appointed to his leadership position in the Missouri State Militia.[5]

Newly elected Republican member of Congress Frank B. Blair Jr. and regular army captain Nathaniel Lyon led the "Unconditional Unionists." Blair's father was a prominent Missouri politician who had been a member of Andrew Jackson's "kitchen cabinet," and his brother, Montgomery, was Lincoln's postmaster general. Thus, Frank Blair had powerful political connections both in Missouri and in Washington, D.C., and the determination to exploit them to the fullest.[6] Nathaniel Lyon, born in Connecticut, graduated from the U.S. Military Academy in 1841 and served in the Seminole and Mexican Wars. His service in "Bleeding Kansas" confirmed him as a passionate abolitionist Republican. His arrival in St. Louis in February 1861 with a company of regulars to protect the arsenal was a propitious event for the Union cause in Missouri.[7] Lyon's arrival was not accidental, as Blair had used his political connections to replace disloyal or unreliable officers of the arsenal.[8]

Prominent "moderates" included Hamilton Gamble and Brigadier General William S. Harney, commander of the Department of the West. Gamble was the former law partner and brother-in-law of Lincoln's attorney general, Edward Bates. Though initially in favor of Missouri neutrality and opposed to any action that might provoke conflict, Gamble became the provisional governor after Claiborne Jackson fled south. Harney, who entered the army in 1818, was a hero in both the Seminole and Mexican Wars and was promoted to brigadier general in 1858 and appointed commander of the Department of the West. As a southern-born supporter of slavery, many ardent Unionists questioned his allegiance. Harney was not disloyal, but he was too easily swayed by those who, through either fear or bad faith, urged him to avoid any "inflammatory" actions.[9]

With the secession of the states of the Deep South, Governor Jackson called for a state convention on the issue. The state convention met in St. Louis from February 28 to March 22, 1861, and decisively voted in favor of remaining in the Union, but it also voted its support for the Crittenden Compromise, which would have guaranteed slavery in the Constitution.[10] Meanwhile, political factions began to marshal their military strength. In St Louis the Republican "Wide Awakes" and German *Turnverein* became the Home Guard, and the Democrat and mostly Irish "Broom Rangers" formed the basis of the paramilitary "Minute Men." Governor Richard Yates of Illinois secretly provided arms to Republican groups. Governor Jackson sought to rally prosouthern support, calling out the Missouri militia and sending representatives to southern states to secure arms.[11]

The attack on Fort Sumter in April 1861 prompted Lincoln to call on the states, including Missouri, to furnish volunteer regiments to preserve the Union and put down the rebellion. The process of raising and mustering into federal service regiments of state volunteers reflected peculiar American patterns of civilian control. While the president appointed officers in the regular army and general officers, state governors raised volunteer regiments and appointed the commissioned officers. Once raised by the governor, the volunteer units were then mustered into federal service. Lincoln pointedly summed up the federal government's dependence on the states in a letter to Governor Hamilton Gamble on July 28, 1862: "You ask for four regiments for Genl. Schofield and he asks the same of the Secretary of War. Please raise them for me, as I have them not, nor can have, till some governor gives them to me." The use of states to raise regiments meant that the Union army was a federal, not a national, army; hence, governors retained many powers of patronage and reward. Moreover, the spirit of democracy limited even the governors' authority by providing that one-third of the company officer positions be appointed from the ranks, based on the recommendation of the regimental commander and approval of the brigade commander.[12]

The War Department assigned an officer of the regular army to muster Missouri volunteers into federal service—Lieutenant John M. Schofield. However, Schofield's mission was frustrated by both the governor and the department commander. Governor Jackson, and many moderates, rejected Lincoln's call as unconstitutional. Jackson did not answer Schofield's request, and through the press he announced his refusal to provide men "to subjugate . . . sister states of the South." The governor denounced Lincoln's action as "illegal, unconstitutional, and revolutionary," as well as "inhuman and diabolical."[13] When Schofield reported to General Harney, his confidence in Harney's vigor was shaken when the old general refused to muster in troops on his own authority. Harney even minimized the crisis by declaring that "the State has not yet passed an ordinance of secession."[14] Unconditional Unionists, such as Blair and Lyon, demanded action to prevent a crisis. Harney, by inaction, sought not to provoke one.[15]

With Schofield's mission stymied by both the governor and the department commander, and the riots against federal troops in Baltimore, Unionist concern for the safety of the St. Louis arsenal rose dramatically. Blair and Lyon desperately sought outside aid and urged Harney to muster in the Home Guard to protect the city. Harney again refused, saying he had no authority to muster in troops independently. Blair frantically wrote his brother, Secretary of War Simon Cameron, and Cameron's political ally, Governor Andrew Curtin of Pennsylvania. To Curtin, Blair wrote that Harney refused to arm loyal men who were prepared to enter federal service and further that "our friends distrust Harney very much. He should be superseded immediately by putting another commander in this district. The object of the secessionists is to seize the Arsenal here with its 75,000 stands of arms."[16]

When on April 20, 1861, Jackson's state militia seized the 1,500 weapons at the federal arsenal at Liberty, Missouri, Blair and Lyon resolved to act, even without orders. The next day, Blair called Schofield from church services and sent him to Lyon. Lyon soon realized that Schofield had no independent authority to muster in the Home Guard and feared Harney would arrest him and undo their efforts. Instead, Blair and Schofield made another unsuccessful appeal to General Harney. In the light of the seizure at Liberty, Harney's continued refusal to act appears perverse. He somehow persisted in the belief that if he did nothing the crisis would dissipate. Late that afternoon, frustrated and desperate, Blair, Lyon, and Schofield arranged to have the 300 loyal men of the Home Guard, mostly Germans, mustered in secretly at the arsenal that night beginning at half past seven. With this action already under way, Lyon, at midnight, finally got a message from the War Department giving him authority to muster in troops. This message was written by Major Fitz John Porter, who had been traveling with Secretary Cameron in Pennsylvania when Blair's message to Governor Curtin had arrived. Porter, on his own authority, approved the mustering of the troops. The next day, Lyon received another message from the War Department informing him that Harney had been relieved of command and directing Lyon to execute the previous order "to arm loyal citizens, to protect public property, and execute the laws."[17] Their conspiracy against the complacent department commander had been affirmed.

By the next day Schofield had mustered in over 600 troops and 3,300 by the end of the month. Lyon expressed no doubt that he could raise the 10,000 authorized by the War Department. In addition to enrolling more troops, the president granted Captain Lyon the authority to declare martial law in St. Louis if six prominent citizens he named agreed. This was an extraordinary delegation of authority to a relatively junior military officer and a combination of public and private citizens. Winfield Scott endorsed the action with the apt comment, "It is revolutionary times, and therefore I do not object to the irregularity of this."[18]

The mustering and arming of the Home Guard did not end the threat to St.

Louis and the arsenal. Lyon's actions worried many moderates, and Governor Jackson's rejection of Lincoln's call for troops was popular with most Missourians who sought to remain neutral. Jackson, however, was anything but neutral. He urged the state legislature to vote for secession and urged passage of a new militia bill. Jackson even requested aid from Jefferson Davis, and Davis responded by sending him four cannon from the arsenal at Baton Rouge. When Davis requested a regiment to defend Virginia, Jackson urged caution, but he assured Davis that Missouri could "put 100,000 men in the field."[19] Brigadier General Daniel Frost of the state militia persuaded Governor Jackson to establish a militia camp outside St. Louis under the pretense of annual training. The state militia at "Camp Jackson," whose very name proclaimed its purpose, had little chance of overpowering Lyon's forces, but it served as a rallying point for secessionists throughout eastern Missouri.[20] Though it was outwardly lawful and peaceful, Lyon knew the militia at Camp Jackson constituted a threat to the Union cause. It was, as Schofield later called it, "an incipient rebel army which ought to be crushed in the bud."[21]

When Lyon learned that Winfield Scott had persuaded Lincoln to reinstate Harney and that Harney was returning on May 11, he decided to move against Camp Jackson. On the morning of May 10, Lyon with Schofield and nearly 10,000 troops surrounded Camp Jackson and demanded that Frost surrender. Shortly after Schofield returned with Frost's response to the surrender demand, a horse kicked Lyon and knocked him unconscious. With no time to waste in completing the surrender, Schofield and Captain Thomas Sweeney concealed Lyon's condition, quickly concluded the surrender terms, and took the formal surrender. The 1,500 prisoners were marched back to St. Louis, where Lyon charged Schofield with the task of paroling them. The object was not to punish the militia but to break it up as an organized force.[22] Once again, relatively junior officers had stepped forward and assumed responsibility while more senior officers had hung back.

Observing Captain Lyon's and Lieutenant Schofield's return to St. Louis with their prisoners were Mr. William T. Sherman and Mr. Ulysses S. Grant. This spectacle turned tragic when a drunken southern sympathizer opened fire on a Union officer. The new, undisciplined troops returned fire. The melee ended with twenty-eight dead civilians, including two women and a child. Sherman and his young son dove to the ground to avoid the gunfire.[23] The affair at Camp Jackson cheered Unionists, enraged secessionists, and frightened conservatives. Grant later observed that with the capture of the camp, the formerly bullying rebels grew quiet, while the Unionists became bolder, and even intolerant.[24]

Harney, upon his return, endorsed Lyon's actions, but he was still reluctant to act aggressively against the obviously prosecessionist state officials. Over the next few weeks, following his own and the public's desire for peace, Harney worked to maintain Missouri's neutrality.[25] Harney's position had support in Missouri and in Lincoln's cabinet. Conservative moderates, like Attorney General Edward Bates, continued to support Harney's policy, hoping that Missouri could avoid civil war.[26] His cabinet divided, Lincoln hesitated.

Lincoln's vacillation can be seen not only as a product of a divided cabinet, but as part of his own desire to respect Missouri public opinion and his conflicting realization that decisive action was needed. Lincoln was groping his way through the difficult task of formulating political-military strategy. The cabinet, wracked by personal and policy quarrels, was one of the few existing institutions to develop and coordinate the war effort. The president and the cabinet secretaries were aided by only a handful of personal assistants. The War Department consisted of staff bureaus that sought to administer their little empires with as little interference as possible. The secretary of war, Simon Cameron, to whom the staff bureaus reported, was a political hack and completely ignorant of military affairs. Lieutenant General Winfield Scott, perhaps the greatest American soldier of the nineteenth century, was a sick old man. His nearly ten years of self-exile in New York had further eroded working relationships with the War Department.[27] Thus, in the early days of the struggle for the Union, Lincoln often relied on trusted associates rather than the formal chain of command.

From a civil-military point of view, this approach is significant. Frank Blair, as an early Lincoln supporter, a local congressman, and the colonel of the newly mustered First Regiment Missouri Volunteers, clearly blurred formal distinctions between civil and military authorities. On May 16, Frank and Montgomery Blair convinced Lincoln to relieve Harney if he proved incapable of handling the emergency. Lincoln transmitted the order through Postmaster General Montgomery Blair to Frank Blair, with the instructions to implement the order if deemed absolutely necessary. Blair prudently waited for ten days, as Lincoln continued to warn Harney of the danger of inaction. Finally convinced that the nation could no longer afford Harney's naiveté, Blair delivered the relief order on May 30.[28]

The moderates still hoped to avoid open conflict, and they urged newly appointed brigadier general Lyon to meet with the state officials. On June 11, with assurance of "safe passage," Jackson and Price met with Blair and Lyon in St. Louis. Jackson and Price spoke of their earnest desire for peace. The tempestuous Lyon listened suspiciously for the first half hour and then began to talk, soon dominating the conversation. The four argued for nearly four hours before Lyon impatiently ended the meeting with a chilling declaration: "Better, sir, far better, that the blood of every man, woman, and child within the limits of the State should flow, than that she should defy the federal government. This means war."[29] Jackson and Price left that night. The next day, Jackson called for 50,000 volunteers to resist the federal troops and made plans for withdrawing the state government to Boonville. By June 15, Lyon occupied the state capital, Jefferson City, and two days later he took Boonville. By the end of the month, the duly elected governor of Missouri was in full flight to southwest Missouri.[30] Civil war had come to Missouri.

The spring of 1861 was certainly, as Winfield Scott said, a "revolutionary" time. The fear of civil war and of the coercive power of a standing army has been an important theme in American military policy and civil-military relations, dating back to the English Civil War. The regular army had been kept small for both ideological and financial reasons. However, the forces that drove Jackson and his followers into exile were not Harney's regulars, but Blair's citizen soldiers. Lincoln, as commander in chief, had precious few military assets at the beginning of the war. Initially, Lincoln could not order operations so much as authorize, delegate, and even acquiesce to the actions of others. He had to rely on state governors to raise troops or, in the case of Missouri, on energetic politicians like Congressman Blair. Further, the president had to rely on the audacious decisions of junior officers like Nathaniel Lyon and John Schofield.

After Camp Jackson, Schofield returned to his assignment of organizing and mustering the newly raised Missouri regiments. Blair's 1st Regiment Infantry Missouri Volunteers elected Schofield regimental major on April 26. Major Schofield divided his time between the mustering duties and helping to organize and train the regiment. On May 14, Schofield was also promoted to captain in the 1st Artillery Regiment, a promotion that seemed impossible a few years earlier. The resignation of southerners, of course, had opened promotions in the regular army. Even so, the U.S. Army was in fact two armies: the regular army, which expanded only slightly during the war, and the volunteer army, which furnished the bulk of the Union forces.

While rank in the regular army would be important for postwar duty, the path to high command led through commanding volunteer units. Many regular army officers, especially those with political connections, requested transfers from their regular units to serve with the volunteers. However, the War Department denied the requests of many unlucky officers, especially those in the specialty corps like engineers, ordnance, and artillery. The continued separation of regular and volunteer forces meant that the Union did not fully tap the officer and enlisted expertise available to it in building the new armies. Again, Schofield was one of the lucky ones. Major Schofield completed his duties as mustering officer on June 24, and on June 26 he joined General Lyon at Boonville, as his adjutant general, or chief of staff.[31]

Though the secessionist government of Governor Jackson was in flight, the struggle for Missouri had just begun. Lyon sought to exploit his momentary numerical superiority by breaking up the secessionist troops organizing in Missouri. Having driven the rebels away from the Missouri River, he now intended to move on southwestern Missouri. On July 3, Lyon, with 2,000 men, marched for Springfield, while 1,500 men under Colonel Franz Sigel marched from St. Louis. Lyon joined Sigel at Springfield on July 13. The July heat and supply difficulties sapped the command's strength. The railroad from St. Louis extended only to Rolla, which was 125 miles from Springfield. Lacking wagons, Lyon could not bring the supplies forward. Unable to sustain an advance, Lyon also faced the prospect of his forces disappearing as their three-month enlistments ended. He had reports that the rebels were massing 20,000 men to confront his 5,000. Unwilling to abandon southwestern Missouri, Lyon pleaded for reinforcements from the new department commander, Major General John C. Fremont.[32]

By August, Lyon's position in Springfield was becoming untenable. Sterling Price's Missourians had joined the Confederate forces of General Ben Mc-Culloch. This force totaled about 10,000, though many were not properly armed or equipped. On August 5, the Confederates advanced to Wilson's Creek, about ten miles southwest of Springfield.[33] Lyon's request for reinforcements had elicited little aid from Fremont. Fremont judged that the possible loss of Cairo or St. Louis was more important than that of the Ozark region, and he had only 15,000 troops available to meet the multiple threats. Fremont further believed that Lyon had enough troops to defend himself and, if not, had the good sense to withdraw. On August 6, Fremont wrote Lyon that if he could not maintain his position at Springfield, he should fall back toward Rolla until reinforcements should meet him. But Fremont did not realize how emotionally committed Lyon was to the rescue of Missouri.[34]

At an August 8 council of war, most of Lyon's senior officers, including Schofield, supported a withdrawal, but at the last moment, the aggressive captain Thomas Sweeney persuaded Lyon to fight. That night, desperately hoping that surprise would overcome his numerical inferiority, Lyon marched his small army out of Springfield. He soon canceled the attack, sensing that he had delayed the march too long and having a premonition of disaster. The next day, Lyon responded to Fremont's message of August 6 that the enemy was ten

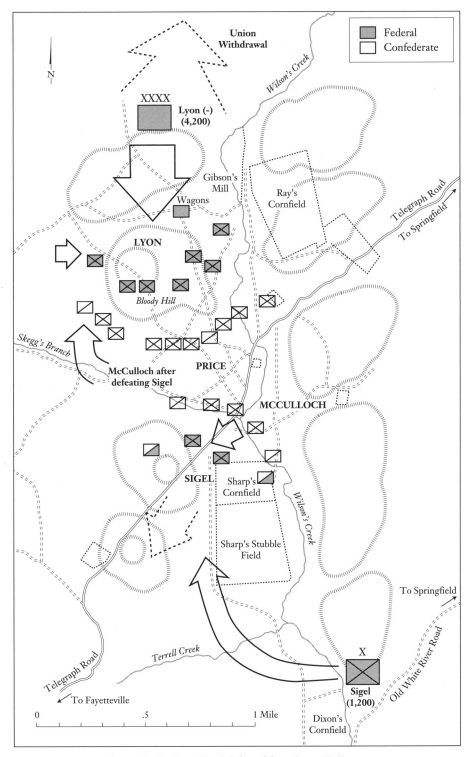

The Battle of Wilson's Creek (adapted from George E. Knapp,
The Wilson's Creek Staff Ride and Battlefield Tour*)*

miles away and that he could resist a frontal assault, but that he would have to retire if the enemy moved to surround him. Lyon gave no indication of his continued intention to attack the Confederate camp.[35]

Lyon was torn by many emotions: his commitment to the Union cause, his loyalty to the Unionists of southwestern Missouri, his concern that a withdrawal would greatly encourage secession, and his fear of personal failure. This fear of failure, combined with political vulnerability, played a role in the plan for an August 10 attack. Shortly after dispatching his reply to Fremont, Colonel Franz Sigel presented Lyon with a plan to divide the army and send Sigel's brigade on a mission to attack the Confederate rear. Sigel was a prominent member of the German community in St. Louis. His background as a graduate of a German military academy in Karlsruhe, as a revolutionist in 1848, and of service in the New York militia inspired many Germans to join his regiments.[36] Over the strenuous objections of Sweeney and Schofield, Lyon adopted Sigel's perilous plan. Lyon had served with Scott and Harney in Mexico and had seen such a plan succeed at the battle of Cerro Gordo.[37] But Lyon was not Scott, Sigel not Harney, and Price not Santa Anna. Sigel's scheme to divide the 5,600-man Union armies in the face of what they supposed was a 20,000-man Confederate army relied not just on surprise, but on blind panic. When other commanders complained of the decision, Lyon responded, "Fremont won't sustain me. Sigel has a great reputation, and if I fail against his advice it will give Sigel command and ruin me." Afraid to retreat, Lyon chose to fight. Fearful of defeat, he adopted a desperate strategy.[38]

As the army marched out of Springfield on the evening of August 9, Lyon's pessimism and depression increased. Schofield, his adjutant, recounted that Lyon rarely spoke except to issue necessary orders. As Lyon and Schofield shared a blanket that night on the rocky ground, Lyon was "oppressed with the responsibility of his situation."[39] In his despondency, he believed "he was the intended victim of a deliberate sacrifice to another's [presumably Fremont's] ambition." Lyon fatalistically told Schofield that he would "gladly give my life for a victory."[40] At dawn, Lyon's troops advanced and ran into the Confederate pickets. Federal troops next confronted rebel cavalry units encamped nearly a mile north of the main camp, who hastily deployed to retard the attack. As the rebel skirmishers withdrew, the Union line slowly advanced to what became known as "Bloody Hill." After taking the hill at about 6:00 A.M., the federal attack halted as rebel artillery opened up on the exposed Union line and General Price unleashed a series of counterattacks.

Meanwhile, to the south, Colonel Sigel had successfully marched behind the Confederates undetected. Upon hearing the firing of Lyon's attack, Sigel began his assault on the Confederate camp through Sharp's cornfield. Sigel caught the rebel cavalry units there by surprise and quickly established a position at the north end of the field that blocked Telegraph Road, the main road between Springfield and Fayetteville. Believing that Lyon had routed the Confederates, Sigel now halted his brigade to await Lyon's men who would sweep the retreating enemy into his arms. Unfortunately, the rebels were not routed and had by no means given up the fight. While Sigel waited, Price and McCulloch rallied their troops. Around 8:30 A.M., McCulloch personally led a charge by the 3rd Louisiana against Sigel. Thinking that these gray-clad troops were the 1st Iowa, Sigel hesitated. The rebels got to within forty yards of his position before he realized his mistake and gave the order to fire. By then, it was too late. The Louisianans charged and Sigel's command disintegrated. Retreating the way they had come, Sigel's brigade hurried back to Springfield. Of his 1,200 troops he lost 35 killed, 132 wounded, and 130 missing, and he lost five of his six guns.[41]

On Bloody Hill, Lyon and his men were unaware of Sigel's rout. The federals were holding their own against the increasingly heavy rebel attacks. Schofield observed that the enemy had made little use of his superior numbers by making frontal, piecemeal attacks. If the leaders displayed no great tactical skill, the raw troops on both sides were showing their courage. Still, the casualties were beginning to mount. By 9:00 A.M., Lyon, whose horse was shot out from under him and who had been wounded in the head and the leg, was becoming dispirited. To Schofield he said, "I fear the day is lost." Schofield replied, "No General; let us try it again." Encouraged, or perhaps shaking off the shock of his wounds, Lyon and Schofield then separated to rally the Union line and lead different regiments in counterattacks. So Schofield and Lyon parted for the last time.[42]

Schofield headed for the right-center of the line. Hoping to shatter the enemy with a bayonet attack, which the American army had used so effectively in Mexico, Schofield placed himself at the head of the 1st Iowa and commanded, "Charge!" Fighting with the bayonet took great courage and discipline; few soldiers were ever killed by the bayonet because one side or the other would generally flinch. The increased range of the rifled musket added to the difficulty of a bayonet attack. The 1st Iowa advanced "splendidly," but when they came under fire, they flinched, halted, and returned the fire. Schofield suddenly found himself "between two fires" and had to make his way back to the line with as much dignity as possible. Upon returning to the firing line, he encountered a soldier "too brave to think of running away, and yet too much frightened to be able to fight." He was rapidly loading and firing his rifle into the air. Schofield shook him and aroused him from his trance.[43]

Meanwhile, on the right flank Lyon was rallying elements of the 2nd Kansas. Waving his hat in the air, he shouted, "Come on my brave boys, I will lead you! Forward!" As he turned, he was struck in the chest and fell from his horse. As the 2nd Kansas repelled the Confederate attack, Lyon's orderly and a few other soldiers carried him to the rear, where he soon died. Lieutenant William M. Wherry, Lyon's aide and Schofield's future staff officer, covered Lyon's face with a coat, hoping to conceal the general's death from the troops. Schofield, after successfully leading the 1st Iowa, encountered Wherry with Lyon. He then captured a loose "secesh" horse and rode to tell Major Samuel Sturgis that as the senior surviving officer, he was in command.[44]

Regular army major Samuel D. Sturgis was a West Point graduate of the class of 1846—the same class as George B. McClellan, Stonewall Jackson, and George Pickett. As Sturgis assumed command, McCulloch and Price prepared for a new assault. Price directed Brigadier General Nicholas B. Pearce's Arkansas Brigade to the left flank for the attack. Thinking that these were Sigel's men, the Union artillery did not fire on this redeployment. Even so, the steady Union line repulsed this latest and heaviest enemy assault. Around 11:30 A.M., in the lull following the rebel assault, Sturgis held a brief council of war with the remaining senior officers. Though the federals had repelled every attack, the troops had been fighting for nearly six hours without food or water, and their ammunition was running low. With the fate of Sigel still unknown and fearing yet more rebel attacks, Sturgis decided to withdraw while he was still able. After retiring to a new position a few miles to the rear, Sturgis learned of Sigel's rout and elected to return to Springfield.[45]

Several officers, particularly Lieutenant Colonel Charles Blair of the 2nd Kansas and Gordon Granger, assistant adjutant general to Lyon and future corps commander, objected to retreat. They thought the battle nearly won.[46] Though he gave no hint of criticism in his official report, Schofield, in his memoirs, concluded that the "retreat was undoubtedly an error." "It was only necessary to hold our ground, trusting to the pluck and endurance of our men, and the victory would have been ours," he wrote.[47] From hindsight, Schofield knew that the Confederates totaled around 10,000, not the 20,000 he and Lyon and Sturgis had believed at the time. He had also learned of the terrible casualties of the Confederates and the dissension between Price and McCulloch over the Missouri campaign. Still, a decision to stand would have been risky. The Union and the Confederates had each suffered 1,200–1,300 casualties, yet this was nearly 25 percent of the Union force and only 13 percent of the Confederates.[48] With more than seven hours of daylight yet remaining, the determined Price had not given up the battle. The Confederates may have employed their superiority in cavalry to turn the Union line and block their retreat to Springfield. Even if the Union had held the field, supply shortages and the impending expiration of the enlistment of many troops would have forced a withdrawal to Rolla. By remaining, the federals hazarded a temporary psychological victory against a truly catastrophic defeat.

Though relatively small, the battle of Wilson's Creek was one of the bloodiest of the war, with a combined casualty rate of 16 percent. Along with Bull Run, it dispelled the idea of easy victory.[49] Two days later the Union forces abandoned Springfield. Sigel, now in command, bungled the march back to Rolla so badly that the other senior officers rebelled and insisted that Sturgis again take charge. Sigel protested but ultimately submitted. The tired command arrived in Rolla on August 19. By then Schofield had relinquished his duties as adjutant general and returned to his regiment, the 1st Missouri. Three weeks later Price, with 10,000 men but without McCulloch's command, which returned to Arkansas, advanced north to the Missouri River, hoping to recruit more soldiers and ignite an uprising. Price gained some success in capturing 2,400 Union soldiers at Lexington, but the general uprising failed, and Price ultimately withdrew into southwestern Missouri.

The Wilson's Creek campaign had been highly instructive to the twenty-nine-year-old Schofield. To begin with, he had passed the first tests of an officer—energy and poise. In camp and on the march, soldiers liked to see energy and efficiency among their officers. One private described Schofield, with perhaps a bit of hyperbole, as "a handsome young man, and was full of steam" and praised his "sleepless" attention to duty.[50] Amid the fear, death, and intrinsic hysteria of battle, soldiers draw courage from the confidence and calm poise of their leaders. In reports of the battle, Fremont commended Schofield for his "cool and conspicuous courage and for his constant effort to inspire confidence among the troops." Sturgis commended Schofield's "coolness and equanimity" and "the confidence his example inspired." The *St. Louis Missouri Democrat* reported that a witness to the battle insisted that "a braver soldier does not live."[51] Schofield would eventually receive the Medal of Honor for his actions at Wilson's Creek.[52]

Schofield also learned important lessons about higher command. Foremost among them was that courage was not enough. He witnessed Lyon's passions descend into reckless fatalism. Despite Schofield's view that they should have held their ground on the battlefield, he considered the entire battle as needless. In his memoirs Schofield noted that "Lyon's personal feeling was so strongly enlisted in the Union cause . . . that he could not take the cool, soldierly view of the situation. The fruitless sacrifice at Wilson's Creek was wholly unjustifiable.

Our retreat to Rolla was open and perfectly safe." Schofield suspected Lyon threw his life away when he realized that he had provoked an "unnecessary battle on so unequal terms." Lyon, like most Americans, believed the war would be short, so any setback was viewed with alarm. In the aftermath of the staggering casualties from the battle, Schofield learned that neither side would give in easily. It was going to be a long and costly war. The Wilson's Creek campaign reinforced the impulses of his cautious and methodical nature.[53]

After the retreat Schofield got a firsthand look at the chaos and confusion of Fremont's headquarters. Fremont ordered him to convert the 1st Missouri into an artillery regiment, and Schofield spent several frustrating weeks attempting to obtain the necessary equipment to accomplish the mission. Several times, he obtained Fremont's personal order for the arsenal to issue him cannon, only to arrive at the arsenal and find that Fremont had been subsequently persuaded to rescind the order. The Blairs also experienced doubts about their handpicked commander. Shortly after Schofield's arrival, he accompanied Frank Blair on a visit to Fremont's palatial headquarters. Schofield was surprised that Fremont did not ask him a single question about the battle of Wilson's Creek. He was then stunned when Fremont directed them to a large map, where he at length outlined a grandiose campaign plan. Fremont "proposed to march the main Army of the West though southwestern Missouri and northwestern Arkansas to the valley of the Arkansas River, and then down that river to the Mississippi, thus turning all the Confederate defenses of the Mississippi River down to and below Memphis." After the meeting Blair asked Schofield what he thought. Schofield replied in words "rather too strong to repeat in print." Blair replied, "I have been suspecting that for some time."[54]

The Blairs, who had sponsored Fremont's appointment, became disillusioned within weeks of the "Pathfinder's" assumption of command. After the defeat at Wilson's Creek, Blair urged his brother Montgomery to support Fremont's demand for money, troops, and the authority to appoint state officers but insisted that Fremont "be held responsible for the results." A week later, the hope that Fremont would bring order to the administrative chaos of the Department of the West was dashed. Fremont, protected by a large staff, was remote and often inaccessible. Frank complained to Montgomery that Fremont "occupied himself with trifles" and had created "a sort of a court." By September 1, Frank Blair wrote his brother that Lincoln ought to replace Fremont. On September 16 the breach became an open scandal, when Fremont ordered Blair's arrest for "insidious and dishonorable efforts to bring my authority into contempt with the Government." Though Fremont released him a week later, the spectacle of a commanding general arresting a congressman (and colonel) added to the turmoil and to Lincoln's frustrations.[55]

The increasingly widespread doubts about Fremont's judgment extended well beyond contracting irregularities and administrative inefficiency.[56] Fremont soon began quarreling with the political leaders of Missouri and issuing politically sensitive proclamations without the approval of the Lincoln administration. Fremont clashed with Governor Gamble about the control of state troops, about Gamble's August 3 proclamation, which promised amnesty to those who had taken up arms with Jackson and Price, and about Fremont's declaration of martial law in St. Louis.[57] Amid these disputes, Fremont issued a proclamation on August 30 declaring martial law throughout the state of Missouri. He argued that circumstances rendered it necessary for him to "assume the administrative powers of the state. All persons captured in arms against the United States were to be shot after a military court-martial."[58]

More provocatively, Fremont announced that the property of those who took up arms against the Union would be confiscated and their slaves freed. Even some Missourians who thought rebels "should be shot summarily by the thousands" recoiled at "Fremont's notion about the negroes."[59] As an abolitionist politician, Fremont saw the conflict as a war to save the Union and end slavery. Fremont's proclamation created a national controversy. President Lincoln learned of the proclamation from the newspapers and immediately dispatched his concerns to Fremont. Dreading Confederate retaliation, Lincoln ordered there were to be no executions without his approval. Fearing the effect on other border states, he then requested that Fremont modify his emancipation order to conform with the August 6 act of Congress, which limited emancipation to those slaves forced to take up arms or actively participate in the war. Responding on September 8, the general told the commander in chief that he would not on his own rescind the order: "If upon reflection your better judgment still decides that I am wrong in the article respecting the liberation of slaves, I have to ask that you will openly direct me to make the correction. The implied censure will be received as a soldier always should the reprimand of his chief. If I were to retract of my own accord, it would imply that I myself thought it wrong."[60]

Lincoln replied that he would "cheerfully" make his request an "open order" and proceeded to do so. By forcing Lincoln to countermand the policy publicly, Fremont was playing to the abolitionist wing of the Republican Party. Fremont's emancipation policy was an attempt to advance Union war aims well beyond those articulated by the president. Lincoln recognized the politics behind the measure and the challenge not only to his policies, but also to his authority. In defending his position, Lincoln wrote to his friend Orville Browning that Fremont's proclamation was "purely political" and "not within the range of military law, or necessity." Further, "the general may not do anything he pleases." This was but the first of Lincoln's many clashes with politically minded generals.[61]

Though Fremont had created political problems for the administration, and he had lost the confidence of most of the important political figures in Missouri, his lack of military success was the ultimate cause of his fall. Lincoln could have overlooked all these problems if Fremont had produced some military successes to demonstrate his effectiveness. While ideology, partisanship, or friendship drove many politicians, Lincoln increasingly adopted the criterion of military effectiveness for the appointment and retention of commanders. By late October, Lincoln was so concerned about Fremont's ability that he issued orders to Major General Samuel Curtis for Fremont's removal. He directed Curtis to forward the orders to Fremont if he had not yet fought, or was on the verge of fighting a battle.[62] On November 3 Curtis's messenger reached Fremont at Springfield, and that evening General David Hunter assumed command of the department. Lincoln, ever the master political juggler, decided to give Fremont another chance and appointed him to command the Mountain Department of Virginia, where he performed dismally against Stonewall Jackson. When he refused to serve under John Pope in June 1862, Fremont sat out the rest of the war "awaiting orders."[63]

On November 9, 1861, the War Department dissolved the Western Department and created the Department of the Missouri, which included Missouri, Iowa, Minnesota, Wisconsin, Illinois, Arkansas, and western Kentucky. To command it, the War Department appointed Henry W. Halleck.[64] High command in Missouri had proven a militarily difficult and politically perilous position. The pace of events and the mingling of political and military questions in the midst of a civil war demanded that a commander have not just military skill, but political acumen. Harney had failed because he too readily listened to those politicians who sought conciliation and counseled caution. He refused to act without authority, yet complacently refused to request authority as the crisis deepened. His desire for peace was heartfelt and even noble, but shortsighted and dangerous for the Union cause in Missouri. Fremont, on the other hand, was only too willing to exert his authority and to make political decisions. He sought to usurp the powers of both the federal and state governments. His self-isolation and grandiose manner further alienated allies. While his policies on emancipation galvanized abolitionists, they repelled the more "moderate" citizens whose support, particularly in the border states, Lincoln so desperately needed.

Schofield had held a ringside seat at these events. He had earned the respect of these fellow soldiers and the confidence of important men. He had seen firsthand the central role that politics played in the art of high command. His political education as a general had begun. The new department commander, Henry Halleck, brought different skills to the job. While not a great battlefield leader, he proved to be an adept military administrator and a politically flexible department and theater commander. Halleck would also have a considerable impact on Schofield's career and his further education as a general.

THREE

Take Care of Missouri

Department commanders in Missouri had to fight on four fronts—a war of southern rebellion, a guerrilla war in Missouri, a war between the states of Kansas and Missouri, and a war among Unionist factions within Missouri. Within six months of Halleck's assuming command, the "war of southern rebellion" was virtually won in Missouri. General Samuel Curtis's victory at Pea Ridge, Arkansas, in March 1862 ended any real threat of a successful Confederate invasion of Missouri. Thereafter, the Confederate invasions were more often large-scale raids to hamper Union operations in other theaters, rather than genuine attempts to "redeem" Missouri for the Confederacy. Still, these rebel incursions generated considerable tension between the state and the federal governments. Missouri state officials were primarily interested in protecting the state, while the national government was more interested in defeating the Confederacy.

As the conventional military threat diminished, the guerrilla war heated up in Missouri. Again, the interests of state and federal officials diverged. State authorities sought to eradicate guerrilla activity, while the national government was content to contain it. To protect Missouri from Confederate raids and guerrillas, most state officials and some military commanders were reluctant to transfer troops to other theaters to prosecute the war. Disputes over how to eradicate or how to contain guerrillas—"hard" war versus "soft" war—further splintered Union strategy.[1]

If the debate over slavery and emancipation was passionate on the national level, it was ferocious in the Department of the Missouri. The border war between Kansas and Missouri did not end with the outbreak of the Civil War. Kansas provided a safe haven for escaping slaves throughout the war. Antislavery Kansans such as Senator James Lane and Colonel Charles Jennison revenged themselves on Missourians with little regard as to whether they were Unionists. To them, all Missourians were "bushwhackers." Some Kansans were motivated by more than political passion. As Schofield archly observed, a number were "not unwilling to steal themselves rich in the name of liberty."[2]

The questions of slavery and emancipation also splintered the Unionist cause in Missouri. Those who initially defended slavery and later advocated gradual emancipation, like Governor Hamilton Gamble, became known as "Claybanks"; those who demanded immediate emancipation, such as Senator Gratz Brown, were called "Charcoals." As the debate on slavery and emancipation intensified, the radicals came to view anyone who did not favor immediate emancipation as "secesh." For military officers, the struggle over guerrilla and emancipation policies entangled them willingly and unwillingly in the nastiest brand of politics. Just as it was difficult for Missourians to remain neutral in the war, few officers could remain neutral in these debates. As the commander of the Missouri State Militia, the District of St. Louis, the Army of the Frontier, and ultimately the Department of the Missouri, John M. Schofield was intimately involved in all of these battles.

Henry Wager Halleck, the new commander in the West, was the antithesis of John C. Fremont. Short and unprepossessing, scholarly and circumspect, he lacked Fremont's flamboyance, yet he was greatly respected in the "old army." Halleck had graduated number three in the West Point class of 1839, and as an instructor he gained the nickname "Old Brains." He had translated Antoine-Henri Jomini's writings on Napoleon and wrote *The Elements of Military Art and Science*, based on Jomini's work. Halleck served in California during the Mexican War. Afterward, he resigned from the army, formed a law firm, and grew rich investing in land, mines, and railroads. In 1861 Winfield Scott recommended him for promotion to major general in the regular army and considered him his eventual successor.[3]

In appearance, intellect, and temperament, Schofield was very similar to Halleck. Lacking charisma, they impressed people by their gravity and intellect. Both were moderate Democrats who had little taste for partisan politics. Schofield embraced Halleck's strategic and administrative ideas, and Schofield's approach to command in Missouri was clearly based on Halleck's thoughtful, methodical, and conscientious example. Schofield so admired the commander that he named his third son, who died in infancy, Henry Halleck Schofield.[4] The respect was mutual. Halleck would often share his troubles and complaints with Schofield. Historian John Marszalek believes that Halleck considered his young subordinate a soul mate.[5]

Yet, there was one major difference in their personalities. Halleck was a solitary thinker. Aloof, suspicious, and brusque, he often created enemies, while Schofield was far more sociable and approachable. Years later, one private recalled his cordial meeting with Schofield and told his grandchildren that he was the "nicest Major General" he met during the war. Schofield had a wide circle of friends, while Halleck had few friends, and even fewer intimates. Nevertheless, Halleck and Schofield developed a close relationship, with Halleck becoming Schofield's mentor and patron.[6]

Halleck's tutelage of Schofield began shortly after Halleck assumed command on November 19, 1861. With the assistance of the Blairs, Schofield was promoted to brigadier general, and on November 27 Halleck assigned him to command the Missouri State Militia. This appointment reflected a novel political compromise. The defense of the Missouri was beyond the resources of the state government, yet the state officials were unwilling to turn the defense of the state completely over to the federal government. To secure federal financial support, Provisional Governor Hamilton Gamble agreed to appoint a federal officer to command the militia and subject it to army regulations and the Articles of War. The department commander became the ex-officio major general of the state militia, and Schofield became his principal deputy in this area. Schofield's job was to raise, organize, and train a force to defend the state. Schofield now possessed three commissions: captain in the regular army, brigadier general of United States Volunteers, and brigadier general of the Missouri State Militia (MSM). Though Schofield was officially a subordinate of the military department commander, Schofield had to be responsive to the governor, who believed he should have a say in the appointments and policy of the state militia. It was a delicate job in which Schofield had to balance carefully local interests with the requirements of the national government.[7]

The MSM would eventually carry the primary burden of combating guerrillas, freeing up many U.S. regiments for duty with the armies invading the South. By April 15, 1862, Schofield had raised and organized a force of 13,800 men and organized them into fourteen regiments and two battalions of cavalry, one regiment of infantry, and one battery of artillery. The preponderance of cavalry in the organized militia was an important part of Schofield's overall strategy. With infantry, he wrote to Brigadier General Benjamin N. Prentiss, one "can do little more than hold a single point." With cavalry, "we can always strike the rebels before they can collect in numbers sufficient to meet us" and frustrate their attempts to organize.[8]

The appointment of general and field-grade officers was especially important. The ability of prominent men to attract recruits played an important role in the appointment to senior command, and thus senior officers were proportionally balanced between conservative Unionists and radical Republicans.

Proslavery men generally commanded in proslavery sections of the state, while abolitionists tended to command in antislavery regions. The political and ideological fissures in the state were thus replicated in the militia. Schofield encouraged Governor Gamble and his subordinate commanders to postpone selection of field-grade officers so that company-grade officers could prove themselves. As the war progressed, Schofield even attempted to dissuade the state government from the election of company officers.[9]

The mixing of volunteer and militia units in Missouri occasionally created conflict and confusion. Those who possessed dual commissions could command both elements, but volunteer and militia officers squabbled over seniority and prerogatives. When in 1862 the state raised a new militia force called the Enrolled Missouri Militia (EMM), the conflict over command authority further increased.[10] Halleck, after becoming commanding general, advanced the theory of federal seniority but concluded, "I agree with you [Governor Gamble] that the commanding officer of a military district can assume no command over the enrolled state militia until the same is brought into service of the United States."[11] Finally, the militia was tied to the state unless sworn into federal service as state volunteers. On several occasions, units mutinied when federal officers attempted to deploy them out of the state.[12] Conflicting authorities and interpretations meant that commanders on the ground could not automatically depend on command prerogatives and frequently had to rely on a spirit of cooperation.

As Schofield organized the militia, Halleck, the lawyer, grappled with the legal implications of guerrilla warfare amid a civil war. During the winter, neither side could sustain large forces in the field, especially cavalry. Bridge burning, which hampered federal movement of troops and supplies, was a favorite tactic of the rebel guerrillas. Beset by numerous acts of sabotage, assault, and murder by an ostensibly civilian enemy, General Halleck, on December 26, 1861, reaffirmed earlier declarations of martial law or the assertion of military jurisdiction in St. Louis and along railroad lines.[13] However, the legal status of various rebels, and the legal authority of the military deal with these rebels and their activities, remained confused.

On January 1, Halleck issued General Order No. 1, which more systematically outlined martial law procedures. The order delineated between the use of military courts-martial for the trial and punishment of military personnel and military commissions for the trial and punishment of civilians for military offenses. Both had similar rules and procedures. Halleck cautioned subordinates that civil offenses would remain the purview of civilian courts, "whenever such loyal courts exist." While military personnel might be charged with the "Violation of the Rules and Articles of War," which was prescribed by statute, civilians would be charged with "violation of the laws of war." Though admittedly general and not fully covered by statute, General Order No. 1 attempted to differentiate the "duly-authorized forces of the so-called Confederate States" and guerrillas. Duly enrolled soldiers, acting under proper authority, would be treated as prisoners of war, whereas "predatory partisans and guerrilla bands are not entitled to such exemptions."[14] The differentiation between combatant and noncombatant, and legal combatant versus illegal combatant, remained a vexed question throughout the war; but Halleck continued with his efforts to create a legal framework. While the partisans decried their treatment as outlaws, Halleck was threading a middle course to prevent all rebels or supposed rebels from being summarily punished. He hoped to suppress guerrillas without descending into atrocity and counter-atrocity.[15]

The use of military commissions was another novel and relatively successful innovation of the Civil War.[16] Historian Mark Neely has concluded that, though imperfect, "trials by military commission restrained United States forces in the Civil War mainly by imposing systematic record-keeping and an atmosphere of legality on the army's dealings with a hostile populace." In addition to requirements for legal representation and record keeping, all sentences had to be reviewed by department commanders and all death penalties reviewed by the president. These requirements were often not found in civilian courts. Neely estimates that nearly 5,000 different civilian prisoners passed through St. Louis's military prisons during the war and that the number held in other portions of the state would be a formidable figure. The thousands of men imprisoned in Missouri were generally not simple "political dissidents." The passions of civil war had erupted into murder well before 1861, and the proximity of Confederate support in Indian Territory or Arkansas fanned the flames of further violence.[17]

In the records of the Department of the Missouri, very few men were charged with simply "uttering disloyal sentiments." Most were charged with "violation of the oath of allegiance" or "violation of the laws of war" by being or aiding rebels. Punishments ranged from fines to banishment to prison. Despite the partisan accusations surrounding the tenures of Curtis and Schofield as department commanders, there was little difference in the number of charges or punishments handed down by their military commissions. After 1862, military commissions in Missouri issued few death sentences.[18] Lincoln's well-known reluctance to use capital punishment penetrated the adjudication process. Criticism of Lincoln's "kind-heartedness" was often bipartisan. Not only did radicals object to coddling treasonous murderers, Governor Gamble complained to Attorney General Edward Bates that Lincoln's pardons deprived Missourians of justice. Bates was unable to change the president's mind and wrote Gamble that real consequences of Lincoln's policies would be to induce Union soldiers not to bother with military commissions. Too often, Bates's harsh assessment was proven brutally accurate. The military commissions were only one tool of the war against the guerrillas, and many "bushwhackers" never made it to trial. Lincoln's disinclination to approve death sentences not only restrained their use by military commission, but also often resulted in a reluctance to take prisoners at all.[19]

While Halleck devised a guerrilla policy, Schofield, assigned to protect the Northern Missouri Railroad, came to grips with the other side of the coin. On the same day that Halleck issued General Order No. 1, Schofield issued a general order decrying the wanton plundering and robbing of peaceable citizens by portions of the militia and reminding commanders of the duty to arrest and punish such crimes. The Germans were a particular problem. As early as August 26, 1861, Gamble complained to Lincoln about the Home Guard. As recent German immigrants, they had little understanding or sympathy of conservative Unionists and considered most of those who did not share their abolitionist views as disloyal. Gamble wanted them placed under state control or integrated into regular U.S. regiments, and consequently deployed out of the state. In January 1862 Schofield lamented that the only cavalry force at his disposal was "a battalion of Germans, utterly worthless for this kind of service. If I trust them out of my sight for a moment they will plunder and rob friends and foes alike." He had already arrested several officers and soldiers and asked Halleck to dismount and disarm the unit. Halleck echoed this complaint to General George McClellan, lamenting, "Wherever they go they convert all Union men into bitter enemies."[20]

Nor was the problem only with "foreign adventurers." As Brigadier General James Totten wrote Schofield, "Private quarrels of long standing, originating out of matters connected with property, county politics, and neighborhood disagreement, are too often the cause of persecution of those in military power, and all is made to appear as connected with the rebellion." The war became an excuse for "personal revenge," and desire for revenge increased as the war continued. Schofield exhorted commanders to "ferret out" both "insurgents and jayhawkers." He ordered commanders to restrain the troops from destroying private property: "The object is not so much to punish the rebels for what they have done as to prevent them from doing injury in the future. This is to be done by putting the incorrigible out of the way, either by death or imprisonment, and by securing the good conduct of others through the obligation of a bond and oath, while many may reclaimed by justice mingled with kindness."[21]

At a time when even many conservatives were advocating rather bloodthirsty recriminations against rebels and southern sympathizers, Schofield's moderate strategy was notable. In dealing with repentant rebel sympathizers, he told Halleck, "It appears to me that by exercising a wise discretion in granting such assurances of protection to men of well-known respectability and influence much good may be done."[22] Of course, Schofield's moderation and "kindness" would be abused by many rebels and would provide grist for his political enemies.[23] But Schofield was not alone. Halleck, Gamble, and Lincoln continued to hope that reconciliation was possible. The early "magnanimous" approach of both Halleck and Schofield to ex-rebels and sympathizers was in accordance with the views of Hamilton Gamble. As early as August 1861 he had hoped to lure many of Price's men back into loyalty by grants of amnesty. As the war continued, Gamble and many other "moderate" officials grew angry and frustrated and eventually endorsed more draconian measures. Yet, Gamble never fully embraced the hard war policy of the radicals. Lincoln, too, preferred offers of amnesty and the oath of allegiance to bring weary or disenchanted rebels back into harmony with their neighbors. As brutal as the war on the border areas would become, it could have been much more barbarous without the restraining hands of men like Schofield, Halleck, Gamble, and Lincoln.[24]

On February 15, 1862, Schofield assumed command of the District of St. Louis, which included the area surrounding St. Louis and, later, parts of southeastern Missouri.[25] Schofield continued to organize militia companies and assign them to the other district commanders when he deemed them ready for service.[26] As Schofield organized the Missouri State Militia, Halleck turned to the war against the Confederacy. In February Ulysses S. Grant's capture of Fort Henry on the Tennessee River and Fort Donelson on the Cumberland River unhinged the Confederate defensive line in Tennessee and Kentucky. At the end of the month, Samuel Curtis forced Price to again abandon Springfield and withdraw into Arkansas. On March 7 and 8 Curtis defeated the Confederate army under Earl Van Dorn at the battle of Pea Ridge in northwest Arkansas. The Confederates withdrew most of their troops from this area to shore up defenses along the Mississippi. On April 6 the Confederate general Albert Sidney Johnston surprised Grant at Pittsburg Landing, Tennessee. The next day, with the aid of Don Carlos Buell's army, Grant counterattacked and drove off the rebel army. The battle of Shiloh was the costliest battle of the war thus far. On April 10 Halleck departed St. Louis to take command of the Union armies that were moving on Corinth, Mississippi, and he told Schofield to "take care of Missouri."[27]

Schofield now assumed responsibility for all of Missouri except the southwest, where Curtis's Army of the Frontier was gradually moving east in an effort to take Little Rock. Throughout April, May, and June, Schofield worked to coordinate Union efforts in Missouri and comply faithfully with Halleck's order to send him "all the infantry within my reach," and later to move all available forces toward the southern border of Missouri to support General Curtis. Schofield repeatedly reminded Halleck that he lacked the formal authority for many actions and requested changes in the department's organization to fit the altered military circumstances. At one point, Schofield's friends approached Lincoln about the issue. Halleck, on being queried by Lincoln, gave a typically scathing answer: "General Schofield has entire command of the Missouri Militia in the United States service, and of the volunteers of two-thirds of the State. He has been informed that his district will comprise the entire State as soon as Major-General Curtis moves south. This is more than his rank entitles him to. If he is intriguing for more he is not honest. I would rather resign than to have him given an independent command in my department. I have yielded much to the importunities of his friends, but they ask still more."[28]

Schofield's importuning, no doubt, reflected his personal ambition, but it also represented his legitimate concern for needed reorganization within Missouri. Throughout his career, Schofield was a shrewd judge of military administrative organization. His status as commander of the St. Louis District gave him no authority to realign the other Missouri district commands to meet the changing guerrilla threat. Schofield used his authority as the state militia commander to allocate and reallocate troops to the various districts, but he had no formal authority over the federal troops assigned to the districts. As the organization of the militia regiments neared completion, the use of Schofield's authority as militia commander in relation to the other district commanders perpetuated a dual chain of command. Schofield also had no authority to review the results of military commissions in other districts or to issue general orders applicable to all Union forces in the state. Further, Schofield needed greater authority in order to protect Missouri from the Department of Kansas. On March 11, 1862, Halleck's command had been expanded to include the Department of Kansas and most of the Department of the Ohio, and renamed the Department of the Mississippi. However, on May 2, 1862, Senator Lane of Kansas had persuaded Lincoln to reestablish the Department of Kansas and place Brigadier General James G. Blunt in command. Blunt was an ardent abolitionist who had been an associate of John Brown. He also served as the lieutenant colonel in Lane's irregular brigade until he was appointed brigadier general of volunteers in April 1862. Blunt and many of his troops saw Missouri as enemy territory.[29]

On May 16, Schofield wrote directly to Secretary of War Edwin M. Stanton to complain about Union troops from Kansas entering Missouri. The specific case concerned two Kansans, a man and a woman, who entered Missouri in early May to claim a horse, which they subsequently took at gunpoint. A body of Missourians gave chase and made a citizen's arrest of the man, Atchison. The local Missouri justice of the peace later dismissed the case based on errors in the papers and released the Kansan. Atchison returned a short time later with a detachment of Union soldiers from Kansas, who, under the orders of General Blunt, arrested all of the men who had apprehended Atchison. Blunt refused the request of Brigadier General Benjamin Loan, Northwest Missouri District commander, to release the Missourians and proposed to try them by military commission. As a department commander, Blunt felt no obligation to cooperate with mere district commanders from Missouri. Loan ominously informed Schofield that he would not permit Blunt to "disregard all laws of the State, the proceedings of the courts, and the rights of the citizens."[30]

In his letter to Stanton, Schofield pointed out that the old feuds along the border often had little to do with "the question of Union or disunion." To mitigate these conflicts, Schofield had endeavored to station troops from other states or from eastern Missouri along the border. He further recommended that since Kansas no longer came under the jurisdiction of Halleck, the only recourse was to forbid soldiers from either department to enter the other's territory. Schofield recognized that this was an imperfect solution. This incident confirmed Schofield's belief in the need for unity of command in the region. To this end, Schofield began to advocate the re-creation of a Department of the Missouri that would include Kansas and, still later, the creation of a District of the Border, which would place this contentious territory under one district commander. This was also Schofield's first collision with the belligerent James G. Blunt, and it colored his subsequent opinion.[31]

On June 4, 1862, despite his earlier fit of pique, Halleck created the District of Missouri and appointed Schofield as its commander. Schofield's new command consisted of all of Missouri except a few counties in the southwest that remained under Curtis. Schofield, in turn, divided his command into five divisions: Northeast Missouri, under Brigadier General Loan with 1,250 troops (volunteer and militia); Northwest Missouri, under Colonel John McNeil with 1,450 troops; Central Missouri, under Brigadier General James Totten with 4,750 troops; Southwest Missouri, under Brigadier General Egbert B. Brown with 3,450 troops; and St. Louis, under Colonel Lewis Merrill with 4,960 troops plus 1,500 at Rolla.[32]

Paradoxically, the Union successes in the spring of 1862 had an adverse effect on the guerrilla war in Missouri. As Union forces moved deeper into the South, Halleck demanded more reinforcements from the rear areas. Schofield's unstinting compliance earned Halleck's favor but at the cost of retaining fewer troops to handle guerrillas. The consolidation of Union gains also permitted the rebels to resume the initiative in Arkansas and Tennessee. Meanwhile, the Confederate authorities infiltrated veterans of Price's forces back into Missouri to recruit guerrilla bands. This, combined with the summer weather and the reduction of federal troops in the state, permitted the guerrillas to operate in groups of 500 to 2,000. These large bands wreaked havoc with the isolated militia garrisons. In his official report, Schofield estimated 30,000 to 50,000 guerrillas were terrorizing Missouri. Schofield's estimate was no doubt exaggerated; the number of active guerrillas was probably closer to 5,000 to 10,000. Since Schofield had approximately 17,360 troops, the guerrillas represented a formidable challenge nevertheless. During the summer of 1862, the Union forces would fight dozens of engagements and undertake numerous grueling pursuits of elusive guerrilla bands.[33]

Schofield's frustration was apparent in his general order of May 29, 1862. While reiterating the government's policy to "be magnanimous in its treatment of those who are tired of the rebellion and desire to become loyal citizens," he declared that those "caught in arms, engaged in their unlawful warfare, . . . will be shot down upon the spot." He required "all good citizens . . . to give their assistance to the military authorities in detecting and bringing to punishment the outlaws . . . and those who give them shelter and protection." Those who failed to do so would be "treated as abettors of the criminals." Finally, he reminded his command: "All officers and men of this command are reminded that it is their duty, while punishing with unmeasured severity those who still persist in their mad efforts to destroy the peace of the State, not only to abstain from molestation, but to protect from injury all loyal and peaceable citizens. All will be held to a strict accountability for the just and proper execution of the important and responsible duties required of them by this order."[34] Brandishing an olive branch and a sword, exhorting his men to destroy the guerrillas with both severity and restraint, Schofield's order reflected the inherent contradictions and dilemmas of guerrilla warfare.

On June 23, Schofield issued an even more drastic order. Schofield declared that "rebels and rebel sympathizers in Missouri will be held responsible . . . for the damages that may hereafter be committed by the lawless bands which they have brought into existence, subsisted, encouraged, and sustained." County boards appointed by the district commanders would assess local rebel sympathizers $5,000 for each Union soldier killed, $1,000 to $5,000 for each one wounded, and the full value of stolen or destroyed property. The government would then distribute the sums collected to the persons so injured, or their heirs. The boards were to immediately "enroll all the residents and property-holders of the county who have actively aided or encouraged the present rebellion." They could drop from the roll any persons who took the oath of allegiance and satisfied the board of their loyalty. In making assessments, the boards would also take into account "the wealth of an individual and his known activity in aiding the rebellion."[35] In a subsequent order, Schofield permitted the use of volunteer or militia officers but urged the use of loyal residents of the county.[36]

Although there had been earlier examples of such fines, Schofield's order was a striking assertion of military authority.[37] Though Governor Gamble endorsed the plan, Schofield issued these orders as the federal commander of the District of Missouri and not as the Missouri militia commander. Schofield, instead, saw the use of local civilian/military boards to levy mass fines as an extension of martial law. That he permitted persons to be dropped from the assessment rolls by demonstrations of loyalty suggests that Schofield's intent was to coerce good behavior as much as punish bad behavior or fund the war.

Laws passed by Congress that called for the confiscation of rebel property did not strictly apply, but they lent Schofield's plan a degree of legitimacy. Yet Schofield's implementation of the congressional confiscation laws was in marked contrast to their radical intent. Since these were laws intended to punish, Schofield interpreted them as requiring execution by normal judicial proceedings. His implementing order called for the provosts marshal to submit the cases and the supporting evidence to federal attorneys for prosecution; condemnation and sale of property would take place after guilt was established by a court of competent jurisdiction. Historian James McPherson notes that the Confiscation Act of 1862 was "confusing and poorly drawn." Despite Stanton's pressure, commanders had considerable leeway in its implementation. George B. McClellan ignored the law, while John Pope used it to justify his "hard war" policies. Schofield's narrow interpretation typically placed him on a middle course. Samuel Curtis would interpret the law far more expansively, and Schofield later attributed Curtis's subsequent troubles in Missouri to his zealous implementation of the confiscation law.[38]

By July, Schofield took an even more revolutionary step. Curtis's advance on Little Rock could not be logistically sustained, so Halleck ordered him to move to Helena on the Mississippi River. Curtis's arrival in Helena on July 14 had opened Missouri's southern border to the threat of Confederate raids.[39] Schofield needed to concentrate more of his troops to meet this threat, but this would leave large portions of the state vulnerable to the guerrillas. Unable to obtain reinforcements from the field armies, Schofield persuaded Governor Gamble to call out the entire militia of the state. Using his authority as commander of the state militia, Schofield's July 22 General Order No. 19 called up for military service most of the free, white, adult males of the state. Not since the American Revolution had there been such an extensive mobilization of the militia.[40]

Schofield acknowledged the "radical" nature of the measure as "the first attempt of the kind in this or any other country under similar circumstances."[41] To differentiate it from the full-time and federally sponsored Missouri State Militia, this force was termed the Enrolled Missouri Militia. Schofield intended the EMM to supplement the MSM, not replace it. Rather than a full-time military force, the EMM was designed to provide local defense and to guard supply depots and bridges. But this mission was not easy. These relatively small and isolated units often became the targets of large guerrilla bands and Confederate raiders. By November 1862, seventy regiments had been formed, and eventually there were eighty-nine. Though this measure eased the manpower crisis, the EMM created problems all its own. If every man were subject to call, what about those who were southern sympathizers? What of civilians who served in critical positions? How would these state units be commanded, sustained, and funded?[42]

Secretary of War Stanton was quick to react to this decree. On July 26, he ordered Schofield to exempt telegraph operators and employees from enrollment. By August 5, Stanton expanded the order army-wide, directing that those engaged in the construction and operation of telegraphs were vital to the war effort and were to be exempted from military service. In a separate decision, he rejected railroad companies' requests to exempt all of their employees and instead ordered exemption just for locomotive engineers. But there were other objections to such an extensive enrollment for military service. Schofield acknowledged that the enrollment prompted many rebel sympathizers either to join the local guerrilla band or run "to the brush." While it increased guerrilla strength, it also unmasked many disloyal men. In heavily secessionist counties, enrollment likewise marked the loyal Unionists and left many of them at the mercy of the guerrillas, particularly while the companies were being armed and equipped. Unfortunately, enrollment also prompted many Unionists, especially in St Louis, to flee the state to avoid militia service.[43]

To avoid the problem of conscripting those who were unwilling to serve,

Governor Gamble suggested that men might buy an exemption for $150 and thus help fund the force. Schofield proposed the far more modest amount of $10 and one-tenth of 1 percent upon all taxable property as shown by the most recent assessment. He calculated that in this way, more southern sympathizers would not serve, but would help pay for those who did. Unfortunately, Schofield misjudged the real effect of the policy. Radicals denounced his exemption because it permitted the rich—slave owners in the eyes of the radicals—to avoid service; many moderates also viewed the $10 exemption as an unfair burden on poor citizens. Schofield hastily withdrew the order.[44]

The call-up of the militia also exacerbated the problem of factional feuding within counties and the militia. Conservatives objected to giving radicals the cloak of military authority with which to intimidate them. Radicals denounced conservative militiamen as secessionists and bushwhackers. They also denounced Schofield for turning over the militia to the enemy while loyal men were excluded or punished. As the commander of the militia, Schofield had to contend with innumerable charges and countercharges of disloyalty or depredation. For example, the commander at St. Charles reported in August 1862 a "private revolution" between the Germans and the "Americans" over the command of the local regiment. The Germans called the nominee, John K. McDearmon, a secessionist and threatened to replace him forcibly with their own candidate. Major Edward Harding, the local army commander, believed that if McDearmon's commission were quickly affirmed, the Germans would back down. In his endorsement Schofield replied, "It is the intention of the Governor to give the Germans a fair proportion of the offices, but they can not expect to control everything."[45] These fights among the countless political, local, and ethnic factions continued throughout the war. When the radicals took control of the state legislature in the fall of 1863, they launched an extensive investigation into the militia and its supposed "inefficiency" and "disloyalty."[46]

If many complained about the call-up, still others detected a political opportunity. Though he initially opposed the enrollment, Frank Blair attributed the Republican success in the elections of 1862 to Schofield's General Order 19. Writing to his brother Montgomery, he acknowledged that "Schofield did not issue the order for that purpose & Gamble did not consent to it with any such idea but it did the work and no mistake." The order, according to Blair, forced the "secesh" to take to the bush, while loyal men were drilled and organized. "Thus many thousands of secession votes were actually lost," he elaborated, "but the great point was that the armed organization was on our side giving protection to our voters."[47]

The most pressing problem of the EMM was how to pay for it. Since these were to remain state troops under state control, the federal government would not foot the bill. Halleck agreed to provide captured arms, but he recommended that the militia be "subsisted by requisitions on rebel sympathizers."[48] Schofield's bounty in place of service had been partially intended as a means to pay for the EMM. Initially, Schofield directed that the enrolled militia would subsist off rebels and, if necessary, Union men, after giving a proper receipt. Schofield later had to amend these orders when the EMM began using any pretense to take provisions, further adding to general fear and bitterness.[49] With the approval of Governor Gamble, Schofield assessed the rebel sympathizers of St. Louis $500,000. To justify this measure, Schofield again switched hats. While acknowledging in a December 5 letter that the funds were to support the state militia, he asserted that the force was called out to "enable me to discharge the important and difficult duty assigned me by the United States Government." He went on to insist that his resort to martial law was based on "my own responsibility as an officer of the United States, and not under the orders of the Governor of Missouri."[50]

By the time he wrote this letter, such assessments by his successors were becoming increasingly common and increasingly unpopular. Schofield's letter gave cover to Gamble while putting responsibility for their continued use on the federal commander, who was now General Samuel Curtis. Schofield also used this line of argument—a state force employed for a federal purpose—to urge the War Department to pay for the EMM while in active service.[51] The War Department eventually agreed to provide the rations and forage for those members of the EMM on active service. This was, no doubt, a great relief to the local commanders. While they could deflect questions of pay or promotion, they could less readily justify feeding the volunteer and MSM units from government supplies, while forcing the EMM to fend for itself. It was a situation tailor-made for dissension and abuse.[52]

As Schofield organized his new force, he admitted to the War Department that "a large part of the State is virtually given up to the guerrillas." He renewed his appeals for reinforcements and repeatedly urged that Curtis's force at Helena either march toward Little Rock to relieve pressure on Missouri or transfer troops to Missouri. Curtis, who hoped to employ his army in an attack on Vicksburg, resisted such orders.[53] On August 10, Halleck responded with substantive aid and somewhat gratuitous advice. Then, almost in passing, Halleck added the stunning news that Schofield's political patron was demanding his head: "A portion of the new troops from Iowa, Illinois, and Wisconsin will be sent to Missouri. Your troops acting against the guerrillas must move rapidly and strike quickly. Do not let them scatter too much. General Curtis will soon make a strong diversion in your favor. There is a deputation here from Colonel Blair and others, asking for your removal on account of inefficiency."[54]

Ironically, Blair walked into Schofield's office within minutes of the thunderstruck commander's receiving the devastating telegraph. A shocked and somewhat angry Schofield handed Blair the message. Blair instantly declared, "That is not true. No one is authorized to ask in my name for your removal." Blair then immediately sent a confirming telegraph to Halleck. In a later, more formal response, Blair stated that he did not seek Schofield's removal, but he added his view that "the State military organization should be abandoned as soon as practicable, and a military commander, in this State, authorized to act without respect to Governor Gamble."[55] Yet, Blair was not entirely innocent in this scheme. The delegation of St. Louis Republicans headed by Henry T. Blow, in addition to demanding Schofield's head, wanted the state militia forces brought under federal control—a position not very different from Blair's. Blow insisted that Blair had expressed dissatisfaction with Schofield. Blair had also attended an early meeting of Blow's group, and many of Blair's friends saw an opportunity to "get rid of Schofield & Gamble" and promote Blair to military governor.[56]

The real issue was not Schofield, nor even federal control. The real target was Governor Gamble, and the real issue was slavery. Blow believed that the rebellion could not be put down while also protecting slavery. To Lincoln he declared, "we have no future with the institution of slavery perpetuated."[57] The question of abolition began to color all public discussions and polarized all policy issues. Here Blair and Blow parted company, for while Blair and Blow agreed on federal preeminence, they profoundly disagreed over emancipation. As Blow became more radical and Blair more conservative, their friendship turned into bitter enmity.[58]

Warned of Blow's purpose, Governor Gamble defended Schofield to Halleck: "I have discovered here a disposition to criticize General Schofield and to have him removed from the command. The persons engaged are of the same class that has opposed and abused General McClellan and yourself. They are zealous in opposing rebellion, but incapable of judging correctly of the measures to be adopted. They have but one idea. General Schofield is doing well, according to my judgment."[59]

A few days later, Schofield wrote Halleck a lengthy explanation of his situation and deployments. He then agreed to place his fate in the hands of Halleck and the president, concluding, "As to the charge of inefficiency, I believe it comes solely from the men who would have me adopt an extreme policy not sanctioned by yourself or by the President. If I thought otherwise I would ask to be relieved at once; and if, upon examination, you think the good of the service will be promoted thereby, I will cheerfully accept a less responsible command."[60]

Halleck responded a few days later, approving of his dispositions and giving his young protégé some encouragement: "I myself never doubted your efficiency, but I wished you to know the charges which were so strenuously urged against you here and the source from which they came." Perhaps referring not only to the Blow delegation but also to Blair and his friends, Halleck went on the say, "It seems impossible for politicians to play a fair or open game. They always keep a trump (as they think) card concealed up their sleeves or in the top of their boots. They cannot get me to assist them in any such a game either against you or any one else."[61]

Characteristically, in the midst of this political fracas Lincoln remained focused on the war effort. While the Blow delegation cooled their heels, Lincoln asked General Curtis if the extension of the railroad toward Springfield would be "of any military advantage" to him. To Lincoln, all other matters were secondary to winning the war. Those who contributed to the war effort had Lincoln's support; those who hampered it, especially for personal or partisan reasons, earned his disdain.[62] After brief reflection, Lincoln rejected the demands of the Blow delegation. But the damage to Schofield had been done; he was politically wounded.

The Confederate activity in Missouri and along the border with Kansas finally galvanized the War Department to reorganize Halleck's old Department of the Mississippi. While grappling with the crisis of Robert E. Lee's invasion of Maryland, Halleck wrote Schofield unofficially that strong political pressures were being brought to bear to get parties appointed to the new departments. Halleck hoped that some western general would do something brilliant so as to prevent the dismemberment of the department based on politics.[63] On September 19, 1862, the War Department recreated the Department of the Missouri, encompassing Missouri, Kansas, Arkansas, and the Indian Territory. A few weeks later, it added the territories of Nebraska and Colorado.[64] Schofield's recommendations had been instrumental in the design of the new department. While combating both the guerrillas and the Blow delegation, Schofield had recommended that Missouri, Arkansas, and Kansas be placed under one command. His repeated suggestions for coordination and cooperation among Curtis's forces in Arkansas and Blunt's forces in Kansas articulated the logic of such a command.[65] Despite Schofield's hopes, the commander of this new department would be Samuel R. Curtis. As Halleck explained, "General Curtis, as the ranking officer, is given the command. This was the only way of cutting the knot."[66]

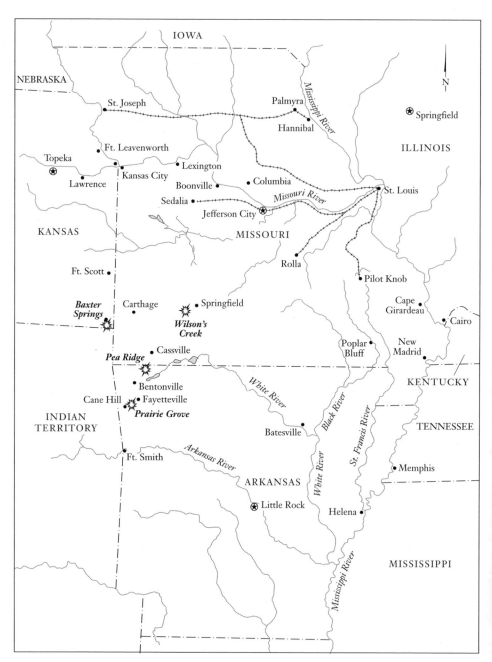

The Department of the Missouri

In reviewing the decision with Schofield, Halleck gave vent to his irritation and complained of his inability to eliminate the role of politics in military decisions. Halleck, like Sisyphus, would be doomed to frustration. The separation of the military from politics was an exercise in futility. The politicians in each state used Schofield's organizational recommendations to pull strings to divide the departments to their benefit. Halleck lamented:

> I have done everything in my power here to separate military appointments and commands from politics, but really the task is hopeless. The waste of money and demoralization of the Army by having incompetent and corrupt politicians in nearly all military offices, high and low, are working out terrible results. It is utterly disheartening! Oh, the curse of political expediency! It has almost ruined the Army, and if carried out will soon ruin the country. I have done and will continue to do all in my power to sustain the military officers against this political pressure; but unless we have some successes soon—I mean real and substantial successes—the ultra radicals will force us to yield. . . . The rabid Abolitionists and Northern Democrats of secession proclivities have done all in their power to weaken and embarrass the administration and at the same time to discourage and demoralize the Army. We are now reaping the fruits of their accursed work.[67]

Though Curtis would later be identified with the radicals, at this point Halleck was not so much complaining of Curtis's appointment as he was the process. He feared that the lack of real military success would provoke further political interference. This was not the only time that Halleck would lecture his young subordinate on the benefits of victory. The more successful the general, the less political interference he would suffer. Of course, the more political toes even a successful general stepped on, the more vulnerable he would be if and when he suffered a setback.

Curtis's appointment as departmental commander was perfectly logical. Curtis was a West Point graduate with solid Republican credentials. As the hero of Pea Ridge, he had proved himself an able and courageous field commander. Nevertheless, his elevation rankled Schofield, who believed his service in Missouri merited the position and the promotion. His recommendations had been instrumental in convincing Lincoln and the War Department to create the new department. Schofield certainly blamed Blow and the radicals for maligning him in Washington, and Lincoln's decision to appoint Curtis was probably influenced by the desire to avoid more political strife. In addition to professional disappointment, Schofield felt he had been undermined by Curtis. Curtis had continually complained about a lack of reinforcements from Schofield in July, while Schofield complained about Curtis's failure to launch a campaign from Helena to relieve the threats to the southern Missouri border in August and September.[68]

Upon receiving the bitter news, Schofield wrote a letter to Gamble announcing his decision to resign as district commander and commander of the militia and requesting to command the army in the field. He added, somewhat petulantly, that he would rather leave the department than endure what he considered a demotion, but he was willing to sacrifice his personal feelings. Curtis assigned Schofield to command a reconstituted Army of the Frontier. With Curtis assigned to St. Louis and Schofield commanding in the field, the two generals had, in an ironic way, exchanged positions. And just as Curtis had hoped his command would be employed to take Vicksburg, Schofield, too, hoped that after the threat to the Missouri border was ended, his army would be called on for more vital missions.[69]

Like Schofield, Gamble was not pleased with the new department commander and voiced his objections to Postmaster General Montgomery Blair. Blair responded, "I am well pleased that you know me well enough to know that I had no share in giving Curtis the command of Missouri. It is the work of the Commander-in-Chief Halleck." Blair then vowed, "I will do what I can to get rid of him." If the radicals had targeted Schofield, the conservatives, from the beginning, painted a bull's-eye on Curtis.[70]

By the time Curtis arrived in St. Louis on September 24, Schofield had already departed for Springfield to assume command of what became the Army of the Frontier. At Springfield, he had 10,800 men, of whom 2,500 were required to guard the line of communication from the railhead in Rolla to the depot at Springfield. Curtis now took the threats to Missouri more seriously and used the authority of his new department to place Blunt's Kansas troops under Schofield. With the injection of 7,000 additional troops, Schofield reorganized his little army into three divisions, commanded by James Blunt, James Totten, and Francis Herron. If Schofield hoped to use this opportunity to build a battlefield record, as Curtis had done, he was to be disappointed. As he advanced into southwest Missouri, the Confederates, after a few cavalry fights, withdrew. When he moved into northwest Arkansas, the Confederates again withdrew over the Boston Mountains. No Union army could sustain operations logistically across these mountains, and Schofield had to withdraw reluctantly. Schofield's inability to bring the Confederates to battle prompted some frustrated soldiers to refer to him as "Granny Schofield."[71]

After withdrawing the bulk of his forces back into Missouri, Schofield was struck with typhoid fever and was forced to relinquish command to Blunt on November 20.[72] Schofield and Curtis had assumed that major operations in northwest Arkansas and southwest Missouri had ended for the year. Neither man reckoned on the aggressiveness of James Blunt and his Confederate counterpart, Thomas Hindman. Hindman had ruthlessly drafted men and supplies to again invade southwest Missouri. Blunt's continued presence in northwest Arkansas made him an alluring target. Despite the reports of Hindman's gathering forces and warnings from Curtis, Blunt refused to withdraw. On November 28 Blunt fought Hindman's cavalry forces under John S. Marmaduke. On December 3 Hindman advanced his entire force of nearly 11,000 on Blunt's force at Cane Hill. Warned of the approach, Blunt called on Herron at Springfield for help. Herron marched the 116 miles in an incredible three days. But Herron paid a heavy price in straggling, and only one-half of the command arrived near Fayetteville on the evening of December 6. The next day Hindman decided to strike the weakened Herron and then turn on Blunt. Herron boldly attacked Hindman's troops, and Blunt quickly joined Herron. Despite their numerical inferiority, the Union commanders believed their men superior to Hindman's ragtag force. Hindman's men barely withstood the attacks, and that night Hindman again withdrew over the mountains. The intensity of the fighting can be seen from the casualties. Of the approximately 19,000 men engaged, the Union suffered 1,251 casualties and Confederates more than 1,500.[73]

Curtis hailed the Union victory at Prairie Grove, and both Blunt and Herron were nominated for major general. Schofield was mortified that he had missed the battle and further chagrined that his subordinates were soon promoted over him. Schofield's nomination to major general had languished in the Senate due to radical opposition, while Blunt and Herron were quickly nominated and confirmed. The competition for promotion frequently pitted Lincoln and the War Department bureaucracy against the disparate interests of Congress. Lincoln's recommendations for military promotion were seldom simply rubber-stamped by the Senate. Senators and congressmen attempted to advance their favorites and obstruct their foes. Rank, and especially date of rank, became the object of intense politicking. A few well-placed enemies could seriously impede the advancement of even the worthiest officers.[74]

In the winter of 1862, party and institutional politics further complicated the routine politics of patronage. The Democrats had won House seats in the 1862 election, and Republicans feared for their control of that body in the next Congress, which rendered the lame-duck session a partisan battleground. Congress, exerting its institutional prerogatives, was also upset that the president had exceeded the number of generals permitted by the Act of July 17, 1862.

After much wrangling and politicking among the White House, Senate, and House, Congress agreed to an increase of thirty major generals and seventy-five brigadiers. Still, this was not enough for all of those whom Lincoln had promoted, and thus six were sacrificed. They were N. B. Buford, G. W. Morell, W. F. Smith, H. G. Wright, J. D. Cox, and J. M. Schofield.[75]

Schofield's failure to make the cut was not accidental. The final number selected by the conferees was designed to deny promotion to certain officers. The opposition of Blunt's sponsor, Senator Jim Lane, and Gratz Brown of Missouri produced a nearly year and a half–long struggle to gain Schofield's confirmation to major general. Lincoln promoted Schofield to acting major general several times, pending confirmation, but was forced each time to return him to brigadier general when the Senate failed to act. The humiliated Schofield certainly had much reason to dislike and distrust the radicals. Decades later in his memoirs, the anger still showed. He tried to put a lighter face on it by telling of his Irish enlisted striker, who kept in Schofield's trunk numerous shoulder straps of different ranks. When Schofield asked him about it, the soldier replied, "Ah, General, nobody can tell what may happen to you."[76]

The battle of Prairie Grove was a testament to the fight qualities of the men in the Army of the Frontier, as well as the dash and courage of Blunt and Herron. But Halleck was less thrilled about the unnecessary battle. Halleck had very different strategic priorities. Earlier that summer, Curtis had resisted both Schofield's calls for aid and Halleck's orders to advance on Little Rock. Once in command of the Department of the Missouri, Curtis put a higher priority on protecting the Missouri border. In addition to Schofield's army, Curtis, by withdrawing troops from Helena, had built up a sizable force in southeast Missouri near Pilot Knob. Throughout October and November, he continued to protest Halleck's instructions to advance on Little Rock. Nor was Halleck the only one who saw the large forces assembled in Missouri as unnecessary. John A. McClernard, in attempting to push his river-based attack in Vicksburg, asked Stanton why there were so many troops at Prairie Grove and Pilot Knob. Since Curtis was unwilling to take Little Rock and restore Arkansas to the Union, Halleck began diverting troops to Grant's efforts to take Vicksburg.[77]

The strategic disarray in the department was matched by an increasing hostility among the senior officers. In November the ill and dispirited Schofield wrote a letter to Halleck complaining about Curtis. He grumbled that Curtis had left the border "entirely unprotected," and that his inactivity at Helena had subjected Missouri to "a guerrilla warfare, perhaps never equaled in extent and intensity, and involved me in almost endless trouble and came near ruining my reputation as a successful commander." In December Curtis and Schofield sniped at one another over their official reports, and Schofield asked Halleck for a transfer to another assignment.[78]

Meanwhile, when Curtis directed Schofield to return to the army at Springfield, Blunt complained to Curtis that he, not Schofield, should command the Army of the Frontier. In January Schofield, partly out of jealousy and partly out of professional judgment, criticized Blunt's unnecessarily risky handling of the army and questioned his capacity to lead large units. Letting spite get the upper hand, he groundlessly alleged, "At Prairie Grove Blunt and Herron were badly beaten in detail, and owed their escape to a false report of my arrival with reinforcements."[79] Curtis, in turn, passed these criticisms on to Blunt and Senator Lane, causing even greater suspicion and animosity.

In February Halleck received two letters from Schofield complaining about Curtis and requesting a transfer for himself or his entire command.[80] While Schofield's conduct was not exactly admirable, it is understandable. Having missed the big battle, he saw his subordinates promoted, while the political friends of these subordinates obstructed his promotion. Having been replaced by a man who ignored his pleas for support, Schofield felt that Curtis was now directing him in a bizarre reprise of the arduous and fruitless march of Curtis's army across southern Missouri nearly a year earlier. Schofield believed himself surrounded by enemies.[81]

Finally, in April, when Congress adjourned and his promotion to major general lapsed, Schofield had to be transferred. Halleck reassigned Schofield to a division in William S. Rosecrans's Army of the Cumberland. In thanking Halleck for delivering him from his "military and political" enemies, Schofield wrote, "I am as willing as anybody to be sacrificed when any good is to be accomplished by it, but do not like to be slaughtered for nothing." On what he called "one of the happiest days of my life," Schofield reported to his new commander. Rosecrans and George H. Thomas, who ten years earlier had voted to dismiss Schofield from West Point, welcomed him cordially and assigned Schofield to command the 3rd Division of Thomas's XIV Corps. Schofield could now return to soldiering, where he could shoot his enemies.[82]

At Triune, Tennessee, he contentedly prepared his new command for the coming campaign. He recalled it as "one of the most agreeable parts of my whole military service," where he formed some of his "strongest and most valued army attachments." However, he had not fully escaped Missouri. Less than a month after arriving in Tennessee, the War Department ordered him back to St. Louis as the new commander of the Department of the Missouri. In congratulating him, Rosecrans wrote, "I looked upon you as a prospective corps commander, but your present position is already above that." He added, "Give my best regards to Mrs. S. who doubtless remembers her old Sunday school teacher."[83] Schofield and Rosecrans remained lifelong friends, and ironically, Rosecrans replaced Schofield in Missouri, where he, too, fell afoul of the radicals.[84]

FOUR

If Both Factions Shall Abuse You

Despite Schofield's trepidation at returning "to the scene of unsoldierly strife and turmoil," he also felt a sense of vindication. His reappointment as major general and commander of the Department of the Missouri was a vote of confidence by the president. That he replaced a man whom he felt had undermined his military record probably gave him secret pleasure. Yet, Schofield was shrewd enough to realize that this opportunity could also lead to his own destruction. Curtis, like Schofield before him, had learned the perils and pitfalls of high command in the Missouri theater. Curtis's dismissal was a useful object lesson, and Schofield grasped the importance of gaining not just presidential support, but the support and cooperation of the local political leaders as well.

The fall of Samuel Curtis had been building for months. Governor Hamilton Gamble and the conservatives had been unhappy with him from the beginning. Schofield, in his memoirs, attributed Curtis's problems to his overzealous use of assessments and confiscations. Schofield's assessment of St. Louis had provided the tool that radical district commanders, such as Brigadier General Ben Loan, needed to punish disloyalty. By the autumn of 1862, Loan had assessed various Missouri towns and counties over $85,000. These mass punishments caused many complaints. With Schofield testifying that he had used his federal authority to institute the system, Gamble appealed first to Curtis and then to Lincoln. Curtis, though asserting the right of military necessity, attempted to pass the problem to Halleck. Lincoln ordered the assessment in St. Louis suspended pending further examination; a few days later Halleck, while reserving the right to impose future assessments, permanently suspended the assessment in St. Louis. It was nearly a year before Lincoln repudiated the whole system.[1]

Curtis also interpreted the Confiscation Acts less strictly than Schofield and gave his provost marshal, Franklin A. Dick, more latitude in employing them. Curtis had to backtrack somewhat, as abolitionist commanders had used the acts to free the slaves of men not proven to be disloyal by any court. Still, Curtis was more disposed to protect the slaves who were fleeing to army camps, and he believed the only objections came from "a few officers, a few slaveholders, and a few butternut politicians [who] are constantly trying to make a mountain out of a mole-hill." Curtis and Dick also made more liberal use of banishment. In one notorious case, Curtis ordered the banishment of a conservative Presbyterian minister, Samuel B. McPheeters, based on the allegations of a minority faction of his congregation. Lincoln was once more forced to intervene. While Lincoln suspected the reverend of southern sympathies, there was no overt evidence of disloyalty, and though he left the matter in Curtis's hands, Lincoln advised him that "the churches, as such, take care of themselves."[2]

Governor Gamble and Curtis also fought over Gamble's authority over the Enrolled Missouri Militia (EMM). When Gamble attempted to dismiss an EMM officer for incompetence, the officer appealed to Curtis. Rather than cooperate with the governor, Curtis sided with the officer and appealed the case to the War Department. Lincoln and Secretary of War Edwin Stanton, concerned of the precedent it would set for other state militias, did not want to accede to Gamble's assertion of authority over his own state militia, which had not been formally mustered into federal service. Halleck again had to make the dubious assertion of federal authority over the officers of the EMM, when the very same War Department had insisted that they had no responsibility for paying or sustaining the EMM.

This rather high-handed treatment greatly angered Governor Gamble. Previously, the vague agreements and differing views of state versus federal authority had not mattered as much, because Halleck and Schofield had sought to cooperate with Gamble. Curtis and Gamble, however, viewed each other with suspicion. Stanton tried to placate Gamble by ratifying all past actions of the governor, but he insisted on the right to approve future ones. This did not mollify the governor, and the issue festered. When the War Department levied the departments for troops to support Grant's Vicksburg campaign, Gamble stated that the EMM could safeguard northern Missouri if it were sustained and paid while on active service. Curtis, in contrast, resisted pulling out federal troops immediately and expressed doubts about the EMM's reliability. Charles Gibson, Attorney General Edward Bates's chief aide and Governor Gamble's nephew, condemned Curtis's mismanagement and his attacks on the loyalty of the EMM. "How," Gibson asked the president, "could the troops have confidence in a commander who assailed them as traitors?"[3]

Halleck, too, had become frustrated with Curtis's resistance. On February 18, 1863, he sent Curtis a lengthy letter on the strategic importance of the Mississippi River. Halleck recounted his opposition to Curtis's insistence on maintaining large forces in interior Missouri rather than garrisoning Spring-field, Rolla, and Ironton against enemy raids. Halleck stressed that the orders to send "all available troops" came not just from him, but from President Lincoln as well. The feud between Curtis and Gamble, which Lincoln had heretofore considered a relatively minor annoyance, began to hinder the war effort. Curtis's position began to crumble.[4]

The conservatives renewed their campaign to oust Curtis, and by February 24, 1863, Senator John Brooks Henderson had obtained Lincoln's assurance that he would replace Curtis. Earlier, Schofield had warned Gamble of efforts by Senator James H. Lane to bring the department under the control of Kansas by installing General James G. Blunt in place of Curtis.[5] On March 10, Lincoln appointed Major General Edwin Sumner. The conservatives were pleased with the appointment, but Sumner unexpectedly died en route to his new post. Halleck ordered Curtis to remain in command pending further notice.[6] The radicals then launched a campaign to reinstate Curtis permanently. As Lincoln delayed naming a replacement, the radicals claimed exoneration for Curtis, and the conservatives grew more agitated. Finally, in hopes of ending the distracting complaints from Missouri, Lincoln appointed Schofield and once again promoted Schofield to major general.[7] Lincoln's letter of instruction to Schofield made it clear that political factors, more than military ones, were the reasons for Curtis's removal, as he outlined his expectations for Schofield:

EXECUTIVE MANSION, *Washington, May* 27, 1863.

General JOHN M. SCHOFIELD:

MY DEAR SIR: Having relieved General Curtis and assigned you to the command of the Department of the Missouri, I think it may be of some advantage for me to state to you why I did it. I did not relieve General Curtis because of any full conviction that he had done wrong by commission or omission. I did it because of a conviction in my mind that the Union men of Missouri, constituting, when united, a vast majority of the whole people, have entered into a pestilent factional quarrel among themselves, General Curtis, perhaps not of choice, being the head of one faction, and Governor Gamble that of the other. After months of labor to reconcile the difficulty, it seemed to grow worse and worse, until I felt it my duty to break it up somehow, and, as I could not remove Governor Gamble, I had to remove General Curtis.

Now that you are in the position, I wish you to undo nothing merely because General Curtis or Governor Gamble did it, but to exercise your own judgment, and do right for the public interest. Let your military measures be strong enough to repel the invader and keep the peace, and not so strong as to unnecessarily harass and persecute the people. It is a difficult role, and so much greater will be the honor if you perform it well. *If both factions, or neither, shall abuse you, you will, probably, be about right. Beware of being assailed by one and praised by the other.*

Yours, truly,

A. LINCOLN.[8]

Lincoln's advice to Schofield was sound but difficult to achieve. Just as Curtis had been identified with the radical Republicans even before he took command, Schofield's prior duty in Missouri had linked him with the conservatives. The conservative St. Louis newspaper, the *Missouri Republican*, hailed Schofield's appointment, praised his military education, and reported his "enthusiastic reception." Moreover, it attributed the hostility of the "revolutionists" (the term the newspaper commonly used for the German radical Republicans of St. Louis) toward Schofield to his criticism of Franz Sigel's conduct at Wilson's Creek. The *Columbia Statesman* also welcomed Schofield as "a brave and gallant soldier and an able, discreet, and energetic commander." It added, "He comes to crush out both open and covert treason in this Department; to quicken and invigorate its military policy; to correct disorders and military insubordination; to enforce and not overthrow the laws of the State; and, to aid in vouchsafing order, peace and prosperity to the country." The radical *St. Louis Missouri Democrat*, on the other hand, denounced the anti-Curtis faction as proslavery men, who only "professed to favor emancipation" and opposed the president's proclamation.[9]

Radicals in the militia were also suspicious. In a letter to his sister, one officer said that, though Gamble was an honest man, his desire to become a senator had led him to steer a course between the Copperhead and conservative politicians. He further concluded that since Schofield owed his appointment to Gamble, he would toady toward him and was unlikely to implement a radical guerrilla policy.[10] Nor were radical politicos the only people upset by Schofield's appointment. Francis Herron, now a major general, objected to "Brigadier General" Schofield's assignment and threatened resignation if not reassigned. In a rather gratifying show of support for Schofield, Stanton responded, "He [the President] directs me to say that he is unaware of any valid objection to General Schofield, he having recently commanded the Department of the Missouri, giving almost universal satisfaction so far as the President ever heard. He directs me to add that he has appreciated the services of General Herron and rewarded them by rapid promotions, but that, even in him, insubordination will be met as insubordination, and that your resignation will be acted upon as circumstances may require whenever it is tendered."[11] Herron ultimately got his wish. Schofield assigned him to command the eight infantry regiments and three artillery batteries sent to Vicksburg in early June. Herron served as a division commander in that campaign and then as district commander in the Gulf region until the end of the war.[12]

Even Lincoln's letter of instruction to Schofield afforded the radicals an opportunity for political mischief. When publisher William McKee secretly obtained a copy, he published it in his *Missouri Democrat*. Governor Gamble was highly incensed to have been criticized by the president as the head of a "pestilent" faction. In an angry letter to Lincoln, Gamble indignantly recounted his contributions to the "cause of the Union." He repeated his complaints about the federal government's refusal to support the state militia, while it intruded on his prerogatives by claiming the units as U.S. troops. He reproved Lincoln's humanitarian concern for rebel prisoners of war, while Missourians were murdered in cold blood "upon mere suspicion of sympathy with the rebellion." Lincoln's implication that he would prefer to remove Gamble rather than Curtis was the final, undeserved insult. In his efforts to set a middle course, Lincoln had unfairly maligned the patriotism of Gamble. The governor had taken considerable political risk in creating the EMM to advance the war effort. Lincoln declined to read Gamble's "cross letter" and told the governor that "when I wrote the letter to General Schofield, I was totally unconscious of any malice or disrespect towards you."[13]

Meanwhile, Schofield, fearing the release of the letter reflected a breach of confidentiality on his part, ordered the publisher to his office to reveal the source of the leaked letter, then had him arrested when he failed to appear. McKee was willing to exonerate Schofield's staff, but he refused to divulge his source. Rather than confine him, Schofield ordered McKee paroled pending further action. This distinction was little noted by the radicals, whose cries of tyranny were heard all the way to Washington. Since Lincoln had sent a copy of his letter to Curtis, he probably suspected the leak came from one of Curtis's officers, so he ordered McKee's "release" to spare him further controversy. McKee offered an insincere apology for his failure to respond to Schofield's first summons, and Schofield dropped the matter.[14]

But the politicos were unwilling to have peace. The radicals repeated the line that Lincoln would have preferred to remove Gamble rather than Curtis, and a disgruntled Gamble issued an ultimatum to Schofield in order to reassert his authority. Gamble demanded that Schofield recognize and support the provisional government in all matters, that state law be enforced in all Union camps, that there be no "recruiting of negroes" without authority of the governor, that all violations be punished in state courts, and that all confiscations would go through civil authorities. While Schofield was willing to agree informally and cooperate with the governor, he could not subordinate federal power to state authority. Schofield tactfully deflected the governor's demands, and Gamble ultimately withdrew them.[15]

Halleck's military instructions to the new department commander, if less inflammatory, were no less important. Halleck reviewed his disagreements with Curtis over strategy and reiterated that the correct line to take Little Rock was west from the Mississippi River. Rather than maintaining large forces in southwest and southeast Missouri, several strongly fortified points at Springfield, Rolla, and Pilot Knob should be sufficient, while the remaining forces were pushed south. He told Schofield of his opposition to the large forces maintained in Kansas, which faced little threat and, when sent to Missouri, "were very much worse than useless." Having been overruled in his attempts to transfer these troops south to fight the rebels, Halleck suggested that these units be used to at least protect emigrant wagon trains in Nebraska or Utah.[16]

Halleck also commended to Schofield's "careful attention" the new General Order No. 100 (Instructions for the Government of Armies of the United States in the Field). Despite his pride in this codification of the "laws of war," Halleck acknowledged they were imperfect and did not always answer the thorny questions in the field. He advised Schofield to consult with the best authorities and act with cool deliberation. Prophetically, Halleck emphasized that hasty decisions could lead to serious difficulty and embarrassment. As was his habit, "Old Brains" reiterated that he could not provide detailed instructions and would have to rely on Schofield's good sense and judgment. Halleck declared that the president made the selection on his own, but Halleck concurred with the decision and pledged his "support, assistance, and co-operation."[17]

Upon assumption of command, Schofield moved with dispatch to transfer U.S. troops to Grant. Within two weeks, he had dispatched Herron's division to the front. Schofield's efforts to advance the war effort, despite the risks in his own department, commended him to Grant as they had to Halleck and Lincoln.[18] Halleck had assured him that once Vicksburg was taken, he would push for a renewed effort to take Little Rock and ease the pressure on Missouri's southern border. The correspondence between Grant and Schofield that summer shows a level confidence and cooperation between department commanders little seen in the war thus far. Schofield also took the opportunity to renew the plea for federal support of the EMM while on active service. He noted that the governor had authorized eight regiments, selected for their "efficiency and loyalty," for "continuous active service." A few days later, Secretary Stanton relented and authorized the logistic support of the EMM on active service. The delighted Schofield immediately contacted the governor, the quartermaster general, and the surgeon general to arrange for the transfer of supplies, clothing, and equipment.[19]

Schofield also set about to reorganize his department, in part to implement Halleck's guidance, but also to take care of some internal political problems. In eastern Missouri, Schofield realigned the military districts. He shrank the District of St. Louis and created a Southeastern District under Brigadier General John W. Davidson to concentrate on the defense of this vital area. The District of St. Louis, reduced to the area around the city, acted as a strategic reserve, as well as the administrative and logistical coordinator of the men and materiel flowing through this important transportation center. One of the small, but essential, chores of a supporting military department was to transship supplies for Grant and return furloughed soldiers to their units.[20] It also supervised several prisons and the transport of prisoners to other prisons in the North. With the bulk of the Army of the Frontier transferred to Grant, Schofield organized a cavalry division under Davidson. This force was to fend off Confederate raids and then participate in the Little Rock expedition.

To the outrage of the *Missouri Democrat* and the satisfaction of Governor Gamble, Schofield also took the opportunity to replace Curtis's provost general Franklin A. Dick with the more conservative and well-connected St. Louis lawyer, James O. Broadhead.[21] Finally, Schofield replaced radical Ben Loan in central Missouri with the moderate brigadier general Egbert B. Brown. Loan had been elected to the House of Representatives as an Unconditional Unionist and became part of the anti-Schofield faction in Congress. Loan's combining of political office with military command was, as in the case of Frank Blair, unusual but not unheard of during the Civil War. Dual military and political officeholders were even more commonplace at state level and created complications for military commanders. At one point, both Lincoln and Stanton reprimanded Schofield for refusing to grant leaves of absence for officers who were also members of the Missouri legislature.[22]

Schofield's changes in Kansas were even more consequential. Just as he had recommended the consolidation of Kansas and Missouri into one department, he attempted to integrate command at the district level. He abolished Blunt's District of Kansas and created the District of the Frontier and the District of the Border. He gave Blunt command of the District of the Frontier, which included southern Kansas, Indian Territory, western Arkansas, and nine counties in southwest Missouri.[23] Later in July, Schofield reconsidered this action and returned these Missouri counties to the District of Southwestern Missouri. The District of the Border consisted of northern Kansas and eight counties around Kansas City and bordering on Kansas.[24] Schofield appointed Brigadier General Thomas Ewing Jr. to this sensitive command. Ewing was the brother-in-law and former law partner of William T. Sherman and a member of a politically powerful Ohio family. Though normally assumed to be aligned with the Jim Lane faction, Ewing attempted to keep his balance between the factions of Lane and Kansas governor Thomas Carney. Ewing was no friend of James Blunt and a declared enemy of Jayhawker Charles "Doc" Jennison. Ewing was also a strong supporter of Schofield's efforts to place the border under a single command, rather than creating the separate district or department for Kansas that Lane favored.[25] Schofield hoped that Ewing's moderate attitude and political skills would help defuse the simmering border war between Kansas and Missouri.[26]

Underlying all the factional rivalry and the disputes over "hard" versus "soft" war was the question of slavery and emancipation. In the spring of 1862, many radicals had advocated gradual emancipation, while conservatives preferred to defer the issue until after the war. The Emancipation Proclamation of January 1863, though not applicable to Missouri, pushed the debate further along the road to emancipation. By the spring of 1863, the number of proslavery "Snowflakes" had dwindled. The struggle in Missouri was then between the Republican "Charcoals," who called for immediate emancipation, and the conservative "Claybanks," who now advocated a gradual process. In April 1863 Governor Gamble, who championed gradual, compensated emancipation, recalled the state convention on the topic. Throughout the spring, the delegates wrangled as conservatives proposed amendments to change ultimate emancipation from 1876 to 1866 to 1868 to 1870. In his response to Lincoln's letter of instruction, Schofield had expressed the hope that the state convention would adopt "measures for the speedy emancipation of slaves" and end the factional fighting that divided the Unionist cause.[27]

In June Schofield inserted himself into the debate. Schofield sent a letter to John E. Williams, a friend of his father-in-law and president of the New York Metropolitan Bank, expressing his views on slavery. Williams then published the letter, with Schofield's approval, in the *New York Tribune* on June 6, 1863, with many Missouri papers reprinting it. In the letter Schofield said:

> You are right in saying that I was an antislavery man, though not an abolitionist, before the war. These terms have greatly changed their relative meanings since the rebellion broke out. I regard universal

emancipation as one of the necessary consequences of the rebellion, or rather as one of the means absolutely necessary to complete restoration of the Union—and this because slavery was the great cause of the rebellion, and the only obstacle in the way of a perfect union. The perception of these important truths is spreading with almost astounding rapidity in this State. I have great hope that the state convention, which meets on the 15th instant, will adopt some measure for the speedy emancipation of slaves. If so, our difficulties will be substantially at an end.[28]

Schofield next attempted to influence the convention's deliberations by enlisting Lincoln's support. The president responded cautiously by saying he could accept gradual emancipation if the transition period were "comparatively short" and if the act included protections against selling slaves "into a most lasting slavery."[29] Schofield then visited the meeting hall and personally urged a "speedy" gradual emancipation. Schofield's hope that he could engineer a compromise on emancipation that would heal the factional divisions was a forlorn one. In the end, no compromise was acceptable. The conservatives adopted neither of Lincoln's provisions and approved a plan that would end slavery in 1870. The "Charcoals" continued to press the cause of immediate emancipation and in 1864 won the state election. On January 11, 1865, a new state convention declared the immediate and unconditional emancipation of all slaves.[30]

The festering controversy over slavery was a thorn in the department commander's side as each faction attempted to enlist military authority to its position. Lincoln's cautious approach to emancipation was often not matched in Congress, which in 1861 and 1862 passed laws forbidding the use of the army in apprehending runaway slaves. In Missouri, with most of the state militia federalized, this policy caused great concern among loyal slave owners. Military commanders were often caught between federal law, state law, white public opinion, the initiative of daring runaway slaves, and their own political beliefs. The court-martial of Colonel W. P. Robinson, commander of the 23rd Missouri Infantry, for disobedience of orders is a good example of this problem. On July 11, 1863, Constable John McBride came to arrest an enslaved woman named Lethe at Camp Edwards. McBride had a lawful warrant and letters from Generals Curtis and Schofield. Colonel Robinson refused McBride entry, stating that doing so would be a violation of congressional law in assisting with the apprehension of runaway slaves. The court-martial found Robinson guilty. In reviewing the case, Schofield confirmed the finding and sentence, saying, "Officers are prohibited from employing their forces for the purpose of returning fugitives from service or labor, but they are not required to employ their forces to prevent such return." Schofield, balancing on the side of the barrel, then remitted Robinson's sentence and restored him to duty.[31]

By the summer of 1863, recruiting for African American regiments became another point of contention between the state and federal governments. The manpower shortage had already resulted in the institution of a highly unpopular draft. A special project of Secretary of War Stanton, the recruiters often did not know or did not care about the status of African American recruits. Governor Gamble had granted permission, so long as there was no "interference with the slaves of loyal owners" and no "violation of state laws." Typically, Schofield had to undertake yet another careful balancing act between the interests of Missouri conservatives and the more radical policies of the federal government. When Gamble subsequently complained of violations of state law, Schofield pledged to look into the recruiting of slaves of loyal men. In a letter he reminded the War Department of the sensitivity of the situation in Missouri. However, the status of slaves, even of loyal men, was becoming increasingly uncertain. Kansans, radical Missourians, and now federal officials sought to evade the laws of Missouri and strike a blow against slavery. Caught in the middle, Schofield requested further guidance directly from Stanton, while, to mollify the Missouri conservatives, he temporarily suspended African American recruitment.[32]

Schofield explained to the War Department that experience had shown that "recruiting officers make little discrimination between slaves of loyal and disloyal men." He went on to suggest that the president had the authority "to receive negroes for service without regard to the loyalty of their masters" and that he would "cheerfully" carry out such instructions. In yet another letter explaining the Missouri situation to the War Department, Schofield suggested a program of compensated emancipation. "I believe the able bodied negroes in Missouri will be worth more to the government as soldiers than they are to their masters as laborers. . . . Moreover, I believe it would be a great benefit to the state as well as to the Negro to have him transformed from a slave into soldier." He then recommended recruiting all able-bodied African American men and giving their masters receipts for the value of services lost.[33]

This was Schofield's way of pushing for compensated emancipation, which had become the position of "moderates" like Hamilton Gamble and Edward Bates. By stressing military necessity, Schofield could inject his political beliefs. Yet this proposal was also a typical Schofield straddle. He assuaged the local state officials and passed the problem to the War Department. Naturally, the War Department threw the problem back in his lap, and black recruitment continued. Neither Stanton nor Lincoln was disposed to instruct Schofield officially to disregard state laws in recruiting black troops. Nor was Congress disposed to underwrite compensated emancipation; Lincoln had already given up on the idea. By the end of the year, more than 2,400 African Americans had been recruited in Missouri.[34]

Schofield's journey from Stephen Douglas Democrat to advocate of compensated emancipation to immediate emancipation was a slow trek marked more by the demands of military necessity and political expediency than principle. Despite his generally racist views about the rights and capabilities of African Americans, he occasionally displayed a scrupulous sense of fairness. Schofield treated black soldiers as soldiers. He, for example, fervently endorsed a request to pay certain black troops for their services, even though they had not yet been officially mustered into federal service. Schofield believed that basic fairness required that the War Department give "these brave men their pay." Another example of Schofield's sense of justice was when, despite his manpower problems, he requested permission to send a small military force across the Mississippi River to the Illinois town of Brooklyn "to protect 300 colored people from attack by evil minded men who have already attempted to burn the church and the school."[35]

Like many white Americans, Schofield did not think much of—or about—African Americans until he was forced to do so. Unionists' measures to undermine the Confederacy's use of slaves inevitably had effects on loyal slave states. High casualties and manpower shortages encouraged northerners to resort to "Colored Troops" to fight the war, especially since the burden fell most heavily on border and southern states. Schofield saw that the war to save the Union had inevitably become a war to end slavery.

In July 1863 the fall of Vicksburg finally began to pay dividends for Schofield, when Grant, true to his pledge, transferred forces to Helena, Arkansas, to begin the long-delayed campaign to take Little Rock. By the end of July, Davidson's cavalry division had moved into eastern Arkansas and established communications with Helena. On August 10, Major General Frederick Steele, nominally under Schofield's direction, began his march. Schofield's instructions during and after the campaign, like those of his mentor Halleck, were general and permitted much flexibility on the part of the field commander. With Steele's supply line to Helena secured by General Stephen A. Hurlbut, there was little the Confederates could do to halt Steele's 13,000-man force, and on September 10 it captured Little Rock. This feat, combined with Blunt's capture of Fort

Smith, Arkansas, nine days earlier, gave the Union control of the Arkansas River and half of Arkansas.

Though Schofield hailed Steele's achievement at the time, he mentioned this long-sought objective only in passing in his memoirs. The capture of Little Rock was overwhelmed by a much greater crisis. William Quantrill's raid on Lawrence, Kansas, renewed the debate over guerrilla policy, reignited the war between Kansas and Missouri, and prompted another delegation to demand Schofield's removal. Schofield could hardly relish Steele's military success because he faced the political fight of his life.[36]

On the morning of August 21, 1863, the notorious William Quantrill and nearly 450 men attacked the town of Lawrence. Shooting most of the men they saw, the raiders quickly overran two small detachments of Union recruits and looted and burned the town. Without suffering a single casualty, they killed 150 Kansans and burned 185 buildings. Quantrill's raid relied on boldness and luck. His guerrilla force was the largest assembled since the summer of 1862, and even so he had been fortunate to accidentally encounter 150 others along the way to Kansas.[37] Quantrill was further aided by an incompetent Union commander who had spotted Quantrill's force the evening before but failed to notify the interior towns or to closely pursue.[38] Though Lawrence was the "citadel of Kansas abolitionism" and had been the target of three "bushwhacker" attacks in the 1850s, the townspeople had grown overconfident, and the home guard and picket system had disintegrated. Schofield's transfer of units to support Grant, Rosecrans, and Steele thinned the troops stationed in the region. When the Union pursuit force of perhaps 200 did catch up with Quantrill's retreating band, their horses were near exhaustion, and the better-armed and better-mounted guerrillas easily fended them off. Once in Missouri, Quantrill's men dispersed into small groups and hid. Over the next week Union commanders claimed to have tracked down and killed 100 of them.[39]

The massacre at Lawrence horrified the nation and enraged Kansans. Radical Republican senator James Lane, who barely escaped death in the raid, declared war on Missouri and called for Kansans to make "a large portion of western Missouri a desert waste." The local commander, Brigadier General Thomas Ewing, under pressure from Lane, issued the notorious General Order No. 11 on August 25, which required all inhabitants in four western Missouri counties—Jackson, Cass, Bates, and Vernon—to move within fifteen days to a military post, if loyal, or to leave the district, if not. While selective banishment or expulsion had long been practiced, the depopulation of entire counties was a radical step. Yet, Union policy had been drifting in that direction even before the massacre. On August 18 Ewing issued two general orders designed to turn the screws on the rebels. General Order No. 9 provided for the confiscation of slaves belonging to those aiding the rebellion and their safe escort to Kansas. General Order No. 10 called for the deportation of disloyal persons to the South, while former rebels who had laid down their arms were required to leave the district. Though it prohibited unauthorized destruction of property, it mandated the eradication of blacksmith facilities outside military stations.[40]

Ewing was not acting on his own. He had fully informed Schofield of his intentions two weeks earlier. Schofield, in turn, employed Frank Blair to approach Lincoln informally on these issues. At an August 12 meeting, Lincoln responded by telling Blair the story of the Irishman who asked for a glass of soda water, then adding that he would be glad to have a little brandy in it "unbeknownst to him." Blair inferred that Lincoln would be glad to have Schofield undertake these policies and that he would later justify them as military necessity. Lincoln's "hidden hand" approach to guerrilla policy enabled him to stay above the fray while his commanders took much of the political heat. Under pressure from the radicals yet fearing the reaction of the conservatives, this informal support gave Schofield confidence in pursuing more drastic means.[41]

On the same day Ewing issued General Order No. 11, Schofield sent him a draft of his own proposal, which was remarkably similar to Ewing's plan. Schofield's plan called for the expulsion of all disloyal persons and the destruction of houses and provisions that could be used by the guerrillas. To prevent retaliation against loyal persons, Schofield advised Ewing to remove them temporarily to places of safety. Schofield's willingness to resort to such harsh measures was in part due to the sting of radical condemnation. In an informal diary of the time, he lamented the unfairness of the criticism and recounted the stern measures he had decreed, such as shooting guerrillas, banishment, and assessments.[42]

While General Egbert B. Brown and Missouri lieutenant governor Willard P. Hall complained of Ewing's failure to control the Kansas border ruffians, known as "Redlegs," Senator Lane continued to incite Kansans to retaliate against Missouri. Schofield hurried to Leavenworth to forestall a full-fledged invasion. He met with Ewing, Kansas governor Thomas Carney, and later with Senator Lane. Carney pledged to help Schofield defuse the situation and then reneged. Lane feigned a willingness to cooperate with Schofield but continued to call for a punitive expedition. Schofield shrewdly recognized the partisan games played by these leaders. Schofield believed Lane's insinuations of making Ewing the scapegoat were for show, and that as long as Schofield commanded the department, Ewing was the most pliant district commander Lane could expect. Schofield sensed that Lane's attacks on Ewing were really directed at him and that Lane would renew his efforts to get rid of him. Carney, as Lane's rival for the Senate, saw the senator's bloodthirsty calls for an invasion as a political opportunity for him. Since he knew Schofield would never permit such an action, he had no interest in helping Lane save face. Nor did he want to be seen as obstructing Kansas's righteous vengeance. Carney also criticized Ewing for his support of Lane's candidacy in the Senate.[43]

Despite the complaints of Lane, Carney, and the radical press about Ewing, Schofield seems to have never considered making Ewing the scapegoat. Ewing complained that "my political enemies are fanning the flames, and wish me for a burnt offering to satisfy the just and terrible passion of the people." Schofield attempted to reassure Ewing, advising him that a board of inquiry would exonerate him. Though Schofield would have preferred a less political commander, he believed that Ewing was still the best man for the job. A new man would quickly fall prey to the snares and quicksand of border politics. Since in Missouri Ewing was condemned by the radicals as a Schofield man, and by the conservatives as a Kansas man, Schofield felt a degree of empathy for his embattled subordinate.[44] With both sides abusing him, Ewing conformed to Lincoln's model of proper command.

Schofield's continued support probably contained another political dimension. Though Ewing's relationships with Lane were deteriorating, he was a member of a powerful political family and remained well connected enough to aid in Schofield's promotion to major general. Furthermore, Ewing also had powerful military connections, as the brother-in-law of William T. Sherman. Schofield's staunch support of Tom Ewing undoubtedly contributed to Sherman's good opinion of his future subordinate.[45]

While at Leavenworth, Schofield also attempted to conciliate yet another delicate problem of civil-military relations by making peace between Ewing and the town mayor. Leavenworth had become the center of a vast "fencing" operation for Redleg looters. One of Ewing's detectives, ironically named Jennison, had confiscated horses stolen by runaway Missouri slaves. Mayor Daniel R. Anthony ordered Jennison's arrest for disturbing the peace. The local court fined Jennison $50 and costs. Ewing objected to Anthony's attempt to use the local courts to obstruct his officers and declared martial law. The mayor challenged Ewing's authority to impose martial law, responding, "our people prefer to have all violations of city and state laws settled by the civil authorities." Yet few Kansas courts were disposed to punish those who committed crimes against Missourians. Schofield was able to negotiate a truce, if not a peace, in which Mayor Anthony pledged not to obstruct federal authorities, and Ewing agreed to lift martial law.[46]

During this trip Schofield's anger cooled, and he began to have second thoughts about some of the draconian measures in both his and Ewing's orders. Schofield still believed that given the passions aroused in Kansas, General Order No. 11 was necessary, but he ordered Ewing to modify it to exclude the destruction of property. He believed that the destruction of crops and buildings would do little to harm the guerrillas but would hamper the return of loyal persons. While the order was still severe, perhaps its greatest problem was its implementation. Though Schofield had given him additional Missouri units, Ewing employed too many Kansas troops, who had little interest in discriminating between loyal and disloyal Missourians. He even permitted the notorious "Doc" Jennison to participate in the operation. Schofield's amendment and cautions did not prevent much unnecessary destruction of property and a few outright murders. Instead of unbridled devastation, Ewing conducted a kind of controlled mayhem, which only somewhat mitigated the destruction.[47]

By November, Ewing suspended the unpopular order, and by March, many inhabitants began returning to their homes.[48] As extreme as the depopulation order was, it demonstrated the political contradictions and limits of radical antiguerrilla policies. Although Missourians to this day denounce the order, Schofield and Ewing, both during and after the war, defended the order as an act of military necessity—to rid the area of guerrilla sympathizers and forestall Kansan retaliation.[49] Lincoln again gave his after-the-fact support: "I am not now interfering, but am leaving [matters] to your own discretion."[50]

The judgments on the order's effects were equally mixed. Guerrilla activity certainly diminished, but some opponents and later historians have argued that it was the approaching winter that curtailed guerrilla activity or that the guerrillas simply moved to other areas, like central Missouri.[51] More supportive was the assessment of Confederate general Joseph O. Shelby, who years later said that without General Order No. 11, "the Confederates would shortly have found their way through the district into Kansas. . . . It not only cut off a large amount of supplies, but it removed a large number of our friends and sympathizers. . . . The order was fully justified and Ewing did a wise thing when he issued it."[52] Neither the Confederates nor guerrillas raided Kansas towns again, but the 20,000 Missourians forced from their homes paid a high price for this "peace."

Quantrill's raid and General Order No. 11 symbolize the brutality of war in the Department of the Missouri. And yet their very rarity says something else about the war. Despite a rather bloodthirsty rhetoric employed by many of the parties, the guerrilla war did not degenerate into ever-escalating atrocities. The American Civil War was neither a battle of chivalrous knights nor an explosion of homicidal frenzy. Appalling as many incidents were, violence in Missouri and Kansas never reached the levels seen in the Vendée during the French Revolution or the guerrilla war in Spain, much less the staggering savagery of twentieth-century civil wars. Despite the passions unleashed by the war, most Americans, especially the leaders, kept their heads.

Halleck had warned Schofield that at the first disaster, the politicians would attack "like a pack of hungry wolves," and again Halleck was proven correct. In the sulfurous political environment of the department, the radical Republicans denounced Schofield as the "bushwhackers' best friend" and no better than a secessionist. The conservatives called the radicals "revolutionists" and "Jacobins." In his memoirs Schofield alleged that he scotched several radical plots to kidnap himself and Governor Gamble. In September 1863 two delegations of Missouri and Kansas radicals met with Lincoln to demand Schofield's replacement by radical Republican general Ben Butler. The radicals did not help their cause by the petty, mean-spirited attacks they made on Schofield, whom Lincoln defended.[53]

In addition to Schofield's removal, the radicals wanted the EMM disbanded and replaced with federal troops, and they wanted federal supervision of state elections. They had also not helped their cause when, two weeks earlier, some had incited two St. Louis EMM regiments to mutiny rather than go to New Madrid to replace a volunteer unit marked to reinforce Steele in Arkansas. Radicals would get local judges to issue writs of habeas corpus to sabotage the EMM, as judges in other states sought to obstruct the draft. Lincoln backed up Schofield and other commanders by a September 15 proclamation that suspended writs concerning members of the military, deserters, or military prisoners. With these events fresh on his mind, Lincoln understood that the radical delegations' real motives were to overthrow Gamble's government. While Lincoln approved of their emancipation policies, he condemned their methods: "They are utterly lawless—the unhandiest devils in the world to deal with—but after all their faces are set Zionwards."[54]

Meanwhile, conservatives like Governor Gamble, Frank Blair, James Rollins, and Attorney General Edward Bates came to Schofield's support. Gamble wrote Lincoln, "Without attempting then to dictate to you who shall be Commanding General of this Department, I do demand as I have a right to demand, that you will finally and boldly discountenance the revolutionists who are about to involve this state in anarchy."[55] Thomas Gantt, a prominent St. Louis lawyer, in warning Montgomery Blair of the delegations from Missouri and Kansas to remove

Schofield, wrote, "This would be a surrender of every conservative man in Missouri to persecution as fierce as that which is the lot of rebels in arms against the United States."[56] Despite his public support, Gamble was not entirely happy with Schofield. In a letter to Edward Bates, he called Schofield a "timid, time serving man. He is afraid to do what he knows is right." Gamble chafed under Schofield's prolonged use of the Provisional Regiments on active service and strongly desired their replacement with federal units.[57] Schofield's public embrace of emancipation and General Order No. 11 had no doubt angered his conservative friends while eliciting no support from the radicals. The radical hostility was implacable and generated much fear among conservatives.[58] Though Schofield sent several lengthy letters to rebut the charges, he perceived that the issue was a matter of politics and that "nothing but an absolute political necessity" would cause Lincoln to remove him from command.[59]

Lincoln soon allayed the conservatives' fears. The day after meeting with the delegations, Lincoln sent Schofield a supportive letter of instruction that affirmed previous policies. He reiterated that Schofield should efficiently employ his forces to bring peace and continue to be prepared to contribute to other forces. He also affirmed Schofield's order of martial law in St. Louis related to inciting mutiny but cautioned him to employ it only against those who had palpably injured the military efforts. He left mass removals of inhabitants to Schofield's discretion. Lincoln enjoined Schofield to prevent his command from either returning or enticing fugitive slaves and not to allow enlistment of "colored" troops without Schofield's orders. He directed that no confiscation of property should take place without orders from Washington. Finally, the president ordered Schofield to permit voting only by those who were eligible under the laws of Missouri.[60] Schofield had already encountered the problem of officers who interfered with political meetings and had several of them dismissed.[61]

Lincoln replied to the radicals a few days later with a long letter that defended his and Schofield's actions in Missouri. "Without disparaging any, I affirm with confidence that no commander of that department has, in proportion to his means, done better than General Schofield," the president wrote. Lincoln commended Schofield on his creation and use of the EMM, especially how it permitted the use of federal troops elsewhere. He highlighted the prompt transfer of Herron's troops to Grant. Concerning Quantrill's raid, far from condemning the department commander, Lincoln approved of Schofield's order to prevent a "remedial raid into Missouri."[62]

Lincoln's letter to Schofield and his reply to the radical delegation were all that Schofield and his supporters could have hoped for. Lincoln viewed the dispute as pure political factionalism. Though Lincoln was more philosophically attuned to the radicals, he considered their tactics "utterly lawless." Lincoln stood by his beleaguered commander, despite the fact that the president's political interests lay with the radicals, and some of these men became permanent enemies.[63] Lincoln recognized that Schofield had faithfully attempted to follow his guidance and had assumed responsibility for implementing distasteful policies. Schofield's conscientious efforts to provide reinforcements for Grant and Steele, notwithstanding the risks that this entailed for the guerrilla war in Missouri, particularly commended him to Lincoln. Winning the war came first. While Lincoln wished the radicals and conservatives would get along, he reminded them, "I hold whoever commands in Missouri responsible to me, and not either the radicals or conservatives."[64] Schofield had again been affirmed by the commander in chief, but it was only a temporary victory. The Constitution afforded a determined opposition other avenues of attack.

The next month produced a period of relative calm, with both sides pretending to make peace. Through an intermediary, Lane announced that he had stopped his war against Schofield because Lincoln had told him that to war on Schofield was to war on him. However, this was only a brief truce. Barely a month later, Representative Ben Loan accused Schofield of arming rebels to drive out loyal men in the Platte and St. Joseph areas. Schofield rebutted the charges by pointing out that 5–10 percent of the militiamen in that region were indeed ex-rebels, but that the officers were all "original Union men," who had all served faithfully. He observed, "I take no little satisfaction in making these men guard the property of their more loyal neighbors, and in holding their own property responsible for their fidelity."[65]

On the military front, a raid by Confederate general Joe Shelby was repulsed through the coordinated efforts of Generals Egbert Brown, John McNeil, and Thomas Ewing. Meanwhile, Blunt was embarrassed when Quantrill's band surprised him with a small escort at Baxter Springs, Kansas. Schofield, who had been attempting to remove Blunt for financial and administrative malfeasance since September, saw his opportunity and replaced Blunt with John McNeil as commander of the District of the Frontier. Schofield also transferred most of Kansas to Ewing. To further press his advantage and solidify his grip on the officers of his command, Schofield also rather imprudently requested the authority to dismiss all officers in the department. Stanton and Halleck wisely rejected the idea, saying that Schofield had enough to worry about without the burden of such authority. By the end of November, with Joseph Shelby, William Quantrill, and Bill Jackman all withdrawn south of the Arkansas River for the winter, Schofield was feeling rather confident.[66]

In December Congressman E. B. Washburne of Illinois accused Schofield of interfering in Missouri legislative affairs. Washburne said that he had attempted to persuade Schofield to harmonize the factions by supporting both conservative John Brooks Henderson and radical Gratz Brown for the Senate. Washburne said Schofield refused, saying he would never support Brown. Lincoln summoned Schofield to Washington to explain. In Schofield's account of the conversation, he said he told Washburne that "union of the radicals and conservatives was impossible" because the two sides were too bitterly opposed. Yet he would not stand in the way of agreements and had even asked conservative James Broadhead, Schofield's provost marshal general, to withdraw his candidacy for the Senate. According to Schofield, Lincoln, after hearing his account of the conversation, replied, "I believe you, Schofield; those fellows have been lying to me again."[67] But Lincoln was still faced with the delicate problem of having to publicly question the veracity of one side or the other.

In the next few days Schofield agreed that he saw no way to reconcile the various factions in Missouri and Kansas. Believing that Schofield's retention would be a continuing source of trouble, Lincoln had also concluded that the Department of the Missouri was just too fractious for a single command. With Steele's success in Arkansas and Blunt's gains in Indian Territory, the strategic rationale for the department had diminished. By giving Kansas to Samuel Curtis and Missouri to William Rosecrans, Lincoln hoped to take care of these officers and to arrange a deal that would secure Schofield's promotion to major general. Lincoln hoped that if he could get Senators Brown and Henderson to agree on this arrangement, it would help heal Missouri. He even succeeded in lining up Senators John Sherman of Ohio, Henry Wilson of Massachusetts, Ira Harris of New York, and James R. Doolittle of Wisconsin to support the deal. But Lincoln's hand was forced by Lane, Brown, and other senators who refused to support Schofield's nomination to major general of Volunteers. Without confirmation, Schofield would again revert to the rank of brigadier general and would again be outranked by several other officers in the department. Just as Lincoln found it easier to replace Curtis than supplant a governor, it was easier to remove Schofield than depose the Senate. Without obtaining Schofield's promotion, Lincoln reluctantly decided to divide the department into three separate departments with Rosecrans going to Missouri, Curtis to Kansas, and Frederick Steele to Arkansas.[68]

Professor Bartlett, ever the faithful father-in-law, suggested that to soften the blow Schofield be promoted to brigadier general in the regular army. Since Schofield remained a captain in the regular army, this would have been an extraordinary consolation prize. Lincoln wisely avoided raising a new ruckus with the sponsors of many, more senior, volunteer major generals and ignored this suggestion. Instead, Lincoln appointed Schofield to command another department—the Department of the Ohio. Schofield's enemies did not relent even after his departure from Missouri, however, and Schofield and his friends had to continue lobbying for his promotion. On May 12, 1864, the Senate finally approved Schofield's promotion to major general of Volunteers with a date of rank of November 29, 1862. Schofield got his promotion and, just as important, a field command—the Army of the Ohio.[69]

In assessing Schofield's contributions in Missouri, one should begin by emphasizing the continuity between Schofield and Halleck. Halleck and Schofield, to their credit, attempted to mitigate the horrors of civil war. They tried, often vainly, to discriminate between enemy soldiers and guerrillas, between organized guerrillas and "freebooters," between Confederate sympathizers and conditional Unionists, between "bushwhackers" and ordinary Missourians, and between lawful military action and partisan reprisal. Schofield shared Halleck's view that Missouri was a supporting theater. He readily responded to Halleck's troop levies for the fighting armies, even at the risk of weakening defenses in Missouri. Schofield's bold call-up of the enrolled militia and his determined efforts to secure federal financial assistance greatly reduced the number of federal troops needed to safeguard Missouri. Schofield did not end the guerrilla war, just as the capture of Little Rock did not end the Confederate raids that periodically spawned turmoil throughout the department. However, Schofield did build up the defensive infrastructure of the state. He raised, equipped, trained, and sustained thousands of Missourians to defend their state.[70] In the summer of 1862, guerrilla bands in the thousands operated freely; in 1863 they were reduced to operating in the hundreds; and by 1864 these bands generally consisted of several dozen men. Though the hard-fighting, hard-riding district commanders and troops deserve the bulk of the credit, Schofield had energetically directed and coordinated their efforts. His choice of cooperation rather than confrontation with Governor Gamble enabled him to tap the military resources of Missouri better than Curtis had.

Schofield had faithfully tried to implement the policies of the commander in chief and was rewarded for his loyalty. Nevertheless, he proved unable to remain above the political factions. His position demanded that he make politically contentious decisions nearly every day. His appointment and promotion of senior officers in the department displayed a rough balance among the various factions. In negotiating the minefield of conflicting laws on confiscation and slavery, Schofield genuinely attempted to hew a middle path that avoided needless partisan explosions. Yet efforts to conciliate the radicals, such as advocating early emancipation and enlisting African American troops, seldom assuaged his enemies and disconcerted his friends. Success required that the commander satisfy not only the president but local politicians as well. However, the bitter divisions among local politicians made harmony impossible.

The Department of the Missouri was inherently a political command, and no commander could have remained pure for long. In breaking up the department, Lincoln acknowledged that fact. Schofield's involvement in the cross fire of Missouri politics was a foretaste of what he would face during Reconstruction. Lincoln's sage advice, steadfast support, and example of calm perseverance were indispensable in Schofield's political education. But in the interim, John Schofield, the professional soldier, had escaped to the front; and while politics did not disappear, it did recede. This new assignment also placed him in a perfect position to advance his career. Henry Halleck had schooled him on departmental administration, and now, under the tutelage of William T. Sherman, his education as a field commander would begin. If Halleck had sponsored him and Lincoln sustained him in Missouri, his new bonds with Sherman and U. S. Grant would support and sustain him for many years thereafter.

FIVE

Escape to the Front

Schofield's assignment to the Department of the Ohio was a golden opportunity, and he made the most of it. One year later, when passing through
Washington, D.C., on his way to North Carolina, Schofield encountered Lincoln for the last time. The president greeted his young general with the words,
"Well, Schofield, I haven't heard anything against you for a year." Though
Schofield's Army of the Ohio was no more than the smallish XXIII Corps with
a large cavalry division, Sherman gave him an important role as the "left wing"
of his "grand" army in the Atlanta campaign. Frequently given secondary
missions, Schofield nevertheless displayed a commendable coolness when operating on the army's flank with his small force. Already a conscientious military
administrator, he became a reliable, if not dazzling, corps commander. However, being the most junior of the army commanders had its additional pitfalls,
as more senior corps commanders in the other armies frequently questioned
Schofield's authority. While Schofield had escaped the brutal partisan politics
of Missouri, he had not eluded all political entanglements. Party politics had
been largely replaced by army politics—the politics of command, of rank, and
especially of dates of rank.[1]

Schofield turned over his command in Missouri to General William Rosecrans on January 30, 1864, and assumed command of the Department of the
Ohio from the ailing general John G. Foster at Knoxville, Tennessee, on February 8, 1864. Schofield gave credit for his assignment to Grant, but Grant had
suggested several candidates and noted that generals already in the department
outranked Schofield. Grant had also proposed William F. "Baldy" Smith,
whom he had known at West Point. Smith, however, had an even more difficult
problem with Senate confirmation than Schofield. Smith's close association
with George McClellan and his open criticism of Ambrose Burnside had enraged many Republicans in Congress. The real credit for Schofield's appointment, however, goes to Lincoln. Grant's endorsement meant that Lincoln could
reward Schofield and settle the Missouri situation without waiting for confirma-

tion from the Senate. Secretary of War Edwin M. Stanton, who shared Lincoln's opinion of Schofield, told a friend that Schofield "was earnest, faithful, and able, and had failed in nothing he had undertaken, and that the opposition to him had been unreasonable and groundless."[2]

Despite the good opinions of Lincoln, Stanton, and Grant, Schofield's position was not secure. He still needed to have his promotion confirmed by the Senate. In response to Halleck's question as to whom he would want if Schofield were not confirmed, Grant listed in order of preference: James B. McPherson, Philip H. Sheridan, and O. O. Howard. As the spring campaign drew near, Halleck warned Sherman, "I fear that General Schofield will be rejected by the Senate. He is a good officer, and you will find it difficult to supply his place." Sherman was loath to displace Schofield because he had gained the confidence of both Grant and his troops. Sherman also considered Schofield's political difficulties as a sort of badge of honor because Schofield "did not allow himself to be used by a political faction"; Sherman had written his brother, Ohio senator John Sherman, in support of Schofield's appointment. On May 14, one week after the Atlanta campaign began, Schofield finally received news of the Senate's confirmation of his promotion to major general. Grant's elevation to lieutenant general in March and his great prestige enabled him to put his stamp on the army. His endorsement finally tipped the balance in getting both Smith's and Schofield's promotions to major general through a balky Congress.[3]

William T. Sherman's famous disdain for politics is ironic, given the powerful political connections of the Sherman family. Without politics, many former officers, such as Sherman or Grant, would not have been appointed to general so quickly. Without politics, Schofield, like hundreds of other regular army officers, would have languished at the rank of captain or major. Samuel Sturgis and George Stoneman, both veterans of the Mexican War and senior to Schofield in the regular army, were now his subordinates in the Department of the Ohio. Many older regular army officers, like George Thomas, resented the meteoric rise of many of these junior officers as much as they resented the political officers. For them, promotion should be by regular order until an officer proved unfit for further promotion. Nor were politics or outstanding military merit the only paths to general's stars. Colonel James B. Fry, assistant adjutant general in Washington, told the story of Lincoln's being lobbied by the wife of a regular army officer to have him made a brigadier general of Volunteers. Lincoln wrote, "She is a saucy little woman, and I think she will torment me till I have to do it." Fry mordantly added, "It was not long till that little woman's husband was appointed a B.G."[4]

Schofield's new command was in woeful condition. Confederate general

James Longstreet's siege of Knoxville had sapped its strength so that its two corps, the IX and XXIII, were mere skeletons, with 2,800 and 3,000 troops present for duty, respectively.[5] During the siege, the army had to be supplied through the arduous passes over the Cumberland Mountains. Although the reopening of the railroad between Chattanooga and Knoxville greatly helped, the army was still dreadfully short of supplies, especially of horses and forage.[6] Within days of assuming command, Schofield was forced to return a 4,000-mule pack train to Kentucky before they starved to death from lack of forage. Grant's primary instructions were to prepare the army for the spring campaign. Though he initially ordered Schofield to engage Longstreet, Grant soon rescinded that command and instructed Schofield to annoy Longstreet as best he could without prompting a debilitating battle. Grant recognized the problem of logistically supporting a large force out of Knoxville and told Schofield to conserve his strength in order to build up supplies for the spring.[7]

Grant's acceptance of logistic realities was in accord with Schofield's own assessment, if not his own interest. In February, with his promotion still stalled, political friends urged him to "whip somebody anyhow." But Schofield was neither temperamentally nor professionally disposed to act rashly, even to further his promotion. He indignantly wrote Missouri senator John Brooks Henderson that too many officers had sought "newspaper notoriety," while he had sought only to do his duty and earn the confidence and approval of his superiors—Lincoln, Stanton, Halleck, Grant, and Sherman. Hitching his stars firmly to Grant, he declared that not the senator, nor the House, nor the newspapers, nor the people could command an army. Let Grant alone, and "he will end the war this year." Schofield later admitted that this seemingly impolitic remark was not so indiscreet because he knew it reflected the opinion of Henderson and others in the Senate.[8]

Another task as pressing as logistical preparation for the spring campaign was the filling out of his badly depleted divisions. Schofield needed time to train the new recruits, especially in brand-new regiments. Even more important, Schofield needed to furlough his veteran troops. With the initial three-year enlistments due to end, the government offered generous furloughs to induce the veterans to reenlist. Experienced troops would be crucial for the upcoming campaign, and the Army of the Ohio was already balefully short of veterans. Sherman deemed veteran troops so vital that the XVII Corps, now commanded by Frank Blair, missed the first month of the Atlanta campaign while it awaited the return of the veteran regiments from their reenlistment furloughs.[9]

In addition to resupplying and refurbishing his army, Schofield needed to do some administrative housecleaning. Almost immediately, he had to a find a "competent and reliable man" to "correct the evil" of major malfeasance and corruption at Camp Nelson, Kentucky, the principal depot for the department.[10] Schofield rapidly lost confidence in his inherited chief of staff, Brigadier General E. E. Potter, due to his "careless interpreting of orders" and "apparent bad memory." He relieved Potter and temporarily replaced him with Jacob D. Cox, who had impressed Grant as an intelligent and energetic officer.[11] Cox would become Schofield's most trusted subordinate, as he eventually rose to succeed Schofield in command of XXIII Corps.[12]

Schofield had also brought along his own trusted team of staff officers. This was common practice, as the absence of a common doctrine or training meant that generals trained their own staffs and greatly relied on their judgment. His younger brother George Wheeler Schofield, who had served as an artillery officer in the Vicksburg campaign, would become chief of artillery for the army. William Wherry was Schofield's extended eyes and ears. The "lithe, graceful, and genial" senior aide was the general's "incessantly active personal representative," entrusted with oral orders, examinations, and investigations, whose judgment the commander had learned to trust "as his own." Major J. A. Campbell, as army adjutant general, rounded out the team. "Accurate, systematic, and untiring," he was admirably fitted for the job of coordinating the operational and administrative orders of the command.[13]

This staff soon tightened the administrative screws on the subordinate units. During the campaign, Schofield took part of his staff to the field, while leaving others to run the departmental headquarters at Knoxville. Ever the conscientious administrator, Schofield kept a fairly tight grip on the administration of the department even after he deployed from Knoxville for the campaign. For example, he was still approving and signing all court-martial recommendations well into July. He eventually delegated most of this administration to the department's rear headquarters, but later he had reason to regret the decision.[14]

Upon Grant's promotion to the rank of lieutenant general and his departure east, William T. Sherman assumed command of the Division of the Mississippi. In preparation for the upcoming campaign, Sherman visited Schofield at Knoxville on March 29. The small size of the Army of the Ohio surprised Sherman. With the transfer east of the IX Corps, Schofield only had the XXIII Corps and a cavalry division. Even the XXIII Corps strength of 19,000 was deceptive, because over 11,000 men of the corps were assigned to protect the District of Kentucky from Confederate raiders. Sherman immediately sought to rectify the problem by assigning to XXIII Corps the 5,000 replacements recruited by Indiana politician and brigadier general Alvin P. Hovey.[15] After the meeting with his junior army commander, Sherman expressed satisfaction with Schofield's reputation for "steadiness, courage, & soldierly qualities" and told his brother that it was a pity Schofield "got mixed up in politics."[16]

The manpower problems of the Army of the Ohio reflected the Union predicament in 1864. The ability of men like Alvin Hovey to recruit new troops was vital to the war effort. Even with the enlistment bonuses, the institution of the draft, and African American recruitment, providing men for the ever-expanding army requirements remained difficult. The strength of veteran regiments became desperate since governors preferred to raise new ones, where they could appoint new officers, rather than provide replacements to existing units. New recruits also preferred new regiments, where they knew their officers and fellow soldiers, to being anonymous fillers. The federal government could not completely resist the pressure to create new units; but by 1864, a majority of the new call-ups went to fill existing units, often by the technique of raising new companies to go into veteran regiments. Recruiting parties from veteran regiments also helped fill out the older units, and successful recruiters were often rewarded with commissions.[17]

But the Union army had another manpower dilemma. The Federals, as they drove more deeply into the South, had a longer supply line and more of the newly conquered territory to control. This vast area was susceptible to raids, and Confederate raiders became quite skillful. When Sherman launched his great campaign in May 1864, his military division had a present-for-duty strength of more than 240,000 men, yet his grand army consisted of about 100,000 effectives. Of the 37,227 troops in the Department of the Ohio, Schofield deployed with about 13,565 men. While his effective strength was depleted by the hundreds of men who were sick, injured, furloughed, detached, on recruiting duty, or had deserted, the bulk of the department's strength remained behind to protect Kentucky and eastern Tennessee. Nor was Schofield alone in this predicament. General George Thomas's Department of the Cumberland had over 127,000 troops, but he deployed with 60,773. General James B. McPherson's Department of the Tennessee reported a strength of more than 77,000 men, yet his army consisted of about 24,500. Despite the huge drain on the available manpower, Sherman's army was still a formidable force. Arrayed against him was Joseph E. Johnston's Army of Tennessee, with about 60,000 men and 144 guns. Johnston's army contained more veterans than Sherman's force, but the Union army was better equipped and supplied.[18]

Schofield, in his memoirs, expressed satisfaction in the size of his army— "not too large for my experience"—and claimed he felt no jealousy of his fellow army commanders. Schofield, however, went on to say that "the organization of Sherman's army during the Atlanta campaign was extremely faulty, in that the three grand divisions were very unequal in strength," with Thomas's army having five times the infantry strength of Schofield's and more than twice that of McPherson's army. This seeming contradiction is explained by the fact that Schofield's account of the Atlanta campaign in his memoirs was both a narrative of his role in the operation and a didactic analysis by a mature officer: "I write not for the present, but for the future."[19]

Well aware of the controversy engendered by Sherman's memoirs, Schofield sought to offer a balanced assessment of Sherman's generalship, warts and all. That Schofield waited until after he retired from the army and had assistants diligently search the military records for source materials is further illustration of his having learned from Sherman's example. Yet Schofield's version of the campaign is no less idiosyncratic, if less controversial, than Sherman's own rendition in his memoirs. Schofield's critique reflects some of his own trials and tribulations and was sometimes more a product of his after-the-fact reflections than perhaps his contemporary opinion.[20]

Schofield attributed many of the "partial failures or imperfect successes" in the campaign to the faulty organization. His chief complaint was that "Thomas's command proved too unwieldy and slow from being larger than one man could handle in a rough and in many places densely wooded country, while the others were frequently too small for the work to be done." The need for more troops frequently prompted Sherman to assign a division or even a corps from the Army of the Cumberland to "cooperate with" or "support" the smaller commands. Schofield, the mature senior officer and doctrinal reformer, then blasted the terms "cooperate" and "support" as useless. Commanders who were given such orders frequently refused to act unless the "requests" were "in accord with their own views." Furthermore, such corps commanders, being unfamiliar with Sherman's plans and intentions, could not act with sufficient confidence or anticipation. To modern military officers, Schofield's arguments for standardized units and precise delineation of command and operational control appear unexceptionable, yet nineteenth-century practice lacked the organizational and doctrinal uniformity of the modern military, especially at the higher echelons.[21]

Sherman's combat organization of his command was the result of complex personal and historical factors. Sherman's army group bore a clear resemblance to Grant's arrangements at Chattanooga—the large Army of the Cumberland, the smaller Army of the Tennessee, and an independent "corps." At Chattanooga, this last element had been Hooker's "corps"; for the Atlanta campaign, it was Schofield's "army."[22] However, Sherman's organization was not simply an imitation of Grant's. The evolution of military organization in the Civil War, especially for corps and higher-level units, was not defined by any doctrine but by personal, military, and political expediency. Just as politics permeated the creation and appointment of department commands, politics even influenced the organization of tactical formations. The scale of the Civil War demanded military organizations heretofore foreign to American experience—specifically the army corps and the army group.

Despite the fame of Napoleon's *corps d'armée*, the creation of corps in the U.S. Army became entangled in politics. Secretary of War Edwin Stanton and Republican congressmen persuaded Lincoln to create corps organizations in March 1862, over the objections of Commanding General George B. McClellan. In this struggle to provide places for Republican and Democratic generals, the Army of the Potomac grew to an unwieldy seven corps. Napoleon could control such an army, but McClellan and his successors were not Napoleons. Ambrose Burnside experimented with the concept of two-corps "Grand Divisions," but Hooker returned to the seven separate corps arrangement. By 1864, after detachments, casualties, and bitter experience, George G. Meade consolidated the Army of the Potomac into three corps—fewer, but larger.[23]

In the West the creation of corps was only slightly less political as politician-generals like John A. McClernand, Stephen A. Hurlbut, John Logan, and Frank Blair maneuvered for commands. Through most of 1862, the western armies lacked a corps structure. As the war progressed, the span of control of senior command was reduced as divisions were consolidated into corps, corps into "wings," and armies into army groups. The size and structure of each army evolved based on unique operational demands and the individual inclinations of commanding generals. The consolidation of cavalry and artillery was dramatically slower in the West as commanders grappled with their large areas of operation. This slow evolution of the cavalry arm led to another of Schofield's organizational criticisms. The decentralized nature of the cavalry during the Atlanta campaign, with separate divisions rather than a cavalry corps, which reported directly to Sherman and operated in coordination with the flanking armies, produced much confusion.[24]

Further complicating the problem of organization and command were the internal army politics of seniority. Unlike the Confederates who had four general officer ranks—brigadier general, major general, lieutenant general, and general—the Union army only had two, until Congress reestablished the lieutenant general rank for Grant. Thus, for example, Major General David Stanley (U.S. Military Academy class of 1852; major general of U.S. Volunteers [MG USV], effective November 29, 1862) commanded a division in Major General O. O. Howard's (academy class of 1854; MG USV, November 29, 1862) corps of Major General Thomas's (class of 1840; MG USV, April 25, 1862) army in Major

General Sherman's (class of 1840; MG USV, May 1, 1862) army group. The relative rank of the "old army" and the politics of promotion and congressional confirmation were further complicated by the politics of demotion. So, for example, the former Army of the Potomac commander, Major General Joseph Hooker (class of 1837; MG USV, May 5, 1862) of the XX Corps, could not be assigned to just any army since he outranked everyone but Thomas, and technically, Thomas—"Old Pap"—had greater seniority as a major general over even Sherman.[25]

The seemingly elementary army principle of the senior officer present assuming command grew quite complex in such circumstances. Sherman, in his memoirs, accused Hooker of acting independently of Thomas in order to gain glory but asserting his seniority over Schofield or McPherson in the event of a battle. Later in the campaign, when Sherman placed John M. Palmer's XIV Corps to operate under Schofield's command, Palmer protested to Thomas, who ordered him to merely "cooperate" with Schofield. When Sherman telegraphed Palmer directly to follow Schofield's orders, Palmer, claiming seniority, flatly refused. Still later, Sherman at Jonesboro ordered Schofield to follow IV Corps commander Stanley's orders. Schofield did so, though both Stanley and Schofield knew it was a mistake and that Schofield was senior.[26]

Sherman was also reluctant to "balance" his armies because he did not view them as interchangeable elements, but as living entities. Their components and character had evolved in grueling campaigns and hard-fought battles. The localism and loyalty of the Civil War soldier did not just attach to his state and regiment. As the troops soldiered their way through the war, their brigades, divisions, corps, and armies also became a source of pride and identity. The attachment was also personal and went both ways. The men of the Army of the Cumberland fought for "Old Pap" Thomas, and "Old Pap" had an abiding affection for his army and especially his XIV Corps. Sherman's emotional attachment to his Army of the Tennessee and his trusty XV Corps was just as strong.

Sherman was as ill disposed to break up these soldierly communities as the soldiers were to be divorced from them. Just as replacements often found themselves outsiders amid highly cohesive veterans, whole units could find themselves strangers in a new command. Hooker's XX Corps, created by the consolidation of the old XI and XII Corps and composed of mostly eastern troops, were the orphans of the grand army. Their outsider status, combined with Hooker's unpopularity with the other senior commanders, meant that XX Corps often got the unpleasant tasks, like being last in the march order, fixing attacks, and detachment to the other armies.[27]

Finally, Sherman's army group organization matched his assessment of the strengths and experience of each army commander and his vision of each commander's role in the upcoming operation. George Thomas was a West Point classmate and Sherman's most experienced senior commander. "Old Pap," or "Old Tom," had been nicknamed "Old Slow Trot" as an instructor at West Point, and in 1863 he earned the name the "Rock of Chickamauga." These various nicknames aptly capture his strengths and weaknesses. Thomas was calm and deliberate, though he was sometimes criticized for being cautious and slow. He was also well organized and tenacious, especially on the defensive. He was the perfect person to command the center, or base, of Sherman's army group. Thomas's job was to fix the bulk of the Confederate army while the wings maneuvered on the flanks and then deliver the coup de grâce. Schofield, the least experienced commander with the smallest and least experienced force, was given carefully circumscribed missions. His role was to deceive and distract Johnston, as well as to protect the left flank of the grand army. The brilliant and personable James B. McPherson was Sherman's handpicked successor for his beloved Army of the Tennessee. Sherman had immense confidence and pride in both, and they were to be his main striking force.

The first clashes of the campaign, at Dalton and Resaca, were a perfect illustration of both Sherman's vision and Schofield's critique of the campaign's organization. At Dalton, Sherman confronted the strongly entrenched Confederate Army of Tennessee. Rather than attack such a position, Sherman decided to send McPherson's army around Johnston's left flank through Snake Creek Gap and threaten the important rail junction at Resaca. Such turning movements of well-prepared enemy defensive positions became the hallmark of the campaign. George Thomas had originally suggested sending his army through this gap, but Sherman decided on the Army of the Tennessee. Sherman's decision was based in part because McPherson, as the "right wing," was best positioned to use the approach undetected, in part because of doubts about the speed with which Thomas could move his large forces through the rugged terrain, and in part because Sherman favored his old army.[28]

McPherson's orders did not require him to take Resaca but to destroy the railroad line and then fall back to a defensive position and prepare to attack Johnston's flank when he withdrew from the Dalton front. McPherson successfully moved through Snake Creek Gap, and though the appearance of the Union troops surprised Johnston, the prudent Confederate commander had stationed a brigade to defend Resaca. Uncertain of the terrain and the state of Confederate defenses, McPherson withdrew into a defensive position at the mouth of the gap, rather than provoke a battle. Meanwhile, Thomas and Schofield conducted strong demonstrations against the Dalton defenses.[29]

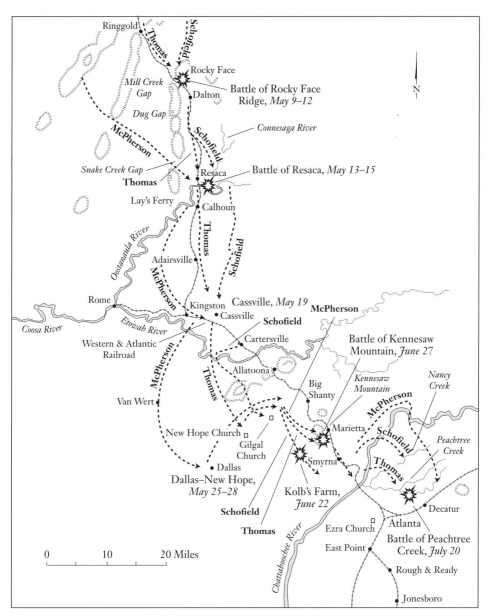

Atlanta Campaign: Advance to Atlanta (adapted from William R. Scaife,
The Campaign for Atlanta*)*

Upon hearing that McPherson was within two miles of Resaca and that Johnston still seemed to be concentrated at Dalton, Sherman was exceedingly hopeful that he had trapped Johnston. On May 10 Sherman, expecting that Johnston would remain in Dalton, changed plans and decided to swing Schofield and most of Thomas's army through the Snake Creek Gap. This move would place the bulk of his army between Dalton and Johnston's vital rail link to Atlanta. However, Johnston, upon learning of the Union troops near Resaca, ordered reinforcements from John Bell Hood's corps near Dalton and from Leonidas Polk's newly arrived corps to Resaca the evening of May 9. Once Johnston determined that Sherman was moving the bulk of his army through Snake Creek Gap, he, having the shortest and easiest path, was easily able to redeploy his army to Resaca to counter this threat. Sherman was again faced with an entrenched opponent, although this time the position was not so formidable.[30]

Sherman was keenly disappointed that he had missed this chance to destroy Johnston at the outset of the campaign.[31] Though recognizing that McPherson acted well within his orders, Sherman, in his memoirs, lamented that he seemed to have been "a little too cautious." From hindsight, Sherman was probably correct that McPherson could have taken Resaca and held it until reinforcements arrived. Schofield, from hindsight, was equally correct that McPherson's confidence would have been increased had his army been strengthened with Hooker's corps from the beginning. In defending his old roommate, Schofield shrewdly observed that Sherman's original orders—to break the railroad and then fall back—were profoundly flawed. Simply breaking the rail line would not have been sufficient. Johnston would have simply repaired the railroad line and prepared new defenses at Resaca. Thus, the results would have been essentially the same. To trap Johnston, McPherson needed to take and hold Resaca. Sherman's orders were tailored more on the size and strength of McPherson's force than the real military requirements. If Sherman had followed Thomas's plan to send the entire Army of the Cumberland, there would have been ample force to hold Resaca. Though Schofield acknowledged that Thomas might not have been able to move fast enough to take Resaca before Confederate reinforcements arrived, this plan had better prospects than Sherman's original.[32]

There is another crucial difference between Sherman's concept of the operation and Schofield's critique. Sherman's idea was to attack Johnston while he was in the process of redeploying; Schofield preferred to place a strong force along Johnston's line of retreat and force the enemy to attack. Sherman's approach often relied on feints and fixing attacks, while other forces maneuvered to make flank attacks. These attacks were intended not so much to crush the enemy in place as to prompt an enemy withdrawal. He could then use his superiority to fight a series of maneuver battles. Sherman's approach demanded exquisite timing. As Grant discovered at Cold Harbor, even an hour's delay could result in horrendous casualties. Sherman's approach also required speed, and his plans were often thwarted by the difficulty of the terrain in northwest Georgia and by the standard practice of withdrawing at night.

Schofield's approach, which was often similar to recommendations made by George Thomas, required speed and surprise to turn the enemy, but envisioned a more traditional set-piece battle. Schofield's concept also demanded enemy cooperation. Even if the Union army had taken Resaca, it may have soon found itself in a race for other key junctions at Calhoun, Adairsville, or Cassville to the south. As generations of generals had discovered, when maneuvering armies in ample terrain, it generally takes the agreement of both sides to make a battle. Both Sherman's and Schofield's methods sought to employ maneuver to avoid costly attacks against prepared defenses, yet both required the enemy to offer battle. But even battle did not decide the issue. Defending or attacking, it was exceptionally difficult to destroy a Civil War army, as most soldiers had learned at Gettysburg, Chickamauga, and Chattanooga.

The maneuver through Snake Creek Gap had been a lost opportunity, but war is filled with chances and missed chances. Sherman chided his young protégé, but he did not engage in the kind of recriminations that ravaged the Army of Tennessee under Braxton Bragg, and later under Hood. It was early in the campaign, and he anticipated other opportunities. Sherman, instead, turned his attention to the new situation. Thomas, thinking that a substantial part of Johnston's army was still moving down from Dalton, recommended using Palmer to trap them; meanwhile, McPherson feinted at Resaca and crossed the Oostanaula River at Lay's Ferry to threaten Johnston's line of retreat to Calhoun. When Sherman realized Johnston was much more concentrated at Resaca and prepared at Calhoun, he chose to keep up the pressure on Resaca, while threatening Johnston's rear with a one-division crossing at Lay's Ferry and a deeper cavalry raid to break the railroad between Calhoun and Kingston.

Sherman's intentions are unclear. He may have intended to conduct a major flanking movement once he had completed the pontoon bridges at the Lay's Ferry lodgment; or, he may have wanted to keep his armies well in hand to strike when Johnston attempted to withdraw. Sherman's cavalry failed to threaten Johnston's rear seriously, but on May 15 McPherson's men had managed to place artillery overlooking the bridges at Resaca. Johnston, sensing the precariousness of his position, successfully crossed his entire army over the Oostanaula River the night of May 15 and burned the railroad bridge behind him.[33] Though unable to trap Johnston, Sherman had forced him to retreat from

Dalton to Cassville without having to stage a costly general assault on Johnston's entrenched troops. However, Sherman's probing and pressuring tactics were not without cost, with probably about 600 casualties at Dalton and another 2,000 around Resaca.[34]

So far, Schofield and his Army of the Ohio had performed creditably. Schofield faithfully followed his orders and was generally where he was supposed to be, when he was supposed to be. Although there were no major battles, his army had fought a number of sharp engagements, generally with Cox's and Henry M. Judah's divisions leading and Hovey's in reserve. Nevertheless, not all was happy in the little Army of the Ohio. Within days of beginning the campaign, Schofield requested Sherman's permission to relieve General Hovey as "utterly inefficient and worthless as a division commander." Recognizing Hovey's past heroism at Champion Hill, Schofield attributed the problem to "some sort of mental disease. He seems incapable of comprehending an order or of having any definite idea of what is transpiring around him." Sherman, also knowing Grant's regard for Hovey, turned down the request.[35]

The 2nd Division commander, Brigadier General Henry Judah, was not so lucky or so well protected. On May 18 Schofield replaced him with Brigadier General Milo S. Hascall, after investigating the conduct of Judah's attack at Resaca on May 14. The XXIII Corps, after a lengthy approach through enemy skirmishers, finally confronted the Confederate main defenses along Camp Creek. Without waiting for reconnaissance or support, Judah ordered his division forward. His troops even passed through the lines of Absalom Baird's division of the XIV Corps as it paused to assess the enemy defenses. Seeing Judah plunge forward into the creek, Baird on the right and Cox on the left attempted to support him. Judah, then Baird, ended up pinned against the steep fortified ridge. Only Cox was able to take a small portion of the enemy line, which he held for three hours until Charles G. Harker of IV Corps came up to relieve them. Despite suffering heavy casualties, Judah wanted to renew the attack until he was dissuaded by his brigade commanders.

Schofield had not witnessed the debacle. He had positioned himself with Cox on the left flank in order to coordinate with Howard, who was due to arrive on his left. Schofield had ordered Judah to align his movements on Cox. Since he had not seen Judah fight, Schofield had to rely on the reports of others, which showed that many of Judah's subordinates had lost faith in him. Already saddled with one unreliable division commander, Schofield could not afford another. Grant, Sherman, and many others had been given second chances early in the war, but now all aspects of the war had become more unforgiving. The aggressive but inexperienced Judah was not to get a second chance.[36]

On the move from Resaca to Cassville, Schofield again operated on the left flank. Poor maps, bad roads, rivers, and congestion with other Union units were more of an impediment than were the Confederates. Without a pontoon train, he forded some rivers and built simple trestle footbridges at others. Meanwhile, he was forced to laboriously ferry across his artillery and trains. He also had to contend with an assertive Hooker, who commandeered the crossing sites allocated for the Army of the Ohio. Still later, Schofield had to make way for George Stoneman's cavalry to pass through on his only good road south. To keep up with the other armies, Schofield resorted to a night march to reach Adairsville on schedule.[37]

As Sherman turned his forces southeast toward Cassville, Schofield, on the left flank, suddenly had the shortest march and approached the Confederates well ahead of the other armies. Johnston, recently reinforced to 70,000–74,000, sensed an opportunity to strike the advancing Union troops before the rest could intervene. On May 19, as Schofield, with Hooker a mile or so to his right, advanced south down the roads from Adairsville to Cassville, Hood would strike them in the flank, while Polk was prepared to support from the front. Just as Hood was about to move into position, Confederate scouts reported an enemy cavalry column advancing on them from the northeast. The Confederate cavalry, for a change, had failed to alert Johnston to the approach of Stoneman's and Edward M. McCook's divisions. Hood hastily pulled back to a new position, and Schofield escaped a nasty surprise. Stoneman had done Schofield a good turn, and Schofield would repay the debt before the year was out.[38]

Schofield's vulnerable position was not entirely accidental. The night before, Sherman had written to Schofield, "If we can bring Johnston to battle this side of [the] Etowah we must do it, even at the hazard of beginning battle with but a part of our forces."[39] Again, he was disappointed. As Sherman's columns converged, Johnston pulled back into defensive positions and, that night, crossed the Etowah River and burned the bridges. Rather than conduct an opposed river crossing, Sherman swung his armies south of the Etowah between Kingston and Cassville to converge on Dallas. Schofield, whom Sherman had ordered to pursue the retreating Confederates as far as Cartersville, had to countermarch to get to the crossing sites. Once again, Schofield had to contend with Hooker's using the bridges allocated to Schofield. This time, however, Hooker had been directed to the site by Thomas, and since Sherman had ordered Thomas to move first, Schofield did not interrupt Hooker's crossing. However, the delay put him a day behind schedule.[40]

At Dallas, the XXIII Corps again assumed a position on Thomas's left and pressed against the skirmishers until they reached the main Confederate lines.

For the next few days, Schofield's troops remained in position as Thomas and McPherson hammered Johnston at New Hope Church, Pickett's Mill, and Dallas. This was fortunate because on May 25 Schofield was put out of action for two days with sickness and an injured leg, after his horse fell into a gully as he was riding forward to get instructions from Sherman on a dark, stormy night. After making little progress at Dallas or New Hope, Sherman needed to reconnect the army to the railroad at Ackworth, and so, on June 2, he sent Schofield to the left to find Johnston's right flank.[41]

After a tough march over broken and heavily wooded terrain in a driving rainstorm, beating back skirmishers, and dodging artillery fire, Schofield's men succeeded in pushing the Confederates back across Allatoona Creek near Gilgal Church. Cox, with Hascall on his left, succeeded in making a lodgment in the Confederate lines but could not break through. Hascall reported that he had nearly flanked the enemy. Hovey's small division was too far to the rear, but Sherman had sent Daniel Butterfield's division of XX Corps to support Schofield. Sensing a chance to outflank the rebel army, Schofield went to "Dan the Magnificent" Butterfield and requested a brigade to help him turn the Confederates' flank. Butterfield, having already declared that he outranked Schofield and reflecting the disdain that Hooker's easterners had for most westerners and especially the tiny Army of the Ohio, refused. He stated that his orders were to "support," not attack.[42]

Hovey was too far away to bring up by dark, so with no other choice, Schofield ordered his men to entrench. Schofield's chances of turning Johnston's flank were in reality slim, since he actually faced not only Patrick Cleburne's division but William H. T. Walker's uncommitted division as well. This "missed opportunity" still rankled Schofield over thirty years later. The next day, the cautious Hovey advanced eastward so slowly that he took most of the day to cover the two miles to the Ackworth road, where he discovered that the Confederates had withdrawn south of Gilgal Church.[43]

Hoping to both outflank Johnston and restore connections to his railroad supply line, Sherman next leapfrogged first Thomas, and then McPherson, past Schofield. Unfortunately, the elusive Johnston had again sensed Sherman's move and realigned his defenses. After a brief respite, Sherman began two weeks of steady pressure that caused Johnston to contract his lines into a very strong semicircular position around Marietta, centered on Kennesaw Mountain. Adding to Sherman's problems was the steady rain that filled the streams, made the hills and gullies slippery, and turned the roads into quagmires. The campaign had literally bogged down.

During the pause, Schofield had two bits of good news. First, his old friend

Frank Blair finally arrived to add his XVII Corps to the Army of the Tennessee, and they had a warm reunion. Second, Schofield finally got rid of Hovey. Hovey, disgruntled over the size of his command and not being promoted to major general, submitted his resignation, and Sherman forwarded it to the War Department, recommending approval. Hovey's 3,000-man division consisted of only six regiments, even though he had recruited five infantry and five cavalry regiments. The cavalry regiments had arrived late and without horses. Unwilling to mix even unmounted cavalry with infantry, Sherman had assigned them to guard the railroad. Schofield, perhaps willing to suffer Hovey if he could get five more regiments, asked Sherman if he could not give Hovey five regiments in replacement. Again Sherman was unwilling to break up another division for Hovey. After Hovey's departure, Schofield broke up the 1st Division, giving Cox the 1st Brigade and Hascall the 2nd Brigade. Schofield's two-division corps was not that unusual. Blair had only two in his corps, while Grenville Dodge commanded two divisions of the XVI Corps. Hovey's division of green troops had been an accident waiting to happen. By integrating them into experienced units, they were less likely to break in a crisis. At least now, Schofield had two strong divisions with two reliable division commanders.[44]

Now on the right flank, Schofield began pushing south down the Sandtown road. Sherman, who had just written Grant that Schofield "does as well as I could ask with his small force," was again attempting to stretch out the Confederate defenses in the hope of provoking another withdrawal that would enable McPherson to strike. Yet progress was slow. In addition to the heavy rains, he was also restrained by the need to keep in contact with Thomas and by the difficulty of transporting supplies from the railhead to his location on the far right flank. By June 20, Sherman's forces were closing on Johnston's strong position at Kennesaw Mountain. The next day, Sherman ordered Hooker's corps to move further down the Sandtown road to support Schofield's flanking movement.[45]

Joe Johnston was also watching Schofield's progress down the Sandtown road and the threat he presented to the rebel left flank. That same day, he redeployed Hood's corps from his right flank to the left, centered on the road from Marietta to Powder Springs. The next day, as Hooker and Schofield skirmished their way south along the Sandtown road, Hood detected an opportunity for an attack. Schofield, while reconnoitering with Hooker, "discovered that the enemy was advancing in heavy force to attack us." The two corps commanders immediately halted their men and ordered them to prepare hasty defenses. Schofield placed Hascall's division to the right of Hooker's right flank division commanded by Brigadier General Alpheus S. Williams. Their line met at Kolb's Farm, with Hooker's men occupying positions north of the Powder Springs road and Schofield's troops located to the south. Schofield then ordered Cox to link up with Hascall but refused his line to the rear so as to protect the army's flank.[46]

Hood launched his attack late in the afternoon, with Carter Stevenson's division on the left, and Thomas Hindman's on the right, and Alexander Stewart's in reserve. Despite the near surprise and a strong attack that focused primarily on two Union brigades, the federals defeated Hood's attack with relative ease. Hindman was arrayed against John W. Geary's division of XX Corps and the left part of Williams's line. Two of Stevenson's four brigades faced Williams's right, and the other two brigades confronted Silas Strickland's brigade of Hascall's division. While Hooker's troops repulsed the Confederates with a massive artillery barrage, the two brigades that attacked Strickland were beaten by virtually a single regiment. Hascall had ordered Colonel George W. Gallup's 14th Kentucky Infantry forward to delay the enemy as the corps prepared its defensive positions. Using the woods in front of the position and giving up ground only when their flanks were threatened, Gallup's men disrupted the oncoming Confederates with withering fire. When Hascall finally ordered them to withdraw to the Union main defenses, the disorganized rebels did not pursue them and fled in the face of Union canister fire. Hood's casualties numbered about 1,500, while Hooker and Schofield combined suffered about 250.[47]

This one-sided victory nevertheless produced great controversy on the Union side and exposed the personal antipathy between Sherman and Hooker. That evening, Hooker sent a report to Sherman saying, "We have repulsed two heavy attacks and feel confident, our only apprehension being from our extreme right flank. Three entire corps are in front of us."[48] This astounded Sherman. How could Johnston's entire army be in front of Hooker? What had happened to Schofield, who was ordered to protect Hooker's flank? When he learned that Schofield was where he was supposed to be, Sherman grew angry. In his memoirs he recounted a confrontation the next day with Hooker, in the presence of Schofield, who supposedly became equally angry upon hearing about Hooker's slight of his corps. Schofield, in his memoirs, insisted that he was not present at such a meeting and suggested that the angry general was really Hascall. Schofield, for his part, was not disturbed by Hooker's message to Sherman because having been with Hooker much of that afternoon, he realized that the "we" meant Hooker and Schofield and that the "extreme right flank" included the Army of the Ohio.[49]

This episode reflected the barely concealed animosity between Hooker and

Sherman. Schofield had first observed the intense rivalry at Resaca. While Sherman, Schofield, Thomas, Hooker, and several general officers conferred on a hilltop, they came under Confederate artillery fire. As Schofield and the rest "scattered" to safer locations, Sherman and Hooker both stood their ground, staring at one another and waiting for the other to make the first move for cover. Sherman distrusted Hooker's motives and later accused Hooker of attempting to position himself so that he could use his seniority to take command from "junior" army commanders like Schofield or McPherson. Schofield was less concerned about that threat than "Hooker's habit of swinging off from the rest of General Thomas's army, and getting possession of roads designated for McPherson or me." Schofield attributed this problem primarily to the size and unwieldiness of Thomas's army.[50]

The personal chemistry among senior commanders is always tricky. As Schofield had learned at West Point, the habit of subordination does not come easily to some men. Hooker's energy and aggressiveness had occasionally irritated the others, but Hooker and his corps had performed admirably. The relatively ascetic Sherman despised Hooker's arrogance and his reputation for debauchery. Meanwhile, Hooker resented the favoritism shown to the western units and especially to the Army of the Tennessee. While Thomas's impassive nature may have occasionally irked the voluble and excitable, high-strung Sherman, he still had a high regard for Thomas's judgment. On the other hand, Sherman distrusted Hooker. Hooker's slightly hysterical and rather egocentric assessment that he faced the entire Confederate army probably reminded Sherman of Hooker's performance at Chancellorsville. In that battle, Hooker, after making a bold turning movement, grew tentative and then timid in the face of the counterattack of Lee's much smaller army.

Even Schofield gently chided Hooker's concern: "being habitually on the flank, I had got used to that sort of thing, while Hooker, having been habitually in the center with his flanks well protected, was more nervous about having them exposed."[51] Constant alarms and importuning for reinforcements become distracting and undermine a subordinate's credibility. The squeaky wheel may get the grease, but the troublesome subordinate may find himself lubricated out of a job. So it was with the quarrelsome Hooker. When McPherson was killed, Sherman passed over his most experienced—and arguably, ablest—corps commander to give the Army of the Tennessee to O. O. Howard. The humiliated Hooker quit in protest.[52]

After the battle at Kolb's Farm, Sherman decided that the Confederates might be stretched thin enough to risk a frontal assault, and he launched the ill-fated assaults on Kennesaw Mountain. Attacks, primarily by Thomas and

McPherson, made no gains, and their losses were considerable—Union casualties numbered 2,000–3,000, and Confederates lost about 450–750.[53] While not comparable to the staggering casualties in the East, the battle of Kennesaw Mountain became the most highly criticized aspect of Sherman's handling of the campaign. General Cox, in his narrative of the campaign, defended Sherman's decision that, as in the cases of Lookout Mountain and Missionary Ridge, seemingly impregnable defenses caused the enemy to become careless. Sherman's frustration with the problems of the weather, supply, and yet another indecisive flanking maneuver further reinforced the hope of duplicating the battle of Missionary Ridge.[54]

While in his memoirs Sherman rather ambiguously suggested that all the army commanders agreed that there was no other option than to attack, Schofield firmly rejected that interpretation in his own memoirs. Schofield deemed another flanking maneuver in order, and he believed that Thomas and McPherson opposed the frontal assault as well. The intensity of Schofield's assessment was again colored by the didactic objectives of his memoirs. Writing in 1897—a time of smokeless powder, repeating rifles, and the first machine guns—military officers were vitally concerned with the effects of increasing firepower on battlefield tactics. Most armies were experimenting with open order tactics, but they had reached few conclusions. The 1894 French regulations still called for infantry to attack elbow to elbow. Meanwhile, the work of the tactics board that Schofield, as commanding general of the army, had created to revise U.S. infantry tactics was being slowed by objections and changes from his successor as commanding general, Nelson Miles.[55]

While some theorists emphasized training and discipline to breach fortified positions, Schofield stressed maneuver. Although some military experts remained skeptical of the capabilities of citizen armies, Schofield reaffirmed the traditional American faith in the courage and resourcefulness of the citizen soldier:

> But we lose one of the most important lessons of the war if we fail to remember and appreciate the fact that our veteran troops are very loath to make an attack where they believe they have not a fair chance of success. This feeling must be attributed, not to a lack of high soldierly qualities, but to intelligence and good sense. The veteran American soldier fights very much as he has been accustomed to work his farm or run his sawmill: he wants to see a fair prospect that it is "going to pay." His loyalty, discipline, and pluck will not allow him under any circumstances to retreat, much less run away; but if he encounters a resistance

which he thinks he cannot overcome, or he thinks it would "cost too much" to overcome, he will lie down, cover himself with a little parapet, and hold his ground against any force that may attempt to drive him back. The general who, with such an army, would win the full measure of success due to greatly superior numbers, must maneuver so as to compel the enemy to fight him on approximately equal terms, instead of assaulting fortifications where, against modern weapons, numbers are of little or no avail. In the days of the bayonet successful tactics consisted in massing superior force upon some vital point, and breaking the enemy's line. Now it is the fire of the musket, not the bayonet, that decides the battle. To mass troops against the fire of a covered line is simply to devote them to destruction. The greater the mass, the greater the loss—that is all. A large mass has no more chance of success than a small one. That this is absolutely true since the introduction of the breech-loaders is probably not doubted by any one; and it was very nearly true with the muzzle-loading rifles used during our late war, as was abundantly demonstrated on many occasions.[56]

Schofield had a high regard for the common sense of the average soldier, and he certainly would not have agreed with the mass offensive tactics for conscript troops being developed by Ferdinand Foch in the French army. Schofield reflects a particularly American style of leadership that relies on persuasion more than blind obedience.[57]

One of the great ironies of the June 27 assault was that Schofield's corps, which was ordered to simply make a demonstration, made the greatest gains and opened the way for the next flanking movement. On the day of general assault, Schofield ordered Hascall to demonstrate strongly against the enemy, while he ordered Cox across Olley Creek to press the rebel flank. While Hascall distracted the enemy, Cox managed to drive back rebel cavalry and occupy a ridge, which, he discovered, dominated Johnston's left flank. Schofield promptly informed Sherman of the situation and brought up both Hascall's troops and Stoneman's cavalry to secure the crucial position. After the failure of his attack on the Confederate center, Sherman took advantage of XXIII Corps's progress to swing McPherson's army around the Confederate left flank. Again Johnston was forced to withdraw, this time to the Chattahoochee River, the last major obstacle between Sherman and Atlanta.[58]

Swollen by the heavy rains, the Chattahoochee River was a formidable barrier. Nevertheless, Johnston kept the bulk of his army on the west bank in a vain effort to provoke Sherman into another frontal assault. While Thomas and

McPherson confronted Johnston, Schofield's little army, finding itself again on the left flank, moved upstream to gain a crossing. On July 8, in a well-managed operation, XXIII Corps established a bridgehead near the mouth of Soap Creek, at Phillips Ferry. Schofield's scouts had discovered an underwater dam that the troops could use to storm across the river, and his personal reconnaissance confirmed the weakness of the enemy defenses. Through careful planning, the assault troops were able to surprise and drive off the Georgia militia and cavalry guarding the site. By the evening, one pontoon bridge had been constructed, and Cox's entire division was across. The next day, the Union cavalry under Kenner Garrard crossed at Roswell, farther to the north. With these crossings, Sherman swung his armies to the left to approach Atlanta from the north, while Johnston abandoned his defensive position along the river.[59]

After crossing the Chattahoochee, Sherman rested and resupplied his troops. In the meantime, Confederate president Jefferson Davis, his patience exhausted, made a fateful decision. Annoyed with Johnston's unwillingness to communicate his views and plans, and frustrated that Johnston seemed to have no other plan than to continue his Fabian tactics, Davis replaced Johnston on July 17 with his polar opposite, the young and aggressive John Bell Hood. Upon hearing of the change, Sherman consulted with Hood's two former classmates, McPherson and Schofield, and with a former instructor, George Thomas. Schofield told him that Hood was "bold even to rashness, and courageous in the extreme."[60] McPherson and Thomas agreed, and all expected Hood to attack. O. O. Howard, one year behind Hood at the academy, had an even harsher assessment. To his wife he wrote, "He is a stupid fellow, but a hard fighter, does very unexpected things."[61]

The Civil War was distinctive for the intimate knowledge that the senior officers of each side had of one another. Both Schofield and McPherson had helped their academically weaker classmate, Hood. Schofield recalled in their first year at the academy how he had encouraged a depressed Hood to apply himself to his impending math exams rather than return to a life of farming in Kentucky. Though he several times thought he had made a mistake in offering that encouragement, Schofield must have later secretly thanked his lucky stars. Without his West Point education, Hood's natural abilities would have likely propelled him to command a division, but probably not a corps and certainly not an army, for which he was wholly unsuited. McPherson, too, had freely lent his intellectual and drafting skills to many cadets, including Hood. McPherson, however, would have cause to regret this assistance to Cadet Hood.[62]

Expecting Hood to attack, Sherman, in his orders for July 19, advised, "Each army commander will accept battle on anything like fair terms." Sherman's

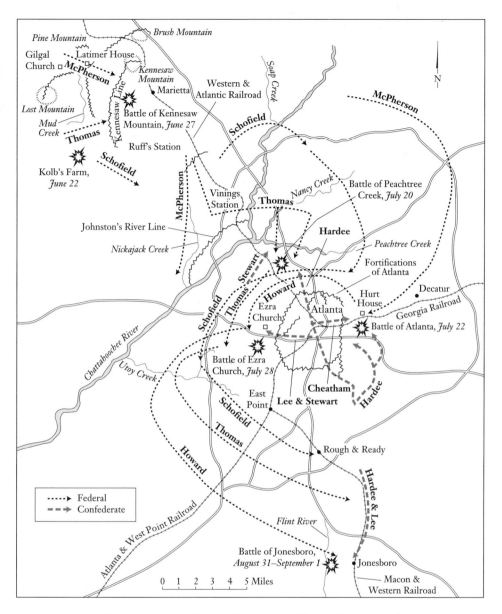

Atlanta Campaign: Isolating Atlanta (adapted from William R. Scaife,
The Campaign for Atlanta*)*

dispositions almost invited attack. With Thomas advancing south across Peach-tree Creek, Schofield in the center moving on Decatur, and McPherson on the far left breaking the railroad well east of Decatur, the Union forces were rather widely separated. Sherman did not have long to wait—that day Hood attacked. Hoping to catch Thomas in exposed positions with an unfordable Peachtree Creek to his rear, Hood attacked with William Hardee's and Stewart's corps. The Confederate assaults were poorly coordinated, and the "Rock of Chick-amauga" bloodily repulsed them.[63]

Frustrated on Sherman's right flank, Hood next attacked the Union left. On July 22 Hood sent Hardee's corps around McPherson's left, or southern, flank and then ordered Benjamin F. Cheatham's corps to support from the west as Hardee rolled up the Union army. With McPherson's left flank dangling in the air and little cavalry for security, Hood's men nearly got around the Union flank. McPherson was surprised, but his fortunate posting of Thomas Sweeney's division to protect the southern flank prevented disaster. Nevertheless, the Army of the Tennessee was in the fight of their lives, with the brunt of it falling on Frank Blair's corps. McPherson's death early in the battle further added to the Union turmoil. Eventually, Hood's furious assault was stopped by the hard fighting of the Army of the Tennessee and the massed fires of Schofield's artillery, directed personally by Sherman.

When Schofield recommended that his and Howard's IV Corps join in the Union counterattack, Sherman rejected the idea, saying, "let the Army of the Tennessee fight its own battle."[64] Sherman later rather strangely suggested that the Army of the Tennessee would have been jealous had the other armies intervened. Schofield criticized Sherman for missing an opportunity to hammer a large part of the Confederate army while it was out in the open and, perhaps, cut them off from Atlanta entirely. Though attacking down a corridor between the Atlanta defenses and the Union line would have been difficult, such an attack would have badly damaged Cheatham's corps. Sherman, for his part, said that he hoped that this attack would give Thomas a chance to breach the Atlanta defenses, but even at reduced strength these fortifications remained too strong, and Sherman never issued any orders to storm the Confederate works. Even with Thomas possessing a four-to-one superiority over Stewart's corps, the success of such an assault was not assured. Perhaps Sherman's romanticism and his attachment to the Army of the Tennessee blinded him to an opportunity to crush a portion of Hood's army, but his decisions also suggest that Sherman was more interested in taking Atlanta than destroying Hood.[65]

The death of McPherson was a severe blow for Sherman, who had great respect and great affection for the intelligent, handsome, and dashing young army commander. In selecting O. O. Howard to replace McPherson, Sherman also made several permanent enemies. Hooker, the "army group's" senior corps commander, angrily requested relief and denounced Sherman's handling of the campaign to the northern newspapers.[66] The Howard selection was doubly insulting to Hooker because of Howard's role as corps commander in Hooker's defeat at Chancellorsville. Logan, who was the senior corps commander of the Army of the Tennessee and had gallantly assumed command of the army after McPherson's death, was also disappointed.[67]

Sherman greatly desired comity and cooperation among his army commanders, and the antagonistic Hooker created too much discord. The quest for harmony also influenced his passing over Logan. Sherman's preference for Howard stemmed, in part, from Thomas's opposition to Logan, in part from the rivalry between Logan and Blair, and in part from his own suspicion of politicians. Sherman valued Howard's modest, conscientious, loyal, and uncomplaining attitude toward duty. Howard's West Point training was decisive. Sherman believed, not without reason, that West Pointers were generally better suited to handle the administrative and logistical demands of department command. Logan returned to his corps and led it valiantly in the Carolina campaigns, but he never forgot this slight; in the postwar years, as a United States senator, he became "the scourge of the regular Army" and a vociferous critic of the West Point "aristocracy."[68]

While both sides bound their wounds and buried their dead, Sherman considered his next move. Having destroyed much of the railroad that linked Atlanta to the east, he shifted his forces back to the west side of the city, in order to cut its remaining railroad links to the south. On July 27 the Army of the Tennessee moved behind Schofield and Thomas to the west side of Atlanta. The next day, Hood again attacked the Army of the Tennessee at Ezra Church. Howard repelled the attack handily, and Hood had little to show but casualties for his offensive policy.

Shifting to defense, Hood was able to thwart Howard's move on the last railroad links to Atlanta and forced Sherman to again shift his entire army group. But Hood's offensive-mindedness had produced an effect on Sherman. As he brought Schofield's corps around, Sherman ensured that it was closely tied to Howard's position and positioned two of Thomas's divisions to support XXIII Corps if Hood attacked again. A few days later, on August 4, Sherman attempted to flank Hood's entrenchments with Schofield's command and to place his forces across Atlanta's last lifeline. Meanwhile, Thomas and Howard, in the hope that the enemy would make an error, were to look for opportunities to gain a lodgment in the city's defenses.

To ensure success, Sherman assigned John M. Palmer's XIV Corps to assist and operate under Schofield's orders. Palmer, insisting he was senior to Schofield, refused. Schofield argued that he was senior because of his commission as brigadier general and his presidential appointment as an army commander. Palmer contended that although Schofield's promotion to brigadier general had occurred nearly a month before his own, both had the same effective date of rank as major generals; since his commission was confirmed earlier than Schofield's, he was senior. Sherman insisted that Palmer follow Schofield's orders, saying:

> The movements for to-morrow are so important that the orders of the superior on that flank should be minutely followed. General Schofield's orders for movement to-morrow must be regarded as military orders and not in the nature of co-operation. I did hope that there was no necessity of making this decision, but it is better for all parties interested that no question of rank should occur during active battle. The Sandtown road and the railroad, if possible, must be gained to-morrow if it costs half your command. I regard the loss of time this afternoon as equal to the loss of 2,000 men.[69]

Claiming that this was an affront to his self-respect, Palmer wrote, "I respectfully ask, therefore, that some officer be designated to whom I may turn over the command of the Fourteenth Army Corps." Sherman, who had never thought Palmer up to the job, genuinely attempted to mollify him. But Palmer was adamant, and Sherman had no choice but to turn command over to the senior division commander, Brigadier General Richard W. Johnson, who proved to be no more energetic.[70] After two frustrating days attempting to get the XIV Corps to move forward, Schofield had elements of the XVI Corps replace his divisions on the line and swung them around the rebel flank. However, it was too late; he found the Confederates well entrenched to block his move. For the next few weeks, the campaign deteriorated into a siege, with bombardments and sap and counter-sap, as each side sought to extend their lines. Even without Palmer's recalcitrance, the chances of outflanking Hood's defenses were not good, but the episode greatly added to Schofield's and Sherman's frustration.[71]

If Sherman was frustrated by the slowness of his infantry maneuvers, he was doubly frustrated by the ineffectiveness of his cavalry. Even before Schofield began his move around the flank, Sherman had launched his own cavalry toward Jonesboro, fifteen miles south of Atlanta, in an effort to wreck Atlanta's last rail line. The cavalry divisions of McCook and Stoneman were to cooperate in taking Lovejoy's Station, several miles south of Jonesboro. McCook would destroy the rail line, while Sherman authorized Stoneman to conduct a raid to free the thousands of Union prisoners who were suffering at Macon and Andersonville. The operation became a complete debacle. Stoneman never linked up with McCook and instead rode on to Macon, where he was surrounded by Confederate forces and forced to surrender with 700 of his men. McCook, after taking Lovejoy's Station and causing some damage, was nearly surrounded by the Confederate cavalry of Joe Wheeler. McCook and his men had to fight their way out.

Later in August, Sherman launched Hugh "Kill Cavalry" Kilpatrick on yet another cavalry raid to make a lasting break of the Macon railroad. This, too, ended in failure, as Kilpatrick was blocked by defending militia, hounded by pursuing cavalry, and finally forced to escape to the east toward Decatur. At this juncture, Hood also attempted to use his cavalry to break the impasse. After his success against McCook and Stoneman, Hood launched Wheeler on a deep raid to interdict Sherman's supply line. This raid also failed and left Hood without much of his cavalry for the rest of the month. Cavalry, which played such an important role in many western campaigns, had remarkably little influence on the Atlanta campaign, to the great frustration of both commanding generals.[72]

Sherman, recognizing that the cavalry was insufficient to break the Confederate rail line, now committed his entire army to the task and once more abandoned his railroad tether. On August 26 Sherman ordered Howard on a long swing around the Confederate lines, first to the Atlanta-Montgomery line near Fairburn and then to the Atlanta-Macon line at Jonesboro. Schofield advanced around East Point toward Rough and Ready on the Atlanta-Macon line, between Atlanta and Jonesboro. Thomas covered the space in between. As Howard's forces closed on Jonesboro, Hood sent Hardee's and Lee's corps to push the Union troops back from this crucial junction. The attack on August 31 against an entrenched XV Corps failed miserably. That afternoon, Sherman also received word from Schofield that he had Cox's division firmly established across the railroad south of Rough and Ready, and Stanley's IV Corps was coming up to secure his right flank.[73]

With Atlanta's lifeline finally severed, Sherman wanted to ensure that it was wrecked permanently, so he ordered Schofield to advance south breaking track as he went, while having his cavalry screen north. Sherman, through Thomas, gave the same instructions to Stanley, who was on Schofield's southern flank. Since Stanley and Schofield both had the same date of rank as major generals, but Stanley had the earlier commission as brigadier general, Sherman placed

Stanley in overall command. Schofield, who believed his appointment as department/army commander gave him precedence, nevertheless placed himself under Stanley's orders.

Sherman's decision in favor of Stanley may have been based on his genuine belief that date of rank was determinative, but he may also have had other motives. He may have thought that the prickly Stanley might respond like Palmer, whereas Schofield, regardless of his views, would follow orders—and Schofield did. Responding to Sherman, Schofield wrote, "I will waive for the time being my own opinion on the question of rank, and act heartily in accordance with your decision." This was the kind of loyal and principled subordination to duty that Sherman admired.[74]

After the campaign, Sherman invited Schofield to state his position on seniority, and Sherman conscientiously submitted the case to the War Department for adjudication. Schofield noted that the Congressional Act of April 4, 1862, gave the president authority to assign officers to command "without regard to seniority of rank," and that the sixty-second article of war established command by seniority "unless otherwise specially directed by the President." From this he concluded that the president's appointment of an army/department commander gave that individual precedence over other major generals, "creating, in effect, another grade in the army, viz. that of Department or Army Commander." A month later, Halleck wrote Sherman on Stanton's decision affirming Schofield's interpretation. To Schofield's great delight, Halleck added, "Although General Stanley's claim to the command of the joint forces, on the occasion alluded to, is not sustained, it was nevertheless General Schofield's duty to acquiesce in your decision and obey General Stanley's orders and the Secretary of War is gratified to find in his conduct on the occasion and in the tone of his protest the spirit and subordination so commendable in the good soldier." By standing on their "honor," Hooker and Palmer propelled themselves into obscurity, while Schofield, by dutifully acquiescing, raised his stock with his military and political superiors.[75]

The morning of September 1 found Howard confronting Hardee at Jonesboro, but the bulk of Thomas's and Schofield's troops were committed to destroying the Macon-Atlanta railroad. Sherman's eagerness to demolish the railroad, however, temporarily blinded him to the opportunity he had to destroy a major part of Hood's army at Jonesboro. It was not until the afternoon of September 1 that Sherman ordered Blair's corps to attempt to cut off Hardee's retreat south to Lovejoy's Station and ordered Stanley to cease the railroad destruction and join in an attack on Hardee's left flank. That night while Sherman was planning the envelopment of the rebels, Hardee slipped away to the south. Early the next day Hood and the rest of his army evacuated Atlanta and marched southeast along the McDonough road, before linking up with Hardee at Lovejoy's Station. On September 2, troops of the XX Corps finally entered Atlanta.[76]

Three days later, still angry over yet another lost opportunity at Jonesboro, Sherman lashed out about the campaign in a private letter to Halleck. Though the letter celebrated the success in taking Atlanta, Sherman nevertheless accused Stanley and Schofield of being slow and permitting Hardee to escape in the night. In assessing the army commanders, he added that Schofield "leaves too much to others." This reproach no doubt colored some of Schofield's later criticisms of the campaign. Stanley also bitterly resented Sherman's contention that his slowness permitted Hardee to escape. Stanley, rightly, blamed his late arrival at Jonesboro and Hardee's escape on Sherman's delay in changing his orders. Stanley was following his orders to demolish the railroad lines thoroughly. Neither Thomas nor Sherman changed them in a timely fashion. By the time Stanley's men came up, Hardee had shifted an unengaged division on his left flank to confront Stanley on the right flank of the Confederate line. Hardee was able to do this because of the ineffectiveness of Howard's army in threatening Hardee's left flank, and because Blair's corps had gotten lost when it attempted to interdict the road south to Lovejoy's Station.[77]

A problem for Sherman at this point was the many, newly appointed senior commanders who were still adjusting to their new level of responsibility. Moreover, Sherman had never inculcated the idea of "marching to the sound of the guns" into his standing orders. He frequently focused on terrain or material objectives over enemy forces. Sherman's sharp pen was one of his least attractive attributes and frequently caused much trouble. Seldom one to back down, Sherman nevertheless included a lengthy addition by Stanley and others about this episode in the appendix of the 1886 revision of his *Memoirs*.[78]

On September 3 Sherman reported to Halleck, "Atlanta is ours, and fairly won."[79] After a brief pursuit, Sherman turned his forces back toward Atlanta to celebrate their victory, to rest and refit after a long and grueling campaign, and most important, to enable Sherman to ponder what he should do next. Sherman offered a shape of things to come when he expelled the civilians from Atlanta. Seeking to avoid the burden and potential trouble of a large civilian population, Sherman wanted to turn Atlanta into "a pure Gibraltar." This permitted him to contract the defenses for a smaller, more efficient garrison. Sherman also sought to remind southerners that their support for the Confederacy put their personal property and fortunes at risk.[80] This expulsion, combined with the damage caused by Hood's destruction of his own ammunition train and some ancillary looting, contributed to the myth of the burning of Atlanta, depicted in southern lore. As with General Order No. 11 of his brother-in-law Thomas Ewing, the stories of atrocity and carnage grew more vivid over time.

Even though Sherman had not destroyed Hood's army, the fall of Atlanta proved to be a resounding military and—more important—political victory. After the carnage and stalemate before Petersburg of Grant's campaign in Virginia, Sherman's capture of Atlanta with relatively low casualties was hailed throughout the North. The capture of Atlanta and Philip Sheridan's success in the Shenandoah Valley renewed the North's confidence in ultimate victory and assured Lincoln's triumph in the 1864 election. Lincoln's reelection sealed the Confederacy's fate.

Although few Confederate leaders were willing to admit defeat, many southerners were increasingly pessimistic about their prospects. More than their stalwart leaders, more than their ragged veteran armies, continued resistance depended on the will and spirit of the southern people. The attack on the popular support for the cause of secession marked the next phase of the war.

Comparing the losses of the two armies is extremely difficult. Sherman reported approximately 35,000 Union soldiers killed, wounded, and missing, of which the Army of the Ohio suffered about 4,000 casualties. At 11 percent of the total, this is slightly less than its proportional strength and reflects its secondary role in the hard fighting at Kennesaw Mountain and the battles around Atlanta. Confederate casualties are harder to assess, given the poor documentation and volatility of Confederate strength, especially the Georgia militia. Confederate casualties under Johnston's tenure were probably slightly less than Union casualties, while Hood's casualties were certainly much more. Sherman's armies reported capturing over 12,000 prisoners and missing less than 5,000 men of their own. The desertion rate of the Confederates would have been considerably higher, though it was often not permanent. Therefore, one might conservatively estimate total Confederate losses at 30,000 to 40,000 —men the Confederacy could ill afford to lose, especially in an unsuccessful effort to repel invasion.[81]

The Atlanta campaign, even more than the famous "March to the Sea," secured Sherman's postwar military reputation. Americans remembered how, in that summer of 1864, their great hopes had bogged down in the trenches of Petersburg until Sherman and his men revived their spirits with the capture of Atlanta. Sherman's achievement lifted their morale and restored their belief in ultimate victory. Schofield's criticism of the missed opportunities to destroy the rebel army, and his conclusion that the Confederate armies, not fortified places, were the true object of military operations—a view shared by George Thomas and his supporters—did not dim the achievement. In the twentieth century, writers such as Basil Liddell Hart, who experienced the brutal trench warfare of World War I, hailed Sherman as a master of maneuver. These disillusioned veterans of the first truly industrial war viewed Sherman's avoidance of bloody battles as a testament to his skill.[82]

As for Schofield and his reputation, he was now an experienced and reliable corps commander. He had shown steadiness and skill in handling his tiny army. Though not demonstrating any special offensive élan, he had energetically performed many flanking movements. He had attentively husbanded his command's strength through prudent deployment of troops, logistical acumen, and the discreet management of replacements. The XXIII Corps actually ended the campaign with more troops than it had at the beginning. Though Schofield's fighting regiments steadily shrank, he brought up new ones to fill out his divisions. He did this despite the ongoing guerrilla war and Confederate cavalry raiders in eastern Tennessee and Kentucky, which sapped his army's strength. The success in Georgia was followed a few days later with more good news, when Schofield reported to Sherman that General Alvan Gillem had surprised and killed Confederate raider John Hunt Morgan at Bull's Gap on September 4, 1864. However, this good news from the rear was soon followed by more disturbing reports, and on September 14, Schofield requested Sherman's permission to return to Knoxville.[83]

Hood remained dangerous, but Hood's 40,000-man army was not Johnston's 60,000, and Sherman's vision extended well beyond the battered Army of Tennessee. Yet while Sherman was looking forward, Schofield was looking rearward. Schofield's concerns resulted in his remaining in Tennessee as Sherman undertook his great march to Savannah. By remaining behind, Schofield would participate in two of the most lopsided battles of the war—two battles that nevertheless reaffirmed how difficult it was to destroy a Civil War army.

The Franklin-Nashville Campaign

Despite the lost opportunities to destroy Hood's army, John M. Schofield had watched the Atlanta campaign unfold much as Sherman had anticipated. The subsequent operations were largely unanticipated. In preparing for his "March to the Sea," Sherman believed, or perhaps hoped, that Hood would be forced to follow him. But Sherman was equally confident that if Hood did not follow him, George Thomas could handle any threat in Tennessee, especially after he sent back XXIII Corps at Schofield's urging. In hindsight, the failure of Hood's invasion of Tennessee appears foreordained. Yet the Nashville campaign could never be described as going according to anyone's plan. Through relatively short, it was marked with unanticipated perils, tantalizing opportunities, narrow escapes, and forlorn hopes. The campaign became a psychological roller coaster as successes and failures produced unexpected and sometimes bizarre reactions. Although Schofield was loath to admit it, luck played a huge role in the outcome. Schofield, the careful planner and prudent calculator of the odds, proved to be incredibly lucky, while the increasingly frustrated and desperate Hood came to rely solely on luck to save his army and his reputation.[1]

After the capture of Atlanta and while Sherman considered his next moves, Schofield and his XXIII Corps settled themselves northeast of Atlanta in Decatur, Georgia. As the troops relaxed and the regimental bands nightly serenaded the corps staff and the unhappy local citizens, Schofield and his officers counted the costs, wrote their reports, recommended promotions, and tackled the dozens of other administrative tasks needed to keep even a stationary army running.[2] Though Schofield had managed to keep his corps up to strength by adding new regiments, his veteran regiments were slowly disappearing. In April the average strength of his regiments was over 550, but by September it averaged less than 400 soldiers. Sherman himself lamented the policy of keeping "our old troops so constantly under fire" and the discouraging effects on the men of their ever-shrinking units. "If we could have a steady influx of recruits," Sherman believed, "the living would soon forget the dead." To that end, Schofield wrote the governors of each state that had provided him with units to plead for replacements for his depleted regiments in order to meet minimum standards. These requests totaled 6,557 men, or the strength of an entire division. Although he received some individual replacements, the bulk of his reinforcements came from new regiments.[3]

In recommending the promotion of his division commanders, Schofield wrote of Jacob Cox, "I have never seen a more able efficient division commander"; Milo Hascall "handled his division with skill, energy, and discretion." Schofield also recommended the promotion of several brigade commanders: Colonels John Bond, J. A. Casement, and Silas Strickland. Cox, Hascall, and most of the brigade commanders served one grade below the rank authorized for the position, and their performance merited promotion. Yet Schofield and other senior commanders had great difficulty in getting their combat leaders promoted. There were three reasons for this. First, there were congressional limits on the number of generals. Second, promotions were generally made up to the limits, leaving little room for future promotions, except through death or resignation. Finally, and most important by this stage of the war, officers who had tired of or failed in combat were seldom eliminated from the service. As Jacob Cox complained, "the political influences which determined the appointment were usually powerful enough to prevent dismissal." Dozens of generals filled the rear area with nominal jobs, while those who were junior led brigades and divisions in battle. Aware of the problem, the War Department began to cull the rear area and order many of these "shelved" generals to assignments at the front, or to resign. Hascall, angry at the politics and delay, shocked Schofield by submitting his resignation in September. The ill-used, but patient, Jacob Cox finally got his well-deserved promotion to major general in December; and he succeeded Schofield in command of XXIII Corps in January 1865.[4]

Long after the war, Jacob Cox, rather ironically, claimed the Union system was superior to the Confederate one, which linked rank to a given level of command—brigadier general at brigade, major general at division, lieutenant general at corps, and general at army. Many, like John Bell Hood, were given temporary rank at the new level of command. Cox argued that the Union system permitted Lincoln to give temporary precedence to major generals who commanded corps or departments, without requiring them to lose their rank if relieved.[5] While this protected the sensibilities of the displaced generals, it was cold comfort for those leaders who were frustrated in their merited promotions. It created needless bottlenecks in appointments and wasteful disputes over seniority. Furthermore, the system of precedence that Cox commended took three years to emerge, largely due to the tribulations of John Schofield. Ironically, the modern army has aspects of both systems. Brigadier and major generals are promoted by list, while lieutenant generals and generals hold their rank by virtue of appointment to specific positions.

Within days of his promotion recommendations, Schofield discovered a more cutthroat brand of promotion politics. On September 9, Schofield learned that the War Department had dishonorably dismissed from the service Colonel John Bond, 111th Ohio Infantry, for disobedience of orders and disrespect to the governor of Ohio. Bond had commanded the 2nd Brigade of Hascall's 2nd Division during most of the Atlanta campaign, and Schofield had just recommended him for promotion to brigadier general. Schofield was stunned to discover that the dismissal of "one of the best brigade commanders in the Army" was due to the bungling of his department's rear headquarters. Without the knowledge of Schofield, Hascall, or Bond, the rear headquarters had sent the request for an inquiry from the Ohio adjutant general directly to the 111th Ohio and its acting commanding officer, Isaac Sherwood. Schofield thundered, "It put a weapon into his [Sherwood's] hands, which he could easily use to the overthrow of Col. Bond and thus secure his own advancement."[6]

John Bond's troubles began in March 1864, when he refused to muster Sergeant John M. Woodruff of the 111th Ohio into service as a lieutenant. The governor of Ohio had granted Woodruff a commission based on his having recruited thirty volunteers for the regiment. Since Woodruff had been absent for more than five months and could name only nineteen of the men he had supposedly recruited, Bond referred the case to Brigadier General Henry M. Judah, then commander of the 2nd Division, XXIII Corps. Judah, without referring the case to the War Department, agreed that Woodruff was not entitled to a commission. Bond's explanation to the Ohio adjutant general in April was apparently lost or captured, and in June the state adjutant general complained to the War Department of Bond's refusal to commission Woodruff.[7]

The War Department demanded a report, but the Department of the Ohio assistant adjutant general at Knoxville sent the request directly to the commander of the 111th Ohio. By that time, Bond was commanding the brigade, and the request fell into the hands of the regiment's acting commander, Lieutenant Colonel Isaac Sherwood, who had also participated in the earlier downfall of General Judah. Bond and Sherwood had already clashed in 1862, when Bond followed the orders of Brigadier General Jeremiah T. Boyle and expelled all slaves from camp. The abolitionist Sherwood complained to the War Department that this was a violation of the Congressional Act of July 17, 1862, concerning fugitive slaves. Since Henry Halleck had issued similar orders, the complaint did not go far. However, in the summer of 1864, Sherwood's hostile report about the Woodruff affair was forwarded to the War Department through the rear headquarters of Schofield's department, without Bond's or Schofield's knowledge. To salvage Bond's career and to knock heads in the rear, Schofield quickly requested Sherman's permission to return to Knoxville and Kentucky to "attend the affairs of my Department." Despite detailed explanations and strong letters of support from both Schofield and Sherman, Governor John Brough of Ohio refused to be mollified, and John Bond departed the army.[8]

But the wheel of fortune turns. In 1866 the new governor of Ohio, Jacob D. Cox, successfully petitioned the War Department to rescind its order of dismissal and grant Bond an honorable discharge. Bond was also given a commission as brevet brigadier general of Volunteers. Lieutenant Colonel Isaac R. Sherwood commanded the regiment to the end of the war and later received a brevet brigadier generalship for his service in the North Carolina campaign, but he was never mustered into federal service as colonel of the 111th Ohio. Schofield thus got some measure of revenge for John Bond. As for John Woodruff, he was commissioned as a first lieutenant effective April 12, 1864, severely wounded during the battle of Peachtree Creek, mustered out with the regiment on June 27, 1865, and returned to Ohio to live to a ripe old age.[9]

After a week in Knoxville and Louisville, Schofield spent a few days in Freeport, Illinois, to take care of some family business and to declare publicly his support for Abraham Lincoln in the upcoming election. Schofield later confided to John Bigelow that he had only twice publicly supported a presidential candidate, Lincoln in 1864 and Grant in 1868. Of the 1864 election Schofield wrote, "Under those circumstances, I thought it my duty to say a few words to my townsmen in Illinois, where I was known as a democrat, explanatory of my view on the great question."[10]

Schofield's brief visit home was quickly interrupted by still more trouble in his department. His trusted adjutant, Major J. A. Campbell, wrote to him at Freeport, "Political-military affairs here are in as bad a state as they ever were in Missouri, and there is but little to be heard except criminations and recriminations on all sides."[11] The guerrilla war in east Tennessee and Kentucky was nearly as ferocious as the one in Missouri. Guerrillas regularly assailed isolated posts, attacked trains, and interrupted traffic on the Ohio River. Even the death of General John Hunt Morgan and the near blinding of Adam R. Johnson did not greatly diminish the rebel activity. Men like Colonel George Jessee or Marcellus Clarke, curiously known as "Sue Mundy," continued the war inside Kentucky, while Confederate commanders in western Virginia continued their raids. A prime reason for the weakness of Sherman's cavalry was the drain of experienced riders to fight the partisan war.[12]

As in Missouri, the level of brutality steadily increased. In July Brigadier General Stephen Burbridge, commanding the District of Kentucky, issued General Order No. 59, which announced that for every unarmed Union man the guerrillas killed, Burbridge would execute four guerrilla prisoners. Burbridge's troops executed at least thirty prisoners in the next few months.[13] The increasing numbers of African American troops also raised the extent of atrocity, as Confederate soldiers murdered members of the Colored Troops who were wounded or taken prisoner. These outrages had a perverse effect on the combatants. As Union officers noted, black soldiers, instead of becoming frightened, fought with even greater ferocity and fortitude and would bear any pain rather than fall into the hands of the enemy. As murder and hostage-taking increased, the faraway Schofield ineffectually warned that "retaliation will only beget retaliation."[14]

Adding to Schofield's problems were reports of corruption. Having seen charges of corruption blight the careers of John C. Fremont, Samuel Curtis, and James Blunt, and unwilling to hand a weapon to his political enemies, Schofield took the reports very seriously, delaying his return to the front to tackle the problem. For example, Schofield initiated an investigation of the Louisville provost marshal's office and had several federal detectives arrested. The charges included accepting bribes to release prisoners, while others, unable or unwilling to pay, languished in jail. There were also allegations of extorting fines for petty offenses and trading in African American substitutes to avoid the draft. The investigation expanded to other posts and even implicated General Burbridge. Schofield, however, was reluctant to initiate an investigation of Burbridge since he had been personally appointed by Grant. But Grant, too, was becoming disenchanted with Burbridge, as Burbridge repeatedly quarreled with Kentucky governor Thomas E. Bramlette. Burbridge, however, retained the support of Secretary of War Edwin Stanton, due to the general's more politically congenial policies on slavery and the recruiting of African Americans.[15]

The Department of the Ohio, which had been expanded in August by adding the District of Western Kentucky, required full-time direction. Schofield's presence at the front prevented him from exercising the necessary attention to and authority over the complex and politically sensitive issues. To solve this dilemma, Schofield appointed George Stoneman as the deputy department commander. Stoneman, who had been exchanged after his capture at Macon, was out of favor with Grant and Stanton. Schofield hoped to use this appointment to rehabilitate Stoneman's reputation. As a West Pointer, Stoneman, Schofield believed, would bring more military and administrative competence to the department. As a professional soldier, he could provide some restraint on the more political district commanders. Although Stoneman had failed in Georgia, he was, nevertheless, a more experienced cavalry commander than any of the others. Stoneman went on to conduct relatively successful cavalry raids into southwestern Virginia in December 1864 and into North Carolina and Virginia in March–April 1865.[16]

Stoneman served as the de facto department commander from November 17, 1864, until the department was discontinued and incorporated into the Department of the Cumberland in January 1865. In another ironic twist, George Thomas replaced Burbridge with John M. Palmer as commander of the re-created Department of Kentucky. Palmer achieved some measure of success against guerrillas by creating special cavalry units whose job was to run down guerrilla bands wherever they went. Authorized to requisition whatever horses and supplies they needed, they angered many local civilians but kept the pressure on the enemy. One of these units caught and fatally wounded the notorious William Quantrill on May 10, 1865.[17]

While Schofield was in Tennessee and Kentucky, the Confederacy attempted to regain the initiative in the West. Sterling Price, with 12,000 cavalrymen, launched a raid into Missouri. Although marching 1,454 miles and causing great commotion, Price lost nearly half of his force and accomplished little of lasting value. However, Price's raid did delay the transfer to Thomas in Tennessee of two veteran divisions of the XVI Corps commanded by A. J. Smith. In Tennessee Nathan Bedford Forrest launched a raid into the western part of the state, while Hood attacked Sherman's supply line from Chattanooga to Atlanta. Forrest's raid so perturbed the Union high command that Sherman ordered Thomas back to Nashville to coordinate the defense and directed Schofield to halt General Burbridge's raid into western Virginia. Unfortunately, the order came too late, and, adding to Schofield's troubles, the Confederates badly handled Burbridge's command. In the midst of the scramble for troops to counter Forrest's raid into Tennessee, politics reared its head when Schofield discovered that Governor Oliver P. Morton of Indiana had ordered leave extensions for an Indiana cavalry regiment so that its members could vote in the federal election. As Schofield made his way back to his command, elements of Hood's army nearly captured him, and Thomas ordered him to take charge of the Chattanooga defenses until the crisis was over.[18]

Sherman had reluctantly turned to follow Hood and drive him away from the Union supply line. He had already suggested to Grant that he cross Georgia and capture Savannah. The experience of chasing Hood and Forrest confirmed Sherman's view that the Union needed to seize the initiative by undertaking a raiding strategy of its own. Pressing his plan to Grant, Sherman insisted, "I can make the march and make Georgia howl." Grant was more concerned about Hood's army and did not believe that Hood would attempt to follow Sherman, should he "cut loose." Sherman explained his position: "I hold Atlanta with the Twentieth Corps, and have strong detachments along my line. These reduce my active force to a comparatively small army. We cannot remain now on the defensive. With 25,000 men, and the bold cavalry he [Hood] has, he can constantly break my road. I would infinitely prefer to make a wreck of the road and of the country from Chattanooga to Atlanta, including the latter city, send back all my wounded and worthless, and, with my effective army, move through Georgia, smashing things to the sea."[19]

Deftly plucking a resonant chord with the offensive-minded Grant, Sherman then argued, "Hood may turn into Tennessee and Kentucky, but I believe he will be forced to follow me. Instead of being on the defensive, I would be on the offensive; instead of guessing at what he means to do, he would have to guess at my plans. The difference in war is full 25 per cent." Forcing the enemy to react to the Union's plans was a telling argument with Grant, and he finally agreed on October 11, 1864, saying, "If you are satisfied the trip to the sea-coast can be made, holding the line of the Tennessee firmly, you may make it, destroying all the railroad south of Dalton or Chattanooga, as you think best." In the coming weeks, he would remind Sherman to leave sufficient forces with Thomas to handle Hood. A jubilant Sherman began formulating his plans.[20]

After Schofield rejoined the army, Sherman briefed both him and General Cox on the proposed march and the participation of the XXIII Corps in the operation. Schofield's corps was again to be the third component of Sherman's army, along with the Army of the Tennessee, consisting of XV and XVII Corps, and the Army of Georgia, consisting of XIV and XX Corps. Schofield objected to Sherman's plan and, specifically, to the role of XXIII Corps. At first, Sherman interpreted Schofield's objections as his unwillingness to give up departmental command and offered to leave Schofield in command of the Department of the Ohio, while Jacob Cox took command of the corps. To the "forward-looking" Sherman, Schofield's "rearward" orientation was troubling, and Cox had performed excellently as acting corps commander. Moreover, Cox was quite eager to go with Sherman. While Sherman believed that Hood would most likely follow him, Schofield was convinced that Hood would invade Tennessee. Schofield made the case that although Thomas had many thousands of soldiers in his command, he had few who were trained or equipped for immediate field duty. Furthermore, during the winter the enlistments for many of Thomas's regiments would expire, and his corps would "disappear" by spring if it were not replenished.[21]

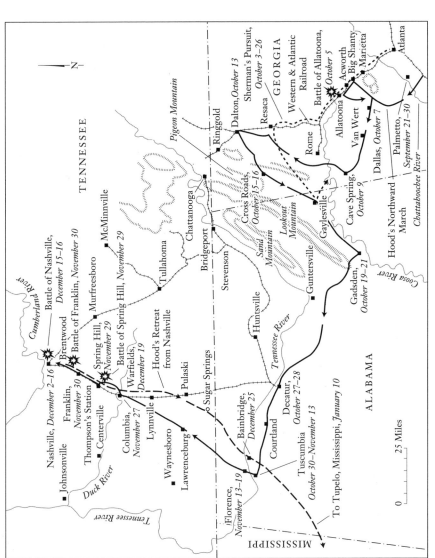

Hood's Tennessee Campaign (adapted from William R. Scaife, Hood's Campaign for Tennessee)

At length, Schofield convinced first Cox, and then Sherman, that Thomas needed XXIII Corps as well as IV Corps, if he were to contend adequately with Hood's diminished but still potent force. On October 30, Sherman ordered Schofield and his corps to report to Thomas. Schofield's success in persuading Sherman to leave XXIII Corps behind was Schofield's greatest contribution to the Nashville campaign—even greater than his generalship during the campaign. Without Schofield's 10,000 veteran troops, Thomas would have had to cede much of Tennessee immediately to Hood, Forrest, and the numerous guerrillas who were still active in the state. He would also have had greater difficulty in assembling the forces necessary to confront and decisively expel Hood from the state.

Schofield reported to Thomas in Nashville as his troops followed from Georgia. After a brief mission to Johnsonville, west of Nashville, where Forrest threatened to cross the Tennessee River, Thomas ordered Schofield and most of his corps to join David Stanley and the IV Corps at Pulaski, where they were already keeping watch on Hood's forces at Florence, Alabama. Schofield's arrival added Cox's division to Stanley's three divisions, which were commanded by Nathan Kimball, George Wagner, and Thomas J. Wood. Brigadier General Thomas Ruger, who now commanded the 2nd Division of XXIII Corps after Hascall's departure, remained at Johnsonville with two brigades.

Thomas appointed Schofield to overall command and instructed him to delay Hood's advance as long as possible, to enable Thomas to assemble reinforcements in Nashville. Upon Schofield's arrival at Pulaski on November 13, Stanley pointed out the problem of stationing the entire army there. With Hood at Florence to the southwest, Pulaski was well positioned to cover the railroad between Decatur and Nashville and any advance on Chattanooga. But, if Hood got a sufficient head start, he could march directly on Columbia and reach Nashville ahead of Schofield's command. Schofield, therefore, stationed Cox's division four miles north of Pulaski, where they could move on Columbia or Pulaski, depending on Hood's actions. He also stationed Strickland's brigade from Ruger's division at Columbia and would later order Ruger there with Orlando H. Moore's brigade.[22]

Schofield, with roughly 20,000 infantry and approximately 3,500 cavalry, awaited Hood's next move.[23] As the campaign began, General Edward Hatch calculated Hood's infantry strength between 30,000 and 35,000, and cavalry about 10,000.[24] This was a relatively accurate estimate. Though Schofield was outnumbered, his chief concern was not annihilation, but being cut off from Nashville and reinforcements. If Hood could prevent Thomas from consolidating his forces, Hood could retain the initiative. The nearly two to one infantry disadvantage was not that serious if Schofield were in prepared positions, but it afforded Hood the opportunity for flanking maneuvers or turning movements.

An even more serious threat to Schofield's flanks was the disparity in cavalry. The superior numbers, leadership, and fighting qualities of Forrest's cavalry enabled him to intimidate and overwhelm the Union cavalry routinely. Even when James H. Wilson took command of the cavalry and brought reinforcements, Forrest still dominated them. Forrest's cavalry constantly threatened to isolate Schofield's force from Nashville. The Union's weakness in cavalry prompted Thomas to order the last of Schofield's brigades (Cooper) at Johnsonville to hold the Duck River fords at Centerville. Cooper's isolated troops would never link up with Schofield's, but they successfully made their way back to Nashville by December 2, one day after Schofield arrived. Surprisingly, amid the scramble to gather troops at Nashville to counter Hood's movements, Schofield, Thomas, and even Lincoln continued to demonstrate great concern with the troop strengths and dispositions in Kentucky and eastern Tennessee, especially cavalry. As dangerous as Hood's invasion was to the Union cause, the government could not politically afford to abandon these areas to guerrillas and Confederate raiders.[25]

On November 15, when Sherman abandoned Atlanta and began his march, Hood not only refused to follow, but he made no move at all. Hood's delay in beginning his invasion of Tennessee would be costly. It had no effect on Sherman's operations and gave Thomas more time to prepare. On November 19, Schofield began to wonder if Hood would "attempt to move his infantry in this state of roads, but Forrest may make a raid on our railroads." The next day, however, General Hatch and his cavalry reported that Hood's infantry was on the move and marching toward Lawrenceburg. A day later, Hatch confirmed the size and direction of Hood's forces. Schofield needed little prompting from Thomas to understand the significance. He immediately ordered Ruger and one more brigade to move from Johnsonville to Columbia. He then alerted Thomas he was preparing to move two divisions to Lynnville, leaving Stanley to follow with the remaining two.[26]

The "race to Columbia," recounted in some memoirs—with Cox's arrival on November 24, just in time to drive off the Confederate cavalry from the harried troopers of Horace Capron's cavalry brigade—makes an exciting but overly dramatic story.[27] Though Forrest's men had energetically pushed back the Union cavalry, he had no chance of taking Columbia because Thomas Ruger, with two brigades, safely controlled the town and the vital bridges. Hatch had provided Schofield timely warning, and the march to Columbia had proceeded much as Schofield and Stanley had planned. By the end of November 24,

Schofield's little army was safely ensconced in Columbia's defenses, and it was another two days before Hood's infantry arrived on the scene.

Schofield delayed his crossing to the north side of the Duck River in the hopes that he might tempt Hood into a rash attack against his prepared defenses. He also hoped to maintain a lodgment on the south side of the river in the event that Thomas arrived with the reinforcements. When Hood did not attack, and knowing he could not secure the lodgment as well as cover the other crossing sites, Schofield ordered his troops across the river on the night of November 27.[28]

Schofield was well satisfied with the initial phases of the operation, but the next few days would prove more frustrating and nerve-racking. Schofield's orders from Thomas were to delay Hood's advance for as long as possible, while "Old Pap" assembled reinforcements and advanced to join him. However, at this vital time Schofield's communication with Thomas began to break down. First, W. C. McReynolds, the civilian cipher clerk assigned to Schofield's command, fearing capture, abandoned his post and moved to Franklin on November 27. This meant that all of Schofield's communications with the rear had to be couriered to and from Franklin, which resulted in eight- to forty-eight-hour delays. Because delaying operations are all about trading space for time, the disruption of his communications to the rear severely hampered Schofield's sense of timing.[29]

The other communications problems were more subtle. Schofield was operating under the assumption that George Thomas was well on the way to assembling substantial reinforcements and preparing to march from Nashville to join him. On November 20, Thomas telegraphed Schofield that A. J. Smith's two divisions were on the way but would not get there before November 25. On November 24, Thomas anxiously asked Schofield if he could protect a bridgehead on the south side of the river "so as to preserve the bridge for crossing whenever we get ready to advance." Schofield's messages from Columbia clearly reflected his anticipation of Smith's approach. On November 28 at 10:00 A.M., Thomas sent Schofield a message that Smith would not arrive for three more days; yet given the need to courier the telegraphs from Franklin, it is uncertain when Schofield received the news. Schofield's telegraphs of 4:00 P.M. and 6:00 P.M. that day suggest he still expected Smith's imminent arrival.[30]

If Thomas's optimism about Smith misled Schofield, it also blinded Thomas to the need for urgency in assembling other troops. General James Steedman had assembled a force of 5,000–7,000 men at Chattanooga. Thomas, still uncertain as to Hood's objective, delayed bringing these troops to Nashville and, on November 27, toyed with sending them to Decatur to destroy Hood's bridges across the Tennessee River at Tuscumbia, Alabama. Steedman did not arrive in Nashville until after the battle at Franklin on November 30. In his memoirs Schofield, perhaps reliving some of the fear he felt during those tense days, rebuked Thomas's delay in recalling these critical reinforcements. While he agreed with Thomas's decision not to completely abandon the railroads to raiders, he argued that if Steedman's troops had been sent immediately to Columbia, Schofield's forces could have held the Duck River fords for several more days.[31]

One final communications difficulty arose while Schofield confronted Hood at Columbia. After using a pontoon bridge across the Duck and no longer having the wagons for transport, Schofield ordered the pontoons destroyed. On November 28 Schofield requested that Thomas place a pontoon bridge at Franklin to replace the washed-out wagon bridge. Thomas rather complacently told Schofield to use the pontoon bridge he had used at Columbia, never considering that Schofield would have done so if he still had it. For Thomas's part, he was already trying to find Steedman replacement pontoons for those that General Robert S. Granger had destroyed a few days earlier as he departed Decatur, Alabama. When Schofield arrived at Franklin, he found some newly arrived bridging material but no bridges immediately ready to carry his troops, artillery, and wagons to safety. The delay to repair and improve the bridges triggered the ensuing battle at Franklin and would fan discord and suspicion between Thomas and Schofield.[32]

Once on the north side of the Duck River, Schofield's task was to hold the numerous fords across the river. He deployed his infantry to many of the crossing sites without spreading them too thinly. He relied on Wilson's cavalry to cover the fords to the east. In messages to Thomas, Schofield apologized for having to abandon the southern bridgehead, but he insisted it was necessary. He was even skeptical about his long-term prospects to hold the north side of the river, telling Thomas, "I do not think we can prevent the crossing of even the enemy's cavalry, because the places are so numerous. I think the best we can do is to hold the crossings near us and watch the distant ones."[33] This statement unfortunately proved prophetic as Forrest's cavalry again overpowered their Union opponents.

By noon on November 28, Schofield was receiving disturbing reports from Wilson of Forrest's cavalry, and possibly rebel infantry, forcing crossing sites seven to ten miles to the east along the Lewisburg Pike. Forrest's cavalry initially drove back the Union cavalry at Hardison Mill along the Lewisburg Pike, then near Huey's Mill. While Wilson attempted to confirm these reports and rally his forces to strike back, Schofield apprised Thomas of the situation and the implications for his link-up with reinforcements. In an effort to react to the crisis along the Lewisburg Pike, Wilson withdrew forces that were supporting the other crossings. This permitted the Confederates to take several of the crossing sites nearer Columbia by attacking the Union pickets from the rear.[34] Meanwhile, as the cavalry screen to the east disappeared, subordinate commanders like General T. J. Wood, hearing of the Confederate crossings, grew anxious about remaining at Columbia.[35]

In a vain hope that the cavalry reports were exaggerated, or that Wilson could retrieve the situation, or that reinforcements were on their way, Schofield delayed any movement to the rear on the afternoon and evening of November 28. After holding the bridgehead around Columbia for three days, he was stunned by the speed of the rebel advance and the deterioration of his position on the north side of the Duck River. Schofield, the careful planner and not the intuitive leader, badly needed information. While he waited anxiously for news, Schofield's communications again broke down, as messengers got lost in the dark or had to take circuitous routes to avoid Confederate cavalry.

Without word from Wilson, Schofield ordered infantry patrols, but they did not accomplish much before dark. Unlike Napoleon, with his large *maison* of aides, or Bernard Montgomery, who relied on a band of intelligent, young officers to augment his electronic communications, the small staffs allocated to Civil War commanders did not permit such redundant means of intelligence and communications. Still, Schofield's relatively few aides provided good service as his eyes and ears. They conducted reconnaissance and carried vital messages. It was important and dangerous work. Three of Schofield's aides were killed in the Atlanta and Nashville campaigns (at Resaca, Atlanta, and Franklin).[36]

Finally, on the morning of November 29, Schofield's worst fears were confirmed when one of Wilson's messengers turned up with an hours-old report. Wilson reported that Confederates had indeed crossed in force and were building pontoon bridges that night for the infantry to cross. Even worse, Forrest was between Schofield and Wilson, for Wilson had withdrawn his forces to Hurt's Crossroad, while Forrest was concentrated at Rally Hill. With Schofield's flank completely uncovered, Wilson unabashedly advised Schofield to withdraw by 10:00 A.M. to Spring Hill, a tiny village of a dozen houses. Even more brazenly, Wilson asked for the one cavalry brigade, under Colonel John Hammond, located at that critical junction. Wilson ended his message rather peremptorily with, "Get back to Franklin without delay, leaving a small force to detain the enemy. The Rebels will move by this road [the Lewisburg Pike] toward that point."[37] Shortly after receiving Wilson's dismaying report, Schofield received another long-delayed message from Thomas, which ordered him to withdraw to Franklin while leaving a delaying force at Spring Hill. It also informed him that Smith's men had still not reached Nashville.[38]

The alarmed Schofield now had a dilemma. He was in danger of being outflanked and possibly cut off from Nashville, but how? Was the entire enemy force swinging to the east and advancing to Franklin along the Lewisburg Pike, as suggested by Wilson? If so, why were so many Confederates still in Columbia with most of their artillery? Or, was Hood preparing a flank attack on the Duck River defenses? Or, were the forces at Columbia a diversion, and was Hood attempting a more significant flanking maneuver by advancing on Spring Hill? With his enormous 800-wagon train and 20,000 soldiers and only one good road, Schofield could not simply "bug out." The Confederates had established a bridgehead, but with the poor roads, they could not rapidly march around Schofield, nor could they easily cross their artillery. If Schofield immediately abandoned the defense of the fords near Columbia, he risked giving Hood an easy opportunity to cross his artillery and trains and march on him that day. Yet, if Hood did block his path to Franklin, Schofield would have to undertake a more difficult route to the northwest in order to get to Nashville. This would leave the path to Nashville open for Hood.

Schofield's decision was a risky straddle. He sought to hold the enemy at bay at Columbia until nightfall while establishing a defensive position at Spring Hill, thirteen miles away. Schofield assigned Cox to defend along the Duck until nightfall and ordered Wood to conduct a brigade-size reconnaissance to the east to see if Hood was attempting to envelop the river defenses. Colonel P. Sidney Post's brigade would discover Hood's troops crossing at Davis Ford and advancing up the Rolla Hill road toward Spring Hill. Schofield also ordered Stanley to take two divisions, Kimball's and Wagner's, north with the wagon train. Wagner was to advance all the way to Spring Hill, while Kimball would peel off several miles to the south to guard an enemy approach along Rutherford Creek. Schofield had initially ordered Ruger's division to follow Stanley immediately, but within the hour he countermanded that order so that Ruger could continue obstructing the fords and covering the Duck. At this point, Schofield still viewed an enemy crossing at Columbia as his most serious threat. He did not advance to Spring Hill with Ruger's division until nearly 3:00 P.M. and arrived at Spring Hill around 7:00 P.M.[39]

On the morning of the November 29, John Bell Hood was full of confidence. His plan was to leave most of S. D. Lee's corps and the artillery at Columbia to distract and deceive Schofield, cross the Duck with Benjamin Cheatham's and Stewart's corps, and then march to cut the Union army off at Spring Hill.

Forrest, meanwhile, was to drive back the Union cavalry and then secure Spring Hill until Hood's arrival. But if the "race to Columbia" had been a foregone conclusion, the race to Spring Hill was marked by a curious lack of urgency on both sides. Schofield's piecemeal moves toward Spring Hill were matched by a certain sluggishness on the part of Hood and the Confederates. Hood's first surprise that morning was the discovery that his map was inaccurate and had deceived him on the length of his route. The march was further slowed when Post's brigade seemed to threaten his flank, so he had some units march on a difficult and wearying parallel route. By noon the Confederate army was still miles away from Spring Hill.[40]

By noon, Stanley, after a rather slow march, arrived at Spring Hill just in time to drive off Forrest and the rebel cavalry who were approaching the town from the north and east. After the departure of Hammond's brigade, the defense of the town fell to a small cavalry regiment, the 12th Tennessee, and a detachment from the 103rd Ohio Infantry who were guarding the wagon train—less than 500 men. Fortunately, some lost and isolated cavalry units turned up to aid in the defense. Upon hearing gunfire, Stanley rushed his men forward: Emerson Opdycke's brigade headed straight through the town, John Q. Lane's brigade deployed to his right facing east, and Luther Bradley's moved on Lane's right flank. Forrest's men had had a busy day. In the morning they attacked Wilson's cavalry and so rattled him that Wilson withdrew north toward Franklin and Nashville. By the afternoon, the Confederate cavalry was running low on ammunition and in no position to confront a veteran infantry division. After a spirited fight against Stanley's troops, Forrest fell back.[41]

Stanley had a few hours to prepare defenses before the Confederate infantry arrived on the scene around 4:00 P.M. Given the short winter days, there were less than two hours of daylight remaining. Cheatham's corps, consisting of Patrick Cleburne's, William Bate's, and John C. Brown's divisions, deployed immediately from the march and attacked in a piecemeal fashion. Upon sighting Spring Hill and the turnpike, Hood changed his plan of attack. Instead of moving directly on Spring Hill, he ordered Cleburne and Bate to attack *en echelon* due west so as to interdict the turnpike south of Stanley's position. Thus, Bradley's right flank took the brunt of the attack from the right flank of Cleburne's division. Unfortunately, Hood did not tell Cheatham, his newest corps commander, about the change in plan, nor did he remain forward to observe the execution.[42]

As Cleburne redeployed his division to assault Bradley's exposed right flank, Cheatham halted Bate, who was on Cleburne's left, and realigned his battle line to the northwest with Cleburne. In the fight Bradley was severely wounded; his

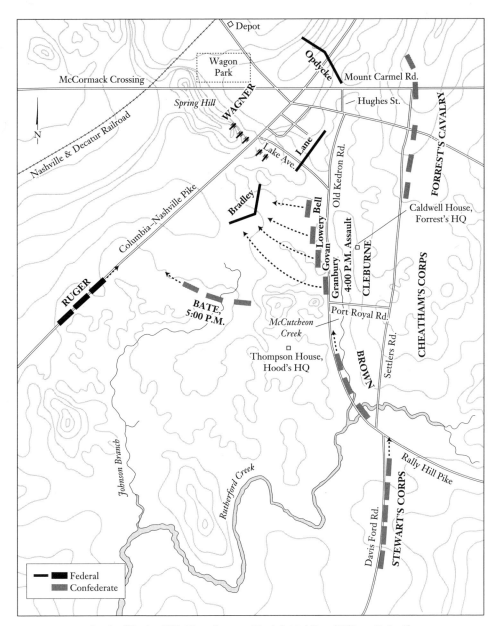

Battle of Spring Hill, November 29, 1864 (adapted from William R. Scaife,
Hood's Campaign for Tennessee*)*

men could not hold such a position long, and they fell back to link up with Lane's position. As the Union forces regrouped for the next assault, six Union batteries, nearly all of IV Corps's artillery, caught the Confederates in a withering fire.

While Bate moved up on Cleburne's left, Brown's division prepared to attack on his right. However, in a bold move Colonel Lane had sent a single regiment far to the east to threaten Brown's right flank. As Brown moved up, his scouts noted the Union troops on his right flank. Uncertain about the enemy position and strength, Brown halted and awaited instructions from Cheatham, who had gone looking for Bate. With neither Cheatham nor Hood present to clarify orders, the Confederate and Union troops waited as darkness mercifully descended on the battlefield.[43]

Despite this debacle, Hood remained optimistic. He ordered Stewart's corps moved up to block the turnpike with its right flank while linking up with Cheatham on the left. In the darkness a staff officer from Cheatham's corps arrived to place Stewart's command. But since Brown's right flank was canted away from Spring Hill, he positioned Stewart parallel to the pike. Believing this an error, Stewart went to Hood's headquarters for confirmation. When Hood finally realized Stewart was not blocking the pike, he rather listlessly told Stewart that it was not material and to let the men rest. He then asked Forrest to block the turnpike, and Forrest, reminding Hood of his ammunition shortages, said he would try. Hood believed he could still finish Schofield off in the morning and predicted Schofield's surrender the following day. Hood took some laudanum for the pain in his amputated leg and went to bed early, as the cold and weary Confederate soldiers huddled by their campfires.[44]

When Hood discovered the next morning that his old classmate had escaped in the night, he was furious. Poor coordination, lack of command presence, and a certain intellectual lethargy had caused Hood to miss another opportunity. In the tradition of the Army of Tennessee, the commanding general castigated his subordinates, especially Cheatham. Cheatham in turn tried to pass some of the blame on to Brown and Cleburne. The stories of Hood's anger began to trickle down the chain of command. The rebel army commander had demeaned their courage, impugned their honor. Each vowed that the next time Schofield would not escape. The angry recriminations and the sense of failure would set the stage for an even greater disaster later that day.[45]

As the rebels withdrew a short distance and bivouacked for the night, their camp paralleling the federal line along the Columbia-Franklin Pike, Schofield finally arrived with two of Ruger's brigades and one of Wood's. Upon hearing that rebel cavalry still occupied Thompson's Station a few miles up the pike,

Schofield's and Ruger's troops advanced to drive the enemy away. Surprisingly, Schofield found only smoldering fires. The path to Franklin seemed clear. To make sure, he rather cold-bloodedly ordered one of his young aides, Captain William J. Twining, and his small headquarters troop to ride at full gallop to Franklin to check on the status of troops there. Schofield then waited in the dark to hear if the aide's mission was cut short by gunfire. Hearing nothing but the fading clatter of hooves, Schofield returned to Spring Hill.[46]

Captain Twining reached Franklin safely and sent a status report to General Thomas. Twining said in part, "General Schofield's troops are pushing for Franklin as rapidly as possible. The general says he will not be able to get farther than Thompson's Station to-night, and possibly not farther than Spring Hill. He regards his situation as extremely perilous, and fears that he may be forced into a general battle to-morrow or lose his wagon train." This reveals that Schofield was far more worried than his later accounts of the campaign admitted.[47]

Upon returning to Spring Hill near midnight, Schofield found Cox's and Wood's divisions arriving from the Duck River and decided to continue the march to Franklin. With Cox in the van followed by the huge wagon train, Ruger, Kimball, and Wood, the Union army marched up the road with the Confederate campfires just a few hundred yards away. Wagner and his men held their positions until the Union column passed and then took up the mission of rear guard. During the march, there was only one brief clash with Confederate cavalry. The officers and men were dead tired, but fear pushed them on. Once they were past the Confederate camp, Schofield's anxiety diminished, and he even slept a bit in the saddle as they marched north. As dawn broke, the weary soldiers hobbled into Franklin. Schofield and his army had escaped by the skin of their teeth.[48]

Even decades later, Schofield continued to claim that his force was never in great danger and minimized the role of luck at Spring Hill. In his memoirs he quoted Hood's claim that Hood hoped to catch Schofield napping, but claimed that "in fact I was watching him all day." While Post's reconnaissance had spotted Hood's movement, and the deployment of Kimball's division at Rutherford's Creek was reaction to that threat, Schofield continued to be fixated on Lee's demonstration at Columbia. Had he been tracking Hood's progress that closely, he would have launched Ruger toward Spring Hill before noon. While Schofield was worried about a possible flank attack, Post's skirmishers had, in turn, worried Hood. More aggressive skirmishing by Kimball would have further slowed Hood's advance on Spring Hill.[49]

Though Schofield might be excused for not anticipating the rout of Wilson's cavalry at Hurt's Crossroads and Mount Carmel, he underestimated the threat that Forrest's cavalry presented to his escape route. Letting Hammond's cavalry leave Spring Hill was a mistake, and only the fortuitous arrival of miscellaneous cavalry units saved the day until Stanley's men came up. Schofield also minimized Forrest's potential threat to Union escape that night. He rather blandly asserted that had Forrest blocked the road, he could have easily gone cross-country to Franklin. The prospect of his army, burdened with heavy wagons, crossing the still soft fields in the dark strains credulity. He would have lost more than a few wagons, and the potential for troops getting lost in the dark was quite high. Schofield's army could have escaped, but not easily.[50]

Stanley later dismissed Schofield's claims to superior foresight and anticipation as "merest bosh." And bosh it was. Schofield had tried to cover all bases. However, his gamble just barely succeeded, due mostly to unforeseen circumstances rather than shrewd calculation. He had been lucky, very lucky, but his vanity refused to accept it. Schofield's claim incensed Stanley, in part, because it minimized Stanley's contribution to the army's escape. While Schofield believed the battle of Franklin was his greatest contribution in the war, Stanley regarded his own efforts at Spring Hill as "the biggest day's work I ever did accomplish for the United States." Stanley, with Wagner's division and the IV Corps artillery, had put up a bold defense and kept the road to Franklin open. If he did not save the army from certain destruction, he spared Schofield a dangerous retreat that would have exposed Nashville, the probable loss of much of his trains, and the possibility of battle under very unfavorable circumstances. Yet Stanley, too, had been aided by fortuitous circumstances, notably the confusions among the Confederate high command. If the Confederate failure at Spring Hill would have fatal consequences at Franklin, the Union success would also have tragic repercussions.[51]

One final consideration about Spring Hill: Schofield had slipped through Hood's grasp, just as Joe Johnston had repeatedly foiled Sherman with timely night withdrawals. Hood, through overconfidence or lack of imagination, seems to have disregarded having the tables turned on him. Hood seriously underestimated his old classmate, whom he knew was no fool. Schofield, for his part, may have been indecisive on November 29, but there was little complacency. Schofield's problem was too much imagination about what Hood might do, and he tried to cover all possibilities. Yet finding himself in a tight spot, Schofield did not panic. He did not fall victim to paralysis or frenetic activity. He and his men kept their heads as they crept by the Confederate army in the dark.

When Schofield, Cox, and their tired troops staggered into Franklin in the early morning hours, Schofield immediately went to check on the status of the bridges. Finding the turnpike bridge washed out and no pontoon bridge, Schofield ordered Cox to take charge of creating a defensive perimeter with XXIII Corps and Kimball's division as they arrived. Taking temporary command of the corps, Cox positioned the three divisions in a shallow horseshoe around the town, with each flank resting on the Harpeth River. Cox placed his division, now led by Brigadier General James Reilly, on the far left, covering the area from the river to the Columbia Pike; he placed Ruger's division in the center between the Columbia and Carter Creek Pikes; and he positioned Kimball's division on the far right extending to the river in the west.

Meanwhile, Schofield returned to the river to supervise the hasty repair of the washed-out turnpike bridge, turning it into a footbridge for soldiers. He also ordered the planking-over of the railroad bridge to permit the wagons and artillery to cross. Shortly after the engineers completed their work, a train arrived with the pontoon bridge sent by Thomas. Now unnecessary, Schofield ordered it back to Nashville. By noon, the wagon train and much of the artillery began to cross to the north side of the Harpeth River.[52]

Wilson's cavalry was also on the north side of the Harpeth, to the east of Franklin. Schofield, who was worried that Forrest would again defeat the cavalry and threaten his flank, crossed Wood's division to back up Wilson at around 1:00 P.M. This was not an imaginary threat. Forrest had advised against a direct attack and begged Hood for infantry support to turn the Union flank. A Confederate cavalry brigade later forced a crossing, but without infantry support, Wilson's men held.

At the same time that Wood was crossing the river, Wagner, as rear guard, sighted Confederate troops marching up the Columbia and Lewisburg Pikes. As the Confederates advanced, the divisions of Reilly, Ruger, and Kimball continued to improve their defensive position, while Wagner's division, as a covering force, gradually pulled back to occupy a ridge less than half a mile from the main entrenchments.

By 3:30 P.M., when the Confederates began to appear on the hill two miles south of the main defenses, Schofield was feeling quite secure. He had his heavy equipment across the river, and he had one division on the north side to prevent another cavalry threat to his left flank. Three divisions held excellent defensive positions, with orders already issued for their withdrawal after dark. And, finally, he had one division covering his defensive position to give him early warning, to force the enemy to deploy prematurely, to threaten Hood's flank if the rebels decided to cross the river east of Franklin, and to dissuade the enemy from advancing his artillery too close to the breastworks. The farther away the Confederates camped, the easier it would be to slip away at night.

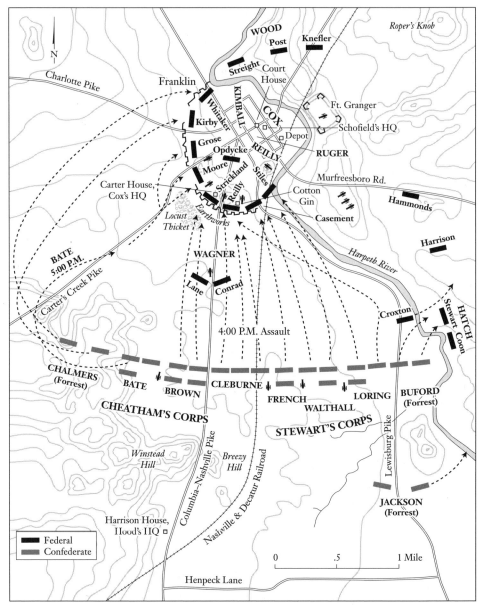

Battle of Franklin, November 30, 1864 (adapted from William R. Scaife,
Hood's Campaign for Tennessee*)*

Finally, if the enemy pressed Wagner's division too hard, Wagner had orders to withdraw behind the main defenses and become the army reserve. Neither Schofield nor Stanley, who was visiting with Schofield at his headquarters on the north side of the river, thought that Hood would attack such a formidable position so late in the day.[53]

At 4:00 P.M., when the Confederate brigades deployed for battle and began to advance, Schofield, Stanley, and most of the Union army were astonished. Stanley immediately got on his horse and rode to his command on the south side of the river, while Schofield rode to nearby Fort Granger, which overlooked the town defenses. Schofield has been unfairly criticized for remaining there rather than going to the front lines. However, this was his logical position. The corps and division commanders had their orders, and his greatest concern was another collapse of his left flank by Wilson's cavalry. Finally, Wood's division, the only reserve with which he could influence the action, was nearby. Nevertheless, Schofield's careful plans went awry almost immediately.[54]

Only one of Wagner's brigades had withdrawn behind the main defenses to act as a tactical reserve as the plans had envisioned. From the high redoubt, Schofield watched in horror as, instead of withdrawing into the defensive works, two of Wagner's brigades remained in their exposed position until they were overwhelmed by the attack of Cheatham's and Stewart's corps. Schofield saw the men fleeing for the main defenses, closely pursued by the rebels, and thus hindering the fire of those defending the entrenchments. His "heart sank" as the enemy seemed to break through. Immediately, Schofield ordered Wood to cover the withdrawal of the fleeing troops across the river. Then, he saw Opdycke's brigade and other reserve regiments rush in to counterattack. Gradually, smoke engulfed the entire defensive line. As the smoke obscured the battle line, Schofield held his breath. The firing continued, but the number of fleeing soldiers abated. A relieved Schofield knew the line had held.[55]

The Confederates had nearly broken through, but after having an almost impossible victory snatched from their grasp, they were unwilling to give up so soon. General Stewart later said it was "the most furious and desperate battle of the war in the West." One of Cox's officers thought it was the "hardest fought battle" in the war, and the rebels "charged and fought like perfect fiends."[56] The Confederates launched repeated attacks along the Union line and especially at the juncture of Ruger's and Cox's divisions, where the initial rupture had occurred. The rebels achieved some toeholds in the breastworks, but they could not exploit them. Union commanders sent reserves to the danger points to throw back the enemy.

Stanley had arrived just in time to join Emerson Opdycke's brigade as its fiery commander led his troops in the desperate counterattack. Within a few minutes, Stanley was wounded in the neck and departed the battlefield. Cox was left as the senior officer directing the fight. Reilly's division, in a rather formidable position, battled Stewart's corps and part of Cheatham's. In doing so, one regiment, the 104th Ohio, captured eleven Confederate battle flags. Ruger's two-brigade division, with the assistance of Opdycke and a few regiments from Kimball, contended with the bulk of Cheatham's corps. Kimball's division was lightly engaged, primarily by the late-arriving troops of Lee's corps. Meanwhile, Wagner desperately and unsuccessfully attempted to re-form with the refugees of his broken brigades, who were huddled by the river. The fighting was fierce, and often hand to hand. The next morning, many adversaries were found locked together in death's embrace.

Rebel units attacked, were repulsed, then regrouped and attacked again. In the meantime, many Confederate soldiers sought cover at the base of the breastworks where the Union soldiers could not fire on them. Eventually, most of these men surrendered. Not even darkness halted the struggle. For five furious hours, the battle raged. Around 9:00 P.M. the assaults slackened, but sporadic firing continued for several hours more. Later that night, the Union divisions slipped across the Harpeth and continued their retreat to Nashville. Hood had captured the battlefield, a traditional measure of victory, but as daylight revealed the carnage from the previous evening, the achievement was lost on his army.[57]

The costs and consequences of the battle of Franklin were frightful, especially for the Army of Tennessee. Casualty reports, always tricky, were difficult because the Union army departed the field that night and the Confederates shortly thereafter. In fact, Confederate reports do not give specific casualty figures for the battle. In his report Hood admitted to 4,500 casualties, but a comparison of the present-for-duty strengths of his army between November 6 and December 10 suggests 6,000 to 7,500.[58]

Schofield reported Union casualties as 189 killed, 1,033 wounded, and 1,104 missing (presumed captured), for a total 2,326. Over half of the casualties came from Wagner's division, which lost 1,241 men, including 670 captured. Schofield's initial estimate of enemy losses was 5,000–6,000. Upon reoccupying Franklin, he reported enemy losses as 1,750 buried on the field, 3,800 disabled in the hospital at Franklin, and 702 captured, for a total of 6,252, not counting the more lightly wounded.[59] Such casualties constituted 10–12 percent of Schofield's infantry strength and 18–25 percent of Hood's infantry strength.[60]

Beyond these grisly statistics, many units were ruined, and the command structure devastated. One Confederate captain wrote, "Our army was a wreck. I can safely say that just two such victories will wipe out any army the power of man can organize." Another Confederate veteran in Stewart's corps later recounted that Cockrell's brigade had only three officers and about a hundred men fit for duty the next day. The Confederates lost thirteen generals (six killed, six wounded, and one captured), including the death of the most able combat leader in the entire army, Patrick Cleburne. More than fifty brigade and regimental commanders were killed, wounded, or missing. Stewart's corps lost three brigade and twenty-four regimental commanders. A comparison between the November 6 and December 10 strength reports reveals a staggering loss of perhaps 800–1,000 officers.[61]

At Franklin, the fighting heart had been torn out of the Army of Tennessee. A Confederate officer later wrote, "General Hood has betrayed us. This was not the kind of fighting promised us. . . . [I]t can't be called anything else but cold blooded murder."[62] The battle has been compared to Pickett's Charge, yet another Confederate forlorn hope, but it more precisely resembled Cold Harbor, where another frustrated commander hoped a direct assault would overcome the hasty defenses of the enemy. After the meat grinder of Cold Harbor, Grant's army lost its aggressiveness. At Petersburg, it hesitated and missed a golden opportunity to capture the weak city defenses before Lee's army arrived. After Franklin, Hood's army would trudge on to besiege Nashville and fight a battle there, but the offensive spirit of the army was gone, forever.

Why did Hood attack such a formidable position? In his report Hood claimed he feared Schofield would fortify Franklin or escape to the works at Nashville. And though Schofield feared most for his flanks, Hood also insisted that "the nature of the position was such as to render it inexpedient to attempt any further flank movement, and I therefore determined to attack him in front, and without delay." To be fair, a flanking maneuver would have accomplished little, as Schofield would have withdrawn all the way back to Nashville. Hood's opportunity to strike the isolated Union force was slipping away. His anger and frustration over Spring Hill, combined with his natural aggressiveness and his sheer lack of any better idea, produced the desperate and deadly gamble. Due to a Union blunder, he almost succeeded. This tantalizing near-victory, like the siren song of the Lorelei, would spur Hood on to the ultimate disaster at Nashville.[63]

The destruction of Wagner's division not only put the entire army in jeopardy; it also cast a huge shadow over the victory. Again, the human factor unraveled Schofield's careful planning. Stanley had assigned the rear-guard mission to Wagner's division. All day, Wagner and his men had the unpleasant task of observing and hindering the Confederate advance. They were quite successful; Hood later acknowledged that he lost much time as they forced him to interrupt his march to deploy against them.[64] As the men approached Franklin around 11:30 A.M., Wagner hoped to move into the safety of the entrenchments. Schofield, however, in the hope of keeping Hood at a distance, ordered Wagner to "hold the heights [Breezy and Winstead Hills, two miles south of Franklin] you now occupy until dark, unless too severely pressed."[65] An irritated Wagner complied, but as Hood maneuvered Stewart's corps on his flank, Wagner withdrew his troops back to Privet's Knob, an open field on a small spur along the Columbia Pike, about a half-mile from the main defenses. Since the brigade commanders did not expect to remain there long, they did not entrench.[66]

By mid-afternoon, the men of Wagner's division were extremely tired from the fighting of the day before and the constant marching. The tempers of their commanders were also frayed. When Wagner ordered Opdycke's brigade back from its exposed position on Breezy Hill to join the rest of the division in line, the hot-tempered brigade commander continued to march into the defensive perimeter, stopping a few hundred yards behind the lines. Wagner followed Opdycke, angrily insisting he obey orders. Opdycke was widely known as a fierce fighter, but he was extremely volatile and willful. His brigade had been the rear guard of the rear guard; his troops had had to stand in position while the others cooked breakfast. He was determined to rest his men. As Opdycke's troops settled down to brew some coffee, Wagner gave up and prophetically shouted, "Well, Opdycke, fight when and where you damn please; we all know you'll fight."[67]

Wagner discussed his situation with Cox, who probably expressed doubt about an enemy attack, but repeated his orders to retire if attacked. Wagner, still angry, returned to his two forward brigades and ordered Lane and Conrad to dig in and even have the sergeants use bayonets to keep the men in position. Wagner then returned to Cox's headquarters, at the Carter House, which was less than one hundred yards behind the main defenses along the Columbia Pike. From this position, the dip in the terrain and his own troop formations obscured his view of Hood's activities. Thus, less than an hour later, when urgent messages arrived from brigade commanders Lane and Conrad that the enemy was advancing and threatening their flanks, Wagner was unprepared. Wagner was not only out of position; he was also emotionally off balance. His frustration with his seemingly thankless mission, his anger with Opdycke, and the pain in his leg from a riding accident, now possibly combined with whiskey, disturbed his judgment. Having boldly defied the rebel army the day before, he dismissed the alarms. Despite the pleading of Cox's staff officers, Wagner angrily sent orders to his brigade commanders to "stand there and fight them." To an anxious messenger, he said, "Tell Colonel Conrad that the second division can whip all Hell, and for him to hold his position." Even the lowliest privates knew this was a mistake, but the brigade commanders followed their orders.[68]

Wagner's act of bravado destroyed his division and his career. After the battle, Thomas quietly relieved and reassigned Wagner. Schofield said he favored a court-martial, including charges against Lane and Conrad for foolishly obeying Wagner's rash order. A court-martial of two officers for obeying orders would have been a fascinating spectacle. Neither Schofield, Stanley, nor Cox would have come out completely unscathed. For if Wagner bore the primary responsibility and was guilty of reckless vainglory, Stanley, Cox, and Schofield were guilty of complacency. Their experience, especially at Columbia and Spring Hill, had lulled them into thinking they were secure and that Hood would dare not attack. They serenely assumed that Wagner's troops would smoothly withdraw into the main defenses, when withdrawing in the presence of the enemy is really a very difficult operation. As Cox rather sadly remarked years later, it was not uncommon for brave officers to lose the "power of calm self-control" when under fire.[69]

Had Hood's attack succeeded, Schofield, as the commanding general, would have been blamed regardless of the circumstances. Even so, decades later former captain John K. Shellenberger of Conrad's brigade wrote angry accounts of the battle that blamed Schofield for the blunder and demanded that the War Department investigate Schofield's conduct during the battle. After the war, Cox and Stanley had a major falling out when Cox, in his account of the battle, referred to himself as "commandant of the line." Stanley viewed this as Cox's attempt to take credit for the victory and diminish his role, especially in Opdycke's counterattack. Both appealed to Schofield, who tried to mollify the two men by suggesting that Cox's unfortunate phrasing only referred to the initial placement of troops. Revealingly, neither general argued about command over Wagner's division.[70] Still, despite the complacency of the senior officers and blind obedience of the brigade commanders, George Wagner must still bear the primary responsibility for recklessly ordering his men to stand and fight.

When Schofield's army arrived at Nashville on December 1, the extremely weary commander was greatly relieved. After directing the disposition of his troops, and before going to sleep for a day and a half, the exhausted Schofield met with George Thomas. It was not a happy meeting. Thomas was displeased with Schofield. He had hoped Schofield could hold the Harpeth line for three days. He had expected that Schofield would immediately withdraw to the north side of the river, but he had just learned that Schofield had fought the battle on the south side of the Harpeth.[71] Finally, he had learned that Schofield's initial report of 500–600 Union causalities was far too optimistic.[72]

Schofield, for his part, received Thomas's typically "undemonstrative" congratulations, but he later reflected, "I may not have shown due appreciation of his kindness at that moment, for I did not then feel very grateful to him." Schofield was angry with Thomas for seemingly misleading him about the arrival of reinforcements, for the delay in the arrival of the pontoon bridges, for the delay in concentrating the Union forces, and for Thomas's remaining in Nashville while Schofield and the bulk of the army confronted Hood. As Thomas had delayed his assault on Hood, Schofield was further rankled at the risks he took based on Thomas's instructions to hold Hood as far south as possible.[73]

For most of the next two weeks, Schofield, like a portly Achilles, would "sulk in his tent." Other aggravations added to his discontent. Schofield had to resume his battle with Burbridge, Stanton, and even Grant to retain Stoneman as second in command of the Department of the Ohio. Though Stanton considered Stoneman "worthless" and Grant viewed him as a failure, Schofield got them to back down by arguing, "If the general can send there an officer in whom he has more confidence, I shall be much gratified to have him do so."[74] Schofield was further irritated when Thomas forced him to displace Ruger for Major General Darius Couch. Couch had been a corps commander in the Army of the Potomac before quarreling with Hooker and being put on the shelf with a rear area job. Now that the War Department was trying to force the use or resignation of these generals, Couch had chosen to return to the front and was originally intended to replace Kimball in IV Corps. Couch's seniority also meant he displaced the trusted Jacob Cox as Schofield's senior subordinate. To mollify Schofield, Thomas agreed to help reinforce XXIII Corps and reconstitute its first division under Ruger's command.[75]

Hood followed Schofield to Nashville, partly out of encouragement from Schofield's hasty withdrawal, and partly out of desperation. Without fully realizing the overwhelming Union strength now concentrated in Nashville, Hood attempted to "besiege" the city with his badly battered army. As one historian has noted, Hood, like McCawber, "seemed to be waiting for something to turn up." Hood seems to have pinned his hopes on Thomas's doing to his army what Hood had done to the Confederate army at Franklin. To further provoke Thomas, he sent Forrest's cavalry and one infantry division to besiege the garrison at Murfreesboro. But the methodical Thomas would not be provoked.

As the ragged and hungry Confederates huddled in their entrenchments, the comfortable Union troops rested and prepared.[76]

The chief reason for Thomas's delay was to remount Wilson's cavalry, nearly half of whom had spent November awaiting new horses. The respective reports of Wilson and Schofield about the superiority of the Confederate cavalry and the ineffectiveness of the Union cavalry clearly influenced Thomas's decision to delay any attack until the bulk of his cavalry could be refitted. Thomas told Grant that Forrest outnumbered Wilson's cavalry four to one, and this superiority was an important reason for his decision to withdraw Schofield's command all the way back to Nashville. Thomas's wild overestimate of Forrest's strength demonstrated how the rebel's skill and ferocious reputation continued to intimidate Union commanders.[77]

As Thomas delayed his assault on Hood to refit his cavalry, his superiors became extremely worried that he would lose the opportunity to crush Hood. On December 2 Stanton relayed to Grant Lincoln's fear of a return to "the McClellan and Rosecrans strategy."[78] Grant warned Thomas that delay would give Hood an opportunity to destroy the vital railroads. Grant, who was himself locked in an enervating siege at Petersburg, also feared that Hood would have time to make his position impregnable. As the days wore on, Grant became almost frantic and told Halleck, "If Thomas has not struck yet, he ought to be ordered to hand over his command to Schofield. There is no better man to repel an attack than Thomas, but I fear he is too cautious to ever take the initiative." Halleck resisted Grant's efforts and the lieutenant general relented, for a time. Thomas was well aware of Grant's irritation. When an ice storm prompted a further delay of his planned December 10 attack, Thomas telegraphed Grant about the postponement, and then in a very dignified manner concluded, "Major-General Halleck informs me that you are very much dissatisfied with my delay in attacking. I can only say I have done all in my power to prepare, and if you should deem it necessary to relieve me I shall submit without a murmur."[79]

On December 13 Grant ordered General John Logan, who happened to be at his headquarters, to proceed to Nashville and, if Thomas had not yet attacked the enemy, to take command and attack. Since Logan was outranked by both Thomas and Schofield, Grant might have thought better of this, and two days later, while Logan was still en route, he decided to go to Nashville himself. By the time he got to Washington, D.C., he learned of Thomas's assault that day. Grant proceeded no further and signaled Logan at Louisville to stop. To Thomas he wrote, "I congratulate you and the army under your command for to-day's operations, and feel a conviction that to-morrow will add more fruits to your victory."[80]

The battle of Nashville was a relatively straightforward affair. Unlike some of Thomas's suggestions during the Atlanta campaign of turning maneuvers and other devices to shift the Confederates out of their defenses, he chose the direct approach for this engagement. On December 15 Steedman, on the far left, demonstrated against the Confederate fortifications. At the same time, A. J. Smith's troops conducted the main attack on Hood's left flank, with Wood's IV Corps supporting on Smith's left and Wilson's cavalry supporting on his right. Schofield was held in reserve. The original orders called for Schofield to cover Wood's left flank, but Schofield convinced Thomas to change them to support Smith's main attack.

Hood had spread his meager forces too thinly, allowing the Union troops to make good progress against his fortifications. Hood attempted to shift reinforcements from his right flank and center, but it was too late to stop the Union advance. In the late afternoon Thomas committed Schofield on the right flank of Smith to press the retreating Confederates, but Schofield's troops were only lightly engaged before darkness halted the Union advance. Though the day's fighting had not been conclusive, the Union troops had, nevertheless, advanced several miles and forced the Confederates out of their main defenses.[81]

That night, Hood consolidated his troops in a more compact position, with Lee anchoring the right flank on Overton Hill, Cheatham the left flank on what became known as Shy's Hill, and Stewart in the middle. James R. Chalmers's single cavalry division covered Hood's eastern flank along the Granny White Pike. On November 16 the Union advance continued, but with agonizing slowness. It took Wood and Steedman most of the morning to approach the new Confederate positions. In the afternoon they conducted a coordinated attack on Overton Hill, but they were bloodily repulsed. On the opposite flank, Wilson's cavalry, after a period of uncertainty concerning enemy intentions, began to advance east to cut off the Granny White Pike and threaten Hood's rear. By late afternoon, they had defeated Chalmers's cavalry division and were battling hastily deployed infantry units from the main Confederate line.[82]

The Union efforts around Shy's Hill were cautious and tentative throughout most of the day. Schofield, snakebit by Franklin, feared a Hood counterattack that morning and was initially more concerned about defending himself. Later, he was reluctant, as was Smith, of taking on the fortified rebel position. Smith looked to Schofield to take the initiative, while Schofield looked to Wilson to outflank the enemy defenses. So Smith and Schofield spent most of the day

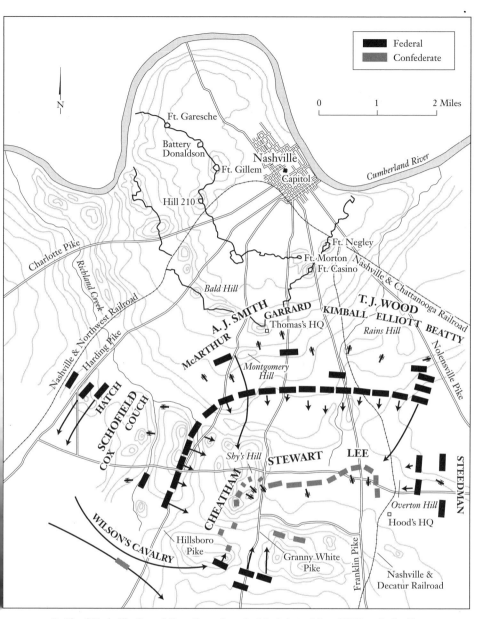

N

| Federal |
| Confederate |

0   1   2 Miles

Ft. Garesche

Battery
Donaldson

Ft. Gillem

Nashville

Capitol

Cumberland River

Hill 210

Charlotte Pike

Richland Creek

Nashville & Northwest Railroad

Harding Pike

Ft. Negley

Ft. Morton

Ft. Casino

Nashville & Chattanooga Railroad

Bald Hill

A. J. SMITH

GARRARD

Thomas's HQ

T. J. WOOD

KIMBALL   ELLIOTT   BEATTY

Rains Hill

Nolensville Pike

McARTHUR

Montgomery
Hill

HATCH

SCHOFIELD   COUCH

COX

Shy's Hill   STEWART   LEE

STEEDMAN

Overton Hill

Hood's HQ

WILSON'S CAVALRY

CHEATHAM

Hillsboro
Pike

Granny White
Pike

Franklin Pike

Nashville &
Decatur Railroad

Battle of Nashville, Second Day, December 16, 1864 (adapted from William R. Scaife,
Hood's Campaign for Tennessee*)*

shelling the rebel position in a crossfire: Smith from the north and Schofield from the west.

Finally, around 3:00 P.M., division commander John A. McArthur prevailed on Smith to let him attack Shy's Hill. Thomas, upon learning of this, immediately went to coordinate the attack with Schofield. Couch's division was to support McArthur, while Cox's division assaulted the west side of the position. McArthur's assault against this seemingly formidable position was surprisingly and spectacularly successful. Shy's Hill was very steep and, like Missionary Ridge, had many dead zones, where defenders could not place effective fire. Moreover, Cheatham's position, manned by his battered and depleted regiments, had been further weakened by the transfer of units to stem Wilson's advance. Bombarded from the north and the west and hearing Wilson's cannon to their rear, the rebels broke and ran. Couch's division had little to do but watch McArthur's victorious advance; in Cox's division, only Doolittle's brigade joined in the attack, encountering even less opposition as the Confederate troops panicked. The rout of Cheatham's corps spread to Stewart's and then to Lee's. A single rebel division on the far right remained formed to provide the fleeing Confederates some cover from the triumphant Union troops.[83]

Ironically, the continuous pressure on the rebel flanks and center was what Sherman had often attempted to do against Johnston. This time it worked. It worked in part because Thomas's nearly 50,000 troops were far superior to Hood's less than 25,000, especially in cavalry, since Forrest was still near Murfreesboro. It worked, too, because Hood stubbornly stayed and fought rather than withdrawing, as Johnston would have. Finally, it worked because the Army of Tennessee was no longer the same army. The hungry, shivering remnants of that summer army had lost hope. The invasion of Tennessee had not been the glorious reversal of Confederate fortune they had anticipated. An embarrassed Colonel Andrew J. Kellar, whose brigade ran from Doolittle's assault, wrote, "It was not by fighting, nor the force of arms, nor even numbers, which drove us from the field."[84]

That evening, Schofield reported to Thomas that "Hood's army is more thoroughly beaten than any troops I have ever seen." Schofield was sure that the battle at Franklin had taken the spirit out of the rebels, and the fact that it was Cheatham's corps—battered at Spring Hill, Franklin, and Murfreesboro—that finally cracked gives some credit to this notion. The relative ease with which Thomas dislodged the Confederates from their prepared fortifications on December 15 must have further dispirited them. Nevertheless, the defense of Overton Hill by Lee's largely unscathed corps demonstrated that the Army of Tennessee was still a fighting force. Ultimately, however, it took the boldness of John A. McArthur to crack this veneer of courage and fortitude, now eggshell thin.[85]

Despite the decisiveness of the victory, it was still difficult to destroy a Civil War army completely. Darkness again gave the defeated forces an opportunity to escape. Wilson attempted to remount his cavalrymen and block the Franklin Pike, but rebel cavalry barricaded the road. Hood got across the Harpeth first and destroyed the bridges behind him. When Forrest rejoined him, his cavalry gave Hood's beleaguered army the protection it needed in its retreat. On December 28 Thomas halted the pursuit when he learned that the Confederate army had crossed the Tennessee River. Two days later, he announced the successful end of the campaign and his plans for posting his army to winter quarters.[86]

Thomas received the "Thanks of Congress" for this great victory.[87] And while Schofield deserves credit for his delay of Hood and the battle of Franklin, Thomas also deserves much credit for the campaign as a whole and the battle of Nashville in particular. Thomas, like Bernard Montgomery later at El Alamein, courageously resisted the pressure from his superiors to attack before he was ready. Thomas's plans, especially for the first day of the battle, skillfully avoided the bloodbath on which Hood's hopes rested. Careful reconnaissance had enabled the Union troops to assail the Confederate strong points with relatively small losses. The casualties for the battle are uncertain, but they seem to have been relatively light on both sides, especially compared to the losses at Franklin. Thomas reported 3,061 casualties, with 387 killed. Rebel casualties may have been about 2,300 killed and wounded. Thomas reported capturing 4,462 Confederates during the battle. This slightly more than two to one ratio does not truly measure the scale of the victory. Thomas reported 13,189 Confederate prisoners and more than 2,000 rebel deserters for the entire campaign.[88]

The Nashville campaign was a devastating blow to the Confederacy. Hood's tenure in command of the Army of Tennessee had been disastrous. The 65,000-strong army had been reduced to 40,000 by the end of the Atlanta campaign and was less than 20,000 after Nashville. The army had little confidence in its commander. As one soldier informed his wife, "Our army was badly whipped and it seems that they are not going to get over it soon, especially if Gen. Hood remains in Command." On January 23 Richard Taylor replaced Hood, and the army was broken up to provide reinforcements to other hard-pressed fronts.[89]

Beyond the destruction of the Army of Tennessee and the elimination of any further threat to Tennessee, the Nashville campaign was part of a larger strategic disaster for the Confederacy. Sherman's march across Georgia, virtually unopposed, and his capture of Savannah on December 21, 1864, demonstrated that the Confederacy could no longer threaten Union territory or protect its own. Jacob Cox, in his 1882 book *Sherman's March to the Sea—Franklin and Nashville*, rightly linked the Georgia, Tennessee, and Carolina campaigns as part of a greater strategic plan, and he rightly credited Sherman as the author of the plan. Though Hood's army remained intact, Sherman boldly, and against all advice, divided his own army. He forced Hood to choose between chasing Sherman through Georgia or attempting to take on Thomas in Tennessee. Sherman had changed the psychological dynamic of the war. Rather than the slow and expensive task of conquering and occupying portions of the Confederacy or the pursuit of the main rebel armies, Sherman launched a large-scale strategic raid. It carried the war to the Confederate people and proved to them that their armies could neither harm Union territory nor protect them from Union forces. Schofield and his Army of the Ohio would demonstrate that fact to the people of North Carolina.[90]

SEVEN

To the East—to the End

Thomas's great victory at Nashville and Sherman's triumphal entry into Savannah marked the beginning of the end for the Confederacy. The two events also prompted Schofield's transfer to the East and his reunion with Sherman. This transfer placed Schofield in an ideal position to witness the transition from the politics of war to the politics of peace. However, these great victories also sparked controversies that extended decades beyond the war, controversies that would divide old comrades. In refighting the war, Schofield's behavior was, in one way, characteristic of his prickly pride and his recognition that his relative lack of military acclaim placed him in the second or third tier of wartime heroes. Yet, the highly public squabbles were also uncharacteristic of Schofield's approach to controversy. Schofield normally preferred to assume the posture of detached reasonableness, earnest moderation, and calm judiciousness. Such qualities served him well in the later phases of his career as a soldier-statesman. In matters related to the Nashville campaign, however, Schofield's normal circumspection too often gave way to his vanity.

Anticipating General George Thomas's plans to go into winter quarters after the Nashville campaign, Schofield was not ready to sit idle in Tennessee until spring. On December 27, 1864, he sent an unofficial telegraph to Grant suggesting that his newly reinforced corps would better serve the Union cause "in Virginia or elsewhere, where decisive work is to be done," rather than waiting for Thomas's spring campaign into Alabama or Mississippi. Schofield declared that "Lee's army is virtually all that is left of the rebellion" and should be the focus of attention. Finally, Schofield noted that this move would deprive him of departmental command, but he candidly admitted, "Nominally, I command both a department and an army in the field; but in fact, I do neither." Schofield also wrote Sherman to ask if he could rejoin him. Referring to the arguments he had made to Grant, Schofield told Sherman that he was certain that Thomas no longer needed him, and it was better to concentrate against Lee.[1]

Schofield had shrewdly anticipated the views of the Union high command. A few days later, Halleck wrote Grant that Thomas seemed ready to suspend operations until spring, and that Schofield's or Smith's troops might be better employed with E. R. S. Canby's campaign against Mobile. Grant responded that he had did not intend to keep troops idle, but he did not want to withdraw troops prematurely from Thomas before Hood's intentions were determined. A week later, satisfied that Hood afforded neither opportunity for continued pursuit nor threat, Grant ordered Schofield's corps east to assemble at Annapolis, Maryland. He also directed that the Departments of the Ohio and the Cumberland be combined under Thomas's command as soon as Schofield departed. On January 15, 1865, Schofield began moving his freshly reinforced corps, nearly 16,000 strong, down the Tennessee, up the Ohio, and finally by rail to the East.[2]

Schofield's reasons for requesting transfer were personal and professional, opportunistic and strategic. He clearly no longer had a good working relationship with Thomas, and his mediocre performance during the battle of Nashville had not improved the situation.[3] Schofield's relations with Thomas had always been correct, but never cordial. Though Schofield claimed to have not learned about Thomas's vote in his West Point court-martial until he became secretary of war in 1868, Thomas probably remembered the young cadet's "dereliction of duty." Thomas was austere and taciturn, while Schofield was outgoing and garrulous. Thomas was very "Old Army" and had very rigid views of propriety and seniority, while Schofield, fifteen years junior, had elbowed his way up to departmental command. Both were ambitious and jealous of their reputations, yet Thomas would silently fume about slights, while Schofield actively politicked.[4]

Beyond the purely personal, Schofield had professional reasons for the transfer. He realized that, with the destruction of Hood's army, the focal point of the war had shifted to the East. Rather than sitting idle, both Halleck and Grant would want to continue to put pressure on the Confederacy. Though the rebels could cobble together some forces, Lee's army was their last hope. By going east, Schofield and his corps could play an active role in the closing stages of the great war. He could again serve under Grant or Sherman, two men who Schofield knew would dominate the postwar army.

Schofield's poor relations with George Thomas extended beyond the war, and even after Thomas's death, to "Old Pap's" friends and supporters in the Society of the Army of the Cumberland. In 1869 Schofield's ambition clashed with Thomas's sense of honor and propriety. After Schofield's stint as the secretary of war, President Grant was going to reward the junior major general of the army with the Division of the Pacific. Thomas, still commanding the Department of the Cumberland, objected that he, as the senior major general, should have the more prestigious assignment. Thomas had actually preferred the Division of the Atlantic or the Division of the Missouri, but the former had gone to the more senior George Meade, and the latter had been given to the newly promoted lieutenant general Philip Sheridan, another fact that galled Thomas.[5]

Schofield, upon hearing of Thomas's interest in the position, said that he went to Grant and withdrew himself from consideration. Schofield may not have had much choice since Grant had only given Schofield the job because he assumed Thomas did not want it. Thomas thus replaced the cantankerous Henry Halleck in San Francisco, who stirred up trouble at a farewell dinner by tweaking Thomas that this was the second time Schofield had nearly taken his place. Halleck then recounted the story of Grant's orders to replace Thomas with first Schofield and then Logan before the battle of Nashville. To add injury to insult, Halleck took Thomas's old job, whereupon Grant expanded the department to a division. Thomas need not have moved to get his division.[6]

Less than a year later, Schofield and the battle of Nashville would again vex George Thomas. In 1870 the *Cincinnati Gazette* published Grant's orders concerning the relief of Thomas. Halleck's revelations ironically precipitated this article. John Logan, fearing he would be accused of intriguing against Thomas, arranged with Grant to have journalist and Army of the Cumberland veteran Henry V. Boynton publish an account of Thomas's near relief. Grant also agreed to release his messages on the subject.[7]

The editorial comments that accompanied the Grant telegraphs championed Thomas and contended that replacing him would have been disastrous. As Thomas's projected replacement, Schofield took this as an affront to his own military reputation. Rather than graciously ignoring the slight, Schofield permitted his aide William Wherry to write an anonymous letter, published in the March 12, 1870, *New York Tribune*. Schofield later admitted to Jacob Cox his role in the publication of this inflammatory letter, which he "deeply regretted." Ironically, some of Thomas's supporters accused Cox of being the author of the letter.[8]

The letter, entitled "Secrets of History—The Battle of Nashville—Was Grant's Order a Blunder?" and signed "One Who Fought at Nashville," praised Schofield's command of the army before Nashville. It criticized Thomas's original plan of battle relating to the XXIII Corps, the lack of specific orders by Thomas on the night of December 15, the lateness of the attacks on the sixteenth, and the slowness of the pursuit. It also revealed the letter that Schofield had sent to Grant after the battle of Nashville that suggested the transfer of his corps to the East. Finally, the *Tribune* letter concluded that the replacement of Thomas with Schofield might have been a great injustice to a "faithful and efficient" officer but would have resulted in little "serious detriment" to the nation.[9]

Though intending to defend Schofield's reputation, Wherry unduly and needlessly disparaged Thomas. Unsurprisingly, the letter deeply offended Thomas and his friends. Thomas reportedly told his aide Colonel Alfred L. Hough that the criticism made for "funny reading" and was easily refuted. He attributed the anonymous letter to Schofield and told Hough that he suspected Schofield had intrigued for Thomas's removal, which was why Schofield returned to Tennessee rather than accompany Sherman on his march. Thomas seemed surprised and shocked at the revelation of Schofield's December 27 letter to Grant that proposed the transfer of his corps east. Thomas contended that this disloyal act of a subordinate had weakened his command and scuttled his own plans to march across north Georgia and into North Carolina to join Grant in Virginia. Thomas then speculated that if Schofield could do such a thing, "is it not also reasonable to suppose that he had written letters previously to General Grant, so commenting on affairs at Nashville as to suggest to him the propriety of substituting Schofield for me?"[10]

Thomas's suspicions of Schofield would have a lasting effect on Schofield's reputation. On March 28, 1870, Thomas sat down to write a response to the *Gazette* and *Tribune* revelations. A few hours later, he collapsed, and that evening he died of a stroke. Many of his friends believed the letter killed him, and they blamed Schofield. Rumors of Thomas's suspicions of Schofield's perfidy circulated among the veterans of the Army of the Cumberland. With each telling, the suspicions began to take on the air of truth. Sherman's memoirs and other histories further stimulated the controversy, and ten years later Schofield reopened the old wounds with a rather insensitive paper submitted to the Society of the Army of the Cumberland.[11]

Schofield began the September 15, 1880, paper by highlighting his own role in the campaign that culminated with the battle of Franklin. He set out his reasons for requesting that his corps not accompany Sherman, writing "that Thomas would have fighting to do, while Sherman's march would be practically unopposed." To counter some assessments that Schofield's actions from Pulaski to Franklin were merely a response to Thomas's orders, Schofield also underscored his own independence and initiative. Finally, he emphasized that the battle of Franklin occurred not as the result of some order from Thomas, but by Schofield's own decision to save the wagon train and thus delay the crossing of all of the troops until the evening.[12]

Schofield then turned to the controversial matter of Grant's relief orders. He blandly insisted that given his seniority as department commander, any relief of Thomas would have meant his elevation. Even Grant's instructions to Logan would have meant Schofield would succeed Thomas, as he was senior to Logan. He shamelessly maintained that Grant had greater confidence in him than Thomas. Given these "obvious facts," Schofield went on to describe the meeting of December 9, where he had immediately and magnanimously supported Thomas's decision to delay the attack, despite his belief that he would benefit from Thomas's relief. As Schofield remembered the episode, when Thomas said he was ordered to attack immediately, Schofield waived his right as the most senior of Thomas's subordinates to speak last and said, "General Thomas, I fully sustain you in your decision not to fight until you are ready. I believe you are right, and I will support you."[13]

This account tallies with what Schofield wrote Sherman about the episode in 1868. At an Army of the Cumberland reunion that year, Sherman had been the only speaker to mention Schofield and his little army. Clearly irritated, Schofield explained that while Thomas was "honest and true," his subordinates had poisoned his mind against Schofield. These subordinates never understood how the risks incurred at Franklin and earlier had contributed to the victory at Nashville. Schofield insisted that he had always served Thomas loyally—that it was he who had come to Thomas's support when threatened with relief, that it was he who had persuaded Sherman to send him back to aid Thomas. By 1880, the slights from Thomas's men had been festering in Schofield's mind for some time.[14]

The problem with Schofield's account was that some of the other senior officers did not quite remember the December 9 meeting the way Schofield did. James Steedman and James Wilson recollected Schofield as being rather quiet. Wilson claimed that he spoke first. Schofield's, Steedman's, and Wilson's memories of the meeting—or possibly meetings, since there were several during those crucial days—were expressed years after the events and reflected their rather subjective perspectives. While the truth can never be known, it is highly probable that given the severe ice storm, Schofield at this point did agree with a delay. But it is also probable that he tendered his opinion so mildly, or even grudgingly, that few recalled it. Since Schofield himself admitted that he had been previously impatient to attack, it is hardly surprising that the others had no clear memory that Schofield had supported the postponement at this particular meeting.[15]

The paper stirred the controversy and dredged up the rumors that had been circulating privately for years. Sanford Kellogg, one of Thomas's staff officers, complained to David Stanley in January 1881 that it was Schofield who had been slow to attack on December 16. Echoing Thomas's suspicions, Kellogg wrote that he had heard that Schofield had sent Grant a telegraph critical of Thomas prior to the battle, and it almost got Thomas relieved. Kellogg told Stanley that he had attempted to find the telegraph, but he believed Schofield destroyed it when he was secretary of war.[16]

On June 22, 1881, the *New York Times* published sensational allegations by James B. Steedman. In "Robbing the Dead," Steedman called Schofield a liar and dismissed the idea that Schofield had influenced Thomas's Nashville plans. He claimed that he, Wilson, T. J. Wood, and A. J. Smith could attest that Schofield did not speak first but at the end, and then only to say he would obey orders. More seriously, Steedman insinuated treachery and cowardice. Again raising the rumors that began with Thomas's own suspicions of Schofield, Steedman contended, "the character of Schofield as an ambitious, unscrupulous intriguer caused suspicion to fall upon him as the person who was disparaging General Thomas at Washington." He alleged that Thomas knew three days before the battle that Schofield was sending disparaging telegraphs to Grant in the hopes of replacing Thomas. Steedman even purported to quote from the incriminating telegraph. He hinted that while Stanley, Cox, and Opdycke fought on the line, Schofield skulked two miles away on the north side of the river. "We do not say that Schofield is a rank coward, but we can, from personal knowledge, safely state that he possesses the 'rascally virtue called caution' in an eminent degree."[17]

When Steedman went public with his accusations, Schofield was at a low point in his career and traveling in Europe. He had been relieved as superintendent of the U.S. Military Academy as a result of the Johnson Whittaker hazing controversy. He spent a year touring Europe and awaiting the retirement of General Irwin McDowell, so that he could resume command of the Division of the Pacific. On July 12, 1881, he sent a letter via Wherry to U. S. Grant, in which he asked Grant to corroborate his denial of having attempted to influence Grant to remove Thomas. Grant responded that, though writing from memory, he could "say with great positiveness" that he never received a dispatch from Schofield disparaging Thomas at Nashville.[18]

Perhaps because he was overseas, or perhaps because he had belatedly learned discretion, Schofield (though he may have shown Grant's letter to such Thomas supporters as J. S. Fullerton and Henry V. Boynton) did not continue the public fight. The storm blew over, although Schofield's reputation had been stained forever. When Philip Sheridan died in 1888, Schofield prudently took his name out of the running for the new president of the Society of the Army of the Cumberland. In his 1897 memoirs Schofield renewed many of his criticisms of Thomas's generalship, though he included some fulsome praise. The passage of years and Schofield's own criticisms of Sherman diminished some of the hostility of the Thomas supporters. Had Schofield been a bit more candid and self-critical, he might have avoided even more controversy.[19]

Schofield's first biographer, James McDonough, concludes that Schofield had probably sent messages critical of Thomas prior to the battle. He bases this conclusion on the facts that Schofield had written similar letters to Halleck complaining about Samuel Curtis, that Steedman had no reason to lie, and that Grant had the capacity to lie for Schofield. McDonough also considers Schofield capable of manufacturing or even destroying evidence. But the proof for these charges is very weak and relies mainly on a negative assessment of the characters of both Schofield and Grant.[20]

The allegation that Schofield destroyed the evidence while secretary of war also does not satisfy. Even if he could have destroyed the War Department records, Schofield could not have destroyed Grant's copy, and since this message would have been relayed to Grant at City Point, there may well have been other copies. Even if the message had been encoded, the War Department's telegraphers, who controlled the codes, could have known of its existence. One of these telegraphers so strongly supported Thomas that he delayed sending the official War Department order relieving him until subsequent events prompted its revocation.[21]

The evidence for Grant's capacity and willingness to lie for Schofield is thin. While Grant played some of his political maneuvering pretty close to the vest and was loyal to his friends, he was also unusually candid about his military career. Grant's near relief of Thomas was a minor embarrassment, which Grant admitted and explained in his usual frank fashion. If Schofield had sent him a message, Grant probably would have mentioned it, not to excuse himself, but to more fully explain his thinking. Moreover, Grant's closest aides, like Adam Badeau or Horace Porter, would have known the truth and would have had no interest in lying for Schofield at the expense of their chief.[22] For Thomas's supporters, blaming Schofield for treachery was a way of not directly criticizing the still widely popular Grant. For them, Schofield must have seemed like the perfidious Iago who turned the noble Grant against the stalwart Thomas.

Without branding James Steedman a liar, as he did of Schofield, it is fair to say that Steedman was certainly a man of fiery temperament. His insinuation of cowardice was undeniably a low blow. The men of the Army of the Cumberland took the slights against their chief very personally. Diminishing Thomas diminished them and their contribution to the war. Steedman probably came to believe the rumors that had been circulating since at least 1870. Those who claimed to have seen Schofield's incriminating message may well have confused it with his "disloyal" message to Grant of December 27 or the more innocuous status reports transmitted by Captain J. C. Van Duzer of the War Department in the days before the battle.[23]

Schofield's complaining letters to Halleck about Curtis clearly demonstrated his capacity for intrigue, but he knew that these criticisms reflected Halleck's own views; Schofield felt himself aggrieved at Curtis for displacing him at St. Louis. Schofield knew that both Sherman and Grant considered Thomas slow on offense, so he could have played to those convictions, but there is no indication that Schofield coveted Thomas's command. He was clearly angry with Thomas, but there is no contemporary evidence that Schofield was especially adamant about an immediate attack. Also, any backdoor criticism of Thomas could have easily backfired. While Halleck had a taste for intrigue, Grant did not. Finally, Schofield was probably too prudent to send such a message out of Thomas's own telegraph office in Nashville.

Given Thomas's great service during the war and his eclipse by younger officers after the war, Schofield's unseemly refighting of the Civil War deservedly mired him in controversy. His rather uncharitable criticisms of Thomas's great victory, especially in the light of his own lackluster performance at the battle of Nashville, did him little credit. But Thomas's suspicions of Schofield's request to return to Tennessee were also uncharitable, especially given his urgent need for veteran troops. Schofield had correctly assessed Hood's probable reaction and placed himself where he was most needed. While neither general was brilliant, they were both highly effective. Just as Schofield narrowly escaped at Spring Hill, Thomas barely completed consolidating his army, despite the risks Schofield undertook. Thomas procrastinated in massing his forces and unintentionally misled Schofield about the immediacy of reinforcement. Finally, Schofield's unexpected fight at Franklin had greatly damaged the Army of Tennessee, setting the stage for its destruction at Nashville.

The resentfulness each displayed in defending his military reputation is even more disappointing when one considers that both commanders benefited from enemy blunders, the initiative of subordinates, and unusual turnabouts. Hood's lapse at Spring Hill caused him to blunder at Franklin, propelling him to a greater disaster at Nashville. At Spring Hill, Franklin, and Nashville, the daring and pluck of regimental, brigade, and division commanders saved the day. George Wagner helped save the army at Spring Hill, but he nearly destroyed it at Franklin. Wilson and his cavalry were routinely whipped during the delay; but rested and refitted, they redeemed themselves at Nashville. The XXIII and

IV Corps divisions, who bore the brunt of the fighting at Franklin, played relatively minor roles in the victory at Nashville.

Schofield, in his memoirs, dispatched his North Carolina campaign in a few paragraphs. When compared to the importance and high drama of the Atlanta and Nashville campaigns, this treatment may have seemed appropriate. Nevertheless, the campaign was not without interest. The operations of the Army of the Ohio in North Carolina symbolize a kind of bridge between Winfield Scott's Anaconda Plan and the raiding strategy of Grant and Sherman. Schofield's assignment in North Carolina was to continue the strangling of the Confederate ports while creating a logistical safe harbor for Sherman's raid through the Carolinas. Schofield's operations exemplified the essential features of the Union military strategy—a system that required energetic efficiency more than tactical brilliance, a military machine that relied on continuous and ever-increasing pressure—a seemingly irresistible force.[24]

Schofield and his XXIII Corps departed Clifton, Tennessee, on January 15, 1865, and arrived at Alexandria, Virginia, by January 31. This 1,400-mile journey took them down the Tennessee River and then up the Ohio River to Cincinnati by steam transports. At Cincinnati they transferred to rail, which took them to Washington and then on to Alexandria. Earlier in the war, senior officers would have been deeply involved in arranging and coordinating such complex transportation requirements; by 1865, however, the War Department had become quite adept at moving troops. Schofield was little more than a passenger during this lengthy journey; Assistant Secretary of War Charles A. Dana and Colonel Lewis Parsons of the Quartermaster Department supervised the movement.[25]

While waiting for the rest of the corps to arrive and for the ice in the Potomac to abate in order to permit loading the naval transports, Schofield went to Fort Monroe to see Grant. Together, they sailed to the Cape Fear River on the North Carolina coast to consult with Admiral David D. Porter and Major General Alfred H. Terry. Terry had replaced Benjamin Butler after Admiral Porter had convinced Grant that, with the proper leader, the Union could take Fort Fisher and Wilmington, one of the Confederacy's few remaining ports on the East Coast. The industrious Terry received his orders on January 3 and captured Fort Fisher on January 15, just three days after landing his troops. Although the Union now controlled the mouth of the Cape Fear River, Terry's forces were too small to take Wilmington in the face of a reinforced Confederate division under General Robert Hoke.[26]

Grant appointed Schofield as commander of the Department of North Carolina and commander of the Army of the Ohio, which now consisted of XXIII Corps and Terry's troops. Schofield's primary mission was to create a base of supply and to link up with Sherman's army as it advanced north through the interior of the Carolinas. Specifically, Schofield was to capture Wilmington, then to advance on Goldsboro with a rail connection extending from either Wilmington or New Bern, and finally to link up with Sherman's army in the vicinity of Goldsboro. Grant optimistically expected Sherman to reach Goldsboro between February 22 and 28.[27]

On February 8 Schofield arrived at Cape Fear with Cox's division. Though the Union controlled Fort Fisher, the Confederates blocked the advance toward Wilmington, on the east bank of the Cape Fear River, with a strong position on Sugar Loaf Hill between the river and Myrtle Sound. Unwilling to launch a direct assault, Schofield landed Cox's and Ames's divisions on the west side of the Cape Fear River to take Fort Anderson. The Confederate forces were small, but they were well positioned behind rivers, with their flanks covered by swamps. Rather than directly assail these positions, Cox chose to march around the swamps. On the night of February 18, the rebels evacuated Fort Anderson, and two days later Cox enveloped the Confederate position on Town Creek, capturing 400 prisoners and two guns.[28]

Meanwhile, General Terry was making little progress against the bulk of Hoke's forces on the east side of the river. On December 19 Schofield recrossed Ames's division to assist Terry and two nights later ordered Cox to follow. However, after taking the enemy position along the Town River, Cox had rapidly advanced two brigades up the road toward Wilmington and was threatening the city from the west. Sensing that the enemy was about to abandon the city, Cox requested that he retain at least two of his brigades on the west side of the river. In the difficult terrain the messages took some time to reach army headquarters, but once Schofield was apprised of the situation, he quickly countermanded his previous orders and approved Cox's initiative. Cox knew he would. He later remarked, "By long service with General Schofield, I knew he was no martinet, snubbing any independent action, but an officer of sound and calm judgment, fairly considering the reasons we might have for departing from the letter of an order."[29] The next day, as expected, Cox crossed the river and entered Wilmington, and Terry marched through the city in pursuit of Hoke's retreating Confederates.[30]

Rather than advancing to Goldsboro from Wilmington, Schofield elected to advance from New Bern along the Neuse River. He had sound reasons for doing so: New Bern was thirty miles closer, and the harbor at Morehead City was

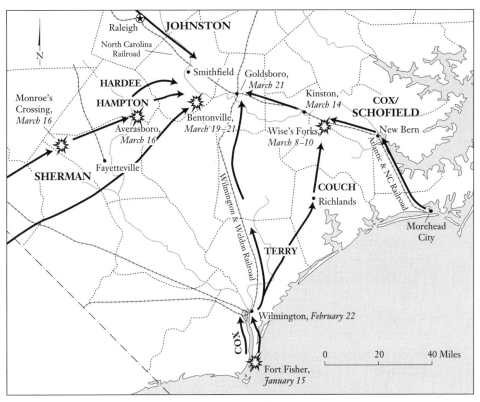

The Carolinas Campaign, January–March 1865 (adapted from Mark L. Bradley, This Astounding Close: The Road to Bennett Place)

better. The rail line, moreover, was less damaged; New Bern already had loco-motives and cars, while the rebels had destroyed all of the rolling stock in the Wilmington area. On February 25 Schofield sent Cox to take command at New Bern. Cox's forces consisted of Thomas Ruger's newly arrived division and two provisional divisions under Generals I. N. Palmer and S. P. Carter. Cox's mis-sion was to advance and repair the railroad across the Dover Swamp from New Bern to Kinston. Meanwhile, Schofield remained at Wilmington to organize a wagon train that was needed to move Darius Couch, with the 2nd and 3rd Divisions, north via Richlands to Kinston. Transport and cavalry were Scho-field's greatest deficiencies during the campaign, which meant that Terry's com-mand remained relatively immobile around Wilmington for several weeks.[31]

On March 6 Couch began his march north toward Kinston, while Cox had advanced through the swamp to a position nearly seven miles from Kinston. Hoping to get through the quagmire before encountering real opposition, Cox hurried his hastily organized command forward. But, hearing that Braxton

Bragg had moved Hoke and other reinforcements into Kinston, Cox instead established a defensive position with Palmer on the right, Carter on the left, and Ruger's division in reserve. Schofield arrived at New Bern on March 8, just in time to hear a Confederate attack on Carter's left flank. The rebels surprised and captured most of Charles L. Upham's brigade of new recruits. Cox ordered reinforcements from Ruger forward to stabilize the line. Over the next two days Bragg continued the attacks, but the now fully prepared Union troops repulsed them all. As Couch and the two veteran divisions of the XXIII Corps approached Kinston, Bragg withdrew. Union casualties, at 1,337, were relatively heavy, but most came from the 810 men captured from Upham's brigade. Confederate losses may have been approximately 500–800. The rebel losses were irreplaceable; moreover, their capture of 800 Union soldiers further strained their dwindling supply and transport resources.[32]

With the bulk of Bragg's forces withdrawing toward Smithville, only natural obstacles and railroad repairs slowed Schofield's advance to Kinston and Goldsboro. On March 14 Cox's troops entered Kinston, and by March 21 they had reached Goldsboro. Terry's command departed Wilmington on March 15 and by March 22 had secured Cox's bridge over the Neuse River, thus affording Sherman's army an easy crossing into Goldsboro. On March 23 Sherman joined Schofield at Goldsboro, and over the next few days the Army of the Ohio reunited with its comrades in the Army of the Tennessee and the Army of the Cumberland, now called the Army of Georgia.

As the armies rested and resupplied, Sherman consulted with Grant and reorganized his grand army. While Slocum's and Howard's armies retained their designations as the left and right wings, Schofield's army became the center of the new grand army. Terry's troops were redesignated the X Corps, and Cox was appointed the commander of the XXIII Corps. For the persevering Cox, this was especially gratifying. Though Cox had at last been promoted to major general, effective December 7, 1864, Darius Couch still outranked him.[33] Cox's assignment to command the provisional corps at New Bern had been yet another display of Schofield's confidence in him. The presidential appointment to corps command now made him senior to Couch, who continued dutifully to command the 2nd Division.[34]

Schofield also had much to be happy about. Not only was he reunited with Sherman, but he was again a department commander and now commanded a real two-corps army. During the next few days, while Sherman was consulting with Grant and Lincoln at City Point, Virginia, Schofield was left in charge of the grand army. When Lincoln expressed concern about Sherman's absence from his army, Sherman assured him that Schofield was "fully competent to command."[35] More important for his future, Schofield had been promoted to brigadier general in the regular army. Grant nominated him for the promotion shortly after the capture of Wilmington, adding that Schofield should have gotten it for the battle of Franklin. The War Department concurred and awarded him a date of rank of November 30, 1864. Aside from his initial promotion to brigadier general of U.S. Volunteers, this was the most important promotion in his career. His regular army rank was still that of captain; this advancement meant that he would remain a general officer when the war ended. Many of Schofield's peers, such as David Stanley, Eugene A. Carr, and William Carlin, would wait decades before reattaining their wartime ranks. Of Schofield's forty-six years in the army, he spent four as a cadet, another eight as a lieutenant, and thirty-four as a general officer.[36]

Even this promotion, however, did not come without a minor political controversy. When Schofield initially arrived at Cape Fear, he and his staff had no horses. Because he was directing operations on the Atlantic Ocean and on both sides of the Cape Fear River, Schofield requested a boat, and the quartermaster suggested the idle steamer *S. R. Spaulding*. This oceangoing steamer was large enough that Schofield made it his headquarters for several days, as he sailed back and forth to communicate with Terry and Cox. After the capture of Wilmington, he permanently moved ashore.

Schofield's use of a War Department vessel did not sit well with Secretary of War Edwin Stanton, however. Stanton responded to Grant's request for Schofield's promotion with a display of temper all too typical of this secretary of war:

> Schofield's nomination will be made, as requested, subject, however, to his obedience to orders. I am not satisfied with his conduct in seizing the hospital boat Spaulding, to make it his own quarters. I have directed him to give it up. If he obeys the order promptly I will send in his nomination, otherwise I will not. I wish you would instruct him as to the impropriety of an officer using hospital boats for their own personal accommodation, or using or employing transports for their quarters at a vast expense to the Government. There has been too much of such practice already, and he takes rather an early start in such irregularities.[37]

Since Grant's aide had just returned from Wilmington, Grant immediately sought to reassure Stanton that Schofield's actions were necessary, temporary, and authorized by the local quartermaster. Stanton relented.[38]

Schofield had been unaware that there was a February 8 general order that prohibited the diversion of such vessels and had no idea of the commotion his use of the ship had caused until well after he had relinquished the use of the *Spaulding*. On March 14 he sent a lengthy letter of explanation and apology to Secretary Stanton. The incident, which began with the complaint of the idle assistant surgeons whom Schofield had temporarily inconvenienced, illustrated the occasional conflict between the field commanders and the staff departments. Secretary Stanton jealously guarded his prerogatives at the War Department and defended the staff bureaus. Stanton's threat and Grant's immediate defense of Schofield are also illustrative. Despite the obvious respect and cooperation between Grant and Stanton, there was sometimes an undercurrent of friction as both strove to control what they saw as their rightful spheres of authority.[39]

The Confederate attacks at Kinston and the battle at Bentonville between Sherman and Johnston on March 19–21 constituted the last desperate attempts by the Confederates to stave off a junction between Sherman and Schofield. With corps that were little more than divisions, the Confederates threw the pitiful remnants of the Army of Tennessee in front of the advancing Union armies. Combined with state militias and other reinforcements, Johnston could only muster 35,000 troops against Sherman's nearly 90,000.[40] Confederate desertions in the last weeks of the war were enormous, as Grant's army closed in on Lee in Virginia and Sherman's troops advanced toward Johnston in North Carolina. The end was near, and most soldiers knew it. On April 9 Lee finally surrendered to Grant.

Schofield noted a certain disappointment in Sherman and his veterans when Lee's surrender denied them the opportunity "to share in the glory of capturing Richmond and Lee's army." Ironically, though Sherman saw the combining with Grant against Lee as the culmination of his great march, Grant was more interested in having Sherman prevent a union of Johnston and Lee. To Schofield, Sherman's march through Georgia and the Carolinas was little more than "a grand raid." The defeat and virtual destruction of Hood's army had really paved the way for the capture of Lee's army and a speedy end of the war. Thus, Schofield concluded, "In military history Sherman's great march must rank as auxiliary to the far more important operations of Grant and Thomas."[41]

Schofield's view that the destruction of the enemy's armies was, or always should have been, the chief objective of the war marked Schofield as a very conventional military strategist. The Napoleonic concept of the decisive battle against the main enemy force permeated nineteenth-century military thought. To Schofield, Grant's operations epitomized this strategy of confronting and defeating the main rebel armies. By contrast, Schofield criticized George McClellan's quest to capture Richmond, and he described Henry Halleck, somewhat unfairly, as "the chief of the 'territorial strategists' of our civil war." He argued that the capture of major cities hurt the Confederacy, but it was not decisive. In a major way, capturing cities drained resources for the field armies to provide garrisons and protect lines of supply.[42]

Henry Halleck, as a translator of the prominent European military theorist Antoine Jomini, certainly understood the role of the decisive battle in military strategy; but he also understood, as most Civil War generals came to understand, that pitched battles too often produced costly and indecisive results. Halleck comprehended the logistical requirements to engage successfully in such battles. The Confederacy was too large simply to send armies to engage each other, especially if one side decided to avoid battle. The idea of dismembering parts of the Confederacy, especially through the control of the rivers in the West, was not unique to Halleck, but he was the strategy's foremost advocate. Unlike McClellan and many others, Halleck always saw the West as the decisive theater. Union control of the Mississippi, Cumberland, and Tennessee Rivers, as well as the Atlantic and Gulf coasts, gave the Union enormous advantages in mounting and sustaining offensive operations.[43]

Schofield never recognized how important raids were to Grant's overall strategy. He viewed raids as ancillary to the operations of the main armies (and in some ways they were), but raids were also a way of keeping pressure on the Confederates without assembling the resources necessary for permanent conquest. The nature of Grant's raids also changed as he gained more authority. Whereas Benjamin Grierson's cavalry raid was certainly auxiliary to Grant's Vicksburg campaign, Sherman's Meridian campaign and Sheridan's Shenandoah campaign were strategic raids and part of Grant's emerging logistic strategy. Carrying the war to the enemy and making the enemy pay had long been a desire of Union leaders. At the beginning of the spring 1864 campaigns, Grant sent instructions to all major commands ordering, "Generals commanding armies and army corps in the field will take the proper measures to supply, so far as may be possible, the wants of their troops in animals and provisions from the territory through which military operations are conducted." The destruction of the southern railroad system became an important objective, just as safeguarding his own was one of his chief reasons for pushing Thomas to attack at Nashville.[44]

Sherman's Atlanta campaign was an extension of this strategy. By expelling much of the population, destroying the factories, and ripping up its railroads, he had rendered the city militarily useless. However, Sherman's goal went beyond Grant's. Sherman sought to remind southerners that their support for the Confederacy put their personal fortunes at risk. Rather than defeat or degrade Confederate armies, Sherman strove to attack the morale and commitment of the population to continue the war. While Schofield hailed Sherman's genius and proclaimed that his "campaigns stand alone, without a parallel in military history," he failed to give much credit to Sherman's strategic approach. Schofield instinctively shrank from the psychological strategy of terror that Sherman embodied.[45]

Schofield, Thomas, and Grant had all opposed Sherman's plan to march through Georgia. All believed in the conventional idea that the object of military operations should be the destruction of the enemy army—that Sherman should have destroyed Hood's army before marching to the sea. Grant, however, demonstrated his strategic acumen by finally agreeing to Sherman's plan, while Schofield more than thirty years later continued to insist that Hood's army should have been the first priority. He argued that Sherman should have sent another corps to Thomas (in addition to IV and XXIII Corps) and delayed his departure from Atlanta until Hood's probable invasion of Tennessee was repulsed. But would even the aggressive Hood have launched an invasion under such circumstances? He might have continued Forrest's cavalry raids, while he nibbled at isolated Union garrisons like Decatur. Sherman's abandonment of Atlanta and his march east, combined with Thomas's perceived weakness, helped lure Hood to his doom. Though Sherman only vaguely alluded to this possibility, his "March to the Sea" forced Hood's hand.[46]

Paradoxically, Schofield offered a different assessment of the campaign in 1877 than the one in his 1897 memoirs. In a paper entitled "Introductory Remarks upon the Study of the Science of War," delivered to the U.S. Military Service Institution, Schofield argued that Sherman's decision was a masterful example of the science of war. The "science of war" involved the assessment of the hazards and opportunities, the costs and the benefits, based on the accumulation of knowledge, but to the mathematically inclined Schofield, this boiled down to the calculation of force, time, and distance factors. Using Tennessee in the fall of 1864 as his example and omitting his own role, Schofield praised Sherman's estimate of how much force and how much time Thomas needed to cope with any threat from Hood. Despite the criticism and the delays, Thomas did have sufficient force to defeat Hood.[47]

In this paper Schofield was not really evaluating Sherman's strategy; he was using it as convenient example to make the case for a corps of professionally trained staff officers who could estimate the complex factors of force, time, and distance. Even so, he darkly remarked that the result of Sherman's plan was so close, "another day might have turned the tide of war against us." Schofield's later critique of Sherman, which emphasized the needless risks that Sherman took in his haste to carry out his grand plan, reflected Schofield's natural prudence and conventional approach to war. In judging the Atlanta and Savannah campaigns, Schofield argued that "the public lost sight of the fact that it was armies in the field, and not fortified places, which gave strength to the rebellion." What Schofield lost sight of—or could not accept—was that it was the enemy population that gave the armies their strength.[48]

Another postwar paper, "Notes on the 'Legitimate in Warfare,'" which Schofield delivered at the U.S. Military Service Institution in 1879, affords further insight into Schofield's concept of war. In this paper Schofield argued that efforts to limit the "killing power" of modern weapons were based on "the erroneous theory that the prime object of military weapons is to kill." He argued that killing is "but one means necessary to the end" and that the "object of war is to conquer an honorable, advantageous, and lasting peace." He considered war the temporary interruption of peace, frequently caused by "temporary rulers or political factions having temporary ascendancy." Hence, "it is of the utmost importance to the future welfare of both nations that this temporary passion of the people be not converted into lasting hatred." While accepting the fact that an unjustly assailed weaker power may rightfully use different means from the stronger power, wanton and unnecessary destruction should be condemned. "The only legitimate objects of attack are the military power and resources of the enemy." In Schofield's concept, it was the targets, not the weapons, that should be limited; thus, modern weapons were a way of producing "short, sharp, and decisive" conflicts.[49]

By way of contrast, the editors of the *Journal of the Military Service Institution*, which published this paper, appended to Schofield's article a letter by Count Helmuth von Moltke. While Schofield reflected the liberal Anglo-American concept of war and peace, von Moltke expressed the darker vision of a European conservative. "Perpetual peace is a dream," von Moltke declared, "and it is not even a beautiful dream. War is an element in the order of the world ordained by God." He continued, "Without war the world would stagnate and lose itself in materialism." Like Schofield, von Moltke doubted philanthropic efforts to mitigate warfare, but he suggested that the brutal elements could be reduced by the incorporation of the "educated classes" into armies through compulsory military service. He also stressed strict discipline and the proper subsistence of armies in the field. Like Schofield, he also believed in short wars and that "the greatest kindness in war is to a speedy conclusion." Based on his experience with France in 1870–71, von Moltke warned of a revolutionary government that would prolong and embitter the conflict.[50]

The idea of "revolutionary" governments' invoking a "people's war" was a great fear among most conventional military officers in the nineteenth century, and remains so today. Antoine Jomini, the great interpreter of Napoleon, re-coiled at the prospect of "National Wars," especially those like the Peninsula War. He wrote that, as a soldier, he preferred "loyal and chivalrous warfare" to "organized assassination," the "good old times" of ferocious pitched battles, such as Fontenoy, to "the frightful epoch when priests, women, and children throughout Spain plotted the murder of isolated soldiers."[51] Nationalism had changed the face of war more alarmingly than modern weapons. Schofield, who had experienced "organized assassination" firsthand in Missouri, was justifia-bly concerned about the implications of Sherman's war against the Confederate people. He, too, recoiled from the revolutionary implications of Sherman's concept of war.

Yet despite their philosophic differences, both Schofield and Sherman shared a common fear: the degeneration of the war into a prolonged guerrilla conflict. Although Sherman sought to terrify the southern population with the consequences of further resistance, Schofield feared that Sherman's tactics would embitter them and foster continued conflict. In the end, both were correct. When, on April 14, Johnston requested a meeting to discuss terms with Sherman, both Sherman and Schofield sought an agreement that would ensure that Johnston's army would peacefully surrender and not break up into small bands of marauders. Yet within a few years, armed marauders would appear in the form of the Ku Klux Klan and other bands.[52]

Although the fear of continued guerrilla warfare was real, Sherman went well beyond that consideration in his first agreement with Johnston. Johnston strove to negotiate terms not just for his army, but for the entire Confederate military. He also sought to gain some measure of recognition for the Confederate govern-ment—which the U.S. government had thus far been unwilling to grant—and political rights for the officers and soldiers of the Confederacy. Sherman even-tually agreed to permit Johnston's men to march to their state arsenals where they would turn in their weapons, to recognize the existing state governments, and to guarantee no punishment and the political rights of all former Confeder-ates.[53] Although the boundaries between the military and political spheres are often faint, Sherman had intruded well into the political realm.

When the national government emphatically rejected his agreement, Sher-man readily admitted his "folly in embracing in a military convention any civil matters." However, Sherman was unprepared for the firestorm that engulfed him. He later claimed that his terms were in keeping with the discussions he had engaged in with Lincoln a few weeks earlier, but it is doubtful that even Lincoln would have accepted such a sweeping agreement.[54] Moreover, Lincoln was now dead, and in the aftermath of his assassination, many in the federal government were enraged, profoundly distrustful, and ill disposed to be so generous. Secretary Stanton acrimoniously denounced Sherman's agreement and his intrusion into "political and civil questions." Stanton expressed to the newspapers his characteristically harsh criticism and insinuated that Sherman was colluding with the Confederates. Even Halleck joined in the attack on Sherman and ordered other commanders to ignore Sherman's orders. Sherman never forgave Stanton or Halleck for the insults to his reputation and patriotism. From then on, he regarded these former friends as dishonorable enemies.[55]

Schofield considered Sherman's first agreement politically unwise, especially given Grant's example and the attitudes of the Republican Party, but he thought the personal attacks and insinuations of treason heaped on Sherman were "utterly inexcusable." Schofield believed the high officers of the government had become "completely unnerved and lost their heads under the terrible strain produced by President Lincoln's assassination." He believed that Sherman failed to appreciate the difference between Lincoln's "humane purposes toward individual Confederates and his political policy." Schofield, however, defended his chief by pointing out that Johnston's army, unlike Lee's, was not surrounded, and the danger of its breaking up into guerrilla bands was very real.[56]

Stanton ordered Grant to go to Raleigh, take command of the army, and continue the war. Grant, showing more tact than Stanton, arrived unobtrusively at Sherman's headquarters to advise his friend to keep to the terms of Grant's agreement with Lee. When negotiations between Sherman and Johnston resumed on April 26, Schofield, who had not been party to the previous discussions, attended the meeting. All parties were concerned about the orderly return of the Confederate troops to their homes. Lee's men, without food, transport, or arms to maintain order, had become desperate scavengers as they returned to their homes. With Sherman constrained to keep to the Grant-Lee agreement and Johnston not surrounded like Lee, the negotiation soon reached an impasse.

At this point, Schofield entered the discussion and offered a diplomatic compromise. He suggested that Sherman and Johnston sign a general agreement, while Johnston's particular concerns would be addressed in a separate arrangement with Schofield as department commander. These supplemental terms, drafted by Schofield, included provisions for transportation and for one-seventh of the troops to retain their weapons until they reached their state capitals. Schofield also provided 250,000 rations and the wagons to haul them, "to prevent the troops from robbing their own people" on their way home. When Sherman and Schofield returned to Raleigh, Grant quickly read, approved, and forwarded the agreements to Washington, where they were duly approved. John M. Schofield had received his first lesson in the tactics and politics of peace.[57]

New brigadier general John M. Schofield. (Library of Congress)

Major General John M. Schofield. From the cartes de visite *album of the James Wadsworth family. (Library of Congress)*

Schofield and his staff before the Atlanta campaign. Back row, left to right: *Archibald H. Engle (killed at Resaca), Charles Bartlett, George W. Schofield;* front row: *J. A. Campbell, John M. Schofield, William M. Wherry. (Don Enders Collection, United States Army Military History Institute)*

William T. Sherman and his major subordinate generals. Clockwise from the top:
*George Thomas, Henry W. Slocum, Oliver O. Howard, Lovell H. Rousseau,
James B. McPherson, John M. Schofield. (Library of Congress)*

Battle of Franklin, November 30, 1864. This 1891 lithograph, though not strictly accurate, symbolically depicts John Bell Hood's attack on the Union lines, the federal artillery firing from the heights, and Schofield's wagon train escaping across the river. (Library of Congress)

"The New Military Commanders in the [In]surrectionary States." Left to right, in the foreground: *Daniel E. Sickles, John Pope, George H. Thomas, Ulysses S. Grant, John M. Schofield, Philip H. Sheridan, and E. O. C. Ord.* Harper's Weekly, *April 6, 1867. (Library of Congress)*

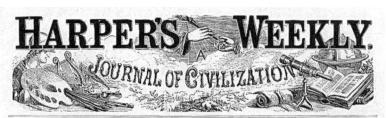

HARPER'S WEEKLY.

JOURNAL OF CIVILIZATION

Vol. XXIII.—No. 1181.]   NEW YORK, SATURDAY, AUGUST 16, 1879.   [WITH A SUPPLEMENT. PRICE TEN CENTS.

Entered according to Act of Congress, in the Year 1879, by Harper & Brothers, in the Office of the Librarian of Congress, at Washington.

"Stop Hazing in Toto: Five Points to West Point—'Don't put on airs. When it comes to
Hazing, Deviling, and Blackguardism, I am as good as you, perhaps better.'"
Thomas Nast's antihazing cartoon compares cadets to New York City thugs.
Harper's Weekly, *August 16, 1879. (HarpWeek)*

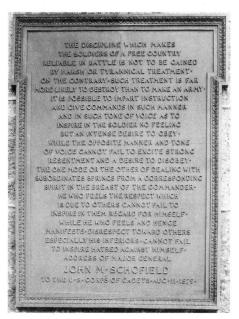

United States Military Academy plaque of Schofield's "Definition of Discipline." (United States Military Academy Archives)

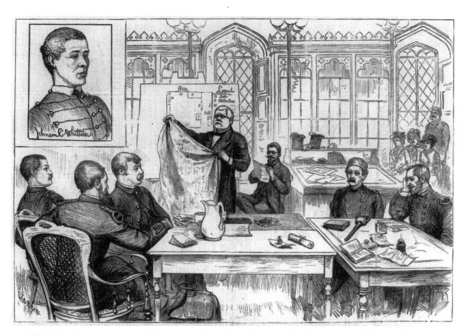

"The West Point Outrage—The Court of Inquiry in Session." In this cartoon, Johnson C. Whittaker is portrayed in the inset box and Schofield is depicted observing in the upper righthand corner. Harper's Weekly, May 1, 1880. (Library of Congress)

Lieutenant Colonel George Wheeler Schofield. (Library of Congress)

Lieutenant General John M. Schofield. (United States Military Academy Archives)

John M. Schofield's grave at Arlington National Cemetery. To the right is the grave of his brother, Captain Charles B. Schofield. To the left are the graves of the general's daughter Mary and her husband, Brigadier General Avery D. Andrews. (Photo by Donald B. Connelly)

EIGHT

Soldier-Statesman

Just as the bloodshed had begun before the firing on Fort Sumter, the conflict did not end with the surrender of the armies of Lee and Johnston. The fight only shifted to different arenas, and the army would remain central to this continued struggle for over a decade. Schofield, too, moved on to new arenas. His transfer to the East had not only rejoined him with Sherman, but it also afforded him an opportunity to forge a closer association with U. S. Grant, a connection that secured Schofield's future and propelled him on a diplomatic mission to France. The transfer also placed him in a position well suited to his political instincts and military skills. As the commander of a military department at the end of the war, as the commander of a military district under Reconstruction, and as secretary of war under Andrew Johnson, Schofield and his army grappled with the political and social consequences of the war and the end of slavery. Again, Schofield would be challenged to balance himself on the side of a barrel.

With the surrender of Johnston's army and the conventional war now all but over, Sherman marched his army north to participate in the Grand Review in Washington, D.C. Schofield and his Army of the Ohio stayed behind to complete the surrender and maintain order in North Carolina. Naturally, they were disappointed that they could not participate in the Grand Review. As Schofield confided to Sherman, "I shall never be quite reconciled to my lot of being deprived of the privilege of exhibiting my command with the rest of your grand army."[1] But Schofield had already become immersed in the politics of peace. Lincoln's death had left Reconstruction policy up for grabs. Sherman's failed attempt to shape policy and Stanton's irate reaction were but the opening shots in the intensified debate over Reconstruction policy. Lincoln had purposely left much of his views about Reconstruction vague until after the end of war. He had hoped to keep the policy in his hands and thus avoid interference from "the disturbing elements" in Congress. Even his own cabinet was divided: Salmon Chase and Edwin Stanton advocated black male suffrage and stern enforcement measures, and William Seward and Gideon Welles desired few conditions beyond emancipation. Montgomery Blair, who had left the cabinet in 1864, favored the forced deportation of freed blacks. Lincoln leaned toward African American suffrage, but he also preferred a policy of no retaliation against the ex-Confederates.[2]

The Unionist Party consensus on Union and emancipation that Lincoln had so painstakingly forged fell apart with the advent of peace. Much like during the early phases of the war, politicians on all sides attempted to use the military to tip policy in their direction. Though the issue of slavery had been decided, several problems continued to divide the nation. These included questions on the status of the existing state governments, the standards for restoring these states to Congress, legal action against ex-Confederates, and above all, the legal and political status of the new freedmen and women.

As Schofield was grappling with the problems of North Carolina, Salmon Chase, now chief justice of the Supreme Court, wrote Schofield to urge universal black suffrage. He argued that since the old North Carolina Constitution recognized freedmen as voters and the new Confederate one did not, Schofield should employ the standards of the old constitution and thus permit all freedmen to vote in the organization of new governments. Schofield tactfully replied that he hoped he would shortly receive guidance from President Johnson. Schofield's vague response impressed Chase sufficiently for him to recommend to Johnson that Schofield be appointed the military governor of North Carolina.[3]

To Grant, Schofield wrote more candidly that Chase's policy would "lead to disastrous results"; of "the absolute unfitness of the negroes, as a class, for any such responsibility"; and, "we certainly ought to teach them something before we give them an equal voice with ourselves in Government." Chase had made similar overtures to Sherman, who responded more emphatically: "I am not yet prepared to receive the negro on terms of political equality, for the reason that it will arouse passions and prejudices at the North" and "will revive the war and spread its field of operations." Additionally, Sherman continued, "we cannot combat existing ideas with force."[4]

Chase further recommended Jacob Cox as a man on whom Schofield could rely for advice in such matters. Given Chase's views on black suffrage, this was ironic. After the war, Cox ran for governor of Ohio. The issue of African Americans divided the Republican/Unionist Party, so Cox, reluctantly, had to state his views. His position was that black suffrage would only inflame racial tensions. He believed that white southerners would never accept political equality with blacks and that most white Union troops agreed with the white southerners. Since racial division was incurable, Cox advocated separation by setting aside the coastal sections of South Carolina, Georgia, and all of Florida for African Americans. Paradoxically, Cox also argued that if his plan were not adopted, he would favor the enfranchisement of black Ohioans. One historian has cogently argued that Cox's eccentric positions were based more on his pessimism about race relations than on his antipathy toward blacks. He considered African American "inferiority" more of a historical than a natural condition, but still a condition that thwarted any happy resolution. As a laissez-faire liberal, Cox recoiled from the massive federal intervention that would be necessary to secure freedpeople's rights. This pessimism about racial harmony influenced many prewar abolitionists to move to other concerns in the postwar years.[5]

In the spring of 1865, these thorny issues were far from resolution, and commanders in the field, like Schofield, needed to get on with the business of restoring peace and order in the conquered South. On April 27, 1865, one day after the agreement with Johnston, Schofield proclaimed hostilities in the state at an end and urged the people to "cultivate friendly relations with the same zeal which characterized our conduct of the war." On the same day, to remove any doubt in the minds of North Carolinians about slavery, he issued General Order No. 32, which declared all slaves in North Carolina free. War and emancipation, however, had created a serious refugee problem. Schofield exhorted former owners to employ the freedmen and women at reasonable wages. Confronted with the problem of feeding thousands of displaced persons, he urged people to return to their homes and moved immediately to break up the freedmen camps that had grown up around the army. While these actions demonstrated a certain cold-hearted attitude about the plight of the former slaves, wars of the twentieth century amply demonstrated how temporary refugee camps could become permanent ghettos.[6]

Schofield inundated his superiors with a stream of policy queries. What was the policy toward the existing state government? Would a military governor or provisional governor be appointed? And most important, "What is to be done with the freedmen?" Though perhaps less momentous, Schofield pressed the need to reestablish the postal system, appoint or confirm justices of the peace, repair the railroads, restore commerce, and even feed the destitute. Sherman, still smarting from the official reaction to his peace terms, offered little advice and referred Schofield to Stanton and Grant. Though the administration lifted the embargo on southern products relatively quickly, it initially remained obsessed with Lincoln's assassination and the apprehension of Confederate leaders. Although the government permitted Joseph Johnston to leave the country,

Stanton directed Schofield to arrest the Confederate governors of both North and South Carolina and ship the Confederate War Department archives that his men had captured.[7]

Schofield anticipated the functions of the Freedmen's Bureau, which Congress had created in March 1865 but which had yet to be organized. Just days after President Johnson appointed Schofield's friend O. O. Howard as commissioner of the Freedmen's Bureau, Schofield issued his own rules concerning the former slaves. His general order of May 15, 1865, affirmed parental authority over minor children and mandated that former owners remain the guardians of minors and the aged and infirm in the absence of relatives who were capable of supporting them. He stressed the need for all able-bodied persons to work for wages and suggested that, given the shortage of currency, laborers ought to accept a fair portion of the crops raised. Originating out of temporary necessity, sharecropping, however, would become an insidious system of economic control. Schofield further directed that each district commander appoint a superintendent of freedmen, whose chief responsibilities would be to find suitable homes and employment for their charges. These "jobs programs" would also become the basis for coercive labor contracts, as legitimate and essential efforts to restore the southern economy grew into mechanisms to restore traditional southern political and social relations.[8]

Schofield freely offered his political views in a revealing letter to Lieutenant General Grant. Although the war had settled the question of secession and freedom, Schofield argued, "the United States cannot make a negro, nor even a white man, an elector in any State. That is a power expressly reserved by the Constitution to the several States." Like Sherman, Schofield opposed Chase's advocacy of black suffrage: "They [African Americans] can neither read nor write; they have no knowledge whatever of law or government; they do not even know the meaning of the freedom that has been given them, and are much astonished when informed that it does not mean that they are to live in idleness and be fed by the Government." Like Sherman and Cox, he believed that no Union man in North Carolina would willingly accept "the immediate elevation of the negro to political equality with the white man," and that to do so would only provoke greater trouble. But unlike Sherman, Schofield did not argue that the African American condition was permanent: "It is true they are docile, obedient, and anxious to learn, but we certainly ought to teach them something before we give them an equal voice with ourselves in Government." While Schofield modified his views on black suffrage during Reconstruction for politically expedient reasons, Sherman did not change his opinions until much later, when he saw the consequences of a solid Democratic South.[9]

Despite his later views, Schofield in 1865 went on to propose to General Grant that the best policy for the South would be to appoint military governors with the power to make provisional appointments of justices of the peace, sheriffs, and other officers normally under the purview of the governor. Meanwhile, the military governor would enroll all electors who met the president's amnesty oath. He would then call an election for delegates to a state convention for the revision of the state constitution to repudiate slavery and the doctrine of secession. If the delegates failed to do so, the military governor would dissolve the convention, as the delegates would have violated their oaths. In his memoirs Schofield listed three principles underlying his proposal:

> First. The Constitution and laws as they were before secession, modified to embrace the legitimate results of the war—namely, national integrity and universal freedom.
>
> Second. Intelligent suffrage, to be regulated by the States themselves, and
>
> Third. Military governments, in the absence of popular civil governments, as the only lawful substitute, under our system, for a government by the people during temporary inability, from whatever cause, to govern themselves.[10]

At the same time Schofield was making this proposal to Grant, he wrote Sherman privately that "the people are perfectly quiet and exceedingly anxious for peace and restoration of civil government. . . . [T]he appointment of a Provisional Governor relieves me from all responsibility as to civil affairs, which is highly satisfactory to me."[11] This contradiction between Schofield's personal preferences and his audacious assertion of military authority in civil affairs was an expression of his pragmatism, his political philosophy, and his sense of military professionalism, rather than a quest for personal power. Pragmatically, by maintaining military authority and martial law, the army could protect itself from retaliation from ex-rebels who were, even in 1865, using the state courts and the largely rebel, all-white juries to harass and indict Union soldiers. Grant's ultimate alienation from President Johnson stemmed, in part, from Johnson's seeming support of these intimidating actions in order to prevent army officers from implementing the Freedmen's Bureau legislation.[12]

In boldly insisting that a military governor appointed under the authority of martial law, rather than a civilian provisional governor appointed by the president, was the only constitutional form of authority in the absence of a popularly elected governor, Schofield was also rejecting the argument of the Republican radicals. The radicals claimed such authority based on the theory that the rebellious states had reverted to the status of territories. For Schofield, the worst possible outcome for the army was unelected and unpopular civilian appointees backed up by federal military power. Knowing that military governors would also be unpopular, he calculated that military government would spur the speedy return to elected civilian governments.[13]

Finally, by using military officers rather than appointed politicians, Schofield hoped to keep Reconstruction simultaneously under the executive branch and beyond partisan politics. Schofield later blamed party passions for the failure of Presidential and Congressional Reconstruction, which led to "twelve years of misrule in the South." Unfortunately, Schofield's conservative attitude about African American rights and his grudge against the radicals blinded him to the party passions and misrule that dominated the South for decades and decades after Reconstruction.[14]

President Johnson, the former provisional governor of Tennessee, did not adopt Schofield's idea of military governors, and on June 5, 1865, he appointed William W. Holden the provisional governor of North Carolina. With the state "perfectly quiet" and Governor Holden's relieving him of many of his responsibilities, Schofield requested a thirty-day leave to visit his family and rest after four years of war. However, Grant had a new mission for Schofield and instead ordered Schofield to meet with him in Washington. On June 13, 1865, Schofield bid farewell to the remnants of the Army of the Ohio, which had largely demobilized. In his message to the troops, he lamented the comrades lost but celebrated the "hardships and dangers bravely met" that had saved the Union from destruction, a Union "more firmly re-established on the basis of freedom for all." He hailed XXIII Corps's victories in the West, X Corps's achievements in the East, and their shared victories in North Carolina. These sacrifices and victories should remind them all of the "priceless value of our free institutions" and the "faithful discharge of our duties as citizens."[15]

Schofield's new mission was a tricky problem of foreign affairs deferred by the war. While the United States was preoccupied with the Civil War, the French emperor Napoleon III, dreaming of a "Latin League" to unite the Mediterranean and Latin American peoples, seized an opportunity to create a puppet regime in Mexico. Under the guise of collecting international debts, Napoleon in December 1861 sent a French army to overthrow the government of Mexico and install Austrian archduke Maximilian as ruler.[16] Most Americans saw the imposition of a European monarchy in America as a threat to the United States and an insult to their republican principles. Francis P. Blair Sr. rather quixotically proposed that peace between the Union and Confederacy could be arranged in order to conduct a joint expedition to expel the French. His son Montgomery Blair suggested that Jefferson Davis lead the expedition, with Sherman and Lee as his major subordinates.[17]

As the Civil War ended, the republican government of Mexico authorized their minister to the United States, Matias Romero, to enlist the aid of a prominent Union general to recruit and lead an army of Union and Confederate veterans to help the Mexicans expel the French. Romero first sought out Grant. Grant declined but became an enthusiastic supporter of the project. Grant, who had fond memories of Mexico and its people, hoped perhaps that a combined force of Union and Confederate veterans would help reunite the nation. Romero next attempted to recruit Sherman, who also declined. Grant then suggested Schofield, who came to Washington to discuss the matter with Grant and then Romero.[18]

In June 1865 Romero and Schofield negotiated an agreement. Its major elements included the following: Schofield agreed to a commission as a major general in the Mexican army and to command the American volunteer forces; the American force, to be recruited along the border, would consist of three infantry divisions, one cavalry division, and nine artillery batteries; Schofield would appoint the officers and use U.S. Army regulations for organizing the force; the Mexican government would determine pay and bonuses; upon discharge of a three-year enlistment, soldiers would be eligible for Mexican citizenship; both the president of Mexico and the commander of the corps could grant commissions; and financial support would come from a loan negotiated with the United States.[19]

Grant had already dispatched Philip Sheridan and a force of some 50,000 soldiers to the Mexican border to intimidate the French, but there was no intention of using this force. Such an action by the U.S. Army might have provoked a war between the United States and France; and besides, these soldiers had enlisted for the War of Rebellion, not a war in Mexico. Grant, however, sent a letter of instruction to Sheridan that outlined Schofield's mission and reminded Sheridan of his authority to permit the discharged to retain their weapons and equipment, which would thus facilitate the recruiting and equipping of those soldiers willing to volunteer for the Mexican force. To further aid the outfitting of Schofield's force, Sheridan would also make available captured Confederate equipment.[20]

President Johnson supported—or at least acquiesced—to Grant's efforts to assist the Mexican government, but Secretary of State William Seward was adamantly opposed. Seward agreed that the French must leave, but he was confident that diplomacy would succeed. He anticipated that Napoleon III would grow weary of the expense and recognize the futility of his Mexican adventure. Seward feared that inflammatory American actions would offend the emperor's honor and only deepen his commitment. To derail Grant's aggressive policy, Seward met with Schofield and enticed him with the prospect of going "to France, under the authority of the State Department, to see if the French emperor could not be made to understand the necessity of withdrawing his army from Mexico." Seward appeared to place the future of American relations with France on Schofield's shoulders. Schofield cited his "natural love of peace" and the slow progress of the loan negotiations as his chief reasons for finally deciding to go to France, but his natural prudence was also a factor. The Mexican expedition was fraught with uncertainty and difficulty, while a trip to Paris would be less risky and far more comfortable.[21]

Schofield notified Seward of his decision to undertake the trip to France on August 4, and the War Department assigned him for duty with the State Department on August 19; however, Schofield did not depart for Europe until November.[22] Seward found reasons to postpone Schofield's departure with various discussions, diplomatic notes, and entreaties to wait for responses from the French government. This was all part of Seward's strategy of delay. As Seward later told John Bigelow, the American minister to France, who had been offended by Schofield's mission: "I sent General Schofield to Paris to parry a letter brought to us from Grant insisting that the French should be driven head over heels and at once out of Mexico. It answered my purpose. It gave Schofield something to do, and converted him to the policy of the Department by convincing him that the French were going as fast as they could. That pacified Grant and made everything easy. Schofield seemed entirely satisfied with you [Bigelow]."[23]

On November 15, 1865, Schofield finally departed New York for Europe. His brother Brevet Brigadier General George W. Schofield and his trusted aide Brevet Brigadier General William Wherry accompanied him. After spending a few days in London with the American minister, Charles Francis Adams, Schofield went on to Paris. Soon after his arrival, Schofield hosted his own American Thanksgiving–style dinner at the Grand Hotel. With diplomatic aplomb, Schofield observed to his guests that the great lesson of the Civil War was how a relatively limited government of a great people could raise vast armies and navies whose physical and moral qualities, discipline, and mobility "have never before been equaled." And then, "this vast army, as soon as its work was done, was quietly disbanded and every man went to his home, as quietly as the Christian goes back from church on the Sabbath morning." Thus having reminded his guests of both his nation's great strength and its desire for peace, he closed with a toast to "the old friendship between France and the United States: may it be strengthened and perpetuated."[24]

News of Schofield's mission had percolated through the diplomatic community and the French press, producing much interest.[25] The three young generals made the rounds of largely ceremonial meetings with dignitaries, banquets, and private dinners. Rather than attempt to compete with the finery of European soldiers, Schofield dressed modestly, as befitting a republican soldier. He eschewed his ornate epaulets and hat for a simple sash and sword—a weapon, he wryly wrote his wife, whose chief purpose seemed to be to snag the dresses of the ladies.[26] Schofield had neither charter to negotiate nor authority to alter American policy. While avoiding provocative references to the Monroe Doctrine, he reiterated the policy that Americans would never accept the French-backed government in Mexico and that the French troops must withdraw. Schofield was a sociable, dignified stalking horse for the American position.

Schofield's initial meeting with French minister of war Marechal Randon was chilly, but once Randon discovered that Schofield was not going to make threats and demands, relations improved dramatically. Schofield met only once with Napoleon III, at a formal ball on January 17, 1866. After Schofield was presented, the emperor asked a few questions "about our late war" and the campaigns in which Schofield had participated. The emperor was particularly interested in how the United States had supplied its armies so far from a base of operations. Perhaps Napoleon was preoccupied by his own supply difficulties, or perhaps he was testing Schofield on how he would supply an army in Mexico. Finally, as Schofield told his wife, the emperor asked "if I intended to remain long in Paris and said he should see me again."[27] Schofield had a longer, more candid interview with Prince Napoleon at a private dinner, which was undoubtedly reported to the emperor. The prince, who was somewhat out of favor with the empress, expressed great friendship with the United States. Unlike the emperor, the prince seemed to realize that Maximilian's government could never survive without French support. Schofield had come to Seward's conclusion that the French were destined to leave, and they only needed gentle, face-saving pressure.[28]

The French intervention was also becoming increasingly unpopular with many of the French elite. Supporting 35,000 troops was expensive, and many understood that Mexican resistance showed no signs of abating. The French government was overextended, and war clouds between Prussia and Austria were gathering. Napoleon III, looking for a graceful way out, hoped at first that he could extract U.S. recognition of Maximilian in exchange for a withdrawal of

French troops. Later, he hoped for at least a declaration of American neutrality. Though Johnson and Seward had been firm but soothing, the emperor, and especially the empress, worried about how Congress might act. On January 22, 1866, Napoleon issued a proclamation that hinted at an eventual withdrawal. By March, opposition in the French legislature had intensified. Dissidents circulated resolutions condemning the Mexican expedition and demanded the troops brought home. In April the government announced the emperor's decision to evacuate the French troops from Mexico in three phases beginning in November 1866, to end by November 1867.[29]

On April 24, 1866, Seward wrote Schofield that, as his mission had "been sufficiently accomplished," he should come back to the United States. Schofield returned, wrote his report, and by June 4 had reported for duty with the War Department. All the French troops departed Mexico by March 1867. Maximilian, disastrously, decided to fight on with a few Austrian troops and local draftees. On May 15, his troops surrounded and starving, Maximilian surrendered. On June 19 the Mexicans executed Maximilian and two of his generals. The Mexican people, with a bit of material and diplomatic help from the United States, had restored their republic. Schofield, by wittingly or unwittingly falling in with Seward's scheme, had gained valuable friends in Seward and Bigelow while not unduly antagonizing Grant.[30]

Schofield the diplomat had very little impact on the ultimate results. His mission to France was largely symbolic. He was, at best, a physical embodiment of American policy, and his presence offered an opportunity for critics of the Mexican adventure to express their opinions. Schofield's greatest contribution was his decision not to go to the border and raise an army to enter Mexico. A foreign army, even in the aid of the legitimate government, would have been dangerous to the Mexican republic. Even Minister Romero admitted that Seward's diversion of Schofield "was the best in the end, and accomplished its object without entailing on Mexico the curse which usually falls on nations who call in a more powerful neighbor to relieve them from a present danger."[31] Schofield's contract with Romero had included a reward of up to $100,000. When Schofield attempted to claim some portion of this, Romero and the Mexican government rightly decided that Schofield's trip to France did not merit such a bounty. Ironically, had Schofield's army entered Mexico, they would have gladly paid twice that much to ensure his departure.[32]

By the time of Schofield's return to the United States, General Grant's fear that President Johnson would treat ex-Confederates too harshly had completely reversed. Johnson was now making common cause with the ex-Confederates to take control of the southern governments and pass the Black Codes, which stripped African Americans of any civil rights. The 1866 elections set the stage for a showdown on Reconstruction policy between the conservative Republicans and Democrats, led by President Johnson, and the radical and moderate Republicans in Congress. This confrontation was also one of the greatest crises in American civil-military relations.[33]

Reconstruction was, first of all, a military occupation of the South. The president and, later, the Congress gave military district commanders unprecedented powers over the civil governments of the South. Military commanders appointed and dismissed civilian officials, remanded civilians for trial by military commission, and supervised elections. Second, and most important, Reconstruction precipitated a fight over control of this army of occupation—a fight between the commander in chief on the one hand and the Congress, the secretary of war, and the commanding general on the other.[34] Subordinate generals, like the nation, were divided. Some, such as Philip Sheridan and John Pope, supported the congressional Republicans; others, like John Schofield and Winfield Scott Hancock, tilted toward President Johnson and the Democrats. In typical American fashion, the crisis was not between the civilians and the military, but between contending groups of civilians, each with supporters in the military. Third, Reconstruction represented a dilemma of democratic government. In a highly decentralized polity, the army was one of the few instruments for implementing or imposing the national will on a recalcitrant region. However, what role should an army play in restoring or reforming popular democracy? More significant, how can a just, popular government be achieved when a majority insists on oppressing a minority?[35]

Martial law and the Reconstruction Acts gave military district commanders tremendous discretionary authority, yet these commanders acted with remarkable circumspection. This circumspection is partially explained by the slender resources available, professional concerns about political repercussions, and lack of commitment to African American equality. Most officers, like their northern civilian counterparts, did not consider blacks the intellectual or social equals of whites. Moreover, conservative officers like Schofield believed the traditional elites were better suited to reestablish order in the South. Most officers found the use of military authority in civil affairs contrary to their professional principles. As Winfield Scott Hancock said, "I have not been educated to overthrow the civil authorities in time of peace."[36] Finally, most officers believed that there were severe limits on what the army could impose on recalcitrant white southerners. General William T. Sherman, who predicted the failure of Reconstruction in a letter to his brother on September 21, 1865, perhaps best summed up the army's attitude: "No matter what change we may desire in the feelings and thoughts of people south, we cannot accomplish it by force. Nor can we afford to maintain there an Army large enough to hold them in subjugation. All we can or should attempt is to give them rope to develop in an honest way if possible, preserving enough military power to check any excesses if they attempt any."[37]

John M. Schofield, as the military commander in Reconstruction Virginia and later as secretary of war, was at the center of this civil-military crisis. In August 1866 Schofield assumed command of the Department of the Potomac, which consisted of Virginia and West Virginia. The governance of the state of Virginia was rather murky. President Johnson curtailed the use of martial law when he declared the end of the insurrection in April 1866. Congress, however, had not yet recognized the state government. Authority was rather uncertainly divided between the provisional government of Governor Francis H. Pierpont and Schofield under the authority of the Freedmen's Bureau. Congress had reinforced the authority of the Freedmen's Bureau by the Act of July 16, 1866, which permitted military jurisdiction over all cases and questions concerning employment, equal benefit of the laws, personal liberty, and security without respect to race and color.[38]

During Schofield's tenure, Virginia had fewer of the civil disturbances that created such national controversy. This was partly due to the energetic actions of Alfred Terry, Schofield's predecessor in Virginia. Terry garnered the hostility of white Virginians as he defended the rights of the new freedmen and women. He had taken immediate action to nullify the vagrancy laws that sought to return the freedpeople to virtual slavery. Terry also quelled the riots in Norfolk in the spring of 1866, as celebrating African Americans clashed with white "roughs." The official army report reiterated the continued need for federal troops to guard against violence "by a certain class toward the colored population."[39] Thereafter, most racial disturbances were between blacks and white police, rather than black and white civilians.[40]

Richmond, as both the capital and major industrial center, was a focal point of political, racial, and labor tension. To stop the influx of unemployed freedpeople into Richmond, the federal authorities instituted a pass system. The hundreds of arrests produced much hostility between the police and the African American community. Schofield worked with O. O. Howard of the Freedmen's Bureau to ease the problem by providing free transportation elsewhere for job seekers without needing to provide the unrealistic proof of a job guarantee that had been previously required by the bureau.[41]

Political rallies were also a continuing source of potential trouble. Some would involve civil rights protests against segregation, while others might be brawls between various Republican factions.[42] The federal troops immediately quelled these small-scale clashes and regularly patrolled the city with cavalry. In May 1867 Schofield intervened in the dispute between African Americans and the Richmond streetcar company, which refused to accept black passengers. Schofield negotiated an agreement to integrate four of the six cars. Schofield's modest integration efforts, however, had few lasting effects. By 1870, ten of the twelve Richmond streetcars were "white only." As one historian has remarked, "Jim Crow's career in Richmond began on the day slavery ended, if not before."[43]

One of the flash points for violence throughout the South was the continuing presence of black regiments of the U.S. Army. White southerners feared and hated these blue-clad soldiers as the embodiment of the Confederacy's defeat. Local whites retaliated against these federal troops with physical attacks and indictments in local courts. Virginia, however, had no black troops stationed there, and the army therefore encountered less resentment by local officials than elsewhere. Schofield cautioned his officers to exercise restraint in employing troops: "It is hoped that the simple presence of troops will be sufficient to secure the object to be obtained."[44] Relations between the military and white Virginians were so good that Schofield frequently yielded jurisdiction to local civilian courts for soldiers accused of civil offenses. By December 1866, Schofield thought Virginia was so peaceful that he could relinquish troops for service elsewhere.[45]

Although there were no black troops in Virginia, there were many freedmen who had acquired weapons, and, as Schofield noted, their right to "bear arms [was] guaranteed by an act of Congress." With the disarming of the Confederate army and the old state militia, which used to enforce slave laws, the white population felt vulnerable. Responding to this "general feeling of insecurity among whites," Schofield proposed the organizing and equipping of local militia companies. The units would "enroll only men who are loyal to the U.S. government and properly disposed toward freed people." The president approved the proposal over the objections of Grant and Stanton. This attempt to placate Governor Pierpont and mollify white Virginians was risky—few whites, even among loyal men, were favorably disposed to the freedpeople. Fortunately, the white militia did not provoke violence.[46]

By December 1866, Pierpont had begun rethinking his strategy to appease conservatives and also authorized the formation of five black militia companies in Virginia. In March 1867 Congress ordered the disbanding of all southern state militias until Congress granted new authority. Though informal militias, both white and black, were periodically formed, they did not end up in the pitched battles that were experienced in Louisiana. Schofield directed his subordinates to closely monitor any secret societies and discourage their "military character." They were to permit no drills, parades, or appearances in public with arms.[47]

While Virginia did not suffer from the widespread or systematic violence of such groups as the Ku Klux Klan or the Knights of the White Camellia, African Americans continued to suffer from sporadic violence. The most notorious case was the murder of a black man by Dr. James L. Watson of Rockbridge County. In November 1866 Watson had a carriage accident on a narrow road with a local freedman of acknowledged good character. The damage was minor, but Watson considered the man's attempt to pass him on the road an insult to his wife and daughter. The next day Watson found the man and began beating him with his cane; when the man ran, Watson shot him. The local justices of the peace reviewed the case and released Watson without a trial. Schofield ordered Watson arrested and tried by military commission.[48]

As the military commission proceeded to try Watson, a federal circuit court judge in Richmond issued a writ of habeas corpus. Schofield refused to honor the writ and release Watson. In a memorandum to the president of the military commission, Schofield argued that under the authority of the Act of July 16, 1866, which provided for the "full and equal benefit of all laws," the decision of the local justices endangered the personal security of all those within their jurisdiction. Schofield also contended that since Watson had not been "tried and acquitted by a jury but simply 'examined' and 'discharged,'" Schofield had the right to try him. Finally, Schofield argued that though the president had declared the rebellion at an end, the Senate had not yet consented; therefore, Congress, through the Act of July 16, 1866, "has declared that martial law still exists." This last argument was particularly bold. Once again, Schofield found himself between the president and Congress and this time seemed to side with Congress.[49]

The sheer lawlessness of the Watson case undoubtedly aroused Schofield, but he had additional reasons for resisting the circuit court writ. The Supreme Court, in *ex parte Milligan*, had recently declared that military commissions were impermissible where civil courts continued to operate. Schofield was testing the authority of the Freedmen's Bureau military commissions in this new environment. In the end, President Johnson sided with white southerners and, relying on the opinion of Attorney General Henry Stanberry, ordered the military commission dissolved and Watson released. The president had earlier that fall permitted writs of habeas corpus to free six white South Carolinians who had been convicted of killing three Union soldiers on guard duty. Incidents like these had driven a wedge between Grant and the president and reinforced the congressional Republicans' determination to implement stronger measures to protect both freedpeople and soldiers.[50]

The next contest over the differing approaches to Reconstruction came with the fight to ratify the Fourteenth Amendment. Though the Thirteenth Amendment, which abolished slavery, had been ratified in December 1865, the white South's use of "Black Codes" and violent intimidation meant this newfound freedom was extremely precarious. President Johnson had pardoned thousands of ex-Confederates, and some southern legislatures refused to repudiate the Confederate war debt. In June 1866 Congress passed the Fourteenth Amendment to guarantee the rights of the new freedpeople. Section 1 affirmed that all freedmen and women were citizens and prohibited the states from abridging their rights "without due process of law" and from denying them "equal protection of the laws." Section 2 provided for equal apportionment in the House of Representatives based on citizenship, unless a state abridged the right to vote of any portion of the male citizens over age twenty-one, in which case, the state's representation would be reduced.[51] Section 3 barred from federal or state office any person who had given an oath to support the Constitution and then participated in insurrection. This prohibited most ex-Confederate leaders from holding office. Moreover, only a two-thirds vote of Congress could pardon such individuals, which thus invalidated the pardons granted by President Johnson. Section 4 repudiated all monetary claims due to rebellion or emancipation.

In order to be restored to the Union, Virginia and the other former Confederate states had to ratify the Fourteenth Amendment. The amendment, which had passed Congress over Johnson's veto, was an important step in Congress's assumption of Reconstruction policy. While President Johnson urged the southern states to reject the amendment, provisional governor Pierpont and General Schofield urged Virginians to accept it or risk more draconian measures. Although they were hopeful of passage, the "Unionist" provisional legislature in Virginia overwhelmingly rejected the amendment (unanimously in the Senate, and 74 to 1 in the House). Of the Confederate states, only Tennessee ratified the amendment. In March 1867, as Pierpont and Schofield predicted, Congress passed the first Military Reconstruction Act and raised the price of readmission.[52]

In his memoirs Schofield related how his recommendation to the Virginia government was not predicated on his agreement with the amendment; it was based on his calculation of the power and strength of intent of the Republican-dominated Congress. In the course of making his appeals to the Virginia legislators, Schofield even went to Washington, D.C., to get the assurance of congressional Republicans that ratification of the amendment would result in the recognition of the state government and its representatives' restoration to Congress. Schofield believed that he had convinced a majority of the wisdom of ratifying the amendment, until President Johnson intervened and it was rejected. "Virginia was thus," as he later wrote, "doomed to undergo 'congressional reconstruction' in company with her sister states."[53]

Schofield, however, left behind a remarkable document on his personal views about the Fourteenth Amendment that casts doubt on the strength and persuasiveness of his appeal to Virginian legislators to ratify the amendment. The draft in Schofield's handwriting was probably written in December 1866 or January 1867, while the Virginia legislature debated the amendment. It appears to have been written to clarify and summarize his views and as a "memorandum of record" for the future. The document reveals Schofield's innate elitism and, at best, his paternalism toward the freedmen and women. It also reflects Schofield's and many Unionists' continued attachment to states' rights. The war had settled the question of secession, but it did not end the localistic outlooks of most Americans.[54]

Schofield began his private memorandum by declaring the proposed amendment to be "unjust and unwise." He then launched a sustained critique of Section 3, which "excludes from office, both State and federal, nearly every man in the South whose social position, intellectual attainments and known moral character entitle him to the confidence of the people." By banning most of the traditional leaders, the North was inflicting "bad government" on the South; and if these men could not be trusted to return to loyalty, then "there is nothing left but to hold the Southern States under military government until a new generation can be educated."[55]

Despite his recent experience with the Watson case, Schofield went on to argue that disfranchising the aristocracy would place the former slaves in the hands of their real enemies, "the inferior class of whites." He contended that while "the colored man is habitually respectful to his recognized superior," he "will not . . . bow to one who [sic] he knows is in no wise his superior, simply because he has a whiter skin." "The low white," Schofield declared, "calls the colored man an 'impudent nigger' because he shows his independent manhood, and knocks him down to 'teach him his place.'" He continued, "The third article of the amendment condemns the poor colored man to seek redress from a magistrate of the same class as the culprit." To Schofield, only the courts of the Freedmen's Bureau and the higher courts dominated by the "impartial" upper classes could offer impartial justice in conflicts between blacks and whites. Though the street violence between blacks and whites generally involved lower-class whites, Schofield chose to overlook the fact that the upper class had instituted the notorious Black Codes. Schofield's faith in the impartiality of the upper classes was as misplaced as that of the later populists who underestimated the racist attitudes of lower-class white southerners.[56]

Schofield believed the section related to suffrage was "not unjust to the South." The Constitution had reduced the power of the slave-owning states by reducing representation based on the number of slaves, and if the freedpeople were now to be denied suffrage, Schofield thought it wrong to let the South "gain political power as a consequence of the rebellion." But he went on to argue that the federal government's imposition of universal suffrage violated the rights of the states to set their own standards. He declared universal suffrage an "absurdity." Again, the elitist Schofield lamented the illiteracy not just of the former slaves, but also of many rural southern whites. Self-government was too important to be left in the hands of "ignorant and vicious masses."

Schofield disguised his hostility to black suffrage in universal terms. He argued that while "ignorance or crime" were grounds for disfranchisement, "the color of a mans [sic] skin ought to have no more to do with it than the color of his hair. Nor has any question of equality or inferiority of races. The difference between individuals of the same race is *immensely greater* than the average difference between any two races. Yet we now permit the most ignorant of one race to vote, and deny the right to the most intelligent of another." Schofield's seeming acceptance of black voting rights was qualified. He rejected universal suffrage for qualified suffrage based on education. This would have left the vast majority of freedmen and a smaller minority of whites disfranchised.[57]

In disfranchising the bulk of the former southern elite and pressing universal (male) suffrage, Schofield argued, Congress had "fallen far short of its high mission." Though Congress had retained the power to remove the disfranchisement clauses, he doubted it would do so. In his concluding paragraph, Schofield hoped that the South's rejection of the amendment would cause it to fail, giving Congress another opportunity to consider the matter, one in which it "will think less of 'punishing traitors' and more of securing the future rights, welfare, and property of the whole people." This memorandum was yet another Schofield straddle. Publicly he expressed tepid support for the amendment on pragmatic grounds while privately recording profound disagreement and misgivings.[58]

On March 2, 1867, Congress passed, over President Johnson's veto, the first of a series of acts to wrest control of Reconstruction policy from the president. The first Reconstruction Act declared that since no legal state government that was adequate to protect life and property existed in the former rebel states, they were to be divided into military districts. These were to be commanded by a general officer with sufficient military force to enforce his authority and were authorized to use military commissions and tribunals. The act further mandated the convening of state constitutional conventions to implement the provisions of the Fourteenth Amendment. Until the former Confederate states accomplished these tasks and were readmitted to Congress, all state governments were deemed provisional.

Congress passed two further measures on March 2 to take control of the army, or more specifically, the occupation army in the South, from the commander in chief. The first was the Tenure of Office Act, which was designed to prevent the dismissal of Stanton. The second, the "Command of the Army" provision of the Army Appropriations Act, stipulated that the general in chief's headquarters be fixed in Washington and decreed that he could not be removed, suspended, or assigned elsewhere without Senate approval. It further required that all orders issued to the army from the president and secretary of war go through the general in chief. This measure was also significant because it was one of the few statutory provisions in the nineteenth century that defined the role and authority of the general in chief. These two acts were clearly intended to buffer the army from Johnson's control. Although of dubious constitutionality, they were a sweeping assertion of congressional supremacy, even in an era of congressional preeminence.[59]

In accordance with the Reconstruction Act, President Johnson made the following military appointments: First Military District (Virginia), Brevet Major General John M. Schofield; Second Military District (North Carolina, South Carolina), Major General Daniel Sickles; Third Military District (Georgia, Florida, Alabama), Brevet Major General John Pope; Fourth Military District (Mississippi, Arkansas), Brevet Major General E. O. C. Ord; Fifth Military District (Louisiana, Texas), Major General Philip H. Sheridan. George Thomas had originally been slated for the Third District, but he remained at the Department of the Cumberland at his own request.

Much to the disgust of conservative secretary of the navy Gideon Welles, President Johnson had left the district assignments to the hated Edwin Stanton. Since most of the new district commanders continued in their departmental positions, politics played little role in the initial slating. The *Army and Navy Journal* considered all the selections reliable officers, though it acknowledged that Ord was the most conservative and Sheridan the most radical-leaning. The *Journal* labeled Schofield a "conservative Republican" and "a safe man." These were all rather moderate men, though Schofield and Ord were the most conservative and sympathetic to the president's policies, while Sickles, Pope, and Sheridan had more sympathy with the objectives of the moderate Republicans in Congress. Over time, they were all displaced for various reasons, but politics played a prominent role in the replacement of Sheridan, Pope, and Sickles with the more conservative Winfield Hancock, George Meade, and E. R. S. Canby.[60]

On assuming command of the First District, Schofield attempted to reassure Virginians by announcing that all officials of the provisional government would continue their duties. He emphasized that civil officers would not be interfered with as long as they strictly obeyed the law and rendered impartial justice. Though Schofield preferred an early return to civil government, he took his new responsibilities seriously and acted with his usual administrative energy. He immediately suspended all elections until the registration specified in the Act of March 23, 1867, was completed. He organized his command into subdistricts and appointed military commissioners to begin the registration process. Military officers from the army units or the Freedmen's Bureau assumed the role of justices or police magistrates and possessed the power to take jurisdiction of civil cases where the civil authorities might fail to render protection or suppress violence. President Johnson, through the legal opinions of Attorney General Stanberry, attempted to limit military authority, but Congress reasserted military power over the civil authorities in the Act of July 19, 1867.[61]

In his memoirs Schofield proudly declared, "No case arose in Virginia in which it was found necessary, in my opinion, to supersede the civil authorities in the administration of justice." This is somewhat misleading. He had clearly intervened in the notorious Watson case before the passage of the Reconstruction Acts. One historian has also counted twenty-one such interventions between July and December 1867, after the third Reconstruction Act of July 19, which reaffirmed military authority. The Freedmen's Bureau in Virginia routinely handled hundreds of cases, chiefly those involving whites and blacks, by military commission. Schofield recognized the difficulty of blacks' getting fair hearings in white courts, especially with white-only juries. Rather than fight the battle of integrating the juries, Schofield took the course of least resistance by relying on the military commissions.[62]

Schofield and his Freedmen's Bureau chief, General Orlando Brown, took the congressional mandates to secure justice for the freedpeople seriously and endeavored to enforce an equal application of the laws, though they often failed. Schofield also chastised officers for brutal punishments of freedmen and women and for forcing them into labor. Still, Schofield's interventions were not as flamboyant as those of General Dan Sickles, who even challenged the authority of federal courts and provoked a rebuke from the United States Supreme Court. Schofield insisted his subordinates report immediately and justify fully their decisions to intervene, occasionally reproving some of them for taking jurisdiction from the civil authorities.[63]

Schofield also used his powers of appointment and removal sparingly. He replaced few civil officials and often preferred leaving a position vacant. When he did replace officials, he generally dismissed radicals or conservatives and installed moderates, or those he thought were moderates. In his 1867 annual report, he documented the removal of five officials and the appointment of 105 individuals to fill vacancies. In March 1869 General Stoneman, Schofield's successor in Virginia, reported that 2,613 of 5,446 state offices were vacant. Schofield had made 532 appointments; by comparison, Stoneman made 1,972.[64] Schofield's frugal use of his appointment power was primarily due to his narrow criteria for appointment. The test oath of July 22, 1866, and the Fourteenth Amendment disqualified most prewar officeholders. Schofield's elitist and racial attitudes eliminated uneducated whites and all blacks—he appointed no black officials. Finally, his political inclinations caused him to reject both radicals and ultraconservatives, which therefore limited his options to a quite small group of non-rebel, educated, white, "moderate" Republicans.[65]

Schofield defended his policy to Grant by asserting that his preference for "respectable Republicans" over "lower class men who have acquired control over the mass of colored voters" would rebut charges of partisanship. The sparsity of civilian officeholders, especially justices of the peace, meant that the military officers assumed greater responsibilities. This seeming circumspection thus produced a subtle retention of military control, which probably comforted Schofield. However, it added to provisional governor Pierpont's irritation with Schofield, for it undermined the governor's power of political patronage.[66]

The most conspicuous removal during Schofield's tenure in Virginia was, in fact, that of Governor Pierpont. Francis H. Pierpont had been a Whig politician from what became West Virginia. During the war, he established a precarious Unionist state government in Alexandria. When West Virginia became a state, his thin base of support grew even more tenuous. After the war, Pierpont initially attempted to establish a conservative government, based primarily on Unionist Whigs. This government had imposed the Black Codes that General Terry nullified. As Pierpont's attempts to build a strong moderate Republican Party failed to gain support, he made overtures to the radicals. He irritated Schofield by feuding over the general's relatively conservative appointments and issuing numerous pardons for African Americans. Pierpont's term expired on December 31, 1867, though the state supreme court ruled he could continue in office until a new election. Schofield toyed with the idea of removing him in January without naming an immediate replacement, but he decided against it.[67]

By March 1868, Schofield began to reconsider his decision. Pierpont was politicking with the radicals at the constitutional convention to change the state constitution to permit him to succeed himself. Meanwhile, moderate Republicans sought to improve their chances in the next election by urging Henry H. Wells to replace Pierpont and run as an incumbent.[68] Though somewhat troubled about the constitutional issue, Schofield chose to replace Pierpont because he believed that Wells was more moderate and thus offered the best opportunity to continue the moderate policies Schofield favored. On April 4, 1868, after obtaining Grant's acquiescence to the move, Schofield announced the appointment of Henry H. Wells as the new provisional governor of Virginia.[69]

Pierpont attempted to get both Grant and Johnson to overturn Schofield's decision, but failed. Pierpont's wife, Julia, wrote an angry letter to a friend defending her husband's patriotism and denouncing Schofield as a "Copperhead General who oppressed the loyal people of Missouri during the war." She accused him of seeking to "defeat Reconstruction," "prevent the Black man from voting," "form a white man's government," and "rule as long as he can by the power of the *Sword*." She lamented the seeming failure of Grant to "oppose treason in the Army." She concluded that Schofield was "not a friend of universal suffrage." Mrs. Pierpont's charges illustrate how, having lost the center, Governor Pierpont's only hope lay in gaining support from Schofield's radical enemies in Congress.[70]

In his efforts to promote moderate politicians, a month after replacing Pierpont, Schofield replaced another official—this time a conservative. Schofield replaced the conservative mayor of Richmond, Joseph Mayo, with a young Republican from New York, George Chahson. Schofield later advised his successor to also replace the Richmond city attorney, whom Schofield saw as "one of the most malignant rebels in the state."[71] In the end, however, Schofield failed in his efforts to create a moderate Republican/centrist government—there were just too few genuine centrists. Both Wells and Chahson turned out to be more radical than Schofield had supposed, as both were persuaded that their political survival depended on consolidating their radical base of support. In 1869, for example, in order to keep radical support, Governor Wells insisted on a disfranchising test oath provision in the new constitution. He nevertheless lost the election to newly energized conservatives who adopted the mildly centrist position of "universal suffrage" and "universal amnesty." This "centrist-Conservative" party became ever more conservative as it regained the levers of political power in Virginia.[72]

One of Schofield's chief responsibilities under the Reconstruction Acts was to register voters for the election of delegates to a state constitutional convention. Though Schofield personally opposed black suffrage and officeholding, he nevertheless performed this task with his usual efficiency. Schofield issued detailed instructions to the registration boards based on his interpretation of the Reconstruction Acts, after once again inundating his superiors with questions concerning what state positions were to be included in the disfranchising clauses. The assembling of sufficient loyal and competent men for these boards was a problem, so Schofield again relied on military officers as his principal instruments. He next gave preference to those who had served in the Union army during the war and, finally, to those "rare birds known as Southern loyalists," as one officer described them.[73]

One anonymous Union officer's account, "A Military Missionary in Virginia," is illustrative of the attitudes and problems encountered by the registration boards. The officer was stationed in the mountains of western Virginia. Despite the presence of a number of loyalists, it was only with great difficulty that he assembled five men who were sufficiently literate to do the work. The officer was appalled at the ignorance and isolation of the mountain population. One "clan patriarch" whose aid he had secured admitted that he had not voted since the election of William Henry Harrison in 1840. "Free schools are unknown among them, and not one man in fifty reads a newspaper," the officer remarked. Inciting resentment of these poor people against the traditional elites was easy, yet this did not translate into support for Congressional Reconstruction. He observed that the black minority in the mountains was more intelligent and better behaved than that in the lower counties, and the local whites had kindly feelings for the blacks. Yet, "the instant the first negro registered, a change came over the white population. Their kind feelings departed as quickly and as surely as Othello's love changed to hate under Iago's conjuring."[74]

This Union officer also shared the elitist and racist attitudes of his district commander. He mocked newfound expressions of loyalty among the whites, and he wryly remarked that he had "not met more than a half dozen original secessionists." His disdain for the ignorance of the local whites intensified for the uneducated blacks. He derided the spectacle of African Americans' taking oaths that "not one in twenty understood." He had originally thought that "the South deserved to have negro suffrage forced upon it, for rejecting terms which seemed to us so reasonable." However, his experiences had produced a new sympathy for white southerners, and he concluded that black suffrage would "prove a dangerous if not disastrous experiment."[75]

Though many officers, especially in the Freedmen's Bureau, were more sympathetic to universal suffrage, this officer's disenchantment with the politics of Reconstruction was common. It was not simply a reflection of their racial aversion toward African Americans and their elitist disdain for poor whites. Nor was it simply a matter of military men being accustomed to hierarchy and order. Democracy can be a messy and sometimes ugly enterprise, where noble principles coexist with pettiness and the pursuit of personal gain. The radical championing of universal suffrage was rife with racial hypocrisy and crass political opportunism. The Democrats, in addition to arousing racist and antimilitary passions, skillfully exploited the perception that Reconstruction was just partisan politics.

In the late nineteenth century many Americans began rejecting the traditional system of political spoils. They resented the "grasping" of new men. While Republicans castigated the Irish political organizations in the North, Democrats denounced the alliance of blacks and Republicans in the South. The corrupting nature of machine politics gave rise to demands for civil service reforms. Abolitionists like Horace Greeley would abandon Reconstruction in reaction to corruption in the Grant administration. Mugwumps would similarly abandon the Republican Party for Grover Cleveland in 1884. This conservative reformist mood, combined with the quest for independence from party politics, would also animate many military reformers. Just as there were political and economic mugwumps, Sherman, Emory Upton, and even Schofield might be classified as military mugwumps.[76]

Mugwumps, both civilian and military, aspired to an ideal of public service beyond interest and ambition. This ideal of selfless service had been inculcated into many senior officers as cadets at West Point. Sherman's antipathy to politicians was based on his suspicions of their motives. More tolerant of politicians, Schofield still yearned for a purer, more systematic approach to government. While Sherman, Schofield, and most other army officers could be blind to how their own interests and ambitions influenced their judgments, the efforts they made to divine a public, or a national, interest was real.

Despite the misgivings of Schofield and many of his officers, voter registration in Virginia was remarkably efficient and scrupulous. The boards registered 114,700 whites and 101,512 blacks. They rejected 1,816 whites and 241 blacks. When compared to the tax rolls, the registration appears relatively thorough. The tax rolls for 1866–67 listed 134,000 whites and 87,000 blacks. Thus, about 19,000 whites on the tax rolls were not registered, and about 15,000 blacks not on the tax rolls were registered. Beyond the pure numbers, Schofield's report included perceptive analysis of the apportionment of delegates. Whites constituted an overall majority in the state and constituted a majority in 52 of the 102 counties and cities. However, since the population of the black-majority counties was greater than that of the white-majority counties (125,895 to 90,555), the black-majority counties would elect 61 delegates and the white majority counties 44 delegates to the constitutional convention.[77]

The election for the constitutional convention was conducted on October 22, 1867. The Virginia voters approved a constitutional convention by a decisive 107,342 to 61,887. Approximately 88 percent of the freedmen voted, while only 63 percent of whites voted. Accordingly, Republicans constituted a clear majority of the convention's delegates, which included 24 African Americans. An ominous sign for the future was that only 12 percent of white voters gave their support to Republicans. With no fixed party structure, the exact political alignment of each delegate was somewhat obscure; but Schofield, in analyzing the delegates, identified 51 "Radicals," 22 "Republicans," 13 "Conservatives," and 19 "Unreconstructed."[78]

The "Radicals," in addition to supporting equal rights, public schools, and the disfranchisement of Confederate leaders according to the Fourteenth Amendment, sought to ban from officeholding virtually all those who had voluntarily supported the Confederacy. The "Republicans" tended to be those moderates who favored black suffrage but opposed the sweeping disfranchisement of ex-Confederates and integrated schools. The "Conservatives" opposed black suffrage and favored the Black Codes, though they considered the questions of slavery and secession settled. The "Unreconstructed" refused to accept even those results.

The "unreconstructed" remained a powerful force in politics through their domination of many of the state's newspapers. While many conservatives were grateful to Schofield for his moderate policies and had urged Johnston to retain him as First District commander, the "unreconstructed" newspapers pummeled Schofield as if he were a radical Republican. Edward A. Pollard, editor of the *Richmond Examiner*, published his famous, or infamous, book *The Lost Cause* in 1866. When General Orlando Wilcox banned a lecture by Pollard, Schofield sustained his subordinate in this case. Perhaps remembering the reprimand he received in Missouri from Lincoln, Schofield counseled Wilcox to interfere with "freedom of speech and the press as little as possible" and refer the question to him in advance.[79]

No good deed goes unpunished, and J. Marshall Hanna, editor of the *Southern Opinion*, lampooned Schofield in a series of essays collected as *The Acts of*

Kings: Biblical Narrative of the Acts of the First and Second Kings of the First Province, Once Virginia. The author recounted how the "Great Mogul Ulysses" appointed "King Schofield" to rule by the "Radical Koran," and how "King Schofield" gave preference in registration to the "sons and daughters of Ham, who are of the tribe of Ethiopia" over those who are "fair of skin and of Saxon blood." Hanna conceded that "the Ethiopians murmured with the [Radical] Saints against the King, for they, too, had great expectations, which were come to naught." The Radical Saints accused King Schofield of being "janus-faced and looketh two ways," which "playeth into the hands of the lukewarm and half-way men."[80]

The constitutional or Underwood convention, named for its leader, Judge John C. Underwood, met from December 1867 to April 1868. With a radical plurality, it produced a highly reformist constitution. It adopted universal male suffrage. It adopted a township system of local government that provided for the election of local officials, rather than appointment. It created a "homestead exemption," which lowered the taxes on small landholdings. It created Virginia's first public school system, though a majority rejected the African American call for school integration.[81] After rejecting a disfranchising provision that would have gone well beyond those of the Fourteenth Amendment, the convention approved the controversial "test oath" that prohibited most men who had supported the Confederacy from holding public office.

This last provision outraged the conservatives and worried many moderate Republicans. Though he had doubts about several provisions, Schofield strongly opposed the "test oath." On the final day of the convention, April 17, Schofield personally appealed to the delegates to remove the requirement. The next day, he wrote Grant criticizing the convention's action. Schofield feared that the radical nature of the convention would be replicated in the state legislature and executive offices since so many men were unfit for office. He recommended that "the wisest course would be to let the thing fall and die where it is—not submit it to the people at all" and convene another convention at a later date. Anticipating that Grant would run for the presidency, Schofield argued that the endorsement of such a punitive constitution by the Republican Party would do damage to party's image in the North.[82]

Schofield usually displayed a certain caution when it came to intrusion into civil affairs, but he exhibited little reluctance when his conservative principles were at stake. The "test oath" offended his conception of good governance. In his mind, it would expel disinterested statesmen and promote self-interested opportunists. The radical strategy of disfranchisement in order to eke out a narrow majority to retain power affronted his centrist instincts. It was these principles, more than party, that animated Schofield. Throughout his career Schofield was quite comfortable with both moderate Republicans and Democrats. To thwart the distasteful provisions of the Underwood constitution, Schofield energetically employed his military authority over the government of Virginia and undertook an intense lobbying campaign of the War Department, the president, and the moderates in the U.S. Congress.[83]

Schofield's first move was to refuse to schedule a ratifying election for the new constitution. The Virginia legislature had appropriated $100,000 for the constitution process; the first delegate election and the convention had consumed the entire amount. Schofield declared that he would not sanction another raid on the state treasury and argued that the federal government should provide for the expenses of the election, since Congress had mandated the new constitutions. Next, Schofield urged that the election should give the voters an opportunity to vote separately on the "test oath" and other controversial provisions. The impeachment crisis, Schofield's own elevation to secretary of war, and the election of 1868 delayed the resolution of this issue, but Schofield substantially achieved his goals.[84]

On April 7, 1869, now president Grant, at the urging of Schofield, requested that Congress provide the money for the ratification election in Virginia and authorize Schofield to submit certain clauses to the electorate in a separate vote. The Congress overwhelmingly approved the new president's request. Though many conservatives also wanted a separate vote on the township and homestead provisions, Grant decided to limit the election to the disfranchising and test oath clauses. In the election on July 6, 1869, whites turned out in larger numbers, while black participation declined slightly. The constitution passed by an overwhelming 96 percent, while the disfranchising and test oath clauses lost with only 40 percent of the vote. The ploy of replacing Governor Pierpont for the seemingly more electable Wells also failed. The "True Republican–Conservative" candidate Gilbert Walker won with 54 percent of the vote. Republicans held a few offices in the next few decades; however, they would not regain the governorship for over one hundred years.[85]

Although the views of Sherman and Schofield on Reconstruction were initially very similar, they began to diverge in the ensuing decades, based primarily on their political leanings. Schofield, who had during Reconstruction accepted "black suffrage" as distasteful but inevitable, became more reconciled to it as it became clear that it would not interfere with control by the Bourbon Democrat elites. Schofield was not especially concerned when the Redeemers and their Progressive Era successors restricted black voting rights. As a Cleveland Democrat, Schofield was also comfortable with the later view that Reconstruction was a huge mistake that imposed a tyranny on a prostrate South. By the time Schofield's memoirs appeared, this interpretation was becoming the mainstream view of the emerging historical profession. Schofield was far more disposed to emphasize reconciliation and amity with the former rebels.[86]

By contrast, Sherman's Republican connections, as well as the continued southern hostility to his great "March to the Sea," prompted Sherman to worry increasingly about the endurance of the Union victory. In 1875 the pessimistic general lamented to his brother the senator that the army could not long protect southern Republican regimes that lacked popular support. He was "always embarrassed by the plain, palpable fact, that the Union whites are cowardly, and allow the rebel element that loves to fight, to cow them. Until the Union whites, and negroes too, *fight* for their own rights they will be down trodden." Ten years later, he encouraged his brother to use Section 2 of the Fourteenth Amendment to make an issue of the voting rights of African Americans in the South: "My notion is that the negro himself will have to fight for his right of suffrage, but the laws of the United States for electing Members of the House should be made as strong as possible, to encourage the negroes in voting for their candidates, and if need be, fighting for their right when they have an undoubted majority."[87] The belief that the people needed to fight for their political rights was as old as the republican idea. Nevertheless, just as Schofield recoiled from Sherman's concept of war, Schofield would have recoiled from the prospect of blacks' fighting for their rights. Sherman's well-known distaste for politics was based in part on his view of democratic government and politics as a battle among self-interested parties. Rights were not so much granted as earned through struggle or manipulation, and this was why politics often repelled him. Schofield had a more orderly expectation of democratic government, where rights were granted and enforced by a paternalistic elite.

Secretary of War

While John Schofield was jousting with the Underwood convention, a more titanic battle was taking place in Washington. The struggle between the president and Congress over Reconstruction had degenerated into a clash over control of the primary instrument of Reconstruction policy—the United States Army. As Congress passed the Reconstruction Acts over the president's veto, Andrew Johnson attempted to limit their effect through his powers of appointment. Schofield's conservative approach in Virginia reassured the president, but other commanders faced Johnson's displeasure. The president replaced Daniel Sickles with E. R. S. Canby in September 1867, John Pope with George Meade in December 1867, and most controversially, Philip Sheridan with Winfield Hancock, also in September 1867. The fight over control of the army would provoke the impeachment crisis and, ironically, propel John Schofield into the cabinet.[1]

President Johnson attempted to use the immensely popular Grant for his own purposes, while Grant, for a time, rather skillfully resisted many of the president's efforts without creating a public rupture. In August 1867, in an effort to dislodge Edwin Stanton, the most radical member of the cabinet, Johnson suspended Stanton and appointed Grant acting secretary of war. General Grant, who had been given wide latitude during the war and who had chafed under Stanton's efforts to take greater control of the War Department, accepted the duty. Stanton, having the strong backing of Congress through the Tenure of Office Act, refused to resign. As Stanton dug in, Grant began to have second thoughts about the issue, especially as he saw this action as a preliminary move in the replacement of many district commanders. Johnson considered the possibility of replacing Grant with Sherman, but Sherman resisted. By the fall of 1867, reports of an open breach between Grant and Johnson were spreading.[2]

In February 1868 Johnson again moved against Secretary of War Stanton.

This time the president ordered Adjutant General Lorenzo Thomas to replace Stanton. The old soldier informed Stanton of his orders and his intention to displace the secretary. The next day, Thomas found himself under arrest by the orders of Secretary Stanton. Stanton had made it clear he would not be so easily removed. Congress came to Stanton's defense and accused President Johnson of violating the Tenure of Office Act. So began the first presidential impeachment in American history. The impeachment crisis combined a momentous constitutional clash between the president and the Congress with a less noble scramble for partisan and personal advantage. Too often forgotten is that this political and constitutional drama began as a crisis in civil-military relations.[3]

In his 1897 memoirs Schofield portrayed the impeachment crisis as originating in a fight over control of the army between Stanton and Grant. While somewhat overstated, Schofield's depiction reflected the central theme of his book—the command of the army. Grant and Stanton did struggle for control of the War Department staff, but Grant's differences with Johnson eventually eclipsed the disagreements he had with Stanton. Grant's initial willingness to succeed Stanton in August 1867 reflected the tension between the two strong-willed men. Schofield recounted how Grant at this time complained about Stanton's behavior, telling Schofield he contemplated resignation if Stanton were not removed. In January 1868 Grant attempted to convince the president to replace Stanton with Jacob D. Cox, Schofield's friend and former subordinate. Historian Brooks Simpson has suggested that Johnson declined this option in order to "smoke out" Grant. Johnson wanted to force Grant to choose sides. If the general did not cooperate with the president, Johnson would undertake a campaign to publicly discredit Grant and diminish his presidential prospects. Although it is possible that Johnson was motivated by such perverse guile, it is more probable that his rejection of the Cox compromise reflected his obtuse intransigence. Either way, President Johnson had made a serious miscalculation.[4]

Throughout the fall of 1867, many radical Republicans had been exploring grounds for impeaching the president, and now they had the weapon. Three days after General Thomas's abortive attempt to displace Stanton, the House of Representatives impeached President Johnson. Eight of the eleven articles of impeachment were related to the Tenure of Office Act and one to the Command of the Army Amendment. The trial in the Senate lasted from March 5 to May 26, 1868. As the trial began, Johnson hoped that the justice of his cause and the unpopularity of the man who would succeed him, radical Republican Benjamin Wade, the president pro tem of the Senate, would save him. By April 16, a less confident president authorized his chief legal advisor—and future attorney general—William Evarts to quietly assure moderate senators that if acquitted, the president would no longer obstruct Congressional Reconstruction.[5]

A week later Evarts requested that General Schofield meet him at the Willard Hotel, near the executive mansion, on the afternoon of April 21. At this meeting Evarts offered Schofield the position of secretary of war. Evarts, after some reluctance, agreed to let Schofield discuss this proposal with General Grant. That evening after dinner, Schofield broached the offer with Grant. According to Schofield, "General Grant replied that he had supposed that there was no reasonable doubt of the President's removal, but if that was not the case, or if it were, he (General Grant) would be glad to have me as Secretary of War during the remainder of the term."[6]

Later that same evening, Schofield met with Evarts again. Evarts expressed confidence that the Senate would not convict the president. He said that several Republican senators were doubtful about removal and were looking for a way "to get out of the scrape." Evarts intimated that this proposal actually originated with several moderate Republicans because Schofield's nomination would be satisfactory to Grant and would reassure the Republicans about the president's future actions. When Schofield pressed Evarts to reveal who some of these senators might be and suggested some names, Evarts only replied that if Senators William P. Fessenden (R-Maine) and Lyman Trumbull (R-Ill.) voted for conviction, he, Evarts, would have no hope for acquittal. Schofield said he would discuss the matter again with Grant and would give Evarts a definite answer the next day.[7]

In seeking Grant's advice that night, Schofield recounted the general substance of his conversations with Evarts, though he mentioned no names. Schofield strongly signaled his willingness, indeed duty, to accept the nomination as it came from both Johnson and the Republican senators. Grant, according to Schofield, seemed sympathetic to this position, but he made it clear that he thought Johnson should be removed. Grant feared that once Congress adjourned, the president would once again "trample the laws underfoot and do whatever he pleased." In the end, Grant advised Schofield that he should not "enter into any project to compromise the impeachment question," but he agreed that Schofield "could not well do otherwise than to acquiesce in the nomination."[8]

The next day, April 22, Schofield communicated to Evarts that he remained concerned about Johnson's future policies should he remain in office, especially those related to his sending orders to military officers outside of regular channels. Schofield wanted assurance that Johnson would not bypass the military command. Evarts could not offer any promises, and Schofield thought it improper to meet with Johnson in order to extract such a pledge, so Schofield merely told Evarts that he was prepared to accept the appointment, if the president were informed of these conditions. Schofield returned to Richmond on the following day, and on April 24 President Johnson submitted Schofield's nomination to the Senate. On April 25 Grant wrote Schofield a confidential letter requesting that he withdraw his nomination. Schofield assumed that Grant's change of opinion was based on a revised appreciation of the effect Schofield's nomination would have on the impeachment. Schofield responded that he regretted that Grant's change of advice came too late and that he could not in good conscience withdraw at that stage. He suggested, perhaps a bit disingenuously, that his nomination might not be confirmed.[9]

On May 16 the Senate voted 35 to 19 to convict on the broadest article of impeachment. Needing a two-thirds majority to convict, the president was acquitted by one vote. Seven Republicans had joined the Democrats to save Johnson. Later votes on the other articles produced a similar result. On May 26 Stanton resigned, and on May 29 Schofield was overwhelmingly confirmed, though there was a bit of partisan squabbling about the wording of how and why he was displacing Edwin Stanton. On June 1, 1868, President Johnson personally escorted Schofield to his new office.[10] John M. Schofield, as a serving brigadier general, became secretary of war.[11]

Schofield's nomination may not have been decisive in Johnson's escape, but given the closeness of the decision, it was certainly a factor. It can also be seen as more of an effect than a cause. As Evarts hinted, several wavering senators were looking for a way "out of the scrape." Johnson, who had rejected Grant's attempted compromise of the nomination of Jacob Cox, was now eager to compromise. Just who suggested Schofield is unclear, but it was a shrewd choice.[12] Members of the Blair family, Schofield's former sponsors, were now among President Johnson's closest advisors.[13] Though Schofield had experienced a few run-ins with Johnson, as in the Watson case, the First District commander had been much more sympathetic to the president's point of view than many others. By hewing to a cautious policy of supporting "moderate" Republicans in Virginia, Schofield had also not antagonized the radical Republicans in Congress. Finally, though he had disagreed with Grant on certain policy questions, notably black suffrage, he retained Grant's trust and confidence. Grant generally responded to people on a personal rather than ideological level. While Sheridan more closely shared Grant's views on Reconstruction, Grant remained loyal to friends like Sherman and Schofield, whose perspectives differed from his own.[14]

The unreconstructed Richmond editor J. Marshall Hanna depicted the motivations of each side with characteristic mockery. The "Chief Ruler [Johnson]" hit upon replacing "Stanton, that is Satan," with "King Schofield" because "he knew that the people of the Province had been mightily put upon by Schofield and would be glad to be ridden of his rule. . . . Then the Select [Senate radicals] took counsel together, and anointed Schofield. . . . 'He is one of us,' they said, 'and we will circumvent the traitor of the White House.'" Nevertheless, unreconstructed Virginians were soon lamenting that, with the arrival of General Stoneman in Richmond, "We have swapped the devil for a witch."[15]

As secretary of war, Brigadier General Schofield was in a unique and delicate position. Although many former generals became secretaries, several secretaries became generals, and some commanding generals, like Grant and Sherman, served as acting secretaries, Schofield was the only actively serving general officer to hold the position formally. Schofield was the second West Pointer to hold the office and the first and only professional soldier.[16] Jefferson Davis had been the first academy graduate to serve as secretary of war, from 1853 to 1857. It was characteristic of the American system that a West Pointer turned politician would head the War Department before the first academy graduate would command the army. Secretary Schofield's position between the commander in chief and the commanding general was also very delicate. Though not overtly disloyal to Johnson, Schofield conformed to Grant's wishes. Grant's authority increasingly rested less on his four stars and more on his status as the future commander in chief.[17]

Several historians have described Secretary Schofield as a "dignified" or "glorified" clerk, ferrying messages back and forth between the army headquarters and the White House.[18] There is some truth to this depiction, in that Schofield had little independent power and did not undertake policy positions at odds with both the president and the commanding general. Yet between a defeated, embittered president and a commanding general who was increasingly preoccupied with a presidential campaign, Schofield carried out his duties with his usual diligence and discretion. Johnson, true to his pledge, no longer interfered in southern affairs, while candidate Grant was reluctant to intrude too greatly in the actions of the district commanders. If "Let Us Have Peace" was Grant's campaign slogan, keeping the peace was Schofield's paramount mission. This task was made more important as the Democrats, especially vice presidential candidate Frank Blair Jr., harangued audiences about military despotism.[19]

In July 1868 Grant left the capital for St. Louis and then Galena, Illinois, where he spent much of his time before the election. Grant did take, along with

Sherman and Sheridan, a military-related trip to the Rocky Mountains, which gave him a better idea about the western posts and Indian territories. While Grant "campaigned" for president, Schofield largely exercised the duties of both secretary of war and commanding general, primarily through Grant's aide John A. Rawlins. In September Grant wrote Schofield a heartening letter: "I presume military affairs are getting along well without me. . . . I feel very grateful that the War Department has fallen where it has, where I not only can communicate with the department freely, but feel that it is administered entirely in the interest of the nation. It is a rare thing that Govt. Depts. are so administered. They are generally administered in the interest of a political party and not to serve the public interest."[20]

Schofield believed his mission and greatest contribution as secretary of war was keeping the peace during the election of 1868. He later bragged that "the Presidential election in the Southern States was conducted with perfect good order." Yet, the peace of the 1868 election was only relative and by no means perfect. In his annual report that year, Schofield more candidly admitted that the army kept order "only in an imperfect degree," though he still claimed the "comparative good order" throughout the country. Three states—Virginia, Mississippi, and Texas—had not yet been readmitted to the Union, and so did not vote in the federal election, and were therefore relatively peaceful. As the election approached, well-founded fears of violence in the South increased. In the remaining former Confederate states, uneasy Republican governors inundated the War Department with requests for assistance. Schofield, Grant, and the local military commanders had to undertake delicate balancing acts to reassure black and white Republicans without inflaming and seeming to confirm the charges of military dictatorship hurled by the Democrats.[21]

In Missouri General Schofield had learned the difficulty of directing and controlling a war against guerrillas; Secretary Schofield again experienced the same predicament in keeping the peace in an atmosphere of political intimidation and violence. Obtaining accurate and unbiased assessments was especially difficult, so in addition to regular reports from and directives to the district commanders, he sent his own observers. Among these was Brigadier General O. O. Howard, who visited many southern states. In August Howard reported that he believed General Orlando Brown "would keep matters quiet in Virginia," and he expected that North Carolina would "get through the political campaign with only little if any violence." Later that month, Howard reported to Schofield that while Georgia and Mississippi seemed quiet, he observed "more irritation in Tennessee than elsewhere" and predicted outbreaks were most likely to occur there. To anxious legislators in Tennessee, Schofield wrote that the army stood ready to protect the law-abiding citizens of the state and directed Major General George Thomas to report immediately on any additional troops he required.[22]

Howard's warning about Tennessee was timely, but his assessment of Georgia proved overly optimistic. With the state restored to the Union, Major General George Meade relinquished most of his authority over the civil government. By September, the Democrats had thrown the black delegates out of the state legislature, a local sheriff had led a murderous attack on a black political meeting, and the Ku Klux Klan was terrorizing much of the Republican electorate. President Johnson and his cabinet blamed the anarchy in Georgia on the "dissatisfaction of the people with their local governments. . . . [T]hey are taxed without their consent, and governed by a few intruders from abroad, and the negroes." Johnson was quite willing to turn a blind eye to the intimidation of Republican voters in Georgia and all other southern states. Secretary Schofield, appalled by the violence and disorder, was the lone voice in the cabinet to express the opinion that the return of full civil authority in some southern states had been premature. He believed that the military governments should have been maintained and would have to be restored. Six months later Meade's successor, Brigadier General Alfred Terry, would make that same recommendation, and by the end of 1869, Congress had granted Terry renewed powers over the civil authorities of Georgia.[23]

In October 1868 Secretary Schofield sent his trusted aide J. A. Campbell to Tennessee and then Arkansas to assess the situation. Campbell reported that though the Ku Klux Klan, headed by Nathan Bedford Forrest, was active in Tennessee, he agreed with military authorities that peace could be maintained for the election. Arkansas was more worrisome. Arkansas governor Powell Clayton was perturbed by recent murders and a riverboat hijacking of arms that were intended for the Arkansas militia. Campbell believed that the crime had been committed by some kind of secret society operating out of Memphis, but he was uncertain if it were part of a larger conspiracy. Campbell also concluded that the assassination of Republican congressman James Hinds on October 22 was politically motivated, though probably unpremeditated, and not connected with the destruction of the arms for the state militia.[24]

Governor Clayton feared that Hinds's assassination was but a precursor to a general attack on state officers to seize control of the government and the polls prior to the election. To safeguard the state government, Clayton wanted federal arms for the "colored militia" in Little Rock, though not for the rural areas he could not control. Brevet Brigadier General Charles H. Smith, the military commander in Arkansas, maintained that he had enough troops to keep the peace, but he reluctantly agreed that arming the militia would do no harm. Campbell advised Schofield against the idea, as he thought arming the black militia would be provocative and prompt retaliation, especially in the unprotected, remote regions. He warned Schofield that Clayton's intention to set aside registration in eleven counties was equally unwise. In November Governor Clayton's fears proved exaggerated, and the election took place without insurrection. Grant won Arkansas with more than 53 percent of the vote.[25]

In Louisiana it was a different story. As the election approached, the state experienced several race riots and Democratic attacks on black political meetings. Brevet Major General Robert C. Buchanan, the Louisiana commander, had conscientiously kept peace during the gubernatorial election in April 1868, but the readmission of Louisiana and other southern states had prompted a reorganization of military districts. President Johnson was able to replace Buchanan with the more conservative Brevet Major General Lovell H. Rousseau, a former congressional supporter of Johnson.[26] By October, the specter of violence and intimidation had reached an unprecedented scale, and Rousseau reacted ineffectually to prevent violence. Meanwhile, Rousseau was sending predictions to Johnson of a Democratic electoral victory. With Rousseau's inaction and his rejection of Republican governor Henry C. Warmoth's request to form a state militia, Warmoth and the state legislature created the Metropolitan Police to counter the New Orleans city police force, which was cooperating with the Democrats in suppressing the Republican vote.[27]

Rousseau attempted to shift the burden of responsibility to the War Department, and Schofield just as quickly put it back on him. Knowing he could not give meaningful commands so far removed from the scene, Schofield replied, "You are authorized and expected to take such action as may be necessary to preserve peace and good order."[28] Rousseau brokered an agreement to support the Metropolitan Police, but the accord immediately began to unravel. Schofield forthrightly advised Rousseau that he could not evade his responsibility concerning the rival police organizations. More strongly Schofield declared, "It is your duty to support the lawful police [the Metropolitan Police]; or if necessary, you may temporarily replace it by your troops. . . . It looks to me, at this distance, as if your troops would be good substitutes for the rival police forces."[29] Rousseau had been reinforced with 550 additional troops from Mississippi. Although he was unwilling to replace the police with soldiers, he did position the soldiers to forestall violence at the polls.[30]

Though not without some sporadic violence, election day in Louisiana turned out to be surprisingly peaceful. Using the October disturbances and the danger of pitched battles between rival police forces as the pretext, the military commander had pressured the governor into discouraging black voters in New Orleans. Though Republican Warmoth had gotten 69,000 votes in April, Grant got only 33,263 to Horatio Seymour's 80,225. The Democrats and General Rousseau accomplished their objective. The Democrats won only one other southern state, Georgia, where pervasive Democratic violence also helped suppress the Republican vote. Three other former slave states—Kentucky, Maryland, and Delaware—went to the Democrats. Grant won the White House carrying twenty-five of thirty-three states, but the relative narrowness of the war hero's victory in the popular vote, 52.7 percent to 47.3 percent, symbolized the enduring divisions of the nation and the still formidable organizational abilities of the Democrats.[31]

Schofield's relations with President Johnson were always correct, but wary. In an effort to stir up trouble for candidate Grant, Johnson requested that Schofield provide him with copies of Grant's military correspondence related to Nathaniel Banks's Red River campaign, and the removal of General Benjamin Butler from command of the Army of the James (both Banks and Butler were then Republican congressmen). Schofield complied with the request, but not before informing Grant, who demonstrated his imperturbability by voluntarily including confidential letters not available to the War Department.[32]

Schofield's sense of duty and decorum denied him the opportunity to see his friend and sponsor Ulysses S. Grant sworn in as president. For the inauguration, Grant had refused to ride in the same carriage as President Johnson. Johnson instead called a cabinet meeting to consider the bills that Congress was still forwarding to the executive mansion. Schofield loyally attended the president until Johnson finally ended the meeting at 12:30 P.M., the time Grant was to be sworn in. The president and his cabinet, except for Evarts, who had departed earlier, then said their farewells and got in their carriages.[33]

Secretary Schofield's relations with the other cabinet secretaries were more cordial. He had already established a friendly relationship with Secretary of State William H. Seward. Schofield's closest cabinet colleagues were William Evarts, who had become the interim attorney general, and Secretary of the Interior Orville Browning. Schofield frequently turned to Evarts for legal advice, and Evarts, in turn, found Schofield genial, sympathetic, approachable, and unostentatious. Schofield and Orville Browning had many friends in common. Schofield's former subordinate General Thomas Ewing was a close Browning family friend, and Jacob Cox served as Browning's chief assistant at the Department of the Interior. Although Browning and Schofield disagreed on many Reconstruction policies and on the candidacy of U. S. Grant, Browning thought Schofield was sensible and fair-minded. In balancing his loyalty to

Grant and President Johnson, Schofield was guided ultimately by his loyalty to the army. Even his fellow cabinet members noted this devotion, as Schofield invariably defended the army against charges from all sides and took any questioning of military proceedings as a personal attack.[34]

Historian Harold Hyman has regarded the impeachment and its aftermath as a military victory.[35] Though many soldiers feared Johnson's alliance with ex-Confederates to harass the army and frustrate Reconstruction, most did not embrace impeachment. Some, such as U. S. Grant and Philip Sheridan, were gratified by Johnson's "humbling." Others, like Schofield and William T. Sherman, considered the situation more tragic than triumphant. Still others, such as Winfield S. Hancock and Lovell Rousseau, were Johnson supporters. The military was no more a monolithic institution than Congress or the president's cabinet.

For the army as an institution, Reconstruction and impeachment proved to be a Pyrrhic victory. Congress would soon take back many of the powers it had given General Grant to fight President Johnson. While some congressmen were sympathetic to the army and its needs, most northern and western representatives returned to politics as usual. Southern congressmen would remain hostile to the army for nearly thirty years, and a few northern congressmen, like John Logan of Illinois, nursed personal grudges that had first developed in the war. Congress had protected the army from southern retaliation during Presidential Reconstruction, but not for the sake of the army. Just as the restoration of congressional supremacy played an important role in the fight over Reconstruction, it would constrain President Grant and his ability to aid his friend and successor, William T. Sherman.

Like the question of slavery, Reconstruction was a minefield about which military officers learned to step carefully. The struggle over a "hard" or "soft" Reconstruction, like the tussle over "hard" or "soft" war, was a question that required national will as much as governmental or military unity. The national will to save the Union and end slavery enabled General Grant to lead his armies to victory, but the lack of national will over defending the rights of African Americans doomed Grant's efforts as general and president.

The Democratic accusations of military tyranny and complaints of Republican partisanship undermined northern support for protecting the rights of the freedpeople. The outrages of the Ku Klux Klan could inflame northern opinion, but so could reports of trials by military commission and the military supervision of elections. American antipathy toward the military in politics was as deep as its racism. Efforts to disfranchise many ex-Confederates, which Schofield had strenuously opposed, smacked of party politics. Democracy through martial law was a difficult policy to defend. Most Americans wanted, according to a more modern refrain, to "move on," even if it meant sacrificing the rights of African Americans. The army was too crude a tool for the political and social revolution envisioned by the radicals and the new black citizens. In wresting control of the army from Johnson, Congress had won the battle, but in losing popular support, they lost the war.[36]

Today we would view Schofield as racist and extremely conservative, but in his day he was generally regarded as a moderate.[37] As in Missouri, he achieved this reputation by steering a course between the radical Republicans and the ultraconservatives. Although personally opposed to the Fourteenth Amendment, the pragmatic Schofield unsuccessfully urged Virginians to ratify it in 1866. He scrupulously supervised the registration of eligible voters, including blacks. Concerned about the radical potentialities of the constitutional convention, he nevertheless kept the polls open several days more to give blacks an adequate opportunity to vote. Opposed to social integration, he brokered an agreement that integrated two-thirds of the Richmond streetcars. While he replaced very few officials, he tended to pick "moderates" over both radicals and conservatives. As secretary of war, he tried to hew to a principled path between an administration willing to turn a blind eye to political violence and the provocative use of military force.

U. S. Grant was appreciative of Schofield's performance and gave him a double reward. First, on assuming the presidency, Grant promoted William T. Sherman to his former position of general, Philip Sheridan to the rank of lieutenant general, and John M. Schofield to major general in the regular army. Sheridan's elevation to lieutenant general irritated many of the supporters of George Thomas and George Meade, but Grant was putting his stamp on the army. Grant was also looking to the future, as Sheridan and Schofield were both only thirty-seven years old. Second, Grant delayed the appointment of his chief of staff and trusted friend John Rawlins as secretary of war to permit Schofield to be Grant's first secretary of war.[38]

President Grant retained Schofield as secretary of war, in part, to complete some unfinished business. With generals and West Point graduates as president, secretary of war, and commanding general, there now existed a rare unanimity for long-sought army reforms. Chief among the desired changes was command of the army. As commanding general, Grant had shared his predecessors' displeasure over the independence of the staff bureaus. Now, as president, he sought to remedy that situation for his successor. President Grant directed Secretary Schofield to prepare an order that General Sherman would command the entire army—the staff as well as the line. But this unanimity proved short-lived, and within weeks, Rawlins, as the new secretary of war, persuaded Grant to rescind the order. The military victory had been overturned by a rapid political counterattack.[39]

The War Department reflected the American pattern of checks and balances among competing institutions. In theory, the commanding general commanded the army, while the secretary of war administered the army. However, the delineation between administration and command is as difficult as that between political and military questions. The commanding general believed the "General Staff" should operate under his supervision.[40] The staff chiefs preferred to report directly to the secretary. Dependent on the staff, the secretary of war generally sided with the bureaus. Without control of the staff, each secretary feared he might become a glorified clerk, dependent on the commanding general for all information. The staff bureaus preferred the temporary and often inexperienced secretary, who would become reliant on them and grant them greater autonomy. Further, many of the chiefs of the bureaus had long experience in Washington, D.C., and had established close contacts with Congress. Thus, the conflict between the secretary and the commanding general also involved the interests of other military and civilian institutions.[41]

A year earlier, in January 1868, Sherman had headed a board of officers to develop new army regulations. Its recommendations included stationing the army headquarters permanently in Washington, requiring all orders issued by the president and secretary of war to go through the headquarters of the army, and placing all parts of the army under the orders of the commanding general, to act only by his authority. Since Congress had directed a review and report on army regulations and since these new regulations included the Command of the Army Amendment of 1867, which mandated that President Johnson's orders go through Grant, the new regulations were submitted to Congress for approval. Secretary Schofield, however, persuaded the heads of the Military Affairs Committees, Senator Henry Wilson and Representative James A. Garfield, that "it would be unwise to subject a code of General Regulations for the Army to the formal action of Congress" and thereby tie the hands of the president. All concluded a presidential directive was the most appropriate instrument.[42]

On March 5, 1869, the day after the inauguration, Schofield issued the following instructions, which were published as General Order No. 11. This portentous order was only three sentences long:

> By direction of the President, General William T. Sherman will assume command of the Army of the United States.
> The chiefs of the staff corps, departments, and bureaus will report

to and act under the immediate orders of the general commanding the army.

Any official business which by law or regulation requires the action of the President or Secretary of War will be submitted by the General of the Army to the Secretary of War, and in general all orders from the President or Secretary of War to any portion of the army, line or staff, will be transmitted through the General of the Army.[43]

On March 13, 1869, Schofield stepped down as secretary of war, and on March 26 the new secretary of war, John Rawlins, issued the equally short directive, published as General Order No. 28:

By direction of the President, the order of the Secretary of War, dated War Department, March 5, 1869, and published in General Orders No. 11, headquarters of the army, Adjutant-General's Office, dated March 8, 1869, except so much as directs General W. T. Sherman to assume command of the Army of the United States, is hereby rescinded.

All official business which by law or regulations requires the action of the President or Secretary of War will be submitted by the chiefs of staff corps, departments, and bureaus to the Secretary of War.

All orders and instructions relating to military operations issued by the President or Secretary of War will be issued through the General of the Army.[44]

Both Sherman and Schofield were stunned by the rapid turnabout. Schofield was chagrined at this failure and rather naively told Sherman that had he remained secretary a bit longer, the new rules might have been accepted. Both underestimated the degree of political resistance to the new arrangement at the War Department. The moment Schofield issued the new order, other interested parties began bringing pressure to bear on Grant. Grant initially told Sherman that Rawlins's worries had been the primary reason for the reversal, but gradually he admitted other political pressures.[45]

Grant's popularity did not translate into power over the Republican Congress. The Senate initially rebuffed Grant's efforts to repeal the Tenure of Office Act. Former general, future president, and congressional advocate of military reform James A. Garfield flatly opposed the law's repeal. The ceding of so much power to a military officer as independent and mercurial as Sherman did not improve the congressional mood. Grant's rapid backtracking on command of the army reflected his political realism. On April 5, 1869, the Senate finally agreed to a compromise that surrendered the ability to compel the retention of a suspended cabinet officer.[46]

The staff departments, which had opposed Schofield's order and proposals to consolidate various departments, had rallied their supporters in Congress. These departments were an extremely important source of political patronage. For example, the quartermaster general maintained a force of 10,494 civilians at a cost of $442,592 per month. The chief of ordnance had 1,543 civilian employees, the chief of engineers had 2,782, and the surgeon general had 400. The Army Corps of Engineers was responsible for millions of dollars in construction and river navigation projects. Control of the staff department by the commanding general would lead to greater control by departmental commanders of staff activities in their commands. The Washington-based staff chiefs were therefore far more responsive to congressional influence, especially through a politically appointed secretary, than a remote departmental commander.[47]

That spring Sherman and Schofield also saw the collapse of their once bright hopes for other reform measures. Representative James A. Garfield of the Military Affairs Committee and Secretary Schofield had become close collaborators in proposing sweeping reforms of the army. In his annual report Schofield pressed the army's case for transferring the Bureau of Indian Affairs to the War Department. He argued that appointing army officers as the Indian agents would be more economical and afford greater fiscal control and accountability. It would also make one authority responsible for safeguarding local whites from Indians and protecting the Indians from lawless whites. When the House passed the bill, Schofield confidently told Sherman that the Senate was sure to do the same. Schofield, however, was too optimistic. The Senate majority instead accepted the humanitarian argument that Indians would receive better treatment from the Interior Department and its civilian agents. The Senate not only refused to authorize the transfer, but later it also halted Grant's informal use of army officers as Indian agents.[48]

Testifying before Garfield's committee in February 1869, Secretary Schofield endorsed the consolidation of the Quartermaster, Commissary, and Paymaster Departments. According to Schofield, such consolidation would also permit the more systematic selection and education of the regimental officers routinely detailed to such duties. Schofield went on to explain that the detailing of regimental officers as bonded paymasters would permit the more timely payment of troops and would greatly improve morale. Under the general theory that consolidation fostered greater unity of effort, Schofield even astonished the committee by suggesting the consolidation of the War and Navy Departments. He argued that in defending against a foreign enemy, the army and navy would be forced to work together, so one person should command in any operation. Schofield was careful not to attribute great financial savings to consolidation, as most functions still had to be performed. Over the next decades, dozens of bills to "increase the efficiency of the army" were introduced. For Schofield and other military reformers, "efficiency" meant improved military effectiveness, while for most congressmen it meant lower costs. This conflicting definition would scupper many reform efforts.[49]

Another obstacle to reform was internal division within the army. Congressional opponents of almost any measure could find officers who also opposed it. Although Schofield had objected to the effort to incorporate Sherman's proposed regulations into federal law, he understood the need to develop consensus within the officer corps. In a letter about a proposed military prison, Schofield laid out the need for the senior officers to present a solid front before their political masters and the public: "the views of leading officers of the army shall be discussed among themselves, differences compromised and plans of organization harmonized; so that we may stand before Congress and the country [as] a unit. Thus we can secure what is necessary for the military service. Without it the army will be a prey to intrigue and individual interest or whim."[50]

Despite the favorable report by Garfield's committee, which supported nearly all of the reforms advocated by Sherman and Schofield, the effort failed, and the only substantive measure in the Act of March 3, 1869, was to reduce the army from forty-five to twenty-five infantry regiments. The opposition of the General Staff and the broad desire in Congress to return to the antebellum status quo undermined the unique impetus for reform. For Sherman, the situation would grow worse. John Rawlins would die within a few months and be replaced by the domineering and ultimately corrupt William Belknap. Grant's "betrayal" over General Order No. 11 and failure to aid Sherman in his struggles with Belknap would create a breach between Sherman and Grant. They remained cordial, but the absolute trust that Sherman felt during the war had largely dissolved.[51]

In Congress, James Garfield soon surrendered the chairmanship of the Military Affairs Committee to John Logan, who vividly remembered Sherman's passing him over for command of the Army of the Tennessee. Logan succeeded in reducing the pay of general officers, and particularly that of Sherman. Meanwhile, the Democrats, who were generally hostile to the army, would gradually increase their strength in Congress until they took over the House in 1875, holding it for eight of the next ten Congresses. The army and its commanding general were politically on the defensive.[52]

TEN

The Rocky Road of Reform

After years of intense involvement in the nation's great political questions, Major General John M. Schofield returned to the army and for the remainder of his life would pursue army reform. Though less momentous than the questions of Union, slavery, and Reconstruction, the issue was no less political. Not everyone, either in the army or in the political institutions that regulated and shaped the army, shared General William T. Sherman's vision of professional reform of the army. Schofield became Sherman's right-hand man in his quest to transform the United States Army. Sherman, the intense and fiery advocate, appreciated Schofield's judicious temperament. Schofield's scholarly, methodical, and open-minded approach to problems engendered reassurance and promoted consensus. On issues like command of the army, professional education, updating regulations and tactics, military reorganization, and politically delicate inquiries, Sherman would turn to Schofield. But even the brilliant Sherman, assisted by the shrewd Schofield, could not overcome many of the institutional and personality-based obstacles that made the politics of army reform such a difficult and seemingly quixotic quest.[1]

Upon Schofield's relinquishing the War Department, Grant assigned the major general to the Department of the Missouri, with headquarters in St. Louis, in place of Lieutenant General Philip Sheridan, who assumed command of the Division of the Missouri in Chicago. Schofield's new department consisted of the states of Illinois, Missouri, Kansas, Oklahoma, Colorado, and New Mexico. Schofield's return to St. Louis was certainly far more felicitous than his departure five years earlier. Even many of his former enemies, such as Charles Drake, attended a welcoming banquet. However, Schofield's return to the department was short-lived. With the death of George Thomas, Schofield was reassigned to command the Division of the Pacific in the spring of 1870.[2]

Schofield's brief tenure in the Department of the Missouri prevented any chance of his gaining the fame as an Indian fighter that his predecessor Sheridan had attained. Schofield's plans to continue winter operations against the remaining nonreservation Indians were cancelled in accordance with President Grant's peace policy. (Rather than simply drive the Indians off lands whites coveted, Grant, responding to eastern humanitarians, launched a program that sought to settle Indians on protected reservations under the supervision of Indian agents, often from religious organizations.) However, during his short time in the Department of the Missouri, Schofield made an early contribution to what became a central feature of Sherman's efforts to professionalize the post–Civil War army.[3]

The creation of postgraduate service schools was one of the most important reforms of the Sherman era. One early historian of the army marked the end of the "Army's Dark Ages" and the beginning the "Army's Renaissance" with the creation in 1881 of the School of Application for Infantry and Cavalry at Fort Leavenworth, Kansas. For decades, most officers received their formal military training at West Point and on the job in their units. The Artillery School at Fort Monroe, Virginia, founded by John C. Calhoun in 1824, was revived in 1867. The Army Corps of Engineers formed an engineering school at Willets Point, New York, after West Point was transferred from the control of the chief of engineers in 1866. Despite a rocky beginning, the school at Fort Leavenworth grew in stature as it expanded its course of study from elementary tactics to the in-depth study of the science and art of war. In time, it became a vital center for the development of military professionalism.[4]

Though Schofield had only served a few years as an artillery officer, he nevertheless had an abiding affection for and affiliation to the branch. As the artillery returned to its peacetime role of coastal defense, light or field artillery atrophied through lack of use and training. At the suggestion of Henry J. Hunt, the former chief of artillery for the Army of the Potomac, Schofield formed a school for light artillery at Fort Riley, Kansas, out of the four light batteries assigned to his department. He also issued them carbines so that they could act as cavalry in protecting the neighboring settlement from Indian raids. The school was disbanded shortly after Schofield departed for command in California, but when he returned as the Division of the Missouri commander, he helped create the School for Cavalry and Light Artillery at Fort Riley in 1887. Through the remainder of his career, Schofield kept a protective eye on the school.[5]

Schofield took command of the Division of the Pacific in May 1870. The division included the newly created Department of Arizona. President Grant stunned and angered many more senior officers when he appointed Lieutenant Colonel George Crook, who had recently distinguished himself in the Paiute War, to command the department as a brevet major general in June 1871.[6]

Schofield had little experience with Indian warfare and even less inclination to micromanage an on-site commander. With the tenacious and unconventional Crook, Grant had given Schofield just the right man. While Crook initially looked to Schofield for guidance about the political environment, he soon earned his division commander's full support and confidence.[7] When peace negotiations with the Apache failed in the fall of 1872, Crook conducted a brilliant and relentless winter campaign. Led by Indian scouts drawn from Apaches' tribal enemies, Crook's columns kept up a remorseless pursuit of the various raiding bands. Unable to hunt or cook, or even sleep securely, the demoralized Indian bands soon returned to the reservations and professed their desire for peace. Lieutenant Colonel Crook's dazzling victory brought him a brigadier general's star in 1873 and relative peace in Arizona for nearly ten years.[8]

Crook's promotion tragically came at the expense of another of Schofield's brigadier generals, Edward R. S. Canby.[9] Canby's assassination on April 11, 1873, which occurred while he was conducting peace negotiations with the Modocs, was just one more dismal episode in tragic history of the Modocs. The Modocs lived in northeastern California near the Oregon border. In the early nineteenth century the Modocs developed a reputation as fierce raiders who would steal slave girls from the Shasta and Paiute tribes and sell them north, often using the Klamaths as middlemen. By 1864, they had been induced into a treaty to go to the Klamath Reservation in southern Oregon. Starved, oppressed by the more numerous Klamaths, and longing for their own territory, many Modocs by 1869 had returned to the area around the Lower Klamath, Tule, and Clear Lakes, where they requested their own reservation. As Schofield wrote, "they would die rather than go to live with the Klamaths again."[10]

The local whites, who feared the Modocs and coveted their lands, and the Bureau of Indian Affairs were united in their ambition to move the Modocs back to the Klamath Reservation. Canby, Schofield, Sherman, and the War Department had opposed such requests, but in November 1872 the local Indian agent, Thomas Odeneal, persuaded a local army officer, Major John Green, to take action against the Modocs under an old army regulation that mandated assistance to civilian authorities.[11] Canby, having received a request for reinforcements and mistakenly thinking the action had been approved by the War Department, then reinforced the local units, and the escalation of the hostilities began. The army assembled nearly 1,000 regular and volunteer troops to deal with the several hundred Modocs. The Modocs, under their leader Captain Jack, withdrew into the natural fortress of the Lava Beds and easily defeated the army's attempts to ferret them out. By March 1873, the secretary of the interior reluctantly ceded to General Canby the authority to negotiate with the Modocs.[12]

Meanwhile, the Modocs had their own factional conflicts. Another band under Hooker Jim had, before joining Captain Jack in the Lava Beds, repelled a posse of local civilians and retaliated by attacking local ranchers, killing perhaps fifteen. While Captain Jack advocated peace, Hooker Jim and other militants urged continued resistance. With Canby's refusal to make the Lava Beds the Modocs' reservation and Captain Jack's refusal to turn Hooker Joe over to the whites, the militants gained the upper hand. They shamed Captain Jack into a desperate attempt to destroy the whites' morale by killing their leaders. At the peace negotiations on April 11, Captain Jack pulled a pistol and killed General Canby, while another Modoc killed commissioner Reverend Eleazar Thomas. This treacherous act destroyed any hope of public sympathy and doomed the Modocs. Yet years later, Schofield would write with compassion, "The brave and noble-hearted Canby strove in every possible way to make peace with the Modocs without further shedding of innocent blood. But the savage red man, who had never been guilty of breaking faith with a civilized white man, would no longer trust any one of the 'treacherous race.'"[13]

The army renewed its efforts but continued to stumble into deadly ambushes by the hard-pressed Modocs. An obviously exasperated Schofield told the new commander, Jefferson C. Davis, "Let there be no more fruitless sacrifices of our troops. . . . We seem to be acting somewhat in the dark." Colonel Davis finally turned to faithless Modocs, among them the perfidious Hooker Jim, who offered to hunt down Captain Jack in return for amnesty. On June 1 troops cornered a starving and despondent Captain Jack with his family and a few remaining followers. Before Davis could summarily hang nearly all of the Modocs, Schofield and Sherman intervened and ordered trials of those responsible for the murder of General Canby and Reverend Thomas. In a trial that was a foregone conclusion, the military court convicted Captain Jack and five others. President Grant pardoned two, and the rest were hanged in October 1873. To the fury of the local whites, who sought to try and then hang the remaining Modocs, Grant also ordered the 153 Modocs transported to other reservations in the East. In 1909 the government permitted the 51 surviving Modocs to return to the Klamath Reservation.[14]

In his memoirs Schofield wrote that, while the Indians who had killed Canby had been tried and justly executed, "those white men who, in no less flagrant disregard of the laws of civilization, brought on the war were not called to any account for their crime." Just as Schofield defended the role of military government during Reconstruction, he forthrightly advocated military government on the frontier. "A little military justice," he wrote, "in the absence of any possible civil government, in what was so long called the Indian country would have saved many hundreds of millions of dollars and many thousands of lives."[15]

Nor was this an after-the-fact opinion. In his 1869 testimony before Congress, Secretary of War Schofield outlined his Indian policy. In urging the transfer of the Indian Bureau from the Interior Department to the War Department, he embraced the old adage that it was cheaper to feed the Indians than to fight them. In the preceding year, he told the House committee, the army had spent more than the bureau to feed them and more to fight them than it would cost to feed them for five years. Schofield believed that Canada had fewer Indian wars because the rights of Indians were given greater respect. He told the committee: "The great evil on the frontier is that there is existing no administration of civil law. If a man commits an outrage on an Indian he is entitled to a jury and you might ransack the whole district around him to find twelve men to sit upon a jury and they would be his confederates in the same business. It is an attempt to carry out the principles of a republican government in a condition of society where it is simply impossible."[16]

Again, Schofield confronted the question of how to protect the rights of a despised minority. Given his experience with Reconstruction, he might have been less sanguine. It is doubtful that the army would have been much more successful in protecting the rights of the Indians than the Indian Bureau. While most westerners wanted the Indians eliminated or moved, easterners had more mixed reactions. The pre–Civil War concept of the Indian tribes as separate nations was waning. Many Americans sympathized with the plight of the Indians, but not at the expense of national development. They hoped to assimilate the Indians but differed in their approaches. Some believed the tribal system should be abolished and the Indians integrated into American population, while others believed that the reservation system was necessary in order to educate and train them as ranchers and farmers. To have provided genuine protection for the rights of Indians, the army would have needed strong backing from the national government in order to overcome the militancy of western voters. Again, not enough eastern voters would have cared. The army could not have sustained Indian rights in the face of southern and western congressional hostility.[17]

Aside from the frustrations of Indian policy, Schofield's tenure in California was relatively peaceful. Schofield participated in the first U.S. military survey of the Hawaiian Islands and the Pearl River in 1872–73 and even found time to apply for a patent for a new method of cooling and ventilating mines. During this time, he kept up a busy correspondence with Sherman on various military topics, especially army reform. In the spring of 1876, Sherman finally persuaded Schofield, against his better judgment, to give up his comfortable position in San Francisco and take on the task of reform from the position of a proposed Department of West Point. As Schofield later characterized it, "I committed the mistake of my life."[18]

In the spring of 1876, Sherman's prospects to command the army and institute major reforms had rebounded. Secretary of War William Belknap had politically overwhelmed the commanding general, and Sherman had even let himself be driven out of town, first on a European tour in 1872 and then to establish the army headquarters in St. Louis in 1874. In Sherman's absence, Belknap ran the War Department unmolested, until his impeachment for corruption in the spring of 1876. Sherman returned to the capital in March 1876, and in April, Grant agreed to issue an order placing the adjutant general and inspector general under Sherman's command. With these renewed hopes for reform, Sherman wrote to Schofield of his plan to enhance the status of the military academy by appointing Schofield as superintendent.[19]

The U.S. Military Academy had been under the supervision of the chief of engineers until 1866, when control passed to the War Department, and the position of superintendent opened to officers of the line. In 1876 infantry colonel Thomas Ruger, Schofield's old comrade, commanded the academy. Citing Admiral David Dixon Porter's revitalization of the U.S. Naval Academy, Sherman sought to enhance the stature of the military academy and place it under his authority. Schofield was very reluctant to give up his division command for a colonel's command. Though Sherman claimed that Schofield would elevate the status of West Point, Schofield feared the new command would degrade the officer assigned. He suggested that the position of superintendent be added to the duties of the commander of the Atlantic Division. Both Sherman and Grant rejected this suggestion, but Sherman promised a position worthy of Schofield's rank.[20]

Schofield assumed command at West Point in September 1876 and immediately began his efforts to reform the institution. Unlike the peerless Robert E. Lee, who had passed through the academy without a single demerit, the young Schofield had squeaked through with 196 demerits. Four more and he could have been dismissed. He had piled up this dangerous number of demerits because of his court-martial and reduction to cadet private in his senior year. Hence, within weeks of becoming superintendent, Schofield secured Grant's approval to revise the demerit system, providing for a reduction of previous demerits based on subsequent good conduct.[21]

For a soldier, even an astute political soldier like Schofield, the governance of the military academy was a nightmare. Although the academy was nominally under the secretary of war, the adjutant general often administered routine matters. Additionally, Congress supervised the academy through the Board of Visitors, made up of prominent politicians and educators who annually visited the academy and made an official report. Finally, there was the Academic Board, composed of the senior faculty, who controlled academic policy and decisions on dismissing cadets for academic failure. Schofield's first task was to assert his command prerogatives; he quickly complained to the secretary about War Department attempts to interfere with his authority as a general officer to grant leaves of absence. The secretary quickly backed off, and Schofield took the opportunity to propose the creation of a Department of West Point.[22]

Schofield's proposal to make West Point a military department was vital to his overall agenda. It would give Schofield the status of other major generals and place the Department of West Point under the direct supervision of the commanding general. The impending end of the Grant administration troubled both Sherman and Schofield. The disputed election of 1876 placed a further pall over their plans, as the capital and the nation were absorbed by the extraordinary political drama. Schofield feared that Grant's promise to create the Department of West Point would be sidetracked or deferred until the new administration took over, and he even considered resigning as superintendent. His perseverance won out, and on March 2, 1877, Secretary of War James D. Cameron, one day before he left office, issued the orders creating the Department of West Point.[23]

The electoral crisis of 1876 also prompted an exchange of interesting and characteristically revealing letters among Sherman, Schofield, and Winfield Scott Hancock. Having seen an election plunge the nation into civil war, Sherman did not have a high regard for politicians. While Sherman believed that Samuel Tilden should have been declared the victor based on the popular vote, his chief concern was about what would happen if no decision were made before President Grant was forced to relinquish office in March. Could the cabinet members stay on? Who could lawfully give Sherman orders to employ military force?[24]

General Hancock believed that if no president were selected by March 5, the secretary of war might continue in office. But, he added, since "the Secretary of War is only the mouthpiece of a President," Sherman was not bound by his authority and would have to act on his own responsibility. Hancock thought the matter would be readily settled in Tilden's favor; but even a staunch Democrat like Hancock thought that if the decision went the other way, he had "no doubt Governor [Rutherford B.] Hayes would make an excellent President." Hancock viewed the rumors of armed uprisings rather skeptically, and, consistent with his views on Reconstruction, he advised that the army should stand clear of any involvement. Hancock had not favored the army's role in protecting the polls and Republican governments in the South. He believed the army would be punished for it, and he was soon proved correct, as the Democrats in Congress held up the Army Appropriation Bill and army pay for more than six months in 1877.[25]

Schofield, characteristically, chose to analyze the abstract legal and constitutional issues and then outlined to Sherman some rules for counting the votes. At first, Schofield rather naively suggested that since neither party wanted a tainted victor, a new election might be held. Like Sherman, he worried that an "unfair" process might lead to conflict. In subsequent letters he suggested to Sherman a complicated process for counting the disputed ballots that might give the appearance of fairness and legality. Schofield contended that as long as the people believed constitutional principles were being adhered to, they would accept any decision. Though Schofield also leaned toward Tilden, his suggestions were made more as a fascinated kibitzer than a partisan.[26]

Notwithstanding their political preferences, these officers were more concerned about institutional integrity than who won the election, though the electoral outcome could certainly influence their military careers. In the end, Sherman's fears of governmental paralysis proved unfounded. The politicians acted like politicians and made a political deal, devising a system wholly different from Schofield's. Hancock, the most politically engaged, most correctly judged the situation, though he got the ultimate winner wrong.[27]

While the electoral crisis was high political drama, Superintendent Schofield had to contend with a more mundane brand of politics. Despite his new status as a department commander and his generally good relations with President Hayes and Secretary of War George McCrary, Schofield still had to grapple with numerous political interventions. The most common were the appeals from prominent citizens or their congressmen when their sons or constituents either failed to pass the entrance exams or were about to be dismissed for academic or disciplinary failure. Sometimes these appeals came directly from the secretary or the president. Schofield was relatively softhearted and often sympathetic to such appeals. At other times, he acceded to the appeals in order to spare the president the problem. However, there were limits to the superintendent's authority. The Academic Board, of which he was a member, was the statutory authority for academic qualifications. The board, which was dominated by senior professors who were relatively invulnerable to outside pressure, was the chief bulwark against reducing academic standards.[28]

However, the Academic Board's power to resist political influence also enabled it to frustrate academic reform measures. The military academy was no longer the premier engineering school of the nation, but the senior faculty in the mathematics, engineering, and natural sciences departments were loath to change the orientation of the institution. One of Schofield's earliest academic goals was to improve the English composition skills of the cadets. This weakness had long been a source of criticism by the Board of Visitors as well. It took Schofield most of his first year as superintendent to persuade the Academic Board to enhance the English instruction for first-year cadets at the expense of Spanish instruction, which had been placed in the curriculum as a result of the Mexican War and the expanded five-year curriculum instituted in 1854.[29]

The Academic Board also attempted to extend its authority to the military side of the curriculum. Schofield fought a continuing battle with the board members over their assertion of the power to dismiss cadets who were "deficient in discipline." Schofield appealed to Sherman and the secretary of war that the superintendent and his commandant of cadets should have primary authority in this arena. Writing the secretary in 1880, Sherman empathically supported his superintendent, insisting that "the prescribed academic course was not meant to embrace 'Discipline,' which is the province of the Superintendent, who has the power at all times to remit or pardon the breaches of discipline which go to make up the Conduct Roll." The secretary agreed, but the board continued its protracted struggle for power with Schofield's successors.[30]

On the military side of training, Schofield attempted to update the practical aspects of the instruction. He brought in several experienced frontier cavalry instructors to improve cavalry training. He stressed marksmanship. He combined the first- and second-year classes in order to permit battalion-level drill. Perhaps remembering his embarrassing reduction from a cadet lieutenant to a cadet private after his court-martial, Schofield instituted a system by which all the third- and fourth-year cadets would assume the duties of noncommissioned officers and officers, instead of continuing as privates. At the expense of close-order drill, he introduced swimming instruction and boat handling. These were not racing boats, which were the new craze in the elite colleges, but the barges and transports that an officer would need to transport supplies and equipment. For the young military faculty, Schofield created a "postgraduate course" to keep them abreast of professional developments, and he encouraged their participation in the newly formed United Services Institution of the United States, which was based in New York City.[31]

Schofield frequently challenged the Academic Board and sought to reduce its power and independence. Working with Sherman, Schofield attempted to gain greater control over the military officers assigned as assistant instructors by limiting their tenure. As Schofield knew from personal experience, these positions in a peacetime army were highly coveted and served as stepping-stones for promotion to permanent professor. By establishing a four- to five-year tour of duty, the superintendent could have more influence in their selection. This also facilitated a greater rotation of officers to these plum jobs. The institutionalization of assignment rotation and selection became one of the major impulses of military reform. Even reformers did not want to totally dispense with the old system of personal patronage; however, most officers endeavored to imbue the system with greater "fairness," which was variously defined by the setting of relatively impersonal and objective selection standards and procedures for assignment.[32]

Perhaps going too far, Schofield also took a swipe at the permanent professors themselves by suggesting that they, too, have their tenure limited and that they also periodically return to regular army duty.[33] Doubtlessly Schofield's father-in-law, Professor William H. C. Bartlett, was not pleased with this impertinent idea. Despite Schofield's admiration and affection for him, Professor Bartlett in some ways typified the difficulty of reforming West Point. Bartlett had served as professor of natural and experimental philosophy for thirty-seven years (1834–71). Along with his colleagues Dennis Hart Mahan (professor of military and civil engineering, 1830–71) and Albert E. Church (professor of mathematics, 1837–78), Bartlett dominated the curriculum and kept its heavy orientation on mathematics and science. Bartlett's successor, Peter S. Michie (1871–1901), would become the next champion of West Point traditions.[34] Congress added to Schofield's problems by attempting to add a permanent professor of law. Fearing he would be saddled with "a political theorist" rather than "a sound constitutional and military lawyer," Schofield urged Sherman to use his influence to defeat all such "special legislation."[35]

The longevity of the senior professors meant they could wear down and outwait the superintendent. However, the superintendent and the Academic Board were not always at odds. Both shared the desire to improve the educational standards for admission to the academy. Just as the intervening decades had seen universities surpass the academy as the premier engineering school of the nation, dramatic changes had also taken place in secondary education. The Board of Visitors routinely commented on the academy's relatively low admission standards when compared to major universities. Unfortunately, these new standards of academic preparation were available to only a very small portion of the population. Efforts to raise admission standards were met with howls of elitism and charges of "military aristocracy" by some members of Congress. Politicians did not relish answering the complaints of constituents whose sons were rejected. No amount of explanation that poorly prepared cadets would merely flunk out later helped; indeed, the pressure increased on both Schofield and the Academic Board to recycle those dismissed for academic failure.[36]

Schofield's even more radical proposal that the academy create a two- to three-year program for the training of officers for state militias affords a glimpse into Schofield's view of the importance of West Point and the army for the nation.[37] "The Military Academy at West Point," he wrote to Representative James Garfield, "is the one institution of the country which is, above all others, eminently national in its character and influence." He explained that the population, except in times of war, is generally preoccupied by their local, sectional, and party interests, but "a nation, however free, requires the services of a certain number of men whose ambition is different from, if not higher than, that for personal wealth or station." To educate such a body of young men was "the primary object of the national school." The military training was merely incidental to this national education, where states and sections are "almost forgotten" and party strife "scarcely heard." Noting the failure of many militia organizations during the recent Great Strike of 1877, Schofield proposed that militia officers also be trained at the national institution. Thus, "the true mission of the Military Academy" was not only to provide officers for the national army but to furnish states with a body of scientifically trained young men—young men inculcated with the principles of public service and "a high sense of duty to the state and the nation."[38]

While the Gilded Age would create the basis for a genuinely national economy, it was not until the Progressive Era that many national institutions were formed or transformed. The United States Army was one of the very few truly national institutions of the nineteenth century. And though Schofield's argument for the expansion of West Point was perhaps a bit self-serving, it captured some of the thoughts and concerns of the larger society as well. Even in the greatest of commercial republics, it is not surprising that many longed for ideals and aspirations beyond those of the marketplace. Many veterans and non-veterans yearned for the sense of great national purpose embodied in the Civil War. The mugwumps were one manifestation of this desire and the Social Darwinists another. Schofield, who shared some of the tendencies of the mugwumps, rejected "survival of the fittest" as unchristian and uncivilized. However, not everyone agreed with Schofield's benign view of a West Point education as a way to reduce party or sectional friction. For those who saw the world in terms of class conflict, the "nationalization" of the militia was simply another ploy of the vested interests. Schofield's legislative recommendations received little interest or support in Congress.[39]

As if wrestling with Congress, the War Department, and the Academic Board were not enough, Schofield even had to battle the cadets. Hazing had always been a part of the West Point experience, but by the 1870s it far exceeded the kind of hazing engaged in by Schofield and his classmates. The senior cadets, primarily of the Third Class, or sophomores, had become more abusive, and the period of abuse extended into the academic year. Each new class seemed resolved to impose on the new cadets all that they had endured and more. While a certain amount of hazing had become traditional in private universities, it was especially problematic at an institution like the academy. Many parents and politicians complained loudly about abuses; yet others protested punishments for the abusers. Hazing was also the dark side of the inculcation of military discipline and authority. To learn the art of military command, the academy gave cadets a certain amount of authority over their juniors to teach them the rules and regulations of the institution and the military service. Too often, the young men abused their authority, and often in embarrassingly juvenile ways.[40]

After taking command, Schofield issued an order against hazing and made his position crystal clear; the repudiation of such behavior was a matter of honor: "For the comparatively intelligent and strong to take unfair advantage of the inexperienced to harass and annoy them is an act unworthy of a civilized man, and much more unbecoming an officer and gentleman. On the other hand, to secure justice and protection to the defenseless is the office of the gentle and brave. The honor of the Corps of Cadets, as well as that of the officers of the Academy, requires that the unkind treatment of new cadets shall be wholly eradicated." There had always been a certain code of silence about the hazing among the cadets, but Schofield's order rejected that tradition and made the reporting of such incidents obligatory.[41]

Over the first few years, Schofield attempted to balance punishment with mercy in controlling the problem, but by the summer of 1879, he faced open rebellion. In July 1879 the Third Class cadets descended on the new cadets with curses, demands for physical stunts, and even physical violence. The superintendent asked the War Department for authority to dismiss the culprits summarily. While the War Department pondered the matter, Schofield, mistakenly thinking the problem solved, went on vacation to New London, Connecticut. Within days, his trusted assistant William Wherry hastily telegraphed him that the academy was in a state of near mutiny. The Third Class cadets were attempting to impose the code of silence about the hazing and had retaliated against two of their classmates who had testified about earlier episodes. The problem had gone beyond youthful horseplay; as Schofield wrote the secretary, "the main difficulty results from a combination of the members of the Third Class to screen their comrades from punishment by refusing to testify against them."[42]

This time Schofield insisted on severe action: "The discipline of the Academy requires prompt dismissal of every cadet who has been guilty of hazing or of shielding the principals." He wrote Sherman that he hoped the president would sustain his efforts to enforce obedience, but that "unfortunately the cadets rely upon the President's well-known kindness to save them from extreme penalties." Of course, Schofield was often just as kindhearted, though in some instances he may have reduced punishments to spare the president the political repercussions. In this case, however, the secretary authorized the dismissal of six cadets. This course of action had the desired effect, and recalcitrant cadets began cooperating. To ensure that cadets did not get the wrong message from the episode, Schofield resisted all efforts to reconsider the cases of the dismissed cadets for the next year. Schofield believed that by holding the fate of these former cadets hostage to the good behavior of their fellows, he could break the hazing cycle.[43]

Schofield also took other actions. He strengthened rules that required regular officers to supervise the training activities of the cadets and at least one to sleep in the cadet bivouac. He strengthened the authority of the commandant of cadets and made it clear that refusal to answer the commandant's questions constituted "disobedience of orders" and was thus punishable by dismissal. Schofield also gave on August 11, 1879, a formal address to the Corps of Cadets on hazing and military discipline. Schofield characterized hazing as a "venerable vice," one like slavery that was now condemned throughout the civilized world. "The practice of hazing," the superintendent declared, "is both injurious and humiliating to its victims and degrading to those who engage in it. . . . You can never be a 'brother officer' to him whom you once degraded."[44]

Schofield also linked the poisonous behavior to military discipline in a democratic republic. "The very foundation of civil society is mutual respect for individual rights," and military honor demanded not only obedience to orders but also detection and punishment of those who abuse their authority. He went on to advise the cadets:

The discipline which makes the soldiers of a free country reliable in battle is not to be gained by harsh or tyrannical treatment. On the contrary, such treatment is far more likely to destroy than to make an army. It is possible to impart instruction and to give commands in such manner and in such tone of voice as to inspire in the soldier no feeling but an intense desire to obey, while the opposite manner and tone of voice cannot fail to excite strong resentment and a desire to disobey. The one mode or the other of dealing with subordinates springs from a corresponding spirit in the breast of the commander. He who feels the respect which is due to others cannot fail to inspire in them regard for himself, while he who feels, and hence manifests, disrespect toward others, especially his inferiors, cannot fail to inspire hatred against himself.[45]

This last section became known as Schofield's "Definition of Discipline." After Schofield's death, a superintendent directed that it be inscribed on a bronze tablet and placed at a barracks sally port for the edification of the cadets. Eventually, the upperclassmen required the new "plebes" to memorize Schofield's words as part of their initiation ritual. That his speech on hazing would become a device for a more civilized form of hazing is an irony that would have prompted even Schofield to laugh. He probably would have observed that this was superior to vulgar insults and physical assaults or the memorization of nonsensical ditties like "How's the Cow." As a final irony, most modern West Point graduates know little about Schofield, the Civil War general and army general in chief, but they can still recite his "Definition of Discipline."[46]

Schofield succeeded in diminishing but not eradicating hazing from the academy. Perhaps part of his difficulty was the distorted reputation that his cadet court-martial had earned him. As one cadet later wrote, "We used to hear that John M. Schofield was turned back a class for deviling plebes." Schofield also had to contend with other forms of youthful rebellion and high spirits. On New Year's Eve of 1879–80, cadets set off illegal fireworks and blew horns to ring in the new year. The cadets fondly remembered "Old Scofe" storming into the barracks square and calling the corps to formation, then confining them to barracks the next day, which was a holiday.[47] While the cadets thought of the incident as an expression of high spirits, Schofield had a darker interpretation. He believed that the recent announcement of clemency for one of the July culprits had encouraged further "reckless deviltry and love of mischief." "Commandant of Cadets," he confided to Sherman, "is nearly broken down by the weight of responsibility to which he does not feel equal."[48] The strains on the academy leadership and a perceived lack of support by civilian authorities would have disastrous consequences a few months later, when the Whittaker case threatened to tear the institution apart.

Despite Schofield's emphasis on discipline and his somewhat reserved nature, most cadets seemed to feel a genuine affection for him. Looking back on their cadet days, they wrote:

> Schofield, a fine man, perfectly fair to the boys.
> Schofield was a gentleman.
> Schofield was a real man, with a fine sense of justice.

> As superintendent of West Point Schofield was captain of a great and noble ship. You can not think of one thing in which he could have been changed for the better. He had an understanding of cadets as if he were still in the Corps. He was calm in action. But I will not go on and try to recount his good qualities, for how do I know all the qualities that made him the best, ablest, strongest, wisest, sternest, truest, kindest of all possible superintendents?

> He was all discipline, all justice, all good will, all wisdom. And he had such a way with him that, for all his dignity and aloofness, it would not have been difficult to think that he would have been well content to leave the high place over at the Adjutant's Office and leave his noble quarters, and come running across the Plain to be a cadet again. When I come to think of it I am sorry that General Schofield left West Point without some worthy tribute to him.[49]

General Sherman had brought Schofield east in 1876 not simply to reform West Point, but to aid him in general army reform. Yet, as discouraging as Schofield's efforts to reform the academy were, he and Sherman faced even greater frustrations in their efforts to reform the army. In the summer before assuming command at West Point, Schofield worked on another effort to revise and consolidate the army regulations. Schofield went about the task with enthusiasm, hoping that the new regulations would define and unify army administration— to make the separate armies of the line, the staff, and the specialist corps into one army. His efforts quickly stepped on the toes of the entrenched bureaucrats, who went to their allies in Congress. Even as Schofield was writing his first draft, Congress passed a resolution that called for yet another commission to study army reorganization and that requested the matter of new regulations be deferred until the commission reported in December 1877.[50]

Schofield's proposals, nevertheless, marked a small milestone in the evolution of Sherman's thinking. Before assuming the task, Schofield made his thoughts on the matter clear to General Sherman. Schofield reiterated his view that the commander in chief's constitutional authority could not be restricted by "law, much less by regulations." Furthermore, the secretary of war, at the discretion of the president, "exercises 'supervision,' 'control' or 'direction' over *all branches of the military service*, while the General-in-Chief, subject to such supervision, control and direction, exercises command over all parts of the Army." Schofield admitted that achieving the ideal of unity in administration and command would require combining the position of secretary and commanding general. However, he rejected that solution as "politically impossible" and ultimately bad for the army because of "the lack of sympathetic connection with the party at any time in power."[51]

Though still troubled by the question of restrictive statutes, Schofield yielded to the Sherman position and six months later proposed an act to cover the legality of the proposed army regulations. Schofield's proposal began with an acknowledgment "that the Secretary of War, under the direction of the President, shall exercise supervision and control over all branches of the military service." But, it directed that the "the Chiefs of the several staff Corps, Departments and Bureaus of the Army are the Chiefs of Bureaus of the War Department and also Chiefs of Staff to the General Commanding-in-Chief." Thus, the proposal forthrightly recognized the secretary's control over the entire army, while it still contained the enduring problem of distinguishing between administration and command and having the staff serve two masters. This ambiguity did not assuage concerns. However, in appointing Schofield and endorsing his work, Sherman at least tacitly accepted the view that the commanding general's authority was not independent of the secretary of war.[52]

That fall the secretary of war, as part of the congressionally directed review, also requested Schofield's views on general army reorganization. Schofield's main theme was that "what the Army most needs is not 'reorganization,' but an adjustment of its administration and command," and he focused his paper on the relationship of the secretary, the commanding general, and the General Staff. Here, in his effort to stress the unity of command and to justify his proposed regulations, Schofield blurred issues that he declared so forthrightly in his correspondence with Sherman. Rather than clearly reiterating the secretary's supervision of the entire army, Schofield stressed the difference between the civilian secretary who administered the army and the general who commanded it. He did, however, raise the issue of a Chief of Staff, but in the context of the Civil War experience: "A perfect military system requires a 'chief of staff' of the army, and also of every large command." Nevertheless, he acknowledged that the position might be unnecessary in the small peacetime army, but that the general in chief should still exercise authority over the General Staff officers. Schofield also maintained his stress on the need for subordinate commanders to control the staff officers in their commands. Schofield, in fact, was always more concerned about the command prerogatives of field commanders than the relative powers of the secretary and commanding general, even when he was the commanding general.[53]

Schofield's efforts on the army regulations succeeded no better than Sherman's nine years earlier. Army regulations had become a political football between the executive and legislative branches. The Army Regulations of 1861, with a few additions in 1863, remained the governing instructions for the army. In 1866 Congress had redirected that the secretary of war report on necessary changes that resulted from the experiences of the war. Congress ignored the work of Sherman's board, yet in 1870 it required that Congress approve any revised army regulations. By 1875 Congress had revoked that requirement and authorized the president to publish new regulations—hence Schofield's project. However, since Schofield's regulations mandated that the General Staff serve both the secretary and the commanding general, the staff chiefs used their influence to once again thwart the promulgation of new regulations. They convinced Congress to direct yet another joint commission on army organization. The Cameron Commission, named for Secretary of War James D. Cameron, included representatives from the Senate, the House, the line army, and the staff.[54] However, this effort fared no better than other efforts and was soon overtaken by a more bitter partisan struggle over Reconstruction, the election of 1876, and the railroad strikes of 1877. These disputes placed the very existence of the army in jeopardy.[55]

As Democrat "redeemers" took over more southern states and northern voters recoiled from the turmoil in the South, the Democrats gained power in Congress. In the 1874 elections the Democrats gained control of the House of Representatives. The new chairman of the Military Affairs Committee, Henry B. Banning (D-Ohio), led the Democratic charge against the army. In Banning, the Democrats had the perfect leader for their agenda. Banning had enlisted in the Union army in April 1861 and was shortly commissioned as a captain. He rose to command an Ohio regiment in the Atlanta campaign and was breveted a major general of Volunteers in 1865. Elected to Congress in 1872 as a Liberal Republican, he joined the Democrats in 1874. As chairman, Banning advocated both military economy and reform, though he was most wedded to reductions in army size and pay.[56]

The electoral crisis of 1876 generated a new issue for the Democrats. The role of the army in protecting the Republican governments and guarding the polls in the South had united the Democratic Party in intense antipathy for the regular army.[57] The Democratic majority in the House attached to the Army Appropriation Bill restrictions on the role of the army in aiding civil authorities. The Republican-dominated Senate refused to accept the amendment. Neither house would capitulate on the issue, and Congress adjourned in March 1877 without passing an army appropriation bill. With Congress not scheduled to reconvene until the fall, the weakened president Hayes refused to call for an emergency session, which prompted some to question whether the army could continue to exist when the new fiscal year began on July 1, 1877.

While some claimed that the army must disband, Congress had, at least partially, anticipated such a circumstance. Section 3732 of the *Revised Statutes* provided that "no contract or purchase on behalf of the United States shall be made, unless the same is authorized by law or is under an appropriation adequate to its fulfillment, except in the War and Navy Departments, for clothing, subsistence, forage, fuel, quarters, or transportation, which, however, shall not exceed the necessities of the current year." Thus, the soldiers could still be fed and clothed by the government, but officers had to provide for themselves. Soldiers and officers housed on military posts, like Schofield, retained their quarters, but those on detached duty or assigned to major headquarters, who usually rented private accommodations, were unprotected. New York bankers Drexel, Morgan and Company offered to advance money to officers, but enlisted soldiers were excluded from this plan. Later that July, the government deployed its unpaid army against striking railroad workers who were protesting pay reductions. The forsaken soldiers responded as the professionals they were and kept order without excessive violence.[58]

That fall, when Congress reconvened, a simple appropriation bill passed both houses, but the partisan battle over the army was far from settled. Army supporters had anticipated that the Nez Perce War and the railroad strike would end the call for major reductions in the army.[59] Sherman boldly proposed to increase the army by fifty companies and more than one hundred field grade officers. Schofield agreed, writing Sherman, "what is needed is not new organization, but more men."[60]

Once again, the hopes of Sherman and his supporters were dashed. Despite the widespread support for the army's role in the Great Strike, the use of federal troops further galvanized some Democrats. They argued that "strike-breaking" was yet another federal military intervention in local civil affairs. The Democrat-controlled House Appropriations Committee, over the objections of its Texas delegation, again proposed to reduce the army to 20,000. The Senate, however, remained adamant about maintaining the army at 25,000, and this time the House blinked. The army was permitted to soldier on for another seven months.[61]

Yet, Henry Banning (D-Ohio) in the Military Affairs Committee had not relented and continued to propose major reductions in army strength and pay.[62] The committee bill included such reform ideas as lineal promotion, or promotion based on seniority in one's entire branch—infantry, cavalry, artillery—rather than seniority in one's regiment;[63] compulsory retirement at age sixty-two or after forty-five years of service, except for those who had received the thanks of Congress by name;[64] and the establishment of designated recruiting districts for each regiment, thus linking each regiment to a geographical region.

The bill also cunningly combined seemingly progressive reform with regressive qualifications. A three-battalion infantry regiment could have only two battalions on active service. The detail of officers to the staff was designed to actually reduce the number of field grade officers in the army. The consolidation of the Quartermaster and Subsistence Departments reduced the total number of officers. The bill crippled the ability of the army to convene military courts and commissions by abolishing the Department of Military Justice, but it retained one judge advocate general with the consent of the Senate. It reduced the number of generals in the army. It also eliminated the law that had created the black army regiments. While some interpreted this last change as a move to integrate the army, it was more probably intended to exclude African Americans from serving in the combat arms branches of the army.[65]

Another duplicitous measure to strike at the army was Section 41 of Banning's bill, which provided that if Congress failed to appropriate money for the army, it would be "deemed equivalent to an express act for the abolition of the military establishment, and the Army shall forthwith be abolished." Banning could simultaneously project historical images of brave parliamentarians opposing a tyrant and claim that such drastic consequences would negate the possibility of another failure to appropriate money for the army. Republicans and army officers saw it as a loaded pistol pointed at the heart of the army, with not a few Democrats perfectly willing to pull the trigger.[66]

When Schofield read the contents of the Banning Bill, he was appalled and told Sherman he was "inclined to wash my hands of the whole business." Schofield was particularly incensed that Banning had quoted him as supporting the bill; Schofield included for Sherman's review a letter of protest to the congressman. In this letter Schofield denounced Section 41, which "provides for the total extinction of the army upon the failure—however temporary, of the usual appropriations." He then criticized the reduction of the army's strength as risking "disaster on some portion of our extended frontier." Finally, he suggested that Congress appoint a board of officers who, with congressional guidance, could then work out the details for army reorganization.[67]

Banning's "anti-army" bill, like various "pro-army" bills before it, soon bogged down in partisan wrangling, personal assaults, regional conflicts, and niggling arguments over side issues. While some Democrats, such as Banning and Edward S. Bragg (D-Wisc.), had pinned their political prospects on substantial reductions in the army, the true goal of a vast majority of congressional Democrats soon became apparent—remove the army from law enforcement. Southern Democrats wanted the army out of protecting the polls, and many northern Democrats wanted the regular army out of labor disputes. The election and the two years of incessant attacks on the army had weakened the Republican resolve to keep the army as the "Bulwark of Law." In the joint committee on the Army Appropriations Bill, the House Democrats dropped the reductions in exchange for the *posse comitatus* provision.[68]

The southerners who had cheered the use of the army as a *posse comitatus* to enforce the fugitive slave laws now congratulated themselves for protecting the nation from military tyranny.[69] House Appropriations Committee chairman Abram S. Hewitt (D-N.Y.) exulted, "Thus have we this day secured to the people of this country the same great protection against a standing Army which cost a struggle of two hundred years for the Commons of England to secure for the British people." While the Republicans were unhappy, the act was in fact anticlimactic. President Hayes had already withdrawn federal troops from Louisiana and South Carolina, and the Supreme Court would overturn some of the rulings that had afforded such broad latitude for the use of federal troops. Schofield, Sherman, and most army officers were remarkably quiet about the act. The *Army and Navy Journal* announced the army should be "profoundly grateful." Weighing the possibility of new missions in quelling labor unrest against the unpopularity and retaliation that the missions might produce, most regulars thought they were better off without these highly unpleasant assignments.[70]

The Posse Comitatus Act of June 18, 1878, restricted the use of the army as a posse to enforce civil law. The army could still be employed in some domestic roles as "expressly authorized by the Constitution or by act of Congress." For example, the president could call on the army and the militia to suppress rebellion and protect federal property. However, this meant that the use of the army required presidential approval. No longer could U.S. marshals or local commanders use the army at their own discretion. While the law reduced the army's intervention in domestic disturbances, it did not eliminate all of them, as the army continued to become entangled in "peacekeeping" actions in the territories or protecting federal property during strikes in the East.[71]

Although it was not the Democrats' true intent, the Posse Comitatus Act was a symbolic turning point for the regular army. First, the act spurred the development of the National Guard. Unable to call out the regulars swiftly, local officials were forced to create another, more reliable force than the old and largely unorganized militia system. The National Guard not only displaced the army as the primary force to handle domestic unrest; it also embodied the ideal of the "volunteer soldier," who, in many American minds, constituted the real source of American military strength. The power of the National Guard would severely hamper the regular army's efforts to create an "expansible army" or an "army reserve." Moreover, by limiting the army's role in enforcing the power of the federal government, the law forced the federal government to develop its own civilian law enforcement agencies. This process was slow in the nineteenth century but accelerated during the twentieth century.[72] Finally, the Posse Comitatus Act declared that soldiers who pledged to "defend the Constitution against all enemies, foreign and domestic," should focus their attention on foreign enemies.

Meanwhile, on the issue of army reform, the Army Appropriation Bill also directed the creation of yet another special commission. Schofield's suggestion of a board consisting of serving general officers was given short shrift. Congress, with its throng of former generals, was not about to leave so important and sensitive a subject to the professionals. Reflecting their intensely political approach to the subject, the House Democrats opposed any military representation on the board and succeeded in restricting the commission entirely to members of Congress. The Burnside Commission, named for its chairman, Senator Ambrose E. Burnside (R-R.I.), consisted of three senators and five representatives, four Republicans and four Democrats.[73] The conscientious Burnside also requested input and testimony from most of the senior officers of the army, and his committee report incorporated much of the historical record on army organization.

Schofield's response to the committee was meticulous and lengthy, as it included his proposed changes in army regulations. He reiterated his view that army strength needed to be maintained at 25,000, as well as his long-standing support for lineal promotion, promotion exams, and limited staff consolidation without significant reductions. He proposed that the duties of the adjutant general and inspector general be combined into a new entity called the General Staff of the Army. Even more novel was his idea to create a standard promotion pattern for officers, in which, assuming successful completion of promotion exams, an officer should reach colonel in about thirty years.[74] Schofield's proposal for the U.S. Military Academy included his plan for making the members of the Board of Visitors permanent rather than annual appointments and his suggestion that future superintendents have the temporary rank of at least brigadier general.[75]

The joint committee's proposed bill, known as the Burnside Bill, was a true piece of committee sausage. It included many of the real—and mischievous— reforms originally proposed by Banning, without the draconian troop reductions. The authorized army enlisted strength would remain at 25,000. However, the bill also called for significant officer reductions. Specifically, the army was to have the same number of soldiers, but significantly fewer officers. It was to have stronger, but fewer, regiments. The bill also included consolidations and major reductions in the staff corps and required the rotation of line officers to staff positions. It reduced the number of regiments: infantry to eighteen from twenty-five, cavalry to eight from ten, and artillery to remain at five with officer reductions. It authorized the four-battalion infantry regiment with two battalions remaining unmanned. It provided for mandatory retirement at age sixty-two, sixty-five for general officers. It also reduced the number of general officers from eleven to six (two major generals and four brigadier generals), through attrition. Finally, while it authorized communication between staff chiefs and staff officers in departmental commands, it required that all orders be issued through the headquarters of the army, a considerable boost to the power of commanders over the staff.[76]

Schofield's response to the new plan was largely positive. The bill included many of his own suggestions and incorporated most of his revised regulations. Schofield had initially been reluctant to tell Sherman of his true feelings about the bill because "this plan appears to be closer to mine than yours."[77] Though troubled by the officer cuts and some of the details, he concluded that the bill "merits the cordial support of the Army." Schofield was especially heartened by the provision that strengthened the commanding general's control over the staff. To Schofield, the requirement that orders to subordinate commanders and even staff officers in subordinate commands go through the commanding general was such an important step forward in creating a true "military system" that he was willing to overlook the flaws. While he assumed the staff departments would not support the measure, he predicted that the rest of the army would support the bill. Other reform-minded officers, such as Emory Upton and William Hazen, agreed with this assessment.[78]

Since the bill weakened the staff by simultaneously reducing its numbers and restricting its autonomy, Sherman and Schofield took for granted that the greatest opposition would come from the staff. The sections on the War Department and the headquarters of the army closely followed the language of Schofield's proposed regulations. Section 76 of the Burnside Bill established that the commanding general "shall, under the direction and during the pleasure of the President, have command of the entire army, command and staff." Section 79 prescribed that the chiefs of the bureaus shall act under the immediate supervision of the secretary of war in "all matters of accountability and administration not connected with military operations," while they would also act as "Chiefs of Staff to the Commanding General," reporting directly to him on matters "appertaining to the command of the Army."[79]

Anticipating that the staff would again raise the specter of the commanding general's encroaching on the authority of the secretary of war, Schofield, in a subsequent letter to Sherman, stressed the importance of Section 75 of the proposed bill, which also closely followed Schofield's proposed regulations:

> Section 75. That the Secretary of War, under the direction of the President, shall exercise supervision and control over all branches of the military service, not only in these cases where his supervision and control are specially required by law, but in all cases embraced within the functions of the President as Commander-in-Chief of the land forces; and such supervision and control may be exercised by the Secretary of War as circumstances may require, either directly or through the Commanding General of the Army, or through such agents as the Secretary may appoint in accordance with law.

Schofield argued that this section, in establishing the secretary's authority over all of the army, ended the controversy between the secretary of war and the commanding general. "Under that section the Secretary is the President's representative in every military matter. The Commanding General of the Army is his subordinate in all things. Just as much as is any staff officer."[80]

In one of his most eloquent letters on the subject of command of the army and the relationship between commanders and staff, Schofield contended that the perennial problems had been based on the "old fallacy" that the military functions of the president are divided between the secretary of war and the general in chief. This resulted in endless controversy and repeated attempts to draft special legislation designed to fortify the secretary or, more accurately, his administration subordinates against the supposed encroachment of the general in chief and his subordinates. With Section 75 the principle was fully established that the secretary of war, under the president, was "supreme over all in the Army." The other sections of the bill relating to the commanding general and other officers merely specified the cases in which the secretary should exercise his authority through one officer or another: "The naming of such subordinate agents does not take one jot nor tittle from the Secretary's authority."[81]

Warming to his subject, Schofield then argued that just as the commander in chief's twofold military authority—administration and command—was impossible to divide, so too was the authority of subordinate commanders. "No officer can command an Army nor any separate portion of an Army unless he has some administrative authority," he wrote. But in asserting that a certain amount of administrative authority was necessary, a commander need not, and should not, have total administrative authority. Hence, the necessity that staff officers also have a dual responsibility, one to their commanding officer and the other to their staff superiors. "This dual responsibility must exist through all grades of the staff, as well as through all grades of command," Schofield concluded.[82]

Moreover, the existing system created the absurd situation where all subordinate commanders had a staff except the general in chief. To those who claimed that the General Staff was really the president's staff, Schofield reminded them that the "President *does not command in person*, that he *delegates* his military command to a general officer who has been educated, appointed, commissioned and assigned by him for that purpose." While the solution to this state of affairs could have been to create a separate staff for the general in chief, Schofield thought that prospect extremely remote. Therefore, the dual role of the staff as prescribed in Section 79 was logical.[83]

Schofield accurately observed that in peacetime the president rarely communicated with the military, except through the secretary, and that the secretary was the personification of the authority of the constitutional commander in chief. But Schofield went a bit too far in arguing that no commanding general had ever questioned the authority of the secretary of war. He also exaggerated the secretary's ability to "decapitate" a commanding general who presumed to disregard his instructions, since it was very difficult to sack commanding generals. One might argue, however, that Belknap effectively "incapacitated" Sherman until he himself was impeached. Schofield more shrewdly noted that the secretary's power and authority derived from the confidence the president placed in him as his personal representative—power that an inherited commander in chief usually lacked. The recognition that the secretary was the president's man at the War Department was a central element of Schofield's view of civil-military relations. While generals should not be seen as the proponents of any given administration, the secretary was an overtly political figure, whose power derived from his political status. Finally, Schofield noted that the true source of opposition to these measures came from those in the staff departments who only sought to advance their own power, by maintaining their autonomy and unfettered access to the secretary.[84]

As Schofield expected, the staff departments were the leading military opponents to the Burnside Bill, and their supporters in Congress continued to frame the issue in terms of the commanding general's encroaching on civilian authority. However, the staff officers were not the only critics within the army. In addition to Schofield's letter of support for the bill, Sherman also passed on Philip Sheridan's and John Pope's letters about the bill to the *Army and Navy Journal*. Sheridan heartily agreed with the sections that described the authority of the secretary of war and the commanding general, but he was less supportive of the reorganization, especially the reduction in cavalry regiments. He also expressed concerns about the staff and general officer cuts. Pope was even more critical. He opposed most of the changes to the staff, including the rotation between line and staff. Pope worried that the measure would reduce the expertise necessary for effective staff departments.[85] The Washington correspondent of the *Army and Navy Journal* noted that while the staff department opposition was organized and vocal, there were many line officers who privately considered the bill too radical. Most officers decried the bill for its requirement to reduce the army by more than three hundred officers.[86]

Amid the criticism, Sherman, again through the *Army and Navy Journal*, let it be known that he would take no active measures to support or defeat the Burnside Bill. However, he also declared that the bill, overall, was the best the army could expect, and if it were defeated, the next bill would be even worse for the army.[87] The three years of legislative battles over the army had deepened Sherman's natural pessimism. Both Sherman and Schofield saw the Burnside Bill as an opportunity to advance their case on the control of the staff departments and worth the price of the other more disagreeable provisions. Yet, even Schofield acknowledged that the suffering the bill's provisions would impose on officers forced out or denied promotion gave its staff opponents an important advantage in defeating the overall bill.[88]

Schofield also admitted that the matter was beyond him, and anyone in the army, and was in the hands of Congress. In marked contrast to the intense interest and energetic public debate the Burnside Bill received in the army and the military press, it was greeted with much less fanfare and enthusiasm in Congress. The bill languished for weeks in the Senate; in the House, Representative Banning attempted to resurrect his old bill and attach to the Army Appropriations Bill only those portions of the Burnside Bill that reduced the army. Despite Senator Burnside's hard work and conscientious efforts to achieve compromise, it was business as usual in Congress.[89]

A "distinguished Senator, interested in the Army," told the *Army and Navy Journal* that the future of the bill depended entirely on its manager in the Senate. According to this old hand, it took a "very old stager" to know how to combat all of the opponents of a bill. He feared that Burnside, in a desire to accommodate, had too often given in to opponents of reform and that it was then too late in the session to recover the lost momentum. The anonymous senator marveled at the way the enemies of the bill had managed their fight. They were able to divert attention from their own self-interests by dwelling on the supposedly "unconstitutional" efforts to give power to General Sherman at the expense of the president and the secretary of war. Although he knew this was false, he also knew the charge resonated, especially with the southern members of Congress.[90]

Ultimately, the Burnside Bill died. Senator Burnside valiantly defended the bill, offered stripped-down versions of it, and even tried the tactic of placing portions in the appropriations acts. The most significant obstacle to the bill's passage was the commission's decision to propose a mammoth 724-section bill that combined both new and controversial ideas, making the legislation a fat target for numerous and diverse opponents. Its sheer comprehensiveness was a profound handicap. Everyone found something to dislike. Burnside strove gallantly, and almost alone, to defend the integrity of the joint committee's work. During the debates, one could sympathize with the old general as he endured personal attacks and tried to fend off the blizzard of amendments—amendments that Burnside may well have personally approved. In the end, Burnside had too many opponents and too few allies.[91]

The intense and skillful opposition of the staff departments to both severe cuts in their departments and restrictions on their autonomy was a major factor in sowing confusion and dissatisfaction with the bill. The staff chiefs had cunningly turned an effort to place greater restrictions on their independence into a conflict between the secretary and the commanding general. By portraying the issue as a question of civil-military relations, they diverted attention from their own agenda, which included fending off the staff department consolidations and reductions. Additionally, they fought to retain their power to issue orders to adjutants, quartermasters, commissaries, and judge advocates of the military divisions and departments, without regard to the desires of the commanding generals at any echelon.

The staff chiefs' relative autonomy to direct projects and contracts also gave them political influence in Congress. It was easier for congressmen to establish cozy relationships with the Washington military bureaucrats than with field commanders. Schofield's complaint that "this total separation of the Staff

Corps from the Army is the fundamental defect in our military administration" afforded opportunities to those devoted to economies in the army budget.[92] The ability of the chiefs of the staff departments to direct the activities of their staff officers in the military commands had a direct bearing on expenditures. If construction were required at a military post, it was easy for them to require the use of troop labor. If fresh vegetables were expensive, it was easy to direct that troops plant their own gardens. These staff officers had no need to worry about the other missions demanded of an already overextended and undermanned military force. They did not have to look the troops in the eye or listen to the complaints of their company and regimental commanders. For the staff corps, economies at the expense of the line army were much less painful.[93]

Internal opposition to reform measures came from diverse interests. Most reform measures created winners and losers: the staff opposed any reduction in their authority; the specialty corps, such as the engineers and ordnance, rebuffed intrusions into their autonomy; and officers in high turnover regiments opposed lineal promotion. The internal division was only part of the explanation for the failure of American army reform in the late nineteenth century. The less intense but more diffuse opposition of many line officers to various aspects of the bill further weakened its political support. Congressmen who lacked specific convictions about the reorganization plan could point to the lack of consensus as a reason for rejecting it. Further doubt about the bill arose as Sherman refused to lobby for the bill, even departing on an inspection tour of the western posts in the middle of the congressional debate. Schofield, too, seemed to lose his enthusiasm for the bill, and the general level of dissatisfaction increased. After January 1879, he wrote few letters about the bill and did not address it in his memoirs at all.

The most significant obstacle to reform was that there was simply no compelling need. Even with an internal consensus, the army would have only achieved substantial structural reform with the support and cooperation of its civilian masters. Yet, Congress was just as divided as the army. More important, the legislators were largely uninterested. Just as there was no external pressure on the army to reform, there were no external pressures on Congress to take up the complex and controversial issues of army reform. Civil service reform was a more salient issue than army reform. The tariff policy was more important than military policy. Most congressmen and most Americans had other, more important concerns, like tremendous geographic, demographic, economic, and technological expansion. Just as the nation enjoyed the strategic luxury of maintaining only a tiny army, it enjoyed the luxury of an antiquated army.

In retrospect, the failure of the Burnside Bill and the failure of army reform in the late 1870s was both a short- and long-term blessing to the future of the army. The proposed reductions of either the enlisted or officer strength of the army would have dispirited the army greatly. The demands of Indian warfare were diminishing but not extinguished. The battalion structure meant little to an army still scattered in numerous one- and two-company posts. Austerity programs increasingly required the diversion of the present-for-duty strength to troop gardens or post maintenance. The greater lethality of weapons made massed formations much too vulnerable, and the complexity of the new extended formation tactics demanded more, not less, training. Individual marksmanship training became more important in order to bring effective fire on these disbursed formations.

The severe reduction in the officer corps would also have had a devastating effect, especially on morale. Another decrease would have further reduced the dismal promotion prospects of many officers. The fact of fewer officers would have diminished the chances for officers to escape dreary little garrisons by reducing the numbers available for temporary assignments to staffs, as military instructors at universities, or for foreign travel. The reduction would have hindered the army's ongoing nation-building missions and would have made it more difficult to assume new ones. Army engineers dredged rivers, built dams and public buildings, and conducted geological surveys. In the absence of federal civilian agencies, the Army Signal Corps formed the nation's first weather service and, anticipating the future National Parks Service, took over the administration of Yellowstone.

A dramatic reduction in the officer corps would also have severely hampered the creation of army professional schools, for which Congress provided few additional resources.[94] It would have been far more difficult to form the new military professional organizations and journals.[95] These institutions were vital to the army during these years of uncertainty and rapid technological advances. The tiny army, with few resources with which to experiment, needed to think and argue about the future of war.

A longer-term impact of the failure of the Burnside Bill was the survival of the staff corps. The battles between the commanding general and the secretary and the staff and the line officers over the command of the army obscured other philosophical clashes between the line and staff officers. Staff consolidation and line officer rotation to the staff threatened to undermine the functional expertise that the staff corps provided. The staff officers emphasized their expertise, but over the decades, selection for staff assignments also became a way of rewarding aging, but still intellectually active, officers. The proposals for line officer rotation to staff jobs assumed that most line officers could acquire the requisite expertise relatively easily.

Finally, the death throes of Burnside's reorganization of the army produced a fitting anticlimax in the publication of two wildly divergent army views on "Command of the Army" in the military journal *Field Glass*. Writing for the staff, Colonel James B. Fry of the Adjutant General Department boldly asserted that the president's command of the army was a personal responsibility. It could only be delegated to the secretary of war as the single, constitutionally valid organ. Two persons could not command the same force at the same time, and therefore the general in chief could not possibly command it. William M. Wherry, Schofield's aide, defended the logical necessity of a military commander of the army and consigned the secretary of war to strictly administrative responsibilities. The articles attest to how polarized and unedifying the debate over the command of the army had become.[96]

While Fry's argument was absurd, Wherry's was equally troubling. Wherry's rehashing of the old debate cast doubts on Schofield's commitment to the secretary's authority to control the entire army. Instead of accepting the secretary as a "deputy" commander in chief and putting the commanding general between the secretary and the staff, this position enabled the General Staff to continue to position itself as the defender of civilian control of the military. It would be another decade before Schofield would have another opportunity to tackle the issue. As commanding general, he would forthrightly subordinate himself to the secretary of war and attempt to forge an alliance with the secretary in the quest for military reform.

As with general army reform, reform at West Point failed through lack of consensus and lack of interest. Most of the West Point reform proposals were either relatively minor or potentially harmful. The idea to create a Department of West Point in order to bring the academy under Sherman's control was somewhat shortsighted. The political dimension of West Point could not be ignored or evaded. Sherman had little inclination to replace the secretary of war as the buffer between the superintendent and the importuning of congressmen and their constituents. Since most of the governing rules of the academy were enshrined in statute, any reform needed to pass through Congress, where enemies of the academy would have had opportunities to attach damaging, faux reforms.

Even more shortsighted were Schofield's efforts to diminish the autonomy of the Academic Board. The board was a genuine obstacle to many academic reforms, and even minor changes prompted fierce bureaucratic fights. Yet, the board was also the bulwark that maintained academic standards. Its very auton-omy gave the superintendent, the secretary of war, and even the president cover against irate congressmen and their constituents. The engineering curriculum was becoming antiquated, but it was in many ways secondary to the real purpose of the school. West Point had always been more about building leaders than producing trained engineers. The curriculum and the West Point system continued to instill the need for intellectual application and responsibility for one's conduct.

At West Point in the 1870s, Sherman and Schofield attempted to wrest the army from their institutional adversaries. Twenty years later, Schofield used these same institutions to promote his reform views. This experience illustrates that the nature, speed, and direction of military reform and professionalization were dictated primarily by the need to conform to the nation's deliberately fragmented and contentious constitutional system—its intentional rocky road of reform.

(ELEVEN)

The Mistake of My Life

Schofield's tenure at West Point was notable for more than just assisting Sherman with academy and army reform. In addition to assigning him to serve as a presidential troubleshooter during the Great Railroad Strike of the summer of 1877, Sherman employed Schofield for other politically sensitive chores. Noteworthy among these was chairing a board to review the Civil War court-martial of Fitz John Porter. The Fitz John Porter case was a political minefield in which the partisan passions and personal rivalries of the war were carried well into the postbellum era, with sometimes surprising alliances. Sadly, Schofield's skill, fortitude, and diligent efforts to uncover the truth in this task stood in marked contrast to his later efforts in the notorious Johnson Whittaker case. In the Whittaker inquiry, Schofield, usually the sober and fair-minded judge, abandoned all appearance of fairness and joined the posse against the academy's only African American cadet. The fallout from his behavior would later cause him to lament, rather self-pityingly, that accepting the assignment at West Point was "the mistake of my life."[1]

On April 12, 1878, the War Department, at the direction of President Rutherford B. Hayes, appointed a board of officers to examine the 1862 court-martial of Major General Fitz John Porter and report its conclusions and recommendations to the president. The board consisted of Major General John M. Schofield, Brigadier General Alfred H. Terry, Colonel George W. Getty, and Major Asa B. Gardner as recorder/prosecutor.[2] This board was the result of a fifteen-year campaign by Porter to overturn his court-martial conviction and dismissal from the army. The Porter trial had been quite controversial in 1862, and Porter and his friends had sedulously kept the issue alive. President Hayes instituted this board despite the strong opposition of his Republican allies and friends in Ohio. Hayes was motivated in part by the continued appeals of Porter's friends, in part by his sense of fairness, and in part by a desire to accommodate the Democrats.[3]

Fitz John Porter's court-martial and disgrace came in the aftermath of the Union defeat at Second Bull Run.[4] In August 1862, after it became clear that General George B. McClellan was ending his peninsula campaign, General Robert E. Lee quickly turned his Confederate army north in the hopes of smashing Union general John Pope's Army of Virginia. In one of Lee's most daring campaigns, he sent half of his army under Stonewall Jackson to take Pope's supply depot at Manassas Junction. As the Union commander focused on Jackson, Lee brought up James Longstreet, who launched a crushing attack on the Union left flank on August 30. Pope's army was sent reeling back toward Washington, D.C.[5]

Pope was discredited, and McClellan was restored to command. Yet, McClellan's failure to follow up his nominal victory at Antietam prompted Lincoln to sack him. Pope took the opportunity to press his case that McClellan and his supporters, most notably Porter, had sabotaged the campaign at Bull Run. Pope's allegations were not simply a matter of personal clashes between Pope and McClellan; they reflected a bitter political debate over war strategy. Pope was a proponent of the "hard war" strategy, which would lead to the defeat of the South and the abolition of slavery favored by most radical Republicans; Democrat McClellan favored a "soft war" or "conciliatory" strategy, which would lead to a negotiated peace that maintained slavery.

After a preliminary investigation of Pope's allegations, Porter was charged under the Ninth Article of War for disobeying a lawful command of his superior officer and under the Fifty-second Article for misbehavior before the enemy.[6] The court-martial included many irregular elements. Based on supposed military necessity, the court consisted of nine, rather than the traditional thirteen, officers. The same officers who were appointed to the initial board of inquiry that recommended the charges were reappointed to the court-martial. Two of the officers, Rufus King and James Ricketts, had participated in the battle as division commanders of Irwin McDowell, whose conduct during the battle was also under investigation. Several of the judges had Republican political connections, and fierce Republican partisan James A. Garfield had an intense hatred for George McClellan, which carried over to McClellan's protégé Porter.[7] Though Porter did not challenge the judges, he observed to a friend, "I have too many personal enemies and enemies of Gen. McClellan on the court." Porter's supporters believed that Secretary Edwin Stanton had stacked the court against him; however, there is no credible evidence that Stanton did so, though his hatred for the McClellan claque was well known.[8]

The evidence presented about Porter's conduct during the battle was relatively weak.[9] Although Porter had hardly distinguished himself at Second Bull Run, Pope's orders to him were vague and often contradictory. Porter's failure to obey the letter of his orders, especially those concerning march times, was well within the discretion accorded to other commanders during the campaign. The general order to attack on August 29 was also vague, couched with qualifications and assumed cooperation between Porter and McDowell. Porter was certainly hesitant, even lethargic, in reconnoitering the forces confronting him, but in little else. Porter's defense, however, was hindered by the highly selective memory of Irwin McDowell, who met with Porter at crucial times during August 29 and through whom Porter sent many of his reports to Pope. Several of these reports were missing during the trial, only to reemerge years later. Under investigation himself, McDowell clearly sought to avoid any blame and shift responsibility.[10]

Moreover, the prosecution's theory of the case depended less on the exact orders and responses than on Porter's adherence to the spirit of his orders. The prosecution argued that Porter's animus toward his commander was such that he refused to energetically and faithfully execute his military responsibilities. To Pope and the Republicans, Porter had colluded with McClellan to sabotage Pope. Porter's attitude and motives—more than his specific actions—were on trial. Unfortunately, Porter had handed his opponents much ammunition to substantiate that position. In the days before the battle, Porter sent many of his reports through his old friend Ambrose Burnside at Fredericksburg, who maintained a telegraph to the rear. In between routine reports and requests for information, Porter made many disparaging remarks about Pope, which Burnside casually passed on to the War Department. Though some of these remarks were made before Porter officially came under Pope's command, he nevertheless displayed a mind-set of disdain and an expectation of Pope's ultimate failure.[11]

In the end, the court agreed with the prosecution's accusation of animus and chose to believe Pope and his witnesses rather than Porter and his witnesses. They found Porter guilty of three of the five specifications in the first charge and all three of the second set of charges, sentencing Porter "to be cashiered, and to be forever disqualified from holding any office of trust or profit under the Government of the United States."[12] The case was then submitted to President Lincoln for review. Judge Advocate Joseph Holt's summary of the case for the president was unsurprisingly very one-sided and began by emphasizing that Porter's alleged animus toward Pope "must largely affect the question of his criminality."[13]

By January 1863, the theory that Porter was motivated by personal, professional, and political animus to undermine his military superior resonated with the president. At the same time Lincoln was reviewing Porter's conviction, he was faced with yet another command crisis in the Army of the Potomac. In December 1862, McClellan's successor, Ambrose E. Burnside, had bungled an attack on Fredericksburg. Lincoln was again forced to appoint a new Army of the Potomac commander amid the finger-pointing, bickering, and politicking of the army's general officers. Though it is doubtful that Lincoln based his decision on political calculations, affirming Porter's conviction would nevertheless send a clear warning to his contentious generals.[14]

For the next fifteen years Porter attempted to overturn this conviction. Both Presidents Andrew Johnson and Ulysses S. Grant rebuffed his appeals. In 1868 Porter had approached Secretary of War Schofield for a rehearing. Schofield, who exhibited no knowledge of the merits of the case, rejected this appeal as premature. He concluded that the passions of the war were still too fresh for an impartial hearing, and that since Grant seemed to be against Porter, there was little to be gained. Schofield was probably also reluctant to stir up such a political hornet's nest that would cast doubt on a military court-martial, even as the army was under siege for its use of military commissions to implement Reconstruction. Ten years later Schofield could not evade the issue.[15]

When Porter saw the composition of his long-sought review board, his heart must have sunk a bit. All three officers were known as Grant men, and Grant had already expressed his opinion on Porter's guilt. Terry believed Porter was guilty and attempted to be relieved of the duty. Though George Getty had served under Porter in the peninsula, Getty had been a classmate of Sherman, and Porter knew Sherman opposed reopening the case. Finally, Porter would have recalled how he had been one of two officers at Schofield's 1852 court-martial to recommend that the cadet be dismissed from the academy, and by 1868, Schofield knew this as well.[16]

Whatever fears Porter had about the members of this board, they proved groundless, especially of Schofield. Although Schofield could hold a grudge, he was not a vindictive man. He most likely relished the idea of granting "clemency" to one who had denied it to him. Given Schofield's own troubles with radical Republicans in Congress, he was also somewhat sympathetic to Porter's plight. Even if he thought Porter had acted badly, Schofield recognized the punishment was too severe. As secretary of war, Schofield had supported Andrew Johnson's proclamation of general amnesty and even argued for the pardon of Jefferson Davis, which the rest of the cabinet thought politically inexpedient.

Almost from the opening of the board's work, Porter had reasons to be optimistic. Though the board indicated that the burden of proof rested on Porter, it would not limit the review to the testimony heard at the court-martial, and new evidence could be presented. Over the intense objections of recorder/prosecutor Asa Gardner, Schofield and his fellow board members insisted on recalling those who had testified at the original court-martial. Thus, in addition to new map surveys, Confederate documents, and witnesses, the board attempted to get additional testimony from Porter's leading accusers. Irwin McDowell was mercilessly cross-examined, especially over how messages that Porter had sent him during the battle had been discovered in his possession well after the original trial and over his subsequent distortions of the facts of the case. Pope's nephew Douglas Pope continued to insist that he had delivered the August 29 attack order before 5:30 P.M., but defense witnesses seriously undermined his credibility. John Pope refused to testify, and the War Department declined to compel his appearance. While it saved Pope an intense grilling by Porter's attorneys, it did not inspire confidence in his position among the board and the disinterested observers of the proceedings.[17]

The inquiry also produced many ironic twists. Veterans of the V Corps like Republican governor of Maine Joshua Lawrence Chamberlain and Gouverneur K. Warren rallied to Democrat Porter. Engineer Warren was the first witness and submitted a new survey of the battle site, which showed that Porter was miles from where Pope and the court-martial thought he had been—there was almost a two-mile gap between Porter and the main federal army. The board considered this new map vital in understanding what really happened during the battle. Warren had been the V Corps commander in the closing days of the war, when Philip Sheridan rather arbitrarily relieved him. The Schofield Board encouraged Warren's efforts to gain a review of his relief. In November 1882 a court of inquiry exonerated Warren, but a bitter Warren had died a few months earlier, having directed that he be buried in civilian clothes and without patriotic emblems.[18]

The next major witness was ex-Confederate turned Republican James Longstreet. Longstreet attested that his 25,000-strong command had been in position on Jackson's right before noon on August 29, well before the major attacks on Jackson by the Union right and hours before Pope's attack order to Porter. Longstreet also related that the presence of Porter's force along the Manassas-Gainesville road had prompted Lee to strengthen that flank and agree to a reconnaissance, which forestalled an immediate attack by Longstreet's corps. Finally, Longstreet testified that he had detected no retreat by Porter's troops before darkness that day. Despite Major Gardner's best efforts, he could not shake Longstreet's assessment that an attack by Porter's 9,000-man corps on his position would have been useless.[19]

The Schofield Board studied dozens of maps, listened to 142 witnesses, and read mounds of documents to recreate a detailed account of the battle.[20] On January 3, 1879, it concluded the hearing, and on March 19, 1879, the board submitted its report to the secretary of war. The conclusions were everything Fitz John Porter could have hoped for. While deploring Porter's "indiscreet and unkind" language toward his superior officer, the board concluded that "the evidence of bad animus in Porter's case ceases to be material in view of the evidence of his soldierly and faithful conduct." It unanimously recommended that the findings and sentence of the court-martial be set aside and Porter restored to the military service, effective his date of dismissal.[21]

As to the specific charges, the board concluded that Porter's decision to delay his march on the night of August 28 was prudent and well within the discretion of a corps commander. Regarding Porter's actions on August 29, the board chose to believe Porter and his staff officers rather than McDowell. It accepted that McDowell had indeed positioned Porter along the Manassas-Gainesville road; that Porter had reported enemy activity to his front to McDowell; that Porter made repeated efforts to link up with McDowell's troops, who he assumed were deployed to his right; and that Porter did not retreat until ordered to report to Pope's position. Moreover, the board agreed that Pope's attack order had arrived too late for execution and went on to offer the assessment that such an attack against the rebel right wing would have been "fruitless of any good result." Finally, the report hailed the vigorous defense conducted by Porter's troops during Longstreet's decisive attack of August 30.[22]

Although the board's report attempted to excuse the decision of the court-martial by stressing the inaccurate maps, incomplete documentary evidence, and contradictory testimony, its conclusions were a stinging rebuke of both Pope and McDowell. Pope was portrayed as largely clueless as to what was happening, especially in his complete ignorance of Longstreet's presence on the battlefield. Meanwhile, in choosing to believe Porter and his officers, the board cast doubt on the honesty and integrity of Irwin McDowell and Douglas Pope.[23]

Perhaps to compensate for the injustice done to Porter or to speed his complete exoneration, the board exaggerated Porter's contributions. They argued that "Porter's faithful, subordinate, and intelligent conduct that afternoon [August 29] saved the Union army from . . . defeat." To the board, Porter's presence on Longstreet's right flank had prompted Lee to hesitate that afternoon, and given the gap between Porter and the rest of the Union army, an attack by Longstreet would have been devastating. Porter's presence on the Confederate right flank was more happenstance than "intelligent conduct." One could equally claim Porter's lucky positioning was also due to McDowell and Pope.[24]

The board also credited Porter's "wise and judicious" conduct that afternoon because it thought that he alone "understood and appreciated the military situation." This, too, is dubious. Porter knew he was confronted with a large force, but he made little effort to discover the identity and size of this force. Porter simply waited for orders. The problem was that few senior officers on the Union side deserved much credit at Second Bull Run. The board could not report that Porter was no more incompetent than the rest of the army and corps commanders, so they magnified his achievements.[25]

Historian Stephen Sears argues that Porter's behavior made him a "not entirely undeserving victim," and that given the poisoned atmosphere in the Army of the Potomac, an example needed to be made. Sears is correct that a nation at war is ill served by destructive personal and political rivalries among its leaders. However, at a time when accusations of treason were on too many people's lips, the court-martial of military leaders could be equally dangerous. There is no evidence that Schofield read Thucydides, yet some of the more classically educated leaders of the time must have recalled the disastrous consequences of Athens's prosecuting its unsuccessful generals. Purging the Army of the Potomac of both McClellan and Pope partisans was necessary and should have been achieved without the unending bitterness of the Porter trial.[26]

Despite the complete exoneration, Porter's ordeal was far from over. President Hayes, without recommendation, passed the problem on to Congress for action. Republicans, led by Senator John Logan, invoked the memory of Lincoln and continued to condemn Porter and McClellan. They insisted that Congress had no power to overturn the results of a court-martial.[27] Porter suffered another blow when James Garfield was elected president in 1880. Even Garfield's assassination in 1881 helped little, as Chester Arthur was not disposed to support what his predecessor had so adamantly opposed. In May 1882 Arthur remitted the sentence that prohibited Porter from holding a federal office but vetoed a bill that overturned the conviction in 1884. In 1886, with a Democrat finally in the White House, Congress passed a bill vacating Porter's conviction and restoring him to the rank of colonel in the army. A few days later, the sixty-four-year-old Porter retired from the army and continued his duties as New York City police commissioner. Fitz John Porter died in 1901. His pallbearers included John M. Schofield and Joshua L. Chamberlain.[28]

Given the partisan rancor of the case, there seems to have been little political retaliation directed at the members of the Schofield Board. Yet, there are some tantalizing ironies. In 1880 President Hayes relieved Schofield of command at

West Point, but this action had little to do with the Porter case. However, Schofield was forced to wait for nearly two years for the retirement of Irwin McDowell to return to his Pacific command. When McDowell retired in 1882, John Pope was promoted to major general, but when Pope retired in 1886, President Grover Cleveland promoted Alfred Terry to major general.[29] George W. Getty retired as a colonel in 1883, despite Schofield's strong appeal to the secretary of war, and a bill to retire Getty as a major general failed, despite the support from Republican Speaker Joseph W. Keifer and Democrat William Rosecrans. Whether it was lack of time and interest or lingering partisan rancor over the Porter case is impossible to say.[30] Within the army, most officers had long ago chosen sides, but the Schofield Board helped to change many minds. The *Army and Navy Journal* hailed the board's decision, and in 1882 U. S. Grant published in the *North American Review* an emphatic reversal of his opinion of the Porter case.[31]

Schofield's position on the Porter case strained his relations with his old friend Jacob D. Cox. Cox, who may have been acting at the behest of his Ohio friend James Garfield, bombarded Schofield with long letters justifying the court-martial verdict. These arguments would find their way into Cox's tendentious book on Second Bull Run. Cox's letters prompted equally long rebuttals from Porter. Schofield patiently defended the board's conclusions without getting mired in the obscure and sometimes pettifogging details addressed by Cox and Porter. Cox, a lawyer in private practice, did not attack Schofield or the board personally and seems to have acted as a zealous advocate of his client's case. Schofield and Cox's disagreement on the Porter case did not prevent them from cooperating on Cox's other historical projects.[32]

Until the Schofield Board review of Porter's court-martial, Schofield had cordial relations with John Pope. This ended forever. Even as Schofield and his colleagues deliberated, Sherman attempted to smooth relations by encouraging Schofield to invite Pope to be the graduation speaker at West Point in June 1879. Though Schofield much preferred to have Terry, he reluctantly agreed. As the event approached and Pope's efforts to derail Porter's exoneration became clear, Schofield complained to Sherman that Pope's presence would be intolerable.[33] Pope saw the situation similarly and interpreted the gesture of conciliation as a "bitter pill" for Schofield, who would be obliged to "eat dirt in the face of the whole corps of cadets as well as of the army."[34] With both President Hayes and General Sherman as Schofield's houseguests for the graduation ceremonies, Schofield and Pope had to be on their best behavior, despite the bad blood.[35]

The animus grew truly personal when Pope ordered court-martial charges against Schofield's brother George. In October 1879 Major George Wheeler Schofield, 10th Cavalry, had been charged with conduct unbecoming an officer and gentleman in attempting to evade duty on a court-martial by claiming a knee injury. Amid mutual recriminations, surgeon J. W. Williams, who had certified Schofield's injury, was also charged. Major Schofield's older brother hastily contacted several friends in order to get a lawyer to Leavenworth in time for the trial. He also advised his younger brother that he should be sure to have all the pertinent facts "clearly and fully" placed before the court.[36]

Before brother John could arrange for a lawyer, George wired him that the case had been closed. Williams had been acquitted, and the prosecutors sought to drop the charges against Major Schofield. However, the departmental commander, John Pope, insisted on a court-martial, and Major Schofield let himself be persuaded that he needed to present no defense because the court would acquit him, which it did. His brother's fears were realized when General Pope forwarded the results to the War Department with ugly innuendos about Schofield's honor that were unrebutted in the court record. General Schofield told his brother that Pope's action was "a dirty fling at me, over your head, or at you on my account." He tried to reassure George, writing, "His [Pope's] character is so well known, and his motives so manifest in view of the past, that all the world will correctly interpret his actions—I will see that the facts are correctly presented in Washington." To Sherman, a bitter John Schofield wrote, "I beg you to read the action of the reviewing authority in the enclosed order from Headquarters Dept. of the Missouri and see what kind of return Gen'l. Pope has made for my efforts, at your instance, to mitigate the humiliation and disgrace which he had brought upon himself. . . . I hope never again to be guilty of the weakness of treating a man of such character otherwise than as he notoriously deserves."[37]

Meanwhile, to his indignant brother, who wanted to retaliate against those who had misled him, General Schofield cautioned discretion: "It often happens both in the army and elsewhere that men who entertain the worst possible feeling toward each other must do their duty side by side. We are not given the right to judge personally of the fitness of our official associates." This advice was easier said than done, as Schofield's outburst to Sherman attested. Moreover, had Pope and Porter taken this advice to heart, they would have spared themselves and many others much grief.[38]

Schofield urged his brother to let the matter rest for the time being and relayed to him that General Hancock and others believed that this episode would not harm him. This appeared to be true when two years later George was promoted to lieutenant colonel in the 6th Cavalry and subsequently posted as commander at Fort Apache, Arizona. Yet a year later, on December 17, 1882, George Schofield committed suicide. His fellow officers had noticed that he had appeared nervous for several days, and in one conversation, he seemed cheerful, but somewhat irrational. Moreover, a few days before, Lieutenant Colonel Schofield had quarreled with a Captain J. P. Walker, 3rd Cavalry, who preferred charges against Schofield, while Schofield arrested Walker for insolence. The post surgeon concluded "a fit of temporary mental aberration . . . probably brought on by fatigue and worry, and the intense pre-occupation of his inventive genius" were the causes of the suicide.[39]

As a forty-nine-year-old lieutenant colonel, George Wheeler Schofield had enjoyed a relatively successful post–Civil War career. He had more frontier and Indian-fighting experience than his brother. As a major in the 10th Cavalry, the "Buffalo Soldiers," he had served in Indian Territory, where in October 1874 he captured a large Comanche war party at Elk Creek. Later, stationed in Texas along the Rio Grande, he chased Kickapoo Indians into Mexico and captured Mexican revolutionaries who had crossed into the United States. Yet, George Schofield had other ambitions as well.[40]

Like his brother, George was quite mechanical and in 1871 began working on designs to improve the reliability of the Smith & Wesson revolver. In 1874 the army agreed to purchase 3,000 Model 3 Schofield Smith & Wesson revolvers for field-testing and evaluation. The Schofield Smith & Wesson, with its hinged, top-break barrel and automatic shell extraction system, enabled a mounted cavalryman to reload seven times faster than one armed with the Army Colt. The Army Ordnance Board, however, still preferred the ruggedness and reliability of the Colt. In 1879 Smith & Wesson ceased production of the Model 3 Schofield, with a total run of 8,969 guns. Equally disappointing had been the rejection of Schofield's application for transfer to the Ordnance Corps.[41]

The disappointments of the Schofield Smith & Wesson, the death of his young wife in 1879, and the lingering effects of the attack on his honor, combined with the loneliness and isolation of winter frontier duty, must have depressed Lieutenant Colonel Schofield sufficiently to prompt the "temporary mental aberration." George Schofield's death reveals another rather macabre aspect of army life. His *New York Times* obituary included not only a brief summary of his career but also the officers who would be promoted as a result of his death. Thus, A. P. Morrow, on Sherman's staff, was promoted to lieutenant colonel; Frederick Benteen, of Little Big Horn fame, was promoted to major; and Charles E. DeRudio and H. G. Sickel were promoted to captain and first lieutenant, respectively. With the great bulge of Civil War officers still on active service, promotion—especially for the postwar generation—had slowed to a trickle. For example, George's younger brother, Charles B. Schofield, graduated from West Point in 1870 and died as a captain in Cuba in 1901.[42] Death and retirement became events for both sorrow and celebration.[43]

In the course of the correspondence between John and George Schofield over the court-martial, General Schofield made a revealing admission about some sentiments toward his brother and the nature of the officer corps. Some officers believed that "Major Schofield became so much interested in his inventions, he took more interest in them than he did his duties in the 10th Cavalry." The general went on to explain that "there is little sympathy in the Army, either high or low, for any efforts an officer may make outside of his regular duties." Given the dismal promotion picture and the prospect of spending years in harsh and isolated frontier posts, many officers were jealous of those with the talent, energy, or connections to escape dreary duties. If this attitude fostered an inward thinking and rather narrow conception of duty among the officer corps, it also produced pressure within the officer corps to normalize special assignments so that all officers had a chance. For reformers like John M. Schofield, the officer corps needed a broader, more expansive view of professionalism. Officers needed to be encouraged, and in some cases forced, to look beyond their immediate duties. With the collapse of army reorganization, the focus for military reformers would become professional organizations, journals, and papers; military schools, lyceums, and military instruction at civilian colleges.[44]

Before turning from the Porter case, there is one final episode that illuminates John M. Schofield's thinking about civil-military relations. In April 1880, as Congress debated the Porter bill, Schofield gave his old friend John Bigelow a letter entitled "The Power of Congress over the Army" and signed "Old Soldier." The essay was designed to advance Porter's cause, especially with the Democratic base. Thus, while Republican senator Logan maintained that Congress had no right to overturn a president-approved court-martial, Schofield argued that Congress had a duty to oversee the executive branch. He noted the vast powers the president possessed in war or national emergency: "In time of war or public disturbance, the President may declare martial law and thus bring military commissions into existence for the trial of civilians. Thus not only officers and men of the Army, but members of Congress, and other citizens may be arraigned before a military court, tried, condemned, and executed, for disobeying an order of the President and obeying in its stead an Act of Congress."[45]

Given Schofield's past troubles with Congress, this support for congressional prerogative was astonishing. Schofield further observed that impeachment had proven extremely difficult, and the power of the purse was ineffective in the short term. Modifying the traditional Democratic rhetoric of the danger of a standing army, he noted the initial advantage of even a small standing army. Though "a standing army of 25,000 or even 100,000 could not permanently endanger the liberty of the American people," he pointed out that 5,000 regulars at Bull Run would have had a decisive effect on the battle, and perhaps the war.[46]

Against this potential power, Schofield asked, "Are officers of the army, high and low, to have no opinions of the law and their duty under it, no authority, under any circumstances, but executive orders, and no possible protection if they should decide to uphold the Constitution and laws rather than obey an unlawful order? Has Congress no power to regulate the use of an army that they have the sole power to raise and support? Not even the power to protect the army in its obedience to the law under which it was raised?" With a reference to the disputed election of 1876, Schofield concluded:

> While every patriotic citizen earnestly hopes no such crisis will ever arise in our country, it would be criminal blindness not to see that it may possibly come, and criminal folly not to be prepared for it. If the two houses of Congress ever admit that they have no power to protect a soldier in his lawful efforts to sustain the constitutional authority of Congress, . . . the President will then have it in his power to decide any doubtful case that may arise as to what man has been elected his successor even though one of the contestants may be himself.
>
> Is this what the people of the United States understand to be the meaning of their Constitution?[47]

Schofield's rhetoric was a bit overblown and dramatically diverged from the Porter case, yet it contained some important and disturbing questions. During the war, officers were constantly juggling the conflicting congressional and administration policies. During Reconstruction, this conflict grew even more intense. Where is a soldier's duty? Must a soldier obey orders he believes to be illegal and have no recourse if punished for disobedience? Has the Congress no authority to redress injustices resulting from the stresses of war or crisis? While Schofield had generally supported Presidents Lincoln and Johnson against Congress, he also possessed rather traditional views of congressional supremacy and the constitutional balance of powers.

At a more practical level, Schofield valued cool reason and detached judgment, yet he understood and accepted, more than Sherman, that most military issues were innately political, involving conflicting interests and agendas. Schofield celebrated his board as an example of impartial judgment, but he had seen its "just" recommendations thwarted by partisanship. If the president would not redress legitimate grievances, then Congress should. Between the contending powers of the president and Congress, the political Schofield was shrewd enough to recognize that a soldier could not and should not look solely to one branch of government.

While Schofield's service on the board to reexamine the general court-martial of Fitz John Porter may have done him credit, his role in the court-martial of Cadet Johnson Whittaker earned him lasting infamy. On April 6, 1880, Johnson Whittaker, the only African American cadet then enrolled at West Point, was discovered bloody and unconscious on the floor with his hands and feet tied to his bed. According to Whittaker's later testimony, three masked assailants had set upon him in the night. He had been choked, hit with a club, his ears and feet cut, and swatches of hair cut from his head. Such an attack went well beyond routine hazing and the fights that periodically erupted among the young cadets. It was even more unusual in that African American cadets were seldom hazed; they were instead subjected to a ceaseless shunning, in which cadets and most faculty had as little contact with them as possible. This perpetual ostracism was far more demoralizing than normal hazing.[48]

From the beginning, commandant of cadets Lieutenant Colonel Henry M. Lazelle doubted Whittaker and made little effort to uncover evidence to verify Whittaker's story. The academy doctor, Charles T. Alexander, who examined Whittaker that morning, believed the cadet had been feigning unconsciousness. They suspected that Whittaker, who was close to failing for the second time Professor Peter Michie's natural and experimental philosophy course, had staged the incident in order to avoid academic dismissal. In the course of the case, academy leaders advanced the notion that if the assault had occurred, Whittaker's lack of resistance demonstrated cowardice unworthy of a future army officer.[49]

Superintendent Schofield initiated an immediate investigation and at Whittaker's request convened a court of inquiry. The newspapers, especially those in New York, covered the story extensively. The publicity resulted in a political outcry and prompted President Rutherford B. Hayes to send a legal representative to ensure that the young African American cadet received a fair hearing. Despite this assistance, the court of inquiry concluded that Whittaker had faked the incident. Whittaker subsequently demanded a court-martial to clear his name. On June 10, 1881, after a lengthy trial, a court-martial found Whittaker guilty, but recommended clemency. After another lengthy review of the case by the judge advocate general, who ridiculed the prosecution's case, and the attorney general, in March 1882 the Arthur administration set aside the court-martial but ordered Whittaker's dismissal for failing natural and experimental philosophy.[50]

In his in-depth analysis of the Whittaker case, historian John Marszalek concluded that it was "a tale of Gilded Age America's attitude toward and treatment of its newly enfranchised black citizens." While many newspapers supported the black cadet, their accounts were generally tinged with "paternalism and racism." Some, like the former defender of freedpeople's rights, *The Nation*, chose to condemn Whittaker in order to protect the reputation of West Point. Most Americans viewed the controversy with detached curiosity. Those who deplored the lack of "fair play" at the academy did not really care about Whittaker's fate. The court-martial verdict and its later reversal prompted little public reaction. Even the political partisans were conflicted about pursuing the case. President Hayes and many Republicans were reluctant to overtly intervene and revive racial and sectional animosities in an election year. Anti–West Point Republicans, such as Senator John Logan, made it a case of Whittaker versus the academy. Meanwhile, the Democrats were willing to use the case to attack the administration and the academy, but they were not eager to champion African American rights.[51]

The Whittaker inquiry and court-martial produced mountains of documents, much speculation, and few undisputed facts. The court-martial verdict was not justified based on the evidence, but there is little in the record to prove Whittaker's version of events either. Even the sympathetic Marszalek judged the young man's guilt as "improbable," based on his entire life. It may have never been possible to prove or disprove Whittaker's account, but the academy officials made no effort in the crucial early days to investigate Whittaker's story. From the beginning, Lazelle and Alexander believed the cadet was faking and acted accordingly. Academy officials initiated no questioning of the activities of other cadets that night, and throughout the controversy there was no serious probe of the Corps of Cadets. While Lazelle's and Alexander's failure to consider other possibilities is deplorable, the ultimate responsibility for the one-sided investigations must fall on the superintendent.[52]

Superintendent Schofield, to his lasting disgrace, had joined the posse against Whittaker. This behavior was rather uncharacteristic for the cautious and judicious Schofield. Only a year earlier in the Porter case, Schofield had been meticulous and fair-minded. In rendering the Porter decision, he risked creating political enemies and alienating friends. In the Whittaker case Schofield was painstaking, but never evenhanded. While declaring his interest in getting to the truth, he had clearly made up his mind in advance. In his memoirs Schofield pretended that he had launched the official inquiry because he was not fully satisfied with Lazelle's initial conclusions, yet his private journal indicates that from the beginning he accepted Lazelle's assessment that Whittaker's wounds were self-inflicted. It was Whittaker who had insisted on an investigation.[53]

Blind to his own prejudices, the superintendent never considered the possibility that Whittaker had been attacked. During the inquiry, Schofield recorded in his journal how he seethed as the lawyer sent by President Hayes attempted to turn the investigation away from Whittaker's actions and toward the actions of others at the academy. Even as the inquiry was getting underway, Schofield told the press that he was sure that no other cadets were involved and suggested that Whittaker had made some false statements. In later comments Schofield declared that since all cadets were honor-bound to expose any complicity in the attack, this proved the Corps of Cadets was innocent. Schofield's prejudicial comments merely stoked newspaper attention and aroused sympathy for Whittaker.[54]

Schofield's statements during the investigations embarrassed the academy. His subsequent annual report, which excused the social ostracism that African American cadets endured and blamed their troubles on their own lack of qualifications, became an enduring disgrace. Even newspapers that suspected Whittaker may have faked the attack, denounced his treatment at West Point. The shunning reinforced for many the elitist, cliquish reputation of the academy.[55]

Schofield's prejudicial conduct in this case was surprising but not inexplicable. Schofield shared what he termed the "universal prejudice" against African Americans. However, as commander in Reconstruction Virginia, Schofield had never let his racial antipathy so openly influence the administration of justice. In too hastily accepting Lazelle's theory of the event, he became committed to proving Whittaker's guilt.[56]

In Schofield's mind, the Whittaker case was simply an opportunistic attack on the academy by its traditional enemies and a personal attack on him by his old radical enemies. While Schofield whined about his unfair political treatment, he never considered that Whittaker had been treated unfairly. Schofield grumbled that he had been very patient with Whittaker, but he remained blind to his own prejudices and to those of the academy. When Whittaker failed the natural philosophy course in 1879, Schofield had recommended his retention. Schofield's letter of support, however, reflected condescension as much as respect for Whittaker's efforts: "In the case of Whittaker, I do not know but I may be influenced somewhat by the fact that he is the only one of his race now at the academy, and has won the sympathy of all by his manly deportment, and earnest efforts to succeed. The Professors do not think he can ever master the course, but I am disposed to give him another chance."[57]

Since scores of cadets over the years had failed at West Point because of mathematics or science, Schofield never even considered the idea that Whittaker's poor grades might be the result of prejudice. More specifically, Schofield, who had often remarked on the academic help cadets provided to one another, never considered that Whittaker's social isolation prevented him from getting any assistance from faculty or classmates. In repeating the suggestions of cowardice, Schofield never considered the dilemma of African American cadets. Those who responded to insults were called hotheads and troublemakers, while those who brushed off affronts were branded as cowards.

Schofield's actions went beyond simple racism, however; they represented a capitulation to the attitudes and prejudices of the Corps of Cadets. Schofield's argument that the military could neither impose social equality nor attempt to enforce rules of social interaction "different from those which prevail among the people of the United States" contained a double message. Even though he did not agree with social equality, he had, in his career, enforced many policies with which he disagreed. His defense that the Corps of Cadets would never lie, although Whittaker apparently would, was clearly something he did not truly believe. In his efforts to stamp out hazing, he had seen too many contrary examples. Schofield once chastised the commandant of cadets, Henry M. Lazelle, for not investigating statements of cadets that the commandant believed to be untrue. To Schofield, the acceptance of "false denials" by cadets tended to "teach the habit of falsehood."[58]

The commandant of cadets had become angry and depressed as he failed to control cadet rowdiness. Schofield considered relieving him from the position but decided to wait one more year. Yet Schofield clearly shared the frustration and growing pessimism over hazing that he attributed to Lazelle. Both the superintendent and commandant preferred to believe in Whittaker's guilt, not just because of their hostility to blacks, but also to avoid another destructive clash between the academy leadership and the Corps of Cadets.[59] The cadets probably did not realize that they had won such a victory over the leadership. The Whittaker case seems to have had little direct impact on their lives, and no one seems to have given Johnson Whittaker a thought as they collected their memories of their academy years.[60]

The controversy and bad publicity that Schofield had brought upon himself soon led to calls for his ouster. The year 1880 was an election year. Judge Manning Force, Union veteran, close friend of President Hayes, and in-law of John Pope, suggested Pope would be an ideal replacement were he not needed in his present job in Missouri. Recognizing the political dangers of stirring up the Porter supporters, the War Department, without Sherman's knowledge, offered the position of superintendent to non–West Pointer Alfred Terry. Terry had been told that Schofield supposedly had made this request for relief, but on visiting West Point, he discovered this was false, and he refused to accept the assignment.[61]

Schofield attempted to shore up his position by enlisting the support of Sherman, Secretary of State William M. Evarts, and other friends. However, after an August 17 meeting with President Hayes, Schofield must have known his days at West Point were numbered. The president, in raising the question of change at West Point, said, "We have neglected our duty toward the colored race." Schofield responded that the rights of African American cadets had been protected, but he reiterated his position regarding the impossibility of imposing social equality between blacks and whites at West Point. Schofield also repeated the slur against Whittaker that the cadet's endurance of insults and assault without resistance showed his cowardice and unfitness for a commission. The general also made it clear to the president that he had not requested an immediate relief from West Pont. Rather ruthlessly, Schofield raised the specter of political repercussions. He told the president that he had learned from Democratic headquarters in New York of the administration's plan to replace him while keeping Sherman in the dark. Schofield then went on to not so subtly remind the president that removal at this time would be denounced as politically motivated by the Democrats and that he, Schofield, could not voluntarily depart under such circumstances.[62]

Denied the political fig leaf of Schofield's acquiescence, the president turned directly to the Whittaker case. In the course of the discussion, Hayes supposedly admitted that he had not read the board of inquiry's report. More astonishing, Schofield told the president that one of the reasons he did not believe other cadets were involved was because Whittaker was not badly injured. The general assured the president that had other cadets committed the offense, they would have beaten or injured Whittaker severely. When asked what he would do with the case, Schofield replied that if there were any doubt about Whittaker's guilt, he would grant the court-martial Whittaker had requested but delay it until December, which is what the president ended up doing.

In an effort to shift the blame for the debacle, Schofield also stated that the experiment of placing West Point under the commanding general had, so far, proved a failure, as the authority of both the commanding general and the general commanding at West Point was continuously undermined and disregarded. More than a change of administration, the academy needed "protection and support." Later that evening, Schofield would learn just how little support he had. During an after-dinner drive, General Sherman informed Schofield that he would not interfere or express any opinion on command at West Point, unless asked. "Thus," recorded a bitter Schofield, "has 'vanished into thin air' all his promises of support and protection." To be fair to Sherman, the commanding general was also making a political calculation. Schofield had put himself out on this limb, and to be seen as acting on his behalf would be counterproductive with the Hayes administration. In the coming months Sherman attempted to aid Schofield by pointing out all of the administrative obstacles to moving him immediately.[63]

Hayes delayed making a decision until after the presidential election. With Representative James Garfield running against General Winfield Scott Hancock, commander of the Division of the Atlantic, there were already enough problems. In the spring of 1880, Schofield had shrewdly anticipated that the Democrats would select a military man after having lost three straight elections to Republican generals. Schofield had even quietly aspired to the Democratic presidential nomination himself and sent feelers to friends, but he saw his admittedly slender hopes vanish in the Whittaker controversy.[64] The Republicans attempted to foment a fight between Hancock and Schofield over Grant's selection of Hancock over Schofield for major general in the regular army in 1866. Though Schofield had been greatly disappointed at the time, he publicly announced that Grant's decision had been correct. Schofield had hoped as early as August that the election would prompt Hancock's retirement from the army and enable him to honorably escape West Point by ascending to Hancock's former command.[65]

With the election of Garfield, Schofield could see the handwriting on the wall. On November 5, he wrote Sherman that he would like to leave West Point when it was convenient, but he did not want to displace another officer. Schofield had hoped that he could delay his departure until at least May 1881, to diminish the appearance of punishment.[66] This offered the administration an interesting puzzle. There were only three commands suitable for a major general—the Divisions of the Missouri, Atlantic, and Pacific, which were occupied by Lieutenant General Sheridan, Major General Hancock, and Major General McDowell, respectively. As Schofield was senior to McDowell, they could return Schofield to his old command, but that would lead to further disruption of command assignments. Besides, Hayes and Garfield would have been reluctant to displace McDowell to accommodate Schofield.

A week after writing Sherman, Schofield wrote a curious letter of explanation to the army adjutant general, presumably to get his views on the record and to send a signal to the secretary of war. Utterly convinced of Whittaker's guilt and the impossibility of imposing social equality at West Point, Schofield inter-preted his troubles as entirely the result of partisan politics, especially by the Republicans. He again outlined the deficiencies of the Department of West Point that still permitted politics to sway academic and disciplinary decisions. He observed that the impositions of the secretary of war had the effect of hampering communications between the superintendent and the War Depart-ment, as the commanding general was not always consulted or apprised of decisions. With a feigned incredulity Schofield declared, "It is difficult for military men to bring themselves to admit that political sympathies must have anything to do with the management of a military institution which should be absolutely non-partisan." Tweaking an administration publicly dedicated to civil service reform, he compared the problems of eliminating the influence of politics at West Point with the resistance to emancipating "the civil service from party servitude."[67]

Admitting that the academy still required the protection of the "dominant party"—the Republicans—from the hostility of the Democrats, Schofield urged that his successor be selected from those officers "who had never had occasion in the discharge of their duties, to come in collision with any faction of the dominant party." Recalling his troubles with the radical Republicans during the Civil War, he declared, "It is a fact well known that, in my official experience of the last eighteen years, I have had the misfortune to incur the relentless hostility, on several occasions, of a certain influential faction of the republican party." Schofield attributed this implacable hostility to recent attacks on the academy that were really aimed at him.[68]

President Hayes was determined to take care of this controversy and some other army problems before Garfield took office. Hayes selected David G. Swaim, Garfield's friend and Civil War army aide, as judge advocate general. General Swaim's later review of the Whittaker court-martial was highly critical of Schofield and the West Point leadership. Over the strenuous objections of Sherman, Hayes forcibly retired E. O. C. Ord instead of Irwin McDowell, in order to promote Nelson A. Miles to brigadier general. Both Ord and McDow-ell were roughly the same age, and McDowell's retirement would have given Ord the opportunity to regain the rank of major general before his retirement. The retirement of McDowell would have also solved the problem of assigning Schofield. Sherman was correct to suspect that politics had played a role in Hayes's decision.[69]

In December 1880 President Hayes also decided to replace Schofield with O. O. Howard. For Schofield, the president created the potemkin Division of the Gulf by rearranging departments. Howard, as one of the foremost supporters of African Americans' rights in the army, had little opportunity to change the racial climate at West Point, however, as no black cadets were appointed during his brief tenure. Hazing continued, and the Department of West Point did not survive Howard's term of office. Howard described the assignment as "the hardest office" he ever had to fill. Five more African Americans were appointed in the nineteenth century, and two graduated—John Alexander in 1887 and Charles Young in 1889. No more would graduate until 1936. Thus, the integration of the United States Military Academy, one of the most significant reform efforts of the nineteenth century, ended in failure. This does not exonerate Schofield, but it reminds us of the difficulty of meaningful reform against entrenched institutional opposition.[70]

In his self-justifying November 1880 letter to the adjutant general, Schofield concluded, perhaps more candidly than he realized, that he could no longer serve as superintendent because "I cannot hope to have that support which is necessary to make my service effective for the public good."[71] He had clearly lost the confidence of President Hayes and the newly elected president Garfield. Schofield's accusations of partisan motivations, though somewhat true, afforded only a limited defense. Schofield's judicious approach to the Porter case and the meticulous documentation of the board's conclusions had helped to muster nonpartisan support and mitigate the potential for overt political retaliation. Schofield's biased conduct in the Whittaker case stands in marked contrast. While his behavior conformed to the racial attitudes of most white Americans, he had seriously misjudged the political reaction, especially in an election year. The appearance of unfairness among a large minority of the public and his refusal to accommodate in any way to the administration's policy in the August 17 meeting with the president made Schofield extremely vulnerable. His willingness to sacrifice Whittaker and his reputation for judicious conduct to protect the cadets and the academy are even more striking, given his previous experiences.

In Civil War Missouri and during Reconstruction, Schofield had learned that only a commander who possessed the trust and confidence of the political leadership could survive, much less thrive. Professional competence alone was not enough for a senior general. Civil authorities would only grant soldiers authority if they could be trusted, and they would only be trusted if they displayed some appreciation of the political implications of military policies. In 1880 John M. Schofield had lost his political balance. In the next two decades he worked very hard to regain his equilibrium and to recover the trust and confidence of the nation's political leadership.[72]

Uncertain Future

In 1881 John M. Schofield faced an uncertain future. He was first assigned to a specially created Division of the Gulf, but everyone soon agreed that this new military division was unnecessary. Schofield toured Europe, while waiting for a suitable command position to become available. Yet by the end of the decade, Schofield's bleak future had been totally transformed. Schofield would not only command in succession the Military Divisions of the Pacific, the Missouri, and the Atlantic, but in 1888 he also unexpectedly ascended to position of the commanding general of the army.

In 1881 the army also faced an uncertain future. The end of the frontier and the Indian Wars was plainly in view, yet the future missions of the army were unclear or lacked national consensus. While some looked to the army to play an increasing role in domestic disorders, others vehemently opposed this course of action. Although the nation did not face any specific foreign threats, technological developments in armaments and shipbuilding prompted a renewed interest in updating coastal fortifications. Rapid technological change and the absence of specific threats produced tremendous uncertainty in the development of tactical doctrine.

Schofield relinquished command of West Point to O. O. Howard on January 21, 1881. He spent the next few weeks in New York, where he testified at the Whittaker court-martial ordered by the War Department. He grumbled to Sherman that its purpose seemed to be "to try me quite as much as the colored cadet." From there, he proceeded to New Orleans to assume command of the newly created Division of the Gulf. President Hayes created this command, consisting of Texas, New Mexico, Louisiana, Arkansas, and the Indian Territory, over the objections of Sherman, who considered it a bungle. Sherman assumed that Garfield would never permit the early retirement of McDowell to accommodate Schofield and had hoped to keep Schofield at West Point until June 1881, then letting Schofield travel abroad for a year until McDowell's retirement. If a new division were to be formed, Sherman had suggested one embracing the new southern railroad and the Mexican border, to consist of Texas, New Mexico, Arizona, and southern California. Schofield's new command lasted only three months, however, as President Garfield soon agreed it was a useless expense. Schofield was placed on "waiting orders" status with full pay and permitted to go abroad.[1]

From May 1881 to May 1882, Schofield toured Europe. Officially, Major General Schofield, Lieutenant Colonel Robert S. La Motte, 12th Infantry, and Captain James Chester, 3rd Artillery, were ordered to French XII Army Corps maneuvers. Accompanying Schofield on his European tour were his aide and brother Lieutenant Charles B. Schofield, his wife, and for a time General Sherman's daughter Rachel. On October 15, 1882, Schofield again assumed command of the Division of the Pacific. Upon the retirement of General Sherman and the elevation of Lieutenant General Philip Sheridan to commanding general, Schofield assumed command of the Division of Missouri on November 1, 1883.[2] With the death of General Hancock, Schofield requested transfer from the heretofore preeminent military command of the Division of the Missouri to the Division of the Atlantic. He assumed this command on April 13, 1886. The emergence of the Division of the Atlantic as the most prestigious command reflected the decline of the frontier and the renewed importance of coastal defense. Finally, on August 14, 1888, with the premature death of Philip Sheridan, John M. Schofield achieved the pinnacle of his profession, commanding general of the U.S. Army.

Schofield's progress from commanding in the Pacific, Missouri, Atlantic, and Washington reflected the changing focus of the army; therefore, rather than discuss Schofield's progress in strict chronological order, it is better to discuss these issues thematically. This chapter will examine how uncertainty and a lack of consensus shaped such major military issues as the end of the Indian Wars, the army's role in domestic disorders, the need to modernize coastal fortifications, and the search for a new tactical doctrine.

For more than a century, the army fought various Indian nations as Americans pushed the frontier westward. Yet, the term "Indian Wars" sometimes obscures the army's role. Schofield's only personal campaign experience was a brief stint as an artillery lieutenant in Florida during a relatively peaceful period of the Seminole Wars. Outright warfare had long been only a small part of the army's mission on the frontier. More often, the soldiers acted like policemen—chasing and arresting culprits. So while John Schofield was never much of an Indian fighter, he had considerable experience as a chief constable or, perhaps more accurately, chief magistrate. As the army's role in Indian affairs became less a military one and more that of a constabulary force, Schofield's experiences in Civil War Missouri and Reconstruction profoundly shaped his attitude and approach.[3]

During Schofield's lifetime, he had seen dramatic changes in the nation's Indian policy. Early in his career, he witnessed the final years of a policy of removal, which transported Indians to "Indian territory" west of the Mississippi. As Americans moved west, as railroads bisected the frontier, and as various western territories were admitted as states, the idea of "Indian territory" steadily shrank into a policy of isolated reservations. The policy of treating the Indian tribes as separate nations was transformed into the goals of "detribalization" and the assimilation of Indians into American society as farmers and ranchers. In one of many sad ironies of American Indian policy, the Indian tribes most amenable to peaceful farming were the most susceptible to attack from both Americans and other Indian groups. They were also the least capable of getting grievance hearings with the government.[4]

The Indian Bureau, which was created in 1824 as part of the War Department, had been transferred to the new Department of the Interior in 1849. Schofield, Sherman, and many army officers sought to transfer the Bureau of Indian Affairs back to the War Department. By the 1880s and 1890s, the army's complaints about the failures and corruption of the Indian Bureau continued, but there were fewer calls for the move. The focus of the debate shifted back to appointing military officers as acting Indian agents.

During the 1860s and 1870s, the army conducted many large-scale campaigns and a number of pitched battles against entire tribes. In the ensuing decades the army operated against increasingly smaller bodies of discontented Indians—their discontent largely due to the reservation system. The two major Indian actions during these years, Geronimo and the Ghost Dancers, symbolize this inexorable change. Both episodes represent the Indians' last gasp to avoid incarceration on reservations. Both reflect the difficulty in transforming hunting cultures and warrior peoples into Jeffersonian citizen farmers.[5]

Geronimo was the last chapter in the centuries of warfare between the Apaches and their Indian neighbors, the Mexicans, and the Americans. Geronimo and his small band were the last resisters to the consolidation of many, sometimes mutually hostile, Apache groups at the desolate San Carlos Reservation. In 1882 George Crook returned to Arizona to track down Geronimo and his band. Crook, using primarily Apache scouts and mule pack trains, wore down the enemy and penetrated Geronimo's mountain fortress in Mexico. In March 1883 the wily Indian leader agreed to return to the reservation for a time. In 1885

Geronimo again broke loose, once more agreed to return, and then escaped again. Sheridan, having lost patience with Crook's reliance on Indian scouts and his reluctance to exile the Chiricahua and Warm Springs Apaches to the East, replaced Crook with Nelson Miles. While Miles made a great show using regular troops, as directed by Sheridan, his methods differed only slightly from those of Crook. The regulars with their pack mules were still led to the enemy sanctuaries by Apache scouts. On September 4, 1886, Geronimo again agreed to surrender, but this time he and his tiny band of some thirty Indians were exiled to Florida.[6]

In the Southwest it took the removal of the Chiricahua and Warm Springs Apaches to bring peace. In the northern plains a different and more tragic example ensued. In 1887 the now routine reservation problems of incompetent or corrupt agents, starvation, and recalcitrant warriors were compounded by the Dawes Act. This legislation disastrously attempted to accelerate the Indians' transition to independent farmers by eliminating the idea of commonly held lands and transferring an allotted amount of land to each Indian. The "excess" reservation land would then be sold off to private interests. This act combined the eastern humanitarians' goal to transform Indian life with the westerners' ambition to wrest even more land from the Indians.[7]

The Great Sioux Reservation, which once comprised half of South Dakota, was cut in half. Congress failed to fulfill treaty provisions and reduced beef rations. The justifiably bitter and distrustful Sioux were ready for a savior. In despair and desperation many Indians turned to their religious traditions for hope and salvation. The mingling of traditional beliefs with a dash of Christianity produced ideas of transcendence. For the warlike Sioux, it brought forth the belief that deliverance from the whites was at hand. The Sioux Ghost Dancers proclaimed that "ghost shirts" would deflect the bullets of the whites. While not all Sioux were influenced by these prophecies, the increasingly defiant actions of some, particularly the Oglala and Brulés, raised fears among the inexperienced and inept Indian agents and the neighboring whites. The army was called in to stem trouble and make arrests, but this in turn heightened the fears and hostility of the Sioux. The killing of Sitting Bull by an agency Indian policeman added fuel to the fire.

Amid the rising tensions, both Miles, rather brashly, and Schofield, more delicately, warned Secretary of War Redfield Proctor and President Benjamin Harrison that no permanent solution was possible unless the government met the just complaints of the Sioux. Miles noted the ration reductions and the broken promises. He argued that in order to restore peace, he needed to give the Indians "some positive assurance that the government intends to act in good faith." Both generals urged their political masters to press Congress to finally approve and fund the provisions of the Crook Commission, which had convinced the Sioux to accept the treaty of 1889, and restore the Sioux beef ration. Such reassurances did not come.[8]

On December 23, 1890, with the 7th Cavalry approaching, the Miniconjous led by Big Foot fled their Cheyenne River Reservation to join the Oglala on the Pine Ridge Reservation. General Nelson Miles, commanding the Division of the Missouri, was determined to prevent the concentration of rebellious and dangerous tribes at Pine Ridge. The department commander, General John R. Brooke, ordered Colonel James W. Forsyth of the 7th Cavalry to capture and disarm Big Foot's entire band. On December 29 at Wounded Knee Creek, the attempt to disarm the surrendering Indians resulted in a horrific tragedy. As the soldiers began to physically search each warrior, a few hotheads opened fire. The surrounding soldiers returned fire, and in the ensuing deadly firefight, many Indian women and children were caught in the crossfire. The 7th Cavalry's losses were high, but the Indian losses were catastrophic. Of the nearly 500 soldiers, 25 soldiers were killed, and 37 soldiers and 2 civilians were wounded. The reported losses among Big Foot's people are less reliable, but at least 84 of the 120 men and 62 of the 230 women and children were killed, while at least 51 more were wounded.[9]

The disaster panicked the other Sioux tribes at Pine Ridge, and they bolted to the hinterland. It took General Miles several weeks and nearly half the infantry and cavalry of the army to coax, pressure, and coerce the Indians to return to the agencies. Miles, who had been criticized by some senior officers for overreacting in the first place, attempted to make Colonel Forsyth the scapegoat and relieved him from command.[10] He accused Forsyth of failing to heed warnings of the desperate and deceitful nature of the Indians and of deploying his men so that many were in the line of fire of others. Miles attributed most of the army's casualties to friendly fire. Many eastern newspapers took up Miles's charges and accused the 7th Cavalry of a deliberate massacre in revenge for Little Big Horn.[11]

Unfortunately for Miles, the officers he ordered to investigate the operation did not corroborate his harsh conclusions. Their report was somewhat critical of Forsyth's deployment, but it rejected accusations of a deliberate massacre. In reviewing the findings, General in Chief Schofield concluded, "The evidence in these papers shows that great care was taken by officers and generally by the enlisted men to avoid unnecessary killing of Indian women and children." Under trying circumstances, the 7th Cavalry showed "excellent discipline" and "great forbearance." In restoring Forsyth to command, Secretary of War Proctor went on in more detail, based in part on Schofield's private assessment.

Proctor noted that Forsyth had been ordered to disarm all the Indians, who "were sullenly trying to evade the order." Proctor also observed that some of the initial Indian fire passed through the intervening soldiers and into the camp where the women and children were and that the Indians continued firing from among their own women and children.[12]

In both the Geronimo and Wounded Knee episodes, Crook and Miles had attempted to use crisis to assert greater military control over the Indian reservations. Miles, in opposition to presidential policy, pressed for the appointment of army officers as acting Indian agents. To most soldiers, the inexperience and incompetence of many Indian agents were due to the political spoils system, which President Harrison showed no signs of abandoning. Through newspaper interviews, however, Miles was able to tap public opinion to pressure the administration into accepting more army officers as acting Indian agents.[13]

Schofield attempted to chart a middle course, emphasizing the temporary nature of the dual assignments and the acceptance that for many routine matters, the officers would report through the Department of the Interior, not military channels.[14] The incoming Grover Cleveland administration chose, for a time, to separate itself from the Republicans by embracing the use of military officers, and by 1893, twenty-seven of fifty-seven agencies were run by military officers. Eventually, the agencies were returned to civilian control, as other pressing demands arose for the small number of regular officers, and the sense of crisis abated. Meanwhile, the humanitarians who generally opposed the use of military officers used the situation to champion placing Indian Service positions under the civil service regulations.[15]

While the tragedy at Wounded Knee confirmed the unsuitability of the army in Indian affairs in the minds of many humanitarian reformers, another incident from the crisis cast in doubt many of their cherished beliefs about rapidly converting the Indians to white ways. As Miles's forces attempted to pressure the Indian tribes into capitulation, Brulé warrior Plenty Horses shot First Lieutenant Edward Casey in the back as he attempted to enter into peace negotiations. An 1873 West Point graduate, Lieutenant Casey was the commander of a company of Indian scouts and one of the army's Indian experts. At his initial hearing Plenty Horses fearlessly announced, "I am an Indian. Five years I attended Carlisle [Indian School] and was educated in the ways of the white man. I was lonely. I shot the lieutenant so I might make a place for myself among my people. Now I am one of them. I shall be hung and the Indians will bury me as a warrior. They will be proud of me. I am satisfied."[16]

While the killing outraged most Americans, a federal judge ruled that Plenty Horses acted as a combatant in time of war, and the jury declared him not guilty.

With the whites thus acknowledging his warrior status, Plenty Horses returned to his people. Nevertheless, Plenty Horses's chilling declaration served as a rebuke of the progressive belief in the power of religion and education to readily transform a warrior culture.[17]

On December 20, 1890, as the storm clouds gathered at the Sioux reservations, Schofield reemphasized to the secretary of war his basic tenets for eliminating discontent: "the means of comfortable subsistence," "satisfactory employment," and "sufficient restraint over the naturally vicious who cannot be controlled by milder means." By employment, he did not simply mean as farmers and ranchers. By restraining the vicious, Schofield did not mean just Indians.[18]

In his 1885 annual report as commander of the Division of the Missouri, Schofield provided his most comprehensive consideration of the "Indian problem." He began by accepting that much progress had been made in civilizing some tribes, but, citing Interior Department numbers, he estimated 122,000 of 175,000 Indians in the Division of the Missouri remained warlike. He further estimated there were more than 25,000 warriors, which constituted two-thirds of the division's military strength and was roughly equal to the size of the entire army. The scattering of the tiny, understrength army over a vast territory in order to dissuade depredations by small raiding bands meant that no single post could deter an entire tribe, which would require the assistance of most of the army. This would leave other areas virtually naked. Therefore, to restrain the "vicious" among the Indians, Schofield, like Sheridan and most of the senior officers, urged a substantial increase in the size of the army, and especially the cavalry.[19]

Just as he had as secretary of war, Schofield stressed the need for equal protection of the law—that Indians needed protection from lawless whites as much as whites needed protection from the Indians. Schofield observed that the seemingly plausible goal of disarming the Indians was fruitless because the Indians could always find individuals who were willing to sell them arms. He argued, "Besides, the free American citizens who roam at will over the plains, and whose right to bear arms is guaranteed by the Constitution of the United States, have no very tender regard for the lives of the Indians, and are not liable to arrest or punishment for any act of war they commit against them, while the Indian who shoots a white man is liable to be shot in turn by the soldiers who overtake him." Thus, fair play and justice demanded that the Indians be left comparatively free on large reservations while sufficient military force deterred them from warlike behavior.[20]

Regarding a comfortable subsistence, Schofield had long advocated the prudence of a generous ration. Moreover, unlike Lieutenant General Sheridan, Schofield did not favor a rapid transfer of title of Indian lands to individual Indians, eventually specified in the Dawes Act of 1887.[21] Schofield's points were rather artfully worded to not directly oppose the emerging consensus that would produce the Dawes Act, but his demurral was clear. Schofield assumed that the warrior culture would persist for many years longer than the sponsors of the bill assumed. He argued that while some farming lands could be apportioned in severalty (separate titles), the grazing lands should be apportioned far more liberally, and the title should be kept inalienable for a much longer period than suggested in the legislative proposals under consideration.[22]

As to satisfactory employment, Schofield proposed that the nation tap the "superior military qualities" of the Indians by permanently enlisting "a large number of Indian warriors" into the regular army. Noting the fidelity and effectiveness of Indians recruited as scouts and agency police, he believed "the best natural soldiers in the world" could fill out the depleted ranks of the cavalry. Incorporating the Indians into the U.S. Army would deflect their martial traditions and spirit to a more peaceful relationship with the army and their neighbors. Though Schofield did not directly address the issue, he may have hoped that an Indian presence in the army would also give Indians greater protection from predatory whites.[23]

Ironically, in 1889 Schofield advised against this idea when another officer proposed it to the secretary of war. He surprisingly argued that the time was past and that Indian soldiers would not be suitable for use in labor unrest. The most likely explanation for this reversal is that early in his tenure as general in chief, Schofield hoped for a general increase in army enlisted strength. Additionally, Schofield's caution may have been prompted by the mixed reaction the proposal received among the senior officers. Some, such as O. O. Howard, Thomas Ruger, and David Stanley, supported the idea. Others, like George Crook and Nelson Miles, were less supportive, arguing that Indians' enlistment as regulars would lessen their effectiveness as irregular auxiliaries. Still others, including John Brooke, Wesley Merritt, and Benjamin Grierson, opposed Indian enlistment completely. Captain Richard Pratt, head of the Carlisle Indian School, was even more opposed to the idea. Pratt contended that enlistment of Indian companies for duty at the respective reservations would do nothing to "detribalize" the Indians.[24]

In the middle of the Ghost Dancer crisis, General in Chief Schofield decided on a double-barrel approach. He reemphasized the manpower shortages of the army and renewed the proposal to recruit Indians. In the two years since he had advised against the idea, the prospects for a general increase in army strength remained bleak. He was also heartened by gaining a powerful ally in the person of Secretary of War Redfield Proctor. Proctor became so enthusiastic about the plan that many thought he was its originator. Since the idea had been kicking about in military circles for years, it would be hard to give credit to a single individual. Secretary Proctor, however, became the program's most zealous sponsor.[25]

The experiment began with the War Department's authorizing the increase of Indian scouts in April 1890. These companies, especially the one commanded by the later assassinated Lieutenant Casey, proved highly successful and encouraged Proctor and Schofield to expand the program. In March 1891, after again failing to get Congress to expand the army, Proctor used his existing authority to recruit Indian soldiers into the existing regiments of the regular army. General Order No. 38 authorized the recruitment of up to fifty-five Indians into cavalry troops and infantry companies that had been skeletonized due to manpower shortages.[26] By the end of the year, local officers had recruited more than 500 Indian soldiers and had reached 780 by 1892. Yet by 1894, the program was clearly on the decline, and it was finally abolished completely in 1897.[27]

Despite the strong support of both the secretary of war and the commanding general, the success of the Indian companies depended heavily on the energy and talents of the company commanders, who confronted many obstacles. Most Indians did not speak any English. Nearly all adult Indians were married, and the army made few provisions for married enlisted men. The commanders faced dissatisfaction when the Indians learned that, because they did not provide their own horses and equipment, they would not be paid as much as Indian scouts. Among the nomadic hunting and warrior tribes like the Apache, Comanche, and Sioux, recruiting went well, but the more peaceful, agrarian tribes had little interest in soldiering. The Indian soldiers were reluctant to conform to white rules such as haircuts and vaccinations and to routine, boring post duties such as guard duty, kitchen police, gardening, and post maintenance. The Indians were often exempted, which bred resentment among the other soldiers. Finally, there were occasional episodes involving alcohol.[28]

The company commanders often faced a lack of interest or even hostility from many in their own regiments. Some argued that the Indian companies undermined the case for strengthening the army. Others resented the special treatment given Indian soldiers. General Schofield often communicated with these junior officers to give them encouragement and support. One of the most talented of these men was future Army Chief of Staff Hugh Lenox Scott. In 1891 the thirty-eight-year-old, professorial-looking lieutenant was one of the nation's foremost experts on Indian customs, languages, and history. He successfully integrated the remnants of Geronimo's band into the Comanche reservation near Fort Sill. His troop of Kiowas and Comanches, L Troop, 7th Cavalry, was probably the most successful and the only one to complete its full term of enlistment. Scott later recalled that though the overall experiment failed, the members of his troop became the leaders on the reservation.[29]

Lieutenant Scott's example also represents one of the major weaknesses of the program. Without talented and dedicated leaders, the units would fail, and there were too few men like Scott. The army was neither intellectually nor institutionally committed to the project. There was little desire by leaders to adjust to the special circumstances of the Indian soldiers, whom officers saw as an "alien" element in the regular regiments. When Redfield Proctor resigned in 1892 to take a seat in the Senate, his successors showed little interest in making the program work. Senator Proctor attempted to get the concept ratified in congressional legislation and failed. Despite the low desertion rates, most Plains Indians did not adjust to the ways of the white soldiers any more rapidly than to farming. Moreover, the army's efforts to reduce desertion rates, together with the depression of 1893, improved its ability to recruit and retain non-Indian soldiers. The manpower crisis, especially in the cavalry, began to lose its salience. Schofield became the last, lone advocate of the program. Even Hugh Scott had become discouraged and asked Schofield to convert his company into scouts, thus removing them from the garrison and the pervasive bias. Writing Schofield's aide, Scott admitted, "I am tired of having to defend myself and them against prejudice." Created by executive order, the Indian soldier program was abandoned in executive apathy.[30]

The experiences of Indians and African Americans in the regular army produce some dramatic and ironic comparisons. African Americans, who spoke English and were acculturated to "white" ways, were nevertheless segregated into separate regiments, while Indians were incorporated into white regiments. White regiments east of the Mississippi River and all black regiments had been excluded from the Indian soldier experiment. Schofield, characteristically, argued both sides of the issue. He contended that while he knew of no difficulty between Indian scouts and black soldiers, the black troops might not exercise the same beneficial influence on the Indians as white units would. He then concluded that since the Indian companies need not be stationed with the parent regiment, all regiments might participate. Beyond simple racial prejudice, black regiments may also have been excluded because they were generally stronger due to low desertion rates.[31]

Proctor and Schofield never even contemplated the creation of an Indian regiment since that would have required congressional approval. Such support was inconceivable, and, besides, the object was to assimilate the Indians. A separate Indian regiment along the lines of the British Gurkha or Indian army units might have succeeded in amalgamating American Indian and army traditions, but it would have been ruinous for eventual Indian assimilation. In the twentieth century there were many legislative proposals for the creation of Indian regiments or divisions, but Indian groups, observing the experience of African Americans, opposed these efforts. Despite the splendid record of black regiments in the West and the Spanish-American War, African Americans only saw segregation intensify. During World War I, the Woodrow Wilson administration denigrated African American martial abilities by shunting the vast majority of black draftees into noncombat service units. Meanwhile, Indians served in white units, often as scouts or telephone operators, and those veterans received American citizenship.[32]

When Lieutenant General Philip Sheridan assumed the position of general in chief in 1883, Schofield replaced him in the army's largest military division—the Division of the Missouri. Sheridan's advancement to commanding general signified a small step in military professionalism. Though two previous commanding generals, like Alexander Macomb (1828–41) and Winfield Scott (1841–61), had been lifelong officers, Sheridan was the first academy-trained, career professional to attain the position. George McClellan (1861–62), Henry W. Halleck (1862–64), U. S. Grant (1864–69), and William T. Sherman (1869–83) had all been West Pointers, but Sheridan was the first academy graduate to rise to that position without a break in service. Schofield, though he nearly left the service, was the second. While politics still played a role in who would rise to the top, Sheridan's career marked the appearance of lifetime professionals at the head of the army. The distinction between military and civil officers of the government now became even more pronounced.[33]

In discussing his command of the Division of the Missouri in his memoirs, Schofield considered the establishment of Fort Sheridan the only significant event of his tenure. Fort Sheridan, twenty-five miles north of Chicago, was created when a group of prominent Chicago businessmen of the Cosmopolitan Club bought over six hundred acres of land and donated it to the federal government for the purposes of building a military fort. These "public-spirited" businessmen, concerned about labor unrest like the Great Railroad

Strike of 1877 and the Haymarket bombing, were investing in security. Schofield correctly saw Fort Sheridan as an important symbol of the changing nature of the army and its missions.[34]

The end of the Indian Wars permitted a major realignment of the nation's military posts. When Schofield became commanding general in 1888, the army had 119 garrisoned posts and 23 armories, arsenals, and depots; when he retired in 1895, it had 82 garrisoned posts and 22 armories, arsenals, and depots. On requests for new posts, Schofield responded that "the present, well mature policy of the War Department is to concentrate the army, as far as practicable, into large posts, not less than a regiment at each." The consolidation of Indian reservations, combined with the use of railroads to concentrate forces rapidly, enabled the army to abandon many smaller western posts.[35] Though the sparsely populated western communities objected, the army's desire to consolidate its units on larger, more comfortable posts received support from politicians from urban districts, who now also claimed a need for military protection. The rapid industrialization and high immigration of the last decades of the nineteenth century greatly exacerbated class relations in the United States. Violent strikes sparked interest, especially among the business and political elite, in locating army posts closer to major industrial areas. More important, domestic disorder produced a dramatic revival in the organized militia and its transformation into the National Guard.[36]

While the army chased Indians and bandits, and dealt with range wars and polygamy laws, the most common domestic disorder involved labor disputes. The Panic of 1873 resulted in an extended depression. On July 17, 1877, as the hard-pressed railroads instituted a new round of wage reductions, the first great labor strike began as even more hard-pressed railroad workers in West Virginia walked out. The Great Railroad Strike of 1877 quickly spread to Baltimore, Pittsburgh, Chicago, and other major cities. Coal miners and many of the urban unemployed joined in the protests, while in California angry American workers attacked Chinese immigrant workers. The state militias proved inadequate to handle the violence. The militias in West Virginia, Ohio, and New York openly fraternized with the strikers, while the National Guard in Pennsylvania and Maryland proved ineffectual. Indiana and Missouri had no organized militia. At the request of many governors, President Hayes deployed the army to support the state militias.[37]

The bulk of the disturbances took place in the Division of the Atlantic, which consisted of twenty-seven of the thirty-eight states. With the frontier army busy chasing the Nez Perce, the 3,300 troops available to General Hancock were spread dreadfully thin. Compounding Hancock's problem was the absence of

General Sherman, who was touring forts in the West and did not return to Washington, D.C., until after the crisis had passed. On July 23, 1877, President Hayes ordered Superintendent Schofield to report to him in Washington. The next day Schofield met with the president and his cabinet. He then proceeded to Philadelphia to meet with General Hancock and Governor John F. Hartranft of Pennsylvania to discuss plans for reopening the Pennsylvania Central Railroad from Philadelphia to Pittsburgh. On July 26 Schofield returned to Washington and assumed command of a mixed collection of soldiers, sailors, and marines who guarded key sites in the capital. To avoid confusion over relative ranks, the various elements reported directly to Schofield. By July 31, the crisis was largely over, and Schofield returned to West Point, though some army units remained at important railroad terminals for several months.[38]

The regulars had been relatively successful in opening the railroads without much bloodshed. The bulk of the nearly one hundred casualties had resulted from the early, bloody clashes between mobs and the police or militia. Few strikers wanted to tangle with the regulars. This was due to Hancock's wise decision to employ his limited resources in large battalion-size formations to intimidate opponents, decisive actions by experienced field officers, and the excellent discipline of the soldiers—soldiers who were no longer being paid because Congress had failed to pass the Army Appropriations Bill. In the emergency Hancock had also been granted extraordinary authority over those organizations that were normally controlled by the staff bureaus and corps.[39]

Over Hancock's objections, however, President Hayes placed control of the army units in the hands of the state governors. This meant that instead of supporting the local forces, the federal soldiers were often placed in the forefront of the struggle. The governors also sought to retain these units for weeks after the crises ended. In St. Louis John Pope skillfully avoided this problem. Rather than appear in person, Pope sent a colonel and several hundred troops to guard the federal arsenal and encouraged local officials to employ their resources. With the regulars in the background, a makeshift militia ended the disorders.[40]

In 1877 President Hayes employed federal forces during the strike based on three rationales: the constitutional requirement to aid states in suppressing domestic insurrection, to protect federal property, and to assist U.S. marshals. After the Posse Comitatus Act, Schofield got his first real taste of the new ground rules in 1885 with the anti-Chinese riots in Wyoming. In the 1870s and 1880s thousands of Chinese came to the United States to work on the railroads and in the mines of the West. Their strange cultural ways, their often temporary residence in the United States, and most important, their willingness to work for lower wages than white American workers produced much hostility between the two communities. On September 2, 1885, anti-Chinese resentment spilled over into violence, as white coal miners and those displaced by Chinese workers attacked the Chinese settlements at Rock Springs, Wyoming. The local sheriff could not protect the Chinese, as most locals supported the rioters and Wyoming Territory had no militia. The Union Pacific officials who ran the coal mines urged the territorial government to appeal to the army for help. Knowing the decision was not theirs to make, Governor Francis E. Warren communicated directly with Secretary of War William C. Endicott and then President Grover Cleveland.[41]

Since General Sheridan, Secretary Endicott, and President Cleveland were out of town, Adjutant General R. C. Drum coordinated the government's response. On September 4 Drum, in the name of the secretary, informed General Schofield in Chicago that, pending an official request from the territorial governor for troops to suppress insurrection, he was to send two companies to Rock Springs to "prevent any interruption to the United States mails or the routes over which they are carried." This provided a temporary fig leaf for military intervention. Three days later, Drum forwarded additional instructions to Schofield. Based on a treaty with China that committed the United States to protect Chinese workers and the inability of the civilian authorities to preserve the peace, the president directed Schofield to send forces to wherever he estimated violence or the threat of violence existed. In addition to protecting life and property and aiding civil authorities, Schofield was authorized, if necessary, to make arrests. The president further directed that each detachment so employed receive their orders directly from Schofield "to make sure that the force is not unnecessarily used" and that Schofield frequently report the situation to the War Department.[42]

Given this broad authority, Schofield issued detailed instructions to his subordinates and stressed the need to limit action only to what was needed to preserve peace. Commanders were to remind troops that "it is no part of their duty to punish offenders," and arrests could only be made at his direct orders. Yet, when Schofield made his reports and requested the War Department to confirm his actions, he received the following reply: "The President regards the instructions already sent you as quite adequate to the occasion and sufficient for the purposes specified in my [Adjutant General Drum] telegram of the seventh of September and directs that these instructions must not be exceeded." To the politically alert Schofield, this was clear signal that he was on his own and he had better not make a mistake. He therefore set out for Wyoming to observe the situation personally. Meeting with Governor Warren on the way, Schofield arrived in Rock Springs on September 22. By the time the division commander arrived, four companies of troops had restored order, the town was quiet, and the Chinese miners had returned to work. By September 25, Schofield had returned to Chicago.[43]

The mobs had killed twenty-eight Chinese and destroyed thousands of dollars in property. It was impossible to impanel an impartial jury for the murders, but Schofield rejected using military commissions to try the murderers. The United States grudgingly paid the Chinese government $147,748.74, without admitting national guilt or responsibility. The Union Pacific Railroad took advantage of the attacks and federal intervention to break the union. The Knights of Labor played into their hands by continuing to strike, making it easy for the company to replace the white workers with more Chinese. Schofield began removing federal troops on October 4, but Governor Warren warned against a drastic withdrawal. Union Pacific agreed to construct buildings for a small post in Rock Springs and nearby Evanston, and several companies remained in the region for fourteen more years.[44]

As commanding general of the army, John Schofield would guide army responses to additional domestic violence in the Northwest and Midwest, most notably during the marches of the "industrial armies" and the Pullman Strike of 1894. Again a financial collapse, the Panic of 1893, produced a depression that set the stage for intense conflict. In the spring of 1894, Jacob S. Coxey, a populist social reformer, conceived of the idea of a workingman's army, the "Commonweal of Christ," to march on Washington to demand that the government implement public works projects to provide relief for the unemployed. Coxey left Ohio with 100 men and arrived in the capital on May 1 with 500 followers, who were vastly outnumbered by police and onlookers. Coxey and the leaders were quickly arrested, they paid a small fine, and Coxey's "army" dissolved. Coxey's march was largely symbolic, but his idea inspired more alarming imitators in the Pacific Northwest. These larger "industrial armies" demanded free railroad transportation to the East and, when they were refused, hijacked the trains.[45]

Since these "armies" had much support among the local population, the militias of the newly formed northwestern states were unresponsive. The railroads, many of which were in federal receivership, again turned to the national government. At the direction of the president, General Schofield ordered his commanders to retake the stolen trains and to guard bridges, tunnels, and railroad property. The army also escorted the prisoners for trial, though only a few leaders were ever imprisoned. Schofield's orders limited military actions to assisting law enforcement and not otherwise obstructing the marchers. Schofield argued that the " 'Commonwealers' have the same right as other citizens to go West or come East at their pleasure, provided they do it in a lawful way." Schofield saw the movement as an understandable and even "laudable desire to get out of a country where they are no longer able to obtain subsistence." In his memoirs the retired general reiterated his sympathy for the unemployed workers stranded on the Pacific Coast and considered the railroads very shortsighted in not offering them free transportation to the East.[46]

Attorney General Richard Olney had decided that, under Revised Statutes Section 5298, the president was authorized to employ troops to assist federal marshals to enforce federal court orders. Schofield agreed with these legal justifications, but he urged that Section 5300 required that the president also issue a proclamation before the use of troops, and he recalled that President Hayes had issued such a proclamation in 1877. Cleveland did not issue a proclamation of this kind. Nevertheless, Schofield was careful to avoid some of the problems of the Great Railroad Strike by issuing General Order No. 15. The order required the use of troops only on orders of the president, and required troops to follow orders issued only by the military chain of command. Schofield concluded his instructions with the warning, "Any unlawful or unauthorized act on their [the troops'] part would not be excusable on the ground of any order or request received by them from a marshal or any other civil officer."[47]

The army had again responded with its traditional decisiveness and restraint, but a greater challenge was just around the corner. The Pullman Strike, much like that of 1877, began with a strike over wage reductions at a single company—the Pullman Palace Car Company—and rapidly spread to other cities and industries throughout the nation. In June 1894 it became a nationwide strike when the American Railway Union (ARU), led by Eugene V. Debs, announced it would boycott all trains pulling Pullman cars. The railroad companies, through the General Managers Association, stood by company owner George Pullman.

The shutdown of the nation's railroads would have been catastrophic, and President Cleveland, like Hayes before him, sided with the railroad companies. The recent labor unrest in the Northwest had provided the administration with the legal tools and rationale it needed for intervention. Federal judges issued injunctions against the ARU for disrupting the U.S. mail, and given the inability of U.S. marshals to enforce the injunctions, the president then authorized the use of troops. Subsequent Supreme Court decisions affirmed the right of the president to employ troops to prevent disruption of the mail and interstate commerce. To these arguments, Schofield added the issue of national defense, as the railroads were also the nation's military roads.[48]

In his memoirs Schofield outlined a general policy for the employment of troops that was very similar to Hancock's 1877 principles. He contended that when the civil power ceased to be effective and the president exercised his authority as commander in chief, "his acts become purely military, untrammeled by any civil authority whatever." Schofield went on to contend that when civil officers and their posse were no longer able to enforce the laws, they needed to stand aside until the military "overcomes lawless resistance to authority"; then, "military duty ends, and the civil officers resume their functions."[49]

The reality of the Pullman Strike was far more complex than this neat division. To avoid some of the jurisdictional problems encountered in 1877, the army performed missions independent of the marshals, police, and National Guard. While others confronted mobs and made arrests, the regulars guarded federal facilities and depots. In the West they served as guards on trains to prevent strikers' interference. To preserve military autonomy, troops were assigned to guard U.S. marshals and their posses as they escorted persons under arrest. The distinction between whether the regulars were guarding the marshals or guarding the prisoners was often lost on those who sought to free their comrades. Again, few protesters wanted to tangle with the regulars.

Two-thirds of the army would be employed during the strike, and again the regulars acted with discretion and restraint. Though the commanders and the soldiers on the spot deserved most of the credit, Schofield made major contributions. Unlike his two immediate predecessors, who had been little involved in directing the army in domestic disturbances, Schofield played an active, and indeed central, role. Schofield was not about to surrender what little authority the commanding general had by permitting the secretary of war or adjutant general to supersede him in issuing military orders to subordinate generals in times of crisis.[50]

Schofield exercised his command authority in two primary ways. He issued specific orders to individual commanders to dispatch troops to various trouble spots, and more important, he established and educated his subordinate commanders on the rules of engagement for civil disturbances. Schofield reiterated the points made in General Order No. 15 and elaborated on them in General Order No. 23. This new order gave specific instructions for dealing with violent mobs. Harking back to the tragic day in St. Louis in May 1861 when undisciplined soldiers fired into a crowd, Schofield noted that at the early stages of unrest, innocent observers were commingled with the lawless. He ordered that "under no circumstances are the troops to fire into a crowd without the order of the commanding officer." He advised that the bayonet was the preferred weapon against mixed crowds and that warnings should be given first. Finally, he concluded that the troops were to use force only to end lawless resistance, and that "punishment belongs not to the troops, but to the courts of justice." Some historians have termed General Order No. 23 "a seminal order that became the foundation of Army civil disturbance doctrine," and it remained virtually unchanged in army regulations until 1937.[51]

The focal point of the Pullman Strike, and Schofield's greatest leadership challenge, was in Chicago. One of the major difficulties was the stark differences among the various civil authorities over what should be done. The striking Pullman workers and their ARU allies had attracted the support of thousands of other workers in Chicago. They also had the sympathy of Illinois governor John P. Altgeld. In June Altgeld deployed 4,700 National Guard troops in various parts of the state to discourage violence but not to act as strikebreakers. Chicago mayor John Hopkins, who controlled about 3,000 city police officers, also sympathized with the strikers.[52] Both men objected to the intervention of federal troops. Unlike the strikes in 1877 and in the western states in 1894, the president could not use the rationale of assisting states with insurrection. Thus, Richard Olney, the attorney general, had pressed President Cleveland to employ federal troops to assist federal marshals in enforcing on the unions the federal court injunctions related to the obstruction of the mail.

The second major problem Schofield had in Chicago was the Department of the Missouri commander, Major General Nelson A. Miles. Miles, the McClellan or MacArthur of his day, was notorious for his almost insubordinate attitude toward orders with which he disagreed. On July 2 railroad officials and federal marshals reported that the situation seemed to be deteriorating, and Schofield alerted Miles of a possible mission to move the garrison of Fort Sheridan to Lake Front Park in Chicago. Unfortunately, General Miles was not in Chicago. After a frantic search, the War Department learned that Miles, who had been on leave in the East, had not returned to his command as the labor troubles increased. Through friends, Miles was discovered to be in Washington. The next day, Schofield took Miles to the White House to meet with the president and the cabinet. According to Schofield, when Miles was apprised of the situation, he showed little concern or inclination to return to Chicago and advised against the use of troops. Upon the president's decision to send in the regulars, Schofield pointedly ordered Miles to return to his command. Miles arrived in Chicago on July 4.[53]

In the meantime, Colonel Robert Crofton had moved eight infantry companies, two cavalry troops, and one artillery battery to Chicago. Unfortunately, Crofton allowed U.S. marshal John W. Arnold to persuade him to break up his command into ten- to twenty-man detachments to augment the police and marshals throughout the city. Such an employment violated the Posse Comitatus Act and Schofield's General Order No. 15. The penny-packet deployment of regulars did not impress the thousands of strikers and simply reinforced their belief that the army was there to break the strike. Of course, the fact that the headquarters of the Department of the Missouri was located in the Pullman Building only heightened the strikers' distrust.[54]

Upon returning to Chicago, General Miles was slow to reconcentrate his badly scattered forces, and he become preoccupied with using troops to break up mobs. The old Indian fighter had abandoned his earlier qualms and was determined to suppress a budding radical revolution. On July 5 Schofield sent a rebuke to Miles over his employment of troops. He angrily wrote, "it is your duty to concentrate your troops. . . . [T]he troops should not be scattered or divided into small detachments." Reminding Miles that his mission was to protect federal property and prevent obstruction of the mails, the general in chief admonished, "The mere preservation of peace and good order in the city is, of course, the province of the city and State authorities."[55]

One of the foremost obstacles in dealing with the disorder in Chicago was the lack of coordination among the various forces of law and order, which by then amounted to more than 13,000 men. The institutional and political divisions of the separate organizations remained strong, as each reported to different civil authorities with their own objectives. Attorney General Richard Olney and his nearly 5,000 U.S. marshals were clearly aligned with Pullman and the railroad owners. Within the limits established by Schofield to protect federal property and keep the rail lines open, Miles's nearly 2,000 regulars coordinated with the federal marshals and the owners. Meanwhile, Governor Altgeld's 4,000 Guardsmen, combined with Mayor Hopkins's nearly 3,500 city and county policemen, attempted to quell pillaging and violence without acting as strikebreakers. This restraint became increasingly difficult as the union tactics of destroying railroad property, combined with outright rioting, produced a backlash among the public.[56]

By July 12, the violence began to abate. The changing public opinion, the antiriot efforts of the National Guard and police, the railroad protection provided by the regulars and marshals, and the arrest of ARU leaders, including Eugene Debs, all helped turn the tide. On July 14 Schofield, over Miles's objections, ordered the regulars to return to their garrisons. During the Chicago strike, the railroads lost $685,308 in property damage and $4,672,916 in earnings, while the workers lost more than $1,748,000 in wages. Twelve people were killed, 515 were arrested, and 71 were indicted by the federal government. Though the U.S. Strike Commission created by President Cleveland severely criticized the intransigence of Pullman and the railroad operators, the strike still proved a devastating blow to the unions. The federal government applied the Sherman Antitrust Act to them and jailed their leaders for violating court injunctions.[57]

During the Chicago strike, General Miles had rather overtly taken the side of Pullman and the railroad owners and regarded the strikers as revolutionaries. While most of the other senior commanders had little sympathy for unions, they were generally more circumspect. With their headquarters in major cities, the army's senior officers were well connected with the local and emerging national elites. Though lacking the wealth of the business elite, they were honored and respected for their positions and past services to the nation. During his time in Chicago, John Schofield developed cordial relations with such men as George Pullman and railroad manager J. W. Doane. The general joined their exclusive Pelee fishing club, traveled in their special trains, and vacationed with them in St. Augustine, Florida, and Bar Harbor, Maine.[58] He and his family received special passes from various railroads.[59] Schofield and his family also owned stock in the Pullman Palace Car Company, before and after the Pullman Strike.[60]

Schofield believed that the officer corps's commitment to public service placed its members apart from the commercial aspirations of civilian society, but it did not put them in opposition to that order. The hierarchical nature of the military had many elements in common with the emerging structures of big business. Just as important, military officers shared the republican values of their fellow citizens. By education and position, they reflected the upper-middle-class values of most other professionals of the day. Like physicians, lawyers, and engineers, the officer corps supported the liberal capitalist order and, through modest business investments, hoped to participate in the growing wealth of the nation.[61] Since the political elites shared a similar relationship with the business elites, the military had little independent impact on business-related policy. For example, Attorney General Olney, a former railroad lawyer, had far more influence on Cleveland's strike decisions than did Schofield. Despite Schofield's stock in the Pullman Company, his actions during the strike did not reflect so much his personal stake as it did his adherence to the laws and orders of the civil authorities.[62]

Army leaders had hoped that an expanded role for the regular army in civil disorders would justify an increase in strength, but it was not to be. Instead, political leaders focused their attention on reforming the militia and transforming it into the National Guard. In this case, the traditional suspicion of standing armies played a factor, but a more significant element was the staunch localism of the American polity. Most governors wanted troops of their own and did not want to rely on the federal government. The National Guard developed a reputation as a strikebreaker, yet as historian Jerry Cooper has shown, fewer than 30 percent of its interventions involved labor disorders. Another frequent mission, especially in the South, was to protect prisoners from lynch mobs. The National Guard's boosters often magnified its industrial constabulary role when seeking funds from the state governments. Just as the regular army intervened in labor disputes far less frequently than the guard, only a few of the thousands of strikes during this period deteriorated into violence that required the use of the National Guard. Though its image as strikebreaker is exaggerated, it broke enough strikes to attract national attention.[63]

The unreliable performance of many militia units in 1877 prompted greater attention to the organization and training of the organized militia. The strength of the National Guard varied from 90,865 members in 1875 to 84,739 in 1885 and 115,699 in 1895. This seeming unevenness actually denoted a broadening of the guard to more states and efforts to turn the organized militia into a more efficient and reliable force. By 1894, the state units of the National Guard, despite meager funding, were much better organized and trained, though nowhere near the standards of the regulars. Army leaders had hoped that this difference in training and discipline would benefit their argument for an increase in strength. In the midst of the Great Strike of 1877, Schofield wrote fellow military reformer Emory Upton that disciplined soldiers were vital in domestic disorders. He observed, "One raw recruit among Gen'l Hancock's troops might do incalculable harm." After the Pullman Strike, Congressman John A. T. Hull led another futile effort to increase the army from 25,000 to 30,000 men. In defeat, Hull opined that the bill "never had a chance of becoming law. There seems to be a deep-seated conviction that 30,000 men, enlisted from citizens of the Republic, would be a menace to 70,000,000 of their fellow citizens." Ironically, the experience and discipline of the regulars made them the most feared force, yet it was the less well trained and less disciplined National Guard that was most apt to employ deadly force.[64]

As the National Guard became better organized, it replaced state volunteer units as the primary way of mobilizing American military strength. The creation of a new and more powerful state-based institution was a severe blow to those army reformers who hoped to fashion a more national military system. The most prominent advocate of such a national system was Emory Upton. Upton was the army's foremost tactical and strategic analyst and the author of most of the tactical manuals used in the post–Civil War era. He had studied and written extensively about foreign armies. Though maligned by some historians as a "militaristic zealot" and opponent of citizen soldiers, Upton was really a nationalist, or even a premature Progressive.[65] He argued that the nation's security should not be left to a decentralized, state-based system of militias and volunteers. Upton would retain state militias for local exigencies, but for national defense he advocated national volunteers, funded by the federal government, to serve as reserve units for the regular army. Regular officers would oversee their training and command at the higher levels. At his premature death in 1882, the political climate was unreceptive to Upton's comprehensive reform and nationalization of military institutions. The revival of his theories in the new century by Secretary of War Elihu Root matched the nationalizing tendencies of the Progressives.[66]

Given how important Schofield and Upton were in Sherman's reform efforts, it is surprising that these two intellectually oriented officers did not have more contact beyond a periodic exchange of letters. Schofield was an academy instructor when Upton was a cadet, but Upton served as commandant of cadets at West Point prior to Schofield's arrival as superintendent. Upton died in San Francisco in 1882, a few months before Schofield's return to command on the West Coast. Schofield shared most of Upton's views about the need for professional officers to train and lead the nation's citizen soldiers. Schofield had also argued that 5,000–10,000 concentrated regulars at the beginning of the Civil War could have had a dramatic effect on the course of the war. During the Spanish-American War, a retired Schofield lent his prestige to the effort to create national volunteer regiments, recruited and officered by the federal government.[67]

Schofield was not a theoretician, however; he was a pragmatic and politically savvy general, who understood that in the contemporary political climate the state-based National Guard could not, and indeed should not, be replaced with a national reserve. Instead, Schofield advocated increasing federal financial support of the guard combined with increasing the regular army's role in inspections and training. This policy was never adopted during Schofield's tenure in the army, but the Dick Militia Act of 1903 provided for increased federal funding of the National Guard in exchange for expanded federal regulation. Ironically, this little-known piece of legislation became a model for twentieth-century extensions of federal power.[68]

The rapid industrialization and technological developments of the late nineteenth century had the greatest effects on the navy. The *Monitor* revolutionized naval warfare, and in the next decades armored, steam-powered ships roamed the seas. Large breech-loading steel guns replaced muzzle-loading bronze cannon. The new naval warships could easily pulverize the existing masonry casement fortresses, which had been mostly built before the Civil War. Coastal defense never elicited the ideological opposition of a standing army, but given the enormous costs to construct and maintain such fortifications, American commitment was sporadic and grudging.[69] In March 1885, after several decades of indifference and neglect, Congress finally took up the problem and created a body that came to be known as the Endicott Board. The Endicott Board's report would provide the basis for coastal defense efforts for the next three decades.[70]

The board was named for its president, Secretary of War William C. Endicott. As prescribed by Congress, its members included two officers of the Engineer Corps, two from Ordnance Corps, two officers from the line of the navy, and two civilians.[71] Significantly, the board included no artillery officers, whose regiments would have to man these fortifications. Completing its report in January 1886, the board envisioned a system of coastal fortifications that would cost $126,377,800, or more than three times the annual army budget. This estimate did not even include the cost of ammunition and the purchase of additional land required for the fortifications. The report recommended an initial appropriation of $21 million, with subsequent annual expenditures of $9 million until completed. The plan provided defenses for twenty-six coastal ports, plus three in the Great Lakes, and 2,362 pieces of ordnance.[72]

Despite the growing federal budget surpluses, the Democrat-controlled House of Representatives was not eager to spend so much on military defense. The difference between the $670,000 proposed by the House and $6 million suggested by the Senate was too great to bridge. As had happened in 1877, the House refused to compromise and made no appropriation for coastal defense for 1887. In 1888 Congress finally approved nearly $5 million to begin work on the development and production of new steel rifled guns and breech-loading mortars. Appropriations generally increased during Republican Congresses and declined under Democratic ones, but even the Republicans preferred to spend the government surpluses on the expansion of Civil War pensions rather than on coastal defense. Appropriations averaged $1.5 million until March 9, 1898, when the threat of war with Spain prompted Congress to approve unanimously $50 million for national defense, and much of the army's $20 million allocation went to coastal defense.[73]

The meager appropriations constituted part of the problem. The new guns, mortars, and gun carriages had to be designed, tested, and put into production.

Though the Endicott Board had recommended armored turrets and casemates, disappearing gun carriages and concrete reinforced earthen barbettes proved especially more effective and cheaper. Yet, these required that the guns and their carriages be engineered before the positions could be constructed. With the fiscal constraints, most of the new weapons did not become available until 1894, and by 1898, the army had installed only 151. In addition to new guns and battery fortifications, modern coastal defense experts also called for the development of floating batteries, submarine mines, and torpedo boats, much of which had to be constructed by the navy.[74]

In the Fortification Act of September 22, 1888, Congress established the Board of Ordnance and Fortifications, with the commanding general John Schofield as its president, to coordinate all of this activity. Schofield attributed the creation of the board to a lack of confidence in the chief of ordnance; and while that may have been true, the board also filled a desperate need. Without a genuine coordinating General Staff, the American military system had great difficulty in managing a project that encompassed the Ordnance Corps's furnishing the guns, the Corps of Engineers's building the fortifications, the artillery's manning the guns and fortifications, and infantry's providing inland protection to the fortifications. Schofield was especially pleased with the creation of the board because it gave the commanding general the statutory authority to supervise preparations for war, rather than simply to command those forces in time of war. Schofield also hailed the inclusion of a civilian representative, normally a member or former member of Congress, who could effectively communicate with congressional committees.[75]

Even this small step toward an integration of military planning was fraught with difficulty, however. The Board of Ordnance and Fortifications, as with most boards, was task-oriented, and specific members were selected to manage specific tasks. For example, the primary ordnance representative on the board commanded the Proving Ground at Sandy Hook, New York. The engineer member was also stationed in New York, where these officers could supervise tests and experiments directed by the board. When their departments reassigned these officers, they lost their usefulness to the board because they could no longer direct the work, and the bureau chiefs were not responsible for the board's mission. A better solution might have been to make the bureau chiefs members of the board, but they generally resisted such a remedy because it would restrict their independence, especially since the commanding general was the board's president.[76]

Another issue that hindered congressional funding was that technological innovation always threatened to render the current systems obsolete. The speed of technological change was a relatively new dilemma for military planners. The Brown Bess musket and Napoleon cannons had remained in military arsenals for decades, with only gradual modifications. The complexity of modern weapons, which took years to develop and refine, combined with the possibility that a new invention would make the expensive weapons outmoded, created enormous uncertainty. Anticipating the modern aphorism that "the best is the enemy of the good," Schofield declared, "If we wait for the best, the next war will be long over before we shall begin to prepare for it." Despite Schofield's hopes, the Board of Ordnance and Fortifications never entirely overcame these worries.[77]

In addition to the financial, technological, and bureaucratic obstacles to coastal defense, Schofield confronted the thorny problem of how to man such expensive fortifications. The general had a special regard for his old branch and its complex requirements.[78] Schofield began his campaign to reform and revitalize the artillery shortly after assuming command of the Division of the Atlantic. Using an article about the artillery and coastal defense by West Point professor Peter S. Michie in the *Journal of the Military Service Institution*, Schofield fostered a public debate among artillery officers. A few months later, on October 3, 1887, he convened an "Artillery Council" at his headquarters on Governor's Island, New York. Consisting of two representatives of the five artillery regiments of the army, the Artillery Council hammered out a report that became a blueprint for artillery reform efforts. Though Schofield had anticipated many of these proposals in his 1887 annual report, the council's report was so comprehensive that it could be read as his agenda as commanding general. Schofield did not fully agree with all of the recommendations, but he incorporated these issues into his annual reports and proposals for legislation.[79]

The council's proposals called for improvements in artillery training and education, a greater integration with the state militias, and a major reorganization of the artillery. The provisions of the plan included (1) the appointment of an inspector general of artillery with rank of brigadier general who would report to the commanding general of the army; (2) the expansion of the five, 530-man artillery regiments to seven, 600-man regiments; (3) the enhancement of promotion prospects by eliminating the extra first lieutenants in each battery, the promotion of lieutenants based on date of rank in branch, not regiment (lineal promotion), and examinations for promotion and transfer into artillery; (4) the institution of increased pay for artillery sergeants and step pay for privates to recognize their technical proficiency; (5) the legal establishment of artillery schools (existing schools were created ad hoc with no separate resources) and artillery representation in the selection of cannon; and (6) suitable provision for instruction of militia artillery units.[80]

Schofield enjoyed his greatest success in improving artillery training. He established a system of annual gunnery practice in the Division of the Atlantic and even conducted in the vicinity of New York City the first joint army and navy training exercise. Shortly after assuming the position of commanding general of the army, Schofield issued General Order No. 108, which standardized heavy artillery training and added an inspector of artillery target practice for the Divisions of the Atlantic and Pacific. In 1891 promotion examinations for all junior officers became required throughout the line of the army.[81]

The other two legs of the artillery reform agenda—regular artillery reorganization and heavy artillery in the militia—fared less well because they were out of the hands of Schofield and the War Department. To man the new coastal defenses proposed by the Endicott Board would require more than 85,000 artillerymen. At a time when an increase of the entire army to 30,000 was proving politically impossible, the use of the militia seemed obvious. While the regulars could maintain the fortresses in peacetime, the National Guard could readily fall in on these posts and units to provide the necessary manpower to operate the guns in an emergency. Yet, most states resisted the expansion of artillery units in the National Guard. The first problem was that artillerymen required greater levels of training than infantrymen. Next, infantrymen were easier to recruit and train and were more suited to the domestic missions of the guard. Further, the linking of National Guard units to reinforce specific regular army units and missions undermined the independence of the guard. Finally, the federal government offered little in the way of incentives to the states, as the federal subsidies remained constant. By 1894, only 5,922 of 117,533 guardsmen were in the artillery, and many of these were in light or field artillery units.[82]

The reorganization of the army artillery branch was a project very dear to Schofield's heart. The artillery had profound structural, technical, and morale problems. By creating two additional regiments, he hoped to increase the strength of the artillery from 2,930 to 4,250. Such an expansion would enable the artillery to minimally man and maintain the new fortifications. Since each regiment contained two light batteries, the expansion would also provide a modest increase in the field artillery. Another important feature was the restructuring of the officer authorizations. Like the cavalry, each artillery regiment had one colonel, one lieutenant colonel, three majors, and twelve captains. However, instead of one first lieutenant and one second lieutenant per troop, each battery had two first lieutenants and one second lieutenant. This structure meant that while new infantry and cavalry officers were promoted to captain in twelve to fourteen years, new artillery officers had to wait twenty to twenty-five years. As a result, in 1891 artillery captains averaged fifty-five years old, and first lieutenants averaged forty-five years old. The Civil War hump—relatively young veterans in the senior ranks—had dramatically slowed the promotion of the entire officer corps, but for the artillery the process was glacial.[83]

In pressing for artillery reform, Schofield also had to fight other bad ideas. One was to transfer the responsibility for coastal defense to the navy, specifically the marines. Schofield, with the able assistance of Tasker Bliss, successfully argued that the army provided "passive defense," while the navy offered "active defense," of the nation's interests. The experience of other countries had shown that navies tended to neglect the passive defenses because such responsibilities hampered the initiative of the active, seagoing fleet. "Therefore," Bliss observed, "England has looked with dread upon any course that tied her Navy to the shore." Schofield noted that coastal fortifications needed the cooperation of armies for inland protection as much as cooperation with the naval fleets.[84]

Another bad idea was to create separate field artillery regiments, similar to those of the European armies. Schofield again contended that the American army and its artillery were too small to create such separate regiments. The expertise gained from the new heavy guns and the light artillery schools needed to be diffused throughout the entire branch. The demographics of the artillery were even more persuasive. Under the current structure, regimental commanders could select young and still vigorous lieutenants to command the regiments' light batteries. The separate field artillery regiments would soon face the problem of aged captains commanding the field artillery.[85]

The paralysis of 1870s retained its grip on any substantive structural reforms, good or bad, until the advent of the Spanish-American War. Schofield's hopes for recognizing and reviving promotion in the artillery would have to wait for the next century. The artillery got two more regiments in 1898 and its own brigadier general chief in 1903. Even then, Major General Joseph Sanger lamented some of the misguided reforms that separated coastal from field artillery and abolished artillery regiments. The grand plan of the Endicott Board would never be completed. Coastal defense would muddle along with limited funding and even more limited manpower. The projects took on the characteristics of other War Department engineering and public works projects, where political considerations were as important as any strategic design. The Spanish fleet proved incapable of threatening American ports, and the United States eventually developed a close friendship with the only naval power, Great Britain, that could be a threat. In the end, the fortifications were less important than the efforts put into engineering and producing the guns. Valuable lessons were learned for the future of heavy artillery.[86]

Just as technological change had dramatically altered coastal defense, it had a profound effect on tactics. Yet, the development of a coherent tactical doctrine suffered from even greater hurdles. In addition to equipment shortages, troop shortages, and lack of structural reorganization, tactical doctrine suffered from a lack of consensus within and among the three combat arms. The most important question was, for what kind of war should the army organize, equip, and train to fight? The debates prompted officers to think deeply about their profession. Rapid technological change and the absence of war made the "correct" answer far from certain. Ironically, an "official" answer imposed on the army would have retarded the professional debate and the growing professional self-examination. With such a dilemma, Schofield attempted to balance the need for authoritative instructions to guide training and inspector general reports with the need to keep the service open to new ideas and developments.[87]

Discussions of tactics and strategy by many late nineteenth-century officers tended to be extremely detailed or very general. For most of the century, tactics, especially at the lower levels, were largely a matter of drill. The detailed drill manuals drove company- through regimental-level training. Discussions of strategy were either lengthy historical analyses or rather vague principles, or both. American officers paid a great deal of attention to developments in Europe, but European practices often did not apply to the United States's strategic concerns. Because the threats to the United States were so remote, many officers, in examining future needs, tended to write about moral qualities and the spirit of the American military. This was not just empty national pride. It was their strategy for preparing for an uncertain future. Rather than a large standing army and navy, American security relied on the nation's location, size, and the fierceness of its people.[88]

In 1869 Sherman had assigned Schofield to be president of the Tactics Board, with the mission to revise drill and tactics for the infantry, cavalry, and artillery. Using the works of Emory Upton as the basis of its work, the board attempted to create a common, or what they called "assimilated," drill and tactics among the three branches. Schofield went about the task with his usual judiciousness, but even his conservatism and ability to compromise did not reconcile all objections. For example, the board rather commonsensically recommended that the rifle and the revolver be the primary cavalry weapons. This prompted cavalry traditionalists to howl about the importance of the saber.

Although seldom used, the saber not only served as the symbol of the cavalry, but it also exemplified the spirit of the cavalry. Infantry officers felt the same way about the bayonet. The saber charge and the bayonet charge symbolized the fighting spirit of the two branches.[89]

Schofield's trip to Europe in 1881 gave him additional insight into the development of modern tactics. As an observer of the French XII Corps maneuvers, he saw that greater depth was required of the new open-order formations that were necessitated by the increase in firepower of cartridge and magazine-feed rifles. Moreover, he noted in the defense the use of separate lines of troops occupying consecutive positions, so that the rear line could fire as the forward one withdrew. Attacks had to be made by small subunits in rushes and, if possible, over covered ground. The rear line would fire until masked by the advancing soldiers. He concluded, "A tolerably well defended line can no longer be carried by the bayonet nor by the rush of a cloud of skirmishers. It must be crushed by a superior and well-directed fire." The tactics relied on accurate, disciplined fire and the judgment and skill of junior officers and even privates. Marksmanship would replace parade-like drill as the cornerstone of infantry training.[90]

At a higher level, Schofield admired the patriotic commitment of the French reservists to serve thirty days in annual military training and the population's willingness to put up with maneuvers over their land. He was thankful that the American strategic position permitted his country to avoid such burdens. One of these burdens was that French troops were billeted in the towns and villages. Schofield believed that while this cantonment system reduced illness in the cool autumn weather, it did inure the soldiers to the hardship of campaigns. In later years Schofield was a strong supporter of regular officers' participating in National Guard bivouacs and the various veterans' encampments. Such events not only taught soldiers how to live in the field but also, just as important, taught the officers the importance of field sanitation and hygiene. World War I would be the first American war where the soldiers killed in action outnumbered those who died of disease.[91]

In March 1889 Commanding General Schofield had boards established at the school at Fort Leavenworth to modernize army tactics, especially in the light of modern weapons. Rather than adapting the ideas of an individual author, these new regulations were the work of a committee. In creating the new tactical regulations, Schofield was again more interested in provoking discussion and building a rough consensus. In January 1891 he had the completed drafts reviewed by three senior officers in each branch. More concerned about substance than speed, he wrote, "My desire is to leave the existing regulations in force until we can be quite sure that a new system will meet in all essential respects the modern conditions." Each reviewer had small reservations but concluded the new regulations were far superior to those in effect. However, in publishing the new regulations, Schofield knew that it was simply one more step to open criticism "with the view to their ultimate perfection."[92]

The title for the new regulations was significant. No longer entitled "Infantry," "Cavalry," or "Artillery Tactics," the new publications were termed "Drill Regulations." The new manuals made a distinction between drill and tactics. They presented "close order" formations for moving troops to the battlefield and "extended order" for combat. They introduced new organizations below company level: the platoon, section, and squad. Extended order formations relied on the movement of squads and placed greater reliance on the combat leadership of sergeants. Ironically, the regulations assumed the three-battalion regiment, though this long-sought reform was still seven years away.[93]

Unlike the French, American officers had no specific threat against which to develop military organization and doctrine and no specific enemy to justify large reserves and annual training maneuvers. The three-battalion regiment existed in tactical theory but not in reality. At the same time, the reality of Indian duty had not disappeared for many officers. While some officers continued to resist the loose or extended order tactics of the new regulations and worried whether such methods could be taught to the militia, other officers sought to extend and elaborate such techniques. The advent of smokeless gunpowder further altered the battlefield environment. Colonel Henry Clossen, whom Schofield had detailed to review the artillery drill, archly observed: "No tactics can ever be a finality until the lion and the lamb, the little child and the leopard, form a set of fours." Tactics were increasingly seen as continuously in flux, and constant study was required to keep up to date.[94]

A military system that relied on rudimentarily trained guardsmen or untrained volunteers and an evolving tactical doctrine that demanded greater training, discipline, and initiative at lower levels of command created a seeming dilemma for American military policy. While in office, Schofield deemed that proper coastal defenses, backed by the small regular army and the National Guard, were sufficient to repel any probable invasion or raid. He admitted, however, that against a large European army, such a force would be "practically worthless." Hastily organized forces could no longer compete with modern, well-organized armies. In retirement, he urged greater preparedness through universal military training in schools and colleges and closer supervision of National Guard training by the regular army. Yet, there was something rather pro forma about his argument. Schofield recognized that, except in instances of insurrection, America's fortunate geographical position generally gave it the luxury of time. Schofield had great confidence in the common sense, loyalty, discipline, and pluck of the volunteer soldier. The ever-greater complexities of modern warfare simply reaffirmed the necessity for highly skilled and dedicated professionals to train and lead these citizen soldiers. The nurturing of a martial interest among the population and a professional commitment among the military were the linchpins of American security.[95]

The decade after his relief from West Point also marked a period of uncertainty and change in Schofield's personal life. His brother George committed suicide in 1882. On December 30, 1888, his wife Harriet Bartlett Schofield died. She was buried at West Point alongside her first son, John Rathbone Schofield, who had died in 1868. In the months before Harriet died, she had seen her husband elevated to command of the army and her daughter Mary married to the general's aide, Lieutenant Avery Delano Andrews.[96] For the sociable Schofield, his wife's death was a double blow. He relished the ceremonial and social life of a commanding general. He loved attending and giving dinner parties. He did not have the reputation of charming the ladies that Sherman had, but he enjoyed their company. Therefore, it was not surprising that on June 19, 1891, Schofield remarried. What was surprising was that the nearly sixty-year-old general married a twenty-seven-year-old woman. Perhaps more shocking, especially to Schofield's daughter Mary, was that Georgia Wells Kilbourne was Mary's best friend. Georgia had been a visitor in the Schofield home since she was fourteen and was the maid of honor at Mary's wedding. The couple would have one child, Georgia Schofield, born in 1896.[97]

During these years, Schofield's relationship with William T. Sherman changed. After Sherman's retirement in 1882, Schofield's correspondence with him naturally diminished. Sherman once bragged that since his retirement he had not "meddled with army matters." Schofield would invite Sherman to stay with him when he visited Chicago or New York, and they would still meet occasionally at reunions of the various veteran societies. These rather serious-minded meetings were not simply excuses for eating and drinking with old comrades, but occasions to relive, review, and analyze the war.[98] One of the important parts of these meetings was the presentation of formal papers about the war. One of these sessions nearly caused a breach between the two men.

In October 1883, at a Cleveland meeting of the Society of the Army of the Tennessee presided over by Sherman, Captain J. Barber read a paper that seemingly disparaged the role of Schofield and his troops at the battle of

Nashville. Schofield, who had not attended but had heard a rumor of the attack, wrote an indignant letter to Sherman demanding to know why he had permitted such an insult to Schofield and his men. Sherman and Schofield traded angry letters, until both men realized this minor matter was getting out of hand, and they agreed to retract their intemperate letters.[99]

This episode is revealing of the prickly nature of both men. Schofield, ever sensitive about his military reputation, reacted defensively to all perceived affronts. Sherman, secure in his reputation, was more blasé but was quite combative about perceived affronts to his personal honor. Yet, their relationship had subtly changed with Sherman's retirement. Schofield, out of propriety and fear, would not have provoked such a dispute while Sherman remained the commanding general. Even after his "betrayal" by Sherman in the Whittaker case, Schofield was always deferential. On this occasion, he felt free to express some of his resentments, though he quickly regretted the outburst.

Soon the two men returned to being old comrades and friends. When Sherman moved from St. Louis to New York City in 1886, they saw more of each other and perhaps discussed some of the army issues they avoided in their letters. Sherman's wife, Ellen, died a month before Harriet Schofield, and his as-yet unmarried daughter Rachel played the social secretary, homemaker, and partner for social occasions. In January 1891 Schofield was hosting a dinner with President Harrison as the guest of honor, and he especially wanted his old friend to attend. Sherman declined the invitation citing the weather and the risk of illness. His fears were justified, and on February 14 William T. Sherman died of pneumonia. The U.S. Army's four-star generals—Grant, Sherman, and Sheridan—were gone. Major General John M. Schofield was now the nation's senior soldier.[100]

Incremental Reformer

While the uncertainty surrounding American national security interests fore-stalled consensus over major changes in military force structure and policy, Schofield's tenure as commanding general produced many seemingly modest— but ultimately significant—reforms. A central theme of these reforms was the reintegration of the army: redirecting its fragmented components from their narrow regimental and branch preoccupations while at the same time building consensus for future reform. Schofield also sought to meliorate the hardships and inequities of military life and perceptively attempted to adapt existing institutions to meet new missions and requirements. In many ways, Schofield was an early Progressive. While military Progressives were often different from other Progressives, they shared an obsession with rationalization, regulariza-tion, and above all, expertise.[1]

Several factors contributed to Schofield's success. First, he substantially changed the tone of debate within the War Department. Rather than simply contending with the secretary of war, Schofield subordinated himself to the secretary and became his closest advisor. In partnership with the secretary, and sometimes with the staff departments, Schofield took advantage of favorable political circumstances to alter army personnel systems by instituting methods that promoted greater "fairness" in promotion and assignments. These innova-tions fostered initiative and encouraged professional development. Taking ad-vantage of post consolidation at the close of the Indian Wars, he helped improve the quality of army life. While rapid technological and economic changes produced tremendous uncertainty, they also fostered an interest in military and international affairs. Schofield took advantage of this interest to promote mili-tary education through post schools, military instructors at civilian colleges, professional associations, postgraduate schools, and journals. Schofield's in-cremental reforms laid the foundation for both a reintegrated army and a mod-ern professional ethic.[2]

Schofield described the condition of the War Department when he succeeded Lieutenant General Philip Sheridan as deplorable. As Schofield related in his memoirs, Sheridan, even before his lengthy final illness, "had long ceased, as General Sherman and General Scott had before him, not only to command, but to exercise any appreciable influence in respect to either the command or administration. The only difference was that General Scott went to New York and General Sherman to St. Louis, while General Sheridan stayed in Washington." The General Staff had succeeded in cloaking its duties with the authority of the secretary of war. This meant that General Sheridan and all the other division and department commanders had to execute the orders of the staff departments as if they came directly from the secretary. The department heads could issue orders to staff officers in the military divisions and departments without informing the secretary or any of the commanding generals. Moreover, they could issue orders in the name of the commanding general without even informing him, much less gaining his approval.[3]

This state of affairs had begun quite early in Sheridan's tenure as commanding general. Sheridan had rather confidently expected to regain the authority lost by Sherman when he decamped from Washington for St. Louis. Sheridan rather naively asserted the principle that, as commanding general of the army, all army officers were subject to his command. When he preemptively gave orders to various staff departments, the staff chiefs once again turned the conflict into one between the secretary and commanding general. When Secretary of War Robert T. Lincoln challenged the lieutenant general's assertions, Sheridan compounded his problem by not responding. Given Sheridan's overt Republican sympathies, the situation grew even worse when Democrats took over the White House a few months later. To put Sheridan in his place, William C. Endicott, Grover Cleveland's secretary of war, sent Lincoln's stinging rebuke to all general officers and the newspapers.[4]

When Schofield assumed command of the army, the staff attempted to draw him as well into a battle with Secretary Endicott. Schofield was far more experienced in the bureaucratic intrigues than Sheridan, however, and avoided the staff's initial traps. Schofield knew that the commanding general's power rested more on influence than command authority. Rather than assert sweeping authority, Schofield defended his prerogatives and fought the staff bureaucrats with their own weapons. Schofield, an inveterate writer, produced a stream of closely argued memorandums that challenged the allegations made by the staff. He also adopted the tone of sweet reason. For example, when the adjutant general issued orders using the authority of the commanding general, Schofield wrote, "It seems to me, that all orders from the War Department which are required to be promulgated through the Commanding General should be shown to him, by the Staff Officer who receives them from the Secretary of War, before they are printed or *made known to any other person.*" Citing a presidential order, he then suggested how such orders could be routed through the headquarters of the army without "appreciable delay." Despite Schofield's efforts to conciliate, the best he could achieve was "an armed truce," as the staff waited to provoke a new battle under the next administration.[5]

At the end of the Cleveland administration, the president had apparently asked General Schofield to submit his thoughts on the administration and command of the army. Schofield's paper came too late in Cleveland's term of office for action. It remained filed in the office of the secretary of war for some years, and it was never officially acted upon. Schofield, however, used this report as his guide for his time as commanding general. This paper renewed some of the arguments Schofield made to Sherman in 1878. Reiterating his position that the secretary of war is "Head of the Army," he argued that the secretary's authority over all of the army was limited only by the president's discretion. Moreover, the commanding general possessed only such authority delegated to him by the president or the secretary of war. This was both a political and politic argument. It assumed that the authority of all officials derived from the trust and confidence in which the president held them, and it acknowledged that the commanding general possessed no authority independent of the president.[6]

Schofield maintained that the solution to the difficulties of command and administration lay in the recognition that the "General Commanding the Army is subordinate, in all things, to the Secretary of War, no less than the President." Furthermore, the commanding general and his subordinate generals "are the assistants of the Secretary and President in the military administration no less than in command."[7] In addition to reiterating Schofield's position on the inextricable linkage between command and administration, this was an especially clever way of claiming that the generals of the army acted under the same authority claimed by the staff chiefs—that of the secretary of war and the commander in chief.[8] This assertion strengthened Schofield's argument that it would be unwise for the secretary to delegate authority to staff brigadier generals to issue orders to major generals.

Schofield suggested that this principle meant that the commanding general, as the senior general, should act as "Chief of Staff" or an "Assistant Secretary of War" for military administration, as opposed to the civil works or nonmilitary responsibilities of the War Department. He also advised that under this principle, the secretary could reserve certain matters or parts of the military establishment for the secretary's direct supervision. Schofield proposed that the fundamental principle of military administration should be based on deference to the "Head of the War Department in all things, coupled with the rule of action that the concurrent opinion of the Commanding General and the Chiefs of Staff Departments is requisite and sufficient in all matters that the Secretary does not choose to concern himself." This principle of coordination, intrinsic to modern staff theory, was remarkably foreign to nineteenth-century military practice. Commanding generals and staff chiefs all sought to maintain their independent decision-making authority. Nevertheless, Schofield optimistically concluded that a regulation acceptable to all parties could be formulated, which would "bring all staff departments and the Headquarters of the Army into harmonious action as a united staff of the Commander-in-Chief, and his War Minister."[9]

With the appointment of Redfield Proctor as secretary of war in March 1889, relations between the commanding general and the secretary of war improved dramatically. Proctor, rather surprisingly, was the first secretary of war since William Belknap to have had any extensive Civil War service. Proctor had served as an officer in the 3rd and 5th Vermont Infantry and commander of the 15th Vermont Infantry at the battle of Gettysburg.[10] Most secretaries had heretofore been lawyers and political advisors who saw themselves as administrative care-takers and, to some extent, spoilsmen. Redfield Proctor was a results-oriented businessman—"a rationalizer and systematizer." He was also a genuine advocate of civil service reform. His military experience, combined with his business background, made him a highly effective leader as the army embarked on a new era. Proctor's managerial approach to the office would become increasing common in the next century, marking him as an early Progressive as well.[11]

Proctor and Schofield forged a genuine partnership dedicated to reforming the army. Schofield, by word and deed, made it clear that he would act as Proctor's subordinate.[12] Aided by his natural sociability, Schofield fostered the relationship with invitations to dinner, club memberships, vacations in St. Augustine, and fishing trips to Schofield's exclusive Pelee Club. Though Proctor did not always accept these invitations, because he preferred to return to Proctor, Vermont, to oversee his business interests, the two developed a real rapport. Schofield became an "assistant Secretary of War," and unlike during the Sheridan years, when the senior staff officer was appointed acting secretary, Schofield served as acting secretary in Proctor's absence.[13]

Schofield's relationships with subsequent secretaries—Stephen B. Elkins, who served from December 1891 to March 1893, and Daniel S. Lamont, who served from March 1893 to March 1897—were neither as close nor as produc-tive as that with Proctor, but they were far more cooperative and cordial than the relations between the other post–Civil War secretaries and commanding generals. Schofield's Democratic connections were especially useful in 1893, when Grover Cleveland returned to the White House.[14] The staff departments would continue to foment division, especially upon the arrival of a new secretary. In the most deferential of terms, Schofield would explain to the new official the history and use of various regulations and procedures, which the staff attempted to transgress. The most common source of contention was when staff officers, especially the adjutant general, issued orders to officers of the line in the name of the commanding general without coordinating with Schofield. A common Schofield refrain was, "I only ask that the chiefs of bureaus shall not presume to decide what may or may not be done in respect to the troops under my command, without my knowledge, and without the approval of the Secretary of War."[15]

Another common controversy was when staff chiefs sought to give orders to the staff officers detailed to the military departments without the knowledge, or over the objections, of the local commanding officers. Schofield defended the prerogatives of his subordinate commanders, not by asserting exclusive authority, but by insisting that these commanders needed to be consulted and, if they disagreed, be permitted to submit their case to the commanding general and the secretary of war. Sometimes when disputes broke out among the staff departments, Schofield would weigh in and none too subtly suggest the remedy of a chief of staff. This was bureaucratic trench warfare, and the staff chiefs discovered that they had a formidable opponent willing to do hand-to-hand, memo-to-memo combat.[16]

Schofield did not always win, but he established a new tone to the debate. For example, Proctor rejected Schofield's effort to restore the 1881 regulation that gave the commanding general some authority over the recruiting service. Nevertheless, Proctor still respectfully sought Schofield's advice and cooperation on the subject. At one point, Secretary Proctor demanded that the adjutant general produce a report describing how the department handled various correspondence, especially routing to the secretary and commanding general.[17] At other times, Schofield could not get a decision overturned, but his meticulous explanations alerted the secretary that his staff chiefs did not always give him the full story or accurately relate regulations and procedures. The quartermaster general, for example, misrepresented his authority to hire and fire departmental employees to the secretary until Schofield exposed the quartermaster's distortions in another lengthy memorandum. Secretary Elkins rather stubbornly refused to overturn the action, but the staff chief had put the secretary in an awkward position. Schofield kept up the pressure by reminding his subordinates to bring orders issued outside proper channels to his attention immediately so that he could make the staff pay a price for such acts.[18]

Although Schofield could be quite touchy over his Civil War record, he generally had the temperament for bureaucratic infighting, where one expects to have one's position challenged and, occasionally, have one's decisions overturned. He once gave valuable advice to General Wesley Merritt when someone complained to the president about one of the younger general's decisions. Detecting a "chip on his shoulder" when Schofield queried Merritt about the situation, the commanding general explained that he could not sustain his subordinates without the facts. In the American system, there was no way to prevent appeals from going to the secretary or the president. "We must be prepared to sustain by appropriate explanation whatever we may do, or else see it undone," Schofield wrote. "Do not presume we are questioning your motives when we make inquires—though different men will come to different judgments upon the same facts, . . . and you cannot expect that your actions will always be sustained." Schofield then reassured Merritt that his views would always be given their "full weight." Schofield realized that military command authority was never absolute and that the power to persuade was just as important.[19]

Despite this protracted bureaucratic warfare, the commanding general, the secretary of war, and the staff departments were able to cooperate on many beneficial reforms. The period between 1889 and 1891 offered a rare window of opportunity for military reform. The Republicans controlled the White House and both houses of Congress. With a reform-minded secretary leading the political charge, many small, but important, reforms were instituted. The commanding general and the adjutant general set aside their antagonisms sufficiently to overcome endemic internal opposition and advanced many long-sought reform measures related to the army's personnel system.

The adoption of lineal promotion was one of the early achievements. The promotion to the grades of first lieutenant and captain within one's regiment had created huge disparities in promotion rates, as some regiments produced greater rates of vacancy by resignation, promotion, or death. The advantages gained by earlier promotion to first lieutenant and captain carried over into field grade promotion (major, lieutenant colonel, and colonel), even though such promotions were made within the entire branch. Some officers, especially in the high-turnover African American regiments, were promoted years before their classmates. A policy that permitted officers with greater seniority and influence to transfer into other regiments, and thus displace those already there, was another source of great friction. For example, Second Lieutenant William H.

Carter, who would become Elihu Root's right-hand man in creating the General Staff, complained to the adjutant general that the transfer of the relatively junior captain Foulk to the 6th Cavalry would significantly affect promotion prospects in the regiment, especially his own.[20]

On October 1, 1890, Congress finally passed the bill providing for lineal promotion in the army. An immediate shift to the new system would have created too many winners and losers, so the bill applied to second lieutenants. This meant that most existing first lieutenants and captains kept their relative place, while the second lieutenants and each new cohort of officers would be promoted in their branch based on their commissioning date. Officers would lose their regimental affiliation, becoming known as a captain of cavalry, infantry, or artillery. This permitted the War Department to assign and reassign officers to regiments based on "the good of the service." What was lost in regimental esprit and loyalty was replaced with greater commitment to their branches. There was a greater sense of fairness about promotion. The army remained wedded to the idea of strict date of rank for promotion up to the rank of colonel. It would take more than a decade before a limited system of early promotion based on merit would overcome the suspicions of political favoritism. More decades would pass before the army established mechanisms for normalizing promotions among the various branches.[21]

Redfield Proctor later suggested that Schofield opposed including all ranks in the new system because his brother Charles was a first lieutenant. This is doubtful since Charles had been harmed by the regimental system. When promoted to captain in the low-turnover 2nd Cavalry in June 1890, Charles B. Schofield had already been superseded by thirty-one cavalry officers who had entered the army after his 1870 commissioning out of West Point. Charles's slow promotion to captain made his promotion to major in the cavalry practically impossible. Despite his brother's position and his service as his brother's aide, or maybe because of them, Charles Schofield was also never able to transfer to a staff corps and be promoted. In January 1901 a board declared him physically unfit for promotion, and he died of a heart attack in Cuba a month later—still a captain of cavalry. The more likely explanation for Schofield's opposition is that retroactive implementation would have created new winners and losers in the promotion process. Too often, Schofield had seen reform thwarted as those harmed by such legislation successfully appealed to their congressmen.[22]

Another component of the legislation was the requirement of a promotion examination up to the rank of major. These noncompetitive exams were intended to weed out those officers who were physically or intellectually unable to hold the next higher rank. By limiting examinations to promotion up to major, the measure was designed to motivate younger officers and not penalize the Civil War veterans approaching retirement. As with many such new policies, this one suffered from growing pains. The War Department appointed examination boards for each branch, but it gave them few specific instructions on the nature of the exam questions. Many officers complained that there should be officially designated questions and texts. This is exactly what Schofield sought to discourage. Aside from army regulations, Schofield did not want to specify official textbooks for the examinations. This was partly because such books were generally written and published privately, and he did not feel that favoritism in a commercial venture was appropriate. Additionally, once a book got on the list, it would be difficult to replace, and its selection would constitute an official endorsement of the author's views. More important, the commanding general did not want the exams to end up as simple memorization drills or to give the appearance that an officer "only need to study one book . . . to the exclusion of all others." Given the rapid pace of change, he did not want to be locked into specific topics and answers. He wanted officers to study and think critically about their profession, and he wanted the boards to have flexibility in formulating their professional questions.[23]

Lineal promotion and promotion examinations were part of a larger effort to regularize the officer appointment, promotion, and assignment system. In 1889 a new system was established for the appointment of second lieutenants. Graduates of the academy would continue to fill the first available positions, but the new rules gave enlisted men with more than two years' service preference for the next available vacancies over appointments from civil life. Both enlisted and civilian candidates had to pass rigorous physical and academic examinations.[24] These rules did not stop prominent men from attempting to get friends or sons appointed directly to the staff corps, but most regular officers were united in opposing such patronage appointments. As Schofield told one petitioner, lieutenants had served nearly twenty years looking for promotion, and "no officer of the army can afford to recommend a civilian for such an appointment in the Army." Proctor and his successors began to accept this policy, tactfully rebuffing much political importuning. The difficulty of obtaining an appointment in the peacetime army was a marked contrast with wartime experience, and thus to outsiders the army often appeared insular or isolated. It was a dramatic culture clash, where civilians advanced by merit, influence, or both, while professional soldiers patiently waited their turn.[25]

In April 1890 the War Department issued General Order No. 41, which established a formal "Efficiency Report" system for the army. This was the first attempt to evaluate the performance of the officer corps annually. The War

Department had established no mechanism for collecting data on the performance and special abilities of all officers. Since promotion was still based on date of rank, the initial purpose for the report was to provide decision makers with vital information needed to select officers for special assignments. As Proctor wrote in his annual report, "This information is required by the Secretary, and by superior military authorities in selecting officers for the varied, important, and often-times delicate duties to which they are frequently assigned."[26]

The original efficiency reports were divided into two parts: officer's individual report and commanding officer's report. The content evolved a bit, but the individual's report included the officer's duty and marital status, leave and detached service in the past year, personal courses of study, foreign language ability, business experience, books or articles published, and lectures given. The commander's report included a general statement of important routine duties, special duties, general conduct, professional zeal, condition and discipline of subordinates, capacity for command, special abilities, and mental, moral, and physical fitness. Though many senior officers still did not attach much value to the report, by 1895 the efficiency report experiment had become accepted as a permanent feature. As the size of the officer corps grew in the twentieth century, the efficiency report took on more importance. It slowly displaced the patronage system for nominations for special assignments, appointments to the staff, and the few merit promotions introduced in 1902. In 1905 President Theodore Roosevelt issued an executive order that henceforth promotion and assignment would be based on the efficiency records.[27]

The systematizing of "fairness" was one of the marks of the gradual professionalization of the army, and the introduction of efficiency reports was but one step in the regularization of promotion and assignments. Politics and personal favoritism still played a role in the appointments to staff departments, where opportunities for advancement were far greater, but increasingly both military and civilian leaders attempted to make the process more objective and impartial. Staff appointments became the de facto method of merit promotion. With promotion prospects in the line so limited, highly qualified officers fiercely competed for openings in the staff departments. For example, the redoubtable Joseph Sanger lost his first attempt for promotion to major in the inspector general's department to the equally renowned cavalryman Henry W. Lawton.[28]

Slowly Schofield and the other army leaders, both staff and line, forged a set of professional standards for merit, and through gentle pressure, these criteria gradually penetrated the largely politician-controlled selection process. While personal reputation and letters of recommendation remained central to the process, the adjutant general added other, more neutral data to the decision-making process. These included the officer's date of rank and relative rank in his regiment, corps, and army, as well as length of service with one's regiment, in schools, and on detached service. Regimental duty came to be seen as an important factor in any selection process—a kind of paying one's dues. Thus, the professional ethic emerged that staff jobs were reserved for the most intellectually energetic of the increasingly middle-aged junior officers.[29]

The much sought-after assignment as a general's aide also became a target for reformers in their efforts to normalize the selection process for prestigious appointments. The number and rank of aides depended on the general's rank, and they were selected at the general's discretion. Again, the professional ethic emerged that these and other coveted jobs should be rotated among the officer corps. In 1885 General Order No. 85 limited the assignment as a general's aide to four years. Unfortunately, this was an area where Schofield opposed reform. Schofield, like Sheridan, Howard, and other senior officers, resented limits on their choices of aides. They frequently used such positions to promote family members and longtime associates. Generals had learned to rely on the loyalty and judgment of these officers in carrying out often delicate and confidential duties.[30]

Schofield grudgingly admitted that there were two schools of thought on aides: one school assumed the purpose was to assist the general, while the other promoted the idea of grooming young officers for the future. Schofield groused, "Instead of an educated staff to assist him in the duties of Command, the principal duty of a general is to educate staff officers for some other undefined purpose." Schofield lost this battle. Aides and other principal staff officers would retain close personal connections to their generals, but a professional development ethic—a collective responsibility to train and groom the future leaders of the army—displaced the idea of patronage and personal loyalty.[31]

The aging officer corps had been a constant concern of Schofield's as commanding general. With Proctor's assistance, the Republican-controlled Congress passed a significant reform of the officer retirement system. Congress had provided for limited disability retirement in the early nineteenth century, but it had provided no general provision for nondisability army retirement until the advent of the Civil War. Suddenly, the government realized it had eighty-year-old officers still on active duty. New statutes gave the president the discretion to retire officers with forty-five years of service or at age sixty-two. An important revision in the 1870s permitted, at presidential discretion, retirement at thirty years of service with 75 percent of pay. However, Congress restricted the number on this retirement list to 400. In 1882 another revision created an unrestricted retirement list that contained those officers who retired with forty or more years of service or were mandatorily retired at age sixty-four. In his memoirs Schofield hailed the support of the senior generals for the mandatory retirement provision as an act of selflessness. Since Lieutenant General Sheridan was only fifty-one, everyone assumed that Hancock, Howard, and Schofield would never reach the position of commanding general. Only the unexpected deaths of Hancock, and then Sheridan, propelled Schofield to the position.[32]

The restricted and unrestricted retirement lists helped a bit, but by 1891 the Civil War generation was clogging the promotion system. Many officers had thirty or more years of service but could not retire because the restricted list was filled, with only a few vacancies or deaths a year. The army carried on active duty nearly sixty infirm officers awaiting retirement. Of the 400 on the restricted list, 143 had been retired for wounds, while nearly 100 were over age sixty-four, the mandatory retirement age. While many in the army wished to eliminate all the restrictions, the pragmatic Proctor suggested that Congress raise the limit to 450. He justified this increase, in part, because many on the list had been volunteer officers who had been transferred to the regular army in order to go on the retirement list. Congress balked at this idea, so Proctor then proposed shifting those on the restricted list to the unlimited retirement list upon reaching age sixty-four. Congress agreed to this adjustment, but it then reduced the restricted list to 350; as a result, the net new retirements were about fifty. Nevertheless, the provision provided continued relief over the next decade as the Civil War veterans reached age sixty-four.[33]

The Civil War weighed heavily on the U.S. Army, perhaps most symbolically in general officer promotions. Since promotion to general officer was based solely on the president's discretion with congressional ratification, politics played an important role. Yet, presidents and secretaries did not want to be seen as issuing promotions based solely on political calculations. In order to avoid such charges, dates of rank were very important. This, however, did not preclude young Indian fighters, such as Nelson Miles and Ranald MacKenzie, from promotion to brigadier general in the early 1880s. As the Civil War generation approached retirement age, pressure increased to restore generals' stars to these heroes. While Schofield's recommendations carefully balanced past versus future service, he clearly leaned toward rewarding his old comrades before their mandatory retirement. As he told President Harrison, "A departure from the rule of seniority in rank may, at least sometimes, be made in favor of seniority in age or length of service, so that two or three officers, instead of only one, may receive the reward due to long and faithful service."[34] Ironically, former Civil War generals like Grant, Hayes, or Harrison were more apt to promote based on future service. By contrast, Grover Cleveland, who did not serve in the military, tended to reward past service and promote based on date of rank.[35]

One attempt at helping old friends blew up in Schofield's face. In 1890 cavalry colonel Eugene A. Carr, who had been a comrade and business partner of Schofield, wrote the commanding general that he feared he would be passed over for promotion to brigadier general because he did not have the political influence of officers like Miles. He also feared his enemies were spreading rumors about his drinking. Schofield tried to reassure his old friend that he had more friends than he thought. In 1892, with the retirement of August V. Kautz, Schofield recommended four officers for promotion, all of whom had "rendered distinguished service in high command": William P. Carlin, Eugene A. Carr, Peter T. Swaine, and Frank Wheaton. The ranking placed the older officers first.[36]

Since President Harrison preferred to promote younger officers, Schofield arranged to have the president promote Carr, who had date of rank over Carlin, and then have Carr retired in order to promote Carlin and the others. When Carr discovered that he would be retired early to make way for Carlin, he cried foul and created such a political commotion that Harrison could not forcibly retire him before his administration ended. Carr criticized Schofield, who had done so much to secure the promotion. A stunned Schofield had to inform William Carlin, who had shown such kindness to Cadet Schofield so many years before, that he would be unable to get him promoted before retirement. Fortunately, the new president Cleveland stepped in and promoted Carlin a scant six months before retirement. Upon Carlin's retirement, Schofield informed him that he owed his promotion to the president. Early in the war, Carlin had drilled a company of young men in Buffalo, a company that had included Grover Cleveland, who had not forgotten his instructor.[37]

The politics of promotion at the highest level was no less difficult. Congress had created the ranks of lieutenant general and general just for Ulysses S. Grant. When Grant was elected president, Sherman had the stature to receive the rank of general without much difficulty. Sheridan's promotion to lieutenant general over more senior major generals like George Thomas and George Meade had created some bitterness but reflected Grant's desires and power. When Sherman retired in 1883, the rank of general was discontinued. Sheridan possessed neither the military stature nor the political connections of Sherman. He had also incurred the enmity of southern Democrats. In 1888, when Sheridan was on his deathbed, Congress relented and promoted him to general.[38]

With Sheridan's death both the ranks of general and lieutenant general lapsed. In the early years of Schofield's tenure as commanding general, his friends made several attempts to restore the rank of lieutenant general. Schofield did not generate the same southern hostility as Sheridan, but many southerners in Congress still rejected the need for a lieutenant general. Even some north-erners thought Schofield did not deserve to be elevated to the rank of George Washington and Winfield Scott. Other old grudges resurfaced. Democratic senator John M. Palmer, recalling his relief as commander of XIV Corps for refusing to take orders from Schofield, opposed the bill. The legislation's prospects were further diminished by the fact that the bill proposed to establish the rank permanently, rather than simply promote Schofield for his past ser-vices. Feigning concern for economy, the House attempted to reduce the num-ber of major generals in exchange for instituting the lieutenant general. Even those who believed that Schofield's service merited the honor were put off by automatically granting this honor to future commanding generals. However, as with most army reforms, lack of congressional interest was the bill's greatest handicap.[39]

Despite this problem, Schofield supported the permanent rank because he believed it was fitting for the commanding general to have a higher rank than the other major generals of the army. It would enhance the professional status of future commanding generals and the overall status of the army. It would also permit another officer to be promoted to major general. One of the most insistent supporters of this approach was Major General Nelson Miles, who, given his age and seniority, was most likely to succeed Schofield and, hence, benefit from the new permanent rank. By 1894, Schofield realized that if he were ever to be promoted to lieutenant general, it would be a personal promo-tion. Miles, meanwhile, continued to urge Schofield and, more important, his supporters in Congress to hold out for the permanent rank. This division nearly scuttled Schofield's chances yet again.[40]

Schofield, the wily bureaucratic infighter, turned the argument around on Miles and his allies. In a memo to Secretary of War Daniel Lamont, Schofield argued that if he, as the last Civil War army commander, were passed over without promotion, the precedent would be set to pass over Miles. Thus, it was in Miles's interest to have his friends join with Schofield's friends to support this temporary revival of the lieutenant general rank. Furthermore, if Schofield were promoted, his friends would join with Miles's friends in Congress to support Miles in the future. In February 1895 Congress finally passed a bill to revive temporarily the rank of lieutenant general for Schofield. On February 5, 1895, after serving nearly twenty-six years as a major general, John M. Schofield became the sixth lieutenant general of the United States Army.[41]

In the progressive tradition, the Proctor-Schofield partnership also produced some notable victories for improving the lives of enlisted soldiers.[42] Central to the effort was the concern within the army over desertion. Desertion had always been a problem, but even with a tremendous growth in the population, the 25,000-man army had considerable difficulty gaining and retaining its recruits. In the early 1870s the army desertion rate averaged a staggering 30 percent of the total enlisted strength, and in the 1880s it remained more than 15 percent. In 1889 it still hovered at a worrisome 11 percent. Secretary Proctor and Schofield, again with considerable support and cooperation from the adjutants general, adopted a three-prong approach to the problem: improve law enforcement, change recruiting and enlistment policies, and improve soldier life. By 1892, their reforms had cut the desertion rate in half to 5.5 percent. By Schofield's retirement in 1895, the desertion rate, aided by an economic recession, was further reduced to 4.6 percent.[43]

Schofield, in his 1889 report, noted that desertion was most common not during periods of intense campaigning but during the long stretches of garrison duty, when the men would become bored, frustrated, or simply discontented with routine post duties. He advocated measures to weed out those who were unsuited for army life early in their recruitment in order to avoid the crime of desertion. Schofield also stressed that company commanders could not leave the discipline of their units to their first sergeants and that they must balance concern for the troops with necessary discipline and efficiency. Finally, Schofield concluded that while penalties need not increase, the apprehension of deserters had to improve if the laws were to provide any deterrent. He recommended granting rewards for civil authorities who arrested and returned deserters. In another memorandum to the secretary, Schofield objected to amnesty for deserters, lamenting the general lack of stigma among the civilian population. He was concerned that a casual attitude toward desertion would carry over in time of war or would translate into soldiers' identification with labor. He contended that it was better to have "15,000 reliable men than 25,000 unreliable" men, and he insisted that the purpose of punishment was not to keep deserters in the army but to deter a deserter class from offering to enlist.[44]

Based on the data provided by the adjutant general, neither location nor climate had any significant influence on desertion rates, though Proctor observed the relatively high rate of the light artillery and the low rate of the "colored regiments." He concluded that reasons for desertion were numerous, including disappointment in service life, restlessness under discipline, poor pay and food, dissipation, and ill treatment. Proctor also stressed the importance of the company commander in deterring desertion: "Every captain should be to his company as a father, and should treat his family, as his children." Proctor also urged improvements in the recruiting service, including regimental recruiting teams, greater recruiting in rural areas, and the assignment of soldiers from the same communities to the same units. He proposed a significant increase in noncommissioned officer (NCO) pay, post schools for the soldiers, shorter enlistments and reenlistments, revision of the military justice system, and the withholding of part of a soldier's pay until the end of enlistment in order to discourage desertion.[45]

In 1890 Congress passed several acts reforming the military justice system. The legislation created new guidelines for punishment under the Articles of War, and the War Department made greater efforts to reduce the variance in punishments from department to department. Another statute created new summary courts to try and then punish petty offenses. This sped up trials and significantly reduced the amount of time spent in the stockade for relatively minor breeches of discipline. The act also rather paradoxically placed a statute of limitations on the crime of desertion. The enforcement of desertion laws had always been difficult, especially in times of peace. Few jurisdictions, particularly in the West, wanted to aid the army in apprehending deserters, especially men who had deserted long ago and had become productive members of the community. By limiting the enforcement span and authorizing the arrest of deserters by civil authorities, the army leadership hoped laws would have greater deterrent effect.[46]

In the June 16, 1890, Act to Prevent Desertion, Congress approved many of Proctor's and Schofield's suggestions. The new law permitted the army to withhold four dollars per month during a soldier's first year of enlistment. This both deterred desertion and partially defrayed recruiting costs should the soldier desert in the first year. Though Schofield and Proctor had both lobbied for three-year enlistments, Congress left the term at five years. However, a soldier could buy his way out of his enlistment after one year, and he would be entitled to a free discharge after three years of faithful service, if desired. These changes afforded soldiers many honorable ways out of the service. The army, however, did not universally hail these new rules. Many officers and noncommissioned officers preferred long-term enlistments and complained that too many recruits bought their way out. Another, better-received provision of the act increased the soldiers' vegetable ration, which helped reduce the need for troops' gardens and the general discontent this chore entailed.[47]

The two reformers were greatly disappointed that the proposal for raising the pay and status of NCOs failed. Enlisted pay remained substantially unchanged from 1872 to 1908. Proctor was especially interested in encouraging a better-educated and more ambitious class of recruit into the army. Although he failed to raise NCO pay, he did open opportunities for educated and enterprising enlisted men to obtain commissions. Proctor and Schofield thus anticipated the emphasis on the education and social uplift of the lower classes that was promoted by the Progressives of the early twentieth century.

In one area Proctor and Schofield had a falling-out. Proctor, in order to create a younger, more active, enlisted force, restricted the reenlistment of older privates. Schofield, more attuned to traditions of the old army, where promotion was slow but demotion could be swift, objected that this restriction would mean that many loyal men would not be able to retire. Later, as a senator, Proctor pushed a bill through Congress that prohibited the reenlistment of privates with more than ten years' service or who were over thirty-five years old. The army protested en masse, and Congress rescinded the law within eighteen months. Given the low pay and poor conditions, the army was very fortunate to have such able noncommissioned officers. With many Civil War veterans, the NCO corps was one of the army's little-regarded strengths.[48]

Schofield and Proctor instituted many other reforms to improve the soldier's life that would shape army service for years to come. In February 1889 the post school system was expanded, and every first- or second-term soldier without a basic education was required to attend. "Modern advances in the art and science of war," wrote Schofield, "require a much higher education, not only of officers, but of all ranks in the Army." This was the beginning of the army's continuing embrace of soldier education, which made the U.S. military one of the largest educational systems in the world. In March 1889 Sunday inspections and parades were abolished. Troops would be inspected on Saturday morning and were then off duty the rest of the day and all of Sunday, except for guard or other such details. Enshrined in a presidential order, this schedule persisted well into the next century. In November 1889 Schofield and Proctor also eliminated the 9:00 P.M. tattoo, when soldiers were forced to stand formation for a bed-check roll call.[49]

Another important reform, undertaken in February 1889 as Secretary Endicott left office, was the replacement of the post sutler, or trader, with the post exchange, or canteen. The sutler system had afforded privileged operators a highly profitable monopoly at military posts, and it naturally bred corruption, high prices, and shoddy goods. Proctor continued the Endicott initiative, and in the 1890s army-run exchanges, or canteens, were created for each post. The canteens sold alcohol and sundries, and the profits were plowed back into comforts for the soldiers. Proctor even persuaded Congress to appropriate $50,000 to construct buildings to house the canteens, recreation rooms, and gymnasiums. The canteens were hugely successful. By 1891, eighty post canteens transacted $1.1 million a year in sales, with a profit of approximately $250,000. Whether they sold alcohol or not, Schofield saw the exchanges, or "clubs," as an important social institution for the enlisted men that needed to be carefully fostered.[50]

The institutionalization of military education was the most important late nineteenth-century development in the professionalization of the United States Army. General William T. Sherman had begun the enterprise with the formation of the Military Service Institution of the United States in 1879 and the establishment of the School of Application for Infantry and Cavalry at Fort Leavenworth in 1881. In the 1890s the Leavenworth school would be transformed under brilliant instructors such as Arthur Wagner, Eben Swift, and John Morrison. The school became a first-rate institution, where ambitious officers were eager to go for the study of the theory, art, and practice of their profession. By the time of Schofield's retirement, the army had four postgraduate schools: the Artillery School at Fort Monroe, Virginia (established 1824, revived 1867); the Engineer School at Willets Point, New York (1866); the Infantry and Cavalry School at Fort Leavenworth, Kansas (1881); and the School for Drill and Practice for Cavalry and Light Artillery at Fort Riley, Kansas (1887). In addition to enhancing the quality and prestige of the existing schools, Schofield sought to establish permanent congressional funding for the instructional activities of these institutions, which had been originally formed by executive order and supported out of regular appropriations.[51]

Schofield had made his own contribution to the establishment of postgraduate schools with the creation of the school for the cavalry and light artillery at Fort Riley. Throughout his time as commanding general, he kept his eye on the school. He needed to pay attention in part because as the school gained status, artillery regimental commanders acceded to the requests of aging captains to be assigned there with their batteries. For a school that stressed drill and practice, most artillery captains were too old for the duties required. Moreover, they could not form the cadre of light artillery officers whom Schofield hoped the school would build for the future.[52]

Schofield also had to watch out because as the school at Leavenworth became more prestigious, the commanders at Fort Riley sought to emulate it. Schofield had to remind the school leadership repeatedly that theirs was a practical, not theoretical, school. Artillery officers received their theoretical training at West Point and the Artillery School, while cavalry officers received similar instruction at Leavenworth. Whole units, not simply individual officers, were rotated through Fort Riley for instruction. Part of the problem was that the term "school" did not fully capture the purpose of the institution. A more accurate term might have been "training center." Schofield envisioned a program that ran units through an "endless variety" of "field exercises and combined maneuvers."[53]

Another major educational initiative of the Sherman era was the formation of the Military Service Institution of the United States, a professional association, in 1879, only one year after the creation of the American Bar Association. This organization, through its regular meetings and especially through its journal, was one of the most important vehicles for professional development in the late nineteenth century. The institution also inspired the creation of other professional associations and journals: *Cavalry Journal* (founded in 1885), the *Journal of the U.S. Artillery* (founded in 1892), and *Infantry Association Journal* (association founded in 1894, journal begun in 1904). The *Journal of the Military Service Institution* published a remarkable array of articles on a wide variety of subjects: tactical and strategic questions, historical and technological issues, and foreign and domestic military affairs. Contributors included junior lieutenants, as well as senior officers such as Sherman, Schofield, and Howard. The association's regular meetings in New York featured the reading of professional papers and commentary before distinguished officers and prominent civilians.[54]

Schofield played a prominent role in the organization throughout his life. He gave the inaugural address for the institution on January 11, 1879. In this address Schofield emphasized the increasing complexity of military affairs, a "diversified knowledge" that had grown beyond the mastery of a single individual. Just as scientists built on the work of colleagues, officers needed to share their experience and expertise. He noted the complex variables of military problems and the need for "never-ceasing" study by the officers of the regular army. The professional officer must study his craft and not simply rely on the discipline and courage of his soldiers.[55]

Though it was nominally a private organization, the senior officers of the army closely directed the affairs of the institution. Headquartered in New York City, the institution was headed by the commander of the Division of the Atlantic, Winfield Scott Hancock. When Schofield succeeded Hancock in command of the Division of the Atlantic, he was also elected the institution's president. Schofield considered the position so important that he retained the presidency during his entire tenure as commanding general. Of special significance to the army leadership was the selection of a topic for the annual Gold Medal essay competition. These questions offer an excellent snapshot of the interests and concerns of the senior leadership. Though some of the subjects focused on relatively narrow military topics, most were very broad policy questions that contained clear political implications.[56]

As the army consolidated itself on fewer and better-constructed posts with larger numbers of officers and soldiers, training and education programs could be enhanced. Schofield expanded the number of professional periodicals available through post libraries, including many foreign language journals.[57] The army created post schools to provide both basic and more advanced education to the soldiers. For the officers, Schofield ordered in October 1891 the formation of "post lyceums," where officers would present papers and discuss professional topics. The lyceum had been a popular vehicle for self-education before the Civil War. Schofield hoped to revive the tradition, but his real model was the Military Service Institution. Schofield's order directed that the lyceums operate four months of each year, generally in the winter, and that each officer write and present a paper on a professional topic to his fellow officers.[58]

Schofield's directive that officers write articles for presentation and publication was a way of shifting their attention from the mundane regimental chores of a peacetime army to the skills of higher command and the challenges of modern warfare. Schofield was wise enough to realize that he could not dragoon the entire officer corps into intellectual and literary pursuits. He acknowledged that he had no intention to condemn or embarrass the many gallant older officers who had not enjoyed early educational opportunities. His real targets were the younger officers, in order to raise the army gradually to a "high standard of professional acquirement." Unsurprisingly, some of the professional debates encouraged within the lyceum spilled over into public discussions of military policy. For example, one captain presented a paper that criticized the Proctor enlistment and desertion policies, which was then highlighted in the *Army and Navy Journal* in the campaign to repeal the law.[59]

Schofield's aspirations for stimulating a high level of intellectual analysis and debate were never fully realized. Schofield looked on the lyceums as forums for original thought, a collegial body where junior officers could impress their seniors and seniors could lend their experience and judgment to juniors. By 1894, other army leaders recommended that the classes should be segregated by rank and that there should be less latitude in the selection of topics. Slowly, the open professional forums were transformed into more prosaic, but no less necessary, post training programs for junior officers, with a prescribed list of subjects, closely related to the responsibilities of officers of their grade and branch. This transformation accelerated after the Spanish-American War with the great influx of new officers. The average lieutenant no longer had more than a decade of service. The complexity of modern warfare and military administration had generated the need for continual practical training, as well as higher levels of education.[60]

Along with postgraduate and post schools, another major component of the expansion of military education in this period was the assignment of military officers to civilian colleges. In 1888 the army had forty officers detailed to civilian colleges and universities to provide military instruction. By 1895, there were nearly a hundred. Schofield considered such duty the "most important detached service which officers of the army can render in time of peace."[61]

One aim of the program was to provide military instruction for those who might become officers in the National Guard. However, a broader goal was to "to give elementary military instruction and discipline necessary to prepare volunteer troops for service in the field in time of war." The army leadership also saw instructor duty at colleges as a way to promote closer relations between military and civilian institutions. The instructors contributed to military awareness among the population, and the position gave army officers an opportunity for intellectual development. Though land grant colleges were the first to receive officers detailed for military instruction, elite private universities soon requested such assignments as well. Harvard and Yale were eager for military instructors, but these institutions wanted practical drill kept to a minimum so instructors could concentrate on "the great military problems that have or may effect [*sic*] the future of the U.S."[62]

Schofield got assistance from various veterans and patriotic organizations in advocating general military education. Although Congress and the public saw little need to expand the regular army, the volunteer tradition remained strong. John Logan's *Volunteer Soldier of America*, in addition to attacking the West Point aristocracy, celebrated the citizen-soldier ideal and advocated military instruction in public schools, colleges, and universities. The Grand Army of the Republic (GAR), the Union veterans' organization, encouraged military drill as a patriotic duty and military service with citizenship. Schofield argued that just as universal education was indispensable to universal suffrage, military education was essential to citizenship. Secretary of War Daniel Lamont also hoped to expand the college instruction program to high schools. The martial nostalgia inspired by the GAR and the Civil War veterans' reunions helped spread an interest in military education, but the efforts remained largely sporadic and voluntary. They did not translate into a dramatic increase in the size of the regular army or the militia or result in the creation of the organized military reserve units, as was taking place in Europe.[63]

While both the GAR and Schofield stressed the citizen soldier and the need for military education among the general population, there were important differences. John Logan and many in the GAR still clung to the idea of volunteer officers leading the volunteer armies, whereas Schofield and the regular officers saw themselves as playing the principal role in the training and leading of American forces. Schofield's emphasis of broad officer education was based on the expectation that relatively junior officers would command major units in times of war. In anticipation of such a temporary exodus of regular officers to volunteer units, he even recommended that the War Department plan to assign volunteer officers to regular regiments as replacements.[64] Thus, without directly challenging the ideal of the citizen soldier, Schofield and his colleagues were slowly, cautiously, making the case for the importance of military expertise and professionalism. Instead of the federal army that fought the Civil War, Schofield and his fellow military Progressives sought to lay the foundation of a national army in time of war.

When John M. Schofield assumed "command" of the army in 1888, the army was administratively, geographically, and generationally fragmented. The internal friction over regimental promotion and opportunities for detached duty only exacerbated the deep divisions between the line and the staff. A lucky few attained comfortable assignments in headquarters, colleges, or foreign travel, but the bulk of the army remained scattered in dozens of small, western posts. The post–Civil War officer corps was entering middle age, yet the Civil War generation still blocked its path to promotion. Although substantive structural reform remained seemingly as remote as ever, Schofield was able to achieve many more modest reforms. By his retirement, Schofield made substantial progress in reintegrating and revitalizing the army. Older veterans were treated with consideration, while the younger generation was given encouragement and hope.

There were three important factors in Schofield's success as commanding general. First, Schofield benefited from important external developments. The end of the Indian Wars enabled the army to consolidate into larger posts. He also benefited from technological changes that focused renewed, if insufficient, attention on coastal defenses. America's increasing economic power and global trade produced greater interest in military affairs, though few concrete programs. Uptonian ideas of a professional army backed by a national reserve were too radical for the average American. However, proposals for postgraduate military schools, professional associations and journals, training exercises, military instructors at colleges, and cooperation with the National Guard did garner increasing public support.

Second, Schofield's accommodation to the secretary of war ended fruitless conflict and forged a partnership for reform. With Schofield orchestrating the military arguments and Proctor directing the lobbying effort, they managed to get through a temporarily Republican-controlled Congress some much needed, though not very glamorous, legislation. The secretary–commanding general partnership presented a more united front in implementing a major post realignment policy. The two men were able, with the help of the staff departments, to reduce the role that political patronage played in military affairs by establishing more "objective" criteria.

Third, Schofield displayed the political shrewdness and sensitivity so necessary for a general in a democratic republic. Sherman's hostility to politics inhibited his ability to push his ideas through the War Department and Congress. Schofield had no such aversion. He understood that politics and military affairs were inevitably intertwined, and if civilians were to accept, or even defer, to military expertise, the soldiers must show respect and understanding for the civilian perspective. His low-key manner and moderate demeanor made his lobbying more subtle and more effective. His willingness to write memo after memo to persuade the secretaries and others, rather than asserting his right of command, not only showed great perseverance but also served as a model of a truly "modern major general."

Arresting stagnation, especially intellectual stagnation, was an abiding concern for Schofield. Lyceums, college assignments, and foreign duty were ways of motivating and rewarding energetic young officers. Schofield's institution of lineal promotion, officer evaluation reports, promotion exams, and assignment rotation was part of his efforts to instill a sense of fairness and hope in an often dispirited officer corps. These seemingly modest reforms were important steps in the reintegration of the army: to raise the sights and the standards of the officer corps, to set aside insular concerns and think about the army and the nation as a whole, and to create a professional ethic. Schofield's small, incremental reforms kept hope alive and laid the groundwork for future reform. In the face of apathy or hostility to major reforms, Schofield realized that small advances still gained ground.

(FOURTEEN)

In Retirement and in Retrospect

During Schofield's tenure as commanding general, major structural reform remained as elusive as in the 1870s. Yet, except for a much-needed reform of the War Department, the army had managed to achieve a certain internal consensus on major reorganization issues. This general agreement included the importance of strengthening the army, revitalizing coastal defenses, restructuring the artillery, and forming three-battalion regiments. Even with army consensus, all these would have to wait for a war to provide the necessary urgency to produce political approval. In retirement John M. Schofield played a supporting role in these efforts, making numerous appearances before Congress and other groups to discuss military policy. His final role in the spotlight came in April 1903, when at Secretary Elihu Root's instigation, Schofield helped lead the way for a major restructuring of the army command system.

On September 29, 1895, Lieutenant General John M. Schofield retired from the army. The sixty-four-year-old general must have had mixed feelings after having served in the military for over forty-six years. Though he publicly supported the mandatory retirement law, there are hints in some of his draft papers that he would have welcomed a law that extended the age restriction for the commanding general. His reluctance can also be seen in his occasional irascible behavior prior to retirement. During his last grand inspection tour of the army in the summer of 1895, some post commanders did not give the appropriate respect to the "lame duck" commanding general. In one incredible instance, Colonel Caleb H. Carleton, 8th Cavalry, at Fort Meade, South Dakota, kept General Schofield and his party cooling their heels, while the colonel reviewed the troops of the post without the commanding general. For this breach of protocol, Schofield relieved Carleton as he left the post. The secretary of war later restored Carleton to command when Carleton explained that one of his regimental officers had wrongly informed him that Schofield had not wanted to review the troops personally.[1]

In another instance, Schofield ordered the arrest of retired captain George

Armes. On September 27, 1895, two days before Schofield's retirement, Armes attempted to see Schofield, and when rebuffed, he had a highly insulting letter passed to Schofield, who was also that day the acting secretary of war. On reading the letter, Schofield ordered Armes's arrest and confinement at Washington Barracks. Schofield and Armes had had a stormy history over the captain's attempts to secure a promotion to brevet lieutenant colonel for actions in an Indian engagement in 1869. Schofield had rejected Armes's brevet based, in part, on the testimony of the African American soldiers whom Armes had commanded, and Armes vilified Schofield for taking their word over his. Armes had had a checkered career in the army, and Schofield's patience with this embarrassingly troublesome officer had run out.[2]

These incidents, however, only slightly marred Schofield's final days in the army, and he retired to general plaudits for his service to the nation. Schofield could take pride in having helped to foster what several historians have called a renaissance. Without major structural reform or significant increases in either strength or funding, the army had repositioned itself to face the modern world. Without repudiating the aging veterans of the Civil War, Schofield had intellectually revitalized the army. While celebrating its accomplishments in the Civil War and Indian Wars, the officer corps was conversant in international military developments. The professional education system and the new personnel policies had been largely accepted and institutionalized. Schofield's personal success became most revealing in the one area that he could not institutionalize— the relationship between the commanding general and the secretary of war.[3]

Schofield and his young wife remained in Washington, D.C., as Schofield focused on writing his memoirs. A year after retirement, the Schofields had a daughter, whom they named Georgia after her mother. Within a few years, however, Schofield gave up his Washington residence and adopted a semi-nomadic existence, spending the summers in Bar Harbor, Maine, and his winters in St. Augustine, Florida. Even before he retired, the general had become a regular visitor to these vacation spots for the elite. In St. Augustine the Schofields were the frequent dinner guests of George Pullman and John Doane, and in Bar Harbor they dined with Grenville Dodge and Daniel Lamont. In addition to fishing, one of Schofield's favorite pastimes was playing poker with his friends. His grandchildren soon learned to watch closely for his return because if he had won, he was usually in a very generous mood.[4]

As for public life, Schofield had toyed with the possibility of political office. Even before his retirement, he had sent out political feelers about becoming the senator for his former home state of Illinois. Writing John Doane, Schofield proclaimed, "I have never ceased to be a democrat, not even during the period of

Civil War and reconstruction; where opposing ideas, politics, and authority were most dominant." Schofield did not want to "enter into any partisan contest," and the office of senator "would be acceptable only as practically the spontaneous gift of my state."[5] There were occasional rumors of a presidential nomination, which Schofield modestly pooh-poohed. Though Schofield dreamed of being "awarded" high political office, he did not really want to run for office. However, the time for electing a "nonpartisan" military hero in the mold of Grant and Sherman was past. Moreover, as a Cleveland Democrat, Schofield was philosophically at odds with the drift of his party. His memoirs delivered a ringing endorsement of the gold standard, while his party standard-bearer, William Jennings Bryan, was leading the crusade against the "Cross of Gold."[6]

In retirement the lieutenant general continued his crusade for coastal defense, primarily as president of the "Coast Defense and Harbor Improvement Convention," a combination of political, military, and business interest groups located chiefly in coastal states, which advocated greater attention to coastal fortifications. The Sino-Japanese War in 1894–95 was an eye-opening example of what a small but technologically superior power could do to a large country. In the 1890s the United States had diplomatic disputes with many European powers, including Britain, Germany, France, and Spain. International commerce had always been important to the United States, and it increased in the late nineteenth century due to the dramatic rise of American agricultural and industrial productivity. Expanding American commercial interests clashed with European imperialism, inspiring suggestions that the United States needed to establish its own colonies, or at least acquire outposts and coaling stations to secure its overseas interests.[7]

While the navy had many officers, such as Admiral Alfred T. Mahan, who advocated a strong overseas presence for the United States, most army officers were more cautious. The army's focus on coastal defense seemed a prudent and conservative response to foreign controversies. The realignment of army posts also reflected a renewed interest in the security of the northern and southern borders of the United States. During one dispute with Britain, Secretary of War Daniel Lamont dispatched Schofield to review the northern defenses. Concerning overseas commitments, Schofield's often elliptical foreign policy pronouncements tended to see the United States as a symbol of freedom and democratic values, rather than its adopting some missionary commitment to bringing those values to the world. He believed in exercising America's growing power with circumspection. As commanding general, Schofield had been embarrassed to prepare an estimate for a possible war with Chile in 1892. He likened it to a man beating a small dog with a club.[8]

One overseas issue in which Schofield took a continuing interest was Hawaii. In 1872 the War Department had dispatched Schofield and engineer officer Colonel B. S. Alexander to accompany Rear Admiral A. M. Pennock on a military survey of the Hawaiian Islands. Schofield and Alexander reported to the War Department that while the port of Honolulu was too small and open for proper defense, the nearby Pearl River estuary would make an excellent and readily defensible harbor and naval base. Since the new king Lunalilo opposed annexation, Schofield proposed that the United States gain rights to a Pearl River naval base in exchange for a reciprocity treaty that would give Hawaiian sugar free access to American markets.[9]

Twenty years later, in 1893, American plantation owners, who chafed under the Hawaiian monarchy, overthrew it, established a republic, and sought annexation to the United States. Schofield had thought that the Hawaiian monarchy would gradually disappear as an anachronism and that annexation was inevitable. Consequently, Schofield was not opposed to annexation per se, but he had developed a strong, almost paternal interest in the Hawaiian people. Representatives of the Hawaiian queen Liliuokalani appealed to Schofield for support. The commanding general entreated President Benjamin Harrison that whatever he decided, he should protect the rights of the native Hawaiians.[10] Incoming president Grover Cleveland decided against annexation, and the issue waned until Republican president William McKinley signed a new annexation agreement and sent it to Congress in 1897. During the debate over the treaty, opponents dragged Schofield into the argument by publishing a pamphlet that falsely portrayed Schofield as an opponent of annexation. Schofield responded by sending a letter to Senator John Morgan, which reiterated the strategic value of Pearl Harbor and concluded that the time had come to accept annexation as Hawaii's "manifest destiny." Schofield concluded, "A little State like Hawaii can not stand alone among the great nations, all of whom covet her incomparable harbor."[11]

Schofield, in another letter to a friend, compared Hawaii to Missouri in 1861, when keeping the territory in the Union was more important than what a majority of the people might have thought. He also noted that statehood had been imposed on the Dakotas regardless of what the Sioux thought about it. In his memoirs Schofield used Hawaii to raise the issues of colonial and military governments. Schofield suggested that small island outposts, with their heterogeneous populations, might not be suitable for immediate self-government or the kind of territorial governments Americans traditionally employed. He argued that despite the bad reputation military government had gained during Reconstruction, it was humane and, citing the example of the Modocs, much more considerate of the rights of native peoples. To Schofield, this "colonialist" rationale was not based on "survival of the fittest" but the "law of Christianity," "of civilization," "of wisdom." It was the obligation of the stronger to protect the weaker. Schofield's optimistic views about the humane and beneficial aspects of military government, or nation-building in a more modern parlance, would be severely challenged in the next few decades in America's imperialist "fling."[12]

After the Spanish-American War in 1898, the United States took control of most of what was left of the Spanish Empire. The new American "empire" transformed the nation's foreign relations and provided the impetus for the transformation of the U.S. Army. The war, while short and successful, exposed the woefully archaic American military system. Once the United States declared war on April 25, 1898, the American people, and soon the president, were demanding immediate military action. Admiral George Dewey's overwhelming victory at Manila Bay on May 1 only added the sense of urgency to get on with the war. Unlike the major European powers, the United Sates had no plans in place for an immediate transition to war.[13]

Under the austere budgets of the last three decades, the army lacked the arms, ammunition, clothing, and equipment for a large army. The National Guard was not sufficiently trained, equipped, or in some cases motivated to assume the role of a reserve for the small regular army. Despite some sporadic articles about overseas military deployments in the military journals, there were no regulations and no doctrine for overseas deployments. Even as war loomed, Congress wrestled with contentious proposals over the size, composition, and sources of the army to fight the war. Battles raged over expanding the regular army, creating national volunteers, and calling out the National Guard, even as the United States declared war on Spain. Compounding these problems was the chaos within the War Department. The friction between Secretary of War Russell A. Alger and General Nelson Miles became outright hostility. Alger, though a Civil War veteran, lacked the expertise to coordinate the staff departments, which were habituated to independent action. Finally, rapid and repeated changes in mobilization plans and military strategy overwhelmed the small department staffs and hastily assembled staffs of the subordinate commands.[14]

As the war clouds gathered in March 1898, John Schofield was appointed the "commander" of the National Military Reserve in New York, an ostensibly private organization that was created to promote the formation of national—as opposed to state-based—volunteer units. Other officials of the organization included Generals James Longstreet, O. O. Howard, G. M. Dodge, Joseph Wheeler, and Alexander McCook. Accepting the post, Schofield predicted in an interview that the campaign in Cuba would not be a long one, with the navy and Cuban insurgents doing most of the fighting. More interestingly, the lieutenant general discounted the problems of invading Cuba in the summer, indicating that with the "military quarantines now required, there would be little danger from yellow fever." He asserted that Spain should disabuse itself of the notion that the United States would not invade in June or July. Schofield may have only intended this statement to convince Spain to accept American ultimatums.[15]

At the end of March 1898, on the way from St. Augustine to New York, Schofield stopped in Washington, D.C., to get Alger's support for his project. A few days later Schofield, at Alger's suggestion, returned and visited President McKinley. The president asked the retired lieutenant general's advice on a number of questions and then requested that Schofield confer with him daily at one o'clock. Over the next few weeks, Schofield consulted with the president daily. His relations with Secretary Alger, however, soon deteriorated. After a few visits, Alger's attitude grew ever more chilly and remote, and soon Schofield stopped coming to see him. The president remained cordial, but eventually he showed little interest in continuing the private discussions with Schofield, instead including him in larger meetings. The oversensitive Schofield took this as a sign that he was no longer needed and announced his decision to return home. McKinley asked him to stay in Washington; and, apparently surprised to learn that Schofield had such poor relations with Alger, he attempted to smooth the matter over. However, Schofield sensed that he was not really needed or wanted, so he left for Bar Harbor on June 4.[16]

Schofield's problems as an advisor to the McKinley administration appear to have several sources. First, Alger and McKinley's attitude about Schofield's successor, Nelson Miles, may have tainted the administration's relations with Schofield. Miles, barely subordinate with superior military officers, refused to subordinate himself to the secretary of war. As a result, the old friction between the secretary and commanding general returned with a vengeance. It was Miles's reactionary attitude, as much as Schofield's progressive example, that finally impelled War Department reform. Moreover, Schofield's presence aggravated the commanding general, who never met with him. Schofield also hoped to be something more than an unpaid civilian advisor. He suggested to McKinley that Congress grant the president authority to recall to duty retired soldiers, and he was angry when he learned that Alger opposed the idea.

Next, Schofield and Alger had some pronounced disagreements about the abilities of some of the senior officers in the regular army. The question of officers may have been further complicated by the fact that both McKinley and

Alger spent a great deal of the time making officer appointments. The Spanish-American War would be the last in which politicians appointed numerous civilians directly to high military command. Politicians such as Theodore Roosevelt and William Jennings Bryan scrambled for commissions, while the appointments of ex-Confederates like Joseph Wheeler and Fitzhugh Lee were appeals to southern support for the war. Although Schofield was savvy enough to understand this angle, he probably pressed the president to give more preference to the long-serving professionals.[17]

Another major source of dissatisfaction may have come from some of Schofield's strategic recommendations. When Alger initially suggested that 40,000 men be called up from the militia, Schofield responded with a wild overestimate of 400,000. In the end, state militia pressure forced the reluctant McKinley to raise the number from 60,000 to 125,000, or nearly the entire strength of the National Guard, regardless of readiness. These unnecessary troops sapped resources from the regulars and the better-organized volunteers. The excess state volunteers, who eventually totaled more than 200,000, would prove a liability when disease ravaged their training camps.[18]

In the midst of the frantic preparations for war, Schofield also proposed a major reorganization of the regular army. Schofield's plan called for a general in chief who would act as Chief of Staff over a newly formed General Staff and the other staff departments. The general in chief would serve at the pleasure of the president and could be retired at the president's discretion. In addition to the four-star general in chief, Schofield proposed three lieutenant generals, six major generals, twelve brigadier generals, and a maximum enlisted strength of the army of 100,000. The sixty-six-year-old lieutenant general also proposed the mandatory retirement age for lieutenant general and above be raised to seventy. Had the government created a General Staff and Chief of Staff six months or a year earlier, it would have dramatically altered the management of the war, but in May 1898 no one had time for such a radical and controversial change in the War Department.[19]

Schofield probably also irritated the president and the secretary of war by agreeing with Nelson Miles on the timing of military operations. On April 20, five days before the United States officially declared war, Schofield implored the president to permit the navy to destroy the Spanish fleet and gain "mastery of the sea" before embarking on an invasion of Cuba. He also counseled that with a naval blockade and an abundant supply of arms, munitions, and rations provided to the Cuban patriots, "there will be no necessity for the landing of an army until after the surrender of the Spanish garrisons." While modern readers might consider this a sound strategy, the prospect of a prolonged siege of Cuba was not what the president and the American people had in mind. Schofield also reversed himself on the advisability of military operations in Cuba during the rainy summer season. Once the navy had bottled up the Spanish fleet in Santiago, he recommended only capturing the town to finish off the fleet and then withdrawing to prevent fever. Meanwhile, the army would conquer Puerto Rico.[20]

However sound the military advice that Miles and Schofield gave McKinley, it did not satisfy the president's political needs and desires. The president was under enormous pressure to get the war over with as soon as possible, and Dewey's early success only whetted the public appetite for instant and overwhelming victory. In rejecting the advice of both Miles and Schofield, McKinley demonstrated another characteristic pattern of American civil-military relations. Regardless of the formal or statutory arrangements of command, the president could readily circumvent them. He easily set aside the commanding general and turned to the modest and efficient adjutant general Henry C. Corbin to provide the military advice and expertise he required. Generals only command as long as they have the support and confidence of the commander in chief, and no law could alter that fact. McKinley did not even need to relieve Miles and precipitate an unpleasant political debate. He could simply ignore the commanding general.[21]

On August 12, 1898, the Spanish-American War ended. The McKinley administration had delivered the quick victory that the American people expected. But the triumph had come at a price. While the battle deaths for the war totaled less than 300, the deaths due to disease were over ten times higher. The volunteer units suffered 3,848 deaths from disease, and while some these were due to yellow fever in Cuba, most died of typhoid and other diseases in their stateside camps. Poor campsite selection and the failure of officers to enforce the basic rules of field sanitation and hygiene caused much of the disease. This medical crisis, combined with inadequate food, unseasonable clothing, and improper camp equipment, produced a firestorm of criticism of the War Department and especially Secretary Alger.[22]

On September 9, 1898, President McKinley asked Schofield to head a commission to examine the failures in the Commissary, Quartermaster, and Medical Departments. Schofield declined, claiming that such a commission would neither "satisfy the public demand" nor "show what legislation is necessary to remedy the defects in our military system." In a personal meeting with the president, Schofield again declined, contending that only a board of inquiry was a suitable vehicle for fixing responsibility. Schofield appears to have been deeply conflicted about the president's motives. He simultaneously suggested that the president wanted a whitewash, a hunt for scapegoats, and a sincere inquiry to identify malfeasance. Since Schofield was still angry over Alger's treatment of him that spring, and because Schofield was convinced that Alger had badly bungled the management of the War Department, he may have felt he could not fairly judge Alger's conduct. Schofield also suspected that the president sought to "obtain a suspension of public judgment until after the approaching election," and as a Democrat this delay would have placed Schofield in an uncomfortable position. Regardless of whether the president wanted a whitewash or a genuine exposure of individual wrongdoing, neither objective would further Schofield's hopes to reform the military system.[23]

The Dodge Commission, named for Grenville M. Dodge, a staunch Republican and friend of Alger's, was not exactly a whitewash, but it was very sympathetic to the conditions and circumstances of Alger's and the War Department's conduct during the war. While it criticized some individual actions, such as the handling of rail and shipping arrangements at Tampa, it also helped to refute the inflammatory allegations of "embalmed beef" made by Nelson Miles. The commission report focused more on systemic rather than individual failures. Amid partisan attacks and cries of whitewash, the commission's reasoned recommendations for comprehensive reform became lost. Schofield's decision to refuse the appointment proved sagacious.[24]

In December 1898, while Miles was attacking Alger and the War Department staff before the Dodge Commission, Schofield was testifying before the House Military Affairs Committee. The focus of Schofield's testimony was the friction between the secretary of war and the commanding general. He reiterated his view that the commanding general really had no command authority. He pointed out that without harmony between the secretary and the commanding general, the adjutant general had become more important than the senior officer of the army. Schofield told the congressmen that it was essential for the president to be given the power to select his commanding general, or as he preferred to call the position, general in chief. He suggested that instead of promoting an officer to permanent lieutenant general, the president should be able to select any major general to hold the rank only as long as that individual held the position of general in chief. Finally, the general in chief would not act as a commander but as an executive officer to the president and the secretary, and he would also act as the Chief of Staff of all of the staff departments. In his turn, the reactionary Miles still pretended he commanded the army and scornfully remarked that no country had their senior general serve as an executive officer.[25]

The debacle of the Spanish-American War had exposed huge flaws in the military system, and the continued requirements of overseas occupation duty and fighting insurgents in the Philippines placed new demands on the antiquated system. Yet the seemingly self-evident need for change was, by itself, insufficient to produce reform. The effort took talented and committed leadership. Although Russell Alger certainly must bear a share of the blame for the many problems and mistakes of managing the war, he became a scapegoat for a generation of neglect. President McKinley forced Alger to resign in August 1899. Alger's ignominious example was not lost on his successor, Elihu Root. Root was an immensely gifted and disciplined corporate lawyer and was not a man to let events determine his fate. Root also benefited from full presidential support and confidence, especially when "Rough Rider" Theodore Roosevelt assumed the presidency upon McKinley's assassination in September 1901.

Lacking any military experience, Root knew he needed professional advice from experienced officers. However, instead of aligning himself with the somewhat discredited staff, he broke with tradition and allied himself with line officers. To be more precise, he took up the reform ideas of many of the young staff officers who had retained their commitment to the line army, most notably Assistant Adjutant General William H. Carter. If Root was not the creator of the reforms, he was their chief advocate and strategist. He shrewdly grasped the nature of the political environment that had frustrated military reformers like Schofield for so long. In a letter to General Leonard Wood on February 23, 1901, the secretary summarized his strategy for getting reform through Congress: "You see Congress will never pay any attention to anything until it has to. Public opinion will never form on any question until discussion commences. . . . [T]he only way to get the country behind us is to bring it up; insist upon disposing of it; make it a matter of present interest."[26]

Root also became skilled in the methods of publicity that Progressives employed to push through their reforms. The annual reports of the secretary of war were not normally popular reading, but Root used them to explain and build support for his policies. Root also had considerable persuasion skills. Congressmen were impressed by his "patient, dignified, and deferential presentations." He fostered close cooperation with fellow Hamilton College alumnus Joseph Hawley, chair of the Senate Committee on Military Affairs.[27] Finally, in shaping public opinion, Root ensured that favorable articles would appear in the popular magazines when he submitted his proposals.[28]

Secretary Root's reform goals can be summarized as reorganizing and permanently increasing the size of the regular army, improving the readiness and reliability of the National Guard to serve as a backup for the regular army, and reorganizing the War Department and the command system of the army. Each of these objectives became the central focus of a major legislative initiative, collectively referred to as the "Root Reforms."[29] The first, the Army Reorganization Act of 1901, finally achieved several of Schofield's most prized objectives. It permanently increased the size of the army, established the three-battalion regiment, reorganized the artillery, authorized the detail of line officers to the staff, and directed the creation of four regional camps for the training of the U.S. Army and National Guard. The bill also authorized one permanent lieutenant general and, as a reward for Henry Corbin, raised the rank of the adjutant general to major general.[30]

The next component of the Root Reforms was the Militia Law of 1903, or the Dick Act, named for Representative Charles Dick (R-Ohio). The Dick Act divided the militia into the reserve militia, which consisted of all able-bodied men between eighteen and forty-five years old, and the organized militia, henceforth named the National Guard. Though Schofield and most regulars preferred a national reserve, the act affirmed that the National Guard would be the primary reserve for the regular army. The act specified the president's authority to call out the organized militia in case of invasion or insurrection, or to enforce federal laws. Its service was limited to nine months and only within the United States. However, the act directed the detail of regular officers to the National Guard to serve as instructors and inspectors. Most important, the act specified training and other requirements for guard units and provided increased federal funding. In many ways, the Dick Act, by providing federal money in exchange for increased federal control, became a model for Progressive extensions of federal power.[31]

The third element of the Root Reforms was the General Staff Bill of 1903.[32] The bill sought to create a General Staff out of portions of the department staffs and replace the commanding general position with the Chief of the General Staff. Since this bill challenged the positions of both the commanding general and the staff departments, it was the most difficult of Root's program. By 1902, Lieutenant General Nelson Miles was virtually at war with the Roosevelt administration, but he retained a great deal of political influence. The failure of the War Department during the Spanish-American War had enhanced the commanding general's standing, and his accusations against military policy in the Philippines resonated in certain political quarters. Seeking a way to counter Miles, Root turned to Schofield for assistance and requested that he testify in favor of the General Staff Bill before the Senate Military Affairs Committee.[33]

Pretending that General Schofield and Major General Wesley Merritt just happened to be in town, Secretary Root persuaded Senator Hawley to have the generals testify before his committee on April 9, 1902.[34] Accompanying Schofield and Merritt was Colonel William H. Carter, Root's chief aide and major author of the General Staff Bill. Schofield recapped the history of friction between the secretary of war and the commanding general and again insisted that the senior general of the army could not act independently of the commander in chief and his war minister. He argued that the seemingly orderly division between administration and command was impossible in practice. He further contended that to expect coequal secretaries and commanders to act in complete harmony with full respect for the limits of their authority was not based on historical experience. Schofield also discounted Miles's charges that the bill would "Germanize and Russianize" the American army. Even though there were significant differences between the governments of the United States and Germany, Schofield declared there should be no difficulty in adapting some of those ideas to "fit our institutions."[35]

Schofield described how in his personal experience there had been such close cooperation and trust around the president's council table that, once the president agreed to a course of action, the secretary might himself write down the military order as the general dictated it, so that it could be dispatched within five minutes. This level of trust and confidence was not automatic, hence the need for the president to be able to choose his senior military officer from all the generals of the army. The four-year appointment of the Chief of the General Staff would permit each president to choose his own man. This also meant that the officer's rank at that level depended on the position, not the individual. Should the president decide to make a change or should the officer not be reappointed after his four-year term, the officer could retire or revert to his previous rank. Schofield did not like this possibility, but he had no solution for it.[36]

The *Army and Navy Journal* reported that Schofield's testimony completely altered the prospects of the bill in the committee. However, it would take many more months of lobbying by Root and his supporters before the bill finally achieved passage on January 7, 1903. Even before testifying, Schofield had greatly strengthened the bill. He insisted to the secretary that the army must have a military head, who under the president and secretary would exercise control over all the staff departments. He also repeated his view that the title for the senior general should be "general in chief." Failing to get that title, Schofield convinced Root to change "Chief of the General Staff" to the less restrictive "Chief of Staff." Root also agreed to let Schofield present an amendment to the General Staff Bill that explicitly gave the Chief of Staff supervision of all staff departments. This amendment survived as Section 4 of the General Staff Act.[37]

The final bill established the position of Chief of Staff upon the retirement of Lieutenant General Miles in August 1903 and created a General Staff Corps of forty-four officers detailed for duty from the line. Schofield's vision of a modern, integrated, coordinating General Staff had at long last been attained, or seemingly so. Though the savvy old soldier probably expected future trials and tribulations, it is perhaps fortunate that he did not live long enough to see the new General Staff's enemies nearly throttle it in the cradle. Although Elihu Root may have intended (and the law asserted) that the Chief of Staff would supervise all staff departments, his concentration on a strategic planning staff, his deliberate vagueness in order to garner support, and his own contradictory thinking helped undermine this goal. Moreover, the department chiefs continued to assert their independence. They claimed that the Chief of Staff only supervised the forty-four officers of the General Staff Corps and was thus just one more department chief.[38]

When Root left the War Department in 1904, his successor, William Howard Taft, reversed course. Instead of aligning himself with the Chief of Staff, the innately conservative Taft returned to the old system that gave greater autonomy to the departments. The military secretary (adjutant general) was even designated as acting secretary in the absence of the secretary of war. In 1911 now president Taft appointed Henry L. Stimson as secretary of war, who returned to the Root concept for reorganizing the War Department. Nevertheless, the staff chiefs, and especially Adjutant General Fred C. Ainsworth, continued to battle and increasingly turned to the Democratic House of Representatives for support. By 1916, the department chiefs and their congressional allies had gutted the 1903 law. The Chief of Staff was forbidden any authority over the departments, and the General Staff Corps was so hamstrung that only nineteen officers were assigned to the War Department when the United States entered World War I. Again, war exposed the deficiencies of the American military system, and it was not until the National Defense Act of 1920 that the General Staff was secure.[39]

In his final years John Schofield kept himself busy with the affairs of his youth. He kept an abiding interest in the United States Military Academy, serving on the Board of Visitors and as the chair of the architectural committee for major expansion and renovation of the school. By selecting the distinctive Gothic architecture so closely associated with the academy, he probably had a greater lasting impact on the academy than by serving as superintendent. The old general also was heavily involved in veterans' organizations, serving as the president of the Society of the Army of the Ohio and commander in chief of the Military Order of the Loyal Legion of the United States (MOLLUS).[40]

On Sunday, March 4, 1906, the seventy-four-year-old Schofield died of a cerebral hemorrhage at his home in St. Augustine, Florida. Both of his sons were overseas—Major William Schofield in Japan and Captain Richmond Schofield in Manila. His aides and old friends Generals Thomas Vincent, William Wherry, and Joseph Sanger took charge of the funeral arrangements. At first, they attempted to get some of the remaining Civil War corps and army commanders to be pallbearers, but time had taken its toll. O. O. Howard was on a speaking tour in Iowa; Daniel Sickles was too ill; and James H. Wilson no longer had a dress uniform that fit. Since Schofield had also been secretary of war, his old friends next contacted former secretaries Redfield Proctor, Stephen Elkins, Russell Alger, and Elihu Root, and all agreed to serve. The services were held in St. John's Church in Washington, near the White House. The church was thronged with dignitaries, including President Theodore Roosevelt, members of the cabinet, the chief justice of the Supreme Court, senators and congressmen, Lieutenant General John Bates, Admiral George Dewey, and other prominent officers and delegations from various veterans' organizations. Schofield was buried in Arlington National Cemetery on a scenic hilltop just off Sheridan Drive. It was everything the proud old soldier could have wished for.[41]

John M. Schofield's reputation rested and continues to rest largely on his service in the Civil War, and particularly on his participation in the Atlanta and Franklin-Nashville campaigns. Schofield considered his repulse of John Bell Hood's army at Franklin his greatest contribution to the war. This assessment reflected Schofield's conventional approach to strategy and his view that defeating the enemy's armies on the battlefield was the primary object of war; and the devastating rebel losses at Franklin certainly contributed to the even greater victory at Nashville. Nevertheless, the entire campaign was rather uncharacteristic of Schofield. He took risks and required a degree of luck not typical of his usual performance. His displays of anger, then and later, about the campaign were at variance to his normal analytical approach to problems. Ironically, it was his more mundane conduct during the Atlanta and North Carolina campaigns that is more representative of his worth as a field commander. As the commander of the Army of the Ohio, he was a reliable battlefield commander. Operating on the wing of Sherman's grand army group or independently in North Carolina, Schofield demonstrated skill, determination, and steadiness. His calm methodical approach put pressure on the rebel commanders without costly frontal assaults. He displayed a high level of competence, rather than brilliance and élan. Although not as celebrated as Grant or Sherman or Sheridan, Schofield was, in many ways, typical of the Union leadership that won the great war.

While the clash of armies has received the bulk of attention from Civil War historians, Schofield's role in Missouri and the role of departmental command during the war merit greater attention and study. In Missouri in the spring of 1861, Lieutenant John M. Schofield, in aligning himself with Captain Nathaniel Lyon and Congressman Frank Blair Jr., became a supporting player in the extralegal mustering of federal troops, the arrest of the lawful state militia, the ouster of the military department commander, and the overthrow of the elected governor of Missouri. Missouri became a meat grinder for commanders as much as the Army of the Potomac. These were not arenas where a soldier could gain much glory, but they nevertheless fully tested a leader's skill and imagination. The Department of the Missouri was an inherently political command. Indeed, all military commands involved in civil war, guerrilla war, or occupation duty were inherently political. The organization and structure of the security forces were political. Commanders were and are required to make politically contentious decisions on a daily basis. Commanders at all levels were buffeted by political factions at all levels and from all sides.

From his role model and mentor Henry Halleck, Schofield learned that such command required a great deal of intellectual energy and flexibility. He learned that solutions, such as the creation of the Enrolled Missouri Militia, bring their own problems and political reactions, and policies must be examined and readjusted continuously. General Schofield also learned a few years later that simply having the support and confidence of the commander in chief was not enough. In the poisonous political atmosphere, Schofield could not maintain his balance between the conservative Unionists and the radical Republicans, either in Civil War Missouri or in Congress. He proved unable to follow President Lincoln's admonition that "if both factions, or neither, shall abuse you, you will probably be about right."[42] Despite his relief, Schofield's command of the Department of the Missouri was relatively successful. With the cooperation of Governor Hamilton Gamble, he was able to mobilize local resources to defend the state without diverting large numbers of troops who were needed for the Union armies. The large guerrilla bands of 1862 declined to smaller, though often more brutal, bands of a few dozen. Flexibility sometimes required that Lincoln replace commanders who had become political liabilities. However, because men like Samuel Curtis or Schofield had faithfully tried to implement the policies of the commander in chief, the president later rewarded them for their fidelity to duty.

Civil War and Reconstruction represent the greatest crises in American civil-military relations. Schofield, and other departmental commanders, instituted martial law, tried civilians before military tribunals, and removed civil officials. Yet despite such military powers, civilian control was never in jeopardy. Notwithstanding the support of President Lincoln and Governor Gamble, Schofield fell afoul of the radical Republicans in Congress and was removed. Reconstruction was even more problematic since it involved not only a military occupation of large portions of the United States, but also an open fight over control of the army of occupation. Schofield, the political soldier, was able to maintain his political equilibrium by maintaining the peace in Virginia and by retaining General Grant's trust while serving in President Johnson's cabinet.

The army's constabulary mission in the West and its involvement in domestic disturbances frequently mired military officers in political controversy. Again, Schofield attempted to tread a middle path. He emphasized the need to both punish Indian transgressions and protect Indians from rapacious Americans. In domestic disturbances Schofield strove to limit the army's missions and minimize its use of force. As in the Civil War and Reconstruction, the debate was generally over which civilians controlled military policy.

Ironically, the intense partisanship of the American political system intensified the cautious nature of Schofield and most military officers. Schofield the military professional and reformer was a political pragmatist—by temperament moderate, by training nonpartisan, by experience practical. All of these characteristics led him to adopt a middle-of-the-road position, to seek safety amid prevailing opinion. Though a man of principle, he was not a crusader. Unromantic, he bowed to the inevitable. Despite his outgoing and avuncular personality, he could be a prickly man and very sensitive to criticism, a characteristic he shared with most of the officer corps. Aversion to politics was due in large part to the inevitable drumbeat of partisan criticism. This sensitivity prompted Schofield to act in highly defensive ways and with much circumspection. The delicate balance of political parties in the late nineteenth century made the political stakes very high and prompted highly partisan accusations of abuse or corruption. To avoid such charges, officers generally acted well within the authorized rules and practices. Thus, politics not only reflected but also reinforced Schofield's conservative nature.

Schofield's repeated defense of the value of military government—in Missouri, North Carolina, Virginia, the western territories, and Hawaii—was a reaction to the partisanship of American politics. Although well aware of the dangers and tribulations of assuming civil authority, Schofield believed that men of intelligence and good judgment could overcome political factionalism. Like Sherman's effort to separate military affairs from politics, this aspiration was unrealistic and naive. Nevertheless, it reflected an aspiration of many Americans. Many mugwumps and Progressives sought to replace the messy tussle of politics with the efficient and orderly direction of dispassionate experts.

Both civilian and military Progressives emphasized professional expertise and bureaucratic processes. As commanding general, Schofield played a leading role in reshaping and reforming the military bureaucracy. More than any of his predecessors, he typified the kind of bureaucratic leadership required of modern Chiefs of Staff. Schofield's political education taught him to value the hidden hand of influence over the sometimes empty assumption of command authority. Schofield was able to build a rough consensus within the army for the increasing bureaucratization of military processes—from education and tactical doctrine to promotions and assignments. This shift was hugely important for developing a modern military because it enabled an army to move from idiosyncratic to systematic inculcation of values and expertise. Schofield the military reformer prepared the army for new responsibilities and a new century.

At Schofield's death, General John C. Bates was the Chief of Staff and the last Civil War veteran to be the army's senior general. Schofield's death and Bates's retirement a few months later reflected the changing of the guard in the army. It was a new century and in many ways a new army. The army was a good deal larger: 10,572 in 1853 when Schofield was commissioned; 27,495 in 1895 when he retired; and 68,945 in 1906 when he died.[43] It was a much younger army, with nearly two-thirds of the officers appointed since 1898. It was an army with nearly half its strength deployed overseas.[44] It was an army now clearly looking outward at the world. It was an army that in the course of World War I would be transformed into a powerful modern army.

The uncertainty with which John Schofield and his fellow officers viewed the army's future role was somewhat clarified by the time of his death. Although the government would still occasionally order the army to intervene in domestic disturbances, the National Guard and more robust police forces would assume most of these responsibilities. The army was no longer a frontier constabulary, but it had assumed new missions as a colonial constabulary. The initiative and small unit tactics of the frontier army were transferred to battling insurgents in the Philippines. Although American military power did not yet match its economic strength, the United States was now a world power. The preparation of the army for general war increasingly preoccupied the officer corps, and they paid close attention to technological and foreign military developments.

In terms of professionalism, the army indoctrinated its new officers with the military ethic—selfless service to the nation—that was forged before the Civil War and instilled in academy graduates. Part of this inculcation was accomplished in the army's enhanced school system and professional associations, but mostly it was done by personal example, especially by the West Point graduates who still composed the bulk of the senior officers. American republican principles increasingly accepted the need for professional expertise in military affairs. Technology and the vast scale of modern warfare demanded educated and trained professionals to lead the citizen soldiers of the nation. The demands of World War I would complete the system of military schools begun by Sherman and Schofield.

The recognition of professional expertise and the military's professional ethic of service resulted in civilian leaders' granting the military much autonomy in military affairs. The military shaped its educational and training programs with little political intrusion. Civilian officials also granted the military discretion in the setting of standards for military appointments, assignments, and promotions. The appointment of "political generals" became the rare exception rather than the norm. Finally, civilian leaders gave the military broad latitude in the formulation of military policy and doctrine. This autonomy was limited and conditioned by the civilian leadership's confidence that decisions were made based on professional considerations.

This did not mean, however, that politics had been totally divorced from military policy. Congress continued to jealously guard its power over military structure and budgets. The historic compromise of making the state-based National Guard the nation's primary military reserve in return for federal funds and supervision did not end the disputes between state and federal soldiers and officials. American involvement in the Great War in Europe divided the nation and its political and military elites. Civil-military conflicts continued to follow the American tradition of disputes between contending coalitions of civilians and soldiers.

Indeed, the new military professionals could not avoid the inevitability of politics in military affairs. A few, such as Leonard Wood, reverted to the old model of overt political partisanship, but more often the senior military leaders were practical men who avoided explicit political leanings. Chiefs of Staff such as Schofield's aide Tasker H. Bliss, Peyton C. March, and John J. Pershing certainly had political connections and were involved in many of the political-military controversies of the day. Yet, the term-limited appointment of the army's senior general did not lead to a succession of partisan Chiefs of Staff. Instead, they were politically astute professional soldiers who understood the Madisonian nature of the American political system and recognized that the efficiency of the army could never be promoted at the expense of the constitutional system. The new professional leaders were political soldiers in the mold of John M. Schofield, and this was his true legacy.

In his classic *The Soldier and the State*, Samuel Huntington described the ideal of objective civilian control through a completely depoliticized professional army. This ideal has blinded us to the strengths of other forms of civilian control that Huntington termed subjective. The social, institutional, and constitutional forms of civilian control in the American context are extremely powerful. Huntington's theory also obscures the inextricable bonds between the political and the military, between citizens and soldiers.[45] While Schofield was dedicated to military subordination and accommodation to civilian authorities, he would have been appalled at the idea that officers should have no understanding of and no interest in the political affairs of the nation.

In a speech at academy graduation in 1892, Schofield expressed his views on soldiers as citizens: "Circumstances will often arise when the higher authority cannot give you instructions in detail to meet possible emergencies, but must leave you to do what is right and lawful in view of all the circumstances that may arise. You should, therefore, cultivate industriously and at all times knowledge of the laws and customs of the country and the fundamental principles upon which the Government of the United States is based."[46]

He went on to discuss the soldier and politics: "While you may wisely abstain from active participation in party politics, you should keep in touch with the people of the country, and [be] thoroughly familiar with all the great political questions that concern your fellow citizens. The American soldier should never cease to be in heart and soul in full sympathy with the citizens of the country. He is no less a citizen because he has become a soldier."[47] John M. Schofield's admonition should remind us that while an army deeply involved in politics is dangerous, so is one completely segregated from the values, institutions, and people of the nation.

NOTES

ABBREVIATIONS

AAG	Assistant Adjutant General
ACP	Appointment, Commission, and Personal Branch of the Adjutant General
A.G.	Adjutant General
BCL	Bowdoin College Library, Brunswick, Maine
CMH	U.S. Army Center of Military History, Fort McNair, D.C.
EMM	Enrolled Missouri Militia
G.O.	General Order
HQ	Headquarters
I.G.	Inspector General
JAG	Judge Advocate General
LC	Library of Congress, Washington, D.C.
MHI	United States Army Military History Institute, Carlisle, Pa.
MHS	Missouri Historical Society, St. Louis, Missouri
MOLLUS	Military Order of the Loyal Legion of the United States
MSM	Missouri State Militia
NARA	National Archives and Records Administration, Washington, D.C.
NYHS	New-York Historical Society, New York, New York
OR	U.S. War Department, *The War of the Rebellion: A Compilation of the Official Records of the Union and Confederate Armies*, 128 vols. (Washington, D.C.: Government Printing Office, 1880–1901).
PFL	Proctor Free Library, Proctor, Vermont
Q.M.	Quartermaster
RG	Record Group
S.O.	Special Order
USMA	United States Military Academy, West Point, New York
WHMC	Western Historical Manuscript Collection, Columbia, Missouri

1. In the interest of space, I have omitted examples of Schofield's writings on Reconstruction, command of the army, and the army and domestic disorder. These can be found in my Ph.D. dissertation, "Political Soldier: John M. Schofield and the Politics of Generalship."

2. Pope quoted in Stanley, *Personal Memoirs*, 214.

3. Stanley rated Schofield as a "pretty fair man," but "his fear of politicians has made him play a very low, mean part in many things." Ibid., 214. According to John McElroy, Schofield's "political views were those of the Douglas wing of the Democracy, and he remained a Democrat ever after." McElroy, *Struggle for Missouri*, 87, 107.

4. For an excellent summary of the historiography of American military professionalism in the nineteenth century, see Grandstaff, "Preserving the 'Habits and Usages of War.' "

5. Hatch, *Professions in American History*, 1–3. Noted theorist of civil-military relations Samuel P. Huntington similarly described a profession in terms of expertise, responsibility, and corporateness. Huntington, *Soldier and the State*, 8–10.

6. The most significant study of the professionalization of the antebellum army is Skelton, *American Profession of Arms*, esp. 238–59, 282–304, 359–62. Skelton's concept of a "new" military professionalism in the late nineteenth century, which was built on the foundations of the old army, is slightly different from this author's view of a lengthy professionalization process that extended into the twentieth century.

7. Ironically, Theodore Crackel traces the origin of the U.S. Military Academy to partisan politics. He notes that the academy was not originally established as an engineering school. He links Thomas Jefferson's creation of the academy not to the advancement of national scientific learning, but as part of his program to wrest control of governmental institutions—the civil service, courts, and military—from the Federalists. Crackel, *West Point*, 50. Also see Crackel, *Mr. Jefferson's Army*.

8. Watson, "Professionalism, Social Attitudes, and Civil-Military Accountability," 1498–526. The works of William Skelton and Samuel Watson provide in-depth analysis of the emerging professionalism of the antebellum army.

9. For excellent accounts of the U.S. Military Academy in the nineteenth century, see Morrison, *"Best School"*; Dillard, "United States Military Academy"; and Crackel, *West Point*.

10. War Department G.O. no. 155, November 27, 1901, CMH, <http://www.army.mil/cmh-pg/documents/1901/wdg0155-1901.htm> (accessed September 17, 2005). The introduction explained the purpose of the army's system of instruction for officers as "maintaining the high standard of instruction and general training of the officers of the Army and for the establishment of a coherent plan by which the work may be made progressive."

11. Karsten, "Armed Progressives," 240–58; Spector, "Triumph of Professional Ideology," 183; War Department G.O. no. 155, November 27, 1901.

12. Huntington, *Soldier and the State*, 10, 16–18.

13. John M. Palmer, the son of Civil War major general John M. Palmer, was a major author of the National Defense Act of 1920 and an advocate of universal military training. He served as

an advisor to George C. Marshall during World War II. For a discussion of John M. Palmer, see Weigley, *Towards an American Army*, 1223–49; and Holley, *General John M. Palmer*.

14. As the twentieth century unfolded, the complexity of warfare increased to the point where the only expertise lay with civilians. While this resulted in military commissions to such civil experts, it also produced a dramatic expansion of the civilian workforce in the War/Defense Department.

15. For example, Russell Weigley, perhaps the dean of American military historians, contrasted a remarkably sanguine judgment that "there was a basic harmony" between President Abraham Lincoln and George B. McClellan with a more severe assessment of Joint Chiefs of Staff chairman General Colin Powell. He then rather gloomily concluded, "The principle of civil control of the military in the United States faces an uncertain future." Weigley, "American Military and the Principle of Civilian Control." See also Kohn, "Out of Control"; and Kohn, "Civil-Military Relations Debated." Both Weigley and Kohn approach civilian control from the point of view of the president. Both, for example, describe Colin Powell's objections to the "gay issue" in terms of a politically partisan effort, and they minimize or ignore the overwhelming support of the public and the Democrat-controlled Congress for the Powell position. One of the central contentions of this study is that the military and military policy have never been the exclusive domain of the president. Weigley's rather benign picture of nineteenth-century civil-military relations is surprising, and he corrects that a bit in a subsequent article. Even in the later article, however, Weigley tends to gloss over important issues raised during the Civil War and Reconstruction to conclude that the 1990s placed a greater strain on civil-military relations "than any time in the past." Weigley, "American Civil-Military Cultural Gap."

16. Paul Hammond has noted that in speaking of civilian control of the military, it is important to identify which civilians one means. Hammond, *Organizing for Defense*, 3. The Truman-MacArthur controversy, arguably the most famous civil-military clash in American history, illustrates this point. The struggle was not simply between President Harry Truman and General Douglas MacArthur. Americans were frustrated and confused over the situation in Korea. MacArthur, with the support of many Republicans, disagreed with the policy of the president and the Joint Chiefs of Staff. Generals George Marshall and Omar Bradley urged Truman to fire MacArthur, while Republicans in Congress sided with MacArthur. When Truman relieved MacArthur, the general did not challenge the president's authority and immediately relinquished command. Republicans brought MacArthur before Congress in a vain effort to discredit Truman's policy. Their failure strengthened Truman's hand. Although most Americans remained frustrated with the war, the MacArthur-Republican alternative was found wanting. The consensus of World War II was relatively unique in American history. American wars have generally produced sectional and partisan divisions.

17. For less alarmist analyses of contemporary civil-military relations, see Hooker, "Soldiers of the State"; and Betros, "Political Partisanship and the Professional Military Ethic." Also see Snider and Carlton-Carew, *U.S. Civil-Military Relations*; Langston, *Uneasy Alliance*; and Feaver, *Armed Servants*.

18. Huntington, *Soldier and the State*, 80–85. For discussions of Huntington's continuing

influence see Coffman, "Long Shadow of *The Soldier and the State*"; and Skelton, "Samuel P. Huntington and the Roots of the American Military Tradition."

19. Russell Weigley has raised the issue of late nineteenth-century military isolation, which separated the army from the American people. Weigley, *History of the United States Army*, 265. Samuel P. Huntington considers this military isolation a prerequisite to military professionalization. Huntington, *Soldier and the State*, 227–30. John M. Gates argues that the army was not as isolated as it has generally been perceived. Gates, "Alleged Isolation of US Army Officers."

20. John M. Schofield to Emory Upton, August 2, 1877, Schofield Letters, vol. 1, 246–47, USMA Archives.

21. Basler, *Collected Works of Abraham Lincoln*, 6:234.

22. Some might argue that the Newburgh "conspiracy" of 1783 constituted a greater crisis in civil-military relations because it seemingly pitted a disgruntled Continental army against Congress. Even this episode, however, reflected the typical pattern of American civil-military relations. Nationalists in Congress hoped to use disaffected officers as tools to create a stronger central government. The officer corps, while unhappy, was very divided over what to do, and the "conspiracy" collapsed completely when General George Washington appealed to the officers' patriotism. Most historians agree the chances of a coup were remote, especially since the soldiers were more interested in getting their pay and going home than intimidating Congress to gain pensions for their officers. Richard Kohn concludes that the significance of the affair is what did not happen. The first national army did not intervene in politics, accepted civilian control, and peacefully disbanded. See Kohn, *Eagle and the Sword*, 17–39; Martin and Lender, *Respectable Army*, 186–94; and Royster, *Revolutionary People at War*, 334–41.

23. Schofield, *Forty-Six Years*, 421–23, 467–83.

24. "Let the President have full freedom of choice, from among those legally eligible, of the officer who he is willing to entrust with military power and then give that officer ample authority, and hold him responsible." Schofield preferred the title "general in chief" to "Chief of Staff." He also saw this officer departing shortly after the rest of the cabinet at each election. Schofield to Elihu Root, March 29, 1902, handwritten draft, Box 38, Schofield Papers, LC.

25. Schofield, *Forty-Six Years*, 536–39. Also see Weigley, "Military Thought of John M. Schofield"; and "John M. Schofield: An American Plan of Command," in Weigley, *Towards an American Army*.

CHAPTER ONE

1. Schofield, *Forty-Six Years*, 6.

2. Ibid., 1–2; McDonough, *Schofield*, 2–4. Genealogical data provided by Schofield Gross of Riverside, Illinois, and John Schofield, of Garland, Texas.

3. Schofield to John L. Schofield, April 8, 1879, Schofield Letters, vol. 3, USMA Archives; Schofield to Frank H. Schofield, February 28, 1880, Schofield Letters, vol. 2, USMA Archives; "In Memoriam: James Schofield," MOLLUS, California Commandery, Cir. 6, Febru-

ary 22, 1888, copy provided by John Schofield, Garland, Tex.; U.S. War Department, *U.S. Army Register*.

4. Schofield, *Forty-Six Years*, 2.

5. Carlin graduated in 1850 and served as a Union brigade and division commander in the Civil War. Schofield went to extraordinary efforts to obtain Carlin's promotion to brigadier general in the regular army just before his mandatory retirement in 1893 (see chap. 13). Garber graduated in 1852 and died at Fort Hoskins, Oregon, in 1859. *Register of Graduates and Former Cadets*, 274, 276; Schofield, *Forty-Six Years*, 3–4.

6. Both Chambliss and Walker resigned to join the Confederacy in 1861 and served as brigadier generals in the Confederate army. *Register of Graduates and Former Cadets*, 277.

7. Schofield, *Forty-Six Years*, 3–5.

8. James, "Life at West Point," 32.

9. USMA Records, USMA Archives; Morrison, *"Best School,"* 87–101, 188–91.

10. Howard, *Autobiography*, 1:57; James, "Life at West Point," 34; Academic Records, USMA Archives.

11. *Library Circulation Records, 1824–1867*, USMA Archives.

12. Morrison, *"Best School,"* 75–86; James, "Life at West Point," 36–37; Schofield, *Forty-Six Years*, 4–5, 7–8. Jerome N. Bonaparte Jr. was the grandson of Napoleon I's brother Jerome Bonaparte. He graduated in 1852, served in the French army from 1854 to 1870, and died in Massachusetts in 1893. *Register of Graduates and Former Cadets*, 276.

13. James, "Life at West Point," 37; Schofield, *Forty-Six Years*, 8–9; Schofield to secretary of war, March 26, 1889, Letters Sent, vol. 45, and Schofield to P. B. Plumb, January 11, 1890, Letters Sent, vol. 46, RG 108, NARA.

14. Schofield to W. T. Sherman, May 29, 1878, Sherman Papers, LC.

15. In a speech at the State Baptist Convention of Florida in January 1897, Schofield recalled how his father had baptized him at thirteen, yet he converted to the Episcopal Church at thirty. Because some members of his family were Catholic, he would not permit any attacks on the church of Rome in his presence. He summed up his attitude by saying, "I am quite sure the Divine Founder of Christianity does not require me to bother my poor head about nice questions upon which the learned doctors are still disputing." *Annual Reunion*, June 11, 1906, 130–31.

16. McPherson was appointed first captain. John Bell Hood and Thomas Vincent (Schofield's USMA roommate and lifelong friend) were also appointed cadet lieutenants. USMA S.O. no. 84, June 16, 1852, USMA Archives.

17. USMA S.O. no. 104, July 17, 1852, USMA Archives; Schofield, *Forty-Six Years*, 9–13.

18. Schofield, *Forty-Six Years*, 10–11; Captain B. R. Alden to adjutant, USMA, June 26, 1852, and John M. Schofield to Alden, June 30, 1852, Letters Received Relative to USMA, 1819–66, RG 94, Engineer Dept., reel 27, USMA Archives.

19. Captain Henry Brewerton to Brigadier General Joseph G. Totten, July 8, 1852, Superintendent's Letterbook No. 2, July 2, 1849–February 5, 1853, USMA Archives.

20. Edward L. Hartz to his sister, June 14, 1851, Hartz Papers, LC; Ambrose, *Duty, Honor, Country*, 158. Ambrose called Schofield "a notorious hazer" who loved to steal plebes'

clothing. While such behavior was not beyond Schofield's capacity, none of the primary sources link Schofield by name to this activity.

21. Fleming, *West Point*, 144.

22. Schofield, *Forty-Six Years*, 4. Schofield's academy obituary also related an incident where Schofield, as a new cadet, crossed bayonets with a corporal of the guard for not challenging promptly. *Annual Reunion*, 1906, 128.

23. James, "Life at West Point," 22. Though seemingly paradoxical, it is not surprising that a West Point graduate would become secretary of war before one became the commanding general. Politics was a far more rapid path to high office than the stagnant peacetime army.

24. Schofield, *Forty-Six Years*, 11–13.

25. HQ Army, S.O. no. 141, September 9, 1852, and S.O. no. 216, December 13, 1852, Orders, vol. 11, 1852, USMA Archives; Schofield, *Forty-Six Years*, 241–42.

26. Post Orders no. 685, May 25, 1852, Post Orders, vol. 3, June 22, 1846–November 14, 1852, USMA Archives.

27. James B. McPherson to brother, October 17, 1852, McPherson Papers, LC; Schofield, *Forty-Six Years*, 13.

28. S.O. no. 216, December 13, 1852, Orders, vol. 11, 1852, USMA Archives.

29. Sheridan, *Personal Memoirs*, 6. Sheridan, in his memoirs, admitted that he had committed a serious breach of discipline. Sheridan also reconciled with Terrill, who died as a Union brigadier general at Perryville in 1862. Hutton, *Phil Sheridan and His Army*, 5.

30. Howard, *Autobiography*, 1:53.

31. Livingston was commissioned in the artillery, served as Sheridan's chief of artillery in the Shenandoah campaign, retired as a colonel in 1895, and died in 1903. *Register of Graduates and Former Cadets*, 277.

32. John B. Hood also had 196 demerits. Sheridan had 189 demerits, McPherson 48, and Vincent 34. *Register of Delinquencies*, USMA Archives.

33. Schofield, *Forty-Six Years*, 13–14.

34. USMA Staff Records, vol. 5, 1851–1854, 281, 301, USMA Archives.

First Class Standings (55 cadets)	McPherson	Schofield	Sheridan	Hood
Engineering	1	3	40	45
Mineralogy and Geology	1	17	28	46
Ethics	3	7	33	52
Fencing	27	37	50	51
Infantry	2	1	42	47
Cavalry	9	35	25	3
Artillery	1	11	40	45
Final Class Standing	1	7	34	44

35. Schofield, *Forty-Six Years*, 15.

36. Ibid., 20, 23.

37. Sherman, "Military Law," 385. Sherman's chief purpose was to delineate the differences between civil and military law.

38. Schofield, *Forty-Six Years*, 24–25; Boatner, *Civil War Dictionary*, 382.

39. Schofield, *Forty-Six Years*, 25–26. Jack D. Welsh says that Schofield might have suffered from yellow fever or typhoid fever. Welsh, *Medical Histories of Union Generals*, 291. In his correspondence Schofield several times suggests malaria. See Schofield's obituary written by Thomas Vincent, *Annual Reunion*, 1906, 172.

40. Schofield, *Forty-Six Years*, 26–27; Ambrose, *Duty, Honor, Country*, 95–96; *Annual Reunion*, 1893, 105–12; Howard, *Autobiography*, 1:55–56.

41. MOLLUS, *Necrology of Companion John M. Schofield*, 65.

42. The Schofields' children were John Rathbone, born West Point, New York, March 22, 1858, and died West Point, August 14, 1868; William Bartlett, born West Point, June 18, 1860, and died San Francisco, California, August 7, 1906; Henry Halleck, born St. Louis, Missouri, November 24, 1862, and died St. Louis, July 29, 1863; Mary Campbell, born Freeport, Illinois, June 10, 1865, and died 1945; and Richmond McAllister, born Richmond, Virginia, March 27, 1867, and died San Diego, California, November 6, 1942. Genealogical data provided by Schofield Andrews Jr. of Nova Scotia and Schofield Gross of Riverside, Illinois.

43. Schofield, *Forty-Six Years*, 27–29; Schofield to James B. McPherson, March 28, 1858, McPherson Papers, LC; Cadet John J. Sweet to sister, October 12, 1856, and Schofield to Mrs. M. P. Sweet, May 9, 1859, Sweet Papers, USMA Archives.

44. *Washington University Catalogues, 1856–1870*, Washington University Archives; Schofield, *Forty-Six Years*, 29–30.

45. Schofield, *Forty-Six Years*, 30–31.

46. Sifakis, *Who Was Who in the Union*, 261, 365.

CHAPTER TWO

1. Schofield's clerk Drennan estimated that of the 1,094 officers in the army on January 1, 1861, 287 (26 percent) joined the Confederacy. Table dated March 4, 1897, Box 38, Schofield Papers, LC.

2. There are a number of remarkably similar accounts of the early "fight for Missouri" written by participants and close observers. These include Anderson, *Story of a Border City*; McElroy, *Struggle for Missouri*; Peckham, *Gen. Nathaniel Lyon, and Missouri in 1861*; Rombauer, *Union Cause in St. Louis*; and Snead, *Fight for Missouri*. More recent studies include an excellent survey by Missouri historian William E. Parrish, *Turbulent Partnership*. Phillips, *Damned Yankee*, provides a detailed depiction of the early days of the Civil War in Missouri.

3. Most contemporary authors, even Confederate Thomas Snead, credited Nathaniel Lyon with saving Missouri for the Union. Many modern scholars have been more critical. William Parrish considers Lyon the single person most responsible for bringing civil war to Missouri. Parrish, *Turbulent Partnership*, 16. Christopher Phillips, who is even more disparaging, concludes that Lyon needlessly polarized the state and provoked the guerrilla war. To Phillips,

Lyon symbolizes the forces of radicalism. Lyon was not only a political extremist; he also engaged in a personal vendetta against secessionists. Phillips, *Damned Yankee*, 262–64. David H. Donald credits Lincoln's support for Lyon and Blair over Department of the West commander William S. Harney with the outbreak of internecine warfare. Donald, *Lincoln*, 300. I disagree with Phillips and Parrish. Missouri governor Claiborne Jackson and Missouri State Militia general Sterling Price were polarizing the issue no less than Blair and Lyon. Just as the Confederacy would not tolerate neutrality on the part of the Indian nations, the United States could not leave free Missouri to sit out the war. Missouri, and especially St. Louis, were too important strategically. Besides, war had already come to western Missouri in the 1850s, and most Kansans did not consider Missouri neutral. Missouri could not avoid the questions of Union and slavery.

4. Rombauer, *Union Cause in St. Louis*, 127; Snead, *Fight for Missouri*, 64. Both sides recognized the coercive power of a "revolutionary" militia. During the Revolutionary War, the local militias played a vital role in suppressing Tories and enforcing revolutionary discipline. See Shy, *People Numerous and Armed*.

5. Parrish, *History of Missouri*, 3:1–6, 17. Parrish concludes that the Camp Jackson affair (discussed below) was the deciding event for Price's support of the Confederacy. Albert Castel agrees. Parrish, *Turbulent Partnership*, 26; Castel, *General Sterling Price*, 14.

6. Parrish, *Frank Blair*, 3, 79–95.

7. Phillips, *Damned Yankee*, 19–26, 81–105, 117–18.

8. Given the need for military arms by both sides, the arsenal in St. Louis, with its 60,000–75,000 stands of arms, became a focal point of contention. Whoever controlled the arsenal controlled St. Louis, and whoever controlled St. Louis dominated Missouri. Secessionists understood this no less than Unionists. Thus, the fight for Missouri began in St. Louis, and the epicenter was the federal arsenal. The commander of the arsenal, Major William H. Bell (academy class of 1820), of decidedly prosouthern sympathies, met secretly with Brigadier General Daniel M. Frost (class of 1844) of the Missouri State Militia. Frost wrote encouragingly to Governor Jackson on January 24, 1861, "I have found the major [Bell] everything that you or I could desire." Bell was prepared to defend the arsenal against "irresponsible mobs," but not against the "proper state authorities." Warned of Bell's disloyalty, Winfield Scott replaced Bell with Major Peter V. Hagner (class of 1836) on the very day Frost wrote to Jackson. Snead, *Fight for Missouri*, 101, 111–17. Both Lyon and Blair considered Major Hagner apathetic and unreliable, and they suspected him of southern sympathies. Blair used his political influence to place Captain Lyon in command of the arsenal, much to the consternation of General Harney, who preferred the compliant Hagner to the headstrong Lyon. Phillips, *Damned Yankee*, 146–50; Parrish, *Turbulent Partnership*, 16–17. Hagner remained in the Ordnance Corps throughout the war and retired in 1881 as a colonel and brevet brigadier general. Boatner, *Civil War Dictionary*, 365.

9. Phillips, *Damned Yankee*, 142–47; Schofield, *Forty-Six Years*, 33.

10. Parrish, *Turbulent Partnership*, 9–14.

11. Rombauer, *Union Cause in St. Louis*, 188–89, 192.

12. Abraham Lincoln to Hamilton Gamble, July 28, 1862, Lincoln Papers, MHS; War Department G.O. no. 15, May 4, 1861, Box 7, Schofield Papers, LC.

13. McDonough, *Schofield*, 13; Parrish, *Turbulent Partnership*, 17 (quotations).

14. Schofield, *Forty-Six Years*, 33.

15. S. Williams to Lyon, April 18, 1861, *OR* I, 1:668; Harney to E. Townsend, April 16, 1861, *OR* I, 1:666–67.

16. Phillips, *Damned Yankee*, 160–63; Blair to Cameron, April 19, 1861, *OR* I, 1:668–69; F. Blair to A. Curtin, April 18, 1861, reel 12, Blair Family Papers, LC.

17. There is some question as to when Lyon received permission to muster troops. Lyon's report of April 27, 1861, says that he got the first (Porter's) message around midnight and commenced mustering the next morning. This would mean that his secret mustering had been underway for several hours before he received the approval message. Rombauer, *Union Cause in St. Louis*, 208–11. Parrish and Phillips imply that Lyon received the approval message from Major Fitz John Porter that afternoon. L. Thomas to Lyon, April 21, 1861, *OR* I, 1:670; Parrish, *Turbulent Partnership*, 18–19; Phillips, *Damned Yankee*, 164–69. Piston and Hatcher also accept the story that Lyon had permission before Schofield began to muster in the volunteers. Piston and Hatcher, *Wilson's Creek*, 31. William R. Brooksher agrees that the mustering began before Lyon received authority. Brooksher, *Bloody Hill*, 47. Schofield glossed over the problem of authority in his memoirs by implying that Lyon already had authority to muster the troops before he called Schofield from church. Schofield, *Forty-Six Years*, 34. Given the illicit nature of the action the night of April 21, both Lyon and Schofield probably sought to obscure the true sequence of events.

18. L. Thomas to Lyon, April 30, 1861, *OR* I, 1:675; Phillips, *Damned Yankee*, 164–69; Parrish, *Turbulent Partnership*, 19–20.

19. J. C. Davis to C. F. Jackson, April 23, 1861, and C. F. Jackson to L. P. Walker, Confederate Secretary of War, May 5, 1861, *OR* I, 1:689–90; Phillips, *Damned Yankee*, 175–77; Parrish, *Turbulent Partnership*, 20–21.

20. *OR* I, 1:689–90; Phillips, *Damned Yankee*, 175–77; Parrish, *Turbulent Partnership*, 20–21.

21. Schofield, *Forty-Six Years*, 36.

22. McDonough, *Schofield*, 17; Adamson, *Rebellion in Missouri*, 60–61.

23. Sherman, *Memoirs*, 191–92.

24. Grant, *Personal Memoirs*, 155–57; McElroy, *Struggle for Missouri*, 58.

25. Harney to L. Thomas, June 5, 1861, *OR* I, 3:383; McElroy, *Struggle for Missouri*, 67.

26. Parrish, *Turbulent Partnership*, 26–28; Nicolay, *Outbreak of the Rebellion*, 120–22. Bates's protégé Charles Gibson counseled the opposite and supported Lyon. C. Gibson to E. Bates, April 22, 1861, *OR* I, 1:672–73.

27. Stohlman, *Powerless Position*, 20–21.

28. Basler, *Collected Works of Abraham Lincoln*, 4:372–73; Parrish, *Turbulent Partnership*, 29; L. Thomas to Harney, May 27, 1861, *OR* I, 3:376. Blair's First Missouri Volunteers was organized on April 27, 1861. Rombauer, *Union Cause in St. Louis*, 196.

29. Parrish, *Frank Blair*, 108.

30. Parrish, *Turbulent Partnership*, 30–32; Parrish, *Frank Blair*, 107–11; Phillips, *Damned Yankee*, 209–14.

31. "Record of Services of Major-General John M. Schofield, July 1849 to June 1893," Box 96, Schofield Papers, LC; Schofield, *Forty-Six Years*, 37; McDonough, *Schofield*, 19; Ganoe, *History of the United States Army*, 253–55. Russell F. Weigley notes Scott's resistance to breaking up the regular army to serve as trainers for the volunteers. Weigley, *History of the United States Army*, 186–87, 197–201.

32. Schofield to Chester Harding, July 26, 1861, *OR* I, 3:408; Report of Brigadier General Lyon, August 2, 1861, *OR* I, 3:47; Schofield, *Forty-Six Years*, 37–38; McDonough, *Schofield*, 19–20; Phillips, *Damned Yankee*, 236–37, 242.

33. Lyon to Kelton, August 4, 1861, *OR* I, 3:47.

34. Parrish, *Frank Blair*, 116–17; Schofield, *Forty-Six Years*, 39–41.

35. Brooksher, *Bloody Hill*, 171; Phillips, *Damned Yankee*, 246–48.

36. Sifakis, *Who Was Who in the Union*, 371–72.

37. Brooksher, *Bloody Hill*, 174–75; Snead, *Fight for Missouri*, 118.

38. Phillips, *Damned Yankee*, 249–51.

39. Wherry, "Wilson's Creek and the Death of Lyon," 293.

40. Schofield, *Forty-Six Years*, 42–43.

41. Knapp, *Wilson's Creek Staff Ride and Battlefield Tour*, 11–12, 51–55.

42. *OR* I, 3:62; Schofield, *Forty-Six Years*, 44.

43. Schofield, *Forty-Six Years*, 44–45.

44. Phillips, *Damned Yankee*, 255–56; Brooksher, *Bloody Hill*, 212–14; Schofield, *Forty-Six Years*, 45–46. Schofield later discovered that one lieutenant colonel remained on the field, but no one questioned Sturgis's assumption of command. In the early stages of the war many of the new colonels and generals still deferred to the experience of the regulars.

45. *OR* I, 3:66–71, 75–78; Phillips, *Damned Yankee*, 255–56; Brooksher, *Bloody Hill*, 214–22; Schofield, *Forty-Six Years*, 45–47.

46. Brooksher, *Bloody Hill*, 223–24.

47. *OR* I, 3:66–71; Schofield, *Forty-Six Years*, 46.

48. Union: engaged 5,400; killed 258; wounded 873; missing 186; total casualties 1,317. Confederate: engaged 10,200; killed 279; wounded 951; total casualties 1,230. Knapp, *Wilson's Creek Staff Ride and Battlefield Tour*, 69.

49. Piston and Hatcher discuss the courage and tenacity of the soldiers in a chapter entitled, "Never Disgrace Your Town." Piston and Hatcher, *Wilson's Creek*, 317–28.

50. Ware, *Lyon Campaign*, 227.

51. *OR* I, 3:55, 69; *Daily Missouri Democrat*, August 1861, quoted in McDonough, *Schofield*, 29.

52. In the early days of the war, officers were ineligible for the Medal of Honor. Schofield received the award three decades later (July 2, 1892) while serving as commanding general of the army. Schofield also sponsored the awarding of the Medal of Honor (October 30, 1895) to his longtime aide William M. Wherry, for his actions at Wilson's Creek. While Schofield's

position certainly had some influence on the awards process, the War Department awarded (and revoked) many of the Civil War Medals of Honor in the 1890s. Arthur MacArthur received the award for his heroic actions at Missionary Ridge on June 30, 1890. Daniel Sickles, who commanded V Corps at Gettysburg, where he lost a leg, received his award on October 30, 1897. Nor were these belated awards just for senior officers; many privates and sergeants received their awards decades later. See CMH, "Medal of Honor Citations," <http://www .army.mil/cmh-pg/moh1.htm> (accessed June 2005).

53. Schofield, *Forty-Six Years*, 39, 42.

54. Ibid., 48–49.

55. Parrish, *Frank Blair*, 124–27. Jessie Benton Fremont had persuaded her husband to arrest Blair. This arrest also confirmed the breach between Blair and many of his radical Republican supporters. The *Missouri Democrat* (a radical Republican paper) supported Fremont, as did the German-language papers.

56. Fremont would later claim that the Blair family's opposition stemmed from Fremont's refusal to give military contracts to Blair cronies. Lincoln began receiving similar reports of political interference, indecision, and inefficiency from newly appointed governor Gamble and prominent Unionist leaders Samuel T. Glover and James Broadhead. Even Fremont's subordinates grew critical. Brigadier General Samuel R. Curtis, a former Iowa congressman, wrote Lincoln on October 12, 1861, that Fremont "lacks the intelligence, the experience & sagacity necessary to his command." He went on to remind the president, "Public opinion is an element of war which must not be neglected." Quoted in Parrish, *Frank Blair*, 127–28.

57. Parrish, *Turbulent Partnership*, 50; Western Department Proclamation, August 14, 1861, RG 393, Pt. 1, E2763, NARA.

58. Parrish, *Turbulent Partnership*, 60.

59. Barton Bates to his father, Edward Bates, September 8, 1861, Bates Family Papers, MHS.

60. *OR* I, 3:477.

61. Lincoln to Fremont, September 11, 1861, *OR* I, 3:485–86; Parrish, *Frank Blair*, 121–22; Parrish, *Turbulent Partnership*, 60–63; Donald, *Lincoln*, 314–17.

62. Earlier on October 7, Lincoln gave Secretary of War Simon Cameron a letter granting him the authority to remove Fremont. Cameron went to Missouri to assess the situation and was persuaded by Fremont to postpone his relief for one more chance to destroy Price. Parrish, *Turbulent Partnership*, 74.

63. Parrish, *Frank Blair*, 133. The disasters at Bull Run, Ball's Bluff, and Wilson's Creek had prompted Congress to create the Joint Committee on the Conduct of the War. Fremont's friends on the committee painted Fremont as a victim—"emancipation's martyr." The committee largely disregarded the testimony of Montgomery and Frank Blair in its efforts to exonerate Fremont. Exasperated by the committee's partiality, Blair prepared a response. On the House floor, Blair attributed all defeats to Fremont. Rather hyperbolically, he declared that Missouri (meaning Lyon and Blair) had enjoyed success before Fremont came, and "as soon as the paralyzing influence of his imbecility was removed, victory came back to the standard of the Union in the West." Schofield played a minor role in these events by providing Blair a copy

of his report on Wilson's Creek. Schofield's report, however, was actually more helpful to Fremont. Schofield confirmed that Fremont's letter to Lyon just before the battle, which Fremont inexplicably failed to provide, indicated that no reinforcements were available and advised Lyon to fall back on Rolla. Frank Blair Jr., "Fremont's Hundred Days in Missouri," speech given in Congress, March 7, 1862, reel 13, Blair Family Papers, LC; Tap, *Over Lincoln's Shoulder*, 81–100; Schofield, *Forty-Six Years*, 39–40; Schofield to Halleck, February 13, 1862, *OR* I, 3:93–98.

64. Welcher, *Union Army*, 2:88.

CHAPTER THREE

1. The terms "hard" and "soft" war are useful expressions for understanding policy differences in dealing with rebellion and guerrilla war. They must, however, be employed cautiously. Different leaders advocated different policies about different issues during the war, most notably slavery. There was no bright line between hard and soft (conciliatory) war policies. Michael Fellman stresses the pragmatic nature and even desperate expediency of many policy decisions. Fellman, *Inside War*, 81–97. Also see Grimsley, *Hard Hand of War*, 1–22.

2. John M. Schofield, "The Border War between Missouri and Kansas," handwritten manuscript, Box 91, Schofield Papers, LC.

3. Ambrose, *Halleck*, 6–10.

4. Henry Halleck Schofield was born November 24, 1862, and died July 29, 1863. He was buried in Bellefontaine Cemetery in St. Louis. Avery D. Andrews, "A Few Family Notes, Genealogical and Otherwise," privately printed and provided by Schofield Andrews Jr., Nova Scotia. Most of Schofield's children were given family names, except for Henry and Richmond; the latter was born in Richmond, Virginia. Naming children for famous and influential people was a common practice. Schofield's naming his son after the commanding general was probably intended as both flattery and sincere admiration.

5. Marszalek, *Commander of All Lincoln's Armies*, 150.

6. Charles P. Draper, "Generals I Have Met," File 96, Draper-McClurg Papers, WHMC.

7. *OR* I, 8:354–56, 389; Schofield, *Forty-Six Years*, 54–56; McDonough, *Schofield*, 29–41.

8. *OR* I, 8:493–94.

9. Schofield to Lieutenant Governor Willard P. Hall, November 21, 1863, RG 393, E2579, NARA.

10. See Schofield to Colonel John Gray, A.G. of Missouri, July 28, 1863, RG 393, Pt. 1, E2571, NARA. Since EMM officers could not command U.S. troops and juniors should not command seniors, Schofield directed Gray to ensure that the U.S. officer was senior where there were combined U.S. and EMM troops.

11. Halleck to Gamble, September 27, 1862, Gamble Papers, MHS.

12. *OR* I, 8:422–23, 13:7–9, 436, 439; Schofield, *Forty-Six Years*, 54–56. For Governor Gamble's complaints about U.S. Volunteer officers' assuming command of state troops and

Halleck's hair-splitting response, see *OR* III, 2:579, 591. Also Halleck to Gamble, September 27, 1862, Gamble Papers, MHS.

13. *OR* I, 8:468.

14. *OR* I, 8:476–79.

15. Later, as commanding general of the army, Halleck issued War Department G.O. no. 100, April 24, 1863, which codified the laws of war. For a discussion of G.O. no. 100 and Halleck's guerrilla policy, see Fellman, *Inside War*, 81–89. Also see Birtle, *U.S. Army Counterinsurgency and Contingency Operations Doctrine*, 32–36.

16. Military trials of civilians were not entirely unprecedented, but the scope of jurisdiction and the scale of the trials were unique. For a brief history of military commissions, see Neely, *Fate of Liberty*, 167–68.

17. Ibid., 32–50, 160–67.

18. General Court-martial Orders, Department of the Missouri, 1861–63, RG 153, NARA.

19. "Our kind-hearted president does not understand the problems created by indefinitely suspending these sentences. They encourage the offenders. Promptitude in executing the sentences is absolutely necessary. . . . Can you help us change the rules to give approval authority to the [commanding general], District of Missouri or Governor of Missouri?" H. R. Gamble to Edward Bates, July 14, 1862, Bates to Gamble, July 24, 1862, Bates Family Papers, MHS. Also see Fellman, *Inside War*, 86–93.

20. Parrish, *Turbulent Partnership*, 55; *OR* I, 8:478, 482, 502.

21. *OR* I, 8:502, 663, 607.

22. *OR* II, 1:254.

23. Schofield's moderation was, in later years, appreciated by ex-guerrillas. Joseph Mudd, who rode with Colonel Joseph C. Porter, observed that Schofield was "not a cruel man," but he was increasingly influenced by the "bloodthirsty press of the state." Mudd, *With Porter in North Missouri*, 71, 336. By the summer of 1862, even many moderates thought the oath and bond system was "played out." They believed that most guerrillas simply laughed at it, not believing the government would retaliate. Surgeon James Martin to Schofield, July 28, 1862, and G. O. Geiser, July 19, 1862, RG 393, Pt.3, E367, NARA.

24. Andrew Birtle argues that the U.S. Army did not develop any new ideas on guerrilla warfare and pacification during the Civil War, but it did validate and codify old ones. They can be summarized as the "firm-but-fair" approach, which stressed restraint but permitted retaliation, and the "hard war" policy, which sanctioned the use of devastation to pacify a population. Schofield was a definite proponent of the "firm-but-fair" method to counter guerrilla operations, and he flinched at Grant's and Sherman's "hard war" philosophy. Birtle, *U.S. Army Counterinsurgency and Contingency Operations Doctrine*, 48.

25. Welcher, *Union Army*, 2:90.

26. *OR* I, 8:582.

27. *OR* I, 13:8.

28. *OR* I, 13:368. Blair wrote Schofield, "Our delegation in Congress would be glad to have you left in command in Missouri if Halleck goes with the army across the Mississippi.

Secretary of War said that [decision] would be left with Halleck." F. Blair to Schofield, March 1, 1862, Box 39, Schofield Papers, LC. These friends also included Schofield's father-in-law William Bartlett, who repeatedly pressed Schofield's case to friend and Missouri representative James S. Rollins. Bartlett also blamed the difficulty in crushing the rebellion on the extremism of the abolitionists. Like Frank Blair and so many of Schofield's political supporters, Rollins was a Republican during the war but later joined the Democratic Party. Bartlett to Rollins, March 13, 1862, April 7, 1862, and April 30, 1862, Rollins Papers, WHMC.

29. *OR* I, 13:398–400. James G. Blunt was born in Maine in 1826, practiced medicine in Ohio, and moved to Kansas in 1856. Shea, *War in the West,* 79.

30. *OR* I, 13:386–88.

31. *OR* I, 13:386–88, 392–93. This incident was not the first, or the most serious, incursion by Kansans into Missouri, but it was important in shaping Schofield's view of department organization and in forming his subsequent relations with Blunt. See *OR* I, 8:507–8, 552–53. Colonel Charles Jennison was the most notorious "Jayhawker." Despite his lawless and insubordinate behavior throughout the war, his ally, Senator James Lane, protected him. See Starr, *Jennison's Jayhawkers;* and Castel, *Frontier State at War.*

32. G.O. no. 1, District of Missouri, June 4, 1862, RG 393, Pt. 3, E367, NARA.

33. *OR* I, 13:7–22. Governor Gamble estimated 5,000–10,000. *OR* I, 13:557. McDonough estimates 5,000. McDonough, *Schofield,* 37. For the most detailed account of these actions see Nichols, *Guerrilla Warfare in Civil War Missouri.*

34. MSM G.O. no. 18, May 29, 1862, *OR* I, 13:402–3.

35. District of Missouri G.O. no. 3, June 23, 1862, *OR* I, 13:446–47.

36. S.O. no. 30, June 29, 1862, RG 393, Pt. 3, E370, NARA.

37. Halleck and John Pope had earlier levied such fines. *OR* I, 3:135, 422, 431.

38. Stanton to Schofield, September 5, 1862, and District of Missouri G.O. no. 19, September 11, 1862, Box 42, Schofield Papers, LC; McPherson, *Battle Cry of Freedom,* 500–501; Schofield, *Forty-Six Years,* 56–58. Mark Grimsley recounts the political compromises that produced the "confusing" law. He also concludes Pope's orders had little real impact. Grimsley, *Hard Hand of War,* 68–71, 75, 78, 90.

39. Sude, "Federal Military Policy and Strategy in Missouri and Arkansas," 58–64, 73–75.

40. MSM G.O. no. 19, July 22, 1862, *OR* I, 13:506–8. Also see Nichols, *Guerrilla Warfare in Civil War Missouri,* 103–5.

41. *OR* I, 13:10.

42. MSM G.O. no. 19, July 22, 1862, *OR* I, 13:506–8. Schofield's report of December 7, 1862, explains and justifies his actions. *OR* I, 13:7–22, 513–15; Schofield, *Forty-Six Years,* 56; Parrish, *Turbulent Partnership,* 92; Lause, "Brief History of the Enrolled Missouri Militia."

43. Stanton to Schofield, July 26, 1862, Box 42, Schofield Papers, LC; *OR* III, 2:294; *OR* I, 13:518–19; Colonel J. M. Glover to Schofield, July 30, 1862, RG 393, Pt. 3, E367, NARA.

44. Gamble to Schofield, July 24, 1862, RG 393, Pt. 3, E367, NARA; MSM G.O. no. 23, July 28, 1862, *OR* I, 13:518–19.

45. Major Edward Harding to Schofield, August 28, 1862, RG 393, Pt. 2, E367, NARA.

46. *Report of the Committee . . . to Investigate the Conduct and Management of the Militia.*

47. Smith, *Francis Preston Blair Family in Politics*, 2:219.

48. Halleck to Schofield, July 30, 1862, Box 40, Schofield Papers, LC.

49. Schofield endorsement to Brigadier General J. Totten to Lieutenant Colonel C. W. Marsh, August 3, 1862, RG 393, Pt. 3, E367, NARA; G.O. no. 23, September 22, 1862, RG 393, Pt. 3, E369, NARA.

50. *OR* I, 22/1:810–11.

51. *OR* I, 22/1:810–11, 827; *OR* I, 13:11–12. One of the complainants was Dr. W. G. Eliot, the president of Washington University, grandfather of T. S. Eliot, and Schofield's former boss. Eliot argued in a December 1 letter that the assessments were often unavoidably arbitrary and created grievances. With the crisis passed, he hoped the assessments would be suspended until other methods for obtaining funds were explored. General Curtis, though asserting the right of military necessity, attempted to pass the problem to Halleck. *OR* I, 22/1:801–3.

52. Halleck notified Gamble of federal support for the EMM on June 3, 1863. *Annual Report of the Adjutant General of the State of Missouri*, December 31, 1863, 27.

53. *OR* I, 13:536; Sude, "Federal Military Policy and Strategy in Missouri and Arkansas," 72–77.

54. *OR* I, 13:532.

55. Schofield, *Forty-Six Years*, 58–60. In his first message to Halleck, Blair wrote, "Nobody is authorized to ask Schofield's removal in my name. I have written to Hon. M. Blair, asking that his powers may be more ample, and that he be disembarrassed from the authority of Governor Gamble." *OR* I, 13:562.

56. Henry T. Blow to A. Lincoln, August 12, 1862, Blow Family Papers, MHS. Blow (1817–75) was elected as an Unconditional Unionist to the Thirty-eighth Congress and as a Republican to the Thirty-ninth Congress (March 1863–March 1867).

57. Ibid.

58. Halleck to Schofield, August 10, 1862, and Halleck to Blair, August 12, 1862, Schofield Papers, LC; Schofield, *Forty-Six Years*, 58–61; Parrish, *Frank Blair*, 154–56.

59. *OR* I, 13:558.

60. Ibid., 561.

61. Ibid., 574.

62. Ibid., 560.

63. Halleck to Schofield, September 9, 1862, Box 40, Schofield Papers, LC.

64. Welcher, *Union Army*, 2:82–84, 92–95.

65. *OR* I, 13:601; Sude, "Federal Military Policy and Strategy in Missouri and Arkansas," 71–84. "I deem it not only important but absolutely necessary, that Missouri and Arkansas be under the same command, in view of future military operations, aside from the fact that Saint Louis is the base of supplies for both. For the same reason Kansas should be added to the department, at least for the present. Harmonious operations on the part of the Kansas and Missouri troops are of great importance at this time, but it seems impossible to secure such harmony between independent commands." Schofield to Halleck, August 12, 1862, *OR* I, 13:562–63.

66. Halleck to Schofield, September 20, 1862, *OR* I, 13:654.

67. Ibid.

68. While sick with typhoid fever and in a deeply depressed mood, Schofield wrote a letter to Halleck recounting his grievances against Curtis. Schofield to Halleck, November 18, 1862, Schofield Papers, LC. Curtis and Schofield bickered over these issues in Curtis's objections to Schofield's December 1862 report; *OR* I, 13:7–29. Curtis underestimated the aid provided by Schofield and the risks Schofield took to provide such aid amid major guerrilla activity. While Curtis was correct that Schofield overestimated the size of the Confederate forces threatening Missouri, Schofield was also correct that the inactivity of the forces in Helena ceded the initiative to the rebels. Sude, "Federal Military Policy and Strategy in Missouri and Arkansas," 77–84.

69. Schofield to Gamble, September 24, 1862, Gamble Papers, MHS.

70. Montgomery Blair to Hamilton Gamble, September 27, 1862, Gamble Papers, MHS.

71. McDonough, *Schofield*, 39. The contested areas of Missouri, Arkansas, and Tennessee were especially hard on local Unionists. They were persecuted by the Confederates and treated as rebels by the Union forces. See William Baxter's account of Unionist travails in Fayetteville, Arkansas, *Pea Ridge and Prairie Grove*.

72. McDonough, *Schofield*, 39, labeled it typhoid fever, based on a report in the *Missouri Democrat*. Schofield termed it "bilious fever," and others called it "camp fever." Schofield, *Forty-Six Years*, 62; Sude, "Federal Military Policy and Strategy in Missouri and Arkansas," 105; *OR* I, 13:787.

73. Shea, *War in the West*, 79–103.

74. Schofield, *Forty-Six Years*, 63–67.

75. Cox, *Reminiscences of the Civil War*, 1:427–34. Lincoln justified the extra generals based on the increases in authorized troops and the 1861 law that provided for one brigadier general for four regiments and one major general for three brigades. Smith, Wright, Cox, and Schofield would ultimately be promoted to major general. Cox attributed his rejection to the fact that he was barely on speaking terms with Senator Benjamin F. Wade and had supported John Sherman's opponent for the Ohio Senate seat in 1860.

76. *OR* I, 22/1:853; Schofield, *Forty-Six Years*, 64, 67.

77. Sude, "Federal Military Policy and Strategy in Missouri and Arkansas," 98–115; *OR* I, 17/2:401.

78. Schofield to Halleck, November 18, 1862, Schofield Papers, LC; *OR* I, 8:23–29.

79. *OR* I, 22/2:6.

80. *OR* I, 22/2:88, 94. In the second letter to Halleck, dated February 3, 1863, Schofield wrote: "I am compelled to say that I believe the interests of the service demand my removal from this command. . . . I do not desire to impugn the motives of General Curtis. He may be perfectly honest and sincere in all his official acts; whether so or not is immaterial. The fact is undeniable that his whole course, while I have been in command of this army, has been calculated to prevent my accomplishing any good result. He has discouraged every advance I have made, and repeatedly ordered me to fall back."

81. Sude has observed that Schofield's complaints were made in ignorance of the orders that placed the troops in Arkansas subject to Grant's orders and therefore reduced the troops

available to Curtis. But Sude concludes that Schofield's criticism of Curtis had merit, especially in Curtis's failure to coordinate the efforts of the Army of the Frontier with the Army of the Southeast. Sude, "Federal Military Policy and Strategy in Missouri and Arkansas," 129–31.

82. S.O. no. 93, April 8, 1863, Department of the Missouri, Box 44, RG 94, NARA; *OR* I, 22/2:208; James Hardie, AAG, to Schofield, April 10, 1863, Box 42, Schofield Papers, LC.

83. Schofield, *Forty-Six Years*, 66; McDonough, *Schofield*, 41–42; Rosecrans to Schofield, May 27, 1863, Box 39, Schofield Papers, LC.

84. Rosecrans (1819–98) was removed as Department of the Missouri commander in December 1864 as the radicals solidified their hold on the state government. He spent the rest of the war awaiting orders.

CHAPTER FOUR

1. *OR* I, 22/1:801–3, 805–6, 810–11, 826–27, 832–33, 888; *OR* I, 13:11–12, 691, 693, 736, 800; Schofield, *Forty-Six Years*, 57–58; Parrish, *Turbulent Partnership*, 113–16.

2. *OR* I, 22/1:877–78; *OR* I, 22/2:6–7, 88–89; Parrish, *Turbulent Partnership*, 110–13.

3. *OR* III, 2:646–47, 658–61, 702–4, 735–36, 955; *OR* I, 22/1:839–40, 878; Parrish, *Turbulent Partnership*, 103–7; Sude, "Federal Military Policy and Strategy in Missouri and Arkansas," 133–34; Charles Gibson to Lincoln, February 23, 1863, Gamble Papers, MHS.

4. Halleck to Curtis, February 18, 1863, Box 40, Schofield Papers, LC.

5. Schofield to Gamble, February 2, 1863, Gamble Papers, MHS.

6. Edward Bates to Sumner, March 7, 14, 1863, Bates Family Papers, MHS; Bates to Gamble, March 19, April 23, 1863, Bates Family Papers, MHS.

7. Hamilton Gamble Jr. to Governor Gamble, March 6, 1863, and Gamble to Lincoln, May 2, 1863, Gamble Papers, MHS; Parrish, *Turbulent Partnership*, 119–21.

8. *OR* I, 22/2:293; Basler, *Collected Works of Abraham Lincoln*, 4:234 (emphasis added).

9. *St. Louis Missouri Republican*, May 25, May 29, 1863; *Columbia Missouri Statesman*, May 29, 1863; *St. Louis Tri-Weekly Missouri Democrat*, May 29, June 1, 1863.

10. Daniel Draper to sister, June 3, 1863, Draper-McClurg Papers, WHMC.

11. *OR* I, 22/2:285.

12. Marsh to Ripley, June 9, 1863, RG 393, Pt. 1, E2571, NARA.

13. Gamble to Lincoln, July 13, 1863, Lincoln to Gamble, July 23, 1863, Gamble Papers, MHS.

14. *St. Louis Tri-Weekly Missouri Democrat*, July 13, 22, 1863; Parrish, *Turbulent Partnership*, 150–52. Schofield was not mollified, however, and decades later insisted that he would have arrested McKee again for the outrage to the president. Schofield, *Forty-Six Years*, 425. Jim A. Hart says the source was generally believed to have been Charles D. Drake, a prominent radical Republican politician. But this does not preclude Drake's getting it from a Curtis man. Hart, *History of the St. Louis Globe-Democrat*, 60–61.

15. Schofield quoted most of Gamble's letter in Schofield, *Forty-Six Years*, 72–74.

16. *OR* I, 22/2:290–92.

17. Ibid. Two recent studies of Halleck's service emphasize Halleck's extreme reluctance to override the judgments of the commanders on the spot, despite the seeming clarity of vision of those in Washington, D.C. Halleck thus sought to protect and insulate field commanders from the demands of impatient politicians. This, of course, worked well with able commanders but less well with incompetents. But then, even the most emphatic orders failed to move some Civil War commanders. While Curt Anders is sympathetic of Halleck's views, John Marszalek is more critical and concludes that Halleck sometimes "refused to command." See Anders, *Henry Halleck's War*; and Marszalek, *Commander of All Lincoln's Armies*, 1–2.

18. Schofield, later, asked Grant as a "personal kindness" to let Schofield retain his brother Captain George W. Schofield as a staff officer. George served on the staff and as chief of artillery until the end of the war. He continued to serve on his brother's staff for much of his career. Schofield to Grant, August 2, 1863, RG 393, E2579, NARA.

19. *OR* I, 22/1:18–24; Schofield to Colonel Kelton, HQ Army, May 30, 1863, Schofield to Gamble, June 3, 1863, Wherry to Brigadier General Allen, Q.M., and Surgeon Magruder, June 5, 1863, RG 393, Pt. 1, E2571, NARA; *OR* I, 22/1:13.

20. Records of the District of St. Louis show hundreds of cases where penniless soldiers were given transportation vouchers to return them to their units, while the units were informed to deduct the money from their pay. RG 393, Pt. 1, E2571, NARA.

21. Ironically, Dick had been a longtime ally of Frank Blair's before the war but was now identified as a Curtis man. Parrish, *Turbulent Partnership*, 27, 110, 155.

22. Welcher, *Union Army*, 2:93–105; *OR* I, 22/2:315. Schofield responded that he did not have the authority to grant leaves except for sickness. He also thought it improper for officers to be absent all winter yet retain their commissions. But he naturally bowed to orders. Lincoln to Schofield, November 10, 1863, Schofield to Lincoln, November 11, 1863, in Basler, *Collected Works of Abraham Lincoln*, 7:8, 10; Stanton to Schofield, November 21, 1863, Box 42, Schofield Papers, LC.

23. "The Indian Territory, the State of Kansas south of the 38th parallel, the western tier of counties of Missouri south of the same parallel, and the western tier of counties of Arkansas will constitute the District of the Frontier, and will be commanded by Maj. Gen. James G. Blunt; headquarters at Fort Scott, or in the field. The State of Kansas north of the 38th parallel, and the two western tiers of counties of Missouri north of the same parallel and south of the Missouri River will constitute the District of the Border, and will be commanded by Brig. Gen. Thomas Ewing, Jr.; headquarters at Kansas City." G.O. no. 48, June 9, 1863, *OR* I, 22/2:315.

24. These counties were Jackson, Cass, Bates, Lafayette, Johnson, Henry, St. Clair, and the northern part of Vernon. On September 23, 1863, after the Quantrill raid and G.O. no. 11, Schofield transferred Lafayette, Johnson, and Henry Counties to the District of Central Missouri.

25. Charles Blair to Ewing, November 18, 1863, Ewing to Jennison, November 25, 1863, Thomas Ewing Jr. to Thomas Ewing Sr., September 22, 1863, H. G. Fant to Ewing, July 18 and 20, 1863, Ewing to Schofield, July 24, 1863, Ewing Papers, LC.

26. After Schofield's removal from command of the Department of the Missouri and Curtis's appointment as commander of the Department of Kansas in January 1864, Ewing was transferred to St. Louis and fought Sterling Price at Pilot Knob on September 27, 1864. Ewing

returned to Ohio after the war and served two terms in Congress (1877–81) as a Democrat. He later practiced law in New York City and died in 1896.

27. Parrish, *Turbulent Partnership*, 126; *OR* I, 22/2:301.

28. Schofield, *Forty-Six Years*, 74–75; *St. Louis Tri-Weekly Missouri Democrat*, June 12, 1863.

29. Lincoln to Schofield, June 22, 1863, in Basler, *Collected Works of Abraham Lincoln*, 6:291.

30. Parrish, *Turbulent Partnership*, 123–48, 200–201.

31. *Daily Missouri Democrat*, September 2, 1863; G.O. no. 87, August 26, 1863, RG 153, NARA.

32. Schofield to Gamble, July 3, 1863, RG 393, E2579, NARA; Schofield to L. Thomas, June 10, 1863, RG 393, Pt. 1, E2571, NARA; "Enlistment of Colored Troops," *Missouri Democrat*, June 10, 1863; Schofield to Stanton, July 17, 1863, RG 393, Pt. 1, E2571, NARA.

33. Schofield to L. Thomas, September 26, 1863, RG 393, Pt. 1, E2571, NARA; Schofield to Townsend, September 29, 1863, RG 393, Pt. 1, E2571, NARA.

34. Schofield to L. Thomas, September 26, 1863, Schofield to Townsend, September 29, 1863, Schofield to L. Thomas, June 10, 1863, RG 393, Pt. 1, E2571, NARA; "Enlistment of Colored Troops," *Missouri Democrat*, June 10, 1863; Schofield to Gamble, July 3, 1863, RG 393, E2579, NARA; *Annual Report of the Adjutant General of the State of Missouri*, December 31, 1863, 531.

35. Schofield to Townsend, November 25, 1863, Schofield to Jacob Ammen, District of Illinois, July 18, 1863, RG 393, Pt. 1, E2571, NARA.

36. Schofield, *Forty-Six Years*, 85.

37. Fifty "bushwhackers" from the Osage River region and a hundred Confederate recruits under Colonel John Holt, who refused to participate in the massacre and looting, joined Quantrill's raid. Castel, *Frontier State at War*, 126.

38. In his report Thomas Ewing faulted Captain J. A. Pike's "error in judgement" for not following Quantrill "promptly and closely." Had Pike done so, Ewing believed that "Quantrill would never have gone as far as Lawrence, or attacked it, with 100 men close to his rear." *OR* I, 22/1:580. While Pike's reluctance to pursue a superior force in the dark is somewhat understandable, his failure to raise the alarm in the area, especially at the two prime targets of Lawrence and Olathe, is less so.

39. Castel, *Frontier State at War*, 124–41; Brownlee, *Gray Ghosts of the Confederacy*, 121–25; *OR* I, 22/1:578–90.

40. *OR* I, 22/1:573; *OR* I, 22/2: 460–62.

41. Neely, "'Unbeknownst' to Lincoln"; *OR* I, 22/2:471–72.

42. *OR* I, 22/2:471–72; "Diary of Events in Department of the Missouri," Box 1, Schofield Papers, LC; Schofield, *Forty-Six Years*, 80–84. According to William Wherry's 1884 note, this diary was dictated by Schofield to his brother and aide George W. Schofield. The Schofield Papers contain several such "diaries" for relatively narrow time periods. Rather than regularly chronicling events, Schofield seems to have felt the need to put his side of controversial events down on paper for future reference.

43. "Diary of Events in Department of the Missouri."

44. Ewing to Schofield, August 25, 1863, T. Ewing to J. R. Usher [secretary of interior], August 28, 1863, and Schofield to Ewing, August 28, 1863, Ewing Papers, LC; "Diary of Events in Department of the Missouri."

45. Concerning his promotion, Schofield requested Ewing's help, writing, "I don't know whether there will be serious opposition to my confirmation, probably not, yet your influence will doubtless aid me and I shall be obliged for it." Schofield to Ewing, December 12, 1863, Ewing Papers, LC.

46. "Diary of Events in Department of the Missouri"; D. R. Anthony to T. Ewing, July 17, 1863, A. H. Jennison to Ewing, July 19, 1863, and Anthony to Ewing, September 8, 1863, Ewing Papers, LC.

47. "Diary of Events in Department of the Missouri"; *OR* I, 22/2:693–94; Castel, "Order No. 11."

48. Schofield told Ewing that "the test of loyalty should be rather liberal than severe, the object being to permit those, and only those, to return who will hereafter be faithful to the Government. Under the reign of terror which has so long existed on the border, active loyalty could not be expected. All who return should be enrolled, and their names registered at the nearest military post." *OR* I, 22/2:693–94.

49. Parrish, *Turbulent Partnership*, 158; "Diary of Events in Department of the Missouri"; Schofield, *Forty-Six Years*, 80–84; Draft review by Thomas Ewing of book on Order No. 11, Ewing Papers, LC

50. Basler, *Collected Works of Abraham Lincoln*, 6:492.

51. For varying analyses of G.O. no. 11 and the border war, see Castel, "Order No. 11"; Gilmore, "Total War on the Missouri Border"; Matthews and Lindberg, " 'Better Off in Hell' "; SenGupta, "Bleeding Kansas"; Crouch, " 'Fiend in Human Shape?' "; Lewis, "Propaganda and the Kansas-Missouri War"; McPherson, "From Limited to Total War"; Hatley and Ampssler, "Army General Orders Number 11"; Cheatham, " 'Desperate Characters' "; Niepman, "General Orders No. 11 and Border Warfare"; Mink, "General Orders, No. 11"; and Castel, "Quantrill's Bushwhackers." For an excellent survey of recent writings on Civil War guerrilla warfare see Sutherland, "Sideshow No Longer."

52. Hunt, "General Orders No. 11," 6. Shelby supposedly made the statement in 1897.

53. Halleck to Schofield, July 7, 1863, Box 40, Schofield Papers, LC; Schofield, *Forty-Six Years*, 86; *Daily Missouri Democrat*, September 11, 1863; *Columbia Statesman*, September 18, 1863.

54. Schofield, *Forty-Six Years*, 84–87; Neely, *Fate of Liberty*, 68–74; *OR* I, 22/2:558, 563; "Enrolled Militia," *Daily Missouri Democrat*, September 9, 1863; Parrish, *Turbulent Partnership*, 166.

55. Gamble to Lincoln, September 30, 1863, Gamble Papers, MHS. Bates reassured Rollins that based on his timely warning about the "Jacobin Delegation," "Schofield would not be relieved." Bates to Rollins, September 26, 1862, Rollins Papers, WHMC.

56. Gantt also admitted that failure of Schofield's nomination had crippled him, but he said if Schofield were removed then "send him to the army of the Cumberland and send Frank

Blair here!" Thomas Gantt to Montgomery Blair, September 30, 1863, reel 22, Blair Family Papers, LC.

57. Gamble to Bates, October 17, 1863, Bates Family Papers, MHS; Gamble to Willard Hall, August 15, 1863, Gamble Papers, MHS.

58. If there were an aura of extremism about the radicals, there was still the whiff of unreality about the conservatives. As late as 1863, Representative James Rollins hoped that Sterling Price would abandon his commitment to the rebellion. Lincoln, with little to lose, told Rollins he would pardon Price if he returned and took the oath of allegiance. Lincoln to Rollins, August 1863, Rollins Papers, WHMC.

59. "Diary of Events in Department of the Missouri," 95.

60. Parrish, *Turbulent Partnership*, 166; Schofield, *Forty-Six Years*, 85–99.

61. "Diary of Events in Department of the Missouri," 88. Schofield issued G.O. no. 120, which outlined the loyalty oaths for voting and the procedures for those in the militia. Those on active service would vote at company polls, while those not on active service could vote at regular polls. *OR* I, 22/2:668–70; Schofield to Drake and Schofield to J. S. Merrill, October 24, 1863, RG 393, E2579, NARA.

62. Lincoln to Schofield, October 1, 1863, and Lincoln to Charles D. Drake and others, October 5, 1863, in Basler, *Collected Works of Abraham Lincoln*, 6:492–93, 499–504.

63. Donald, *Lincoln*, 452–54.

64. Lincoln to Charles D. Drake and others, October 5, 1863, in Basler, *Collected Works of Abraham Lincoln*, 6:504.

65. Basler, *Collected Works of Abraham Lincoln*, 6:543–44; *OR* I, 22/2:666, 670, 680, 698.

66. "Diary of Events in Department of the Missouri," 90–99, 120–21; Schofield to Colonel Townsend, October 3, 1863, RG 393, E2571, NARA; Halleck to Schofield, October 12, 1863, RG 393, NARA; *OR* I, 22/1:12–17; *OR* I, 22/2:677–78, 689. Blunt would regain district command under Curtis, as commander of the District of Upper Arkansas and later South Kansas. Welcher, *Union Army*, 2:74–75.

67. Schofield, *Forty-Six Years*, 107–8.

68. Lincoln to Stanton, December 18 and December 21, 1863, in Basler, *Collected Works of Abraham Lincoln*, 7:61–62, 78–79, 84–85; Dennett, *Lincoln and the Civil War*, 139–40; Schofield, *Forty-Six Years*, 107–12. Senator B. Gratz Brown's January 20, 1864, opposition speech to Schofield's promotion to major general included a petition signed by sixty-four members of the Missouri legislature. The opposition letter was signed by Ben Loan, J. W. McClurg, S. H. Boyd, and Henry T. Blow. "Confirmation of General Schofield," speech of Honorable B. Gratz Brown of Missouri, January 20, 1864, Sampson Family Papers, WHMC.

69. Bartlett to Rollins, December 14, 1863, Schofield to Rollins, February 18, 1864, and Bartlett to Rollins, February 19, 1863, Rollins Papers, WHMC. Schofield was first appointed major general of Volunteers on November 29, 1862, but the Senate failed to ratify him, and his term expired March 4, 1863. Lincoln reappointed him on May 12, 1863. The December 31, 1863, list sent to the Senate included Schofield with a date of rank of November 29, 1862. The Senate finally approved the list on May 12, 1864. Memo by AAG Chalfin, ACP J. M. Schofield 2556, 1883, RG 94, NARA.

70. As of December 31, 1863, Missouri had contributed 104,927 troops (nearly 10 percent of the state's population) to the Union cause. Missouri volunteers: 35,355; MSM: 16,918; EMM: 46,893; sundries: 5,761 (including 2,409 African American troops). *Annual Report of the Adjutant General of the State of Missouri*, December 31, 1863, 531.

CHAPTER FIVE

1. Schofield, *Forty-Six Years*, 110. This chapter focuses primarily on the political, operational, and interpersonal aspects of the Atlanta campaign. For the tactical details of the campaign and Schofield's role, see McDonough, *Schofield*, 70–98. For the most comprehensive analysis of the campaign see Castel, *Decision in the West*.

2. Schofield, *Forty-Six Years*, 109; Grant to Halleck, January 13, 1864, Box 40, Schofield Papers, LC; *OR* I, 31/3:571; Browning, *Diaries*, 1:676. Halleck, probably with Lincoln's approval, had suggested Schofield to Grant on December 29, 1863. *OR* I, 31/3:529.

3. Cox, *Reminiscences*, 2:162; *OR* I, 36/2:746; *OR* I, 32/2:394; *OR* I, 32/3:289, 319–20.

4. J. B. Fry, *Miscellany*, 280–81, quoted in Cox, *Reminiscences*, 1:436. Since Thomas was a Virginian, his resentment was compounded by his own initial lack of political connections.

5. Cox, *Sherman's Battle for Atlanta*, 10–15.

6. Schofield, *Forty-Six Years*, 113–14; Schofield to Rollins, February 18, 1864, Rollins Papers, WHMC.

7. Grant to Schofield, February 11, 13, 16, 17, 21, March 5, 1864, Box 40, Schofield Papers, LC; *OR* I, 32/2:359, 374–75.

8. Schofield, *Forty-Six Years*, 117–19.

9. Ibid., 120; Sherman, *Memoirs*, 488, 519–20.

10. Schofield to W. T. Sherman, March 20, 1864, and Schofield to Potter, March 20, 1864, RG 393, Pt. 1, E3504, NARA. Grant had suggested closing down Camp Nelson, but Schofield wanted it to remain in operation. Kentucky, with its ample forage, was the staging ground for the cavalry forces for the department.

11. Schofield to T. Vincent, March 23, 1864, RG 393, Pt. 1, E3504, NARA; *OR* I, 32/3:105–6. Schofield later gave Cox his choice of continuing as chief of staff or commanding a division. Cox chose command. Cox, *Reminiscences*, 2:158–59.

12. Cox had an up-and-down career, both in war and peace. Having already commanded the IX Corps (September–October 1862) in the East and XXIII Corps (December 1863–February 1864) in the West, he, too, had failed to have his first promotion to major general (October 1862) confirmed. He commanded the 3rd Division, XXIII Corps, in the Atlanta and Nashville campaigns and the XXIII Corps in North Carolina. After the war he was a one-term governor of Ohio and served Grant as secretary of interior, until he broke with the president and resigned. Thereafter, he practiced law in Cincinnati and wrote many books and articles on the war, notably *Atlanta* (New York: C. Scribner's Sons, 1882) and *Sherman's March to the Sea—Franklin and Nashville* (New York: C. Scribner's Sons, 1882).

13. *OR* I, 32/2:359; Cox, *Reminiscences*, 2:159–60.

14. AAG to all division commanders, May 1, 1864, and Bascom, AAG, to Schofield, July 1, 1864, RG 393, Pt. 1, E3504, NARA. In May and June Schofield continued to attempt to direct cavalry raids and counterraids in east Tennessee and North Carolina. J. A. Campbell to J. Ammen, May 16 and June 1, 1864, Box 65, Schofield Papers, LC.

15. *OR* I, 32/3:178, 181, 208–9.

16. W. T. Sherman to John Sherman, April 14, 1864, Sherman Papers, LC.

17. Rappaport, "Replacement System." Many of Hovey's recruits were described as "old men and boys, who had been mustered into service without critical inspection." *OR* I, 38/2:522.

18. The deployed strength of Sherman's army group is from his campaign report, *OR* I, 38/1:62–63, 115. The departmental strengths come from departmental reports of April 30, 1864, *OR* I, 32/3:550–51, 561–62, 569. Also see Schofield's campaign report, *OR* I, 38/2:509; and Castel, *Decision in the West*, 111–14. For a useful discussion of the problems of counting troops and comparing Union and Confederate troop strengths, see Cox, *Sherman's Battle for Atlanta*, 25, 27–29, 241–244; and Sherman, *Memoirs*, 472–87.

19. Schofield, *Forty-Six Years*, 121.

20. Ibid., 120–23. Sherman's *Memoirs*, published in 1875, prompted many debates by or about those he criticized or insufficiently praised. Many with whom Sherman had clashed, like John A. McClernand, Joseph Hooker, and John Logan, were outraged. It particularly upset friends of George Thomas and the Army of the Cumberland. Schofield had hoped for more recognition, but he accepted it as Sherman's nature. Both Schofield and David Stanley published their memoirs after Sherman's death; but while Schofield's coolly analytical account combines praise with candid criticism, Stanley's repeated criticism was highly personal. Stanley, *Personal Memoirs*. Despite the criticism, Sherman's generalship in the Atlanta campaign was largely unchallenged for nearly one hundred years. Albert Castel's recent and very detailed account of the Atlanta campaign, *Decision in the West*, takes a highly critical view of Sherman's generalship and the accuracy of his memoirs. Other Sherman historians are critical but less reproachful than Castel. See Marszalek, *Sherman*, 259–87, 462–67; and McMurry, *Atlanta 1864*. See also Castel, "Prevaricating through Georgia"; and Marszalek, "Sherman Called It the Way He Saw It." For generally favorably views of Sherman's Atlanta campaign, see Jones, *Civil War Command and Strategy*; and McDonough and Jones, *War So Terrible*.

21. Schofield, *Forty-Six Years*, 123–24.

22. Joseph Hooker's command consisted of elements of XI Corps (two divisions) and XII Corps (two divisions) from the Army of the Potomac, but during the battle of Lookout Mountain he commanded divisions from the XII, IV, and XV Corps. In April 1864 XI and XII Corps were consolidated into XX Corps. See Welcher, *Union Army*, 2:166–73, 513–26. Hooker's two-corps "corps" was a combat command, while Schofield's one-corps "army" included a cavalry and departmental responsibilities. Schofield's overall command was larger, but the bulk of it remained in Tennessee and Kentucky.

23. Welcher, *Union Army*, 1:251–81.

24. Epstein, "Creation and Evolution of the Army Corps"; Schofield, *Forty-Six Years*, 123.

25. Sherman outranked Thomas by right of his presidential appointment to command the Military Division of the Mississippi.

26. Sherman, *Memoirs*, 528, 572–73.

27. The XX Corps was originally redesignated as I Corps, which happened to be the corps Hooker commanded in the Army of the Potomac. Two days later (April 6, 1864), Grant ordered the designation changed to XX Corps. Grant's reasons are obscure. Since George G. Meade had also commanded the I Corps, perhaps Grant hoped to one day recreate it in Meade's army. Or, perhaps Grant did not want Hooker to have "pride of place." Or, perhaps because there had been a previous XX Corps in the Army of the Cumberland (deactivated in September 1863), he thought that number more fitting. Regimental lineages had existed for decades, but the Civil War marked the emergence of unique corps lineages. Welcher, *Union Army*, 2:322–28. World War I marked the beginning of distinctive numbered divisions and field armies.

28. As of May 1, Thomas was preparing to move on Ringgold, while McPherson was still at Huntsville, Alabama, directing his troops to Chattanooga for a planned move to Rossville. This meant that Thomas was actually closer to Snake Creek Gap than McPherson. But a direct move by Thomas would probably have been detected by rebel cavalry. Furthermore, Thomas provided the engineers and most of the garrisons to maintain and protect the logistical base of the army group, hence Sherman's desire to move him along the railroad line to Dalton. *OR* I, 38/4:3, 5–9, 34–35. Both Cox and Schofield refer to Thomas's initial proposal. Cox, *Sherman's Battle for Atlanta*, 31; Schofield, *Forty-Six Years*, 129.

29. *OR* I, 38/1:59, 139–41; *OR* I, 38/4:38–40; Sherman, *Memoirs*, 496–500; Van Horne, *History of the Army of the Cumberland*, 2:60–61.

30. *OR* I, 38/1:63–64; *OR* I, 38/2:510–511; *OR* I 38/4:38–40, 56, 65, 70, 84, 86–88, 92–93, 105–6, 111–14, 120–25; Johnston, *Narrative of Military Operations*, 304–9; Castel, *Decision in the West*, 121–50.

31. Sherman was initially quite sanguine about McPherson's not taking Resaca, telling Halleck on May 10: "General McPherson reached Resaca, but found the place strongly fortified and guarded, and did not break the road. According to his instructions, he drew back to the debouches of the gorge, where he has a strong defensive position. . . . I must feign on Buzzard Roost, but pass through Snake Creek Gap, and place myself between Johnston and Resaca, when we will have to fight it out. I am making the preliminary move. Certain that Johnston can make no detachments, I will be in no hurry. My cavalry is just approaching from Kentucky and Tennessee (detained by the difficulty of getting horses), and even now it is less than my minimum." *OR* I, 38/4:111. Sherman did not believe that Johnston would so easily abandon his Dalton position. *OR* I, 38/4:138. Only after he realized that Johnston had thwarted his efforts to place himself between Johnston and Resaca did he fully appreciate the missed opportunity on May 9.

32. Sherman, *Memoirs*, 500; Schofield, *Forty-Six Years*, 124–29.

33. *OR* I, 38/1:664–66; *OR* I, 38/4:189–90, 199; Cox, *Sherman's Battle for Atlanta*, 37; Sherman, *Memoirs*, 500–505. Jacob Cox said Sherman's purpose was to strengthen the line so that major forces could be withdrawn for a flanking movement south of the Oostanaula River.

Cox, *Sherman's Battle for Atlanta*, 47. Castel states that because Sherman did not believe that Johnston would remain long at Resaca, he rejected Thomas's plan for another major flanking maneuver. Castel, *Decision in the West*, 154. Thomas recommended using Palmer to trap Johnston's army, while McPherson feinted at Resaca and crossed the Oostanaula River at Lay's Ferry to threaten Johnston's line of retreat to Calhoun. However, this proposal was based on the assumption that a substantial part of Johnston's army was still moving down from Dalton. *OR* I, 38/4:160–61. Without the installation of pontoon bridges, Lay's Ferry was incapable of sustaining the crossing of major forces. By the time the pontoons were in position, it was too late. The fact that Schofield's men were moved to the left flank, rather than positioned to use the pontoons, suggests that Sherman did not think that Johnston would long remain on the north side of the river.

34. Cox, *Sherman's Battle for Atlanta*, 58.

35. *OR* I, 38/4:121.

36. *OR* I, 38/1:735–36, 758–59, 774–75; *OR* I, 38/2:511, 581–82, 620–21, 715–16; *OR* I, 38/4:182, 243; Castel, *Decision in the West*, 150–60. In his report Schofield stated that Judah was relieved for physical disability. Judah (USMA class of 1843) was given rear-echelon jobs, like court-martial duty, until 1865, when he commanded the District of Etowah in the Department of the Cumberland. He died in 1866. Milo S. Hascall (USMA class of 1852) had resigned from the army in 1853. He was appointed a colonel of Volunteers in 1861 and by 1864 was an experienced brigade commander. Schofield recommended him for major general after the campaign, but Hascall resigned on October 27, 1864. Lieutenant Colonel Isaac Sherwood, 111th Ohio, complained directly to Schofield about Judah the day after the battle. This would not be the last time Sherwood would help depose a superior officer. Sherwood, *Memories of the War*, 105–7.

37. *OR* I, 38/4:210, 225; Cox, *Sherman's Battle for Atlanta*, 51–53.

38. *OR* I, 38/1:65; *OR* I, 38/3:634–35, 682–84; *OR* I, 38/4:216, 233, 244; Castel, *Decision in the West*, 198–202; Cox, *Sherman's Battle for Atlanta*, 55–56.

39. *OR* I, 38/4:242–43.

40. Ibid., 274, 285–86, 290–91, 295–96.

41. Cox, *Sherman's Battle for Atlanta*, 74–80; Howard, *Autobiography*, 1:547–48; *OR* I, 38/2:512, 680; *OR* I, 38/4:386. The exact nature of Schofield's incapacitation is unclear. In his book Cox said Schofield was "severely injured" when he and his horse fell into a gully. O. O. Howard recalls that during this period Schofield came to offer his assistance to Howard and Hooker "in spite of a severe injury to his leg." Both Schofield's and Cox's reports in the *OR* said Schofield was "disabled by sickness." It may be that with the incessant rain, Schofield was both injured and sick.

42. Butterfield had the same date of rank as major general as Schofield (November 29, 1862), but his commission as brigadier general predated Schofield's by two months. Butterfield's report to Hooker cheekily mentioned his timely arrival, but he omitted all mention of Schofield's request for a brigade to attack on Hascall's left. "I rank Major-General Schofield, but informed him immediately upon my arrival that I would support him in any way he might desire, cheerfully and promptly, and ordered my first line to move up at once without waiting

for me, if not at hand, upon an intimation from him that they were needed." *OR* I, 38/4:386; Castel, *Decision in the West*, 256–57.

43. Schofield, *Forty-Six Years*, 130–31; *OR* I, 38/2:512, 542, 651; *OR* I, 38/4:395–96; Cox, *Sherman's Battle for Atlanta*, 89–91.

44. *OR* I, 38/4:433, 438–39, 443–44, 448; Schofield, *Forty-Six Years*, 138–39; Castel, *Decision in the West*, 265–66.

45. W. T. Sherman to U. S. Grant, June 18, 1864, *OR* I, 38/4:507. In this letter Sherman candidly assessed his subordinates. Sherman also commended McPherson, except for his caution at Resaca. He called cavalry commanders Kenner Garrard overcautious and George Stoneman lazy. He particularly complained about the slowness of the Army of the Cumberland and Thomas's large headquarters baggage train. *OR* I, 38/4:508–9, 516.

46. *OR* I, 38/2:513.

47. *OR* I, 38/1:151; *OR* I, 38/2:14–15, 513–14, 569, 646–47, 655, 683; *OR* I, 38/3:814–15; *OR* I, 38/4:551–68; Schofield, *Forty-Six Years*, 132; Cox, *Sherman's Battle for Atlanta*, 108–15; Castel, *Decision in the West*, 288–95; McMurry, *John Bell Hood*, 112–13.

48. *OR* I, 38/4:558.

49. Sherman, *Memoirs*, 528–30; Schofield, *Forty-Six Years*, 134–36; Castel, *Decision in the West*, 295–99.

50. Schofield, *Forty-Six Years*, 136, 139.

51. Ibid., 133.

52. Prior to the Confederate attack at Kolb's Farm, Hooker, upon learning that he faced elements of William Hardee's and Hood's corps, urgently requested that Thomas send forces to relieve Butterfield, so that Hooker could consolidate his corps. Thomas, after examining the situation himself, concluded that Hooker was well positioned and that his reports of facing the entire rebel army were exaggerated. Thomas, too, expressed few regrets about Hooker's departure. Joseph Glatthaar makes the point that effective military partnerships are based on leaders' having complementary capabilities. Ironically, Hooker and Thomas did complement one another, and had Hooker's corps led rather than trailed the Army of the Cumberland, both commanders would have enjoyed greater success. See Glatthaar, *Partners in Command*, 225–36. Also see Castel, "Prevaricating through Georgia"; and Marszalek, "Sherman Called It the Way He Saw It."

53. Castel, *Decision in the West*, 319–20 (3,000 Union and 700 Confederate); McDonough and Jones, *War So Terrible*, 188 (3,000 Union and 750–1,000 Confederate); Hattaway and Jones, *How the North Won*, 596 (1,999 Union and 442 Confederate).

54. *OR* I, 38/1:69; Cox, *Sherman's Battle for Atlanta*, 116–29; Castel, *Decision in the West*, 305–22.

55. Schofield, *Forty-Six Years*, 142–44. In fairness, Miles faced the problem of reconciling the emerging tactics that assumed three-battalion regiments with the continued authorization of one-battalion regiments. With no consensus and without the appropriate organizational structure, the official doctrine of the infantry bore little resemblance to how units really operated in the field. Jamieson, *Crossing the Deadly Ground*, 116–18, 128–30.

56. Schofield, *Forty-Six Years*, 145–46.

57. See Jamieson, *Crossing the Deadly Ground*, 111–20; and Howard, "Men against Fire."

58. *OR* I, 38/2:514–15, 682; *OR* I, 38/4:596–604, 616–22; Army of the Ohio, S.O. no. 36, June 26, 1864, Box 65, Schofield Papers, LC; Castel, *Decision in the West*, 305, 317–18.

59. *OR* I, 38/2:515–16, 683–85; *OR* I, 38/5:76–79; Cox, *Sherman's Battle for Atlanta*, 136–43.

60. Sherman, *Memoirs*, 543–44.

61. O. O. Howard to wife, July 23, 1864, Howard Papers, BCL.

62. Schofield, *Forty-Six Years*, 137–38.

63. *OR* I, 38/5:193.

64. Schofield, *Forty-Six Years*, 148.

65. Sherman, *Memoirs*, 547–58; Howard, *Autobiography*, 2:14–15; Castel, *Decision in the West*, 410–14.

66. Halleck, after the capture of Atlanta, wrote Sherman that Hooker had made a mistake in quitting the army and predicting doom for the campaign. Sherman, *Memoirs*, 558–61, 589–92. Hooker commanded the Northern Department until the end of the war. He retired in 1868 after a paralytic stroke.

67. *OR* I, 38/5:271–73; Marszalek, *Sherman*, 278–79; Castel, *Decision in the West*, 417, 422.

68. *OR* I, 38/5:271–74; Sherman, *Memoirs*, 558–61; Marszalek, *Sherman*, 279; Cox, *Sherman's Battle for Atlanta*, 179; McConnell, *Glorious Contentment*, 197. Schofield may have harbored hopes of commanding the larger Army of the Tennessee, but Sherman probably never considered such an option since it would have necessitated two new army commanders. "Atlanta" notes, Box 93, Schofield Papers, LC.

69. *OR* I, 38/5:356.

70. Ibid. The XIV Corps were known as "Thomas's Pets," and though it was the largest corps, it had suffered the fewest casualties. Sherman complained to Thomas that it was splendid on defense but useless on the offensive. *OR* I, 38/5:371. The most mysterious aspect of this affair was why Sherman relied on telegraphic messages to exert his authority, rather than personally taking charge of the situation. Sherman's use of the telegraph for rapid battlefield communications marked him as a modern general, yet sometimes there is no substitute for personal contact. Sherman's messages, no matter how stinging, could not have the same effect as a personal command. Sherman, who would rightly accuse Schofield of occasionally leaving things to others, was sometimes guilty of the same offense.

71. *OR* I, 32/3:221; *OR* I, 38/5:354–73; Schofield, *Forty-Six Years*, 149–51. Castel concludes the operation had no chance of success, as Hood had ample troops to man the Atlanta defenses and counter the flanking movements. Castel casts this as another of Sherman's failures rather than as an expression of the difficulty of Sherman's task. The major defect in this effort was the lack of aggressive cavalry working on the right flank to screen and deceive Hood about the strength and location of Union flanking efforts. The cavalry, however, was still recuperating from the Jonesboro and Macon debacles. Castel, *Decision in the West*, 454–61.

72. *OR* I, 38/1:75–78.

73. *OR* I, 38/1:79–81; *OR* I, 38/5:732–33; Sherman, *Memoirs*, 578–80; Castel, *Decision in the West*, 485–505.

74. *OR* I, 38/1:82–83; *OR* I, 38/5:733–34, 753. In his memoirs Schofield said that Stanley realized Sherman's decision was wrong and urged Schofield to take command, but Schofield declined, as "Sherman's order was imperative." Stanley's memoirs do not mention his opinion of their relative ranks. Schofield, *Forty-Six Years*, 156–58.

75. Schofield to W. T. Sherman, September 4, 1864, Sherman to Halleck, September 20, 1864, Halleck to Sherman, October 4, 1864, Box 40, Schofield Papers, LC; U.S. War Department, *Revised United States Army Regulations of 1861*, 494–95, 531; Schofield, *Forty-Six Years*, 150–51. In November, after being apprised of Stanton's decision, Stanley wrote that he never disputed Schofield's seniority and that XXIII Corps was never under his orders. This was probably true, but Schofield conformed his actions to those of Stanley and certainly never gave Stanley orders. *OR* I, 45/1:959–60.

76. Schofield, *Forty-Six Years*, 156–58; Stanley, *Personal Memoirs*, 181–83, 214; Sherman, *Memoirs*, 580–83; *OR* I, 38/5:746; Castel, *Decision in the West*, 511, 515, 520–21, 526. Schofield wrote that he urged that he be sent to interdict Hood's retreat from Atlanta, but that Sherman rejected the idea. McDonough is probably correct that there was little chance of Schofield's intercepting Hood. McDonough, *Schofield*, 97; *OR* I, 38/5:771–74.

77. *OR* I, 38/5:791–94; Stanley, *Personal Memoirs*, 181–83, 214. The full assessment of the army commanders was as follows: "George Thomas, you know, is slow, but as true as steel; Schofield is also slow and leaves too much to others; Howard is a Christian, elegant gentleman, and conscientious soldier. In him I made no mistake. Hooker was a fool. Had he staid [*sic*] a couple of weeks he could have marched into Atlanta and claimed all the honors." The reproach of Stanley and Schofield, while ignoring the lack of pressure by Howard's troops and the failure of Blair's flanking maneuver, no doubt irritated Schofield when that volume of the *OR* was published in 1891, while he was commanding general. *OR* I, 38/5:793.

78. Schofield, in agreeing that Stanley, the inexperienced IV Corps commander, could have moved his troops into a line of battle a bit quicker, hinted that if he had been in command, he would have displayed more initiative. Both Sherman and Schofield were unfair to Stanley. Castel suggests that Thomas's recommendation that his army move south of Jonesboro might have worked better, but Thomas's troops were too far away to prevent Hardee's escape. *OR* I, 38/5:746, 792–93; Schofield, *Forty-Six Years*, 156–58; Stanley, *Personal Memoirs*, 181–83, 214; Sherman, *Memoirs*, 580–83; Castel, *Decision in the West*, 511, 515, 520–21, 526. For the Stanley addition to the 1886 edition, see Sherman, *Memoirs*, 965–75.

79. *OR* I, 38/5:777.

80. *OR* I, 38/1:837, 839; Marszalek, *Sherman*, 285–86; Castel, *Decision in the West*, 548–49. The depopulation of Atlanta amounted to about 1,600 people moving south. Castel thinks that more inhabitants may have moved north. That more people might have moved into Union territory is similar to the situation in Missouri, when Thomas Ewing and Schofield depopulated several counties. It suggests that even many southern sympathizers had little confidence in the Confederacy's ultimate success and chose safety over the cause.

81. *OR* I, 38/1:85; Cox, *Sherman's Battle for Atlanta*, 211–17; Castel, *Decision in the West*, 535–36. Neither Cox nor Castel puts a number to overall Confederate casualties. Hood reported casualties during Johnston's and his own period of command as 24,000 and 8,000,

respectively. Hood's estimate of his own casualties is ridiculously low. McMurry, *John Bell Hood*, 156, 222. In *Atlanta 1864*, 194–97, McMurry provides an analysis of the casualty issue and concludes that Confederate casualties for the entire campaign were approximately 35,000, divided equally between Johnston and Hood.

82. Schofield, *Forty-Six Years*, 160; Liddell Hart, *Sherman*; Marszalek, *Sherman*, 287. Modern historians have diverged somewhat from these assessments. John Marszalek, a modern Sherman biographer, while noting the missed opportunities, emphasizes the enormous psychological impact that the capture of Atlanta had on both the North and the South. Hypercritical assessments like Albert Castel's *Decision in the West* stress Sherman's failures, his missed opportunities, and his flawed rendition of the campaign in his memoirs. For Castel, Sherman's single-minded focus on the capture of the city, rather than on the destruction of the Confederate army, undermined and even devalued the achievement. Still other historians, most conspicuously Herman Hattaway, Archer Jones, and Richard M. McMurry, reverse Sherman's legacy to place his "March to the Sea" and his articulation of the strategic raid as his greatest contributions to victory. Given the vast size of the Confederacy and the immense difficulty in destroying Civil War armies, they argue that the Grant-Sherman strategy of exhaustion by continuous pressure and strategic raids was superior to a Napoleonic annihilation of the enemy armies. The Atlanta campaign had weakened the Confederate army, raised Union morale, and set the stage for the great raid. Castel, *Decision in the West*, 539–42, 561–65; Hattaway and Jones, *How the North Won*; Jones, *Civil War Command and Strategy*, 202–4; McMurry, *Atlanta 1864*, 180–83. Hattaway, Jones, and McMurry give Sherman far more credit for his logistical preparations and operations than does Castel. At the expense of his frontline troops, Sherman made his supply line relatively invulnerable and thus negated the effect of Confederate raids or turning movements on him. McMurry also argues that Sherman's mistakes tended to be those of omission rather than commission. He concludes that had Sherman taken greater risks at Snake Creek Gap or Jonesboro, he could have achieved decisive victory and ended the war months earlier. Although McMurry offers an excellent survey of the campaign, Castel's hypercritical analysis, nevertheless, remains the most detailed account of the Atlanta campaign.

83. *OR* I, 38/5:812; Schofield to W. T. Sherman, September 14, 1864, RG 393, Pt. 1, E3505, NARA.

CHAPTER SIX

1. There are many books and articles on the Franklin-Nashville campaign. Schofield's memoirs, *Forty-Six Years*, devoted much attention to it. Jacob Cox wrote extensively about it both in his *Reminiscences* and in *Sherman's March to the Sea—Franklin and Nashville*. The viewpoint of Thomas is contained in Van Horne, *History of the Army of the Cumberland*, and, more recently, in Horn, *Decisive Battle of Nashville*. Like Schofield's, the accounts of James H. Wilson and John Bell Hood are very defensive. Wilson, *Under the Old Flag*; Hood, *Advance and Retreat*. McDonough and Connelly have written a detailed account of the battle of

Franklin in *Five Tragic Hours*. The best single volume on the campaign is Sword, *Confederacy's Last Hurrah*. More recently, Anne J. Bailey has updated Cox by placing the Nashville campaign in the strategic context of both the Atlanta and the Savannah campaigns in *Chessboard of War*.

2. William Wherry to J. Cox, August 20, 1864, RG 393, Pt. 1, E3505, NARA.

3. Sherman quotations in *OR* I, 38/5:793. Kentucky, seven regiments needing 2,369 replacements; Ohio, ten regiments, 1,409 replacements; Indiana, five regiments, 741 replacements; Tennessee, three regiments, 703 replacements; Michigan, four regiments, 692 replacements; and Illinois, four regiments, 643 replacements. Total: 6,557. Schofield left most of his understrength Kentucky regiments behind and took new Ohio regiments to North Carolina in January 1865. Schofield to A.G. of Kentucky, Ohio, Indiana, Tennessee, Michigan, and Illinois, September 13, 1864, RG 393, Pt. 1, E3505, NARA.

4. Schofield to W. T. Sherman, September 12, 1864, RG 393, Pt. 1, E3505, NARA; Cox, *Reminiscences*, 1:171–72, 1:437–38, 2:143; Hascall to Schofield, September 14, 1864, Box 43, Schofield Papers, LC. As a further accolade, the president appointed Cox as corps commander over the more senior major general Darius Couch.

5. Cox, *Reminiscences*, 1:438.

6. Hascall to Schofield, October 9, 1864, Box 43, Schofield Papers, LC; George W. Schofield to G. M. Bascom, September 14, 1864, RG 393, Pt. 1, E3505, NARA. George Schofield was relaying the words dictated by his irate brother, John.

7. Schofield to W. T. Sherman, September 14, 1864, Schofield to Governor Brough, November 1, 1864, Schofield to Major T. Vincent, December 3, 1864, RG 393, Pt. 1, E3505, NARA; Halleck to Schofield, October 21, 1864, Box 40, Schofield Papers, LC.

8. Schofield to Colonel E. D. Townsend, September 14, 1864, RG 393, Pt. 1, E3505, NARA; *OR* II, 5:456–57.

9. ACP Bond, B-483 CB 1866, Roll 241, and 1701 CB 1866, Roll 245, microfilm M1064, 156-01, RG 94, NARA; *Official Roster of the Soldiers of the State of Ohio*, 8:45, 49; Sherwood, *Memories of the War*, 116–17. Sherwood's book is actually a pastiche containing relatively few of his own memories and stories of the war. While he recounted his personal entreaty to Schofield to relieve Judah, Sherwood says nothing about Bond's dismissal. By 1923, when his memoir was published, Sherwood was one of the last remaining brevet generals of the war.

10. Schofield to John Bigelow, October 10, 1880, in "Private Military Journal, 1876–1880," Box 1, Schofield Papers, LC. Schofield's trip home was not exceptional. The administration directed that Generals Logan and Blair and many lesser-known volunteer officers be given leave in order to campaign for Lincoln. *OR* I, 38/5:802, 809.

11. J. A. Campbell, to Schofield, September 22, 1864, Box 39, Schofield Papers, LC.

12. Martin, "Third War," 172–259; *OR* I, 39/1:879–82. For an account of the situation in Kentucky, see the report of JAG Joseph Holt, *OR* I, 39/2:212–14. Also see Harrison, *Civil War in Kentucky*.

13. *OR* I, 39/2:174; Martin, "Third War," 241–50. As in Missouri, Union commanders held family members and local leaders accountable for guerrilla actions. Stephen Ash also describes how the guerrilla war descended into banditry, with locals' organizing "home guards" to hunt

down and kill these desperadoes. Ash, *Middle Tennessee Society Transformed*, 153–60, 164–67; see also Ash, *When the Yankees Came*, 166–69, 205–10.

14. *OR* I, 39/1:461 (quotation), 554, 556. Also see Fisher, *War at Every Door*, 87, 131–44.

15. Bramlette accused Burbridge of arresting men solely because they opposed Lincoln's reelection. Bramlette also opposed the recruiting of African Americans in Kentucky. Stanton naturally favored Burbridge's more "radical" approach. Schofield to W. T. Sherman, Campbell to Hammond, Campbell to Ewing, Campbell to Savaino, October 3, 1864, and Campbell to Ewing, October 6, 1864, RG 393, Pt. 1, E3505, NARA; *OR* I, 39/3:47, 724–25, 739, 749. While Schofield was in the rear taking care of departmental business, Sherman was chasing Hood and had forgotten that he had given Schofield permission to return to the rear. Sherman testily demanded to know where Schofield was. Schofield replied, "My official business here is much more important than at Knoxville, or even at the front while the army is not in motion. . . . I have no desire to be away from the field longer than absolutely necessary and would gladly wash my hands of this whole Kentucky business if I could." Division of the Mississippi to Schofield, September 14, 1864, and Schofield to W. T. Sherman, October 1, 1864, Box 44, RG 94, NARA.

16. Schofield to Stoneman, December 28, 1864, Box 66, Schofield Papers, LC; *OR* I, 45/1:950; *OR* I, 45/2:402. When Schofield appointed Stoneman to run the department, Burbridge complained to Stanton. Grant, however, persuaded Stanton to leave the employment of Stoneman to Schofield's discretion. Burbridge to Stanton, November 27, 1864, Schofield to Townsend, December 2, 1864, and Grant to Stanton, December 5, 1864, Box 66, Schofield Papers, LC. Stoneman's assignment did not relieve Schofield of the responsibility to review and approve courts-martial, which became a significant bottleneck, one that the War Department bureaucrats proposed to solve by granting the authority to the department's JAG, rather than to Stoneman. Halleck to Schofield, December 8, 1864, Box 40, Schofield Papers, LC; Townsend to Schofield, December 10, Box 43, Schofield Papers, LC.

17. Martin, "Third War," 252–56. Andrew Birtle credits George Crook as one of the earliest proponents of specialized antiguerrilla units during the West Virginia campaign of 1861. Birtle, *U.S. Army Counterinsurgency and Contingency Operations Doctrine*, 42–43.

18. Monaghan, *Civil War on the Border*, 343; G. W. Schofield to J. M. Schofield, October 23, 1864, Box 47, Schofield Papers, LC.

19. *OR* I, 39/3:162, 202.

20. *OR* I, 39/3:239–40, 594–95; Marszalek, *Sherman*, 295–96.

21. Schofield to W. T. Sherman, October 27, 1864, RG 393, Pt. 1, E3505, NARA; Schofield to Grant, December 21, 1864, Box 66, Schofield Papers, LC; *OR* I, 39/3:468; Schofield, *Forty-Six Years*, 163–65; Cox, *Reminiscences*, 1:320–25. David Stanley, in his often bitter memoirs, claimed that Sherman sent back XXIII Corps "principally because he thought it did not amount to anything as a fighting force." Stanley, *Personal Memoirs*, 189.

22. Schofield, *Forty-Six Years*, 166–68.

23. Strength estimates for both armies are difficult. In his report Schofield placed his own infantry strength at 18,000; but it is unclear whether he meant the grand total or just those in the vicinity of Pulaski. Three strength reports between November 20 and December 10 show a

combined, present-for-duty equipped strength of IV and XXIII Corps of 24,265, 26,638, and 24,379, respectively. *OR* I, 45/1:52–55, 341. Yet there were many detachments, including Cooper's brigade of Ruger's division, that never linked up with the main army until reaching Nashville in December. While at Pulaski, Schofield sent back to Kentucky four regiments whose terms were about to expire. *OR* I, 45/1:891–92.

24. At Florence, Hood had approximately 40,000 infantry and artillery and 9,000–12,000 cavalry. On November 14 Hatch had estimated Forrest's strength at 12,000–15,000. The Confederate reports show the Army of Tennessee at a present strength on November 6, 1864, of 44,719 (including 3,532 cavalry) and an effective strength of 30,600. Forrest reported a strength of 5,000 cavalry, which probably did not count the cavalry with Hood. Again the vagaries in present and effective strength figures make precise counts difficult. *OR* I, 45/1:663, 678–80, 752, 887, 970–71. A Thomas spy estimated Hood's strength at 55,000. *OR* I, 45/1:1035. For a discussion of the various categories in the strength reports, see McMurry, *Atlanta 1864*, 194–97.

25. *OR* I, 45/1:999, 1007–8, 876–983. Adding to Thomas's problems were the loss of veteran troops and their replacement with untrained recruits. Thomas wrote Grant on November 25, "Since being placed in charge of affairs in Tennessee I have lost nearly 15,000 men, discharged by expiration of service and permitted to go home to vote. My gain is probably 12,000 of perfectly raw troops." *OR* I, 45/1:1034.

26. *OR* I, 45/1:944 (quotation), 954–56, 972–74; Stanley, *Personal Memoirs*, 198–99; Cox, *Reminiscences*, 2:341; AAG Ohio to Cox, November 20, 1864, Box 47, Schofield Papers, LC. The order to Ruger went through Thomas.

27. Cox, *Sherman's March to the Sea*, 66–67; Stanley, *Personal Memoirs*, 199.

28. Cox, *Reminiscences*, 2:341; Schofield, *Forty-Six Years*, 168–69; Sword, *Confederacy's Last Hurrah*, 93–94; *OR* I, 45/1:1017.

29. Schofield, *Forty-Six Years*, 169; Cox, *Reminiscences*, 2:136. The War Department cipher clerks were all civilians and rigorously controlled by Edwin Stanton. The special status of the telegraphers can be seen in McReynolds's punishment. A court-martial on December 11, 1864, found McReynolds guilty of disobeying orders and sentenced him to one month at hard labor. Schofield then remitted the sentence and returned him to duty. *OR* I, 45/2:289–90.

30. *OR* I, 45/1:957, 1018, 1104–8.

31. *OR* I, 45/1:1050–51, 1100, 1167, 1171; Schofield, *Forty-Six Years*, 195–97.

32. *OR* I, 45/1:1107–8, 1084; Schofield, *Forty-Six Years*, 175–77.

33. *OR* I, 45/1:1106–7.

34. The reports of cavalry actions on November 28 are a confusing jumble. Even Cox had trouble sorting them out. Wiley Sword has offered the most coherent explanation of events. *OR* I, 45/1:1109–13, 1121–25; Cox, *Sherman's March to the Sea*, 69–70; Sword, *Confederacy's Last Hurrah*, 97–98, 103–6.

35. Wood wrote Stanley, "It is perfectly patent to my mind, if the enemy has crossed in force, that General Wilson will not be able to check him. It requires no oracle to predict the effect of the enemy's reaching the Franklin pike in our rear." It is difficult to tell when Wood wrote this, but it was probably on the evening of November 28. *OR* I, 45/1:1115.

36. For example, Schofield's aide Captain William J. Twining accompanied Colonel Post's brigade on an important reconnaissance mission the next day, November 29, and reported directly back to Schofield. He later checked the road to Franklin. *OR* I, 45/1:1139; *OR* I, 45/2:445.

37. Wilson's message was written about 1:00 A.M., but Schofield did not receive it until after dawn. *OR* I, 45/1:1143–44; Cox, *Sherman's March to the Sea*, 70. Hammond's brigade of 1,000 green troopers paused at Springfield at 7:30 A.M. to obtain caps for their weapons and then moved east to join Wilson along the Lewisburg Pike. Hammond departed before Stanley arrived on the scene. Incredibly, Wilson saw no problem withdrawing the one cavalry unit that was still in contact with Schofield, and Schofield did not countermand Wilson's orders for Hammond to depart Spring Hill that morning. *OR* I, 45/1:1150–51; Stanley, *Personal Memoirs*, 201.

38. Thomas's civilian telegraphers delayed sending this message due to other traffic and then forgot about it during a shift change. *OR* I, 45/1:1137.

39. *OR* I, 45/1:113, 342, 1138, 1142; Schofield, *Forty-Six Years*, 170–73.

40. The straight-line distance to Spring Hill from Davis Ford was about twelve miles, but Wiley Sword estimates the actual road distance at over seventeen miles. Sword, *Confederacy's Last Hurrah*, 113–17. Wiley Sword agrees that Lee's diversion at Columbia substantially fooled Schofield. Ibid., 141–42.

41. *OR* I, 45/1:113, 753; Sword, *Confederacy's Last Hurrah*, 118–20; Longacre, *Grant's Cavalryman*, 170–72. McDonough and Connelly argue that Forrest's near-capture of Spring Hill constituted the greatest danger to the Union army that day. McDonough and Connelly, *Five Tragic Hours*, 44.

42. Hood, *Advance and Retreat*, 284–86; Sword, *Confederacy's Last Hurrah*, 124–27.

43. *OR* I, 45/1:652–53, 657–58, 670, 708, 712–13, 743, 753; Stanley, *Personal Memoirs*, 195, 200–204; Sword, *Confederacy's Last Hurrah*, 125–37.

44. *OR* I, 45/1:712–13; Glatthaar, "Hood's Tennessee Campaign," 134. McDonough and Connelly posit that Hood did not believe that Schofield's troops at Columbia could make it much past Spring Hill that night, much less all the way to Franklin. They also suggest that Hood may have been more interested in beating Schofield to a presumably lightly defended Nashville than in trapping and defeating his army. McDonough and Connelly, *Five Tragic Hours*, 37–38, 50.

45. While most historians pin the primary responsibility for the debacle on Hood, they agree that Hood had considerable assistance. Cheatham, Brown, and even Forrest get a portion of the blame. The recriminations on the morning of November 30 cut deeply because all echelons shared a sense of failure and missed opportunity. Sword, *Confederacy's Last Hurrah*, 152–59. McDonough and Connelly also conclude that the Union position on November 29 was not weak, and that Ruger arrived well before Stewart could have gotten into position. They also suggest that had Bate interdicted the pike, he would have been in a more precarious position than Stanley. McDonough and Connelly, *Five Tragic Hours*, 53–59.

46. Ruger's men had encountered Confederate pickets on the way to Spring Hill but had little difficulty driving them off. A regiment from Bate's division, which had blocked the road

an hour earlier, had been withdrawn. Even so, Ruger's men would probably have expelled them since they had the greater numbers and incentive. *OR* I, 45/1:342; Sword, *Confederacy's Last Hurrah*, 137; Schofield, *Forty-Six Years*, 173–74.

47. *OR* I, 45/1:1138.

48. *OR* I, 45/1:148–49, 342; Schofield, *Forty-Six Years*, 174.

49. Schofield, *Forty-Six Years*, 172. Though the Confederates did not encounter Kimball's troops, Hood did halt Stewart's corps at Rutherford Creek while Cheatham moved on Spring Hill. Joseph Glatthaar suggests that this was less to protect his flank than to catch Schofield in a three-way pincer between Cheatham in the north, Lee in the south, and Stewart in the east. Glatthaar, "Hood's Tennessee Campaign," 127.

50. Schofield's notes on speech by General J. H. Chambers entitled "Forrest and his Campaigns," given at the Southern Historical Society, August 5, 1879, Box 93, Schofield Papers, LC.

51. Schofield to William B. Dupree, May 4, 1895, Dupree Papers, Duke University Library, Durham, N.C.; Stanley, *Personal Memoirs*, 214, 195, 204. If Schofield minimized the situation, Stanley tended to exaggerate the state of things at Spring Hill a bit.

52. Schofield makes it clear that the battle of Franklin occurred because he had to delay his crossing to repair the bridges. Schofield, *Forty-Six Years*, 176; Sword, *Confederacy's Last Hurrah*, 167.

53. Schofield, *Forty-Six Years*, 177; Stanley, *Personal Memoirs*, 206–7.

54. *OR* I, 45/1:115. For an excellent discussion of the attacks against Schofield for positioning himself at Fort Granger, see McDonough, *Schofield*, 121–22.

55. Schofield, *Forty-Six Years*, 178–79.

56. Sword, *Confederacy's Last Hurrah*, 266.

57. For details of the fighting see Cox, *Battle of Franklin*; McDonough and Connelly, *Five Tragic Hours*; and Sword, *Confederacy's Last Hurrah*.

58. *OR* I, 45/1:653–54, 678–79. The difference in the present-for-duty strengths between November 6 and December 10 for each corps and the army total (not counting Forrest) was: Lee—1,090; Stewart—3,987; Cheatham—3,709; and army total—8,787. These differences generally comport with the levels of fighting for each corps at Columbia, Spring Hill, and Franklin. McDonough and Connelly, *Five Tragic Hours*, 157.

59. *OR* I, 45/1:343–44. Former Confederate captain George L. Cowan wrote that 1,487 Confederate dead were reburied at the McGavock Cemetery in Franklin in 1866. *Confederate Veteran* 18:452–53, quoted in Logsdon, *Eyewitnesses at the Battle of Franklin*, 88. See also McDonough and Connelly, *Five Tragic Hours*, 158. Some of the Confederate wounded later found at Franklin may have been wounded in operations after the battle.

60. Union: 20,000–22,000 infantry, 2,326/22,000 = 10.6 percent; Confederate: 30,000–35,000 infantry, 6,252 / 35,000 = 17.9 percent.

61. Sword, *Confederacy's Last Hurrah*, 262; Logsdon, *Eyewitnesses at the Battle of Franklin*, 79; *OR* I, 45/1:344, 684–86, 678–79; McDonough and Connelly, *Five Tragic Hours*, 168. Hood admitted that the officer losses were proportionally much greater than enlisted losses. *OR* I, 45/2:650. The difference in the present-for-duty officer strengths between November 6

and December 10 for each corps and the army total (not counting Forrest) was: Lee, minus 145 officers; Stewart, minus 528 officers; Cheatham, minus 430 officers; army total, minus 1,104 officers. *OR* I, 45/1:678–79.

62. Logsdon, *Eyewitnesses at the Battle of Franklin*, 81.

63. *OR* I, 45/1:653. Cox saw the attack as an act of desperation. Cox, *Sherman's March to the Sea*, 87. Stanley blamed Hood's anger over Spring Hill. Stanley, *Personal Memoirs*, 206. Others have criticized Hood for attacking the center rather than the weaker defenses in Kimball's sector on the extreme right flank. The problem was that it would have taken even longer for Hood to deploy his corps. McDonough and Connelly, *Five Tragic Hours*, 63.

64. *OR* I, 45/1:658.

65. Ibid., 1174. The specific order probably came from Stanley.

66. The best and most detailed account of Wagner's division at Franklin is by Jacob Cox. Though personally involved in the controversy, he rather fairly and reliably recounts the facts. Cox, *Battle of Franklin*, 64–82, 91–108.

67. Quoted in McDonough and Connelly, *Five Tragic Hours*, 99; Sword, *Confederacy's Last Hurrah*, 171–77.

68. Cox, *Battle of Franklin*, 104, 107; Logsdon, *Eyewitnesses at the Battle of Franklin*, 6, 16; Stanley, *Personal Memoirs*, 206–7; Cox, *Sherman's March to the Sea*, 86–87; Sword, *Confederacy's Last Hurrah*, 188–90.

69. Schofield, *Forty-Six Years*, 181–82; Cox, *Battle of Franklin*, 79. Wagner commanded the St. Louis District from April 8, 1865, to June 20, 1865, and mustered out of the army on August 24, 1865. He died in 1869.

70. Shellenberger to Root, May 20, 1901, Shellenberger to Roosevelt, December 23, 1901, *National Tribune*, September 12, 1901, in ACP J. M. Schofield 2556, RG 94, NARA; Stanley, *Personal Memoirs*, 210–11.

71. In a paper submitted to the Society of the Army of the Cumberland, Schofield acknowledged he could have avoided the battle at Franklin, but only by abandoning much of his trains. Schofield to Henry M. Cist, September 15, 1880, Journal, 1876–80, Box 1, Schofield Papers, LC. This paper is noteworthy because it reflects Schofield's irritation with some George Thomas supporters in the society, who claimed for Thomas the credit for the battle of Franklin and suggested that Schofield was merely executing Thomas's orders. It also rekindled smoldering resentment by Thomas's friends, which is discussed further below.

72. There is a curious discrepancy in the Union casualties in Schofield's November 30 telegram to Thomas. The *OR* twice says, "Our loss is probably not more than one-tenth that number [of Confederate losses]," or 500–600 men. *OR* I, 45/1:1167, 1171. The telegraph records of the Army of the Ohio also show "one-tenth." RG 393, Pt. 1, E3283, NARA. Yet Cox's book, which supposedly extracted the information from the adjutant general's file, says "one-quarter" (1,250–1,500 men), and Schofield used that same percentage in his memoirs. Cox, *Sherman's March to the Sea*, 238; Schofield, *Forty-Six Years*, 225. Schofield admitted that his initial estimate undercounted the number of prisoners taken by the Confederates. Either way, Schofield's 7:10 P.M. report significantly underestimated Union casualties. Since it had been dark, and the battle was still going on, an error was likely. But the rosy report probably

grated on Thomas, especially since he had assumed that Schofield had moved directly to the north side of the Harpeth, as ordered.

73. Schofield, *Forty-Six Years*, 226–27. Smith's and, more significantly, Steedman's troops did not arrive in Nashville until December 1, the same day as Schofield. Sword, *Confederacy's Last Hurrah*, 273–74.

74. *OR* I, 45/1:1109; *OR* I, 45/2:22, 44, 55, 59, 73.

75. *OR* I, 45/2:8, 72, 87, 104; Cox, *Reminiscences*, 2:356–58.

76. McPherson, *Battle Cry of Freedom*, 813; Hood, *Advance and Retreat*, 299–300.

77. *OR* I, 45/2:18. Though Thomas did not make this argument in his messages and reports, Hood's dispatch of Forrest to Murfreesboro may have had a paradoxically reassuring effect on Thomas. In effect, while Forrest was butting his head against that fortified position, he could not be interdicting Nashville's lines of communication. Forrest's continued presence there probably also persuaded Thomas that Hood was not preparing to move farther north or to withdraw to the south. Forrest's absence at the decisive battle would also make Thomas's victory that much easier. Cox, *Reminiscences*, 2:358. Hood's motives for sending Forrest to Murfreesboro are obscure, but he may have hoped to capture isolated garrisons, which would thus enable him to claim some success, even if he were later forced to withdraw. Hood may have remembered that Lee's invasion of Maryland failed, but the capture of the Union garrison at Harpers Ferry mitigated some of the disappointment.

78. *OR* I, 45/2:16.

79. *OR* I, 45/2:15–18, 55, 84–85, 96–97, 114–16.

80. *OR* I, 45/2:114–16, 118, 143, 155, 180, 195–96; Grant, *Personal Memoirs*, 656–60. Grant also sent Thomas a message that was a bit more curt, which said in part, "Push the enemy now, and give him no rest until he is entirely destroyed. Your army will cheerfully suffer many privations to break up Hood's army and render it useless for future operations. Do not stop for trains or supplies, but take them from the country, as the enemy have done. Much is now expected." *OR* I, 45/2:195. In his official report Grant candidly related his apprehensions about Thomas's delay, but he generously concluded, "But his [Thomas's] final defeat of Hood was so complete that it will be accepted as a vindication of that distinguished officer's judgment." *OR* I, 34/1:38.

81. *OR* I, 45/1:37–39; *OR* I, 45/2:201; Schofield, *Forty-Six Years*, 243; Cox, *Sherman's March to the Sea*, 107–15.

82. *OR* I, 45/2:202, 214–15; Cox, *Sherman's March to the Sea*, 116.

83. Stiles's brigade was too slow in supporting the attack, due to difficult terrain. Cox, *Sherman's March to the Sea*, 122; *OR* I, 45/1:345–46, 434–36, 552–53; *OR* I, 45/2:215–17; Sword, *Confederacy's Last Hurrah*, 351–52, 369–80. Schofield noted in his memoirs "the wasting of nearly the entire day" on December 16, yet characteristically he ignored his own caution or lethargy. Schofield, *Forty-Six Years*, 248.

84. *OR* I, 45/2:707; Sword, *Confederacy's Last Hurrah*, 377.

85. *OR* I, 45/2:215; Schofield, *Forty-Six Years*, 246–49.

86. *OR* I, 45/1:40–45.

87. Thomas was also promoted to major general in the regular army, effective December 15,

1864, an honor he said should have been granted after Chickamauga in September 1863. Adding to Thomas's sense of grievance was the promotion of his former subordinate, Philip Sheridan, to major general, USA, effective November 8, 1864, when Sheridan had just been promoted to brigadier general, USA, on September 20, 1864, after his successful campaign in the Shenandoah Valley.

88. *OR* I, 45/1:40, 46, 105; Sword, *Confederacy's Last Hurrah*, 425.

89. *OR* IV, 3:989; W. H. Reynolds to wife, January 15, 1865, quoted in McMurry, *John Bell Hood*, 182; McMurry, *Two Great Rebel Armies*, 131–32.

90. Many modern historians give Grant the bulk of the credit for the emergence of a Union raiding strategy. For the best discussions of Grant, Sherman, and the evolution of Union strategy, see Jones, *Civil War Command and Strategy*, 187–245; Hattaway and Jones, *How the North Won*, 506–10, 518–19, 629–68, 687–702; Weigley, *Great Civil War*, 386–96, 412–22; and Royster, *Destructive War*, 327–52.

CHAPTER SEVEN

1. *OR* I, 45/2:377–78; Schofield, *Forty-Six Years*, 254–55.

2. *OR* I, 45/2:419–20, 530, 557, 567, 587, 603.

3. Wiley Sword suggests that Thomas's dissatisfaction with Schofield prompted him to have Schofield bring up the rear during the pursuit. The need to reorganize and incorporate replacements may have been another reason. Sword, *Confederacy's Last Hurrah*, 386.

4. *OR* I, 45/2:440–41. In another example of the tension between Thomas and Schofield, Thomas thought his recommendation that Schofield be breveted one grade higher in the regular army (i.e., major) for his services in the campaign was appropriate. Schofield, however, was outraged that Thomas had not recommended him for one of the regular army brigadier general vacancies. Schofield did not discover Thomas's promotion recommendation until much later, but it colored Schofield's subsequent relations with Thomas. Schofield, *Forty-Six Years*, 241, 277–80.

5. Schofield, *Forty-Six Years*, 278; Sherman, *Memoirs*, 928–30.

6. Van Horne, *Life of Major-General George H. Thomas*, 433–36, 439–40; Schofield to Henry Cist, September 15, 1880, Box 1, Schofield Papers, LC; Schofield, *Forty-Six Years*, 278. John Marszalek concludes that Halleck did not intend to imply that Schofield had conspired with Grant. Marszalek, *Commander of All Lincoln's Armies*, 239.

7. Piatt, *General George H. Thomas*, 649–50.

8. Schofield to Cox, October 18, 1881, Box 50, Schofield Papers, LC. Most of Thomas's friends suspected Schofield was behind this letter to the *Tribune*, but some did accuse Jacob Cox. R. W. Johnson to D. S. Stanley, December 17, 1889, West-Stanley-Wright Family Papers, MHI. Stanley accused Cox in an 1889 letter to Thomas aide John Hough. Thomas, *General George H. Thomas*, 616.

9. *New York Daily Tribune*, March 12, 1870.

10. Ibid., March 19, 1870; Van Horne, *Life of Major-General George H. Thomas*, 440–42.

11. Henry V. Boynton, a great supporter of Thomas and an acquaintance of Schofield, blamed Grant and his aide Adam Badeau for Thomas's death. When the *Cincinnati Gazette* published Boynton's article, Thomas and his staff complained that many relevant messages were omitted, primarily those of Thomas and Halleck. Boynton later alleged that Badeau and Grant intentionally omitted these messages (all later published in the *OR*) because they cast Thomas's position in a more favorable light. He intemperately called this suppression little less than an assassination of Thomas, yet Boynton curiously made no reference to Schofield and the letter to the *New York Tribune*. Piatt, *General George H. Thomas*, 649–52; Schofield to Henry Cist, September 15, 1880, Box 1, Schofield Papers, LC.

12. Schofield to Henry Cist, September 15, 1880, Box 1, Schofield Papers, LC.

13. Ibid.

14. Schofield to W. T. Sherman, February 16, 1868, reel 12, Sherman Papers, LC.

15. James B. Steedman, "Robbing the Dead," *New York Times*, June 22, 1881, 5; Wilson, *Under the Old Flag*, 100–102. Also see Sword, *Confederacy's Last Hurrah*, 311. Schofield's 1868 letter to Sherman gives credence to Schofield's portrayal of events over Steedman's and Wilson's, which were made decades later. But it may not accurately reflect the forcefulness with which Schofield expressed his views. As with most meetings, people tend to remember what they said better than what others said. Subsequent events can often shape the tenor and tone of these memories.

16. Sanford Kellogg to D. S. Stanley, January 12, 1881, West-Stanley-Wright Family Papers, MHI.

17. Steedman, "Robbing the Dead." Steedman's letter had originally been published in the *Toledo Northern Ohio Democrat*. Schofield, *Forty-Six Years*, 293.

18. Grant to Schofield, August 1, 1881, contained in Schofield, *Forty-Six Years*, 293–98.

19. Schofield to L. P. Bradley, August 22, 1888, Box 4, Bradley Papers, MHI. Schofield also enlisted the aid of Fullerton and Boynton in writing the portions of his memoirs related to Thomas. Schofield to Boynton, January 14, 1897, Box 64, Schofield Papers, LC. But not all Thomas supporters forgave and forgot, and neither did Schofield. In 1898 he challenged James H. Wilson's application for membership in MOLLUS. Suspecting that Wilson had been involved in spreading the rumors contained in Steedman's letter, Schofield requested that Wilson answer these issues before admission. Schofield to Orlando B. Wilcox, January 29, 1898, Box 38, Schofield Papers, LC.

20. McDonough, *Schofield*, 132–34. McDonough also rather darkly notes that the August 1, 1881, letter from Grant to Schofield is not in the Schofield Papers, and that Schofield may have forged the copy in his memoirs. However, copies of the July 12, 1881, letter to Grant appear twice, one in the letterbook and the other a copy, in Box 40, Schofield Papers, LC. The index for 1876–88 Confidential Letters in Box 10 shows a August 1, 1881, letter from Grant on the subject of the Thomas newspaper article. It was labeled item #27, but item #27 is missing from the file, and the surrounding files. This researcher has found a number of items missing or misfiled in the Schofield Papers. The Grant Papers show no evidence of a letter to or from Schofield at this time, but the files are very sparse for this period. Box 14, Correspondence, October 1878–August 1883, Series 10, Grant Papers, LC.

21. Sword, *Confederacy's Last Hurrah*, 345–46.

22. See Porter, *Campaigning with Grant*, 343–53; and Adam Badeau, *Military History of Ulysses S. Grant*, 3:230–81.

23. Sword, *Confederacy's Last Hurrah*, 292; *OR* I, 45/2:19, 45, 57, 97–98, 117, 145, 171, 195, 197.

24. Russell Weigley has characterized this as the "American way of war." Edward Luttwak has suggested that this style of warfare is characteristic of those who are numerically and materially superior. Weigley, *American Way of War*; Luttwak, *Strategy*.

25. Schofield, *Forty-Six Years*, 345; Cox, *Sherman's March to the Sea*, 147.

26. *OR* I, 46/1:43–44. For his accomplishment Terry was promoted to brigadier general, USA, effective January 15, 1865, and became the only non–West Point graduate to be promoted to general officer in the regular army during the war.

27. Grant to Schofield, January 31, 1865, Box 40, Schofield Papers, LC; *OR* I, 46/1:44–45.

28. *OR* I, 47/1:909–11, 927–30; Cox, *Sherman's March to the Sea*, 147–54.

29. Cox, *Reminiscences*, 2:411–18.

30. Cox, *Sherman's March to the Sea*, 147–54; *OR* I, 47/1:910–11, 927–30.

31. *OR* I, 47/1:911–12; Cox, *Sherman's March to the Sea*, 154–56.

32. *OR* I, 47/1:62, 932–33, 1053. Cox later claimed there were 1,257 Union casualties, and he estimated an equal number for Bragg. This is probably an exaggeration, but Confederate reports for this period were fragmentary. Cox, *Sherman's March to the Sea*, 161–62.

33. Cox learned of his promotion to major general on January 15, as he was about to depart for the East. His date of rank was, ironically, December 7, 1864, the very day that Darius Couch reported to XXIII Corps and displaced him as second in command. *OR* I, 45/1:359, 364.

34. *OR* I, 47/3:7, 18, 68–70; Cox, *Reminiscences*, 2:452–53; Welcher, *Union Army*, 1:53–54, 455–57, 653–54.

35. Sherman, *Memoirs*, 810.

36. Grant to Stanton, February 24, 1865, Box 91, Schofield Papers, LC; *OR* I, 47/2:545. Schofield's ever-loyal father-in-law, Professor Bartlett, advanced the claim that since Schofield had been recommended for brigadier general for Franklin, the capture of Wilmington merited promotion to major general in the regular army. W. Bartlett to J. S. Rollins, February 28, 1865, Rollins Papers, WHMC. In 1861 Schofield spent a few months as a regular army captain and major of Volunteers.

37. *OR* I, 47/2:562. The *S. R. Spaulding* was not exclusively a hospital ship. It was a 1,090-ton oceangoing side-wheeler that been used as a troop, prisoner, medical transport, and courier vessel for much of the war. The *OR* contains dozens of references to its various uses. Stanton himself had traveled aboard her. *OR* III, 4:915.

38. *OR* I, 47/2:562.

39. *OR* I, 47/2:342–43, 832–33; Cox, *Reminiscences*, 2:453–54; McDonough, *Schofield*, 155–56.

40. *OR* I, 47/1:43, 1059; Cox, *Sherman's March to the Sea*, 239–43.

41. Schofield, *Forty-Six Years*, 347–48.

42. Ibid., 358–59.

43. For Halleck's contributions, see Ambrose, *Halleck*, 206–11; and Anders, *Henry Halleck's War*, vii–ix, 604–44. Ambrose gives Halleck more credit as an administrator than as a strategist. Anders offers a more positive assessment of Halleck's strategic skills. Among Halleck's contributions, according to Anders, was the "Halleck Doctrine," by which Halleck sought to protect the independence of field commanders from Washington micromanagement. When applied to such men as Grant and Sherman, it worked well. When applied to others, such as Benjamin Butler or Nathaniel Banks, it worked less well.

44. *OR* III, 4:250. For discussions of raiding in the Civil War, see Jones, *Civil War Command and Strategy*, 187–245; and Hattaway and Jones, *How the North Won*, 506–10, 518–19, 629–68, 687–702. For an analysis of the importance of raids in the history of warfare, see Jones, *Art of War in the Western World*.

45. Schofield, *Forty-Six Years*, 356.

46. For Schofield's assessment of Sherman's strategy, see ibid., 329–44.

47. "Introductory Remarks upon the Study of the Science of War," delivered to the U.S. Military Service Institution at West Point, October 11, 1877, Box 89, Schofield Papers, LC.

48. Ibid.; Schofield, *Forty-Six Years*, 160.

49. "Notes on the 'Legitimate in Warfare,'" read by Maj. Gen. John M. Schofield before U.S. Military Service Institution, December 30, 1879, handwritten manuscript in Box 89, Schofield Papers, LC. Also published as Schofield, "Notes on the 'Legitimate in Warfare,'" 1–10.

50. Schofield, "Notes on the 'Legitimate in Warfare,'" 10.

51. Jomini, *Art of War*, 31.

52. Schofield, *Forty-Six Years*, 350.

53. *OR* I, 47/3:243–44.

54. Lincoln's March 3, 1865, instructions to Grant, via Stanton, make it clear that Lincoln would not have welcomed the political portions of the Johnston-Sherman agreement. Stanton wrote, "He [Lincoln] instructs me to say that you are not to decide, discuss, or confer upon any political question. Such questions the President holds in his own hands, and will submit them to no military conferences or conventions." These instructions were belatedly conveyed to Sherman, along with the cabinet's rejection of his agreement. *OR* I, 47/3:285.

55. *OR* I, 47/3:263–64, 285–86, 301–3, 311–12, 582–83; Sherman, *Memoirs*, 810–17, 834–56. John Marszalek suggests that Sherman was simply oblivious to the political implications of his actions. Marszalek, *Sherman*, 334–59. Michael Fellman argues that Sherman's simplistic view of the war shifted from total destruction to total forgiveness. More plausibly, Fellman suggests that Sherman saw little distinction between his military and political opinions and, when offered an opportunity to negotiate a complete Confederate surrender, got "carried away." Fellman, *Citizen Sherman*, 238–56. Also see Badeau, *Grant in Peace*, 120–23. Though often hailed by modern historians, Sherman's "forty acres and a mule" order was also a significant transgression against civil authority.

56. Schofield, *Forty-Six Years*, 349–50.

57. *OR* I, 47/3:263, 320–21, 350; Schofield, *Forty-Six Years*, 351–52; Johnston, *Narrative of Military Operations*, 412–14; Sherman, *Memoirs*, 847–59. Schofield paroled about 30,000

Confederate troops. Many of the North Carolina militia went home without parole, and about 800 cavalry refused parole, marching south, supposedly for Mexico. *OR* I, 47/3:392.

CHAPTER EIGHT

1. Schofield to W. T. Sherman, June 6, 1865, reel 9, Sherman Papers, LC; *OR* I, 47/3:323.

2. Donald, *Lincoln*, 592. For the evolution of Lincoln's thinking on Reconstruction, see ibid., 469–74, 561–65, 582–85, 589–92.

3. Chase to Schofield, May 7, 1865, Box 91, Schofield Papers, LC; Schofield to Chase, May 8, 1865, Generals Papers, Box 44, RG 94, NARA; Niven, *Salmon P. Chase*, 386.

4. *OR* I, 47/3:410, 461–62.

5. Chase to Schofield, May 7, 1865, Box 91, Schofield Papers, LC; Ahern, "Cox Plan of Reconstruction"; Fredrickson, *Inner Civil War*, 171–72, 189–96.

6. *OR* I, 47/3:330–31, 398. Also see Schofield, *Forty-Six Years*, 367–77, where Schofield printed most of his major correspondence during his time in North Carolina.

7. *OR* I, 47/3:405–6, 430, 440, 451, 481–83, 490, 504, 510–11, 602, 616.

8. *OR* I, 47/3:477, 503. President Johnson, based on Stanton's recommendation, appointed Howard the Freedmen's Bureau commissioner on May 12, 1865.

9. *OR* I, 47/3:462. For Sherman's views on African Americans, see Marszalek, *Sherman*, 351, 365–68, 372; and Fellman, *Citizen Sherman*, 70–72, 255–56, 408–9.

10. *OR* I, 47/3:461–63; Schofield, *Forty-Six Years*, 376.

11. Schofield to W. T. Sherman, June 6, 1865, reel 9, Sherman Papers, LC.

12. Hyman, "Johnson, Stanton, and Grant," 88–89.

13. For an analysis of the constitutional status of the defeated Confederates states, see Belz, *Reconstructing the Union*.

14. Schofield, *Forty-Six Years*, 353–55, 376.

15. *OR* I, 47/3:625, 646–47, 649. William Holden had written the president a glowing report of Schofield's performance, saying, "General Schofield, the Department Commander, is acting with wisdom and fairness and giving satisfaction to the true men." W. W. Holden to Andrew Johnson, May 13, 1865, Johnson Papers, LC.

16. Britain and Spain were part of the original expedition to Mexico, but they withdrew when they understood that Napoleon III intended to conquer the entire country. The French did not capture Mexico City until June 1863, and Maximilian did not arrive in Mexico until May 1864.

17. Miller, "Arms across the Border." Also see Schofield, *Forty-Six Years*, 161–66; and Swails, "John McAllister Schofield," 15–58.

18. Miller, "Arms across the Border"; McFeely, *Grant*, 198.

19. Miller, "Arms across the Border," 15.

20. Schofield, *Forty-Six Years*, 379–82.

21. Ibid., 382–83; Miller, "Arms across the Border," 15.

22. Schofield, *Forty-Six Years*, 383–84.

23. Bigelow, *Retrospectives of an Active Life*, 4:42.

24. Reported in the *New York Herald*, December 8, 1865, and quoted in Schofield, *Forty-Six Years*, 386–87.

25. Bigelow, *Retrospectives of an Active Life*, 3:265; Swails, "John McAllister Schofield," 46–48.

26. Schofield to his wife, January 15 and 19, 1866, Box 77, Schofield Papers, LC.

27. Schofield to his wife, January 19, 1866, Box 77, Schofield Papers, LC. During his mission to France, Schofield's escort was Captain Pierre Guzman, who had visited the United States during the war and had written a lengthy report for the French army. The French minister of war was particularly interested in getting details of Sherman's logistical arrangements. Although they never influenced French official doctrine, Schofield and Confederate general P. T. Beauregard were supposedly responsible for convincing Napoleon III of the importance of entrenchments. Luvaas, *Military Legacy of the Civil War*, 92, 150.

28. Schofield, *Forty-Six Years*, 390–92; Schofield to his wife, January 2 and 19, 1866, Box 77, Schofield Papers, LC.

29. Bigelow, *Retrospectives of an Active Life*, 3:265–67, 298–301, 370–71; Swails, "John McAllister Schofield," 39–40, 53.

30. Seward to Schofield, April 24, 1866, Box 77, Schofield Papers, LC. Adam Badeau, Grant's aide, described Grant's frustration at Seward's "stalling" tactics but admitted that public opinion was more with Seward than Grant. Badeau, *Grant in Peace*, 180–89.

31. Miller, "Arms across the Border," 16; Bigelow, *Retrospectives of an Active Life*, 4:274.

32. Schofield to Romero, June 13, 1867, and Romero to Schofield, June 13, 1867, and Schofield to Ambassador Thomas H. Nelson, September 13, 1872, Box 77, Schofield Papers, LC.

33. Military historians, such as James E. Sefton, Joseph Dawson, William L. Richter, and Brooks Simpson, have continued to explore the importance of the army in Reconstruction. Sefton, *United States Army and Reconstruction*; Dawson, *Army Generals and Reconstruction*; Richter, *Army in Texas during Reconstruction*; Simpson, *Let Us Have Peace*. Sefton's account remains the best overall survey of the topic. Dawson provides an excellent in-depth study of Louisiana, a very contentious district. Richter emphasizes the futility of military reconstruction. Military commanders in Texas intervened in support of the radicals, in contrast to Schofield's conservative policies, yet both Texas and Virginia were "redeemed" in 1870. Simpson rehabilitates Grant's political convictions and skill before he became president.

34. Hyman, "Johnson, Stanton, and Grant." This is a seminal article on the struggle for control of the army. Hyman makes a useful distinction between the frontier army and the army of occupation; Congress sought control of the latter.

35. Also see the following Ph.D. dissertations: Alderson, "Influence of Military Rule and the Freedmen's Bureau on Reconstruction in Virginia"; Kirkland, "Federal Troops in the South Atlantic States"; and Ulrich, "Northern Military Mind."

36. Coffman, *Old Army*, 239.

37. Sefton, *United States Army and Reconstruction*, 254.

38. G.O. no. 2, August 15, 1866, RG 393, Pt. 1, E5054, NARA; Annual Report, 1866–67,

First Military District, Box 86, Schofield Papers, LC. The Department of the Potomac included all of Virginia, except Alexandria and Fairfax County.

39. U.S. House, *Riot at Norfolk*, 65–66.

40. Coakley, *Role of Federal Military Forces in Domestic Disorders*, 273–74; Chesson, *Richmond after the War*, 103–4; Sefton, *United States Army and Reconstruction*, 50–54, 261. See also Letters Sent, August 1866–March 1867, Department of the Potomac, RG 393, Pt. 1, NARA, pp. 78, 152, 161, 212.

41. Schofield to Howard, February 14, 15, and 28, 1867, Box 47, Schofield Papers, LC.

42. Rachleff, *Black Labor in the South*, 35–37, 44.

43. Chesson, *Richmond after the War*, 101–2.

44. Schofield to Captain J. C. Bates, November 11, 1866, Box 47, Schofield Papers, LC.

45. See Letters Sent, August 1866–March 1867, Department of the Potomac, RG 393, Pt 1, NARA, pp. 52–53, 59, 63; Schofield to Grant, December 31, 1866, RG 94, NARA; and Kirkland, "Federal Troops in the South Atlantic States," 66, 129–30.

46. Schofield to Major Leet, August 25, 1866, RG 393, Pt. 1, E5047, NARA; Kirkland, "Federal Troops in the South Atlantic States," 109–10. Prior to the passage of the Fourteenth and Fifteenth Amendments, Congress affirmed the rights of freedmen and women by statute.

47. Lowe, *Republicans and Reconstruction in Virginia*, 68; G.O. no. 3, March 15, 1867, RG 393, Pt. 1, NARA; Chalfin to Granger, October 3, 1867, RG 393, Pt. 1, E5047, NARA; Dawson, *Army Generals and Reconstruction*, 164–82. In North Carolina Schofield had successfully created a loyal police force to help preserve the peace and enforce the law. The police turned prisoners over to military commissions. *OR* I, 47/3:396.

48. Schofield to Lieutenant Wm. Cameron, December 1, 1866, Box 47, Schofield Papers, LC; Taylor, *Negro in the Reconstruction of Virginia*, 26.

49. "Memoranda," undated, Box 86, Schofield Papers, LC.

50. McDonough, *Schofield*, 166–67; Swails, "John McAllister Schofield," 62–64.

51. As a way of reducing the power of slave states, Article I, Section 2, of the Constitution had apportioned representation in the House based on all free persons and three-fifths of non-free persons. This section of the Fourteenth Amendment ended that distinction and attempted to penalize states that disfranchised African American men. This nudge toward full black male suffrage proved too weak, and in February 1869 Congress passed the Fifteenth Amendment, which declared that the right to vote could not be denied based on race, color, or previous condition of servitude. The Fifteenth Amendment became an additional condition for the readmission of former Confederate states and was ratified in February 1870.

52. Lowe, *Republicans and Reconstruction in Virginia*, 68–71.

53. Schofield, *Forty-Six Years*, 394–95.

54. "Reconstruction," Box 86, Schofield Papers, LC. For an analysis and complete transcription of the text, see Sefton, "Aristotle in Blue and Braid."

55. "Reconstruction," Box 86, Schofield Papers, LC.

56. Ibid.

57. Ibid.

58. Ibid.

59. U.S. Senate, *Correspondence Relating to Reconstruction*, 3–7; Sefton, *United States Army and Reconstruction*, 109–12. Like the Reconstruction Act, the Tenure in Office Act was passed over Johnson's veto. Johnson reluctantly signed the Army Appropriations Act, though he protested the Command of the Army provision.

60. Thomas and Hyman, *Stanton*, 530–31; *Army and Navy Journal*, March 30, 1867, 514; Sefton, *United States Army and Reconstruction*, 113–18, 256–57; Kirkland, "Federal Troops in the South Atlantic States," 167. William Ulrich classifies Sherman, Hancock, and Schofield as the most lenient toward the South, and Butler and Sheridan as the most "vindictive." He sees Howard, Grant, Logan, and Banks as becoming increasingly radicalized during Reconstruction. Ulrich, "Northern Military Mind," 368–74.

61. U.S. Senate, *Correspondence Relating to Reconstruction*, 26–47; Kirkland, "Federal Troops in the South Atlantic States," 164–67.

62. Schofield, *Forty-Six Years*, 399; Sefton, *United States Army and Reconstruction*, 145; First Military District Annual Report, October 5, 1867, Box 86, Schofield Papers, LC.

63. Brown to Schofield, January 25, 1867, Box 2, Schofield Papers, LC; Sefton, *United States Army and Reconstruction*, 121–22, 145; Kirkland, "Federal Troops in the South Atlantic States," 167–68; Letters Sent, Department of the Potomac, August 1866–March 1867, RG 393, Pt. 1, E5047, NARA; Letters Sent, First Military District, March 1867–January, 1870, 1867, RG 393, Pt. 1, E5048, NARA; Telegraphs Sent, First Military District, RG 393, Pt. 1, E5061, NARA.

64. First Military District Annual Report, October 5, 1867, Box 86, Schofield Papers, LC; Taylor, *Negro in the Reconstruction of Virginia*, 254. One of the reasons that Stoneman appointed so many more officials was because the full implementation of restrictions of the Fourteenth Amendment did not take hold until his tenure.

65. Kirkland, "Federal Troops in the South Atlantic States," 171, 175.

66. First Military District Annual Report, October 5, 1867, Box 86, Schofield Papers, LC; Schofield to Grant, December 18, 1867, Grant Papers, LC.

67. Maddex, "Virginia," 115*n*; Schofield to Grant, December 1867, Schofield Papers, LC. Before 1881, the governor spelled his name "Peirpont," and the records reflect a variety of spellings. "Pierpont" is now the commonly used spelling.

68. Henry Horatio Wells was born in New York and entered the Union army in a Michigan regiment. He served as the provost marshal and commander of the District of Alexandria (Va.) and was breveted to brigadier general at the end of the war.

69. Schofield to Grant, April 2, 1868, and Grant to Schofield, April 3, 1868, Schofield Papers, LC; Alderson, "Influence of Military Rule and the Freedmen's Bureau on Reconstruction in Virginia," 216–22; Lowe, *Republicans and Reconstruction in Virginia*, 141–43.

70. Julia Peirpont [Pierpont] to Anna Dickinson, April 10, 1868, Dickinson Papers, LC; Grant to Schofield, telegraph, April 6, 1868, Box 40, Schofield Papers, LC.

71. Schofield to Stoneman, August 29, 1868, Box 49, Schofield Papers, LC.

72. Chesson, *Richmond after the War*, 96–97; Maddex, "Virginia," 126–50. Maddex contends that poor organizing, especially of mountain whites, and not demographics condemned

Republicans to defeat by a narrow centrist-conservative majority. The centrist impulses of the state, however, kept the Republicans competitive long after other southern Republican Parties collapsed. Lowe underscores the racial hostility of mountain whites as the reason few joined the Republican Party. Lowe, *Republicans and Reconstruction in Virginia*, 183–95.

73. First Military District Annual Report, October 5, 1867, Box 86, Schofield Papers, LC; Schofield to Grant, December 18, 1867, Grant Papers, LC; Schofield to Army A.G., March 22 and April 15, 1867, and Schofield to Grant, April 22, 1867, RG 393, Pt. 1, NARA; "Military Missionary in Virginia," 544.

74. "Military Missionary in Virginia." This article appeared in *De Bow's Review*, published in New Orleans by conservative southerner J. D. B. De Bow.

75. Ibid., 549–51.

76. Keller, *Affairs of State*, 277–78, 550–52; Skowronek, *Building a New American State*, 132–36.

77. First Military District Annual Report, October 5, 1867, Box 86, Schofield Papers, LC; Schofield to Grant, December 18, 1867, Grant Papers, LC. By the time of the election, the registration totals were 120,101 whites and 105,832 blacks. There was a black majority in 50 of 102 districts, which, due to population distribution, elected 59 of the 105 delegates. Lowe, *Republicans and Reconstruction in Virginia*, 122–23.

78. Lowe, *Republicans and Reconstruction in Virginia*, 126–28; "Virginia Constitutional Convention 1868," Box 86, Schofield Papers, LC.

79. Schofield to O. B. Wilcox, May 10, 1867, Box 47, Schofield Papers, LC.

80. Hanna, *Acts of Kings*, 12, 18, 22, 23, 44–46.

81. Some blacks accepted segregated schools as an inevitable compromise to obtain public schools. Lowe, *Republicans and Reconstruction in Virginia*, 138–39.

82. Schofield, *Forty-Six Years*, 400–401; Lowe, *Republicans and Reconstruction in Virginia*, 144.

83. Schofield to Grant, April 18, 1868, Box 47, Schofield Papers, LC.

84. Schofield to Grant, March 21, 1868, Box 47, Schofield Papers, LC; Schofield, *Forty-Six Years*, 402–3; Lowe, *Republicans and Reconstruction in Virginia*, 148–50, 170–77.

85. Lowe, *Republicans and Reconstruction in Virginia*, 177.

86. Schofield, *Forty-Six Years*, 394–405. Named for Columbia University historian William A. Dunning, this came to be known as the Dunning school of Reconstruction historiography. See Dunning, *Essays on the Civil War and Reconstruction*; and Dunning, *Reconstruction, Political and Economic*.

87. W. T. Sherman to John Sherman, February 3, 1875, and W. T. Sherman to John Sherman, October 1885, in Thorndike, *Sherman Letters*, 344, 367–68.

CHAPTER NINE

1. Sefton, *United States Army and Reconstruction*, 141, 153, 156–64, 168–69, 176.

2. Simpson, *Let Us Have Peace*, 190–204; Sefton, *United States Army and Reconstruction*,

154–56. General Sherman insisted that the Mexico gambit had no connection to the final Grant-Johnson quarrel. Sherman marked the date of the final breach as January 14, 1868. On that day, the *National Intelligencer* reported that four cabinet members accused Grant of "prevaricating and deceiving the President." Sherman was present when Grant presented his case to Johnson, who appeared satisfied. "But the newspapers kept it up, and made the breach final and angry." W. T. Sherman to John Sherman, November 8, 1885, in Thorndike, *Sherman Letters*, 368–69. Grant's aide Adam Badeau described the deterioration of relations between Stanton and Grant as the result of personal rather than policy reasons. Grant resented the secretary's caustic and often bullying manner. Badeau, *Grant in Peace*, 77–83. Brooks Simpson marks the final break of relations between Johnson and Grant in February 1868, when they quarreled over authorization for Grant to ignore the orders of Stanton. Simpson, *Let Us Have Peace*, 233.

3. Sefton, *United States Army and Reconstruction*, 180–82.

4. Schofield, *Forty-Six Years*, 406–13; Simpson, *Let Us Have Peace*, 225–31; Hyman, "Johnson, Stanton, and Grant."

5. Foner, *Reconstruction*, 333–36. William M. Evarts (1818–1901) served as counsel for President Andrew Johnson in the impeachment trial before the U.S. Senate (1868). Although he served as attorney general under President Johnson (July 1868–March 1869), Evarts did not abandon the Republican Party: he served as chief counsel for the Republican Party in the disputed Hayes-Tilden presidential election (1876), as secretary of state under President Rutherford B. Hayes (1877–81), and as Republican U.S. senator from New York (1885–89).

6. Schofield, "Memorandum," May 1868, Box 86, Schofield Papers, LC; also reprinted in Schofield, *Forty-Six Years*, 413–18. This chapter of his memoirs also appeared as Schofield, "Controversies in the War Department."

7. Schofield, "Memorandum"; Schofield, *Forty-Six Years*, 413–18. In his handwritten memorandum Schofield indicated the probable involvement of Senators Fessenden and Trumbull in the scheme, but he omitted this portion from his published accounts. Fessenden and Trumbull both voted for Johnson's acquittal. In the memorandum Schofield also refers to himself in the third person, but he changed the references to the first person in the published versions.

8. Schofield, "Memorandum"; Schofield, *Forty-Six Years*, 413–18.

9. Schofield, "Memorandum"; Schofield, *Forty-Six Years*, 413–18.

10. U.S. Senate, *Journal of the Senate*, May 28, 1868, 238–39, 968–70. By May 28, President Johnson was considering appointing another cabinet officer as acting secretary of war, if Schofield were not confirmed soon. Browning, *Diaries*, 2:200. Thomas and Hyman describe how Stanton's resignation produced a certain amount of confusion and intrigue about the interim control of the War Department. Thomas and Hyman, *Stanton*, 606–12. Journalist Henry V. Boynton kept Schofield apprised of the status of his nomination, and Grant sent an immediate telegraph informing Schofield of his confirmation. Boynton to Schofield, telegraphs, May 27, 28, and 29, 1868, Box 39, Schofield Papers, LC; Grant to Schofield, May 29, 1868, Box 40, Schofield Papers, LC.

11. To diminish his military status, Schofield frequently wore an "undress" uniform, which

probably consisted of military frock coat, waistcoat, and tie. William W. Belknap to Schofield, June 30, 1873, Box 39, Schofield Papers, LC. See also Schofield's portrait in Bell, *Secretaries of War and Secretaries of the Army*, 75.

12. Fletcher Pratt suggests that it was Evarts, "one of the best and cleverest lawyers in American history," who proposed Schofield to the Republican senators. Pratt, *Stanton*, 452–53.

13. Hyman, "Johnson, Stanton, and Grant," 88.

14. Simpson, *Let Us Have Peace*, 242–44. Grant's sense of personal loyalty would later cause him problems as president when corrupt associates, such as Secretary of War William Belknap, betrayed his trust.

15. Hanna, *Acts of Kings*, 57–59.

16. One might argue that the first secretary of war, Henry Knox, was a professional soldier, given his service in the militia, the Continental army, and as senior army officer in 1783–84, when he became secretary of war under the Articles of Confederation and later President Washington. I would argue that Knox was more of a citizen soldier–statesman in the mode of many of the Founding Fathers. After retirement, George C. Marshall became the first and only professional soldier to become secretary of defense.

17. Schofield, *Forty-Six Years*, 420. Schofield was well aware of his temporary or caretaker status. To Sherman, who would become commanding general if Grant moved to the White House, Schofield wrote, "I shall, of course, be glad to assist in carrying out your views in regard to affairs in your Division and to serve you personally whence opportunity may offer." Schofield to Sherman, June 25, 1868, reel 13, Sherman Papers, LC.

18. Thomas and Hyman, *Stanton*, 612; Hyman, "Johnson, Stanton, and Grant," 100; McDonough, *Schofield*, 188.

19. Simpson, *Let Us Have Peace*, 248–49.

20. Badeau, *Grant in Peace*, 141–48; McFeely, *Grant*, 278, 280; Grant to Schofield, September 28, 1868, Badeau Papers, LC.

21. Schofield, *Forty-Six Years*, 419–20; U.S. War Department, *Annual Report of the Secretary of War*, November 20, 1868. For a less rosy picture of the 1868 election, see Dawson, *Army Generals and Reconstruction*, 82–92; and Rable, *But There Was No Peace*, 69–80. Rable marks 1868 as the beginning of systematic, rather than sporadic, political violence. Also see Foner, *Reconstruction*, 342–45.

22. O. O. Howard to Schofield, August 8 and 24, 1868, Box 40, Schofield Papers, LC; Schofield to Joint-Select Committee of the Legislature of Tennessee and Schofield to George Thomas, September 11, 1868, Box 86, Schofield Papers, LC.

23. See Rable, *But There Was No Peace*, 73–74; Browning, *Diaries*, 2:214, 222–23; and Sefton, *United States Army and Reconstruction*, 198–206.

24. J. A. Campbell to Schofield, October 22, 26, and 27, 1868, November 9, 1868, Box 39, Schofield Papers, LC; Powell Clayton to Schofield, October 18, 1868, RG 94, NARA.

25. J. A. Campbell to Schofield, October 27, 1868, and November 9, 1868, Box 39, Schofield Papers, LC; Clayton to Schofield, November 5, 1868, Schofield to Colonel G. Moore, November 5, 1869, Horace Porter to Grant, December 26, 1868, Johnson Papers, LC.

26. Lovell H. Rousseau (1818–69) was a Kentucky politician before the war and was

promoted to brigadier general of Volunteers in 1861 and major general of Volunteers in October 1862. He served primarily in the Department of the Cumberland. After the war he became a congressman from Kentucky and a supporter of Andrew Johnson. In 1867 President Johnson rewarded him with an appointment as brigadier general in the regular army. Sifakis, *Who Was Who in the Union*, 344. Rousseau replaced Buchanan on September 15, 1868.

27. Dawson, *Army Generals and Reconstruction*, 80–88.

28. Schofield to L. H. Rousseau, October 27, 1868, Johnson Papers, LC.

29. Schofield to L. H. Rousseau, October 29, 1868, Box 49, Schofield Papers, LC.

30. Ibid.; Schofield to Johnson, October 30, 1869, Johnson Papers, LC; Dawson, *Army Generals and Reconstruction*, 89–91.

31. Dawson, *Army Generals and Reconstruction*, 89–91; Foner, *Reconstruction*, 343–45.

32. Andrew Johnson to Schofield, September 7, 1868, and Schofield to Johnson, September 14, 1868, Johnson Papers, LC. Johnson also requested correspondence on the 1864 campaign plans for George Meade's Army of the Potomac.

33. Barrows, *William M. Evarts*, 178; Browning, *Diaries*, 2:243.

34. Barrows, *William M. Evarts*, 167; Browning, *Diaries*, 2:210, 214, 220, 244. Perhaps still embittered by Grant's victory, Browning noted the appearance of Cox and Schofield on Grant's cabinet list as respectable choices, but he did not find "a statesman or first class man on the entire list" (244).

35. Hyman, "Johnson, Stanton, and Grant," 100.

36. Unlike Eric Foner, who sees Reconstruction as an "unfinished revolution" and an opportunity lost by policies that were too cautious and too conservative, Michael Perman suggests that the problems of emancipation and Reconstruction were too complex and far-reaching for ready resolution. Foner, *Reconstruction*; Perman, *Emancipation and Reconstruction*, 2–4, 128–30. George Rable shares this pessimistic conclusion. His study describes the difficulty of the army's Reconstruction mission. The strength and persistence of white southern resistance and the use of systematic terror and counterrevolutionary guerrilla warfare doomed Reconstruction. Rable, *But There Was No Peace*, 187–91.

37. Both Sefton and Lowe refer to Schofield as a moderate Republican, though he was probably closer to the position of overt Democrat Winfield S. Hancock. Sefton, *United States Army and Reconstruction*, 18; Lowe, *Republicans and Reconstruction in Virginia*, 76.

38. Badeau, *Grant in Peace*, 163.

39. Schofield, *Forty-Six Years*, 421; Andrews, "Years of Frustration," 37–39.

40. The nineteenth-century "General Staff" was far different from a modern General Staff. The adjutant general, quartermaster general, commissary general, judge advocate general, and so forth, were the chiefs of separate staff departments and bureaus. They were not a coordinating staff, and they sought to assert their independence from both other departments and the line army.

41. White, *Republican Era*, 134–53; Hewes, *From Root to McNamara*, 3–6. See also Short, *Development of National Administrative Organization*, 119–39, 236–68. For an excellent summary of the institutional politics of army reform, see "Patching the Army: The Limits of

Provincial Virtue," chap. 4 in Skowronek, *Building a New American State*, 85–120. For an excellent account of the origins of the commanding general position, see Skelton, "Commanding General and the Problem of Command."

42. Schofield to Wilson and Garfield, June 12, 1868, RG 107, NARA; Andrews, "Years of Frustration," 25–29. On January 31, 1868, as Johnson renewed his effort to get rid of Secretary of War Stanton, Sherman suggested that Johnson could simply issue a presidential directive to restrict the secretary's ability to issue orders. Sherman, *Memoirs*, 910–18. William R. Roberts suggests that Congress was likely to pass these regulations and that Schofield's opposition to having Congress ratify them doomed the effort to place the staff under the commanding general. Although the Reconstruction crisis had produced an unusual alliance between the commanding general and Congress, Roberts underestimates the degree of political opposition to placing so much power in the hands of a military officer. The failure of the transfer of the Indian Bureau suggests that the command of the staff question would not have survived in the way Sherman hoped. Further, enshrining regulations into law would have unduly tied the hands of the executive branch, the commanding general included. Schofield reversed himself on this issue in 1878 and 1886, but by 1895, he had reverted to not enshrining the regulations into law. Roberts, "Loyalty and Expertise," 152–57. The transfer of the Indian Bureau from the Interior Department to the War Department is discussed in chapters 10 and 12.

43. Sherman, *Memoirs*, 931. On March 8 Sherman issued his own order to reinforce the new arrangement.

44. Ibid., 932.

45. Schofield to Sherman, April 2, 1869, Box 49, Schofield Papers, LC; Sherman, *Memoirs*, 932–33; Marszalek, *Sherman*, 384–85.

46. White, *Republican Era*, 29–30. The vitriolic Gideon Welles continued to complain about the power Grant had ceded to General William T. Sherman and Admiral David D. Porter. Welles wrongly asserted that Schofield, "a man of more general intelligence than Grant," left the War Department in protest of Grant's directive. Welles claimed that while Rawlins had restored the secretary's authority at the War Department, Aldolph E. Borie and George M. Robeson yielded to Porter. Welles to Samuel S. Cox, February 26, 1870, Grant Papers, MHS.

47. U.S. House, *Report on Army Organization*, February 26, 1869, 2.

48. U.S. War Department, *Annual Report of the Secretary of War*, November 20, 1868; Schofield to W. T. Sherman, December 10, 1868, reel 13, Sherman Papers, LC; Wooster, *Military and United States Indian Policy*, 88–89.

49. U.S. House, *Report on Army Organization*, February 26, 1869, 123–29.

50. Schofield to W. T. Sherman, November 27, 1868, reel 13, Sherman Papers, LC.

51. Wooster, *Military and United States Indian Policy*, 85; Marszalek, *Sherman*, 385; Fellman, *Citizen Sherman*, 280–85.

52. Andrews, "Years of Frustration," 45–62.

CHAPTER TEN

1. For an excellent summary of the institutional politics of army reform, see "Patching the Army: The Limits of Provincial Virtue," chap. 4 in Skowronek, *Building a New American State*, 85–120. For an in-depth examination of Sherman's role, see Andrews, "Years of Frustration." For an internal army perspective on professionalism and reform, see Roberts, "Loyalty and Expertise"; and Thomas, "Army Reform in America."

2. Schofield, *Forty-Six Years*, 424–25. One old enemy, Henry T. Blow, refused to attend.

3. U.S. War Department, *Annual Report of the Secretary of War*, 1869, 67–70; Wooster, *Military and United States Indian Policy*, 134.

4. Ganoe, *History of the United States Army*, 354–55; Weigley, *History of the United States Army*, 273–74. For a detailed account of the Leavenworth schools, see Nenninger, *Leavenworth Schools and the Old Army*.

5. Schofield, *Forty-Six Years*, 426–27.

6. Utley, *Frontier Regulars*, 200. George Crook (1828–90) graduated from the USMA in 1852 (ranked thirty-eighth out of forty-three), a year ahead of Schofield, but he did not rise as rapidly as Schofield. Without much political pull, Crook, though breveted a major general, ended the war with a regular army rank of captain and was promoted to lieutenant colonel in 1866. Charles Robinson has noted that Crook was not excited about being assigned to Arizona and would have preferred to remain in the Department of the Columbia. Robinson, *General Crook and the Western Frontier*, 106–7.

7. Crook to Schofield, September 15, November 14, and December 11, 1871, Box 39, Schofield Papers, LC.

8. U.S. War Department, *Annual Report of the Secretary of War*, 1872, 72; Utley, *Frontier Regulars*, 199–205; Greene, "George Crook," 118–23.

9. Edward Richard Sprigg Canby (1817–73), USMA class of 1839 (ranked thirtieth of thirty-one), had fought in the Seminole and Mexican Wars. Promoted to brigadier general of Volunteers, March 31, 1862, and major general, May 7, 1864, he commanded the Department of Western Mississippi and captured Mobile in 1864–65. Promoted to brigadier general, USA, in 1866, he assumed command of the Department of the Columbia in 1870.

10. Murray, *Modocs and Their War*, 12–13; Schofield, *Forty-Six Years*, 435.

11. In his October 1, 1872, report, Canby expressed doubts about the reservation system and looked favorably on peaceful settlements outside the reservations: "The sooner the tribal organization is broken up and the Indians absorbed into the general community, the better it will be for them and for us." U.S. War Department, *Annual Report of the Secretary of War*, 1872, 71.

12. Murray, *Modocs and Their War*, 79; Utley, *Frontier Regulars*, 205–9. Schofield was absent on a special mission to the Hawaiian Islands (December 30, 1872–April 6, 1873) during most of this period.

13. Waldman, *Atlas of the North American Indian*, 132; Utley, *Frontier Regulars*, 209–11; Murray, *Modocs and Their War*, 200–210, 302; Schofield, *Forty-Six Years*, 436.

14. Murray, *Modocs and Their War*, 241, 273–97, 306, 318.

15. Schofield, *Forty-Six Years*, 437.

16. U.S. House, *Report on Army Organization*, February 26, 1869, 129.

17. Wooster, *Military and United States Indian Policy*, 42–47; Utley, *Frontier Regulars*, 53, 116–17. This author would argue that Canada's centralized government, low immigration, and lack of democratic responsiveness enabled the Mounties to protect Indian rights against expansionist whites in the West.

18. Patent application, July 1876, Box 89, Schofield Papers, LC; Schofield to Sherman, October 28, 1870, July 2, 1871, October 24, 1871, January 26, 1874, March 2, 1874, May 8, 1876, Sherman Papers, LC; Schofield, *Forty-Six Years*, 439. Schofield's later connections with Hawaii are discussed in chapter 14.

19. Marszalek, *Sherman*, 385–88; Sherman to Schofield, March 28, 1876, telegram, Box 42, Schofield Papers, LC.

20. Sherman to Schofield, March 28, March 30, April 8, May 4, May 25, June 1, 1876, Box 42, Schofield Papers, LC; Schofield to Sherman, March 29, March 30, April 7, May 10, 1876, Box 42, Schofield Papers, LC; Dillard, "United States Military Academy," 176–78. Schofield departed California in June but did not assume command at West Point until September. Sherman detailed Schofield to revise the army regulations in a renewed effort to gain control over the General Staff.

21. Schofield to Grant, September 18, 1876, Cullum Files 1585, USMA Archives.

22. Schofield to Secretary James D. Cameron, November 27, 28, December 1, 1876, Schofield Letters, vol. 1, 3–7, 11–12, USMA Archives; Dillard, "United States Military Academy," vi–ix, 177–79.

23. Schofield to Sherman, December 12, 19, 1876, and Schofield to Secretary James Cameron, January 5, 1877, Schofield Letters, vol. 1, 20–21, 37–47, 75–79, USMA Archives; Schofield, "Private Military Journal, 1876–1880," 94, Box 1, Schofield Papers, LC.

24. "The Electoral Count 1876–77," letters between Sherman and Schofield, December 26, 1876–January 26, 1877, Box 93, Schofield Papers, LC.

25. Hancock to W. T. Sherman, December 28, 1876, Sherman to Hancock, January 2 (or 20), 1877, reel 23, Sherman Papers, LC. Also see Hancock, *Reminiscences of Winfield Scott Hancock*, 151–56.

26. "The Electoral Count 1876–77."

27. This correspondence produced one other important observation about political uncertainty and civil-military relations. Regarding the political situation in which the army found itself, Sherman wrote Hancock, "Our standard opinions are mostly formed on the practice of our predecessors, but a great change was made after the close of the civil war, by the amendments of the Constitution giving to the freed slaves certain civil and political rights, and empowering Congress to make the laws necessary to enforce these rights. This power is new and absolute, and Congress has enacted laws with which we are not yet familiar and accustomed." Regarding a soldier's duty in such circumstances, Sherman went on the say: "As a matter of fact, I dislike to have our army used in these civil conflicts, but the President has the lawful right to use the army and navy, and has exercised the right, as he believes, lawfully and rightfully, and our duty has been, and is to sustain him with zeal and sincerity." Given the

importance of the president in directing the army in politically sensitive areas, it is hardly surprising that Sherman would be concerned over who legitimately ought to wield those powers. W. T. Sherman to W. S. Hancock, January 2, 1877, reel 27, Sherman Papers, LC.

28. Dillard, "United States Military Academy," 253–54.

29. Schofield to secretary of war, June 29 (or 30), 1877, Schofield Letters, vol. 1, USMA Archives; Schofield to Vincent, June 22, 1877, Box 42, Schofield Papers, LC; Dillard, "United States Military Academy," 162–63, 267–69. The five-year program was finally abandoned in 1861. Morrison, *"Best School,"* 143–53.

30. Dillard, "United States Military Academy," 163–68, 175.

31. Schofield to Sherman, October 25, 1877, Schofield Letters, vol. 1, 223–31, USMA Archives; U.S. War Department, *Annual Report of the Secretary of War*, 1877, 150–51; Dillard, "United States Military Academy," 283–84.

32. Schofield to A.G., April 14, 1877, Schofield Letters, vol. 1, 171–75, USMA Archives.

33. U.S. War Department, *Annual Report of the Secretary of War*, 1877, 152–54; Schofield to Sherman, November 27, 1877, Box 89, Schofield Papers, LC.

34. Morrison, *"Best School,"* 59–60. Bartlett retired at the age of sixty-seven only because he was enticed by the professional and financial prospects of becoming the actuary for the Mutual Company of New York. He died in 1893 at Yonkers, New York. *Annual Reunion*, June 9, 1893, 105–12.

35. Schofield to Sherman, January 27, 1877, reel 23, Sherman Papers, LC.

36. U.S. War Department, *Annual Report of the Secretary of War*, 1879, 173–75; Dillard, "United States Military Academy," 253–60. The congressional attack on academy standards was part of a general Democratic assault on the army. Efforts to reduce the size and pay of the army were extended to USMA instructors. The *Army and Navy Journal* argued that standards were not too high. Between 1832 and 1876 there were 4,599 appointments made, 3,302 admitted (72 percent), 763 (17 percent) rejected by Academic Board, 145 (3 percent) rejected by the Medical Board, and 389 (8 percent) who did not report or declined appointment. *Army and Navy Journal*, January 27, 1877, 392–93.

37. Schofield, "Suggestions for the consideration of the Academic Board," October 9, 1879, with replies, Box 89, Schofield Papers, LC; U.S. War Department, *Annual Report of the Secretary of War*, 1879, 175.

38. Schofield to Garfield, January 26, 1878, Box 89, Schofield Papers, LC.

39. Schofield, *Forty-Six Years*, 438; Weigley, "Military Thought of John M. Schofield," 77–78; Mallon, "Roosevelt, Brooks Adams, and Lea."

40. Dillard, "United States Military Academy," 89–97, 290–301.

41. *Army and Navy Journal*, July 26, 1879, 939.

42. Schofield to Mrs. John Wendenhall, July 20, 1879, Wherry to Schofield, July 21, 1879, Schofield Letters, vol. 2, 53–56, USMA Archives; Dillard, "United States Military Academy," 295.

43. Schofield to A.G., July 21, 1879, Schofield to Sherman, July 23, 1879, Schofield to President Hayes, August 15, 1879, Schofield to editor, *New York Times*, August 17, 1879, Schofield to Sherman, August 18, 1879, Schofield to A.G., October 2, 1879, Schofield Letters, vol. 2, 57–59, 95–104, 141–44, USMA Archives. For examples of presidential pressure see

President Hayes to Schofield, December 17, 1879, 1585, Cullum Files, USMA Archives; and Schofield to Hayes, December 19, 1879, Schofield Letters, vol. 2, 230–32, USMA Archives.

44. Schofield memorandum for the commandant, July 30, 1879, and Schofield to commandant, August 19, 1879, both in Schofield Letters, vol. 2, 70–72, 105 insert, USMA Archives; "An Address Delivered by Major General J. M. Schofield to the West Point Cadets," August 11, 1879, Box 91, Schofield Papers, LC. Schofield was so proud of this speech that he had it printed and sent copies to General Sherman and President Hayes.

45. "An Address Delivered by Major General J. M. Schofield to the West Point Cadets."

46. Adjutant to Edward Holden, August 11, 1908, Adjutant Letter Book, vol. 20, USMA Archives. While most West Pointers associate Schofield's name with the "Definition of Discipline," most Americans only associate it with Schofield Barracks on Oahu and the 1941 attack on Pearl Harbor. Such are the vagaries of fame.

47. Williston Fish, *Memories of West Point, 1877–1881*, 490, 853, USMA Archives.

48. Schofield to Sherman, January 4, 1880, Schofield Letters, vol. 2, 254–60, USMA Archives. The Whittaker case is discussed in chapter 11.

49. Fish, *Memories of West Point*, 490–93, 820, 853.

50. For a lengthy discussion of Schofield's "regulations," see Andrews, "Years of Frustration," 156–69. The proposed regulations were reprinted in U.S. Senate, *Burnside Report on the Proposed Reorganization of the Army*, 354–65. Large portions of these proposed regulations were incorporated in the unsuccessful "Burnside Bill" for army reorganization.

51. Schofield to Sherman, May 8, 1876, reel 23, Sherman Papers, LC.

52. Schofield to Colonel J. E. Tourtelotte, December 1, 1876, reel 23, Sherman Papers, LC.

53. Schofield to secretary of war, October 13, 1876, printed as *Remarks of Major General John M. Schofield, United States Army, upon the Reorganization of the Army* (Washington, D.C.: Government Printing Office, 1876), Schofield Papers, LC. Also printed in *Army and Navy Journal*, March 24, 1877, 525.

54. In addition to Secretary Cameron, members included Senator Joseph R. West (R-La.), Senator Francis Cockrell (D-Mo.), Representative Henry Banning (D-Ohio), Representative Stephen Hurlbut, (R-Ill.), General William T. Sherman, and Quartermaster General Montgomery C. Meigs. In March 1877 Cameron became a Republican senator for Pennsylvania. U.S. Senate, *Reorganization of the Army*.

55. A year later, the new secretary of war's annual report argued that giving the army regulations the force of law was a mistake and requested that the president have the authority to issue new regulations. "Annual Report of the Secretary of War, 1877," *Army and Navy Journal*, December 8, 1877, 277–78. For Sherman's input to the commission, see *Army and Navy Journal*, March 16, 1878, 507.

56. *Army and Navy Journal*, June 9, 1877, 704. Henry B. Banning was born in Bannings Mills, Ohio, on November 10, 1836, and died in Cincinnati, Ohio, on December 10, 1881. He practiced law both before and after the war. He commanded three different Ohio infantry regiments—the 78th, 121st, and 195th—during the war. First elected to Congress in 1872 as a Liberal Republican, he was reelected as a Democrat in 1874 and 1876. He lost his bid for renomination in 1878 and was defeated in the general election in 1880.

57. The *Army and Navy Journal* defended the army's role during the election and commended the "cool-head and cautious" officers. It rejected the hysterical cries of despotism, though it acknowledged that it was "a misfortune for the Army that it should have been compelled to take so prominent a part in the election disturbances at the South." *Army and Navy Journal*, October 28, 1876, 184, November 18, 1876, 282, December 16, 1876, 296.

58. *Army and Navy Journal*, May 12, 1877, 649, May 19, 1877, 567, May 26, 1877, 669. By October 1, 1877, the bankers had advanced over $400,000 to the officers, but the supposedly "reasonable" rate of interest for these loans caused considerable resentment among the officer corps. Andrews, "Years of Frustration," 184. The Railroad Strike of 1877 is addressed in more detail in chapter 12.

59. *Army and Navy Journal*, July 28, 1877, 813.

60. Schofield to Sherman, October 25, 1877, Sherman Papers, LC.

61. Andrews, "Years of Frustration," 192–95; Skowronek, *Building a New American State*, 99–102.

62. U.S. House, *Consideration for the Reorganization of the Army*. Also reprinted in *Army and Navy Journal*, February 9, 1878, 421–22.

63. At that time, promotion to captain was made based on seniority within one's regiment, while promotion to field grade was based on seniority in the entire branch. This meant that second lieutenants who were commissioned at the same time could have wildly different dates of promotion to first lieutenant and captain, based on the vacancies in their respective regiments.

64. Thirteen officers received the thanks of Congress during the war. By 1879, the only ones remaining on active duty were William T. Sherman, Philip Sheridan, Winfield Hancock, O. O. Howard, and Alfred Terry. Sifakis, *Who Was Who in the Union*, 477.

65. U.S. House, *Consideration for the Reorganization of the Army*, v–x; *Army and Navy Journal*, February 16, 1878, 440. Also see Coffman, *Old Army*, 369–70; and Foner, *United States Soldier between Two Wars*, 138–41.

66. *Army and Navy Journal*, February 2, 1878, 409, February 9, 1878, 421–22, February 16, 1878, 440. Sherman suspected that southern Democrats sought to dramatically reduce or temporarily abolish the army in order to shift the Unionist northerner tilt of the officer corps by later bringing in southerners to replace those officers who were dismissed during the reductions. Andrews, "Years of Frustration," 195.

67. Schofield to Sherman and Schofield to Banning, February 10, 1878, Schofield Letters, vol. 1, 343–48, USMA Archives.

68. *Army and Navy Journal*, June 22, 1878, 744, 746. *Posse comitatus* is literally translated as "power of the county" and derived from the English custom for a sheriff to call on local men for law enforcement.

69. For the role of the army in enforcing fugitive slave laws, see Coakley, *Role of Federal Military Forces in Domestic Disorders*, 128–37.

70. *Army and Navy Journal*, June 22, 1878, 744. The *Army and Navy Journal* pointed out that while Congress and the army had reason to be happy, the various governors who repeat-

edly called on the president for federal troops might be less pleased. *Army and Navy Journal*, June 29, 1878, 761.

71. The act read: "From and after the passage of this act it shall not be lawful to employ any part of the Army of the United States, as a posse comitatus, or otherwise, for the purpose of executing the laws, except in such cases and under such circumstances as such employment of said force may be expressly authorized by the Constitution or by act of Congress; and no money appropriated by this act shall be used to pay any of the expenses incurred in the employment of any troops in violation of this section. And any person willfully violating the provisions of this section shall be deemed guilty of a misdemeanor and on conviction thereof shall be punished by fine not exceeding ten thousand dollars or imprisonment not exceeding two years or by both such fine and imprisonment." Quoted in Hammond, "Posse Comitatus Act," 961*n*52.

72. Today's federal government has multiple law enforcement agencies, many with extensive paramilitary elements. For a discussion of the modern implications of the act, see Hammond, "Posse Comitatus Act"; and Grove, *U.S. Military and Civil Infrastructure Protection*.

73. *Army and Navy Journal*, June 22, 1878, 746; Andrews, "Years of Frustration," 205–6. The bill also appointed a commission to examine again the question of transferring the Indian Bureau to the War Department. The members of the Burnside Commission, 1878–79, were Senator Ambrose E. Burnside (R-R.I.), Senator Preston Plumb (R-Kans.), Senator Matthew C. Butler (D-S.C.), Representative George Dibrell (D-Tenn.), Representative Henry Banning (D-Ohio), Representative Edward S. Bragg (D-Wisc.), Representative Horace Strait (R-Minn.), and Representative Harry White (R-Pa.).

74. Schofield's maximum time in grade guidelines were as follows: second lieutenant, six years; first lieutenant, eight years; captain, ten years; major, six years; lieutenant colonel, four years. This totaled thirty-four years. He proposed that every officer be retired after forty-four years of service or at sixty-six years of age. U.S. Senate, *Burnside Report on the Proposed Reorganization of the Army*, 246. American officers were very aware of the disparity in rates of promotion between the American and European armies. For example, see "Promotion in the German Army—II," *Army and Navy Journal*, May 26, 1877, 670.

75. U.S. Senate, *Burnside Report on the Proposed Reorganization of the Army*, 245–56. The proposed bill included most of Schofield's suggestions for West Point, except the position of brigadier general for the superintendent. It also did not establish his idea for promotion guidelines.

76. Ibid., 1–78. The complete text of the Burnside Bill was also published in the *Army and Navy Journal*, December 21, 1878, 325–41.

77. Schofield to Sherman, December 20, 1878, Schofield Letters, vol. 3, 217–18, USMA Archives. Sherman's plan was more orthodox than Schofield's was. He did not propose lineal promotion, though he did advocate that the general officer positions of the staff be selected from the army at large, rather than from just that staff branch. Clearly, this was an attempt to break up the insularity of the staff branches. Sherman did not propose a formal battalion structure, although his plan could accommodate one. He offered few changes in the staff

structure. He appealed especially for additional regimental first lieutenants to meet the need for staff and other special duty details. He urged the authorization of general officers based on one brigadier general for every three regiments and one major general for every three "brigades." Combat brigades and divisions were not a peacetime formation in the nineteenth century. Sherman's letter to the committee also referred to Emory Upton's *Military Policy of the United States*. Though he expected that it would be in print soon, it would be not accessible before the committee's report had to be submitted in December 1878. Alas, Upton's master work would not see publication for twenty-six years. U.S. Senate, *Burnside Report on the Proposed Reorganization of the Army*, 78–79.

78. Schofield to Sherman, December 20, 1878, Schofield Letters, vol. 3, 217–18, USMA Archives; *Army and Navy Journal*, January 25, 1879, 438. Schofield wrote two letters to Sherman that day. The first reflected his initial qualms about submitting his views; the second was a longer analysis, which he may have assumed Sherman would use to garner further support. Sherman passed the second letter on to William Conant Church, who published it in his *Army and Navy Journal*, December 28, 1878, 359.

79. U.S. Senate, *Burnside Report on the Proposed Reorganization of the Army*, 7–8, 354–55.

80. Schofield to Sherman, December 24, 1878, Schofield Letters, vol. 3, 225–34, USMA Archives; U.S. Senate, *Burnside Report on the Proposed Reorganization of the Army*, 7.

81. Schofield to Sherman, December 24, 1878, Schofield Letters, vol. 3, 225–34, USMA Archives.

82. Ibid.

83. Ibid.

84. Ibid.

85. *Army and Navy Journal*, January 18, 1879, 409–10.

86. Ibid., January 25, 1879, 436.

87. Ibid., January 11, 1879, 398. Despite the close connections between Sherman and editor William Conant Church, the *Army and Navy Journal* dismissed that idea. The *Journal* believed that since previous efforts to harm the army had been defeated, the friends of the military need not accept bad measures out of fear of even worse measures to follow. Ibid., January 25, 1879, 436.

88. Schofield to Sherman, January 21, 1879, Schofield Letters, vol. 3, 253–55, USMA Archives.

89. *Army and Navy Journal*, January 11, February 8, and February 15, 1879.

90. Ibid., January 25, 1879, 438. A week earlier, the Washington correspondent of the *Army and Navy Journal* also noted the effectiveness of the opponents' argument when he predicted that any bill that seemingly gave authority to Sherman at the expense of the secretary would fail. The correspondent also noted the increasing opposition to enshrining in statute West Point as a military department. Ibid., January 18, 1879, 417.

91. *Congressional Record*, 45th Cong., 3d sess., 660, 847–52, 897–926, 963–76, 1034–51, 1132–45, 1707–14, 1755–67, 1809–25; *Army and Navy Journal*, February 15, 22, 1879, March 1, 8, 1879; Thomas, "Army Reform in America," 254. The Democrats also attempted to use the appropriations bill to add further restrictions to the use of the army to protect the polls.

92. Schofield to Sherman, May 8, 1876, reel 23, Sherman Papers, LC.

93. For example, Schofield complained about the Quartermaster Department's refusal to hire blacksmiths, wheelwrights, and saddlers, thus forcing commanders to divert troops to perform these essential tasks. Schofield to A.G., June 12, 1884, Box 52, Schofield Papers, LC. Edward Coffman describes the long tradition of inadequate food, housing, and clothing for the troops and the seemingly never-ending details that sapped the present-for-duty strength of most units. Coffman, *Old Army*, 167–71, 340–46; see also Foner, *United States Soldier between Two Wars*, 16–21. For an enlisted man's perspective on reorganization, see "Wants of the Soldier Versus Reorganization," *Army and Navy Journal*, July 5, 1879, 873.

94. These professional schools were the Artillery School (established 1868), Signal School (1868), School for Application of Cavalry and Infantry (1881), Engineer School for Application (1885), School for Cavalry and Light Artillery (1887), and Army Medical School (1893).

95. The new journals were the *Journal of the Military Service Institution* (established in 1880), the *Cavalry Journal* (1885), the *Journal of the Artillery Corps* (1889), and the *Infantry Association Journal* (1904).

96. James B. Fry, "The Command of the Army," *Field Glass*, May 1879, and William M. Wherry, "The Command of the Army," *Field Glass*, July 1879, reprints in Box 86, Schofield Papers, LC. Schofield wrote a remarkably restrained and friendly reply to Fry about his article. While Schofield begged to disagree with Fry over the extent that the Constitution demanded personal action by the commander in chief, he suggested that his and Fry's views did not radically differ. Schofield to James B. Fry, December 13, 1879, Schofield Letters, vol. 2, 219–21, USMA Archives. For a more direct and scathing rebuttal of Fry's contention that the president as commander in chief cannot delegate his command authority to a general in chief, see *Army and Navy Journal*, June 14, 1879, 803–4.

CHAPTER ELEVEN

1. Schofield, *Forty-Six Years*, 439.

2. George W. Getty was a USMA classmate of Sherman's and a division and corps commander in the Army of the Potomac. He retired as a colonel in 1883, despite Schofield's strong appeal to the secretary of war for Getty's promotion. Foreshadowing his efforts as commanding general, Schofield compared the dreary promotion prospects of the army with the navy's ability to promote nearly all captains to commodore or rear admiral before retirement. He gloomily concluded that "if it is true, as often alleged that many older officers seem to have lost their zeal to a certain extent, is it any wonder that it is true." Schofield to secretary of war, May 29, 1882, Gibson-Getty-McClure Papers, LC.

3. Gabler, "Fitz John Porter Case," 371–79. The major accounts of the Fitz John Porter case are Gabler's and Eisenschiml, *Celebrated Case of Fitz John Porter*. Eisenschiml's account is strongly pro-Porter. Gabler's analysis is less partisan but still sympathetic to Porter. A more recent study by Curt Anders, *Injustice on Trial*, is also strongly supportive of Porter. Also see Sears, "Court-Martial of Fitz John Porter"; and Haydock, "Court-Martial of Fitz John Porter."

For an account sympathetic to Pope, see Cozzens, *General John Pope*, 202–24, 291–92, 297–300, 327–29, 333–37.

4. Fitz John Porter (1822–1901) was born in New Hampshire, graduated from West Point in 1845 (ranked eighth of forty-one), and served in the Mexican War. He was appointed brigadier general, U.S. Volunteers, on May 14, 1861, and made major general, U.S. Volunteers, and commander of V Corps on July 4, 1862. He was dismissed from the service in 1863 and reappointed and retired as colonel in 1886. John Pope (1822–92), USMA class of 1842 (ranked seventeenth of fifty-six), also served in the Mexican War. He was appointed brigadier general, U.S. Volunteers, on May 17, 1861, and major general, U.S. Volunteers, on March 21, 1862. After Second Bull Run, he commanded the Department of the Northwest for the remainder of the war. He retired as major general, USA, in 1886. Boatner, *Civil War Dictionary*, 661, 658–59.

5. The Porter controversy made the second battle of Bull Run among the most written-about battles in the postbellum years. Most notable are Ropes, *Army under Pope*, which severely criticizes Pope; and Cox, *Second Battle of Bull Run*, which unpersuasively attempts to pin the blame on Porter. The most detailed recent account is Hennessy, *Return to Bull Run*, 464–70. Hennessy deems Porter an average officer who lacked energy but certainly no traitor. He concludes that nearly all Union corps commanders were ineffective, but the primary responsibility fell on the high commanders Halleck, McClellan, and above all, Pope. For other modern accounts of the battle, see Cozzens, *General John Pope*; and Martin, *Second Bull Run Campaign*.

6. Under the Ninth Article Porter was specifically charged with (1) disobedience of Pope's order to begin marching to Bristoe Station at 1:00 A.M. on August 28; (2) ignoring Pope's joint order of August 29 and failing to join the battle; (3) failure to execute Pope's 4:30 P.M. August 29 order to attack the Confederate right flank and rear; (4) disobedience of Pope's order to move his corps to Pope's location by permitting one brigade to march to Centerville; and (5) permitting an attached brigade to march to Centerville. Under the Fifty-second Article of War Porter was charged with (1) not engaging with the enemy on August 29 and retreating instead; (2) failing to bring his corps to the field of battle even as the rest of the army could be heard fighting a severe action; and (3) launching on August 30 only a feeble attack, unnecessarily retreating, and making little effort to inspire and rally his troops. *OR* I, 12/2 (Supplement): 824–27. The complete proceedings of the Porter court-martial were published as *OR* I, 12/2 (Supplement). The report of the Schofield Board can be most conveniently found in *OR* I, 12/2:512–36. The complete proceedings are contained in *Proceedings and Report of the Board of Army Officers . . . in the Case of Fitz-John Porter*.

7. Gabler, "Fitz John Porter Case," 207–10, 215–20. The officers of the court were Major Generals David Hunter and Ethan Allen Hitchcock and Brigadier Generals Benjamin Prentiss, Rufus King, James Ricketts, Silas Casey, James Garfield, Napoleon Buford, and John Slough. According to Eisenschiml, *Celebrated Case of Fitz John Porter*, 75, Brigadier General W. W. Morris had protested the legality of the court and was replaced by Slough.

8. Porter to S. L. M. Barlow, December 29, 1862, cited in Sears, "Court-Martial of Fitz John Porter," 60, 62. According to Stephen Sears, when Secretary of War Stanton reputedly showed the court roster to his assistant William Tucker, Tucker remarked, "that court will convict

General Porter whether guilty or not." Stanton nodded in agreement. Henry Gabler relates that Tucker's story came to light years later, with few dates or details. Further, Tucker refused to testify before the Schofield Board. Gabler concluded that Tucker's story was not conclusive. Gabler, "Fitz John Porter Case," 314–15. Thomas and Hyman also maintain there was no evidence that Stanton packed the court. Thomas and Hyman, *Stanton*, 259–60.

9. Both Eisenschiml and Gabler agree that the evidence did not support the verdict. Eisenschiml, *Celebrated Case of Fitz John Porter*, 82–105; Gabler, "Fitz John Porter Case," 315–17.

10. Gabler, "Fitz John Porter Case," 227–55.

11. *OR* I, 12/2 (Supplement): 918–19, 925. In his court testimony, Burnside said that while Porter's remarks may have been indiscreet, he did not consider them disloyal. Furthermore, Porter's lack of confidence in Pope was relatively common, and not simply among officers from the Army of the Potomac. Ibid., 1002–6.

12. Ibid., 1051.

13. Ibid., 1112.

14. Stephen Sears writes that Lincoln probably did not read the entire record of the court but relied instead on the judge advocate's summary and the defense's summation. Seeing no blatant injustice, he approved the sentence. Sears, "Court-Martial of Fitz John Porter," 66–67. During the Schofield Board inquiry, Robert Lincoln testified that his father had been outraged when he read Holt's assertion that Porter had retreated on August 29. That this accusation was false did not seem to matter to young Lincoln. Former New Jersey governor William A. Newall testified that in 1864 Lincoln expressed a willingness to hear new evidence of Porter's innocence. Eisenschiml, *Celebrated Case of Fitz John Porter*, 236–39.

15. Schofield, *Forty-Six Years*, 460; Schofield conversation with artist James Edward Kelly, May 29, 1901, Kelly Papers, NYHS.

16. Schofield conversation with artist James Edward Kelly, May 29, 1901, Kelly Papers, NYHS.

17. Eisenschiml, *Celebrated Case of Fitz John Porter*, 217–18; *Proceedings and Report of the Board of Army Officers . . . in the Case of Fitz-John Porter*, 1:742–811, 1:552–68; Gabler, "Fitz John Porter Case," 394–98; *Army and Navy Journal*, October 19, 1878, 166–67, November 2, 1878, 204, 206, November 9, 1878, 222–23.

18. *Proceedings and Report of the Board of Army Officers . . . in the Case of Fitz-John Porter*, 1:26–29; Sifakis, *Who Was Who in the Union*, 438–39; conversation between Schofield and Chamberlain recorded by artist James Edward Kelly, October 13, 1903, Kelly Papers, NYHS; Trulock, *In the Hands of Providence*, 360, 421 n. 63; Finding aid, Gouverneur Kemble Warren Papers, New York State Library, Albany, N.Y. Chamberlain's 1915 book *Passing of the Armies* was written in large measure to defend the honor of V Corps and its commander, Gouverneur K. Warren. Chamberlain, *Passing of the Armies*, xiv–xv.

19. *Proceedings and Report of the Board of Army Officers . . . in the Case of Fitz-John Porter*, 1:63–74. Also see Longstreet, *From Manassas to Appomattox*, 180–85.

20. Eisenschiml, *Celebrated Case of Fitz John Porter*, 243.

21. *OR* I, 12/2:512–36.

22. Ibid.

23. Schofield had been well aware that a decision in favor of Porter would cast doubt on the veracity of senior officers and hoped an early decision would reduce the "after pains." Schofield to Terry, December 5, 1878, Schofield Letters, vol. 3, 191–94, USMA Archives. When McDowell later attacked the integrity of the members of the board, an irritated Schofield discussed with Terry the possibility of bringing charges against him. Schofield to Porter, February 6, 1880, and Schofield to Terry, February 14, 1880, Schofield Letters, vol. 2, 319–21, 325–34, USMA Archives.

24. *OR* I, 12/2:534.

25. Ibid.

26. Ibid., 533–34; Sears, "Court-Martial of Fitz John Porter," 71.

27. Schofield told Terry that if the Republicans had controlled both houses of Congress, they would have done the right thing and not let the matter become a partisan issue. Given Representative James Garfield's intense opposition to Porter and McClellan, this was a dubious assessment. Schofield to Terry, February 28, 1880, Schofield Letters, vol. 2, 343–47, USMA Archives.

28. Eisenschiml, *Celebrated Case of Fitz John Porter*, 300–307; Gabler, "Fitz John Porter Case," 426–75. In an effort to thank Schofield, Porter urged President Grover Cleveland in 1888 to revive the rank of lieutenant general for Schofield, calling him "a democrat—of the Hancock school." Gabler, "Fitz John Porter Case," 468.

29. Utley, *Frontier Regulars*, 422 n. 7.

30. Rosecrans to Getty, February 12, 26, 1883, Keifer to Getty, February 13, 21, 1883, and Schofield to secretary of war, May 29, 1882, Gibson-Getty-McClure Papers, LC.

31. *Army and Navy Journal*, April 12, 1879, 638; Grant, "Undeserved Stigma." Grant reviewed the Schofield Board record in 1881 at the request of Porter and wrote the president of his belief that Porter had been misjudged. Grant to President [Arthur], December 22, 1881, Box 40, Schofield Papers, LC.

32. Schofield, "Private Military Journal, 1876–1880," 176–78, and "Confidential Record," October 1881–September 1891, 29–33, Box 1, Schofield Papers, LC; Cox, *Second Battle of Bull Run*.

33. Schofield to Sherman, November 23, 1878, and May 27, 1878, Schofield Letters, vol. 3, 179–80, 325–30, USMA Archives.

34. Cozzens, *General John Pope*, 330.

35. Schofield to Sherman, May 26, 1879, Schofield Letters, vol. 3, 350–53, USMA Archives; Schofield to Sherman, April 27, 1879, May 2, 1879, reel 25, Sherman Papers, LC.

36. Department of the Missouri, General Court-martial Order no. 74, November 25, 1879, Box 86, Schofield Papers, LC; Schofield to Terry, October 15, 1879, J. Schofield to G. Schofield, October 15, 1879, and October 23, 1879, Schofield Letters, vol. 2, 147–48, 151–55, 161–62, USMA Archives.

37. J. Schofield to G. Schofield, October 27, 1879, and December 5, 1879, Schofield to Sherman, December 6, 1879, Schofield Letters, vol. 2, 166–67, 204–5, 208–11, 234–41, 262–63, USMA Archives.

38. J. Schofield to G. Schofield, December 20, 1879, and January 8, 1879, Schofield Letters, vol. 2, USMA Archives.

39. ACP George W. Schofield 396, 1874, RG 94, NARA.

40. Carroll, *Black Military Experience*, 84, 176.

41. *Army and Navy Journal*, February 10, 1877, 435–39, April 7, 1877, 566, May 28, 1877, 675; "Three New Versions of Smith & Wesson . . . Schofield Model," <http://customersup port.smith-wesson.com/userimages/Schofield—Model—of—2000.pdf> (August 28, 2005).

42. *New York Times*, December 19, 1882, 5. Twenty-four-year-old Alma Bullock Schofield died on March 27, 1879, at Fort Sill, Oklahoma. Altshuler, *Cavalry Yellow and Infantry Blue*, 294. The couple had married at Fort Concho, Texas, on November 9, 1875. Leckie, *Colonel's Lady on the Western Frontier*, 70–80, esp. 76. While not unique, Charles B. Schofield's career was a bit of an anomaly, in that he frequently served as an aide to his brother John in the grade of major and lieutenant colonel, yet remained a permanent captain. In the 2nd Cavalry, promotion was especially slow, and Charles lost much ground before lineal promotion was instituted. He was not able to transfer to a staff corps and did not transfer to a volunteer unit during the Spanish-American War. *Annual Report of Association of Graduates of USMA*, 146–48; ACP Charles B. Schofield 5075, 1876, RG 94, NARA.

43. This virtual deathwatch was not just the concern of senior officers; the commissions for new West Point graduates also depended on vacancies. In 1878 the *Army and Navy Journal* expressed grave concern about their prospects, since in the past year "there were only sixty-two casualties among the commissioned officers in the army, viz., sixteen resignations, thirty-two deaths, one dropped, twelve dismissed, and one cashiered." *Army and Navy Journal*, March 9, 1878, 470.

44. J. Schofield to G. Schofield, December 29, 1879, Schofield Letters, vol. 2, 234–41, USMA Archives.

45. Schofield, "The Power of Congress over the Army," April 6, 1880, Box 89, Schofield Papers, LC.

46. Ibid.

47. Ibid.

48. For a comprehensive account of the case, see Marszalek, *Assault at West Point*. Also see Center of Military History, "The Case of Johnson C. Whittaker," March 15, 1994, Whittaker File, USMA Archives.

49. H. M. Lazelle to adjutant, USMA, April 7, 1880, Whittaker File, USMA Archives; Schofield, *Forty-Six Years*, 445. Whittaker had failed the course in 1879, and Schofield had permitted him to repeat the year rather than be dismissed.

50. Of the members of the court-martial board, all were northerners, six of ten were not academy graduates (including the presiding officer, Nelson Miles), and one had served in a black regiment. The army JAG wrote a highly critical report of the trial and Schofield's conduct. President Arthur based his reversal on a technicality about the admissibility of certain evidence. Whittaker's dismissal in March 1882 was for his having failed his June 1880 exams, taken just after the first board of inquiry. Marszalek, *Assault at West Point*, 135–36, 153–54, 239–50.

51. Ibid., 74–75, 246–50, 274–80.

52. Ibid., 275–76. Marszalek concludes that Schofield was "notably myopic" and genuinely unconscious of his own prejudices that marred his handling of the situation. Thus, Schofield believed that criticism of his actions was conspiratorially inspired.

53. Schofield, *Forty-Six Years*, 445; Schofield, "Private Military Journal, 1876–1880," 104–28, Box 1, Schofield Papers, LC.

54. Schofield, "Private Military Journal, 1876–1880," 104–28, Box 1, Schofield Papers, LC; Marszalek, *Assault at West Point*, 62–66. John Bigelow, who had visited Schofield two days after the attack, later wrote that Schofield was already quite confident that Whittaker was the real culprit. John Bigelow to Edward Holden, October 24, 1906, John Bigelow Sr. File, USMA Archives; newspaper clippings, Whittaker File, USMA Archives.

55. "Annual Report, Department of West Point, 1880," October 5, 1880, Box 93, Schofield Papers, LC. Schofield had written much of the section on "The Freedman at West Point and in the Army" in May 1880. See Schofield's handwritten draft, "Notes on the Colored Cadet," May 1880, Box 89, Schofield Papers, LC; and Schofield, *Forty-Six Years*, 445–47.

56. "Annual Report, Department of West Point, 1880."

57. Schofield to A.G., January 15, 1879, Whittaker File, USMA Archives.

58. Schofield to commandant of cadets, September 14, 1878, Schofield Letters, vol. 3, 119–20, USMA Archives.

59. Schofield to Terry, January 13, 1880, Schofield to Lazelle, January 20, 1880, Schofield to Sherman, January 26, 1880, Schofield Letters, vol. 2, 283, 299, 311–12, USMA Archives.

60. Williston Fish, *Memories of West Point, 1877–1881*, USMA Archives, 490–93, 820, 853.

61. Hoogenboom, *Rutherford B. Hayes*, 424–27; Schofield to W. T. Sherman, August 14, 1880, reel 26, Sherman Papers, LC.

62. The only account of this meeting comes from a lengthy memo in Schofield's private journal, probably dictated to aide William Wherry by Schofield. Schofield, "Private Military Journal, 1876–1880," 193–209, Box 1, Schofield Papers, LC.

63. Ibid., 207–9. Sherman privately argued, "The relief of Gen. Schofield *now* will embarrass the War Department." Elaborating, he observed that there were only three grand divisions suitable for three major generals, but the army also had Lieutenant General Sheridan. In 1882 General Sherman would retire, and Sheridan would move to Washington, D.C. Then, three divisions could be filled by Hancock, Schofield, and McDowell. W. T. Sherman memorandum, undated [probably August 1880], reel 26, Sherman Papers, LC. Two weeks after Schofield's meetings with Hayes and Sherman, Sherman wrote that he wanted Schofield to hang on until June 1882, when he expected radical changes potentially involving himself, E. O. C. Ord, McDowell, and Pope, because "unless room is made for [Nelson A.] Miles, [Ranald] McKenzie, and some of the Colonels the boiler will burst." Sherman to Schofield, August 31, 1880, Box 42, Schofield Papers, LC.

64. J. D. Broadhead to Schofield, March 1, 1880, Box 37, Schofield Papers, LC; John Bigelow to Edward Holden, October 24, 1906, John Bigelow Sr. File, USMA Archives.

65. Schofield, "Confidential Record, 1881–1891," 2–7, Box 1, Schofield Papers, LC. Schofield resisted requests for the publication of his correspondence with Sherman about the 1876

electoral crisis, but he showed the letters confidentially to friend and prominent Democrat John Bigelow. Schofield, "Private Military Journal, 1876–1880," 189–90, Box 1, Schofield Papers, LC. After the election, Hancock told Schofield that had he been elected president, he would have appointed Schofield to replace him at the Division of the Atlantic. Jordan, *Winfield Scott Hancock*, 308.

66. Schofield to W. T. Sherman, November 5, 1880, reel 27, Sherman Papers, LC.

67. Schofield to A.G., November 12, 1880, ACP J. M. Schofield 2556, 1883, RG 94, NARA.

68. Ibid.

69. Marszalek, *Sherman*, 437–38; Hoogenboom, *Rutherford B. Hayes*, 455–57. Ord (1818–83) was placed on the retirement list as a major general in 1881. McDowell (1818–85) retired in 1882. Boatner, *Civil War Dictionary*, 531, 609–10.

70. Carpenter, *Sword and Olive Branch*, 273; Coffman, *Old Army*, 228–29; Dillard, "United States Military Academy," 213–25, 301–16, 351–55.

71. Schofield to A.G., November 12, 1880, ACP J. M. Schofield 2556, 1883, RG 94, NARA.

72. Shortly before Schofield departed for Washington to assume the position of commanding general, an African American man wrote Schofield and asked for five dollars to pay the installment on his house. The man wrote, "Dear Sir you will please pardon me a poor colored man for venturing to address you but I wish to ask a small favor of you altho people have said you disliking my poor black race, but that come about thrue the Whiticer case." Perhaps out of a sense of guilt over his handling of the Whittaker case, or perhaps in celebration of his promotion, Schofield sent this apparent stranger the money. John H. Davis, Brooklyn, N.Y., to Schofield, August 8, 1888, Box 37, Schofield Papers, LC.

CHAPTER TWELVE

1. West Point G.O. no. 1, January 21, 1881, Box 38, Schofield Papers, LC; Schofield to Sherman, February 8, 1881, Sherman to Schofield, November 12, 27, 1880, reel 27, Sherman Papers, LC; Schofield, *Forty-Six Years*, 447–51.

2. Hancock had been offered the larger Division of the Missouri upon Sheridan's elevation, but he chose to remain in New York. Secretary of War Robert Lincoln to Hancock, October 9, 1883, Hancock Papers, MHI.

3. For an excellent analysis of the army as a constabulary force, see "The Constabulary Years, 1865–1898," chap. 3, in Birtle, *U.S. Army Counterinsurgency and Contingency Operations Doctrine*, 55–98.

4. The most balanced and complete accounts of the Indian Wars in the West are written by Francis Paul Prucha and Robert M. Utley. See Prucha, *Broadax and Bayonet*; Prucha, *Sword of the Republic*; Prucha, *Documents of United States Indian Policy*; Prucha, *Great Father*; Utley, *Frontiersmen in Blue*; Utley, *Frontier Regulars*; and Utley, *Indian Frontier of the American West*. Also see Wooster, *Military and United States Indian Policy*.

5. Utley, *Frontier Regulars*, 191 n. 28; Prucha, *Great Father*, 58.

6. Utley, *Frontier Regulars*, 353–55, 365–66, 379–406; Prucha, *Great Father*, 170.

7. Utley, *Last Days of the Sioux Nation*, is the most detailed account of the events surrounding Wounded Knee.

8. Miles to Schofield and Schofield endorsement, December 20, 1890, reel 29, Harrison Papers, LC; copies in Box 68, Schofield Papers, LC; and RG 108, NARA. Secretary of the Interior John W. Noble forwarded the correspondence to President Harrison on January 2, 1891. For a discussion of the Crook Commission and the Sioux treaty, see Utley, *Last Days of the Sioux Nation*, 40–59, 76.

9. Utley, *Last Days of the Sioux Nation*, 200–230. Utley concludes, "It is time that Wounded Knee be viewed for what it was—a regrettable, tragic accident of war that neither side intended, and that called forth behavior for which some individuals on both sides, in unemotional respect, may be judged culpable, but for which neither side as a whole may be properly condemned" (230). At the direction of the president, Schofield sent Miles a vague response lamenting the deaths at Wounded Knee and vague assurances of friendship with the Indians. Schofield to Miles, January 2, 1891, reel 29, Harrison Papers, LC.

10. *Army and Navy Journal*, December 20, 1890, 279. General Miles later attempted to prefer charges against adjutant general Colonel Chauncey McKeever (USMA, class of 1849) as the source of some of the derogatory comments against Miles. *Army and Navy Journal*, January 24, 1891, 370–71, February 14, 1891, 426. As Miles was assembling his forces, Schofield was attempting to dissuade political leaders from exacerbating the problem by calling out the South Dakota militia. Schofield endorsement, December 29, 1890, Box 68, Schofield Papers, LC; *Army and Navy Journal*, December 27, 1890, 303.

11. Utley, *Last Days of the Sioux Nation*, 229–30, 245–49, 551–54; *Army and Navy Journal*, January 10, 1891, 337–38. Miles was also angry at Forsyth for letting his regiment get pinned down by the Sioux at Drexel Mission and needing the assistance of Major Guy Henry's 9th Cavalry to extricate him. Henry wrote Schofield a personal letter somewhat supportive of Forsyth's actions at Wounded Knee and concluded, "Starvation is at the bottom of the whole affair, and with food, they want agents of good force and character." Henry to Schofield, January 5, 1891, Box 27, Schofield Papers, LC.

12. "The Case of General Forsyth," *Army and Navy Journal*, February 14, 1891, 425–26. Schofield offered a detailed assessment of the action at Wounded Knee in a private memorandum for the secretary's use, and many points were reflected in Proctor's official decision. Schofield, "Notes on Wounded Knee Affair and General Forsyth," Box 91, Schofield Papers, LC. Proctor's biographer Chester Bowie argues that Proctor and Schofield were too lenient and that they simply wanted to put the issue behind them. Bowie agrees with Miles that Forsyth should have placed his entire force between the Indian warriors and the noncombatants. In hindsight, this might have been better, but it ignores the fact that Forsyth's orders were to disarm all Indians and permit none to escape. Bowie, "Redfield Proctor," 244–49. The Wounded Knee disaster and General Miles's continuing hostility to Forsyth did not prevent Forsyth's promotion to brigadier general in 1894 and major general in 1897.

13. Utley, *Last Days of the Sioux Nation*, 38–39, 277–82.

14. Schofield endorsement to Interior Department letter, April 1, 1891, Box 69, Schofield Papers, LC.

15. Schofield to secretary of war, January 10, 1892, March 25, 1892, Box 57, Schofield Papers, LC; Prucha, *Great Father*, 242–51.

16. Quoted in Utley, *Last Days of the Sioux Nation*, 266.

17. Ibid., 257–58, 265–66; *Army and Navy Journal*, January 10, 1891, 335, January 24, 1891, 372.

18. Schofield endorsement to report of General Brooke, December 20, 1890, Box 68, Schofield Papers, LC.

19. U.S. War Department, *Annual Report of the Secretary of War*, 1885, 129–33.

20. Ibid.

21. The allotment of land in severalty idea marked a rare agreement between Philip Sheridan and the humanitarians. Both saw the breakup of the reservations as the way to "detribalize" the Indians. The resulting legislation allocated half the acreage recommended by Sheridan and, as historian Paul Hutton has observed, dispossessed the Indians of their land far more rapidly than Sheridan's military campaigns. Hutton tartly observes that the enthusiastic cooperation of the humanitarians in this vast land swindle justified Sheridan's long-standing contempt for them. Hutton, *Phil Sheridan and His Army*, 343–45.

22. U.S. War Department, *Annual Report of the Secretary of War*, 1885, 129–33.

23. Ibid.

24. Schofield endorsement, November 29, 1889, Box 68, Schofield Papers, LC; Miles to A.G., November 25, 1890, RG 108, NARA; Coppersmith, "Indians in the Army," 174; Richard Pratt to W. C. Church, March 18, 1894, Box 2, Church Papers, LC. For other accounts of Indian soldiers, see White, "American Indian as Soldier"; Tate, "Soldiers of the Line"; and Feaver, "Indian Soldiers."

25. Schofield reported that the events at Pine Ridge showed that a force of 7,300 soldiers was the maximum possible that could be safely withdrawn from other posts in an emergency. The commanding general concluded that the army could not have handled the Pine Ridge crisis and another Indian or domestic emergency simultaneously. He emphasized that the large number of posts occupied by the army meant the average post numbered only 200 soldiers and could not be completely abandoned. This, combined with the need to man the new seacoast fortifications, justified an increase of 5,000 enlisted men to the total of the 30,000 authorized by law, but not provided for in the annual appropriations. Schofield to secretary of war, January 30, 1891, Box 55, Schofield Papers, LC. Also see Schofield to secretary of war, December 3, 1890, Box 55, Schofield Papers, LC; Bowie, "Redfield Proctor," 230–36.

26. Schofield to secretary of war, July 18, 21, 1890, January 22, 1891, Box 55, Schofield Papers, LC; U.S. War Department, *Annual Report of the Secretary of War*, 1891, 67–70. Two of ten cavalry regiments were exempted (9th and 10th) and six of twenty-five infantry regiments were exempted (6th, 11th, 15th, 19th, 24th, and 25th).

27. *Army and Navy Journal*, April 19, 1890, 643, July 5, 1890, 846, February 14, 1891, 426, March 7, 1891, 479, March 14, 1891, 496–97. The total numbers of Indian soldiers (per year) were as follows: 780 (1892), 771 (1893), 547 (1894), 65 (1895), 69 (1869). U.S. War Department, *Annual Report of the Secretary of War*, 1892, 1893, 1894, 1895, 1896.

28. Schofield endorsement, December 1, 1891, January 11, 1892, Box 69, Schofield Papers,

LC; Schofield memorandum, June 13, 1892, Box 56, Schofield Papers, LC; Coppersmith, "Indians in the Army," 171, 179–80; Scott, *Some Memories of a Soldier*, 168–70.

29. Scott, *Some Memories of a Soldier*, 168–70, 186. Schofield frequently used his aides to communicate outside of normal channels. Charles Schofield to Lieutenant S. C. Robertson, October 29, 1891, Box 63, Schofield Papers, LC; Tasker Bliss to H. L. Scott, December 21, 1894, Bliss Papers, MHI.

30. Lieutenant J. C. Byron to Senator Proctor, April 19, 1893, Box 9, Lamont Papers, LC; Captain J. M. Lee to Proctor, September 2, 1893, Lamont Papers, LC; H. L. Scott to Tasker Bliss, December 21, 1894, Letters Received, Bliss Papers, MHI. W. Bruce White has argued that the peacetime army had little appeal for Indians, and army rules were too much of a culture shock. White, "American Indian as Soldier," 19. Clifford Coppersmith suggests the army also lost interest in Indian issues and turned toward other missions. Coppersmith, "Indians in the Army," 184–85.

31. Schofield to secretary of war, January 22, 1891, Box 55, Schofield Papers, LC; U.S. War Department, *Annual Report of the Secretary of War*, 1890, 69; U.S. War Department, *Annual Report of the Secretary of War*, 1891, 91–92.

32. Tate, "Soldiers of the Line," 347–48; White, "American Indian as Soldier," 19–23; Nalty, *Strength for the Fight*, 63–124. One of the greatest obstacles to African American integration into the army was the refusal of so many whites to recognize the status and authority of black officers. Indian units were never expected to have Indian officers.

33. Leonard Wood (1860–1927) was a slight exception to this rule. Wood completed his training as a medical doctor in 1884 and joined the army as a contract surgeon in 1885. As an army surgeon, Wood received a Medal of Honor for his participation in the Geronimo campaign. By 1898, he was the army physician for the president and other senior officials. Wood's career as a line officer began in 1898 as the colonel of the U.S. 1st Volunteer Cavalry (the "Rough Riders"), and by the end of the year he was promoted to major general. Wood served as Army Chief of Staff from 1910 to 1914. Bell, *Commanding Generals and Chiefs of Staff*, 100.

34. Schofield, *Forty-Six Years*, 454–55.

35. Schofield to secretary of war, June 16, 1890, Box 55, Schofield Papers, LC (quotation); U.S. War Department, *Annual Report of the Secretary of War*, 1888, 89–94; U.S. War Department, *Annual Report of the Secretary of War*, 1895, 91–95. In 1888 there were an additional forty-eight ungarrisoned posts; in 1895 there were forty-five ungarrisoned posts. Edward Coffman has argued that the consolidation of the army into fewer permanent posts, where the time spent performing routine maintenance was much reduced, had a greater effect on professionalism than the writings of Emory Upton and other reformers. Coffman, "Long Shadow of *The Soldier and the State*."

36. The major works on this topic are by Jerry M. Cooper: *Army and Civil Disorder* and *Rise of the National Guard*. Other major books include Laurie and Cole, *Role of Federal Military Forces in Domestic Disorders, 1877–1945*; Coakley, *Role of Federal Military Forces in Domestic Disorders, 1789–1878*; and Wilson, *Federal Aid in Domestic Disturbances*. See also Hacker, "United States Army as a National Police Force."

37. Cooper, *Army and Civil Disorder*, 44. For a general account of the strike, see Bruce, *1877*.

38. Laurie and Cole, *Role of Federal Military Forces in Domestic Disorders*, 34; Schofield, "Private Military Journal, 1876–1880," 95, Box 1, Schofield Papers, LC; Schofield to Hancock, July 29, 1877, Schofield to A.G., August 2, 1877, Schofield to Upton, August 2, 1877, Schofield to Breck, August 3, 1877, Schofield Letters, vol. 1, 242–43, 245–47, 249, USMA Archives; Hancock to Schofield, July 30, 1877, Box 40, Schofield Papers, LC.

39. *Army and Navy Journal*, July 28, 1877, 816–17, August 4, 1877, 832–33; Laurie and Cole, *Role of Federal Military Forces in Domestic Disorders*, 31, 41.

40. Cooper, *Army and Civil Disorder*, 50, 62–66; Laurie and Cole, *Role of Federal Military Forces in Domestic Disorders*, 31, 43, 50–52.

41. Laurie and Cole, *Role of Federal Military Forces in Domestic Disorders*, 85–99; Wilson, *Federal Aid in Domestic Disturbances*, 215–18.

42. A.G. to Schofield, September 4, 7, 18, 1885, Schofield to Governor Warren, September 8, 1885, and Schofield to Howard, September 8, 1885, Box 91, Schofield Papers, LC.

43. Schofield to Governor Warren, September 8, 1885, Schofield to Howard, September 8, 1885, Schofield to A.G., September 19, 22, 25, 1885, and Lieutenant Colonel Chipman to Schofield, September 21, 1885, Box 91, Schofield Papers, LC; Schofield, *Forty-Six Years*, 509–10.

44. Laurie and Cole, *Role of Federal Military Forces in Domestic Disorders*, 85–99.

45. Ibid., 113–24.

46. Schofield memorandum to secretary of war, May 18, 1894, Box 57, Schofield Papers, LC (quotations); Schofield, *Forty-Six Years*, 491–92. Schofield's detailed instructions to subordinate commanders can be found in Box 57, Schofield Papers, LC. "Interruption of Traffic on Pacific Railroads" contains extracts of these orders, compiled by Captain Tasker Bliss, and is located in Box 78, Schofield Papers, LC.

47. Schofield to secretary of war, April 28, 1894, Box 57, Schofield Papers, LC; HQ Army G.O. no. 15, May 25, 1894, Box 78, Schofield Papers, LC. For full passages of relevant Revised Statutes, see HQ Army G.O. no. 26, July 24, 1894, Box 78, Schofield Papers, LC.

48. Schofield, *Forty-Six Years*, 507–9.

49. Ibid., 507–8.

50. Hacker, "United States Army as a National Police Force," 261. Schofield was also more active because in 1891 the number of subordinate commanders had increased when the three grand military divisions were abolished, and eight separate departments reported directly to the War Department.

51. Laurie and Cole, *Role of Federal Military Forces in Domestic Disorders*, 146–47. Though the general orders were issued under the adjutant general's signature, which was standard practice, Schofield was clearly the primary author. Schofield proudly reprinted G.O. no. 15, May 15, 1894, and G.O. no. 23, July 9, 1894, in *Forty-Six Years*, 504–6. G.O. no. 26, July 24, 1894, was issued after the many outbreaks ended and served as a compilation of the various statutes defining the army's missions. All general orders are contained in Box 78, Schofield Papers, LC. G.O. no. 23 and no. 26 were incorporated into army regulations under Article 52, "Employment of Troops in the Enforcement of the Laws." U.S. War Department, *Regulations*

of the Army of the United States, 1895, 64–69. For Schofield's streams of orders, see Boxes 57 and 78, Schofield Papers, LC.

52. U.S. Strike Commission, *Report on the Chicago Strike*, xix.

53. Schofield to Miles, July 2, 1894, Colonel J. P. Martin to A.G., July 2, 1894, A.G. to Martin, July 2, 1894, and J. A. Hoyt to A.G., July 2, 1894, Box 72, Schofield Papers, LC; Schofield, *Forty-Six Years*, 494–96. Miles contended in his memoirs, which were written after Schofield's death, that he was in the East on an important mission and that he had immediately supported the use of troops. Miles, *Serving the Republic*, 252–54. Miles's biographer Robert Wooster agrees that Miles was on leave and had initially advised against using troops. Wooster, *Nelson A. Miles and the Twilight of the Frontier Army*, 1198–99.

54. Laurie and Cole, *Role of Federal Military Forces in Domestic Disorders*, 140–41.

55. Schofield to Miles, July 5, 1894, Box 72, Schofield Papers, LC. Also see Schofield, *Forty-Six Years*, 498–501.

56. Miles to Colonel Croft, July 7, 1894, Miles to D. S. Lamont, July 7, 1894, Miles to Schofield, July 9, 11, 18, 1894, Miles to D. S. Robinson, July 10, 1894, and Schofield to Miles, July 14, 17, 18, 1894, Box 72, Schofield Papers, LC; Laurie and Cole, *Role of Federal Military Forces in Domestic Disorders*, 145–48; Cooper, *Army and Civil Disorder*, 149–54.

57. U.S. Strike Commission, *Report on the Chicago Strike*, xviii, xlvi–liv.

58. The Commercial Club, Chicago, to Schofield, May 27, 1887, Box 37, Schofield Papers, LC; Schofield to Pullman, February 29, 1892, Box 62, Schofield Papers, LC.

59. Boxes 37, 38, and 63 of the Schofield Papers, LC, contain numerous requests for railroad passes. Some of these requests were for personal travel, but many were for official travel. For example, the 1895 requests in Box 63 are related to Schofield's grand tour of the army before his retirement. Schofield wanted to both save the government money and travel with his staff in some style.

60. Cooper, *Army and Civil Disorder*, 247–48. Cooper concludes that Schofield sold all of his Pullman stock in June 1893. However, Schofield had transferred some stock to his wife and children several years before, which they might have retained, and he bought a new issue of stock in June 1893. A copy of the 1894 Pullman financial report is also in his papers. In 1895 Schofield wrote Horace Porter, a vice president of the Pullman Company, about the 2 percent federal tax on Pullman dividends. It is probable, therefore, that Schofield still owned some shares. Schofield to William B. Schofield, November 6, 1890, Box 54, Schofield Papers, LC; Schofield to Pullman Palace Car Company, May 1, 1893, May 16, 1893, June 10, 1893, and Schofield to Riggs & Company, May 2, 1893, Box 62, Schofield Papers, LC; Schofield to Homans & Company, September 7, 1894, Box 57, Schofield Papers, LC; Schofield to Porter, April 9, 1895, Box 63, Schofield Papers, LC.

61. Schofield's business dealings appear sporadically in his papers. He was president of the Manassas Panorama Company and probably owned shares in the Shiloh and the Merrimac and Monitor Panorama Companies. A. J. Andreas to Schofield, December 5, 1885, Box 37, Schofield Papers, LC. He owned various railroad bonds. John Devereau to Schofield, May 12, 1870, Box 37, Schofield Papers, LC; John Devereau to Schofield, March 28, 1885, Box 38, Schofield Papers, LC. He financially backed his son William in a cattle ranching venture in

New Mexico in partnership with E. A. Carr. Schofield to Carr, October 24, 1888, August 29, 1889, and Schofield to William B. Schofield, June 7, 1890, September 21, 1890, Box 54, Schofield Papers, LC; Schofield to Carr, June 3, 1890, Box 55, Schofield Papers, LC.

62. One irate Democrat sent Schofield a letter that captured the situation. Schofield, the "Military Autocrat," oppressed the people by obeying the orders of a Democratic president who violated the Constitution by sending soldiers to a "peaceful sovereign State." J. W. Bloom to Schofield, May 25, 1895, Box 23, Schofield Papers, LC.

63. Cooper, *Rise of the National Guard*, 44–64, esp. 47, 58, 59, 62. Cooper's book is the best and most up-to-date account of the National Guard in this period. Also see Mahon, *History of the Militia and the National Guard*; and Dupuy, *National Guard*. Though they focus on the Progressive Era, the following studies recount the National Guard's rise as a political pressure group: Derthick, *National Guard in Politics*; Riker, *Soldiers of the States*; and Cantor, "Creation of the Modern National Guard."

64. Cooper, *Rise of the National Guard*, 23–43; Schofield to Emory Upton, August 2, 1877, Schofield Letters, vol. 1, 246–47, USMA Archives; Hull quoted in Hacker, "United States Army as a National Police Force," 256.

65. Weigley, *Towards an American Army*, 100–117; Ambrose, *Upton and the Army*, 132, 156–59. While Weigley is hostile and regards Upton's views as a threat to civilian control of the military, Ambrose is more equivocal, stressing that Upton's emphasis on nationalization and the professionalization of American military institutions was premature. Both, however, tend to interpret the professional soldier's critique of a highly politicized military system as a rejection of civilian control. Upton's criticisms of political interference into military affairs were well within the American tradition, as factions jockeyed for influence over policy. David J. Fitzpatrick has done much to rehabilitate Upton's reputation and present his ideas in the context of his times. See Fitzpatrick, "Emory Upton and the Citizen Soldier"; and Fitzpatrick, "Emory Upton: The Misunderstood Reformer."

66. Upton, *Armies of Asia and Europe*, 367–70; Upton, *Military Policy of the United States*, xiii–xv.

67. Fitzpatrick, "Emory Upton: The Misunderstood Reformer"; Schofield, "The Power of Congress over the Army," April 6, 1880, Box 89, Schofield Papers, LC; *New York World*, March 28, 1898, Box 96, Schofield Papers, LC.

68. Cantor, "Creation of the Modern National Guard," 288–89.

69. The best survey of American coastal defense through the nineteenth century is Browning, *Two If By Sea*. More general surveys of the topic include Lewis, *Seacoast Fortifications*; and Hogg, *History of Fortification*.

70. Browning, *Two If By Sea*, 150–51.

71. Board members were William C. Endicott, secretary of war; Brigadier General Stephen V. Benét, chief of ordnance; Captain Charles S. Smith, Ordnance Corps; Brigadier General John Newton, chief of engineers; Lieutenant Colonel Henry L. Abbot, Corps of Engineers; Commander William T. Sampson, U.S. Navy; Commander Casper F. Goodrich, U.S. Navy; Joseph Morgan Jr.; and Erastus Corning. U.S. House, *Report of the [Endicott] Board on Fortifications or Other Defenses*, 6–8.

72. Ibid., 6–8, 27–30; Ranson, "Endicott Board"; Browning, *Two If By Sea*, 158–67.

73. U.S. House, *Fortification Appropriation Bill*, copy in Box 91, Schofield Papers, LC; Browning, *Two If By Sea*, 167–70; Ranson, "Endicott Board," 78.

74. Schofield to secretary of war, February 5, 1890, Box 55, Schofield Papers, LC; Ranson, "Endicott Board," 78. The Endicott plan had called for $97,782,800, but by the time Schofield retired, only $10,631,000 had been appropriated. Only three of the twenty-nine had any of the new defenses, and 98 new guns were available. U.S. War Department, *Annual Report of the Secretary of War*, 1895, 19–20.

75. Schofield, *Forty-Six Years*, 459–60, 484–87.

76. Schofield to secretary of war, December 2, 1891, Box 64, Schofield Papers, LC.

77. Schofield, *Forty-Six Years*, 486.

78. Aiding him in his efforts to reform and revitalize the artillery were two of the finest young artillery officers of the day, Joseph P. Sanger and Tasker Bliss. Sanger was commissioned a lieutenant in regular artillery in 1861. He accompanied Emory Upton on his 1875 inspection tour of foreign armies and served on two boards to revise artillery tactics. From 1884 to 1889 Captain Sanger served as Schofield's aide and divisional inspector of artillery. Promoted to brigadier general of Volunteers in 1898, Sanger retired as a major general. Tasker Bliss graduated from West Point in 1875 (ranked eighth of forty-three) and was commissioned in the 1st Artillery Regiment. He served as an instructor at the academy (1876–80) and the Naval War College (1885–88). He was an aide to Schofield from 1888 to 1895, during Schofield's entire tenure as commanding general. Bliss rose to be Chief of Staff of the Army (1917–18) and a delegate to the Paris Peace Conference (1918–19). ACP Joseph Sanger 5091, 1875, and ACP Tasker Bliss 3525, 1880, RG 94, NARA; Bell, *Commanding Generals and Chiefs of Staff*, 106.

79. Michie, "Personnel of Sea-Coast Defense"; Sanger, "Artillery Council"; U.S. War Department, *Annual Report of the Secretary of War*, 1887, 118–23.

80. Sanger, "Artillery Council," 252.

81. Schofield to Endicott, August 31, 1888, Box 54, Schofield Papers, LC; Schofield to secretary of war, January 4, 1890, Box 55, Schofield Papers, LC; Endicott to Schofield, March 5, 1889, Letters Sent, vol. 126, RG 107, NARA; *Army and Navy Journal*, December 15, 1888, 301. After three failed attempts, and with Schofield's pulling as many strings as he could, Sanger was finally appointed a major in the Inspector General Department in 1889. With Sanger in place as inspector of artillery, Schofield was able to further consolidate and standardize artillery training.

82. U.S. War Department, *Annual Report of the Secretary of War*, 1889, 69–73; U.S. War Department, *Annual Report of the Secretary of War*, 1894, 23–24.

83. U.S. War Department, *Annual Report of the Secretary of War*, 1887, 4; Schofield memorandum to secretary of war, June 27, 1890, Box 91, Schofield Papers, LC; Tasker Bliss, "Memorandum for the Commanding General," March 7, 1891, and Tasker Bliss, "Reorganization of the Artillery," [probably October 1891], Box 7, Bliss Papers, MHI; Karsten, "Armed Progressives," 259. Karsten also notes that the youngest captain of artillery in the U.S. Army was older than the oldest captain of artillery in the British army.

84. Hains, "Should the Fixed Coast Defenses of the United States Be Transferred to the

Navy?"; Schofield to secretary of war, November 27, 1894, Box 57, Schofield Papers, LC; Tasker Bliss, "Memorandum for the Commanding General," November 26, 1894, Box 7, Bliss Papers, MHI.

85. Memorandum, March 19, 1894, Box 8, Bliss Papers, MHI.

86. There were rumors that infantry and cavalry officers helped sabotage the Artillery Bill because of the lack of support for the infantry and cavalry reorganization. *Army and Navy Journal*, March 28, 1891, 532. For more on the failure of reorganization bills, see *Army and Navy Journal*, January 31, 1891, 388–89, February 7, 1891, 406–7, March 7, 1891, 478; and Sanger, "Artillery Council," 261–63. Schofield conducted a rather overt public relations campaign to convince the public of the need for coastal defense, providing rationales to sympathetic journalists. Schofield to Kate Field, editor of "Kate Field's Washington," July 17, 1890, Box 91, Schofield Papers, LC; Schofield to Charles Archer, *Boston Journal*, April 23, 1894, Box 62, Schofield Papers, LC. In retirement, Schofield continued to promote coastal defense; see "Seacoast Defenses, Address Before Coast Defense Convention, January 1897, Tampa FL," Box 95, Schofield Papers, LC.

87. The best book on the development of tactical doctrine in this period is Jamieson, *Crossing the Deadly Ground*.

88. Among the most prominent books by American officers on strategy during this period were Bigelow, *Principles of Strategy*; and Wagner, *Elements of Military Science*. Like Upton's *Armies of Asia and Europe*, General William B. Hazen's *School and the Army in Germany and France* was an examination of the French and German militaries.

89. The members of the Tactics Board were Major General John Schofield; Lieutenant Colonel Joseph Potter, 4th Infantry; Lieutenant Colonel Wesley Merritt, 9th Cavalry; Major James Van Voast, 18th Infantry; and Major John Hamilton, 1st Artillery. Army G.O. no. 60, August 6, 1869, Box 42, Schofield Papers, LC; Jamieson, *Crossing the Deadly Ground*, 6–14. For Upton and the assimilated tactics see Upton, *New System of Infantry Tactics*; U.S. War Department, *Cavalry Tactics*; U.S. War Department, *Artillery Tactics*.

90. Schofield, "Report and Observations upon the Maneuvres [*sic*] of the French Army," 156.

91. Small notebook journal, begins September 26, 1881, Box 1, Schofield Papers, LC; Schofield, "Report and Observations upon the Maneuvres [*sic*] of the French Army."

92. Schofield to Thomas Ruger, Wesley Merritt, and Henry Clossen, January 24, 1891, and Schofield to secretary of war, September 2, 1891, Box 55, Schofield Papers, LC.

93. *Army and Navy Journal*, October 10, 1891, 114, October 17, 1891, 131, October 24, 1891, 139; Jamieson, *Crossing the Deadly Ground*, 98–112; U.S. War Department, *Infantry Drill Regulations*; U.S. War Department, *Cavalry Drill Regulations*; U.S. War Department, *Drill Regulations*.

94. Quoted in Jamieson, *Crossing the Deadly Ground*, 129.

95. Schofield to F. W. Archer, *Boston Journal*, April 23, 1894, Box 62, Schofield Papers, LC; Schofield, *Forty-Six Years*, 145–46, 518–28.

96. *Army and Navy Journal*, January 5, 1889, 363. Harriet died at a time when Schofield was also heavily involved in dealing with the alcoholism and financial problems of her broth-

ers, Lieutenant Colonel Charles G. Bartlett and Captain William C. Bartlett. Balancing his family obligations with his military duty, Schofield kept the secretary of war apprised of the situation. William retired in 1892 and Charles in 1896. Alfred Terry to Schofield, September 3, 1886, Box 37, Schofield Papers, LC; Schofield to Major Lord, February 18, 1889, Schofield to Colonel Langdon, November 29, 1889, and Schofield to Charles Bartlett, December 24, 1889, Box 54, Schofield Papers, LC; Schofield to Major Lord, October 27, 1889, and Schofield to Charles Bartlett, December 8, 1889, Box 54a, Schofield Papers, LC.

97. *Army and Navy Journal*, June 13, 1891, 711, 719, June 20, 1891, 730; J. P. Sanger to Tasker Bliss, January 24, 1889, and Frances Sanger to Mrs. Tasker Bliss, July 6, 1891, Bliss Papers, MHI; telephone conversation with Schofield Andrews Jr. (General Schofield's great-grandson), August 9, 1999. Also see "Confidential Record," 99–118, Box 1, Schofield Papers, LC.

98. Marszalek, *Sherman*, 446–47; Schofield to Sherman, December 1, 1883, reel 32, Sherman Papers, LC.

99. Schofield to Sherman, January 25, 28, 1884, February 2, 5, 8, 1884, and Sherman to Schofield, January 23, 26, 31, 1884, reel 32, Sherman Papers, LC.

100. Marszalek, *Sherman*, 484–97; Schofield to Sherman, January 7, 1891, and Sherman to Schofield, January 9, 1891, reel 41, Sherman Papers, LC; Schofield to John Sherman, February 24, 1891, reel 42, Sherman Papers, LC.

CHAPTER THIRTEEN

1. Russell Weigley was among the first military historians to place Schofield in the context of Progressivism. See Weigley, "Military Thought of John M. Schofield"; Weigley, "Schofield: An American Plan of Command," in *Towards an American Army*, 162–76; and Weigley, "Elihu Root Reforms and the Progressive Era."

2. Robert W. Mixon has described Schofield as a "pioneer professional." Mixon, "Pioneer Professional."

3. Schofield, *Forty-Six Years*, 469–70.

4. Robert T. Lincoln to Sheridan, December 9, 1884, January 19, 1885, Box 33, Schofield Papers, LC; Schofield, *Forty-Six Years*, 471–73; Hutton, *Phil Sheridan and His Army*, 349–50. This rebuke of the commanding general prompted Schofield to again recommend going to Congress to establish the commanding general's authority in statute. Report of Major General Schofield in U.S. War Department, *Annual Report of the Secretary of War*, 1885, 133.

5. Schofield to A.G., October 29, 1888, Box 54, Schofield Papers, LC (emphasis in original); Schofield to Proctor, March 8, 1889, Box 68, Schofield Papers, LC; Schofield, *Forty-Six Years*, 470–71. Within a week of Secretary Redfield Proctor's assuming office, the adjutant general attempted to cut Schofield out of the agreed-upon procedures for issuing assignment orders. Schofield to Proctor, March 30, 1889, Box 54, Schofield Papers, LC.

6. John M. Schofield, "Questions and Suggestions Relative to Military Administration and Command," February 1889, and Cleveland to Schofield, March 3, 1889, Box 95, Schofield

Papers, LC; Schofield to R. Alger, handwritten and undated [probably 1897], Box 64, Schofield Papers, LC; Schofield, *Forty-Six Years*, 480.

7. Schofield, "Questions and Suggestions Relative to Military Administration and Command."

8. In modern parlance, the secretary of defense and the president are termed the "National Command Authority."

9. Schofield, "Questions and Suggestions Relative to Military Administration and Command." Schofield even carried the fight over the proper command and administration of the army to West Point textbooks. In a letter to the secretary critiquing Professor James Mercur's academy textbook, Schofield contrasted the U.S. and German military systems. Schofield to secretary of war, September 19, 1889, December 3, 1889, and Schofield to Mercur, February 13, 1890, Box 54, Schofield Papers, LC; Memorandum, typed and undated, Box 94, Schofield Papers, LC.

10. Robert T. Lincoln had served on Grant's staff at the end of the war but had little campaign duty. Of Proctor's successors, Stephen Elkins had served briefly in the Missouri militia, and Russell Alger had a distinguished Civil War record commanding the 5th Michigan Infantry and was breveted to major general. Bell, *Secretaries of War and Secretaries of the Army*, 78–98.

11. For an excellent biography of Proctor see Bowie, "Redfield Proctor," esp. 3–4, 162–68, 271–72. Bowie's biography also provides details on the legislative history of military reform during Proctor's tenure.

12. Schofield went so far in accommodation as to surrender his commander's authority to approve leaves for his subordinate generals, referring all such requests to the secretary. Schofield to Miles, November 6, 1889, Box 54, Schofield Papers, LC.

13. Benjamin Harrison, Executive Order, June 7, 1889, Box 40, Schofield Papers, LC; Schofield to Proctor, June 16, 1889, Box 54, Schofield Papers, LC. The *Army and Navy Journal* suggested that Proctor's military service during the Civil War was an important factor in improving relations. *Army and Navy Journal*, June 8, 1889, 847. Schofield was irritated when Congress finally created, at Proctor's request, a civilian assistant secretary of war. Schofield would still serve as acting secretary when both of these officers were absent. Cleveland to Schofield, April 26, 1893, Box 92, Schofield Papers, LC. Chester Bowie concludes that Schofield served as Proctor's principal advisor and suggests he was "a *de facto* chief of staff." Though Schofield attempted to insinuate himself between the secretary and the staff, he never had the degree of authority over the staff that a true chief of staff would possess. Bowie, "Redfield Proctor," 173–75.

14. Schofield played host during the inauguration to such Democrat luminaries as W. J. Gresham, Cleveland's secretary of state, and Chicago Democrat J. W. Doane. Schofield to Gresham, February 13, 1893, Box 54, Schofield Papers, LC.

15. Schofield to secretary of war, February 27, 1892, Box 56, Schofield Papers, LC (quotation); Schofield to A.G., February 11, 1890, April 3, 1890, Box 55, Schofield Papers, LC; Schofield to A.G., March 7, July 7, 1892, Box 56, Schofield Papers, LC; Schofield to A.G., February 8, 1893, Box 57, Schofield Papers, LC. Civil War general, railroad executive, and

prominent Republican Grenville Dodge commended Elkins to Schofield as "an able, intelligent, straightforward business man. . . . I have said to him that if he wanted to have success in the office, he wanted to keep in full accord with the General of the army, and have told him that he could not go astray with your advice, which I know he fully appreciates. . . . You do not want to allow the Staff Officers to capture him as they generally do any person not acquainted with army matters." Dodge to Schofield, December 22, 1891, Box 39, Schofield Papers, LC.

16. Schofield to secretary of war, December 17, 1889, Box 54, Schofield Papers, LC; Schofield to secretary of war, June 16, 1890, Box 91, Schofield Papers, LC; Schofield to secretary of war, February 23, February 27, December 8, December 24, 1892, Box 56, Schofield Papers, LC; Schofield to secretary of war, January 25, February 24, April 3, August 8, September 7, November 11, 1893, Box 57, Schofield Papers, LC. For general background on "the war between commander and administrator," see chap. 6 of Roberts, "Loyalty and Expertise," 160–207.

17. Proctor to Schofield, December 4, 1889, vol. 6, Proctor Papers, PFL; A.G. to secretary of war, December 3, 1889, Letters Received, Box 501, RG 107, NARA.

18. Batchelder to Tompkins, July 16, 1892, and Henry to AAG, July 22, 1892, Box 86, Schofield Papers, LC; Schofield to secretary of war, August 4, November 9, 1892, and Schofield to O. O. Howard, December 8, 1892, Box 56, Schofield Papers, LC. Sometimes staff officers in the departmental commands joined the line officers in complaining about the micromanagement of the War Department staff. See Lee, "Centralization and Decentralization in Military Affairs"; and Howard, "Comment and Criticism." Also see *Army and Navy Journal*, August 1, 1891, 836, July 30, 1892, 853.

19. Schofield to Merritt, September 3, 1890, Box 55, Schofield Papers, LC.

20. Carter to A.G., November 6, 1878, 3543 ACP 1878—Carter, William H., RG 94, NARA. The ambitious Carter had transferred into the 6th Cavalry a year after his graduation from West Point in 1873. He unsuccessfully applied for transfer to the Subsistence Department in 1881. He received a Medal of Honor for actions against the Indians at Cibicu Creek in 1881. Carter was promoted to major in the Adjutant General Corps in 1897 and brigadier general in 1902, and he retired in 1915 as a major general.

21. U.S. War Department, *Annual Report of the Secretary of War*, 1890, 3–4; U.S. War Department, *Annual Report of the Secretary of War*, 1891, 20–21; Schofield to A.G., December 4, 1890, Box 55, Schofield Papers, LC. See also various memoranda related to lineal promotion in Boxes 92 and 93, Schofield Papers, LC.

22. Proctor to F. C. Ainsworth, February 6, 1908, A.G. Office, 1908, 1337139, RG 94, NARA; ACP Charles B. Schofield, 5075, 1876, RG 94, NARA. Schofield acknowledged that Charles would have been superseded by fourteen more officers, in addition to the thirty-one who had already been promoted past him, if lineal promotion had been applied to first lieutenants. Schofield really preferred the readjustment of all dates of rank based on entry into the regular army, exempting only appointments due to Civil War service. Schofield to secretary of war, April 23, 1890, Box 55, Schofield Papers, LC. For later unsuccessful efforts to extend lineal promotion to first lieutenants, see *Army and Navy Journal*, March 12, 1892, 511, April 2, 1892, 558, April 16, 1892, 592.

23. Bliss memorandum, January 4, 1893, Box 92, Bliss Papers, MHI; Schofield memorandum, February 20, 1895, Box 8, Bliss Papers, MHI; Memorandum for the commanding general, January 2, 1895, Box 7, Bliss Papers, MHI. For the initial implementation of promotion exams, also see *Army and Navy Journal*, October 3, 1891, 96, October 17, 1891, 131, October 24, 1891, 148; Schofield to secretary of war, September 29, 1890, October 9, 1890, Box 55, Schofield Papers, LC; and Schofield to secretary of war, April 29, 1891, Box 69, Schofield Papers, LC.

24. In 1882 appointment priority went to meritorious noncommissioned officers, the academy's graduating class, academy graduates honorably discharged, and finally, those from civil life. War Department circular, July 11, 1882, RG 94, NARA.

25. Burnham, *Roads to a Commission*, 1–2, 58–61, 72, 109–10, 123; U.S. War Department, *Annual Report of the Secretary of War*, 1891, 22; Schofield to Walter Phelps, U.S. minister to Germany, June 30, 1890, Box 64, Schofield Papers, LC; Proctor to Representative H. C. Lodge, August 5, 1889, and Proctor to Senator B. Butler, October 2, 1889, vol. 5, Proctor Papers, PFL. General Schofield's son Richmond McAllister Schofield successfully passed the test and received a commission in the cavalry from civilian life in February 1889. Schofield's elder son William Bartlett Schofield received an appointment in the Paymaster Department in May 1898 as part of the mobilization for the Spanish-American War. ACP Richmond M. Schofield 4269, 1888, RG 94, NARA; Heitman, *Historical Register*, 865.

26. U.S. War Department, *Annual Report of the Secretary of War*, 1891, 21–22.

27. Craig, *History of the Officer Efficiency Report System*; ACP records, RG 94, NARA.

28. "Maj. Gen. Henry W. Lawton," 13. A comparison of the personnel files and letters of recommendation of Schofield aides Joseph Sanger, Tasker Bliss, and Charles Schofield makes clear why Sanger and Bliss were selected for the staff, but not brother Charles. ACP Joseph P. Sanger 5091, 1873, ACP Tasker H. Bliss 3525, 1880, and ACP Charles B. Schofield 5075, 1876, RG 94, NARA.

29. For example, Redfield Proctor expressed the hope that his appointment of Arthur MacArthur to major met with general approval. Proctor to Miles, July 2, 1889, Box 1, Proctor Papers, PFL. Captain Arthur MacArthur, the father of Douglas MacArthur, also lost out to Lawton and was finally promoted to major, A.G., a few months after Sanger received his promotion. Major MacArthur was very active in preparing much of the reform legislation of the Proctor-Schofield period. See Young, *General's General*, 152–67.

30. Endicott memorandum, November 1885, Box 90, Schofield Papers, LC.

31. Schofield memorandum, December 18, 1885, and Schofield undated memorandum [probably 1889], Box 90, Schofield Papers, LC (quotation); Memorandum, April 9, 1889, Box 54, Schofield Papers, LC. Also see Hutton, *Phil Sheridan and His Army*, 140, 153–54, 349.

32. In 1885 enlisted men with thirty years of service were permitted to retire at 75 percent of pay. "History of the Military Retirement System," October 31, 1960, draft, CMH; U.S. House, *Alfred Pleasanton*, 1–3; Schofield, *Forty-Six Years*, 480–81.

33. U.S. War Department, *Annual Report of the Secretary of War*, 1889, 6–7; U.S. War Department, *Annual Report of the Secretary of War*, 1890, 12–13; Bowie, "Redfield Proctor,"

214–15, 217, 220–22. The *Army and Navy Journal* gave much credit for the reform to General Byron Cutcheon, chair of the House Military Affairs Committee. *Army and Navy Journal*, February 14, 1891, 424–25.

34. Schofield to president, July 2, 1890, Box 91, Schofield Papers, LC. Schofield repeatedly raised the general officer situation with his superiors. He compared the promotion rates between the navy and army: the navy was able to promote most of its captains to rear admiral before retirement, while few colonels made it to general. Schofield to Senator Joseph Hawley, December 28, 1888, Box 54, Schofield Papers, LC. He also compared the chances of staff and line officers to make general. Between 1866 and April 1895, forty-one staff officers and twenty-three line officers were promoted to brigadier general. For most of this period, there were nine staff brigadier general positions and six brigadier general and three major general positions for the line. Staff: A.G.—5, I.G.—6, JAG—3, Q.M.—4, Subsistence—5, Pay—6, Medical—5, Engineers—5, Ordnance—2, Signal—1. Line: Infantry—15, Cavalry—6, Artillery—1. Schofield to secretary of war, April 3, 1895, Box 58, Schofield Papers, LC.

35. Grant had promoted many younger officers, including Sheridan and Schofield. President Hayes retired Ord and promoted Miles in 1880 over the objections of Sherman. President Arthur promoted Ranald MacKenzie in 1882 over David Stanley, Gibbon, and Thomas Ruger. President Harrison promoted Frank Wheaton over the older Eugene A. Carr, William P. Carlin, and Peter T. Swaine.

36. Carr to Schofield, September 28, 1890, Box 38, Schofield Papers, LC; Schofield to Carr, April 26, 1890, Schofield to President Harrison, February 21, 1893, Box 54, Schofield Papers, LC; Schofield to secretary of war, December 9, 1891, Box 55, Schofield Papers, LC; Schofield to secretary of war, March 22, 1892, May 2, 1892, Box 56, Schofield Papers, LC. Schofield listed the officers in order of mandatory retirement: Carlin—November 1893; Carr—March 1894; Swaine—January 1895; Wheaton—May 1897. Schofield to secretary of war, December 9, 1891, Box 55, Schofield Papers, LC.

37. Schofield to Carlin, July 20, 1892, Schofield to Carr, July 25, 1892, Box 56, Schofield Papers, LC; Schofield to Carlin, February 23, 1893, June 23, 1893, Box 57, Schofield Papers, LC. Secretary of War Elkins supposedly informed Carr's brother of the arrangement before Carr's promotion. Schofield to secretary of war, February 10, 1893, Box 57, Schofield Papers, LC. Schofield thanked Elwell S. Otis for permitting a delay in his promotion to make way for Carlin, but he had the unpleasant task of informing Peter Swaine that he had failed to secure promotion before retirement. Schofield to Otis, March 5, 1894, Schofield to Swaine, November 22, 1894, Box 57, Schofield Papers, LC. See also *Army and Navy Journal*, February 6, 1892, 418, April 2, 1892, 559, April 23, 1892, 612, February 18, 1893, 433–34, and February 25, 1893, 448–49. Schofield was also unsuccessful in getting his former roommate and close friend Thomas Vincent appointed adjutant general of the army. It is possible that Vincent's close links to Schofield were a reason for his being passed over by Secretary Elkins. Schofield to President Harrison, February 15, 1893, Box 54, Schofield Papers, LC.

38. Hutton, *Phil Sheridan and His Army*, 371–72.

39. As the prospects for Schofield's promotion went up and down, so did the hopes of Civil War veterans such as Miles, Stanley, and Gibbon to regain their second star. Schofield to

Stanley, April 18, 1890, Schofield to Representative Joseph Wheeler, July 4, 1890, Schofield to Senator Hawley, July 28, 1890, Schofield to Stanley, February 6, 1891, Schofield to J. W. Doane, December 15, 1892, Box 54, Schofield Papers, LC; Howard to Schofield, December 17, 1891, January 12, 1892, Box 40, Schofield Papers, LC; Schofield to H. W. Slocum, February 25, 1892, Box 56, Schofield Papers, LC.

40. Schofield to Miles, January 14, 1889, March 2, 1889, Box 54, Schofield Papers, LC; Schofield to C. Gibson, May 21, 1894, Box 57, Schofield Papers, LC. While still the senior brigadier general, Miles was so anxious to have the bill retain three major generals that he accused Major General George Crook and Major General O. O. Howard of using their influence to thwart the bill. Miles to Schofield, January 15, 1889, Box 41, Schofield Papers, LC. At another point, Schofield contacted prominent Chicago businessman and Democrat J. W. Doane to use his influence on Democratic representative W. C. Newberry, who was apparently obstructing the Lieutenant General Bill in the mistaken belief that it would harm Miles's chances to command the army. Schofield to Doane, December 15, 1892, Box 54, Schofield Papers, LC.

41. Schofield to secretary of war, November 22, 1894, Box 79, Lamont Papers, LC; Schofield to Representatives Crisp, Outhwaite, Wheeler, and Grosvenor and to Senators Manderson and Hawley, February 4, 1895, Box 58, Schofield Papers, LC. The five preceding lieutenant generals were George Washington (1798), Winfield Scott (brevet lieutenant general, 1855), U. S. Grant (1864), William T. Sherman (1866), and Philip Sheridan (1869). U.S. House, *Lieutenant General of the Army*, 1–7.

42. For general accounts of enlisted life in this period, see Coffman, *Old Army*, 328–99; Foner, *United States Soldier between Two Wars*; and Rickey, *Forty Miles a Day on Beans and Hay*.

43. Foner, *United States Soldier between Two Wars*, 222–24. One of the significant factors in the desertion rates was the overall economic situation. The high desertion rates dropped dramatically after the 1877 and 1893 panics and resultant economic depressions. Rickey estimates that half of all recruits were unemployed men, who deserted when employment picked up. Rickey, *Forty Miles a Day on Beans and Hay*, 22.

44. U.S. War Department, *Annual Report of the Secretary of War*, 1889, 63–65; Schofield to secretary of war, January 24, 1890, February 24, 1890, February 27, 1890, Box 55, Schofield Papers, LC.

45. U.S. War Department, *Annual Report of the Secretary of War*, 1889, 7–11.

46. U.S. War Department, *Annual Report of the Secretary of War*, 1890, 4–5, 9; U.S. War Department, *Annual Report of the Secretary of War*, 1891, 11–12; Foner, *United States Soldier between Two Wars*, 73–75. Schofield opposed a general amnesty as unfair to those who were already undergoing punishment. Schofield to O. O. Howard, October 25, 1889, Box 54, Schofield Papers, LC.

47. U.S. War Department, *Annual Report of the Secretary of War*, 1890, 9–10; U.S. War Department, *Annual Report of the Secretary of War*, 1891, 63–65; Bowie, "Redfield Proctor," 199; Schofield to secretary of war, January 24, 1890, February 27, 1890, July 1, 1890, Box 55, Schofield Papers, LC. For complaints see *Army and Navy Journal*, January 21, 1893, 364–65, January 28, 1893, 282–83, February 18, 1893, 432–33, March 18, 1893, 499.

48. U.S. War Department, *Annual Report of the Secretary of War*, 1890, 9–10; Schofield to secretary of war, December 23, 1890, Box 55, Schofield Papers, LC; Foner, *United States Soldier between Two Wars*, 151; Coffman, *Old Army*, 397–98; *Army and Navy Journal*, September 30, 1892, October 21, 1893, 141; Schofield to secretary of war, January 15, 1894, Box 57, Schofield Papers, LC.

49. U.S. War Department, *Annual Report of the Secretary of War*, 1890, 61–62; U.S. War Department, *Annual Report of the Secretary of War*, 1892, 49 (quotation); Schofield to secretary of war, March 26, 1889, Box 54, Schofield Papers, LC; Schofield to Senator Proctor, December 3, 1893, Box 57, Schofield Papers, LC; Foner, *United States Soldier between Two Wars*, 91. Schofield recognized that some of the "old soldiers" would not benefit from such instruction, and might be embarrassed by attendance, so he left such matters to the discretion of the local commanders. Schofield to secretary of war, December 19, 1890, Box 68, Schofield Papers, LC.

50. U.S. War Department, *Annual Report of the Secretary of War*, 1891, 76–77; Bowie, "Redfield Proctor," 184–89; Schofield to secretary of war, September 5, 1890, Box 55, Schofield Papers, LC; Schofield to secretary of war, March 29, 1892, May 19, 1892, Box 56, Schofield Papers, LC. Ironically, by eliminating the politically connected trader, the canteen became vulnerable to the temperance movement, which in 1900 succeeded in prohibiting the sale of alcohol in all post canteens. *Army and Navy Journal*, December 8, 1900, 341, January 26, 1901, 513–15.

51. Nenninger, *Leavenworth Schools and the Old Army*, 34–52; Schofield to secretary of war, February 25, 1891, Box 55, Schofield Papers, LC. In 1884 Schofield commended the work of Christopher C. Augur and Elwell S. Otis in starting the course and concluded the biggest need was to detail excellent instructors to Leavenworth. One of the old artilleryman's suggestions was to assign recent Artillery School graduates. Schofield to Augur, May 31, 1884, Box 52, Schofield Papers, LC.

52. Schofield to secretary of war, December 12, 1888, Box 54, Schofield Papers, LC.

53. Schofield to commandant, Cavalry and Light Artillery School, April 7, 1893, Box 57, Schofield Papers, LC; *Army and Navy Journal*, November 19, 1892, 208.

54. Karsten, "Armed Progressives," 263–64.

55. Schofield, "Inaugural Address."

56. Each issue of the *Journal of the Military Service Institution* listed the officers of the institution and frequently contained the essay competition subject and previous winners. Even as president, Schofield could not dictate topic selection. For example, in 1892 he preferred the subject of smokeless powder to the more political topic of army organization and republican government. Major Haskin to Schofield, November 17, 1891, Box 27, Schofield Papers, LC; Schofield to Haskin, November 18, 1891, Box 62, Schofield Papers, LC.

57. Schofield to Holabird, February 11, 1889, Box 54, Schofield Papers, LC. Schofield's list of journals included three British publications, five French, four German, two Italian, and one Belgian.

58. G.O. no. 80, October 5, 1891, in A.G. Office, *General Orders and Circulars*; *Army and Navy Journal*, August 5, 1891, 872, October 24, 1891, 146, November 21, 1891, 221; U.S. War

Department, *Annual Report of the Secretary of War*, 1892, 56. Also see Crackel, "West Point's Contribution to the Army and to Professionalism."

59. Schofield to secretary of war, April 1, 1892, Box 56, Schofield Papers, LC; *Army and Navy Journal*, April 29, 1893, 596–97.

60. U.S. War Department, *Annual Report of the Secretary of War*, 1894, 21–22, 71; War Department G.O. no. 155, November 27, 1901, CMH, <http://www.army.mil/cmh-pg/documents/1901/wdg0155-1901.htm> (accessed September 17, 2005). This general order established the first comprehensive education system for the army, which included post schools, service schools, a staff college, and a war college. For an explanation of the transformation of lyceums into a training program for lieutenants, see Carter, *Creation of the American General Staff*, 5–6.

61. U.S. War Department, *Annual Report of the Secretary of War*, 1888, 204; U.S. War Department, *Annual Report of the Secretary of War*, 1895, 18–19; Schofield to secretary of war, October 2, 1893, Box 57, Schofield Papers, LC.

62. Schofield to secretary of war, October 2, 1893, Schofield to Harvard president Charles Eliot, February 16, 19, 1894, Box 57, Schofield Papers, LC; Memo for commanding general, March 12, 1894, Box 7, Bliss Papers, MHI.

63. Schofield, *Forty-Six Years*, 519–22; U.S. War Department, *Annual Report of the Secretary of War*, 1895, 18–19; Logan, *Volunteer Soldier of America*; McConnell, *Glorious Contentment*, 197–202, 230–32. McConnell notes that part of the interest in military drill for schoolboys was directed at instilling discipline in poor, urban youths. Also see Karsten, "Militarization and Rationalization."

64. Schofield to secretary of war, January 19, 1892, Box 56, Schofield Papers, LC; Schofield to secretary of war, January 26, 1893, Box 57, Schofield Papers, LC; Schofield, *Forty-Six Years*, 522–24.

CHAPTER FOURTEEN

1. "Reorganization of the Army," undated pencil draft, Box 86, Schofield Papers, LC; *Army and Navy Journal*, June 29, 1895, 727, July 20, 1895, 777, 779.

2. Armes had been court-martialed and cashiered in 1870, but through political influence he was restored in 1878. He retired in 1883. In 1889 he was again court-martialed for assaulting the governor of Pennsylvania. In 1895 Armes was released on habeas corpus and gained a brief victory when a federal judge declared that the military had no authority over retired officers. This decision was overturned on appeal. *Washington Post*, September 28, 1895, 1, October 11, 1895; *Army and Navy Register*, October 12, 1895, 2; *Army and Navy Journal*, October 5, 1895, 67, October 12, 1895, 83, 89, October 19, 1895, 99, 105; Schofield to secretary of war, December 13, 1889, March 13, 1890, Box 68, Schofield Papers, LC; Schofield to A.G., February 28, 1895, and Schofield to Lamont, September 28, 1895, Box 58, Schofield Papers, LC; Mixon, "Pioneer Professional," 52–56.

3. *Army and Navy Journal*, October 5, 1895, 70; Ganoe, *History of the United States Army*, 355–56; Skowronek, *Building a New American State*, 86, 120.

4. *St. Augustine Tatler*, January 23, 1897, 11, January 15, 1898; telephone conversation with Schofield Andrews Jr. (General Schofield's great-grandson), August 9, 1999.

5. Schofield to Doane, February 26, 1894, Box 57, Schofield Papers, LC.

6. *Army and Navy Journal*, June 8, 1895, 672, September 7, 1895, 5; Schofield, *Forty-Six Years*, 530–34.

7. "Speech to Coast Defense Convention, January 1897," Box 95, Schofield Papers, LC; newspaper clippings, 1897, Box 96, Schofield Papers, LC.

8. Schofield to secretary of war, January 20, 21, 1892, Box 56, Schofield Papers, LC; Lamont to Schofield, August 16, 1894, Box 29, Lamont Papers, LC; Schofield, *Forty-Six Years*, 489–90. For an excellent analysis of the foreign policy attitudes of American military and naval officers before the Spanish-American War, see Abrahamson, *America Arms for a New Century*.

9. Belknap to Schofield, June 24, 1872, Schofield to Sherman, March 18, 1873, Schofield to Belknap, May 8, 1873, Box 78, Schofield Papers, LC. See also Swails, "John McAllister Schofield," 84–110, 114, 136–42. Schofield went on the expedition, in part, to recuperate from pneumonia. Schofield, *Forty-Six Years*, 431–34. In 1873 the population of Hawaii was 65,000, including 2,500 foreigners, of whom 1,500 were Americans. *San Francisco Chronicle*, January 4, 1873.

10. J. A. Cummins to Schofield, January 28, 1893, April 23, 1893, Box 78, Schofield Papers, LC; Schofield to President Harrison, February 15, 1893, and Schofield to Cummins, February 23, 1893, Box 62, Schofield Papers, LC.

11. J. M. Schofield, A. L. Beardslee, J. C. Breckenridge, and Charles P. Egan, *Important Views on the Annexation of Hawaii* (San Francisco: Hirsh-Judd Co., 1898), 1–2 (quotations), copy available in Special Collections, LC. Hawaii was annexed on July 7, 1898, became a territory in 1900, and achieved statehood in 1959.

12. Schofield to Hiram Barney, February 26, 1895, Box 62, Schofield Papers, LC; Schofield, *Forty-Six Years*, 433–38. Walter A. McDougall uses the term "fling" to describe the foreign policy embodiment of the Progressive impulse to rationalize and reform the world. McDougall, *Promised Land, Crusader State*, 101–21.

13. For an excellent study on how President William McKinley directed the war and its aftermath, see Gould, *Spanish-American War and President McKinley*. For a detailed analysis of army structure, procedures, and performance during the war, see Cosmas, *Army for Empire*. Also see Smith, "'Splendid Little War' of 1898." For a condensed version of the official records, see *Correspondence Relating to the War with Spain*. For an analysis of the impact of the Spanish-American War on military reform, see Zais, "Struggle for a 20th-Century Army."

14. Cosmas, "From Order to Chaos"; Wooster, *Nelson A. Miles*, 215–17. Graham Cosmas makes the shrewd observation that the highly centralized, "top-down" staff procedures were dramatically shifted to a situation where commanders in the field had to assess their needs and forward their requirements to the War Department. However, all levels found it difficult to keep up with the scope of requirements and the pace of operational change. Cosmas also concludes that despite the lack of preparedness and initial confusion, the War Department performed relatively well. Cosmas, *Army for Empire*, 134–36.

15. *New York World*, March 28, 1898, Box 96, Schofield Papers, LC. The mission of the

National Volunteer Reserve was soon overtaken by events as military bills piled up in Congress. With little substantive help from the organization, Congress nevertheless included national volunteer regiments in its authorization of troops. Schofield lamented that people misunderstood the goal of the organization to be the creation of some kind of separate army, when in fact the group was committed only to lobbying Congress. Schofield to Representative John A. T. Hull, April 6, 1898, Schofield to A. McCook, April 15, 1898, and Schofield to W. Washington, April 22, 1898, Box 64, Schofield Papers, LC.

16. Schofield, "Some of My Experiences with the Administration of President McKinley," handwritten thirty-nine-page paper written sometime after September 1898, Box 93, Schofield Papers, LC; Schofield to Senator Elkins, June 2, 1898, Box 64, Schofield Papers, LC.

17. Schofield, "Some of My Experiences with the Administration of President McKinley"; Cosmas, *Army for Empire*, 133–34; Gould, *Spanish-American War and President McKinley*, 70.

18. Schofield, "Some of My Experiences with the Administration of President McKinley"; Cosmas, "From Order to Chaos," 116–19.

19. Schofield, "Some of My Experiences with the Administration of President McKinley"; "Reorganization of the Army," undated, Box 86, Schofield Papers, LC.

20. Schofield, "Memorandum for the President," April 20, 1898, Box 64, Schofield Papers, LC; Schofield, "Some of My Experiences with the Administration of President McKinley."

21. Gould, *Spanish-American War and President McKinley*, 67–69. Despite Nelson Miles's arrogance and impractical ideas, Edward Ranson rightly points out that Miles made a number of important contributions to the war effort, such as getting a dramatically expanded force sent to the Philippines, delaying the hasty dispatch of troops to Cuba in May, and executing a flawless campaign in Puerto Rico. Ranson also makes the observation that Miles was unsuited to his position as commanding general. Lacking any real influence, his official duties were so light that he naturally turned to political intrigue. One might add, however, that Miles's passion for political intrigue was so great that he indulged in it even during arduous military campaigns. Ranson, "Nelson A. Miles as Commanding General," 199.

22. Adjutant General's Office, *Statistical Exhibit*. Despite the high death rate from disease in the war, it was, at 34 per 1,000, still lower than that of the Civil War (71.4 per 1,000) and the Mexican War (103.9 per 1,000). Chambers, *Oxford Companion to American Military History*, 108; Gould, *Spanish-American War and President McKinley*, 68, 91–94.

23. McKinley to Schofield, September 9, 1898, Schofield to McKinley, September 13, 1898, Box 41, Schofield Papers, LC; Schofield, "Some of My Experiences with the Administration of President McKinley."

24. Cosmas, *Army for Empire*, 285–98; Zais, "Struggle for a 20th-Century Army," 166–215.

25. *New York Times*, December 13, 1898, 4; *Washington Post*, December 13, 1898, 1. Schofield also had other major disagreements with his successor. Whereas Miles had recommended that Congress determine the size of the army based on a fixed percentage of the nation's population (1 soldier per 1,000 citizens, which meant an army of about 75,000), Schofield argued the size of the army must be based on need. Given the new overseas responsibilities and the continuing insurgency in the Philippines, the lieutenant general recommended an army of 85,000–90,000.

26. Zais, "Struggle for a 20th-Century Army," 253.

27. Jessup, *Elihu Root*, 1:252, 255.

28. Greene, "Our New Army"; Whepley, "Militia Force of the United States"; Villard, "Army of the United States"; Carter, "Will America Profit by its Recent Military Lessons?"; Carter, "General Staff for the Army." Root also made special appeals for support to the editor of the *Army and Navy Journal*, William C. Church. Root to Church, February 20, 1900, March 26, 1902, May 9, 1902, May 15, 1902, Box 2, Church Papers, LC.

29. There are many accounts of the Root Reforms. Some of the general ones include Weigley, "Elihu Root Reforms and the Progressive Era"; Barr, *Progressive Army*; and Roberts, "Reform and Revitalization." Weigley places Root in the context of the Progressive Era, using Robert Wiebe's *The Search for Order*. Despite the title, Barr focuses on the Root Reforms, especially the General Staff. Roberts focuses on Root and his coterie of uniformed reformers, describing the adjustments Root and Colonel William H. Carter made to appease congressional opponents. For an in-depth examination of the early growing pains of the General Staff, see Raines, "Major General J. Franklin Bell and Military Reform."

30. *Army and Navy Journal*, January 26, 1901, 513–15.

31. Cooper, *Rise of the National Guard*, 108–12. Congress eliminated the nine-month and overseas restrictions in 1908. One of the biggest fights in Congress was the effort of the regular officers to create a national volunteer reserve to reinforce the regular army in emergencies. The National Guard lobby adamantly opposed this effort, and the Dick Act ensured the guard's primacy. In the National Defense Act of 1920, the Army Reserve was created, but it was restricted to noncombat support units. The most comprehensive treatment of the Dick Act is Cantor, "Creation of the Modern National Guard." Other excellent studies are Riker, *Soldiers of the States*; and Derthick, *National Guard in Politics*.

32. In addition to the previously cited works, accounts of the creation of the General Staff include Nelson, *National Security and the General Staff*; Semsch, "Elihu Root and the General Staff"; Hewes, *From Root to McNamara*, 3–21; and Ball, *Of Responsible Command*, 41–78.

33. Root to Schofield, March 27, 1902, Box 38, Schofield Papers, LC; Carter, *Creation of the American General Staff*, 35–36. In 1901 Schofield had served on the prize committee for the Military Service Intuition essay competition on the topic of the General Staff. Significantly, the committee awarded no gold medal, as the contestants merely offered warmed-over rehashes of the status quo. *Journal of the Military Service Institution* 28 (1901): 169–220.

34. The legislative battle over the Goldwater-Nichols Act of 1986 to reorganize the Joint Staff system also saw retired flag officers testify in favor of the bill, while serving generals and admirals, with presidential support, opposed the legislation.

35. Root to Hawley, April 7, 1902, Box 38, Schofield Papers, LC; *Army and Navy Journal*, April 12, 1902. Also see House Committee on Military Affairs, *National Defense*, 77–108.

36. *Army and Navy Journal*, April 12, 1902; *Army and Navy Register*, April 12, 1902, 4–5. Even today, all lieutenant generals and generals hold their rank as long as they hold an authorized position.

37. *Army and Navy Journal*, April 12, 1902, February 21, 1903; Schofield to Root, March 29,

1902, Box 38, Schofield Papers, LC; *Army and Navy Register*, April 12, 1902, 5; Roberts, "Reform and Revitalization," 213; Carter, *Creation of the American General Staff*, 9, 21, 22–29, 45–46.

38. Ronald Barr does an especially good job of describing how the General Staff's supporters nearly sabotaged their own efforts. Barr, *Progressive Army*, 123–75. See also Hewes, *From Root to McNamara*, 3–56; Nelson, *National Security and the General Staff*, 73–186, 274–345.

39. Morison, *Turmoil and Tradition*, 117–38; Deutrich, *Struggle for Supremacy*, 105–22; Nelson, *National Security and the General Staff*, 274–345.

40. Schofield to Root, April 16, 1901, Mills to Schofield, January 3, 1903, June 26, 1903, J. F. Richard to Schofield, January 12, 1904, and J. F. Richard to Mrs. Schofield, April 2, 1906, Box 38, Schofield Papers, LC; Carroon and Shoaf, *Union Blue*, 69–73. Schofield did not abandon all interest in contemporary army issues. The first Chief of Staff, Samuel B. M. Young, asked for Schofield's advice concerning the reorganization of territorial departments. Young to Schofield, November 3, 1903, and Schofield to Young, November 5, 1903, Young Papers, MHI.

41. ACP J. M. Schofield 2556, 1883, RG 94, NARA; *St. Augustine Tatler*, March 10, 1906, St. Augustine Historical Society, St. Augustine, Fla.

42. Basler, *Collected Works of Abraham Lincoln*, 6:234.

43. Weigley, *History of the United States Army*, 567–68.

44. Ganoe, *History of the Unites States Army*, 417, 430.

45. Huntington, *Soldier and the State*, 80–85.

46. Schofield address to the USMA graduating class, 1892, Box 91, Schofield Papers, LC.

47. Ibid.

BIBLIOGRAPHY

PRIMARY SOURCES

Manuscripts

Bar Harbor Historical Society, Bar Harbor, Maine

Bowdoin College Library, Brunswick, Maine
    Oliver O. Howard Papers

Duke University Library, Durham, North Carolina
    Romeyn Beck Ayres Letters
    William B. Dupree Papers

Library of Congress, Washington, D.C.
    Adam Badeau Papers
    John Bigelow Papers
    Blair Family Papers
    William Conant Church Papers
    Anna E. Dickinson Papers
    Thomas Ewing Papers
    Gibson-Getty-McClure Papers
    Ulysses S. Grant Papers
    Henry Halleck Papers
    Benjamin Harrison Papers
    Edward L. Hartz Papers
    Andrew Johnson Papers
    Daniel Lamont Papers
    James B. McPherson Papers
    John M. Schofield Papers
    Philip H. Sheridan Papers
    William T. Sherman Papers

Missouri Historical Society, St. Louis, Missouri
    Bates Family Papers
    Blow Family Papers

    Hamilton Gamble Papers
    U. S. Grant Papers
    Abraham Lincoln Papers
    William T. Sherman Papers

National Archives, Washington, D.C.
    Record Group 94, Records of the Adjutant General's Office
    Record Group 107, Records of the Office of the Secretary of War
    Record Group 108, Letters Sent by the Headquarters of the U.S. Army
    Record Group 153, Records of the Office of the Judge Advocate General
    Record Group 393, United States Army Continental Commands, 1821–1920
    Record Group 404, Records of the United States Military Academy

New-York Historical Society, New York, New York
    Francis Jay Herron Papers
    James Edward Kelly Papers

New York State Library, Albany, New York
    Gouverneur Kemble Warren Papers

Proctor Free Library, Proctor, Vermont
    Redfield Proctor Papers

St. Augustine Historical Society, St. Augustine, Florida

United States Army Center of Military History, Fort McNair, D.C.

United States Army Military History Institute, Carlisle, Pennsylvania

Tasker Bliss Papers

Luther Prentiss Bradley Papers

Winfield Scott Hancock Papers

Nelson A. Miles Papers

West-Stanley-Wright Family Papers

Samuel B. M. Young Papers

United States Military Academy, Archives
and Special Collections, West Point,
New York

John J. Sweet Papers

Washington University Archives, St. Louis,
Missouri

Western Historical Manuscript Collection,
Columbia, Missouri

Charles D. Drake Papers

Draper-McClurg Papers

Henry C. Fisk Papers

James S. Rollins Papers

Sampson Family Papers

Newspapers

Army and Navy Journal

Army and Navy Register

Columbia Missouri Statesman

New York Herald

New York Times

New York Tribune

San Francisco Chronicle

St. Augustine Tatler

St. Louis Missouri Democrat

St. Louis Missouri Republican

Washington Post

Documents

Adjutant General's Office, U.S. Army. *Distribution of Troops of the U.S. Army from January 1, 1866, to June 30, 1909.* Washington, D.C.: Adjutant General's Office Circular, 1909.

——. *General Orders and Circulars: Adjutant General's Office, 1891.* Washington, D.C.: Government Printing Office, 1892.

——. *Statistical Exhibit of Strength of Volunteer Forces Called into Service during the War with Spain; with Losses from All Causes.* Washington, D.C.: Government Printing Office, 1899.

Annual Report of Association of Graduates of USMA. West Point, N.Y.: Association of Graduates, 1901.

Annual Report of the Adjutant General of the State of Missouri, December 31, 1863. Jefferson City, Mo.: W. A. Curry, 1864.

Correspondence Relating to the War with Spain, including the Insurrection in the Philippine Islands and the China Relief Expedition. 2 vols. Washington, D.C.: Center of Military History, 1993.

Hanna, J. Marshall. *The Acts of Kings: Biblical Narrative of the Acts of the First and Second Kings of the First Province, Once Virginia, Including the Doings of the First and Second Tycoons of the City of Richmond from the Surrender to the Present Time.* New York: G. W. Carleton, 1868.

McPherson, Edward. *The Political History of the United States of America during the Period of Reconstruction, April 15, 1865–July 15, 1870.* New York: Da Capo Press, 1972.

Official Roster of the Soldiers of the State of Ohio in the War of the Rebellion, 1861–66. Vol. 8: *110th–140th Regiments Infantry.* Cincinnati: Ohio Valley Press, 1888.

Proceedings and Report of the Board of Army Officers, Convened by Special Orders no. 78,
    Headquarters of the Army, Adjutant General's Office, Washington, April 12, 1878, in the Case
    of Fitz-John Porter. 3 vols. Washington, D.C.: Government Printing Office, 1879.

Report of the Committee of the House of Representatives of the Twenty-Second General Assembly of
    the State of Missouri Appointed to Investigate the Conduct and Management of the Militia.
    Jefferson City, Mo.: W. A. Curry, 1864.

U.S. Congress. House. *Alfred Pleasanton.* 49th Cong., 1st sess., 1886. House Reports, No. 927,
    Serial 2437.

——. *Army Staff Organization.* 42d Cong., 3d sess., 1873. House Reports, No. 74, Serial 1576.

——. *Consideration for the Reorganization of the Army.* 45th Cong., 2d sess., 1878. House
    Miscellaneous Documents, No. 56, Serial 1818.

——. *Correspondence between General Grant and President Johnson.* 40th Cong., 2d sess.,
    1868. House Executive Documents, No. 149, Serial 1337.

——. *Correspondence Relating to Reconstruction.* 40th Cong., 1st sess., 1867. House Executive
    Documents, No. 20, Serial 1311.

——. *Detail of Army Officers for Service with the Militia.* 52d Cong., 2d sess., 1893. House
    Executive Documents, No. 224, Serial 3105.

——. *Disqualification of Certain Civil Officials: Report of General Schofield.* 40th Cong., 2d
    sess., 1868. House Executive Documents, No. 302, Serial 1341.

——. *Expenses of Elections in the First Military District.* 40th Cong., 2d sess., 1868. House
    Executive Documents, No. 244, Serial 1341.

——. *Fortification Appropriation Bill.* 51st Cong., 1st sess., 1890. House Reports, No. 877,
    Serial 2809.

——. *General Orders Pertaining to Reconstruction.* 40th Cong., 2d sess., 1868. House Executive
    Documents, No. 342, Serial 1346.

——. *Grade of Lieutenant General in the Army.* 53d Cong., 3d sess., 1895. House Reports, No.
    1648, Serial 3345.

——. *Lieutenant General of the Army.* 50th Cong., 2d sess., 1899. House Reports, No. 3677,
    Serial 2673.

——. *Lineal Promotion in the Line of the Army.* 51st Cong., 1st sess., 1890. House Executive
    Documents, No. 424, Serial 2752.

——. *Military Officers Detailed to Educational Institutions.* 50th Cong., 1st sess., 1888. House
    Reports, No. 1669, Serial 2602.

——. *The Modoc War.* 43d Cong., 1st sess., 1874. House Executive Documents, No. 122, Serial 1607.

——. *Reorganization of the Artillery and Infantry of the Army.* 52d Cong., 2d sess., 1893. House
    Reports, No. 2354, Serial 3141.

——. *Reorganization of the Artillery Force of the Army.* 51st Cong., 1st sess., 1890. House
    Reports, No. 777, Serial 2809.

——. *Report on Army Organization: The Garfield Committee Report.* 40th Cong., 3d sess.,
    1869. House Reports, No. 33, Serial 1388.

——. *Report of the [Endicott] Board of Fortifications or Other Defenses.* 49th Cong., 1st sess.,
    1886. House Executive Documents, No. 49, Serials 2395–96.

——. *Report on the Proposed Reorganization of the Army*. 45th Cong., 3d sess., 1878. House Reports, No. 3, Serial 1866.

——. *Revised Army Regulations*. 42d Cong., 3d sess., 1873. House Reports, No. 85, Serial 1576.

——. *Revised Army Regulations*. 43d Cong., 1st sess., 1874. House Reports, No. 592, Serial 1625.

——. *Riot at Norfolk, Virginia, April 16, 1866*. 39th Cong., 2d sess., 1867. House Executive Documents, No. 72, Serial 1293.

——. *A School of Instruction for Cavalry and Light Artillery*. 49th Cong., 1st sess., 1886. House Reports, No. 1948, Serial 2441.

U.S. Congress. House. Committee on Military Affairs. *The National Defense, Hearings before the Committee on Military Affairs, House of Representatives, Sixty-Ninth Congress, Second Session: Historical Documents Relating to the Reorganization Plans of the War Department and to the Present National Defense Act. Part 1*. Washington, D.C.: Government Printing Office, 1927.

U.S. Congress. Senate. *Burnside Report on the Proposed Reorganization of the Army*. 45th Cong., 3d sess., 1878. Senate Reports, No. 555, Serial 1837.

——. *Correspondence Relating to Reconstruction*. 40th Cong., 1st sess., 1867. Senate Executive Documents, No. 14, Serial 1308.

——. *Examinations and Promotions in the Army*. 51st Cong., 1st sess., 1890. Senate Reports, No. 832, Serial 2706.

——. *Federal Aid in Domestic Disturbances, 1787–1903*. 57th Cong., 2d sess., 1903. Senate Executive Documents, No. 209, Serial 4430.

——. *Federal Aid in Domestic Disturbances, 1787–1922*. 67th Cong., 2d sess., 1922. Senate Executive Documents, No. 263, Serial 7985.

——. *J. M. Schofield, Remarks on Promotion within the Staff of the Army*. 43d Cong., 2d sess., 1875. Senate Executive Documents, No. 9, Serial 1629.

——. *Journal of the Senate of the United States of America, 1789–1873*. May 28, 1868.

——. *Papers in Relation to the Proposed Reorganization of the Army*. 46th Cong., 1st sess., 1879. Senate Miscellaneous Documents, No. 14, Serial 1873.

——. *Reorganization of the Army*. 44th Cong., 2d sess., 1876. Senate Executive Documents, No. 26, Serial 1719.

U.S. Strike Commission. *Report on the Chicago Strike of June–July, 1894*. 53d Cong., 3d sess., Senate Executive Documents, No. 7, Serial 3276. Washington, D.C.: Government Printing Office, 1895.

U.S. War Department. *Annual Report of the Secretary of War, Vol. 1*.

for 1866, 39th Cong., 2d sess., House Executive Documents, No. 1, Serial 1285.

for 1867, 40th Cong., 2d sess., House Executive Documents, No. 1, Serials 1324–25.

for 1868, 40th Cong., 3d sess., House Executive Documents, No. 1, Serial 1367.

for 1869, 41st Cong., 2d sess., House Executive Documents, No. 1, Serial 1412.

for 1870, 41st Cong., 3d sess., House Executive Documents, No. 1, Serial 1446.

for 1871, 42d Cong., 2d sess., House Executive Documents, No. 1, Serial 1503.

for 1872, 42d Cong., 3d sess., House Executive Documents, No. 1, Serial 1558.

for 1873, 43d Cong., 1st sess., House Executive Documents, No. 1, Serial 1597.

for 1874, 43d Cong., 2d sess., House Executive Documents, No. 1, Serial 1635.

for 1875, 44th Cong., 1st sess., House Executive Documents, No. 1, Serial 1674.

for 1876, 44th Cong., 2d sess., House Executive Documents, No. 1, Serial 1742.

for 1877, 45th Cong., 2d sess., House Executive Documents, No. 1, Serial 1794.

for 1878, 45th Cong., 3d sess., House Executive Documents, No. 1, Serial 1843.

for 1879, 46th Cong., 2d sess., House Executive Documents, No. 1, Serial 1903.

for 1880, 46th Cong., 3d sess., House Executive Documents, No. 1, Serial 1952.

for 1881, 47th Cong., 1st sess., House Executive Documents, No. 1, Serial 2010.

for 1882, 47th Cong., 2d sess., House Executive Documents, No. 1, Serial 2091.

for 1883, 48th Cong., 1st sess., House Executive Documents, No. 1, Serial 2182.

for 1884, 48th Cong., 2d sess., House Executive Documents, No. 1, Serial 2136.

for 1885, 49th Cong., 1st sess., House Executive Documents, No. 1, Serial 2369.

for 1886, 49th Cong., 2nd sess., House Executive Documents, No. 1, Serial 2461.

for 1887, 50th Cong., 1st sess., House Executive Documents, No. 1, Serial 2533.

for 1888, 50th Cong., 2nd sess., House Executive Documents, No. 1, Serial 2628.

for 1889, 51st Cong., 1st sess., House Executive Documents, No. 1, Serial 2715.

for 1890, 51st Cong., 2d sess., House Executive Documents, No. 1, Serial 2831.

for 1891, 52d Cong., 1st sess., House Executive Documents, No. 1, Serial 2921.

for 1892, 52d Cong., 2d sess., House Executive Documents, No. 1, Serial 3077.

for 1893, 53d Cong., 2d sess., House Executive Documents, No. 1, Serial 3198.

for 1894, 53d Cong., 3d sess., House Executive Documents, No. 1, Serial 3295.

for 1895, 54th Cong., 1st sess., House Executive Documents, No. 2, Serial 3370.

for 1896, 54th Cong., 2d sess., House Executive Documents, No. 2, Serial 3478.

———. *Artillery Tactics, United States Army.* New York: D. Appleton, 1874.

———. *Cavalry Drill Regulations, United States Army.* Washington, D.C.: Government Printing Office, 1891.

———. *Cavalry Tactics, United States Army, Assimilated to the Tactics of Infantry and Artillery.* New York: D. Appleton, 1874.

———. *Drill Regulations for Light Artillery, United States Army.* Washington, D.C.: Government Printing Office, 1896.

———. *Infantry Drill Regulations, United States Army.* Washington, D.C.: Government Printing Office, 1891.

———. *Revised United States Army Regulations of 1861, with Changes to June 25, 1863.* Washington, D.C.: Government Printing Office, 1863.

———. *Regulations of the Army of the United States, 1895.* Washington, D.C.: Government Printing Office, 1895.

———. *The War of the Rebellion: A Compilation of the Official Records of the Union and Confederate Armies.* 128 vols. Washington, D.C.: Government Printing Office, 1880–1901.

———. *U.S. Army Register.* Washington, D.C.: Government Printing Office, 1906, 1921.

Badeau, Adam. *Grant in Peace: From Appomattox to Mount McGregor, a Personal Memoir.* 1887. New York: Books for Libraries Press, 1971.

——. *Military History of Ulysses S. Grant: From April, 1861 to April, 1865.* Vol. 3. New York: D. Appleton, 1881.

Baxter, William. *Pea Ridge and Prairie Grove: Scenes and Incidents of the War in Arkansas.* Cincinnati, Ohio: Poe and Hitchcock, 1864.

Bigelow, John. *Retrospectives of an Active Life.* Vols. 3–4. New York: Baker and Taylor Company, 1909.

Britton, Wiley. *Memoirs of the Rebellion on the Border, 1863.* Lincoln: University of Nebraska Press, 1993.

Browning, Orville H. *The Diaries of Orville Hickman Browning.* 2 vols. Springfield: Illinois State Historical Library, 1925.

Carter, William Harding. *Creation of the American General Staff: Personal Narrative of the General Staff System of the American Army.* 68th Cong., 1st sess., Senate Documents, No. 119. Washington, D.C.: Government Printing Office, 1924.

Chamberlain, Joshua Lawrence. *The Passing of the Armies: An Account of the Final Campaign of the Army of the Potomac, Based upon Personal Reminiscences of the Fifth Army Corps.* 1915; New York: Bantam, 1993.

Chase, Salmon P. *Inside Lincoln's Cabinet: The Civil War Diaries of Salmon P. Chase.* Edited by David Donald. New York: Kraus Reprint, 1970.

Cox, Jacob D. *Reminiscences of the Civil War.* 2 vols. New York: Charles Scribner's Sons, 1900.

Dana, Charles A. *Recollections of the Civil War.* 1902; New York: Collier Books, 1963.

Grant, Ulysses S. *Personal Memoirs and Selected Letters, 1839–1865.* New York: Library of America, 1990.

Hancock, Winfield Scott. *Reminiscences of Winfield Scott Hancock by His Wife.* New York: Charles L. Webster and Company, 1887.

Hood, John Bell. *Advance and Retreat: Personal Experiences in the United States and Confederate Armies.* Millwood, N.Y.: Kraus Reprint, 1981.

Howard, O. O. *Autobiography of Oliver Otis Howard.* 2 vols. New York: Baker and Taylor Company, 1908.

Johnston, Joseph E. *Narrative of Military Operations during the Civil War.* 1874; New York: Da Capo Press, 1959.

Logan, John A. *The Volunteer Soldier of America.* New York: R. S. Peale and Company, 1887.

Longstreet, James. *From Manassas to Appomattox.* Secaucus, N.J.: Blue and Gray Press, 1984.

Miles, Nelson Appleton. *Serving the Republic: Memoirs of the Civil and Military Life of Nelson A. Miles.* 1911; Freeport, N.Y.: Books for Libraries Press, 1971.

Mudd, Joseph A. *With Porter in North Missouri: A Chapter in the History of the War.* Washington, D.C.: National Publishing Company, 1909.

Porter, Horace. *Campaigning with Grant.* 1897; Secaucus, N.J.: Blue and Gray Press, 1984.

Rombauer, Robert Julius. *The Union Cause in St. Louis in 1861.* St. Louis: Press of Nixon-Jones Company, 1909.

Schofield, John M. *Forty-Six Years in the Army*. New York: Century Company, 1897.

Scott, Hugh Lenox. *Some Memories of a Soldier*. New York: Century Company, 1928.

Seward, Frederick William. *Reminiscences of a War-Time Statesman and Diplomat, 1830–1915*. New York: G. P. Putnam's Sons, 1916.

Sheridan, Philip H. *The Personal Memoirs of P. H. Sheridan*. 1888; New York: Da Capo Press, 1992.

Sherman, William T. *Memoirs of General William T. Sherman*. New York: Library of America, 1990.

Sherwood, Isaac R. *Memories of the War*. Toledo, Ohio: H. J. Crittenden Company, 1923.

Snead, Thomas. *The Fight for Missouri: From the Election of Lincoln to the Death of Lyon*. New York: Charles Scribner's Sons, 1886.

Stanley, David S. *Personal Memoirs of Major-General D. S. Stanley, U.S.A.* Cambridge, Mass.: Harvard University Press, 1917.

Thorndike, Rachel Sherman, ed. *The Sherman Letters: Correspondence between General and Senator from 1837 to 1891*. New York: Charles Scribner's Sons, 1894.

Wilson, James H. *Under the Old Flag: Recollections of Military Operations in the War for the Union, the Spanish War, the Boxer Rebellion*. 2 vols. 1912; Westport, Conn.: Greenwood Press, 1971.

SECONDARY SOURCES

Books

Abrahamson, James L. *America Arms for a New Century: The Making of a Great Military Power*. New York: Free Press, 1981.

Adamson, Hans Christian. *Rebellion in Missouri, 1861: Nathaniel Lyon and His Army of the West*. Philadelphia: Chilton Company, Book Division, 1961.

Altshuler, Constance Wynn. *Cavalry Yellow and Infantry Blue: Army Officers in Arizona between 1851 and 1886*. Tucson: Arizona Historical Society, 1991.

Ambrose, Stephen E. *Duty, Honor, Country: A History of West Point*. Baltimore, Md.: Johns Hopkins University Press, 1966.

——. *Halleck: Lincoln's Chief of Staff*. Baton Rouge: Louisiana State University Press, 1962.

——. *Upton and the Army*. Baton Rouge: Louisiana State University Press, 1964.

Anders, Curt. *Henry Halleck's War: A Fresh Look at Lincoln's Controversial General-in-Chief*. Indianapolis: Guild Press of Indiana, Inc., 1999.

——. *Injustice on Trial: Second Bull Run, General Fitz John Porter's Court-Martial, and the Schofield Board Investigation that Restored His Good Name*. Zionsville, Ind.: Guild Press/Emmis Publishing, 2002.

Anderson, Galusha. *The Story of a Border City during the Civil War*. Boston: Little, Brown, and Company, 1908.

Annual Reunion. West Point, N.Y.: United States Military Academy Graduates Association, 1893, 1901, 1906.

Ash, Stephen V. *Middle Tennessee Society Transformed, 1860–1870: War and Peace in the Upper South*. Baton Rouge: Louisiana State University Press, 1988.

——. *When the Yankees Came: Conflict and Chaos in the Occupied South, 1861–1865*. Chapel Hill: University of North Carolina Press, 1995.

Bailey, Anne J. *The Chessboard of War: Sherman and Hood in the Autumn Campaigns of 1864*. Lincoln: University of Nebraska Press, 2000.

Ball, Harry P. *Of Responsible Command: A History of the U.S. Army War College*. Carlisle Barracks, Pa.: Alumni Association of the U.S. Army War College, 1994.

Barr, Ronald J. *The Progressive Army: U.S. Army Command and Administration, 1870–1914*. New York: St. Martin's Press, 1998.

Barrows, Chester L. *William M. Evarts: Lawyer, Diplomat, Statesman*. Chapel Hill: University of North Carolina Press, 1941.

Basler, Roy P., ed. *The Collected Works of Abraham Lincoln*. Vols. 4, 6–7. New Brunswick, N.J.: Rutgers University Press, 1955.

Bell, William Gardner. *Commanding Generals and Chiefs of Staff, 1775–1983: Portraits and Biographical Sketches of the United States Army's Senior Officer*. Washington, D.C.: Center of Military History, 1983.

——. *Secretaries of War and Secretaries of the Army: Portraits and Biographical Sketches*. Washington, D.C.: Center of Military History, 1992.

Belz, Herman. *Reconstructing the Union: Theory and Policy during the Civil War*. Ithaca, N.Y.: Cornell University Press, 1969.

Betros, Lance, ed. *West Point: Two Centuries and Beyond*. Abilene, Tex.: McWhiney Foundation Press, 2004.

Bigelow, John. *The Principles of Strategy, Illustrated Mainly from American Campaigns*. 2d ed. 1893; New York: Greenwood Press, 1968.

Birtle, Andrew J. *U.S. Army Counterinsurgency and Contingency Operations Doctrine, 1860–1941*. Washington, D.C.: Center of Military History, U.S. Army, Government Printing Office, 1998.

Boatner, Mark M. *The Civil War Dictionary*. New York: Vintage Books, 1988.

Bogue, Allan G. *The Congressman's Civil War*. New York: Cambridge University Press, 1989.

Brooksher, William R. *Bloody Hill: The Civil War Battle of Wilson's Creek*. Washington, D.C.: Brassey's, 1995.

Browning, Robert S. *Two If By Sea: The Development of American Coastal Defense Policy*. Westport, Conn.: Greenwood Press, 1983.

Brownlee, Richard S. *Gray Ghosts of the Confederacy: Guerrilla Warfare in the West, 1861–1865*. Baton Rouge: Louisiana State University Press, 1958.

Bruce, Robert V. *1877: Year of Violence*. 1957; Chicago: Ivan R. Dee, 1989.

Burnham, W. P. *The Roads to a Commission in the United States Army*. New York: D. Appleton and Company, 1893.

Caro, Robert. *The Years of Lyndon Johnson: Means of Ascent*. New York: Alfred A. Knopf, 1990.

Carpenter, John A. *Sword and Olive Branch: Oliver Otis Howard*. Pittsburgh, Pa.: University of Pittsburgh Press, 1964.

Carroll, John M., ed. *The Black Military Experience in the American West*. New York: Liveright, 1971.

Carroon, Robert G., and Dana B. Shoaf. *Union Blue: The History of the Military Order of the Loyal Legion of the United States*. Shippensburg, Pa.: White Mane Books, 2001.

Castel, Albert. *Decision in the West: The Atlanta Campaign of 1864*. Lawrence: University Press of Kansas, 1992.

———. *A Frontier State at War: Kansas, 1861–1865*. Lawrence, Kans.: Heritage Press, 1958.

———. *General Sterling Price and the Civil War in the West*. Baton Rouge: Louisiana State University Press, 1968.

———. *The Presidency of Andrew Johnson*. Lawrence: Regents Press of Kansas, 1979.

Chambers, John Whiteclay, ed. *The Oxford Companion to American Military History*. New York: Oxford University Press, 1999.

Cherny, Robert W. *American Politics in the Gilded Age*. Wheeling, Ill.: Harlan Davidson, 1997.

Chesson, Michael B. *Richmond after the War, 1865–1890*. Richmond: Virginia State Library, 1981.

Clapp, Margaret A. *Forgotten First Citizen: John Bigelow*. Boston: Little, Brown, 1947.

Coakley, Robert W. *The Role of Federal Military Forces in Domestic Disorders, 1789–1878*. Washington, D.C.: Center of Military History, U.S. Army, Government Printing Office, 1988.

Coffman, Edward M. *The Old Army: A Portrait of the American Army in Peacetime, 1784–1898*. New York: Oxford University Press, 1986.

———. *The Regulars: The American Army, 1898–1941*. Cambridge, Mass.: Harvard University Press, 2004.

Connelley, William E. *Quantrill and the Border Wars*. 1910; Ottawa: Kansas Heritage Press, 1992.

Cooper, Jerry M. *The Army and Civil Disorder: Federal Military Intervention in Labor Disputes, 1877–1900*. Westport, Conn.: Greenwood Press, 1980.

———. *The Rise of the National Guard: The Evolution of the American Militia, 1865–1920*. Lincoln: University of Nebraska Press, 1997.

Cosmas, Graham A. *An Army for Empire: The United States Army in the Spanish-American War*. Shippensburg, Pa.: White Mane Publishing Company, 1994.

Cox, Jacob D. *The Battle of Franklin*. New York: Charles Scribner's Sons, 1897.

———. *The Second Battle of Bull Run, as Connected with the Fitz-John Porter Case. A paper read before the Society of ex-army and navy officers of Cincinnati, February 28, 1882*. Cincinnati, Ohio: P. G. Thomson, 1882.

———. *Sherman's Battle for Atlanta*. New York: Da Capo Press, 1994.

———. *Sherman's March to the Sea: Hood's Tennessee Campaign and the Carolina Campaigns of 1865*. New York: Da Capo Press, 1994.

Cozzens, Peter. *General John Pope: A Life for the Nation*. Urbana: University of Illinois Press, 2000.

Crackel, Theodore J. *Mr. Jefferson's Army: Political and Social Reform of the Military Establishment, 1801–1809*. New York: New York University Press, 1987.

——. *West Point: A Bicentennial History*. Lawrence: University Press of Kansas, 2002.

Craig, Malin, Jr. *History of the Officer Efficiency Report System, United States Army, 1775–1917*. Washington, D.C.: Office of the Chief of Military History, 1953.

Dawson, Joseph G. *Army Generals and Reconstruction: Louisiana, 1862–1877*. Baton Rouge: Louisiana State University Press, 1982.

——. *The Late 19th Century U.S. Army, 1865–1898: A Research Guide*. New York: Greenwood Press, 1990.

Dennett, Tyler, ed. *Lincoln and the Civil War in the Diaries and Letters of John Hay*. New York: Dodd, Mead, 1939.

Derthick, Martha. *The National Guard in Politics*. Cambridge, Mass.: Harvard University Press, 1965.

Deutrich, Mabel E. *Struggle for Supremacy: The Career of General Fred C. Ainsworth*. Washington D.C.: Public Affairs Press, 1962.

Donald, David H. *Lincoln*. New York: Simon and Schuster, 1995.

Dunning, William A. *Essays on the Civil War and Reconstruction*. New York: Macmillan, 1897, 1904; reprint, New York: Harper and Row, 1965.

——. *Reconstruction, Political and Economic, 1865–1877*. New York: Harper and Row, 1907.

Dupuy, R. Ernest. *The National Guard: A Compact History*. New York: Hawthorn Books, 1971.

Eisenschiml, Otto. *The Celebrated Case of Fitz John Porter: An American Dreyfus Affair*. New York: Bobbs-Merrill, 1950.

Feaver, Peter D. *Armed Servants: Agency, Oversight, and Civil-Military Relations*. Cambridge, Mass.: Harvard University Press, 2003.

Feaver, Peter D., and Richard H. Kohn, eds. *Soldiers and Civilians: The Civil-Military Gap and American National Security*. Cambridge, Mass.: MIT Press, 2001.

Fellman, Michael. *Citizen Sherman: A Life of William Tecumseh Sherman*. New York: Random House, 1995.

——. *Inside War: The Guerrilla Conflict in Missouri during the American Civil War*. New York: Oxford University Press, 1989.

Fisher, Noel C. *War at Every Door: Partisan Politics and Guerrilla Violence in East Tennessee, 1860–1869*. Chapel Hill: University of North Carolina Press, 1997.

Fleming, Thomas J. *West Point: The Men and Times of the United States Military Academy*. New York: William Morrow and Company, 1969.

Foner, Eric. *Reconstruction: America's Unfinished Revolution, 1863–1877*. New York: Harper and Row, 1988.

Foner, Jack D. *The United States Soldier between Two Wars: Army Life and Reforms, 1865–1898*. New York: Humanities Press, 1970.

Forsyth, George A. *The Story of the Soldier*. New York: D. Appleton and Company, 1900.

Fredrickson, George M. *The Inner Civil War: Northern Intellectuals and the Crisis of the Union*. Urbana: University of Illinois Press, 1965.

Ganoe, William A. *The History of the United States Army*. New York: Appleton, 1942; reprint, Ashton, Md.: Lundburg, 1964.

Glatthaar, Joseph T. *Partners in Command: The Relationships between Leaders in the Civil War.* New York: Free Press, 1994.

Gould, Louis. *The Spanish-American War and President McKinley.* Lawrence: University Press of Kansas, 1982.

Grimsley, Mark. *The Hard Hand of War: Union Policy toward Southern Civilians, 1861–1865.* New York: Cambridge University Press, 1995.

Groom, Winston. *Shrouds of Glory, from Atlanta to Nashville: The Last Great Campaign of the Civil War.* New York: Atlantic Monthly Press, 1995.

Grove, Gregory D. *The U.S. Military and Civil Infrastructure Protection: Restrictions and Discretion under the Posse Comitatus Act.* Stanford, Calif.: Stanford University Center for International Security and Cooperation, October 1999.

Hammond, Paul Y. *Organizing for Defense: The American Military Establishment in the Twentieth Century.* Princeton, N.J.: Princeton University Press, 1961.

Harrison, Lowell H. *The Civil War in Kentucky.* Lexington: University Press of Kentucky, 1975.

Hart, Jim Allee. *A History of the St. Louis Globe-Democrat.* Columbia: University of Missouri Press, 1961.

Hatch, Nathan O., ed. *The Professions in American History.* Notre Dame, Ind.: University of Notre Dame Press, 1988.

Hattaway, Herman, and Archer Jones. *How the North Won.* Urbana: University of Illinois Press, 1983.

Hazen, William B. *The School and the Army in Germany and France, with a Diary of Siege Life at Versailles.* New York: Harper, 1872.

Heidler, David S., and Jeanne T. Heidler, eds. *Encyclopedia of the American Civil War: A Political, Social, and Military History.* New York: W. W. Norton, 2000.

Heitman, Francis Bernard. *Historical Register and Dictionary of the United States Army, from Its Organization, September 29, 1789, to March 2, 1903.* Washington, D.C.: Government Printing Office, 1903.

Hennessy, John J. *Return to Bull Run: The Campaign and Battle of Second Manassas.* New York: Simon and Schuster, 1993.

Hewes, James E., Jr. *From Root to McNamara: Army Organization and Administration, 1900–1963.* Washington, D.C.: Center of Military History, 1975.

Hindale, Burke A., ed. *The Works of James Abram Garfield.* Boston: James R. Osgood and Company, 1883.

Hogg, Ian. *The History of Fortification.* New York: St. Martin's Press, 1991.

Holley, I. B., Jr. *General John M. Palmer, Citizen Soldiers, and the Army of a Democracy.* Westport, Conn.: Greenwood Press, 1982.

Hoogenboom, Ari. *Rutherford B. Hayes: Warrior and President.* Lawrence: University Press of Kansas, 1995.

Horn, Stanley. *The Decisive Battle of Nashville.* Knoxville: University of Tennessee Press, 1956.

Huntington, Samuel P. *The Soldier and the State: The Theory and Politics of Civil-Military Relations.* New York: Vintage Books, 1957.

Hutton, Paul Andrew. *Phil Sheridan and His Army*. Lincoln: University of Nebraska Press, 1985.

——, ed. *Soldiers West: Biographies from the Military Frontier*. Lincoln: University of Nebraska Press, 1987.

Jamieson, Perry D. *Crossing the Deadly Ground: United States Army Tactics, 1865–1899*. Tuscaloosa: University of Alabama Press, 1994.

Jessup, Philip C. *Elihu Root*. Vol. 1: *1845–1909*. New York: Dodd, Mead and Company, 1938.

Johnson, Virginia Weisel. *The Unregimented General: A Biography of Nelson A. Miles*. Boston: Houghton Mifflin, 1962.

Jomini, Antoine. *The Art of War*. 1862; Westport, Conn.: Greenwood Press, 1991.

Jones, Archer. *The Art of War in the Western World*. New York: Oxford University Press, 1987.

——. *Civil War Command and Strategy: The Process of Victory and Defeat*. New York: Free Press, 1992.

Jordan, David M. *Winfield Scott Hancock: A Soldier's Life*. Bloomington: Indiana University Press, 1988.

Keller, Morton. *Affairs of State: Public Life in Late Nineteenth-Century America*. Cambridge, Mass.: Harvard University Press, 1977.

Knapp, George E. *The Wilson's Creek Staff Ride and Battlefield Tour*. Fort Leavenworth, Kans.: Combat Studies Institute, 1993.

Kohn, Richard H. *Eagle and the Sword: The Beginnings of the Military Establishment in America*. New York: Free Press, 1975.

Koistinen, Paul A. C. *Mobilizing for Modern War: The Political Economy of American Warfare, 1865–1919*. Lawrence: University Press of Kansas, 1997.

Kreidberg, Marvin A., and Merton G. Henry. *History of Military Mobilization in the United States Army, 1775–1945*. Washington, D.C.: Department of the Army, 1955.

LaFeber, Walter. *The American Age: United States Foreign Policy at Home and Abroad since 1750*. New York: W. W. Norton, 1989.

Langston, Thomas S. *Uneasy Alliance: Civil-Military Relations in Peacetime America since 1783*. Baltimore, Md.: Johns Hopkins University Press, 2003.

Laurie, Clayton D., and Ronald H. Cole. *The Role of Federal Military Forces in Domestic Disorders, 1877–1945*. Washington, D.C.: Center of Military History, U.S. Army, Government Printing Office, 1997.

Leckie, Shirley Anne, ed. *The Colonel's Lady on the Western Frontier: The Correspondence of Alice Kirk Grierson*. Lincoln: University of Nebraska Press, 1989.

Lewis, Emanuel Raymond. *Seacoast Fortifications of the United States: An Introductory History*. Washington, D.C.: Smithsonian Institution Press, 1970.

Lewis, Lloyd. *Sherman: Fighting Prophet*. 1932; Lincoln: University of Nebraska Press, 1993.

Liddell Hart, B. H. *Sherman: Soldier, Realist, American*. 1929; New York: Harcourt, Brace and Company, 1958.

Lindsey, Almont. *The Pullman Strike*. Chicago: University of Chicago Press, 1942.

Logsdon, David R., ed. *Eyewitnesses at the Battle of Franklin*. Nashville, Tenn.: Kettle Mills Press, 1996.

Longacre, Edward G. *Grant's Cavalryman: The Life and Wars of General James H. Wilson.* Mechanicsburg, Pa.: Stackpole Books, 1972.

Lowe, Richard. *Republicans and Reconstruction in Virginia, 1856–70.* Charlottesville: University Press of Virginia, 1991.

Luttwak, Edward. *Strategy: The Logic of War and Peace.* Cambridge, Mass.: Harvard University Press, 1987.

Luvaas, Jay. *The Military Legacy of the Civil War: The European Inheritance.* Lawrence: University Press of Kansas, 1988.

Mahon, John K. *History of the Militia and the National Guard.* New York: Macmillan, 1983.

Marszalek, John F. *Assault at West Point: The Court-Martial of Johnson Whittaker.* New York: Collier Books, 1994.

——. *Commander of All Lincoln's Armies: A Life of General Henry W. Halleck.* Cambridge, Mass.: Harvard University Press, 2004.

——. *Sherman: A Soldier's Passion for Order.* New York: Free Press, 1993.

Martin, David G. *The Second Bull Run Campaign, July–August, 1862.* Conshohocken, Pa.: Combined Books, 1997.

Martin, James Kirby, and Mark Edward Lender. *A Respectable Army: The Military Origins of the Republic, 1763–1789.* Arlington Heights, Ill.: Harlan Davidson, 1982.

McConnell, Stuart. *Glorious Contentment: The Grand Army of the Republic, 1865–1900.* Chapel Hill: University of North Carolina Press, 1992.

McDonough, James L. *Schofield: Union General in the Civil War and Reconstruction.* Tallahassee: Florida State University Press, 1972.

McDonough, James L., and Thomas L. Connelly. *Five Tragic Hours: The Battle of Franklin.* Knoxville: University of Tennessee Press, 1983.

McDonough, James L., and James Pickett Jones. *War So Terrible: Sherman and Atlanta.* New York: W. W. Norton, 1987.

McDougall, Walter A. *Promised Land, Crusader State: The American Encounter with the World since 1776.* New York: Houghton Mifflin, 1997.

McElroy, John. *The Struggle for Missouri.* Washington, D.C.: National Tribune Company, 1909.

McFeely, William S. *Grant: A Biography.* New York: W. W. Norton, 1981.

——. *Yankee Stepfather: General O. O. Howard and the Freedmen.* New Haven, Conn.: Yale University Press, 1968.

McMurry, Richard M. *Atlanta 1864: Last Campaign for the Confederacy.* Lincoln: University of Nebraska Press, 2000.

——. *John Bell Hood and the War for Southern Independence.* Lincoln: University of Nebraska Press, 1982.

——. *Two Great Rebel Armies: An Essay in Confederate Military History.* Chapel Hill: University of North Carolina Press, 1989.

McPherson, James M. *Battle Cry of Freedom: The Civil War Era.* New York: Ballantine Books, 1988.

——. *Drawn with the Sword: Reflections on the American Civil War.* New York: Oxford University Press, 1996.

Military Order of the Loyal Legion of the United States. *Necrology of Companion John M. Schofield, Lt. Gen., U.S. Army*. Washington, D.C.: Press of Gibson Brothers, 1908.

Monaghan, Jay. *Civil War on the Border, 1854–1865*. Lincoln: University of Nebraska Press, 1955.

Morison, Elting E. *Turmoil and Tradition: A Study of the Life and Times of Henry L. Stimson*. New York: Atheneum, 1964.

Morrison, James L., Jr. *"The Best School": West Point, 1833–1866*. Kent, Ohio: Kent State University Press, 1998.

Murray, Keith A. *The Modocs and Their War*. Norman: University of Oklahoma Press, 1959.

Nalty, Bernard C. *Strength for the Fight: A History of Black Americans in the Military*. New York: Free Press, 1986.

Neely, Mark E., Jr. *The Fate of Liberty: Abraham Lincoln and Civil Liberties*. New York: Oxford University Press, 1991.

Nelson, Otto L. *National Security and the General Staff*. Washington, D.C.: Infantry Journal Press, 1946.

Nenninger, Timothy K. *The Leavenworth Schools and the Old Army: Education, Professionalism, and the Officer Corps of the United States Army, 1881–1918*. Westport, Conn.: Greenwood Press, 1978.

Nichols, Bruce. *Guerrilla Warfare in Civil War Missouri, 1862*. Jefferson, N.C.: McFarland and Company, 2004.

Nicolay, John G. *The Outbreak of the Rebellion*. New York: Charles Scribner's Sons, 1881.

Niven, John. *Salmon P. Chase: A Biography*. New York: Oxford University Press, 1995.

Palmer, John McAuley. *America in Arms: The Experience of the United States with Military Organization*. New Haven, Conn.: Yale University Press, 1941.

Paludan, Phillip Shaw. *A People's Contest: The Union and Civil War, 1861–1865*. Lawrence: University Press of Kansas, 1996.

Papke, David Ray. *The Pullman Case: The Clash of Labor and Capital in Industrial America*. Lawrence: University Press of Kansas, 1999.

Parrish, William E. *Frank Blair: Lincoln's Conservative*. Columbia: University of Missouri Press, 1998.

——. *A History of Missouri*. Vol. 3: *1860–1875*. Columbia: University of Missouri Press, 1973.

——. *Turbulent Partnership: Missouri and the Union, 1861–1865*. Columbia: University of Missouri Press, 1963.

Pearlman, Michael D. *Warmaking and American Democracy: The Struggle over Military Strategy, 1700 to the Present*. Lawrence: University Press of Kansas, 1999.

Peckham, James. *Gen. Nathaniel Lyon, and Missouri in 1861: A Monograph of the Great Rebellion*. New York: American News Company, 1866.

Perman, Michael. *Emancipation and Reconstruction, 1862–1879*. Arlington Heights, Ill.: Harlan Davidson, 1987.

Peskin, Allan. *Garfield: A Biography*. Kent, Ohio: Kent State University Press, 1978.

Phillips, Christopher. *Damned Yankee: The Life of General Nathaniel Lyon*. Columbia: University of Missouri Press, 1990.

Piatt, Donn. *General George H. Thomas: A Critical Biography, with Concluding Chapters by Henry V. Boynton*. Cincinnati, Ohio: Robert Charles and Company, 1893.

Piston, William Garrett, and Richard W. Hatcher III. *Wilson's Creek: The Second Battle of the Civil War and the Men Who Fought It*. Chapel Hill: University of North Carolina Press, 2000.

Pratt, Fletcher. *Stanton: Lincoln's Secretary of War*. New York: W. W. Norton, 1953.

Prucha, Francis Paul. *Broadax and Bayonet: The Role of the United States Army in the Development of the Northwest, 1815–1860*. 1953; Lincoln: University of Nebraska Press, 1995.

——. *The Great Father: The United States Government and the American Indians*. Abridged ed. Lincoln: University of Nebraska Press, 1986.

——. *The Sword of the Republic: The United States Army on the Frontier, 1783–1846*. Bloomington: Indiana University Press, 1969.

——, ed. *Documents of United States Indian Policy*. Lincoln: University of Nebraska Press, 1975.

Rable, George C. *But There Was No Peace: The Role of Violence in the Politics of Reconstruction*. Athens: University of Georgia Press, 1984.

Rachleff, Peter J. *Black Labor in the South: Richmond, Virginia, 1865–1890*. Philadelphia: Temple University Press, 1984.

Register of Graduates and Former Cadets, 1802–1990. West Point, N.Y.: Association of Graduates of the United States Military Academy, 1990.

Richter, William L. *The Army in Texas during Reconstruction, 1865–1870*. College Station: Texas A&M University Press, 1987.

Rickey, Don, Jr. *Forty Miles a Day on Beans and Hay*. Norman: University of Oklahoma Press, 1963.

Riker, William H. *Soldiers of the States: The Role of the National Guard in American Democracy*. Washington, D.C.: Public Affairs Press, 1957.

Robinson, Charles M., III. *General Crook and the Western Frontier*. Norman: University of Oklahoma Press, 2001.

Ropes, John Codman. *The Army under Pope*. New York: Charles Scribner's Sons, 1881.

Royster, Charles. *The Destructive War: William Tecumseh Sherman, Stonewall Jackson, and the Americans*. New York: Alfred A. Knopf, 1991.

——. *A Revolutionary People at War: The Continental Army and American Character, 1775–1783*. New York: W. W. Norton, 1979.

Sefton, James E. *The United States Army and Reconstruction, 1865–1877*. Baton Rouge: Louisiana State University Press, 1967.

Shea, William L. *War in the West: Pea Ridge and Prairie Grove*. Abilene, Tex.: McWhiney Foundation Press, 1998.

Short, Lloyd M. *The Development of National Administrative Organization in the United States*. Baltimore, Md.: Johns Hopkins University Press, 1923.

Shy, John. *A People Numerous and Armed: Reflections on the Military Struggle for American Independence*. New York: Oxford University Press, 1976.

Sifakis, Stewart. *Who Was Who in the Union*. New York: Facts on File, 1988.

Simpson, Brooks D. *Let Us Have Peace: Ulysses S. Grant and the Politics of War and Reconstruction, 1861–1868.* Chapel Hill: University of North Carolina Press, 1991.

——. *Ulysses S. Grant: Triumph over Adversity, 1822–1865.* New York: Houghton Mifflin, 2000.

Simpson, Brooks D., Leroy P. Graf, and John Muldowny, eds. *Advice after Appomattox: Letters to Andrew Johnson, 1865–1886. Special Volume No. 1 of the Papers of Andrew Johnson.* Knoxville: University of Tennessee Press, 1987.

Skelton, William B. *An American Profession of Arms: The Army Officer Corps, 1784–1861.* Lawrence: University Press of Kansas, 1992.

Skowronek, Stephen. *Building a New American State: The Expansion of National Administrative Capacities, 1877–1920.* New York: Cambridge University Press, 1982.

Smith, Jean Edward. *Grant.* New York: Simon and Schuster, 2001.

Smith, William E. *The Francis Preston Blair Family in Politics,* Vol. 2. New York: Macmillan, 1933.

Snider, Don M., and Miranda A. Carlton-Carew, eds. *U.S. Civil-Military Relations: In Crisis or Transition?* Washington, D.C.: Center for Strategic and International Studies, 1995.

Spiers, Edward M. *The Late Victorian Army, 1868–1902.* Manchester, U.K.: Manchester University Press, 1992.

Starr, Stephen Z. *Jennison's Jayhawkers: A Civil War Cavalry Regiment and Its Commander.* Baton Rouge: Louisiana State University Press, 1973.

Stockdale, Paul H. *The Death of an Army: The Battle of Nashville and Hood's Retreat.* Murfreesboro, Tenn.: Southern Heritage Press, 1992.

Stohlman, Robert F., Jr. *The Powerless Position: The Commanding General of the Army of the United States, 1864–1903.* Manhattan, Kans.: Military Affairs, 1975.

Sword, Wiley. *The Confederacy's Last Hurrah: Spring Hill, Franklin, and Nashville.* Lawrence: University Press of Kansas, 1992.

Tap, Bruce. *Over Lincoln's Shoulder: The Committee on the Conduct of the War.* Lawrence: University Press of Kansas, 1998.

Taylor, Alrutheus A. *The Negro in the Reconstruction of Virginia.* Washington, D.C.: Association for the Study of Negro Life and History, 1926.

Thomas, Benjamin P., and Harold Hyman. *Stanton: The Life and Times of Lincoln's Secretary of War.* New York: Alfred A. Knopf, 1962.

Thomas, Emory. *The Confederate Nation: 1861–1865.* New York: Harper and Row, 1979.

Thomas, Wilbur. *General George H. Thomas: The Indomitable Warrior.* New York: Exposition Press, 1964.

Trulock, Alice Rains. *In the Hands of Providence: Joshua Lawrence Chamberlain and the American Civil War.* Chapel Hill: University of North Carolina Press, 1992.

Upton, Emory. *Armies of Asia and Europe: Embracing Official Reports on the Armies of Japan, China, India, Persia, Italy, Russia, Austria, Germany, France, and England.* 1878; New York: Greenwood Press, 1968.

——. *The Military Policy of the United States.* Washington, D.C.: Government Printing Office, 1917.

——. *A New System of Infantry Tactics, Double and Single Rank. Adapted to American Topography and Improved Fire-Arms.* New York: Appleton, 1867.

Utley, Robert M. *Frontier Regulars: The United States Army and the Indian, 1866–1890*. New York: Macmillan, 1973.

———. *Frontiersmen in Blue: The United States Army and the Indian, 1848–1865*. New York: Macmillan, 1967.

———. *The Indian Frontier of the American West, 1846–1890*. Albuquerque: University of New Mexico Press, 1984.

———. *The Last Days of the Sioux Nation*. New Haven, Conn.: Yale University Press, 1963.

Van Horne, Thomas B. *History of the Army of the Cumberland*. 2 vols. 1875; Wilmington, N.C.: Broadfoot Publishing Company, 1988.

———. *The Life of Major-General George H. Thomas*. New York: Charles Scribner's Sons, 1882.

Wagner, Arthur L. *Elements of Military Science*. Kansas City, Mo.: Hudson-Kimberley Publishing Company, 1898.

Waldman, Carl. *Atlas of the North American Indian*. New York: Facts on File Publications, 1985.

Ware, E. F. *The Lyon Campaign in Missouri: Being a History of the First Iowa Infantry*. Topeka, Kans.: Crane and Company, 1907.

Weigley, Russell F. *The American Way of War: A History of United States Military Strategy and Policy*. New York: Macmillan, 1973.

———. *A Great Civil War: A Military and Political History, 1861–1865*. Bloomington: Indiana University Press, 2000.

———. *History of the United States Army*. New York: Macmillan, 1967.

———. *Towards an American Army: Military Thought from Washington to Marshall*. New York: Columbia University Press, 1962.

Welcher, Frank J. *The Union Army, 1861–1865: Organization and Operations*. Vol. 1: *The Eastern Theater*. Bloomington: Indiana University Press, 1989.

———. *The Union Army, 1861–1865: Organization and Operations*. Vol. 2: *The Western Theater*. Bloomington: Indiana University Press, 1993.

Welsh, Jack D. *Medical Histories of Union Generals*. Kent, Ohio: Kent State University Press, 1996.

White, Leonard D. *The Republican Era: A Study in Administrative History, 1869–1901*. New York: Free Press, 1958.

Wiebe, Robert H. *The Search for Order, 1877–1920*. New York: Hill and Wang, 1967.

Williams, Charles Richard. *Diary and Letters of Rutherford Birchard Hayes, Nineteenth President of the United States*. Vol. 3: *1865–1881*. New York: Kraus Reprint Company, 1971.

Williams, R. Hal. *Years of Decision: American Politics in the 1890s*. New York: John Wiley and Sons, 1978.

Williams, T. Harry. *Lincoln and His Generals*. New York: Alfred A. Knopf, 1952.

Wilson, Frederick T. (Adjutant General's Office). *Federal Aid in Domestic Disturbances, 1787–1903*. New York: Arno Press, 1969.

Wood, W. J. *Civil War Generalship: The Art of Command*. Westport, Conn.: Praeger, 1997.

Wooster, Robert. *The Military and United States Indian Policy, 1865–1903*. Lincoln: University of Nebraska Press, 1988.

——. *Nelson A. Miles and the Twilight of the Frontier Army*. Lincoln: University of Nebraska Press, 1993.

Young, Kenneth. *The General's General: The Life and Times of Arthur MacArthur*. San Francisco, Calif.: Westview Press, 1994.

Articles

Ahern, Wilbert H. "The Cox Plan of Reconstruction: A Case Study in Ideology and Race Relations." *Civil War History* 16 (December 1970): 293–308.

Allen, Henry T. "The Organization of a Staff Best Adapted for the United States Army." *Journal of the Military Service Institution* 28 (March 1901): 169–83.

Berlin, Ira. "Who Freed the Slaves? Emancipation and Its Meaning." In *Union and Emancipation: Essays on Politics and Race in the Civil War Era*, edited by David W. Blight and Brooks D. Simpson, 105–21. Kent, Ohio: Kent State University Press, 1997.

Betros, Lance A. "Political Partisanship and the Professional Military Ethic: The Case of the Officer Corps' Affiliation with the Republican Party." National War College Paper, May 4, 2000.

Boman, Dennis K., ed. "Campaigning through Missouri: The Civil War Journal of Robert Todd McMahan: Part 1." *Missouri Historical Review* 93, no. 2 (1999): 133–48.

Bradbury, John F., Jr. " 'This War Is Managed Mighty Strange': The Army of Southeastern Missouri, 1862–1863." *Missouri Historical Review* 89, no. 1 (1994): 28–47.

Carter, William H. "A General Staff for the Army." *North American Review* 175 (October 1902): 558–65.

——. "Will America Profit by Its Recent Military Lessons?" *North American Review* 174 (May 1902): 658–71.

Castel, Albert. "Order No. 11 and the Civil War on the Border." *Missouri Historical Review* 57 (July 1963): 357–68.

——. "Prevaricating through Georgia: Sherman's Memoirs as a Source on the Atlanta Campaign." *Civil War History* 40, no. 1 (1994): 48–78.

——. "Quantrill's Bushwhackers: A Case Study in Partisan Warfare." *Civil War History* 13 (March 1967): 40–50.

Cheatham, Gary L. " 'Desperate Characters': The Development and Impact of the Confederate Guerrillas in Kansas." *Kansas History* 14 (Autumn 1991): 144–61.

Coffman, Edward M. "The Long Shadow of *The Soldier and the State*." *Journal of Military History* 55 (January 1991): 69–82.

Coppersmith, Clifford P. "Indians in the Army: Professional Advocacy and Regularization of Indian Military Service, 1889–1897." *Military History of the West* 26 (Fall 1996): 159–85.

Cosmas, Graham A. "From Order to Chaos: The War Department, the National Guard, and Military Policy, 1898." *Military Affairs* 29 (Autumn 1965): 105–22.

——. "Military Reform after the Spanish-American War: The Army Reorganization Fight of 1898–1899." *Military Affairs* 35 (February 1971): 12–18.

Crackel, Theodore J. "West Point's Contribution to the Army and to Professionalism, 1877 to 1917." In *West Point: Two Centuries and Beyond*, edited by Lance Betros, 38–56. Abilene, Tex.: McWhiney Foundation Press, 2004.

Crouch, Barry A. "A 'Fiend in Human Shape?' William Clarke Quantrill and His Biographers." *Kansas History* 22, no. 2 (1999): 142–56.

Draper, Arthur G. " 'Dear Sister': Letters from War-Torn Missouri, 1864." *Gateway Heritage* 13, no. 4 (1993): 48–57.

Epstein, Robert M. "The Creation and Evolution of the Army Corps in the American Civil War." *Journal of Military History* 55 (January 1991): 21–46.

Feaver, Eric. "Indian Soldiers, 1891–95: An Experiment on the Closing Frontier." *Prologue: The Journal of the National Archives* 7 (Summer 1975): 108–18.

Fitzpatrick, David J. "Emory Upton and the Citizen Soldier." *Journal of Military History* 65 (April 2001): 355–90.

Gates, John M. "The Alleged Isolation of US Army Officers in the Late 19th Century." *Parameters* 10 (September 1980): 32–45.

——. "The 'New' Military Professionalism." *Armed Forces and Society* 11 (Spring 1985): 425–36.

Garfield, James A. "The Army of the United States." *North American Review* 126 (March–April 1878): 193–216, (May–June 1878): 442–66.

Gerteis, Louis S. " 'A Friend of the Enemy': Federal Efforts to Suppress Disloyalty in St. Louis during the Civil War." *Missouri Historical Review* 96 (April 2002): 165–87.

——. " 'An Outrage on Humanity': Martial Law and Military Prisons in St. Louis during the Civil War." *Missouri Historical Review* 96 (July 2002): 302–22.

Gilmore, Donald L. "Total War on the Missouri Border." *Journal of the West* 35 (July 1996): 70–80.

Grandstaff, Mark R. "Preserving the 'Habits and Usages of War': William Tecumseh Sherman, Professional Reform, and the U.S. Army Officer Corps, 1865–1881, Revisited." *Journal of Military History* 62 (July 1998): 521–45.

Grant, U. S. "An Undeserved Stigma." *North American Review* 135 (December 1882): 536–47.

Greene, F. V. "Our New Army." *Scribner's*, November 1901, 286–311.

Greene, Jerome A. "George Crook." In *Soldiers West: Biographies from the Military Frontier*, edited by Paul Andrew Hutton, 115–36. Lincoln: University of Nebraska Press, 1987.

Hacker, Barton C. "The United States Army as a National Police Force: The Federal Policing of Labor Disputes, 1877–1898." *Military Affairs* 33 (April 1969): 255–64.

Hains, Peter C. "Should the Fixed Coast Defenses of the United States Be Transferred to the Navy?" *Journal of the Military Service Institution* 15 (March 1894): 233–56.

Hammond, Matthew Carlton. "The Posse Comitatus Act: A Principle in Need of Renewal." *Washington University Law Quarterly* 75 (Summer 1997): 953–84.

Hatcher, Richard W., III, and William Garrett Piston, eds. "Kansans Go to War: The Wilson's Creek Campaign as Reported by the *Leavenworth Daily Times*." *Kansas History* 16, no. 3 (1993): 180–99, and *Kansas History* 16, no. 4 (1993): 224–47.

Hatley, Paul B., and Noor Ampssler. "Army General Orders Number 11: Final Valid Option or Wanton Act of Brutality? The Missouri Question in the American Civil War." *Journal of the West* 33, no. 3 (1994): 77–87.

Haydock, Michael D. "The Court-Martial of Fitz John Porter." *American History* 33 (February 1999): 48–57.

Hooker, Richard D., Jr. "Soldiers of the State: Reconsidering American Civil-Military Relations." *Parameters* 33 (Winter 2003–4): 4–18.

Howard, Michael. "Men against Fire: The Doctrine of the Offensive in 1914." In *Makers of Modern Strategy: From Machiavelli to the Nuclear Age*, edited by Peter Paret, 510–26. Princeton, N.J.: Princeton University Press, 1986.

Howard, O. O. "Comment and Criticism." *Journal of the Military Service Institution* 12 (September 1891): 1013–14.

Hunt, R. H. "General Orders No. 11." 15th Kansas Cavalry, Kansas Commandery, Military Order of the Loyal Legion of the United States, February 1908, 6–12, Box 212, Thomas Ewing Papers, Library of Congress, Washington, D.C.

Hyman, Harold M. "Johnson, Stanton, and Grant: A Reconsideration of the Army's Role in the Events Leading to Impeachment." *American Historical Review* 66 (October 1960): 85–100.

——. "Reconstruction and Political-Constitutional Institutions: The Popular Expression." In *New Frontiers of the American Reconstruction*, edited by Harold M. Hyman, 1–39. Chicago: University of Illinois Press, 1966.

James, Joseph B. "Life at West Point One Hundred Years Ago." *Mississippi Valley Historical Review* 31 (June 1944): 21–40.

Karsten, Peter. "Armed Progressives: The Military Reorganizes for the American Century." In *The Military in America: From the Colonial Era to the Present*, edited by Peter Karsten, 239–74. New York: Free Press, 1986.

——. "Militarization and Rationalization in the United States, 1870–1914." In *The Militarization of the Western World*, edited by John R. Gillis, 30–44. New Brunswick, N.J.: Rutgers University Press, 1989.

Kelly, Alfred. "Comment on Harold M. Hyman's Paper." In *New Frontiers of the American Reconstruction*, edited by Harold M. Hyman, 40–58. Chicago: University of Illinois Press, 1966.

Kohn, Richard H. "Civil-Military Relations Debated." *National Interest* 36 (Summer 1994): 23–31.

——. "Out of Control: The Crisis in Civil-Military Relations." *National Interest* 35 (Spring 1994): 3–17.

Langdon, Russell C. "The Organization of a Staff Best Adapted for the United States Army." *Journal of the Military Service Institution* 28 (March 1901): 208–20.

Lause, Mark. "A Brief History of the Enrolled Missouri Militia: Forgotten Citizen-Soldiers of the Civil War." <http://www.geocities.com/CollegePark/Quad/6460/CW/EMM/EMMhist.html> (accessed June 2005).

Lee, J. G. C. "Centralization and Decentralization in Military Affairs." *Journal of the Military Service Institution* 12 (July 1891): 744–54.

Lewis, Lloyd. "Propaganda and the Kansas-Missouri War." *Missouri Historical Review* 92, no. 2 (1998): 135–48.

Maddex, Jack P., Jr. "Virginia: The Persistence of Centrist Hegemony." In *Reconstruction and Redemption in the South*, edited by Otto H. Olsen, 113–55. Baton Rouge: Louisiana State University Press, 1980.

"Maj. Gen. Henry W. Lawton, USA." *On Point: Newsletter of the Army Historical Foundation* 8 (Spring 2002): 13.

Mallon, John P. "Roosevelt, Brooks Adams, and Lea: The Warrior Critique of the Business Civilization." *American Quarterly* 8 (Fall 1956): 216–30.

Marszalek, John F. "Sherman Called It the Way He Saw It." *Civil War History* 40, no. 1 (1994): 48–78.

Matthews, Matt, and Kip Lindberg. " 'Better Off in Hell': The Evolution of the Kansas Red Legs." *North and South* 5, no. 4 (2002): 20–31.

McPherson, James M. "From Limited to Total War: Missouri and the Nation, 1861–1865." *Gateway Heritage* 16, no. 2 (1995): 4–17.

Michie, Peter S. "The Personnel of Sea-Coast Defense." *Journal of the Military Service Institution* 8 (March 1887): 1–17.

"A Military Missionary in Virginia." *De Bow's Review* 5 (June 1868): 542–51.

Miller, Robert Ryal. "Arms across the Border: United States Aid to Juarez during the French Intervention in Mexico." *Transcript of American Philological Society* 63, no. 6 (1973): 13–16.

Mink, Charles R. "General Orders, No. 11: The Forced Evacuation of Civilians during the Civil War." *Military Affairs* 34 (December 1970): 132–37.

Neely, Mark E. "Lincoln and the Theory of Self-Emancipation." In *The Continuing Civil War: Essays in Honor of the Civil War Round Table of Chicago*, edited by John Y. Simon and Barbara Hughett. Dayton, Ohio: Morningside Press, 1992.

———. " 'Unbeknownst' to Lincoln: A Note on Radical Pacification in Missouri during the Civil War." *Civil War History* 44 (September 1998): 212–16.

Niepman, Ann Davis. "General Orders No. 11 and Border Warfare during the Civil War." *Missouri Historical Review* 66 (January 1972): 185–210.

Nye, Russell B. "Comment on C. Vann Woodward's Paper." In *New Frontiers of the American Reconstruction*, edited by Harold M. Hyman, 148–56. Chicago: University of Illinois Press, 1966.

Page, Dave. "A Fight for Missouri." *Civil War Times Illustrated* 34, no. 3 (1995): 34–38.

Palmer, Henry E. "The Lawrence Raid." In *Civil War Sketches and Incidents: Papers Read by Companions of the Commandery of the State of Nebraska*, edited by Military Order of the Loyal Legion of the United States. Wilmington, N.C.: Broadfoot, 1992.

Patrick, Jeffrey L., ed. " 'This Regiment Will Make a Mark': Letters from a Member of Jennison's Jayhawkers, 1861–1862." *Kansas History* 20, no. 1 (1997): 50–58.

Ranson, Edward. "The Endicott Board of 1885–86 and Coastal Defenses." *Military Affairs* 31 (Summer 1967): 74–84.

———. "Nelson A. Miles as Commanding General, 1895–1903." *Military Affairs* 29 (Winter 1965–66): 179–200.

Rappaport, Armin. "The Replacement System during the Civil War." In *Military Analysis of the Civil War: An Anthology by the Editors of Military Affairs*, 115–26. Millwood, N.Y.: KTO Press, 1977.

Roberts, William R. "Reform and Revitalization, 1890–1903." In *Against All Enemies: Interpretations of American Military History from Colonial Times to the Present*, edited by Kenneth J. Hagan and William R. Roberts, 197–218. New York: Greenwood Press, 1986.

Romero, Matias. "The Fall of the Second Empire." *Century Magazine* 54 (May 1897): 138–39.

Sanger, Joseph P. "The Artillery Council of 1887." *Journal of the United States Artillery* 49, no. 4 (1918): 233–63.

Scherer, Louis C. "The Organization of a Staff Best Adapted for the United States Army." *Journal of the Military Service Institution* 28 (March 1901): 184–207.

Schofield, John M. "Controversies in the War Department: Unpublished Facts Relating to the Impeachment of President Johnson." *Century Magazine* 54 (August 1897): 576–83.

——. "Inaugural Address." *Journal of the Military Service Institution* 1, no. 1 (1880): 1–19.

——. "Notes on the 'Legitimate in Warfare.'" *Journal of the Military Service Institution* 2, no. 1 (1881): 1–10.

——. "Report and Observations upon the Maneuvres [*sic*] of the French Army and the Military Systems of France and Other Nations of Europe." *Journal of the Military Service Institution* 3, no. 10 (1882): 151–59.

——. "The Withdrawal of the French from Mexico." *Century Magazine* 54 (May 1897): 128–37.

Sears, Stephen W. "The Court-Martial of Fitz John Porter." In *Controversies and Commanders: Dispatches of the Army of the Potomac*, edited by Stephen W. Sears, 51–73. Boston: Houghton Mifflin, 1999.

Sefton, James E., ed. "Aristotle in Blue and Braid: General John M. Schofield's Essays on Reconstruction." *Civil War History* 17 (March 1971): 45–57.

Semsch, Philip L. "Elihu Root and the General Staff." *Military Affairs* 27 (Spring 1963): 22–26.

SenGupta, Gunja. "Bleeding Kansas." *Kansas History* 24, no. 4 (2001–2): 318–41.

Sherman, William T. "Military Law." *Journal of the Military Service Institution* 1, no. 2 (1880): 129–32; no. 3 (1880): 320–25; no. 4 (1880): 385–90.

Skelton, William B. "The Commanding General and the Problem of Command in the United States Army, 1821–1841." *Military Affairs* 34 (December 1970): 117–22.

——. "Samuel P. Huntington and the Roots of the American Military Tradition." *Journal of Military History* 60 (April 1996): 325–38.

Smith, Joseph. "The 'Splendid Little War' of 1898: A Reappraisal." *History: The Journal of the Historical Association* 80 (February 1995): 22–37.

Spector, Ronald. "The Triumph of Professional Ideology: The U.S. Navy in the 1890s." In *In Peace and War: Interpretations of American Naval History, 1775–1984*, edited by Kenneth J. Hagan, 174–85. Westport, Conn.: Greenwood Press, 1984.

Stephenson, Philip Dangerfield. "'Like Sheep in a Slaughter Pen': A St. Louisan Remembers the Camp Jackson Massacre, May 10, 1861," edited by William C. Winter. *Gateway Heritage* 15, no. 4 (1995): 56–71.

Sutherland, Daniel E. "Sideshow No Longer: A Historiographical Review of the Guerrilla War." *Civil War History* 46, no. 1 (2000): 5–23.

Tap, Bruce. "'Union Men to the Polls, and Rebels to Their Holes': The Contested Election between John P. Bruce and Benjamin F. Loan, 1862." *Civil War History* 46, no. 1 (2000): 24–40.

Tate, Michael L. "Soldiers of the Line: Apache Companies in the U.S. Army, 1891–1897." *Arizona and the West* 16 (Winter 1974): 343–64.

Villard, Oswald Garrison. "The Army of the United States." *Atlantic Monthly*, April 1902, 437–51.

Weigley, Russell F. "The American Civil-Military Cultural Gap: A Historical Perspective, Colonial Times to the Present." In *Soldiers and Civilians: The Civil-Military Gap and American National Security*, edited by Peter D. Feaver and Richard H. Kohn, 215–46. Cambridge, Mass.: MIT Press, 2001.

——. "The American Military and the Principle of Civilian Control from McClellan to Powell." *Journal of Military History* 57 (October 1993): 27–58.

——. "The Elihu Root Reforms and the Progressive Era." In *Command and Commanders in Modern Warfare*, edited by William Geffen, 11–38. Colorado Springs, Colo.: United States Air Force Academy, 1969.

——. "The Military Thought of John M. Schofield." *Military Affairs* 23 (Summer 1959): 77–84.

Whepley, J. D. "The Militia Force of the United States." *North American Review* 74 (February 1902): 275–80.

Wherry, William M. "Wilson's Creek and the Death of Lyon." In *Battles and Leaders of the Civil War*, 1:289–97. Edison, N.J.: Castle, [1887].

White, W. Bruce. "The American Indian as Soldier, 1890–1919." *Canadian Review of American Studies* 7 (Spring 1976): 15–25.

Wolseley, Garnet. "England as a Military Power in 1854 and in 1878." *Nineteenth Century* (March 1878), reprinted in *Army and Navy Journal*, March 23, 1878, 525–27.

Woodward, C. Vann. "Seeds of Failure in Radical Race Policy." In *New Frontiers of the American Reconstruction*, edited by Harold M. Hyman, 125–47. Chicago: University of Illinois Press, 1966.

Dissertations and Theses

Alderson, William T. "The Influence of Military Rule and the Freedmen's Bureau on Reconstruction in Virginia, 1865–1870." Ph.D. diss., Vanderbilt University, 1952.

Andrews, Richard A. "Years of Frustration: William T. Sherman, the Army, and Reform, 1869–1883." Ph.D. diss., Northwestern University, 1968.

Beckenbaugh, Terry Lee. "The War of Politics: Samuel Ryan Curtis, Race, and the Political/Military Establishment." Ph.D. diss., University of Arkansas, 2001.

Bowie, Chester Winston. "Redfield Proctor: A Biography." Ph.D. diss., University of Wisconsin–Madison, 1980.

Cantor, Louis. "The Creation of the Modern National Guard: The Dick Militia Act of 1903." Ph.D. diss., Duke University, 1963.

Connelly, Donald B. "Political Soldier: John M. Schofield and the Politics of Generalship." Ph.D. diss., University of Houston, 2003.

Dillard, Walter Scott. "The United States Military Academy, 1865–1900: The Uncertain Years." Ph.D. diss., University of Washington, 1972.

Fitzpatrick, David John. "Emory Upton: The Misunderstood Reformer." Ph.D. diss., University of Michigan, 1996.

Gabler, Henry. "The Fitz John Porter Case: Politics and Military Justice." Ph.D. diss., City University of New York, 1979.

Glatthaar, Joseph T. "Hood's Tennessee Campaign." M.A. thesis, Rice University, 1980.

Kirkland, John R. "Federal Troops in the South Atlantic States during Reconstruction, 1865–1877." Ph.D. diss., University of North Carolina at Chapel Hill, 1967.

Martin, James. "The Third War: Irregular Warfare on the Western Border, 1861–1865." Ph.D. diss., University of Texas at Austin, 1997.

Mixon, Robert W. "Pioneer Professional: John M. Schofield and the Development of a Professional Officer Corps, 1888–1895." M.A. thesis, Rice University, 1982.

Raines, Edgar Frank, Jr. "Major General J. Franklin Bell and Military Reform: The Chief of Staff Years, 1906–1910." Ph.D. diss., University of Wisconsin–Madison, 1976.

Roberts, William R. "Loyalty and Expertise: The Transformation of the Nineteenth-Century American General Staff and the Creation of the Modern Military Establishment." Ph.D. diss., Johns Hopkins University, 1980.

Skirbunt, Peter D. "Prologue to Reform: The 'Germanization' of the United States Army, 1865–1898." Ph.D. diss., Ohio State University, 1983.

Sude, Barry. "Federal Military Policy and Strategy in Missouri and Arkansas, 1861–1863: A Study in Command Level Conflict." Ph.D. diss., Temple University, 1986.

Swails, Thomas Walter. "John McAllister Schofield: Military Diplomat." M.A. thesis, University of Hawaii, 1966.

Thomas, Donna Marie Eleanor. "Army Reform in America: The Crucial Years, 1876–1881." Ph.D. diss., University of Florida, 1980.

Ulrich, William J. "The Northern Military Mind in Regard to Reconstruction, 1865–1872: The Attitudes of Ten Leading Union Generals." Ph.D. diss., Ohio State University, 1959.

Watson, Samuel J. "Professionalism, Social Attitudes, and Civil-Military Accountability in the United States Army Officer Corps, 1815–1846." Ph.D. diss., Rice University, 1996.

Zais, Barrie E. "The Struggle for a 20th-Century Army: Investigation and Reform of the United States Army after the Spanish-American War." Ph.D. diss., Duke University, 1981.

INDEX

General Staff Bill of 1903, 10, 333–34

Georgia, 209–10, 212. *See also* Atlanta campaign

Geronimo, 271–72

Getty, George W., 249, 252, 399 (n. 2)

Ghost Dancers, 271, 272, 276–77

Gibson, Charles, 22, 64, 351 (n. 26)

Gillem, Alvan, 113

Glatthaar, Joseph, 368 (n. 52), 376 (n. 49)

Glover, Samuel T., 353 (n. 56)

Grand Army of the Republic, 320, 321

Granger, Gordon, 34

Granger, Robert S., 125

Grant, Ulysses S.: Schofield compared to, 1; and civil-military relations, 8; Schofield's relationship with, 10, 68, 83, 84, 85, 86, 99, 147, 148, 153, 155, 159–60, 177, 178, 180, 207, 338, 360 (n. 18), 380 (n. 20); and Missouri State Militia, 27; and Confederate defensive line, 46; and Vicksburg, 60, 64, 68, 73, 161; Schofield transfers troops to, 68, 74, 79, 80; promotion of, 85, 87, 90, 312; and Halleck, 85, 141, 148; instructions to Schofield, 86; Sherman compared to, 89; and delays in battle, 95; second chances of, 96; and Virginia campaign, 112; and election of 1868, 117, 208–9, 211, 212; and Burbridge, 118; and Stoneman, 118, 140, 373 (n. 16); and raiding strategy, 119–20, 155, 161, 379 (n. 90); and Hood, 120; and Cold Harbor, 137; and Thomas, 141–42, 149, 150, 151, 152, 153, 154, 374 (n. 25), 378 (n. 80), 380 (n. 11); and Franklin-Nashville campaign controversy, 149–50, 152–54; and North Carolina campaign, 156; and Sherman's Carolinas campaign, 158; and Lee's surrender, 160, 165; and Sherman's March to the Sea, 162; and Sherman's terms with Johnston, 165; and Reconstruction policy, 179, 207; and Johnson, 181, 186–87, 191, 204, 205, 206, 207, 208, 212, 213, 388 (n. 2); and Schofield's advocacy of military governors, 181–82; and Mexico, 182, 183, 184, 186, 384 (n. 30); and Schofield's foreign affairs mission, 182, 186; and local militia companies, 189; and

Schofield as military district commander, 196, 197, 201, 202; and corruption, 199, 289 (n. 14); as secretary of war, 204; and Schofield as secretary of war, 206, 207, 209, 214; as president, 212, 214–17; and army reform, 214–15; peace policy of, 220; and Indian reservations, 220–22; and election of 1876, 225; and Sherman's promotion, 241; and Porter case, 252, 256, 402 (n. 31); as commanding general, 279; death of, 300; and promotions, 311–12, 418 (n. 35); and hard versus soft war, 355 (n. 24); strategy of, 371 (n. 82)

Gray, John, 354 (n. 10)

Great Britain, 295

Great Sioux Reservation, 272, 275

Great Railroad Strike of 1877, 9, 229, 236–37, 279–81, 289

Greeley, Horace, 199

Green, John, 221

Green, Oliver D., 17

Grierson, Benjamin, 161, 276

Grimsley, Mark, 356 (n. 38)

Guerrillas and guerrilla warfare: and politics in military affairs, 9, 41, 45–46, 55, 74–77, 79–80; in Missouri, 40, 49, 53, 77–78, 209, 337; and Missouri State Militia, 42; and Halleck, 43–44, 45, 82; Confederate army differentiated from, 44; and hard versus soft war, 46, 355 (n. 24); in Tennessee, 117, 122, 123; in Kentucky, 117–18, 119, 123, 372–73 (n. 13); and fear of prolonged conflict, 164; and antiguerrilla units, 373 (n. 17)

Guzman, Pierre, 384 (n. 27)

Hagner, Peter V., 350 (n. 8)

Hall, Willard P., 75

Halleck, Henry W.: as lawyer, 20; and Department of the Missouri, 38, 40; as military administrator, 39; Fremont compared to, 41; relationship with Schofield, 41–42, 46, 47, 48, 49, 50–51, 53–55, 57, 60–61, 68–69, 73, 77, 80, 82, 83, 86, 147, 153, 154, 337, 356 (n. 28), 358 (nn. 68, 80); and mixing volunteer and militia units, 43, 355 (n. 12); and legal implications of guerrilla warfare and civil war, 43–44, 45, 82; and Mississippi, 46; and reconciliation with guerrillas, 46; expansion of command, 47; and Kansas, 48; and Enrolled Missouri Militia, 53, 64; and Blair, 54, 58, 357 (n. 55); and politics in military affairs, 57, 78, 360 (n. 17); strategic priorities of, 60, 64–65, 68, 160–61, 382 (n. 43); and Grant, 85, 141, 148; and Sherman, 110, 111, 165, 366 (n. 31), 369 (n. 66); and slavery, 116; and Thomas, 149; and Sherman's terms with Johnston, 165; as commanding general, 279

Hammond, John, 126, 128, 132, 375 (n. 37)

Hammond, Paul, 345 (n. 16)

Hancock, David P., 17

Hancock, Winfield Scott: and civil-military relations, 10, 187; and Reconstruction policy, 187; as military district commander, 195, 204; and Johnson, 213; and election of 1876, 225–26, 393–94 (n. 27); and George Schofield, 257; and election of 1880, 266, 405 (n. 65); and labor relations, 280–81, 285, 289; death of, 311; and U.S. Military Service Institution, 318

Hanna, J. Marshall, 200–201, 208

Hardee, William, 106, 109, 110–11, 368 (n. 52), 370 (n. 78)

Harding, Edward, 52

Hard war versus soft war, 40, 46, 50, 70, 250, 354 (n. 1), 355 (n. 24)

Harker, Charles G., 96

Harney, William S., 24, 25–26, 27, 28, 29, 32, 38, 350 (nn. 3, 8)

Harris, Ira, 81

Harrison, Benjamin, 272, 300, 311–12, 326, 418 (n. 35)

Harrison, William Henry, 198

Hart, Basil Liddell, 113

Hart, Jim A., 359 (n. 14)

Hartranft, John F., 281

Hartsuff, George L., 20

Hascall, Milo S., 96, 98, 99, 100, 103, 115, 116, 122, 367 (nn. 36, 42)

Hatch, Edward, 122, 123

Hatch, Nathan O., 2

Hatcher, Richard W., III, 351 (n. 17)

Hattaway, Herman, 371 (n. 82)

Havens, Benny, 15

Hawaiian Islands, 223–24, 326–27, 338, 422 (n. 9)

Hawley, Joseph, 332, 333

Hayes, Rutherford B.: Schofield's relationship with, 226, 265, 266, 268; and Army Appropriation Bill, 236; and use of federal troops, 238; and Porter case, 249, 255–56; and Whittaker case, 261–63; and Division of the Gulf, 269; and Great Railroad Strike of 1877, 280, 281; and federal court order enforcement, 284; and promotions, 311–12, 418 (n. 35)

Haymarket bombing, 280

Henderson, John Brooks, 65, 81, 86

Herron, Francis, 58, 59, 60, 61, 66–67, 68, 79

Hewitt, Abram S., 238

Hill, Ambrose Powell, 19, 20–21

Hindman, Thomas, 59, 100

Hinds, James, 210

Hoke, Robert, 155, 156, 158

Holden, William W., 182, 383 (n. 15)

Holloway, Ezekiel, 18

Holt, John, 361 (n. 37)

Holt, Joseph, 251

Home Guard, 24, 25–28, 45

Hood, John Bell: and military education, 14, 15, 19, 348 (nn. 32, 34); and Atlanta campaign, 94, 97, 99, 100, 104–14 passim, 368 (n. 52), 369 (n. 71), 370 (n. 76); and recriminations, 95, 130, 375 (n. 45); and casualties, 112, 370–71 (n. 81); as threat, 113, 148; and Franklin-Nashville campaign, 114, 122–46 passim, 154, 336, 375 (nn. 44, 45), 376 (n. 49), 376–77 (n. 61), 377 (n. 63), 378 (n. 77); and promotions, 115; and Sherman, 119, 120, 123, 162, 373 (n. 15); and Grant, 120; and Thomas, 120, 122; troops of, 122, 374 (n. 24)

Hooker, Joseph: and corps organizations, 89, 90, 91, 365 (n. 22); and Atlanta campaign, 89, 94, 97, 98, 99–100, 101, 365 (n. 20), 367 (nn. 41, 42), 368 (n. 52); and seniority, 91, 101, 110; and Sherman, 100–101, 107, 369 (n. 66), 370 (n. 77); and Couch, 140

Martial law: in St. Louis, 26, 37, 43, 79; during Civil War, 26, 37, 43–44, 50, 53, 79; in Missouri, 37, 43–44, 50, 53; during Reconstruction, 187, 190

Maximilian (archduke of Austria), 182, 185–86

Mayo, Joseph, 197

McArthur, John A., 144, 145

McBride, John, 71

McClellan, George B.: and civil-military relations, 8; and Sturgis, 34; and Halleck, 45; and confiscation laws, 50; and William Smith, 84; and corps organization, 90; and Lincoln, 141; strategy of, 160, 161, 250; and Porter case, 250, 251; as commanding general, 279; relationship with Lincoln, 345 (n. 15)

McClernard, John A., 60, 90, 365 (n. 20)

McCook, Alexander, 327

McCook, Edward M., 97, 108–9

McCrary, George, 226

McCulloch, Ben, 30, 33, 34, 35

McDearmon, John K., 52

McDonough, James, 153, 370 (n. 76), 380 (n. 20)

McDowell, Irwin, 152, 250–51, 253–56, 266, 267, 269, 402 (n. 23)

McElroy, John, 344 (n. 3)

McKee, William, 67, 328, 359 (n. 14)

McKinley, William, 326, 328–29, 332

McMurry, Richard M., 371 (nn. 81, 82)

McNeil, John, 58, 80

McPheeters, Samuel B., 64

McPherson, James, 50

McPherson, James B.: and military education, 14, 15, 18, 19, 348 (nn. 32, 34); promotion to brigadier general, 22; and Grant, 85; and Department of the Tennessee, 88, 89; and seniority, 91, 101; and Atlanta campaign, 92–106 passim, 366 (nn. 28, 31), 367 (n. 33); and Sherman, 92, 368 (n. 45); death of, 106–7

McReynolds, W. C., 124, 374 (n. 29)

Meade, George G., 90, 149, 195, 204, 210, 214

Mercur, James, 415 (n. 9)

Merrill, Lewis, 49

Merritt, Wesley, 276, 306, 333

Mexican army, 183

Mexican War, 24, 32, 33, 41

Mexico, 182–86, 383 (n. 16)

Michie, Peter S., 228, 261, 293

Miles, Nelson: as successor to Schofield, 1; and infantry tactics, 102, 368 (n. 55); and Indian affairs, 272–73, 274, 276, 406 (nn. 9, 10, 11); and domestic disorder, 286–87, 288, 410 (n. 53); and promotions, 311, 313, 419 (n. 40); and Alger, 327, 328, 329; and Spanish-American War, 330, 331, 423 (n. 21); disagreements with Schofield, 331, 334, 423 (n. 25); and Roosevelt, 333

Military Affairs Committee, 215, 218, 235, 237, 331, 333

Military career of Schofield: as U.S. commanding general, 1, 270, 276–77, 285, 294–313 passim, 321, 325, 409 (n. 50); and relationship with Grant, 10, 68, 83, 84, 85, 86, 99, 147, 148, 152, 153, 155, 159, 177, 178, 180, 207, 338, 360 (n. 18), 380 (n. 20); and relationship with Thomas, 17, 18, 61, 148–51, 153, 154, 379 (nn. 3, 4), 380 (n. 19); and artillery, 19–20, 294–95, 412 (n. 81); as U.S. Military Academy instructor, 20, 21; and promotions, 22, 29, 30, 42, 60, 81–82, 84–85, 86, 159, 214, 313, 362 (n. 45), 363 (nn. 68, 69), 379 (n. 4), 381 (n. 36), 418–19 (n. 39); and military leave of absence, 22, 86; and muster of Missouri volunteers, 23, 25, 26, 29, 30, 351 (n. 17); and Missouri State Militia, 27, 42–43, 45, 46, 47, 51–53; and battle of Wilson's Creek, 32, 33, 34, 35, 353–54 (n. 63); poise during battle, 35, 39; and Medal of Honor, 35, 352 (n. 52); and cautious, methodical nature, 36; and politics in military affairs, 39; and guerrilla and emancipation policies, 41; and relationship with Halleck, 41–42, 46–61 passim, 68–69, 73, 80, 82, 83, 86, 148, 153, 154, 337, 356 (n. 28), 358 (nn. 68, 80); and guerrilla warfare, 45–46, 47, 49–51, 53, 60, 74–77, 79–80, 82, 209, 337, 362 (n. 48); and St. Louis district, 47; and military administration, 47, 69, 83, 84, 86–87, 89, 303–4, 415 (n. 9); and Department of the Missouri, 47–49,

Politics in military affairs: and military professionalism, 1–2, 3, 5–6, 10, 11, 344 (n. 7); primacy of, 2; and Schofield's example of military authority, 6; and military promotion, 6, 29, 59–60, 84–85, 86, 90, 115, 116, 358 (n. 75); pervasiveness of, 8–9, 11; and guerrilla warfare, 9, 41, 45–46, 55, 74–77, 79–80; and Great Railroad Strike of 1877, 9, 236–37, 279–80; and officer corps, 11, 396 (n. 66); and federal service regiments of state volunteers, 25–26, 64; and Fremont, 37–38, 353 (n. 56); and state and federal interests, 40; and emancipation, 41; and Missouri State Militia, 42–43, 45–46; and Department of the Mississippi, 55; and Halleck, 57, 77, 360 (n. 17); and Enrolled Missouri Militia, 64; and Department of the Missouri, 65–66, 83; and leaves of absences, 69, 360 (n. 22); and appointments to command, 90; and corps organization, 90; and military organization, 90, 340; and seniority, 90–91, 115; and Sherman's terms with Johnston, 164–66, 177, 382 (nn. 54, 55); and Reconstruction policy, 178, 213; and military district commanders, 195; and army reform, 219, 244; and army appropriations, 226, 236, 237–38, 239; and U.S. Military Academy, 226–27, 229, 247; and commanding generals, 279

Polk, Leonidas, 94, 97

Pollard, Edward A., 200

Pope, Douglas, 253

Pope, John: and Schofield, 1, 256–57; and Reconstruction policy, 10, 187; and Fremont, 38; and confiscation laws, 50, 356 (n. 38); as military district commander, 194, 195, 204; and army reform, 243; and Porter, 250, 251, 253, 254, 255, 400 (n. 6), 401 (n. 11); promotion of, 256; and U.S. Military Academy, 264; and Great Railroad Strike of 1877, 281

Porter, David D., 155, 224, 391 (n. 46)

Porter, Fitz John: and Schofield's court-martial, 17, 18; and muster of Missouri volunteers, 26, 351 (n. 17); and Second Bull Run, 250, 251, 255, 400 (nn. 4, 5); charges against, 250, 400 (n. 6); and Lincoln, 251, 252, 401 (n. 14); evidence against, 251, 401 (n. 9); testimony concerning, 253–54; decision on case, 254–55

Porter, Horace, 153

Porter, Joseph C., 355 (n. 23)

Posse Comitatus Act of 1878, 238–39, 281, 287, 397 (n. 71)

Posse comitatus provision, 238, 396 (n. 68)

Post, P. Sidney, 127, 128, 131

Potter, E. E., 87

Powell, Colin, 345 (n. 15)

Pratt, Richard, 276

Prentiss, Benjamin N., 42

Price, Sterling: as secessionist, 23, 24; meeting with Blair and Lyon, 28; and McCulloch's forces, 30; and battle of Wilson's Creek, 32, 33, 34, 35; and Gamble, 46; and guerrilla warfare, 49; and Missouri raid, 119; polarizing influence of, 350 (n. 3); and Ewing, 360 (n. 26); and Rollins, 363 (n. 58)

Proctor, Redfield: and Indian affairs, 272, 273–74, 275, 277, 278, 279; Civil War service of, 304, 415 (n. 13); and Schofield as commanding general, 305, 314–16, 322, 414 (n. 5), 415 (n. 13); and promotions, 307, 308, 417 (n. 29); and officer retirement system, 310–11; and Schofield's death, 336

Professions: and egalitarianism, 2; definition of, 2, 344 (n. 5); autonomy of, 4–5. *See also* Military professionalism

Progressivism, 7, 290, 301, 304, 316, 321, 328, 338–39, 414 (n. 1)

Prussia, 185

Public opinion: and civil-military relations, 7, 345 (n. 16), 353 (n. 56); and emancipation, 71

Puerto Rico, 330

Pullman, George, 284, 288, 324

Pullman Strike of 1894, 283–88, 410 (n. 60)

Quantrill, William, 74–75, 77, 79, 80, 119, 361 (nn. 37, 38)

Rable, George, 390 (n. 36)

Race relations: and African American suffrage, 178–79, 198–99; and Richmond, 188; and election of 1868, 211; and Whittaker case, 263–64, 268; and Schofield, 268, 405 (n. 72)

Randon, Marchal, 185

Ransom, Edward, 423 (n. 21)

Rawlins, John A., 209, 214, 215, 216, 218, 391 (n. 46)

Reconstruction: and army of occupation, 9, 187, 194, 338; and civil-military relations, 9, 187, 196, 213–14, 337, 384 (n. 33), 390 (n. 36); and Schofield's political involvement, 83; policy on, 177–79, 187, 191

Reconstruction Acts, 193–94, 195, 204

Reilly, James, 133, 136

Republicanism: and officer corps, 2–3, 5–6

Republican Party: Schofield's contacts with, 3; and civil-military relations, 9, 10; and Missouri, 23, 24–25; and Fremont, 37; and Missouri State Militia, 42; and politics in military affairs, 59–60; and Sherman's terms with Johnston, 165; and African American suffrage, 178; and Reconstruction policy, 181–82, 187; and political brawls, 189; and Fourteenth Amendment, 192; and military district commanders, 195; and Pierpont, 196; and centrist-conservative majority, 198, 386–87 (n. 72); and test oath provision, 201; and impeachment of Johnson, 205, 206, 207; and election of 1868, 210, 212; and army reform, 237, 238, 306; and Porter case, 249–50, 251, 252, 402 (n. 27); and election of 1880, 266; and Whittaker case, 267; and military defense spending, 291

Revolutionary War, 350 (n. 4)

Ricketts, James, 250

Roberts, William R., 391 (n. 42)

Robinson, W. P., 71–72

Rolla, Missouri, 30, 35, 36, 65

Rollins, James S., 78, 356 (n. 28), 362 (n. 55), 363 (n. 58)

Romero, Matias, 183, 186

Roosevelt, Theodore, 6, 309, 329, 332, 336

Root, Elihu, 4, 10, 290, 307, 323, 332, 333, 335, 336

Root Reforms, 2, 332–33, 424 (n. 29)

Rosencrans, William S., 61–62, 74, 81, 84, 141, 256, 359 (n. 84)

Rousseau, Lovell H., 211, 212, 213, 389–90 (n. 26)

Ruger, Thomas: and Franklin-Nashville campaign, 122, 123, 127, 130–31, 133, 135, 136, 140, 375 (n. 45), 375–76 (n. 46); and North Carolina campaign, 157, 158; and U.S. Military Academy, 224; and Indian affairs, 276

St. Louis, Missouri: arsenal of, 24, 25, 26–27, 350 (n. 8); political factions of, 24–25; martial law in, 26, 37, 43, 79; and assessments, 63; District of St. Louis, 69, 360 (n. 20)

San Carlos Reservation, 271

Sanger, Joseph P., 295, 309, 336, 412 (n. 78)

Schofield, Caroline McAllister, 12

Schofield, Charles B., 13, 259, 270, 307, 403 (n. 42), 416 (n. 22)

Schofield, George W., 8, 13, 87, 184, 257–59, 299, 361 (n. 42)

Schofield, Georgia, 299, 324

Schofield, Georgia Wells Kilbourne, 299, 324

Schofield, Harriet Bartlett, 21, 299, 413–14 (n. 96)

Schofield, Henry Halleck, 41, 349 (n. 42), 354 (n. 4)

Schofield, James, 12, 13

Schofield, James S., 13

Schofield, John McAllister: military education of, 4, 6, 12, 13–19, 347–48 (n. 20), 348 (nn. 22, 34); diversity of friends, 8, 42; and politics in military affairs, 9, 11; as secretary of war, 10, 148–49, 152, 153, 177, 206–16, 223, 252, 262, 338, 388 (n. 10), 388–89 (n. 11), 389 (n. 12); personal and family life of, 12–13; as superintendent of U.S. Military Academy, 15, 152, 224–31, 249, 264–68, 269; and religion, 15–16, 347 (n. 15); and legal studies, 19–20; good fortune of, 20, 22, 30, 114, 131, 132; health of, 20–21, 59, 98, 349 (n. 39), 358 (n. 72), 367 (n. 41); marriage of, 21; Mexican mission of, 182–84; French mission of, 184–86, 384 (n. 27); and impeachment of Johnson, 205, 207,

177; and African American suffrage, 178, 180; and Blair's Mexican expedition, 183; and Reconstruction, 187–88, 202, 203, 207; as military mugwump, 199; and Johnson, 204, 213, 388 (n. 2); promotions of, 214, 312; and army reform, 215, 218, 219, 223–24, 233–34, 238, 240–41, 243, 244, 245, 290, 397–98 (n. 77), 398 (n. 90); and U.S. Army command, 215–16; and Belknap, 218; and postgraduate service schools, 220; and U.S. Military Academy, 224, 227, 231, 248; and election of 1876, 225, 226, 393–94 (n. 27); and Porter case, 252, 256; and Whittaker case, 265, 266, 269, 300, 404 (n. 63); and Division of the Gulf, 269; as commanding general, 279, 302; and labor relations, 281; and Schofield on Tactics Board, 296–97; death of, 300; and Schofield as commanding general, 303; and hard versus soft war, 355 (n. 24); assessment of subordinates, 368 (n. 45); and logical arrangements of war, 384 (n. 27). *See also* Atlanta campaign

Sherman Antitrust Act, 288

Sherwood, Isaac: and Bond, 116, 117, 372 (n. 9); and Woodruff, 116–17; and Judah, 117, 367 (n. 36)

Sickel, H. G., 258

Sickles, Daniel, 194, 195–96, 204, 336, 353 (n. 52)

Sigel, Franz, 30, 32–33, 34, 35, 66

Simpson, Brooks, 205, 388 (n. 2)

Sino-Japanese War, 325

Sitting Bull, 272

XVI Corps, 99, 119

Slave owners: and militia service, 52; and use of army in apprehending runaway slaves, 71

Slaves and slavery: and politics in military affairs, 9; and Crittenden Compromise, 24; and Harney, 24; and Fremont, 37; and Department of the Missouri, 40, 41; and Missouri State Militia, 43; and Blow, 54; and Curtis, 63–64, 66; and political factions in Missouri, 70; apprehension of runaway slaves, 71–72; and Halleck, 116; and Sherwood, 116; political and social

consequences of ending of, 177, 178; and hard versus soft war, 354 (n. 1)

Slocum, Henry W., 158

Smith, A. J.: and Franklin-Nashville campaign, 119, 124, 142, 144, 378 (n. 73); and Canby, 148; and Franklin-Nashville campaign controversy, 152

Smith, Charles H., 210–11

Smith, William F., 60, 84, 85, 358 (n. 75)

Snead, Thomas, 349 (n. 3)

Social class: Schofield's attitudes toward, 192–93, 196, 198; and domestic disorder, 280; and Progressivism, 316

Social Darwinism, 229–30

Society of the Army of the Cumberland, 148, 150, 152–53

Society of the Army of the Ohio, 335

Society of the Army of the Tennessee, 299–300

South: restoration of peace in, 179; and Democratic Party, 180; economic restoration of, 180; military governors for, 181–82; Reconstruction as military occupation of, 187; and domestic disorder, 289. *See also* Reconstruction

South Carolina, 190–91

Spanish-American War, 6, 279, 290, 295, 319, 327, 329–32, 333

Springfield, Missouri, 30, 32–33, 35, 46, 55, 65

Staff College, 4

Stanberry, Henry, 190, 195

Stanley, David: on Schofield, 1, 344 (n. 3); and seniority, 90, 91, 109–10, 370 (nn. 74, 75); and Atlanta campaign, 109–10, 111, 365 (n. 20); and Sherman, 111, 370 (n. 77), 373 (n. 21); and Franklin-Nashville campaign, 122, 123, 128, 132, 135–36, 137, 139, 375 (nn. 37, 45), 376 (n. 51), 377 (n. 63); and Franklin-Nashville campaign controversy, 152; and promotions, 159; and Indian affairs, 276

Stanton, Edwin M.: and Missouri, 48, 60; and confiscation, 50; and local militia companies, 51, 189; and Gamble, 64; support for Schofield, 66, 85, 86; and Enrolled

Missouri Militia, 69; and recruitment of African American regiments, 72, 73, 118; and Schofield's request to dismiss officers, 80; and corps organizations, 90; and seniority, 110; and Stoneman, 118, 140, 373 (n. 16); and Burbridge, 118, 373 (n. 15); and Franklin-Nashville campaign, 141; and Schofield's use of idle vessel, 159–60, 381 (n. 37); and Sherman's terms with Johnston, 165, 177, 382 (n. 54); and Grant, 165, 204, 205, 388 (n. 2); and Reconstruction policy, 177–78, 179, 180; and military district command assignments, 194; and Tenure of Office Act, 194; and Johnson, 204–5, 391 (n. 42); resignation of, 207, 388 (n. 10); and Porter case, 250, 400–401 (n. 8); and cipher clerks, 374 (n. 29)

State constitutional conventions, 194, 198, 199–200, 387 (n. 77)

State militias: disarming of, 189; training of, 229; and Great Railroad Strike of 1877, 280; and Upton, 290; and technological developments, 293; and McKinley, 329

States: and civil-military relations, 7, 10; and federal service regiments, 25, 29, 64; and dual military and political officeholding, 69; and recruitment of African American regiments, 72; and replacements for XXIII Corps, 115, 372 (n. 3); status of state governments, 178, 179, 192, 194; revision of state constitutions, 181; and suffrage laws, 193; and U.S. Army, 396–97 (n. 70)

States' rights: and Unionists, 192

Steedman, James: and Franklin-Nashville campaign, 124–25, 142, 378 (n. 73); and Franklin-Nashville campaign controversy, 151, 152, 153–54, 380 (n. 15)

Steele, Frederick, 73–74, 78, 80, 81

Stevenson, Carter, 100

Stewart, Alexander, 100, 106, 127, 130, 135–38, 144, 375 (n. 45), 376 (n. 49)

Stimson, Henry L., 335

Stoneman, George: and seniority, 85; and Atlanta campaign, 97, 103, 108–9, 368 (n. 45); as Department of the Ohio deputy commander, 118–19, 140, 373 (n. 16); as

military district commander, 196, 208, 386 (n. 64)

Strickland, Silas, 100; and Schofield's promotion recommendation, 115; and Franklin-Nashville campaign, 122

Sturgis, Samuel: and battle of Wilson's Creek, 34, 35, 352 (n. 44); on Schofield's battle presence, 35; as subordinate to Schofield, 85

Sumner, Edwin, 65

Swaim, David G., 267

Swaine, Peter T., 312

Sweeney, Thomas, 27, 30, 32, 106

Swift, Eben, 317

Tactics Board, 296–97, 413 (n. 89)

Taft, William Howard, 335

Taylor, Richard, 145

Tennessee, 117, 122, 123, 191, 209–10. *See also* Franklin-Nashville campaign

X Corps, 158, 182

Tenure of Office Act, 194, 204, 205, 216, 386 (n. 59)

Terrill, William, 18, 348 (n. 29)

Terry, Alfred H., 155–59, 188, 196, 210, 249, 252, 256, 265, 381 (n. 26)

Test oath provision, 197, 201–2

Texas, 209

3rd Louisiana, 33

Thirteenth Amendment, 191

Thomas, Eleazar, 222

Thomas, George H.: relationship with Schofield, 17, 18, 61, 148–51, 153, 154, 379 (nn. 3, 4), 380 (n. 19); and military promotions, 85, 378–79 (n. 87); troops of, 88, 101, 120; and Atlanta campaign, 89, 92–113 passim, 365 (n. 20), 366 (n. 28), 367 (n. 33), 368 (n. 52), 369 (n. 70), 370 (n. 78); and seniority, 90, 91, 366 (n. 25); and return to Tennessee, 114, 119, 120, 122; and Palmer, 119; and Hood, 120; and Franklin-Nashville campaign, 122–27, 131, 133, 139–49 passim, 161, 374 (n. 25), 377 (n. 71), 378 (nn. 72, 77, 80); and Grant, 141–42, 149, 150, 151, 153, 154, 214, 374 (n. 25), 378 (n. 80), 380 (n. 11); and winter quarters,